# WINCHESTER

## THE GUN THAT WON THE WEST

*Oliver Fisher Winchester*

# WINCHESTER

## THE GUN THAT WON THE WEST

*By* HAROLD F. WILLIAMSON

**South Brunswick and New York: A. S. Barnes and Company**
**London: Thomas Yoseloff Ltd**

(*The Winchester trade mark is used with permission of the Winchester Repeating Arms Company*)



MANUFACTURED IN THE UNITED STATES OF AMERICA

*Library of Congress Catalog No. 52-11409*

SBN: 498 08315 2

**TO EDWIN PUGSLEY**

*Qui Facit Per Alium Facit Per Se*

# PREFACE

Few company names are better known than Winchester. Merchandise marked "Winchester's Repeating Firearms, New Haven, Conn.," "Manufactured by the Winchester Repeating Arms Company," or with a red W, has long been associated with a fine line of guns and ammunition; an association which has been extended in more recent years to other products.

The explanation of the reputation of the Company is to be found in its history. A pioneer in the manufacture of repeating rifles, Winchester products became known and used throughout the world, prized alike by Eskimo and South Sea Islander, by the hunter on the plains and in the Rockies, on the African veldt, and in the Australian bush. They contributed in no small way to the paradox noted by one author that "The least mechanized of all aspects of our [American] society, the lives of men and women on the advancing frontier, depended upon the machine made rifles and revolvers which enabled the pioneers to kill game and outfight Indians." [1]

Winchester's achievements form a significant chapter in the whole development of firearms and ammunition; indeed the name "Winchester" has practically become a synonym for "repeating rifle," and the Company's .30-30 cartridge has taken its place as the most famous of all game-killing ammunition. The evolution of Winchester guns and ammunition, the circumstances that prompted their development, the principal figures associated with their invention and improvement, and the chief uses to which they have been put, make up an important part of the history of the Company.

But the story of Winchester has a significance beyond the fact that it was a gun and ammunition manufacturer. Back of the development of these products was a business organization managed by individuals who had to decide all matters necessary to operate a going business concern. The years from the start of the organization in the 1850s until it came under the control of its present owners in 1931 cover a period when American industry in general grew from the modest beginnings of the early nineteenth century into the giant that has contributed so much to America's material well-being in peacetime and performed so remarkably during two world wars.

Understanding of this period of American history is still incomplete. The favorable combination of abundant natural resources, technology, and expanding frontier, and a growing population has been recognized; but the part played by individual business men or *entrepreneurs* in shaping the industrial and commercial segments of our society needs further examination. It is clear that their role was especially important in an economy marked by a minimum amount of governmental supervision and control, but more studies must be made; studies that may be of particular relevance at a time when social control through governmental agencies seems to be increasing.

It might be supposed that being predominantly a sporting firearm and ammunition producer. Winchester's history would be quite different from the general run of American industrial concerns. A popular conception is that arms and ammunition makers are immune from ordinary business risks and through Government subsidies are supported in good times and bad. The history of the Winchester Repeating Arms Company through 1931 does not fit this pattern. While benefiting greatly from Government contracts during its early years, the real growth and financial success of the Company were based on nonmilitary sales. Set against the greatly expanded plant with which the Company emerged after World War I, even the profits from Government contracts during that conflict proved illusory.

In many respects, therefore, the experiences of the Winchester organization were typical of business operations in general between 1850 and 1931. Its business was subject to most of the broad influences, including the general expansion of markets and fluctuations in economic activity that affected other business concerns. Problems of raising capital, introducing new techniques, labor-management relations, and adapting the internal organization to changing needs, were not dissimilar to those experienced by the majority of its contemporaries. Even the more distinguishing features of the Company were not unique. The fact that it was a metal fabricator, that it followed the principle of interchangeable-parts manufacture, that it was located in New England, that throughout the greater part of its history it was controlled by one family, that it came under investment-banker domination during the 1920s, and even that it went into receivership in 1931, were characteristics shared to a greater or lesser degree by other industrial concerns of the time, especially in New England.

In relating the Company's history the major objective has been, so far as information permitted, to reconstruct the circumstances under which the major policy decisions were made by the management. Fortunately, sufficient material was available to trace the principal developments of the Company and in some instances to give considerable detail on particular phases. It is hoped that the resulting history contributes in a small way to the history of the sporting arms and ammunition industry and to a better understanding of the way business organizations operated during the years covered.

The more detailed history stops with the year 1931. This is appropriate, since after that date the Winchester Repeating Arms Company ceased as an independent organization and became a division of a larger concern. The epilogue traces the major gun and ammunition developments and contributions made by Winchester from 1931 to 1950.

The preparation of this history was made possible through an arrangement between Yale University and Olin Industries, Incorporated, the present owner of Winchester Repeating Arms Company. The Company made a grant to be distributed through the University for the purpose of meeting research expenses. The author undertook the assignment of writing the history with the understanding that he would be given full access to the Winchester records up to the time the present owners acquired the business, and that he would be given complete freedom in preparing the manuscript for publication. Without the complete and enthusiastic cooperation of everyone connected with the Company the task would have been insurmountable.

To the persons who helped in the preparation of this history the author is indebted. George Watrous, George Walker, William Roemer, Paul Beem, John Peck, Roy Parsell, Joseph Fleischer, Harold Steed, and Arthur Arnold, were most patient in answering the questions of a tyro in the field of guns and ammunitions. Paul Foster prepared the appendix on ammunition and Thomas Hall the gun appendices. Edgar W. Taft, William Tobler and John E. Otterson gave generously of their time in clearing up certain questions of management policies, as did William T. Birney and H. F. Beebe respecting the Company's marketing development. Those who read the manuscript at various times and made a number of constructive suggestions include Lucian Cary, S. R. Truesdell, Arthur H. Cole and Kent T. Healy. Marriner Browning very graciously made available a number of letters of John M. Browning, and Mrs. Zara Powers of the Yale Library staff contributed valuable information regarding the background of a number of important figures in the Company's history. Special thanks are due the author's research staff—John Buttrick, Pauline Adams, Robert L. Sucher, Eleanor Steffen and Philip Bishop—for their invaluable aid. The author is particularly obligated to Edwin Pugsley for his part in initiating the study and his continued help at all stages of its preparation.

*Northwestern University*
*November, 1952*

HAROLD F. WILLIAMSON

# PREFACE TO SECOND PRINTING

The favorable reception of this account of the history of the Winchester Repeating Arms Company is a tribute to the general reputation of the organization and its products. Reviews of the volume were generally enthusiastic, while a wide variety of readers, including gun and ammunition collectors, students of Americana, and economic and business historians, have all apparently found something of interest in the volume.

Much credit for the book's favorable reception should go to those who contributed to the preparation of the original manuscript. The author is especially indebted to the members of the Winchester research staff for their technical advice; gun experts and collectors, noted for their detailed knowledge of firearms and ammunition and quick to call attention to errors, have accepted the descriptions and specifications of the company's products contained in the book almost without question.

It is hoped that the volume will continue to attract readers interested in the important role played by the Winchester Repeating Arms Company and its products in American history.

* * * * *

Northwestern University
Evanston, Illinois
June, 1961

Harold F. Williamson

# CONTENTS

## Part 4 CONSOLIDATION OF POSITION: 1881-1889



## Part 5 REWARDS OF LEADERSHIP: 1890-1914

## Part 6 WINCHESTER AND WORLD WAR I: 1914-1918



## Part 7 POSTWAR EXPERIMENT: 1919-1924



## Part 8 RETREAT FROM POSTWAR EXPERIMENT: 1924-1931

# PART 1

# AN INDUSTRY IN TRANSITION

CHAPTER ONE

# FIREARMS PRODUCTION IN THE 1850s

## *Development of Firearms to 1850*

Firearms, the axe and the plow were the three cornerstones upon which the pioneer Americans built this nation. Of the three, firearms were the most dramatic and appealed most to popular imagination. The musket or rifle was a necessity for the pioneer who depended upon his ability as a marksman to provide food and clothing and to protect himself against attack. By 1774 a visiting Englishman could write, "There is not a Man born in America that does not Understand the Use of Firearms and that well . . . it is Almost the First thing they Purchase and take to all the New Settlements and in the Cities you can scarcely find a Lad of 12 years that does not go a Gunning."

The firearms brought from Europe were a conglomerate collection, representing almost every type currently produced in Britain and on the Continent. If the Americans had been content with the weapons they had when they landed it would have taken as long to settle the Ohio Valley as it did the Far West. The European arms failed in every way to meet the requirements of the American environment. Of large bore, clumsy construction, and badly sighted, they were inaccurate and too heavy and unwieldy for long journeys.

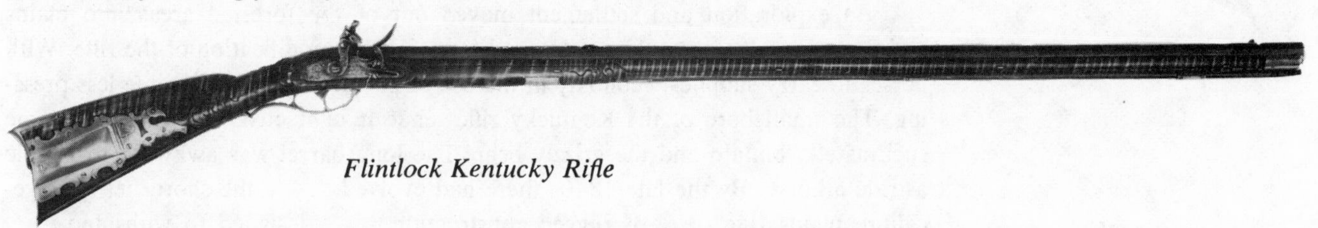

*Flintlock Kentucky Rifle*

Prompted by the complaints of users, the Swiss and German Colonial gunsmiths set to work to develop a rifle that would dominate the conditions found in the New World. Out of this competition among rival gunmakers, chiefly near Lancaster, Pennsylvania, there came about 1725 a new type of weapon which became known as the Kentucky rifle for the region where it first saw extensive use.[1] While certain basic features of the older models were incorporated, the Kentucky rifle was a radically redesigned arm to meet the demands of American shooters.

Compared with the customary European smoothbore musket, the new arm was rifled and smaller in bore and had a longer barrel ranging between 36 and 48 inches. The lead ball was placed in a patch of lubricated buckskin or cloth and both were rammed down the barrel. This patch method not only cut the time of loading and gave greater accuracy, but the patch helped clear the barrel of the unburned black powder from the previous shot. The long barrel gave adequate holding weight (the weight on the left hand while shooting) without adding excessively to the total weight of the gun. The longer distance between the plain, notched, rear sight and the front sight made more accurate shooting possible and because the powder stayed in the barrel longer it burned cleaner and cut down the amount of powder needed. The smaller bore economized on lead and gave higher velocity.

These features made an especial appeal to the earlier pioneers who could take only a limited amount of powder and lead with them into the wilderness or on long hunting trips and could ill afford to miss their targets.

A skilled user of a Kentucky rifle could measure and empty a charge of powder into the barrel, insert the lead ball and patch and ram them down, replace the ram-rod under the barrel, place a few grains of powder in the pan of the flintlock, and be ready to fire in about thirty seconds. He might, with some luck, hit a small target 150 yards away, but would seldom try beyond a hundred yards, and found by experience that between sixty and a hundred yards was the best range.[2]

Interestingly enough, the rifle was practically unknown in New England before 1776. Gunsmiths in this area reflected their English background by concentrating on smoothbore muskets. During the American Revolution several companies of frontiersmen from Pennsylvania, Virginia and Maryland, each soldier armed with his own rifle, joined the Revolutionary forces at Cambridge in 1776. The marksmanship of these men introduced the rifle dramatically to the New England scene.

*Percussion Lock Plains Rifle*

As exploration and settlement moved out of the forested areas into plains and the mountains, there was a demand for a further modification of the rifle. With horses to carry supplies, economy in the use of powder and lead became less pressing. The small bore of the Kentucky rifle made it ineffective against larger game such as elk, buffalo and the grizzly bear. The long barrel was awkward to handle astride a horse. By the late 1840s there had evolved ". . . the short, heavy large-calibre plains rifle . . . of rugged construction . . . designed to withstand . . . ill treatment. . . . It was, in short, a modification of the Kentucky rifle, and was capable of accurately delivering a heavy ball with great shocking power at long range." [3]

Meanwhile, ammunition was being improved. The paper cartridge containing a measured amount of powder with the ball attached, long used in military weapons, became more widely adopted in sporting rifles. In 1807 the Reverend Alexander Forsyth of Belhelvie, Scotland, used fulminate of mercury in a percussion lock to ignite the powder charge. The percussion-lock rifle proved more effective than the flintlock, although the fulminate of mercury, used either loose or in pellets, proved somewhat dangerous to handle. In 1822 Josiah Shaw, of Philadelphia, took out a patent for percussion caps, which were safer and more convenient to use and over the next two decades the percussion cap replaced the flintlock as a method of igniting powder. About 1825, experiments were made with conical bullets which, in a rifled barrel, gave greater range and accuracy than the round ball.

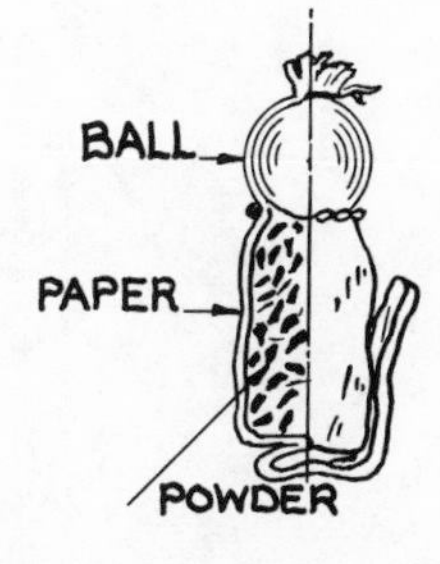

*Paper Cartridge*

While much progress had been made in gun and ammunition development during the preceding decades, there was a demand for a firearm that could be loaded more rapidly and more easily than the muzzle-loader. In the hands of an expert, the muzzle-loader using a paper cartridge with ball attached and a percussion cap could be fired once every twenty seconds, but the average performance was considerably below this standard. There were certain hazards in using the gun. It was awkward to load except from a standing position, which was dangerous during combat; if there were any sparks left in the barrel after firing, reloading was likely to result in a premature explosion that would remove the fingers or hand. It was not unusual in the excitement of battle for a rifleman to place several charges of powder and ball in the gun, often causing it to burst when fired.

For some time prior to 1850 the efforts of inventors had been directed along two closely associated lines. One was to work out a breech-loading weapon; the other to devise a practical repeating mechanism.

The idea of loading a firearm at the breech instead of the muzzle was centuries old. "Gloan," an anonymous American author, in his book, *Breech-Loaders,* calls attention to such a gun in the British Museum of Artillery at Woolwich which dates back to 1471. In the United States, Captain John Harris Hall of Maine had some success with a breech-loader patented in 1811, but his mechanism was complicated and awkward to operate. Although adopted in limited quantities by the United States Army, it never became a popular gun.

Probably the best of the time and certainly destined to become one of the most famous of the single-shot, breech-loading guns, was the one invented by Christian Sharps in 1848. It used a movable breech block that slid downward when the trigger guard was moved forward, and exposed the breech end of the barrel. A paper or linen cartridge with powder and bullet attached was inserted in *breech* of barrel. The sharp edge of the breech block, when it was brought back into firing position, sheared off the rear end of the cartridge, exposing the powder. The arm was fired by the usual percussion cap.

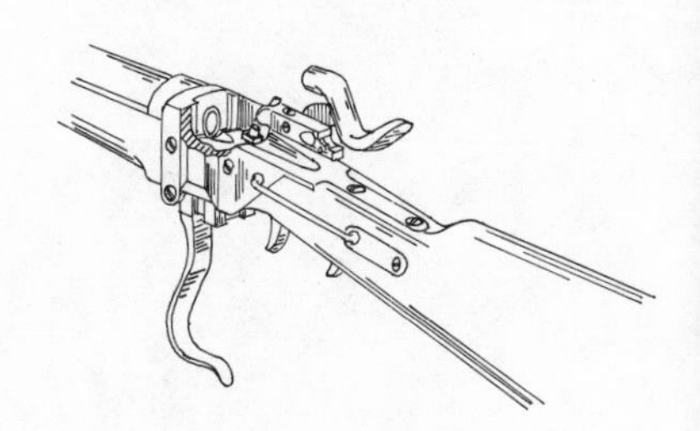
*Sharps Breech Action*

Until it was superseded by the repeating rifle, the Sharps rifle was one of the most widely used guns in America. It soon largely replaced the muzzle-loading type of plains gun and during the 1850s and 1860s ". . . accompanied every wagon train from the Mississippi to the Rio Grande, the Sacramento, or the Columbia, and taught alike Pawnee, Ute, Arapahoe, Cheyenne, Sioux, Crow, and Blackfoot that . . . their Canutelike attempts to check the incoming tide of white men were predestined to be a losing game." [4]

John Brown was equipped by the Northern abolitionists with Sharps carbines for his famous raid on Harpers Ferry, and during the Civil War some 100,000 Sharps rifles and carbines were supplied to the Union troops. "Selected for the famous Berdan sharpshooters—so popularly nicknamed from their preference for it—and equipped with telescopic sights, it taught the world of arms the art of front line sniping." After the war the Sharps became the favorite of the buffalo hunters in whose hands it was largely responsible for the extermination of the vast herds that once roamed the Western plains.

With the Sharps rifle it was possible to load and fire about five times a minute. This was a considerable improvement over the muzzle-loaders, but still fell short of the performance that a practical repeating mechanism would give. A more serious limitation of the Sharps rifle came from a defect that was common to all breech-loading weapons prior to the development of metallic ammunition. This defect was the escape of the gas at the breech when the arm was discharged. Not only was the result unpleasant for the user, but the escape of gas reduced the velocity of the projectile and fouled up many mechanisms so that they failed to function after a few shots. In spite of repeated attempts to solve the problem, it proved impossible to construct a movable breech that would seal off the gases and smoke effectively.

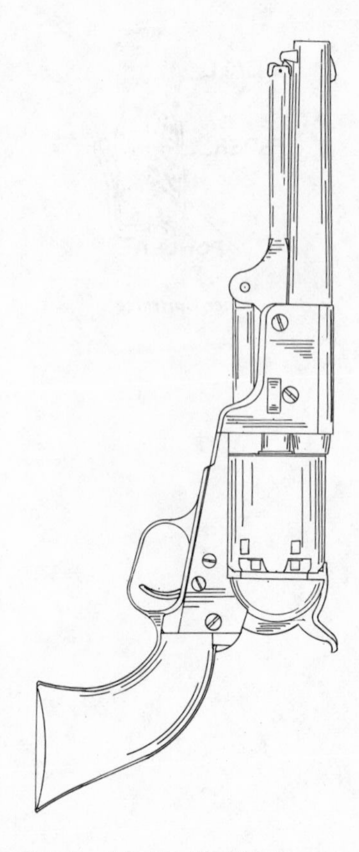

*Colt Revolver Third Model Dragoon*

Notwithstanding these difficulties there was great interest in developing breech-loading weapons. Between 1836 and 1873 over 540 patents were issued in the United States for inventions covering single-shot, breech-loading small arms, not including pistols.[5] A great many of these inventions were patented just prior to and during the Civil War and were used in the manufacture of a considerable number of guns sold to the United States Government during that struggle.[6]

Meanwhile, other inventors had turned their attention to the development of repeating firearms. Some 120 patents were taken out during the same period covering various types of magazine guns.[7] Because of the greater mechanical difficulties involved, however, progress in developing a satisfactory repeating rifle had been slow prior to 1850.

The first, most famous, and successful repeating firearm was the Colt revolver. Samuel Colt had taken out his basic patents in England in 1835 and the United States in 1836. His invention was a rotating cylinder having several chambers containing the ammunition which was discharged through a single barrel. His firearms first were used in military operations on a limited scale in Florida during the Second Seminole War (1835-42) but their first great popularity came in the Southwest in the Mexican War and in the hands of the Texas Rangers.

Colt produced rifles and shotguns as well as revolvers using the same repeating action, but because the escape of gas at the breech caused a loss in velocity, the revolving cylinder was not as well suited to the rifle or shotgun. In a revolver with its shorter range, this was not serious, and was more than offset by the rapidity of fire. To this loss of power in the rifle was added the danger that the flame would jump from one chamber to another and that several charges would be fired simultaneously. This happened not infrequently and the hazard to the shooter who supported the front part of the rifle or shotgun with his hand is obvious.

In 1850 a practical repeating mechanism that could be used in a breech-loading rifle was still to be devised. Colt's success with his revolver gave an indication of the desire on the part of shooters for such a weapon. It was a question as to which of the many inventors tackling the problem would be successful.

### *Changes in Production Methods*

Not only had there been substantial changes in the design of small arms by 1850, but manufacturing methods had been revolutionized by that date. The early gunsmiths were craftsmen filling the individual orders of their customers, and working alone in small shops or at most with the assistance of one or two helpers. Each part of the firearm was made with hand tools and individually fitted. Various components were not interchangeable with those of other weapons.

*Whitney Arms Company in 1825*

While private gunsmiths could adequately supply the market during peace, the demands of war put a severe strain on their capacity. The lack of interchangeability was also critical. The breaking of one part of a gun meant that a new piece had to be fitted by an expert armorer, which added to the problem of military supply. These limitations were particularly serious for the United States Government during the Revolution, in spite of an increasing number of small gunshops. In order to provide a more adequate supply for the future, the Government in 1792 authorized the creation of two national armories and a few years later began subsidizing private contractors on a generous scale.

Manufacturing methods were somewhat elaborated in both the Government armories and the shops of the private contractors, but it was not until Eli Whitney of New Haven, Connecticut, and Simeon North, originally of Berlin and later of Middletown in the same state, began their experiments, that the first steps were made toward interchangeable-parts manufacture. Whitney received a Government contract to make muskets in 1798 and North a similar contract to make pistols the following year. Both men had their employees specialize on various parts of the weapons and both designed tools which made a considerable amount of interchangeability of individual components possible.

Once started, the system spread to other contractors and to the Government armories and less than a half century later the industry was transformed and, as far as general methods of manufacture were concerned, became essentially what it is today.[8]

Both British and American inventors contributed to the machine tools that made this development possible. Roe, in his authoritative work, *English and American Tool Builders,* has pointed out that the modern machine tool had its origin in England and America. But, whereas the general machine tools were developed first in England, Americans took the lead in manufacturing interchangeable parts, and by 1850 this method of manufacture as applied to firearms had become known as the "American System." [9]

Of parallel importance with the invention of machine tools for American manufacture was the growth of the machine-tool industry. When Eli Whitney accepted his Government contract in 1798 to produce muskets, he had to invent, design, and build all of his proposed machinery, and it took him two years to produce his first guns. Nearly ten years passed before he had his plant thoroughly organized and his workers educated to use the machinery and equipment.

By the middle of the nineteenth century the machine-tool industry, spurred by the needs of the firearms producers, had developed to the point where its members were ready to supply standard machinery or build special equipment to meet the needs of their customers.

This development of machine tools and the growth of the machine-tool industry signalled the decline of small gunshops as the chief suppliers of firearms in America. To take advantage of interchangeable parts manufacture, it was necessary to operate a plant of considerable size. The transition, however, was gradual. Census data for 1860 reveal that there were some 239 establishments producing firearms which employed a total of 2,056 workers, or an average of less than nine per establishment. Only in the New England states and especially in Connecticut was there any trend toward large-sized concerns. In the latter state, nine producers employed around 969 workers. Of this number some 369 worked in Colt's factory at Hartford and another 300 in the Sharps factory operated by Robbins & Lawrence in the same locality.[10] But these two factories had only recently been established—Colt's in 1853 and Sharps' armory in 1854.[11]

The stage was set for the large arms factory employing scores and later hundreds of employees. Such plants called for an investment of capital on a substantial scale and for the services of managers who could combine the talents of the skilled mechanic with the ability to supervise the operations of large groups of workers and solve the problem of marketing an enlarged output that would no longer (except in the case of governmental contracts) be sold largely on individual order.[12]

The rewards promised to be substantial. The American Far West was largely unexploited. Settlement had pushed to the western fringes of the prairie country and gold discoveries in California had attracted thousands to the Pacific Coast. But the vast area in between, with its Indians and abundant animal life, including the great buffalo herds, was still to be won. As they had before, the pistol and the rifle were to play an important role in conquest of this part of the American Continent. Other parts of the world, such as South America and Australia, presented similar opportunities. The clouds of the American Civil War were gathering and Europe's national rivalries offered a lucrative, if somewhat erratic, outlet for military supplies, as did revolutions and armed expeditions in Latin America and the Orient. To the individuals or companies that could develop a superior type of firearm and mass-produce it, there awaited a large and expanding market and the promise of attractive financial returns.

CHAPTER TWO

# AN EXPERIMENT IN REPEATING FIREARMS

*The Development of a Repeating Firearm*

Among the many individuals who contributed to the mechanism that was eventually incorporated in the early Winchester repeating rifles was Walter Hunt. Born in 1796, Hunt learned the machinist's trade in his home town of Martinsburg, New York. In 1826 he moved to New York City where he set himself up as an inventor and mechanic. From that date until his death in 1859, Hunt turned out a remarkable number of inventions, including such diverse items as a flax-spinning machine, a heating stove, an iceboat, a nail-making machine, a fountain pen, and the safety pin. Despite his originality Hunt seems to have had no mind for business and was never able to capitalize on his inventions. This is illustrated in the case of the lock-stitch needle which he perfected between 1832 and 1834, but which he failed to patent. Some twelve years later Elias Howe received a patent for a similar needle and Hunt lost his chance at a fortune and general recognition as the inventor of the sewing machine.[1]

It is not astonishing that such a prolific inventor should turn his attention to firearms. His first move was to devise a loaded bullet for which he received a patent in August 1848 (US 5701) and which he described as a hollow-based, conical projectile, filled with powder and with the base closed by a cork wad having a hole in its center to admit the flame from an independent priming unit.[2]

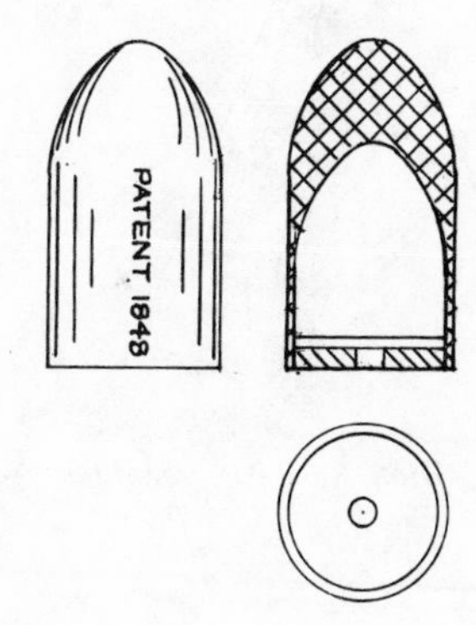


*Hunt Cartridge Patented 1848*

Hunt's next step was to design a gun that would utilize his ammunition, and in August 1849 he was granted a patent (US 6663) for a repeating firearm with a tubular magazine under the barrel, which he called the "Volitional Repeater." In many respects this gun was a brilliant achievement. It had a straight drive, spiral-spring-driven firing pin that was well ahead of the time, and the tubular magazine under the barrel was to become an integral part of the Winchester repeaters. But the repeating mechanism was far too complicated for practical use.

Not having sufficient funds to promote his inventions, Hunt assigned his patents to a fellow New Yorker, George A. Arrowsmith. Arrowsmith was a model-maker and machinist, who had in his employ Lewis Jennings, a skilled inventor and mechanic in his own right. Jennings was put to work on the problem of improving Hunt's rifle, and within a few months had succeeded in simplifying the lock and repeating mechanism which was patented in December 1849 (US 6973).

At this point Arrowsmith interested a New York capitalist, Courtlandt C. Palmer, in the possibilities of the new firearm. Palmer, one-time president of the Stonington & Providence Railroad, and a leading hardware merchant in New

York, bought the Hunt and Jennings patents from Arrowsmith with the idea of manufacturing the gun. In 1850 he contracted with the already famous firm of Robbins & Lawrence, of Windsor, Vermont, to have 5,000 Jennings Patent Rifles produced. It was in connection with this contract that Palmer became associated with Horace Smith and Daniel B. Wesson, who were later to found the well-known firm that bears their names.

While Smith and Wesson made their lasting reputation as revolver producers, they played an important role in the development of the repeating rifle that, had circumstances worked out a little differently, might have carried their names instead of Winchester's.

Daniel B. Wesson, who in 1850 was working at Robbins & Lawrence, was already an experienced gunsmith, having learned his trade in the shop of his older brother, Frank Wesson, of Worcester, Massachusetts. He became interested in the Jennings gun and began some experimental work on the mechanism for Palmer. About the same time, Palmer engaged Horace Smith to make further experiments with the gun. Smith was also an experienced gunsmith. After working for various arms producers, he set up shop for himself in 1846 at Norwich, Connecticut. For the next eight years he experimented with and produced various types of firearms. Of special interest is the fact that during 1851 and 1852 he was manufacturing the small-caliber .22 Flobert pistol which had been developed in France a few years before.[3]

While this pistol was practically a toy and could be used safely for target practice within the confines of the drawing room, it was a breech-loading firearm and used a metallic cartridge, called a BB cap, containing a charge of fulminate in the head which was the only propellant of the lead ball. Smith's early acquaintance with this type of ammunition was an important link in the development of metallic cartridges in the United States.

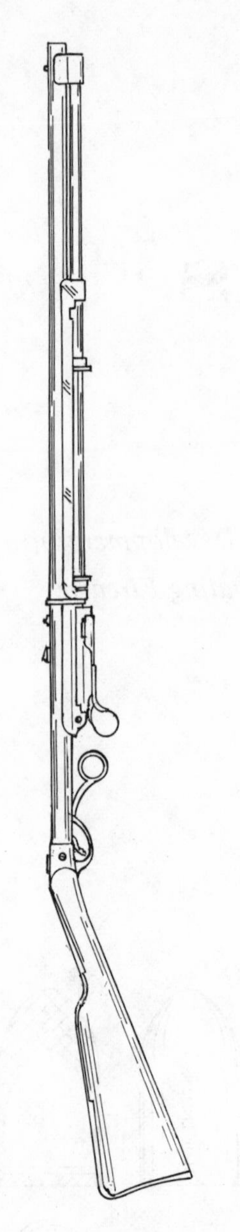

*Hunt Rifle Patented 1849*

In 1851 Smith took out a patent (US 8317) for an improvement of the Jennings rifle and Palmer had hopes that the weapon would be successful. Despite improvements, the gun remained too complicated and not powerful enough for a practical firearm and its production was abandoned in 1852.

The association of the three men continued, however, with Palmer apparently furnishing funds for further developmental work. Out of this experimentation came a new patent (US 10,535) granted to Smith & Wesson in February 1854. The most important feature of this rifle was the mechanism that moved the bolt and locked it in position with its head supporting the cartridge. It was a simple mechanism and, for cartridges of medium power, a highly satisfactory method of obtaining reciprocal movement in the carrier and locking the block in its forward position. This improvement, added to the tubular magazine and the rising breech block of earlier models, completed the essential mechanical features that were subsequently incorporated in the early Winchester rifles.

## *The Smith & Wesson Partnership*

Encouraged by the possibilities of the improved repeating action, Smith, Wesson, and Palmer formed a limited partnership on June 20, 1854, under the partnership name of Smith & Wesson. Manufacturing was carried on in Norwich, Connecticut, apparently at the same location previously owned by Smith. The firm's principal assets included the Hunt, Jennings, Smith, and Smith & Wesson patents already described. In addition, the partners signed an agreement that the partnership was to receive the benefit of any improvements in firearms or ammunition that Palmer or his representatives or Smith & Wesson might patent or acquire.

Production was concentrated primarily on pistols, using the mechanism patented by Smith & Wesson in February 1854.[4] The ammunition used in these arms, which was also produced by the firm, consisted of a cylindro-conical bullet weighing about 115 grains with a deep cavity in the back, filled with a priming mixture. It was sealed off with a copper washer having a cork disk in the center and was discharged by the impact of the hammer on the breech or firing pin. Except for the substitution of priming mixture for compressed powder, this ammunition was almost identical in form with that described by Hunt in his patent taken out in 1848.

For reasons to be noted presently, this type of ammunition was not very effective. Wesson, in particular, appears to have been dissatisfied with its performance, for in August 1854 he was granted a patent (US 11,496) which was assigned to the firm for an inside-primed, centerfire, metallic cartridge, apparently to be used in the arms being produced by the firm. For some inexplicable reason, this ammunition was not utilized or developed further at this time, even though it held the key to the satisfactory operation of the type of firearms under production.

The partnership had been in operation about a year when it was decided to change the nature of the organization. Just why this change was decided upon is not clear. In any event, when a group of New Haven and New York capitalists made a propostion to form a corporation to take over the business, the partners agreed to sell to the new concern.

### *The Volcanic Repeating Arms Company*

With some imagination the sponsors of the newly formed corporation called it the Volcanic Repeating Arms Company. Incorporated in Connecticut in June 1855, the organization was capitalized at $150,000 (6,000 shares of common stock at $25 par value per share). The backers, numbering forty in all, were chiefly from New Haven and nearby towns, although four lived or had their businesses in New York City. Their occupations give an interesting sample of the kinds of business enterprises that were capable of supplying venture capital to new undertakings. Included were seven clock-makers, three carriage-makers, two bakers, two grocers, as well as representatives of shipping, merchandising, shoe manufacture and similar types of business. Of particular interest is the fact that Oliver F. Winchester, then engaged in the manufacture of shirts in New Haven, subscribed to 80 shares of stock. (The list of stockholders is shown in Appendix E.)

In July 1855, Smith, Wesson and Palmer sold, transferred or assigned their various assets to the new corporation, including an agreement made by Smith and Wesson that ". . . it shall have the exclusive use and control of all patents and patent rights which the said Smith and the said Wesson or either of them can or may hereafter obtain or acquire for inventions or improvements in firearms or ammunition or upon the matters already patented as aforesaid, including all power of granting licenses, conveying shares and rights, receiving rents and royalties, and recovering and collecting damages for infringements." [5] The partners received $65,000 in cash paid in three instalments, plus 2,800 shares of stock, for their assets. In addition, Smith and Wesson were given an undisclosed sum for machinery at the Norwich plant.

*Horace Smith and Daniel B. Wesson*

With the formation of the Volcanic corporation the former partners withdrew from active participation. Smith and Wesson went on to form their famous pistol company while Palmer appears to have withdrawn entirely from the firearms business. Although Palmer, at least, held a substantial block of stock, neither he, Wesson, nor Smith appears to have served as an officer or a member of the board of directors.[6] Smith did act as plant manager for a short time during the latter part of 1855, but when the factory was moved to New Haven, early in 1856, he left the company's employment.

Initially the leading personality in the new management seems to have been Nelson B. Gaston of New Haven. Gaston had for a number of years been engaged in mining and processing barytes, a mineral used in paint. Around 1854 he shifted his principal business interests to shipping, and in 1855 became one of the largest stockholders and president of the Volcanic Company.[7] Oliver F. Winchester, although holding only a few shares of stock, apparently became more active in the management during the latter part of the concern's short existence and, when Gaston died, in December 1856, succeeded him as president.

The withdrawal of Smith and Wesson had left no one in the organization with any experience in the manufacture and improvement of firearms. William C. Hicks was picked to succeed Wesson as plant manager. Little is known of Hicks's early life and training, but he appears to have been an experienced mechanic.[8] There is nothing, however, to indicate that he knew very much about guns.



Manufacturing was started in New Haven under Hicks's direction in February 1856, in a small building located near the corner of Orange and Grove Streets. Compared with the Colt and the Robbins & Lawrence establishments at Hartford, operations were on a relatively modest scale. At the same time the labor force which numbered some fifty employees, including four girls making ammunition, and the amount of machinery used, made this plant well above the average size for the industry.

No description of the factory's operations at this time is available, but an inventory made when the Volcanic Company was liquidated gives some indication of the processes used. Included in the inventory were such standard types of machine tools as lathes, millers, drills, reamers, broachers, screw cutters, and the like. More specialized equipment was used in barrel-making and rifling. All of the machinery was apparently purchased from contemporary tool builders.

The machinery on hand was sufficient to permit the fabrication of parts that were reasonably interchangeable. Samples of the pistols and carbines show a considerable amount of file work, but this process was carried only to the point necessary to smooth off machined surfaces so that a more accurate fit was possible. The Company depended upon outside suppliers for frames and receivers, made of brass castings, drilled gun barrels of mild steel, and rough gun stocks.[9] Otherwise the quantity and variety of machinery on hand was extensive enough to have produced practically all of the parts that went into the finished products, plus the making of gauges, jigs, and fixtures.

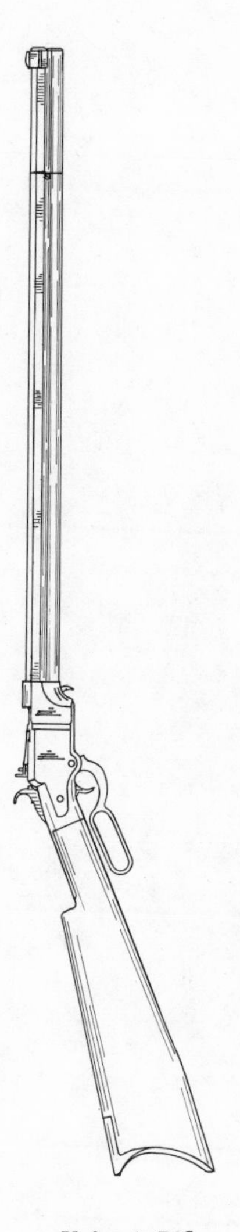
*Volcanic Rifle*

An examination of the names that appear on the payrolls of the Company indicates that almost all of the labor force was of English or Scottish background. The work-day and the work-week were probably typical for the period in the arms industry; that is, six days per week and ten hours per day. There is evidence of the beginnings of the contract system being utilized in the organization, under which agreements were made with individuals to assume responsibility for the production of specific items within the plant of the Volcanic Company. These early contractors were drawn from the more highly paid men already employed, or from outside the firm. Different individuals assumed contractual obligations from time to time, resuming their status as regular employees after the contract had been filled. It was not uncommon for a man to take on such an obligation in addition to his regular employment.[10] As will be noted subsequently, the contract system became a very important feature of the organization of manufacturing under the Winchester Repeating Arms Company.

The Volcanic Company continued to produce the same types of firearms and ammunition begun by the Smith & Wesson partnership. The principal change was the addition of carbines to the line which used the same repeating action as the pistols. An advertisement in the form of a circular, issued in 1856, lists the following models, all of which were caliber .36:

| *Type* | *Length of Barrel* | *Load* |
|---|---|---|
| Navy Pistol | 6 inches | 8 balls |
| Navy Pistol | 8 inches | 10 balls |
| Carbine | 16 inches | 20 balls |
| Carbine | 20 inches | 25 balls |
| Carbine | 24 inches | 30 balls |

*Office of the Volcanic Repeating Arms Company, New Haven*

The Volcanic Company's products received favorable comments from several sources. The New Haven *Journal-Courier* reported on February 9, 1856: "We find in the N.Y. Tribune's notices of new inventions, the following account of two articles manufactured in this city. The Volcanic pistol and rifle seem to be the very perfection of firearms, and must be favorites with the public when they are fully known. We understand that orders crowd in upon the Company from all quarters." There followed a lengthy description of both the firearms and ammunition, and a statement that "about 70 men are now employed in the manufactory."

On November 17, 1856, the same paper, under the headline "Tall Pistol Shooting," noted: "The N.Y. Tribune gives the following account of practice with the Volcanic pistols made by the Volcanic Repeating Arms Co. of New Haven. It shows that they are a wonderful weapon, and that the shooter is an accomplished marksman. Col. Hay of the British Army, tried his hand with the Volcanic Repeating Pistol, a Yankee invention made at New Haven. The pistol used on the occasion was an 8 inch barrel, which discharged 9 balls in rapid succession. The Colonel fired shots which would do credit to a rifleman. He first fired at an 8 inch diameter target at 100 yards, putting 9 balls inside the ring. He then moved back to a distance of 200 yards and fired 9 balls more, hitting the target seven times. He then moved back 100 yards further, a distance of 300 yards from the mark, and placed 5 of the 9 balls inside the ring, and hitting the bull's eye twice. The man who beats that may brag."

This was indeed Tall Pistol Shooting, so tall in fact that there is a strong suspicion that the reporter drew heavily on his imagination and not on fact. An analysis of the accuracy and velocity of the Volcanic ammunition made by the ballistic department of the Winchester Repeating Arms Company shows that Colonel Hay's chances against putting nine out of nine balls into an eight-inch target at 100 yards were about eleven to one. The odds against his score at 200 yards were on the order of seventy to one; while he had about one chance out of 7,140 of making his score at 300 yards.[11]

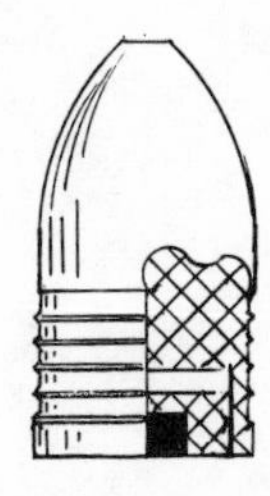

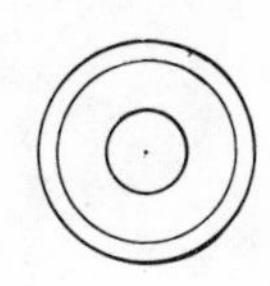

*Volcanic Cartridge*

In fact, the Volcanic firearms were subject to the limitations, previously noted, that affected all breech-loading arms before the perfection of metallic ammunition: the impossibility of sealing off the breech sufficiently to prevent the escape of gas at the moment of firing. Furthermore, the Volcanic ammunition itself was seriously deficient. As one authority has noted: "The self-propelling bullet had many defects. The hollow base could not possibly hold a charge of powder adequate to produce effective velocities and energies. Proper obturation was impossible, and the projectiles [with their heavy charges of fulminate] had the unfortunate tendency to go off, a whole magazine load at a time, at moments most unpropitious. A fine mechanism had been evolved [in the Volcanic arm] but faulty ammunition caused it to fall dismally short of developing its potentialities to the fullest." [12]

Subsequent events showed that the poor performance of the ammunition made it almost impossible to market the Volcanic products in competition with other firearms. This technical limitation appears to have been obscured by the immediate financial and management difficulties that were affecting the concern. The chief basis for this conclusion is that Oliver F. Winchester and a number of the Volcanic stockholders were willing to furnish additional capital to form a new organization to manufacture the same type of firearms and ammunition.

### *Failure of Volcanic Repeating Arms Company*

The proximate causes for the failure of the Volcanic Repeating Arms Company seem to have come from difficulties in connection with manufacturing and from a lack of working capital. The exact nature of the production problem is not known, but a letter written May 18, 1857, stated: "The settlement of the affairs of the Volcanic Repeating Arms Co. is now being delayed by claims at law . . . occasioned by the inferior quality of the workmanship of the arms sent Messrs. Post and Wheeler during the last summer and autumn." Something over $11,000 was involved in this controversy, which must have represented a fairly large percentage of the organization's total sales for the period of operation.

The difficulty in collecting this account undoubtedly added to the financial stringency felt by the management during the latter part of 1856. At best the Volcanic Company could not have had any very large amount of working capital, especially after the last instalment of the total $65,000 cash was paid to Smith, Wesson and Palmer in April of the same year. Of the original 6,000 shares, 2,800 had been turned over to the three partners. On the assumption that the remaining 3,200 shares were fully paid in at their par value of $25, the total subscribed capital would have been $80,000. After deducting the $65,000 already noted, plus an undisclosed amount to Smith and Wesson for machinery, the organization would have left only a small balance.

Whatever the amount, it seems to have been insufficient to carry the organization for more than a short time after April 1, 1856. Additional funds were borrowed from banks and by discounting notes, but the chief suppliers of capital were Gaston and Winchester, whose advances to the Company had amounted to something over $25,000 by August 1856. On the 26th of that month the Company issued a mortgage to Winchester and Gaston for the amount of their loans, pledging the principal assets of the organization as security. Another $10,000 was borrowed from the Tradesman's Bank of New Haven, the payment of which seems to have been guaranteed by Winchester and Gaston.

Even with these funds, the Company experienced increasing financial difficulties and in early February 1857 was unable to pay several notes which fell due at that time. Upon petition of the Tradesman's Bank of New Haven, the Volcanic Repeating Arms Company was declared insolvent on February 18, 1857, and Samuel Talcott and R. B. Bennett were made trustees. Eli Whitney, Jr., Henry Newson, and Charles Ball were appointed by the probate court to make an inventory and an appraisal of the assets of the Company.

Sometime within the succeeding few weeks Winchester made arrangements with the heirs of Gaston, who had died during the preceding December, and the Tradesman's Bank, to take over their claims. On March 15, 1857, by order of the court, the entire assets of the Volcanic Company were assigned to him for a figure slightly in excess of $39,000, which was just about sufficient to cover the secured claims against the organization, now held by Winchester. As a result the stockholders received nothing from their investment.

Thus the pioneer attempt to manufacture repeating firearms utilizing the action developed by Hunt, Jennings, Smith, and Wesson, failed because of immediate financial and managerial difficulties and because of the more basic problem of getting a satisfactory ammunition.

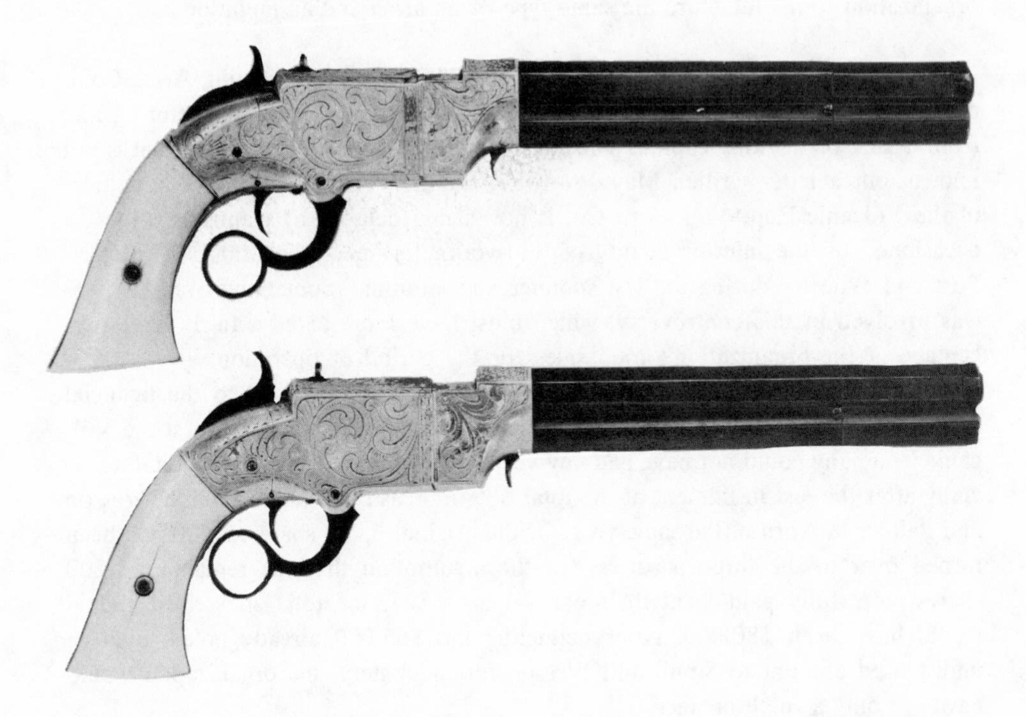

*Pair of Ivory-Handled Engraved Volcanics Made for Oliver F. Winchester*

# PART 2

# GAINING A FOOTHOLD

CHAPTER THREE

# CRISIS AND TRIAL

*Oliver Fisher Winchester*

It is doubtful whether Oliver F. Winchester had any intention of becoming an active gun and ammunition manufacturer at the time he purchased his eighty shares of Volcanic stock in 1855. As a partner in a flourishing business he was well known at the time as a capitalist and this investment was apparently only one of several that gave promise of financial success. The fact that he subsequently lent considerable money to the concern and took over as president, suggests that he soon became very much interested in firearms. Even before he had completed arrangements to acquire the assets of the defunct Volcanic concern, he had organized a new corporation, the New Haven Arms Company of New Haven, to carry on production under his general management.

Forty-six years old at the time he took over the management of the New Haven Arms Company, Winchester had already achieved a substantial business success. This he had accomplished largely through his own efforts, as he began life with few material advantages. He and his twin brother, Samuel C. Winchester, were born on November 10, 1810, in Boston, Massachusetts, the youngest in a family of five children. Oliver's mother was the third wife of his father, Samuel, who had ten children by his previous two marriages.

This branch of the Winchester family had long resided in Massachusetts, being directly descended from John Winchester, who had migrated from England at the age of nineteen and settled in the Boston area in 1635. The family genealogist has noted of the Winchesters: "Looking back . . . I do not find that they were men of note or known for their great deeds to mankind, but I do realize that they were men of strong character, earnest purpose, and deep religious convictions, upright and useful citizens, holding many offices of trust in the communities of which they were members, and helpful in building up the towns they selected for their homes, showing both ability and public spirit." [1]

There is no information about the occupation of Samuel Winchester, Senior, but it appears that most likely he was engaged in farming near Boston. In any case, when he died a year after Oliver and his brother were born, his wife was left with very little with which to raise and educate her children. The limited resources of the family made it necessary for young Oliver, at the age of seven, to go to work on a farm. During the winter months, when the work was slack, he attended school. When he was fourteen he was apprenticed to a carpenter and six years later became a master builder.

Having completed his apprenticeship in 1830, he moved to Baltimore, where, in spite of his youth, he became a building contractor for the succeeding three years. He is credited, among other projects, with having constructed a church in that city. In 1833 he decided to change his vocation and went to work in a local commission store which handled dry goods and men's furnishings. The following year he married Jane Ellen Hope, originally of Portland, Maine, and at that time went into business for himself, opening a small retail store selling men's furnishings in Baltimore.

Three years later he decided to expand operations and opened a downtown store in Baltimore, handling the same type of merchandise. Although this new venture began in the panic year of 1837, it was successful, and for the next ten years he continued in this line of business. It was while Winchester was living in Baltimore that his three children were born: Ann Rebecca, William Wirt, and Hannah Jane.

Some time before the end of 1847, Winchester became interested in improving the construction of men's dress shirts. During the latter part of that year he applied for a patent on his ideas. In his application he pointed out, "The methods of cutting shirts heretofore and at present practiced are accompanied with a disadvantage which all have more or less experienced, *viz*: that of the pull on the neckband."

After reviewing the attempts that others had made to correct this fault, he continued: "The object of my invention is to remedy this evil, and this I effect by making a curved seam on top of and corresponding with the curve of that part of the shoulder which extends from the arm to the neck so that the shirt shall be supported on the shoulder and thereby avoid a pull on the neckband. The bosom is also curved out on each side which aids the effect produced by so cutting the shirt and also serves to make it fit better." [2]

It is interesting to speculate whether Winchester himself had suffered from ill-fitting shirts or whether he was struck by the complaints of the customers who patronized his store. In any case, he was sufficiently impressed by the possibilities of producing and marketing an improved product to sell his business in Baltimore and move to New Haven, where he began the production of shirts in a small building on State Street, a few months before his patent (US 5421) was granted in February 1848.

In placing his product on the market, Winchester had made the acquaintance of John M. Davies, a leading importer and jobber of men's furnishings in New York City, and in 1849 the two men formed a partnership known as Winchester & Davies. The following year the manufacture was moved into a new building which the partners had built on nearby Court Street. Winchester seems to have supervised the production end of the business while Davies handled the marketing and distribution with headquarters in New York.

Initially the manufacture was conducted on what is known as the "putting-out system." The various parts of the shirt were cut out in the New Haven plant and distributed to the homes of workers for hand sewing. At one time the firm is said to have had eight hundred employees in the New Haven plant and another five thousand scattered throughout western Massachusetts, Connecticut, and Long Island.[3]

The advent of the sewing machine made it possible to eliminate much of the hand sewing and to change the production system to the factory form.[4] Some time around 1853 the partners enlarged their plant, installed a number of sewing machines, and increased the number of workers in the factory. The firm's operations were conducted on an impressive scale. According to the Census of 1860, the firm of Winchester & Davies had an invested capital of $400,000 and used 1,500,000 yards of cotton cloth, 400,000 yards of linen cloth, 25,000 spools of thread, 25,000 gross of buttons, 50,000 pounds of starch, and 18,00 pounds of soap. Some 500 foot-pedal sewing machines were utilized, and the average monthly employment included 40 male and 1,500 female workers. The payroll was reported to have been $17,000 per month—$2,000 for the men and $15,000 for the women. The annual output came to around 40,000 dozen shirts, valued at $600,000.[5]

The shirt business was undoubtedly profitable, and by 1855, when he invested in the stock of the Volcanic Arms Company, Winchester was already well-to-do, if not a wealthy man.[6] With the formation of the New Haven Arms Company he divided his attention between the gun and ammunition business and shirt manufacture. He continued his interest with Davies until 1866, at which time he sold out to his partner and devoted full time and energies to firearms.

Winchester represented a new type of *entrepreneur* in the firearms industry. Up to this time the prominent figures, such as Eli Whitney, Eliphalet Remington, and Samuel Colt, had typically been inventors and skilled machinists, who also had a flair for business. Smith and Wesson carried on this tradition, but Winchester's background and experience had been completely foreign to his new interest. His promotion and early administration of the New Haven Arms Company show he knew rather little about the mechanics of firearms and ammunition. His ability lay in his skill as a salesman, his grasp of financial matters, and his choice of subordinates who could advise him on technical matters. In spite of his ability, the New Haven Arms Company barely managed to survive the first four years of its existence. Winchester learned by experience, and after an uncertain start his administration of the Company began to show increasingly favorable results.

### *Organization and Control of the New Haven Arms Company*

The new company was formally organized under the Articles of Association which were signed April 3, 1857. The authorized capital was fixed at $50,000, divided into 2,000 shares with a par value of $25 per share. It is a tribute to Winchester's reputation as a business man and his powers of persuasion that eleven individuals joined him in investing in the new company, seven of whom had been shareholders in the Volcanic Repeating Arms Company. Winchester himself was the largest single stockholder, holding 800 shares, and he became president and treasurer and active head of the organization.

The New Haven Arms Company officially began on May 1, 1857, with the purchase from Winchester of the assets he had acquired from the trustees of Volcanic. He was paid $25,000 for the tools, equipment and fixtures and an additional $15,000 for the right to manufacture firearms and ammunition, under the patents which had been assigned to him and the ownership of which he appears to have retained.[7] This sum, it may be noted, was the approximate value of the claims Winchester had held against the Volcanic Repeating Arms Company. His 800 shares in the new company took half this amount, leaving him $20,000 in cash plus the ownership of the patents.

Besides these patents, Winchester held the beneficial interest in the covenant signed by Smith and Wesson in 1855. It was not until ten years later that he turned over these rights to the newly formed Winchester Repeating Arms Company in return for a substantial block of stock.

The following letter, written on the first day of business, reports the progress that had been made in collecting the subscriptions to the capital stock and the optimism of the management for the future success of the venture.

*New Haven, Conn.*
*May 1, 1857*

CHARLES J. HARRIS, ESQ.
NEW YORK

*Dear Sir:*

Your valued favor of the 29th inst. came directly to hand last evening. In reference to your question concerning the installments called for and payable this day, I would say that already over $33,000 has been paid *in full*; and that by Monday hope for quite a large portion of the balance. It is proposed, in order to accommodate and suit the convenience of all, that such as may prefer can pay 20% cash and balance by note at not to exceed in all ninety days (interest added), from this date.

It is not the purpose of the Treasurer to use the credits of the Company at all in bank at present. The Directors aim to start the wheels cautiously and, believing most confidently that in the present company there are unmistakable elements of success, they hope for satisfactory results.

S. L. TALCOTT
Secretary

*Benjamin Tyler Henry*

Winchester demonstrated his ability to choose personnel by selecting Benjamin Tyler Henry to succeed Hicks as plant manager. Henry, a somewhat neglected figure in the history of firearms, was the grandson of Benjamin Tyler, a pioneer ironmaster and mechanical engineer who lived in the Windsor section of Vermont.[8] B. Tyler Henry, as he invariably signed his name, was born in Claremont, New Hampshire, on March 22, 1821. After attending school until he was sixteen, he became an apprentice in the gunshop of J. B. Ripley & Company, in the same town.

During his apprenticeship he worked on various firearms and gun models, including the so-called "Waterproof Rifle," an early magazine gun patented in 1839 (US 1084), by R. B. Ripley, Lebbeus Baily, and William B. Smith. While this gun never became popular, it represented an intermediate development between Hall's breech-loader rifle and the Spencer repeating rifle, which came out in 1860, and served to familiarize Henry with the problems connected with breech-loading repeating firearms.

Leaving J. B. Ripley & Company, Henry worked in various gunshops, including Springfield Armory, until some time around 1842 when he was employed by N. Kendall & Company, of Windsor, Vermont. When that organization merged the following year to form the Robbins, Kendall & Lawrence Armory, he continued as their expert on guns. In 1850 when Courtlandt C. Palmer made arrangements with the company (now Robbins & Lawrence) to produce the Jennings rifle, Henry was among those who worked on the improvement of the mechanism. It was in connection with this contract that he met Daniel Wesson, and when the latter joined with Horace Smith and Palmer to form the Smith & Wesson partnership, Henry went with them to Norwich.

Henry's name does not appear on the payrolls of the Volcanic Repeating Arms Company, and he apparently returned to Windsor during the period of that concern's operation, because he came directly from Windsor to the New Haven Arms Company. There is no record of how he came to the attention of Winchester. It is said that the two first met when Winchester employed him as an expert mechanic to repair a number of sewing machines used in the shirt factory. It is quite possible that he was also recommended by Smith or Wesson, as their relations with the New Haven Arms Company were friendly. In any event, the choice of B. Tyler Henry was a happy one. He brought to the organization his experience with the improvement and manufacture of repeating firearms and made a major contribution by effecting changes in the Volcanic firearm and ammunition.

*Early Operations of the New Haven Arms Company*

Under Henry's supervision, the New Haven Arms Company continued the production of essentially the same firearms and ammunition that had been manufactured by the Volcanic Company. Two small-caliber .30 pistols, one a four-inch and the other a six-inch model, were added to the line, along with the ammunition to fit them. The ammunition itself was unchanged except for substituting black powder for part of the fulminate in the charge.

By the end of 1857, the full line and list prices of the Company's production were as follows:

| | | |
|---|---|---|
| No. 1 | 4-inch pistol | $15.00 |
| No. 2 | 6-inch Navy pistol | 21.00 |
| No. 2 | 16¼-inch carbine | 30.00 |
| No. 2 | 20-inch carbine | 35.00 |
| No. 2 | 24-inch carbine | 40.00 |
| No. 1 | balls | 11.50 per 1,000 |
| No. 2 | balls | 12.00 per 1,000 |

The bore of the No. 1 arm was approximately caliber .30 while the No. 2 was caliber .36.

Manufacturing was carried on in the same rented building that had been used by the Volcanic Company until June 1859, when the New Haven Arms Company moved into newly leased quarters at 9 Artizan Street, a short distance away. There is no information about the size of the plant before 1860, but in the census returns for that year, the Company reported the average number of employees at sixty-eight, forty of whom were men and the rest women. The monthly payroll came to $1,000, and the annual value of products was stated to be $25,000.[9]

Winchester's personal efforts appear to have been directed toward building up a market for the Company's products. Contacts with dealers were made by letter and through personal calls by himself and W. C. Stanton, who was employed as a traveling salesman about the middle of 1857. The Company was interested in opening an office in New York and on March 4, 1858, Winchester wrote Smith & Wesson: "We have in contemplation to open an office on Broadway, N. Y. for the sale of our arms and should perhaps like to make an arrangement with you to sell yours if we can do so in a manner mutually satisfactory. What do you think of it?" Nothing appears to have come from this proposal, but the Company did make an arrangement with J. W. Storrs of New York to act as its agent.

Dealers were given discounts from list prices which varied according to the volume of orders. On firearms they ranged from 20 per cent on amounts over $100, 25 per cent on sums above $1,000, and 30 per cent on $5,000 or more. The discount on ammunition was 20 per cent on any orders above $100. These discounts applied to settlement by "approved paper" of four months' duration or less, while a cash settlement gave the payer an extra 5 per cent discount. To any interested, responsible party, the Company sold a sample set of its products at regular dealer discounts and stood ready to fill additional orders as they were received. No merchandise was sold on consignment, and Winchester refused several requests of this nature. He was willing and eager to grant exclusive privileges to wholesalers or jobbers and occasionally to large dealers. Even during this early period he was interested in maintaining prices, cautioning one prospect who was interested in becoming a wholesaler, ". . . in selling to dealers you will please adhere to these prices and in retailing them do so at list price and in all cases for net cash."

In advertising the Company's arms Winchester made an early use of testimonials, which was the common practice of the period. In Winchester's case there was an added reason. Machine-made firearms were still a novelty and it was necessary to overcome the prejudice of users who preferred the products of the gunshops. Testimonials could be effective in breaking down their prejudice. A circular printed in 1859 reproduced the following letters from "among the numerous testimonials" received:

*New York, March 10, 1855*

Gent:—I consider the Volcanic Repeating pistol the *ne plus ultra* of Repeating or Revolving Arms, and far superior in many respects to Colt's much extolled Revolver. I have fired, myself, over 200 shots from it without even wiping the barrel—this is an advantage which no other arm I know of possesses. I have had the pistol with me at sea for more than eighteen months, on a voyage around the world, and find that, with the most common care, it will keep free from rust far more so than Colt's. I find the Balls as good now as when I left New York. I have shown the pistol to my friends in San Francisco, Hong Kong, Manila, Canton, and Shanghai, and they were much pleased with it.

C. F. W. BEHM, late of Clipper Ship *Stag Hound*

*New York, 23rd November, 1856*

Gent:—I have used a Volcanic Repeating Pistol for some months, on my last voyage to San Francisco, and in all that constitutes a good Pistol or Firearm, it has no equal and excels all others I have ever seen in rapidity, efficiency and certainly of execution. Its peculiar merit for sea service is the nature of the Ball, which contains the Ammunition, is water-proof and cannot be damaged by any change of climate, but is sure fire even after having been loaded for months.

FRED K. A. STALL, Commander Ship *Star of the Union*

In spite of the enthusiasm with which the New Haven Arms Company was begun and the efforts to make it successful, sales remained small. The financial position of the organization steadily deteriorated after 1857, and by 1861 the Company was virtually bankrupt.[10] The basic difficulty with the Volcanic firearms has already been described; it arose from the use of the self-propelled bullet. It is

# VOLCANIC
# REPEATING FIRE ARMS,

MANUFACTURED BY THE

## NEW HAVEN ARMS COMPANY,

### NEW HAVEN, CONN.

(PATENTED, 1854.)

The above named Company having purchased all the Patent rights on this Arm and its ammunition, (some eight or ten in number,) the inventions of as many of the most ingenious mechanics of the country, who have spent years in bringing this wonderful triumph of genius to perfection, are now prepared to manufacture them in a perfect manner, and offer them for sale as the most powerful and effective weapon of defense ever invented. They are made of all sizes, from a four inch Pocket Pistol, carrying six balls, to a twenty-four inch Rifle, carrying thirty balls.

*The rapidity of execution* of this Arm places it beyond all competition. The thirty shooter can be loaded and fired in less than one minute—a quickness and force of execution which is as much superior to the best revolvers, as they are to the old muzzle loading single shooters.

*The Ammunition is water-proof*, hence it can be used in any weather, or loaded and hung up for months, or laid under water, and then fired with certainty.

*Its safety from accidental discharge* is a great consideration in its favor; for while the magazine (a tube running the whole length of the barrel) may be filled with balls, and thus the gun, in fact, be loaded from breech to muzzle, it is yet impossible, from any carelessness in handling, to discharge it. *Its construction* is simple and its workmanship most perfect, hence it is not easily got out of repair.

*Its proportions* are light, elegant and compact, and the barrels are all rifled with great exactness. It requires no cap nor priming, no bullet mould nor powder flask. The powder and cap is contained in a loaded "minnie" ball of the best form and proportions, and is as sure as the best percussion caps.

*It shoots with accuracy* and *greater force* than any other Arm can with double the powder used in this. Directions for use accompany each Arm. Balls are packed in tin cases, 200 each.

### LIST OF MANUFACTURERS' PRICES.

|  |  |  |  |  |  |  |
|---|---|---|---|---|---|---|
| No. 1, | 4 inch | Pocket Pistol, | $12.00, | Plated and Engraved, $13.50, | Carrying | 6 Balls. |
| " 1, | 6 " | for Target Practice, | 13.50, | " " 15.00, | " | 10 " |
| " 2, | 6 " | Navy Pistol, | 18.00, | " " 20.00, | " | 8 " |
| " 2, | 8 " | " " | 18.00, | " " 20.00, | " | 10 " |
| " 2, | 16 " | Carbine, | 30.00, | " " 33.00, | " | 20 " |
| " 2, | 20 " | " | 35.00, | " " 38.00, | " | 25 " |
| " 2, | 24 " | " | 40.00, | " " 43.00, | " | 30 " |

Plating and Engraving, from $2.50 to $5.00 extra, per Arm.

### AMMUNITION.

No. 1 Balls, 130 to the Pound, $10 per M. No. 2 Balls, 66 to the Pound, $12 per M. (No. 1 Arms, require No. 1 Balls. No. 2 Arms, require No. 2 Balls.)

The numbers 1 and 2 designate the size of the bore, and the Balls are numbered to correspond.

A liberal discount to the trade.

We select the following from numerous testimonials, as the service to which the Arms were subjected was most severe, from the rapid action of salt water upon all metals.

*New York, March 10th*, 1855.

GENT.:—I consider the Volcanic Repeating Pistol the *ne plus ultra* of Repeating or Revolving Arms, and far superior in many respects to Colt's much extolled Revolver. I have fired, myself, over 200 shots from it without even wiping the barrel—this is an advantage which no other Arm I know of possesses. I have had the Pistol with me at sea for more than eighteen months, on a voyage around the world, and find that, with the most common care, it will keep free from rust, far more so than Colt's. I find the Balls as good now as when I left New York. I have shown the Pistol to my friends in San Francisco, Hong Kong, Manilla, Canton and Shanghaie, and they were much pleased with it.

C. F. W. BEHM, Late of Clipper Ship Stag Hound.

---

*New York, 23d November*, 1856.

GENT.:—I have used a Volcanic Repeating Pistol for some months, on my last voyage to San Francisco, and in all that constitutes a good Pistol or Fire Arm, it has no equal, and excels all others I have ever seen in rapidity, efficiency and certainty of execution. Its peculiar merit for sea service is in the nature of the Ball, which containing the Ammunition, is water-proof, and cannot be damaged by any change of climate, but is sure fire even after having been loaded for months.

Signed, FRED'K A. STALL, Commander Ship Star of the Union.

All orders may be addressed to

**NEW HAVEN ARMS COMPANY,**

*October*, 1859. **New Haven, Conn.**

*Broadside Advertising Volcanic Repeating Arms*

somewhat ironic that the Company should have continued to use this type of ammunition, when Winchester owned the Smith and Wesson patent covering a metallic cartridge which was the key to the solution of the problem. The failure, initially, to recognize the faults of the Volcanic products is a reflection of Winchester's limited knowledge of firearms in 1857.

As soon as this fault was recognized in 1858, Winchester put B. Tyler Henry to work to correct the difficulty, but nearly three years passed before his efforts began to show favorable results.

It was only the possibility of getting more satisfactory types of ammunition and adapting the Volcanic mechanism to handle them that kept the concern from being liquidated. Winchester's personal confidence in the future of the Company is revealed by the amount of funds he advanced to the business and his acceptance of responsibility as co-signer, along with the other directors, for the concern's notes payable.

### *Metallic Ammunition and the Rimfire Cartridge*

It is impossible to credit any single individual with the invention of the metallic cartridge. Ammunition development has always proceeded in a series of small steps. It has involved a delicate balance among several variables, including the form and construction of the projectile, the relationships between the amount of propellant and the weight of the bullet, the strength of the cartridge case, and the kind of priming mixture used. The continuing problem of getting satisfactory performance from the ammunition has prompted changes in allied fields; for example, better control of powders, priming materials, and improvements in metallurgy. In some instances an impetus that has come from the outside has in turn affected ammunition production.

The idea of making metallic ammunition was not new in the decade of the 1850s, but interest tended to lag as long as muzzle-loading weapons were predominant. A few Englishmen and Americans took part in the early development, but French inventors showed the greatest initiative. As early as 1812, Pauley, encouraged by Napoleon, patented a cartridge with a priming base and a charge of powder contained in a metal cylinder that was screwed onto a bullet.[11] Between that date and 1860 a number of French patents covering various types of metallic ammunition were granted, including a pinfire cartridge which enjoyed a measure of popularity. This was perfected by Houiller in 1847, who at the same time took a patent for a rimfire cartridge.[12]

With the growing number of breech-loading firearms, more and more attention was given to the development of metallic ammunition. By the late 1850s enough progress had been made to assure its early substitution for the kinds of cartridges currently being used in breech-loading arms. The significance of this development for the history of the industry has been pointed out by W. W. Greener, the famous British authority: "Probably no other invention connected with firearms has wrought such changes in the principle of gun construction as the invention of the expansive cartridge case. It has been used for every description of small firearms, and has been applied with success even to cannon. It has completely revolutionized the art of gun-making and has called into being a new and important industry—that of cartridge manufacture." [13]

The immediate credit for perfecting the rimfire cartridge which brought success to the New Haven Arms Company's weapons, should probably go to Daniel

B. Wesson of the Smith & Wesson Company. Wesson's interest in metallic cartridges dated back at least to 1854 when, during the original Smith and Wesson partnership, he took out his patent on the construction of a centerfire cartridge. Soon after Smith and Wesson established their pistol business in Springfield, Massachusetts, they acquired a basic revolver patent from Rollin White which covered a revolving cylinder with the chambers bored clear through the cylinder. (The chambers in Colt's revolvers at this time did not extend through the cylinder and were loaded from the fore part of the chambers, usually with loose powder from a flask designed to "throw" the proper charge, and a separate bullet. There was a limited use of paper cartridges with the bullet attached, but these were fragile and hard to get for most persons.)

*Pinfire Cartridge*

The White repeating action presented the same problem of checking the escape of gas and fire at the breech that was plaguing the New Haven Arms Company's firearms. Wesson, accordingly, began experimenting with metallic cartridges in the hope of overcoming this difficulty. It will be recalled that Smith, his partner, had manufactured the caliber .22 Flobert pistol which used a metallic cartridge (more accurately a BB cap) containing no powder but propelled by a charge of fulminate in the head. Wesson's initial attempt was to use this type cartridge in the first Smith & Wesson revolver, a caliber .22 model, which was brought out in 1857.[14]

The low velocity of this ammunition, plus the tendency of the head to bulge when fired, made the empty shells difficult to extract and led Wesson to further experimentation. By early 1858 he had worked out a cartridge with the priming mixture in the rim of the head and a powder charge as a propellant which worked satisfactorily in the Smith & Wesson pistols. The following extracts from his patent application, made two years later, show something of other attempts that had been made up to that time:

> We are aware that a metal cartridge for breech-loading pistols . . . has been made, in which the fulminate is spread in a thin layer over the interior of the base of the cartridge and is held in place by a washer of thin metal or other material.
>
> The explosion of the cartridge [in our type of revolver] from the hammer causes the base to bulge out—by which the cylinder is jammed and prevented from revolving freely.
>
> Metallic cartridges have also been constructed with a milled washer inserted in their base and the fulminate contained between the projection and depression around the edge of the washer and the interior surface of the cartridge at its base; but these cartridges are not adapted to the cylinder used in our arm.
>
> Metallic cartridges have also been constructed with a hollow flanged annular base and the fulminate contained in a hollow ring which is inserted in the hollow annular base . . . but this description of cartridge is expensive and the construction dangerous from the difficulty of closing and turning the ring after the fulminate is introduced, without explosion.[15]

Wesson proposed to avoid these various difficulties by making a rimfire cartridge with a projecting flange around its base with an annular recess in which the fulminating powder is placed, the fulminate from the central portion of the head being removed.

An important part of Wesson's invention was a loading tool which consisted of a small arm that spun the fulminate into the recess in the flange of the cartridge head. After the fulminate was in place, a wad was inserted in the head of the cartridge and the case filled with gunpowder. A ball of an "elongated conical form" grooved at the rear was in turn put into the mouth of the case and pressed into place. The final step was to put a light pressure on the head to bring the metal into close contact with the fulminate.

Wesson, it may be noted, made no claim to have invented the rimfire metallic cartridge, but he did claim priority in making it in the form and manner described. Actually, he made the first cartridges of this type in January 1858, and they were used in the caliber .22 revolver that his company had introduced the year before.

*The Henry Rimfire Cartridge*

In testimony given some years later, B. Tyler Henry stated that he began experimenting with metallic ammunition in the fall of 1858.[16] By the end of the year he could produce flanged rimfire cartridges almost identical with those of Wesson's except that they were larger in size. It is possible that he developed this type of ammunition independently, but it seems more likely that he had seen some of Wesson's products and realized their applicability to the problem of the Volcanic firearms. The fact that Henry did not take out a patent on ammunition might be taken as evidence that he recognized Smith & Wesson's prior claim. It appears much more probable that he and Winchester did not believe such a cartridge was patentable, for on April 20, 1863, the latter wrote Smith & Wesson:

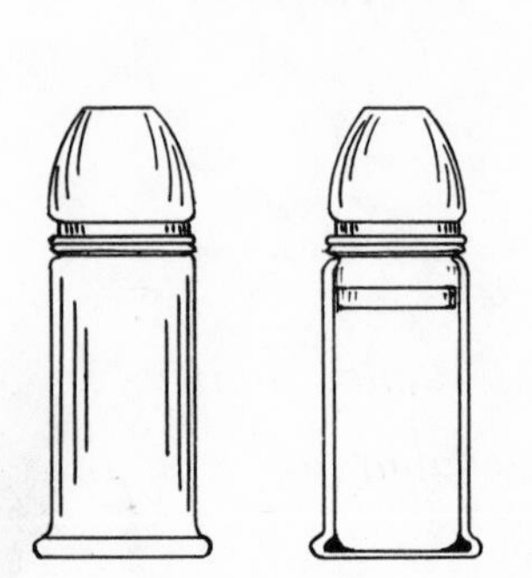

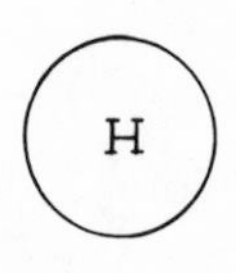


*44 Flat Rimfire Cartridge*

*Gentlemen:*

After I saw you on Friday last, I saw Mr. Leete and, in course of the conversation, he asked me if you had said anything to me about your patent on cartridges. I replied that you had not, that I was not aware that you had one, and if you had I presumed you would not say anything to me about it for the reason that by virtue of certain agreements with the Volcanic Arms Company to which I fell heir, you would doubtless consider me entitled to make them. On this subject, however, it is best we should have a fair understanding, to this end please give me the facts and your views.

Yours Respectfully,
O. F. WINCHESTER

In any event, at the time the letter to Smith & Wesson was written, the New Haven Arms Company had been turning out caliber .44 rimfire cartridges in some quantity for well over a year and a half. Stamped on the head with the letter H, in honor of Henry, these cartridges carried a pointed, conical, spherical bullet weighing 216 grains and a powder charge of about 26 grains. About a year later the Company brought out a cartridge with a flat-nosed bullet, designed to lessen the danger of explosion in the magazine. These cartridges became known as the Henry .44 Flat. Some measure of their superiority over the Volcanic ammunition is indicated by the fact that they developed a muzzle velocity of about 1,200 feet per second compared with the maximum of 500 feet per second for the former.

*The Henry Rifle*

As soon as he had produced a satisfactory cartridge, Henry turned his attention to adapting the Volcanic repeating mechanism to the use of the new ammunition. Specifically, his improvements consisted in adapting the bolt and firing pin to loading, firing, and extracting the rimfire cartridge. A special feature was the design of the firing pin, which was divided at the fore end so that it indented both sides of the rim of the cartridge head and reduced the possibility of misfires. There was no question as to the patentability of these improvements, and in October 1860 Henry was granted US Patent 3446, which he assigned to the New Haven Arms Company.

These changes were incorporated in a new model rifle, bearing Henry's name, which in external appearance showed its relationship to the Volcanic. The magazine was the same, consisting of a slotted metal tube under the barrel, parallel with it, and holding fifteen cartridges. A section of the magazine, near the muzzle, which swung to one side to permit loading, contained a spiral spring that forced the ammunition to the rear against the carrier block. The barrel was twenty-four inches long with a bore of caliber .44. Complete, the gun weighed about ten pounds.

The choice of the caliber .44 bore for the new rifle raises an interesting question. While not an uncommon size, this bore was smaller than the standard military arms which were all above caliber .50. At the same time, it was larger than the Volcanic caliber .36 rifle and, therefore, its manufacture required the use of new equipment. It seems most probable that the Company adopted the larger bore in an attempt to tap the military market, but could not go beyond the caliber .44 without redesigning the repeating action to handle the longer ammunition. Even if this had been possible or practicable in 1861, it would have made the arm heavier and would have cut down on the amount of ammunition that could be carried in the magazine.[17]

*Importance of Henry's Contribution*

Some evidence of the significance of Henry's contributions to the New Haven Arms Company is contained in a brief submitted for an extension of his patent to the Patent Office in September 1874. According to this document

> In 1860 the Volcanic arm as fully shown by all the witnesses for applicant, had become a failure, and the company insolvent, which state of affairs led applicant to make the improvements in the arm.
>
> That the invention was of great value and importance is clearly shown by each and all of the witnesses on the part of the applicant.
>
> It is impossible to estimate the real value of the invention made by the applicant.
>
> The Mechanism of the arm remains the same as the original arm, the patents for that mechanism are the foundation of all subsequent improvements, and to those patents, in this arm, applicant's patent was and still is subservient. The arm was a failure till the applicant's improvements, but it would be folly to say that the value of the arm made successful by such improvements is the real value or ascertained value of the invention of the applicant.
>
> The witness, Winchester, fully explains the difficulties of estimating the real value of the invention . . . and fixes one dollar per gun as the money value of an improvement of that kind, and he stated that one hundred forty thousand arms have been made and sold to 1874, hence one hundred and forty thousand dollars is a reasonable estimate of the real value of the invention to the manufacturer, some portion of which should properly be credited to the inventor.
>
> The Winchester Repeating Arms Company have agreed to pay the applicant for the patent for the extended term, the sum of twelve thousand five hundred dollars.[18]

The same document gives the details of the way in which Henry was compensated for his improvements:

> Applicant's salary as superintendent was fifteen hundred dollars per year, and as in all manufactures, his ingenuity and talent were expected to be exercised for the good of

his employer without special agreement to that effect, leaving the question of the right of any patentable invention that he may make open, to be settled between the inventor and Company that employed him as they can agree.

Rather than pay Henry a cash settlement or royalty, Winchester, on behalf of the New Haven Arms Company, gave him a contract to manufacture five thousand arms "but in this contract no extra price was allowed applicant, above what other parties would have received from the same." (This is an example of the inside contract system, which will be discussed in some detail in Chapters Seven and Twelve. In brief, under this arrangement Henry was to produce the guns in the New Haven Company's factory, using the fixed plant and equipment and raw materials supplied by the Company. He was to employ, supervise and pay the workers himself. The difference between his costs and the contract price to the New Haven Arms Company was his income.) Furthermore, under this contract, although Henry continued to act as superintendent, his pay was discontinued. The arrangement ran for five years during which time Henry made some $15,000, or more by $7,500 than he would have received from his salary as superintendent.

In view of the importance attached to Henry's improvements, that amount does not appear to be overly generous. As the brief relates, if a deduction is made from Henry's income of a reasonable allowance for his attention and services under the contract, little or nothing remains as compensation for his invention which made a complete success of the arm and which, but for his improvement, was a failure.

This statement was made in an attempt to get a renewal of the patent and after the new gun had proved itself. In 1861, when the future of the rifle was still uncertain, Winchester's unwillingness to make a cash payment to Henry is understandable. Evidence is lacking as to whether the question of a royalty payment was raised, but it is significant to note that Winchester and his successors in general followed a rule of never granting royalties on inventions they acquired.

*"Gentlemen's Agreement"*

With the introduction of the Henry improvements, the New Haven Arms Company dropped the production of pistols and concentrated on the manufacture of rifles. The fact that the New Haven Arms Company and its successor, the Winchester Repeating Arms Company, never again manufactured pistols or revolvers, has given rise to an interesting speculation about an agreement between Winchester and Smith & Wesson. Chinn and Hardin, in their book on American hand arms, state, without documentation, that when Winchester and Smith & Wesson came to terms about the patents, they entered a gentlemen's agreement

> . . . that was verbal, but has never been violated by either company in their many years of active existence. Oliver Winchester pledged that his company would never compete in the revolver business by manufacturing them; likewise the Smith and Wesson Company agreed never to produce rifles. And this agreement has been recognized by each succeeding generation having proved more binding than lots of contracts have that were legally perfect and elaborately drawn.[19]

Such an agreement may have been entered into, and, being a "gentlemen's agreement," might not have been made a matter of record. There is, however, no mention of such an arrangement in the existing documents of either Smith & Wesson or the Winchester Repeating Arms Company, although the latter company did make a similar agreement with another concern.

Furthermore, the timing of the alleged agreement is wrong, because the patents were transferred to the Volcanic Company in 1855 and that company continued to produce pistols until almost 1860, several years after Smith & Wesson had started operations. In any case, the decision to specialize after 1860 can be accounted for largely on other grounds. If Smith & Wesson had wished to produce repeating rifles, it would have been necessary for them to develop an action not covered by the patents turned over to the Volcanic Repeating Arms Company and now held by Winchester. Moreover, any such invention would have reverted to Winchester under the covenant signed by the two at the same time. The Rollin White patent acquired by Smith & Wesson did not fall within the covenant although Winchester seems to have had his lawyers explore the possibility.

Of course, Winchester could have continued the manufacture of pistols using the toggle-link action. But at this time the revolving action popularized by Colt was well known and liked by shooters. This was largely because the revolver was easier to manipulate than the finger-lever action of the Volcanic which required both hands. As the Rollin White patent covered the revolving mechanism with the chambers bored through, in which metallic ammunition could be used, it would have been extremely difficult for the New Haven Arms Company to develop a patentable revolving action during the life of the Rollin White patents.

Whatever may have been Winchester's inclination toward the production of pistols, there is no doubt that by the middle of 1862 the prospects for the future of the New Haven Arms Company looked promising. The improvements in the rifle had been completed and the organization was tooled up and ready for production. The Civil War had begun the year before, and the tremendous demand for military supplies of all kinds offered the prospect of a substantial market for the New Haven Arms Company's new rifle.

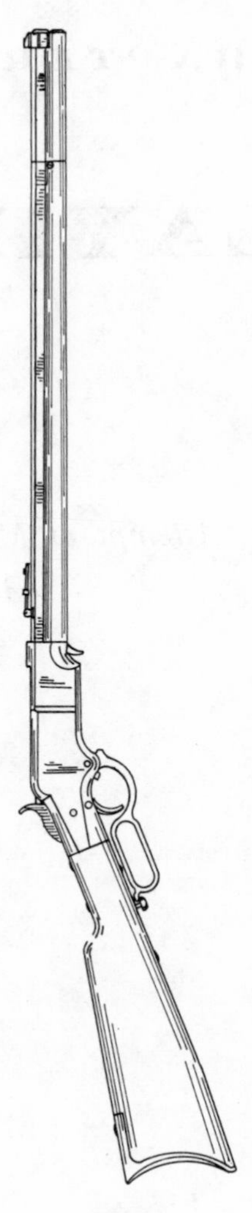

*Henry Rifle*

CHAPTER FOUR

# LAYING THE FOUNDATION

*Attempt at Military Adoption*

The Henry improvements marked a turning point in the history of the New Haven Arms Company and in the career of Winchester himself as a gun and ammunition producer. The latter had stated in a communication of October 17, 1862, that the new rifle would "if pressed with vigor retrieve [the Company's] past losses." Actually, this claim was too modest. Production of the new firearm not only enabled the New Haven Arms Company to recover its previous losses, but to develop into a profitable organization during the succeeding four years. In this accomplishment, the management was considerably aided by external conditions, but even so, no small amount of energy had to be expended before success was achieved. It was to this task that Winchester devoted an increasing amount of his attention after 1861.

NEW HAVEN ARMS COMPANY,
NEW HAVEN, CONN.,
U. S. A.,
Manufacturers of
Henry's Repeating Rifles,
CARBINES, MUSKETS AND SHOT GUNS,
AND
FIXED AMMUNITION
FOR THE SAME.
HENRY A. CHAPIN, Sec'y. O. F. WINCHESTER, Pres't.

*Trade Card of New Haven Arms Company*

Like every other gun and ammunition manufacturer at the time, Winchester was interested in supplying the military demand. With the firing on Fort Sumter in April 1861, the Nation had plunged into its grim civil conflict. At the outset neither side was adequately prepared to supply its armed forces with military equipment. This was especially true in regard to small firearms. So great was the need that all types, ancient and modern, foreign and domestic, were pressed into service. This demand for firearms, coupled with the fact that the arms and ammunition themselves were undergoing extensive modification, resulted in the use of a greater variety of guns during the Civil War than in any other major conflict in history.

In the new gun the New Haven Arms Company had a product that might be expected to sell readily, and Winchester made early arrangements to have the Henry rifle tested by the military authorities. The results of one such trial made by an officer of the United States Navy, in May 1862, give a good impression of the gun's performance. During the test, 187 shots were fired in 216 seconds, which did not, however, include the time spent in reloading the magazine. For comparison with the rapidity of fire of other rifles, 120 rounds were fired in an elapsed time of 340 seconds, including reloading, or an average of 1 shot every 2.9 seconds. Compared with the best performance of the muzzle-loader of around 20 seconds per shot, and the single-shot breech-loader, which could be fired once every 10 or 12 seconds, this was a substantial improvement. The Henry was shot for accuracy and range, and in the hands of a relatively inexperienced shooter placed 14 out of 15 shots in a target 18 inches square at a distance of 348 feet. The rifle was also tested for endurance, and after being fired 1,040 times without cleaning, developed no mechanical difficulties, although the barrel was considerably leaded and very foul.[1]

In spite of the need for firearms, the reaction of the United States military authorities to the use of a repeating firearm was not enthusiastic. The following extract from a letter written by Brigadier General James W. Ripley, Chief of Ordnance, to Secretary of War Simon Cameron on December 9, 1861, illustrates the official attitude. Referring to tests that had been made of the Henry and the Spencer rifles, he admitted that both guns had performed well, but continued: "... it is impossible, except when arms are defective in principle, to decide with confidence, in advance of practical trials, on their value, or otherwise, as military weapons. I regard the weight of the arms with the loaded magazine as objectionable, and also the requirement of special ammunition, rendering it impossible to use the arms with ordinary cartridges or with powder and ball. It remains to be shown by practical trial what will be the effect on the cartridges in the magazine of carrying them on horseback, when they will be exposed to being crushed or marred possibly to such an extent as to interfere with their passage into the barrel, and whether they will be safe for transportation with the fulminate in the cartridge; also, what will be the effect on the spiral spring of long use and exposure in the field. I do not discover any important advantage of these arms over several other breech loaders, as the rapidity of fire with these latter is sufficiently great for useful purposes without the objection to increased weight from the charges in the arm itself, while the multiplication of arms and ammunition of different kinds and patterns, and working on different principles, is decidedly objectionable, and should, in my opinion, be stopped by the refusal to introduce any more unless upon the most full and complete evidence of their great superiority. In view of the foregoing, of the very high prices asked for these arms, and of the fact that the government is already pledged on orders and contracts for nearly 73,000 breech-loading rifles and carbines, to the amount of $2,250,000, I do not consider it advisable to entertain either of the propositions for purchasing these arms." [2]

Apparently General Ripley's attitude remained unchanged until sometime in June 1863, when he authorized a Government order for some 250 Henry rifles.

In a letter to General Ripley dated June 24, 1863, Winchester took the occasion to point out the virtues of the Henry rifle and to bring a little pressure on the Ordnance Department by concluding: "If these arms are used as efficiently by the men who are to receive them as they have been by our Union friends in Kentucky the country will have no cause to regret the expenditure. We are having many more orders than we can fill, those from Europe are the most profitable owing to the Exchange, but prefer and anxiously desire that they may be used against the Rebellion, but cannot afford to refuse other orders upon an uncertainty. We trust, therefore, that the Government may find its interest in using them and place orders with us early that we may be able to meet them in time."

At this point Winchester determined to make a strong bid for the Government orders. He wrote Messrs. W. G. Woodman, of New York City, in 1863: "We are preparing to make Rifles and Carbines on the principle adapted especially to Infantry and Cavalry using the same size cartridges and one with a barrel 30 inches long and the other 20 or 22 inches carrying a ball nearly twice the weight of the one sent, the bore to be 50/100. Many experiments have been recently made by gun men in this country and by the English Government all which result in establishing the fact that a rifle with a small bore of 46/ to 50/100 of an inch carries with more accuracy and greater effect than the larger ones heretofore in use of 56/ to 60/100 inches or more in the bore. Other incidental advantages also arise from the use of the smallest practicable size bore in the diminished cost and weight of the ammunition both of which increase in a rapid ratio with the increase of size."

Sometime within the next few months he opened negotiations directly with Assistant Secretary of War R. C. Watson, suggesting that the New Haven Arms Company be given a contract. Winchester's hopes were temporarily dashed when he learned that the armory he proposed to rent from Wheeler & Wilson, in Bridgeport, was already spoken for. He wrote Watson that it would take longer to make sizable deliveries than he had anticipated because at least eighteen months would be needed to construct a new building and get production under way. A further investigation, however, revealed that Colt's Patent Firearms Company at Hartford had sufficient idle capacity to take care of his needs. At the same time the Wheeler & Wilson armory was also offered to him. With these plants available Winchester reopened negotiations with Assistant Secretary Watson and offered to deliver as many as forty thousand Henry carbines in about eight months at $26 each.[3]

But Winchester was doomed to disappointment. Assistant Secretary Watson apparently presented his proposals to the Ordnance Department. While the new head, Brigadier General George D. Ramsay, was more favorably inclined to the repeating rifle than his predecessor, General Ripley, had been, he was not impressed with the Henry rifle. In a report to Assistant Secretary Watson, dated April 5, 1864, he stated: "Repeating arms are the greatest favorite with the Army, and could they be supplied in quantities to meet all requisitions, I am sure that no other arm would be used. Colt's and Henry's rifles and the Spencer carbines and rifles are the only arms of this class in the service. Colt's is both expensive and a dangerous weapon to the user. Henry's expensive and too delicate for service in its present form, while Spencer's is at the same time the cheapest, most durable, and most efficient of any of these arms."[4]

General Ramsay's report apparently caused Assistant Secretary Watson to limit severely the orders for the Henry rifle. Ordnance Department records show a contract for eight hundred was made with the Company on December 30, 1863.[5] This order was followed over a year later by a second contract for eight hundred Henrys on April 7, 1865, and by a third for an additional 127 rifles on May 18 the same year.[6] These contracts, plus sales made earlier, made the total number of Henry rifles supplied to the U.S. Government during the war come to 1,731. The total amount collected from the Government for these arms came to $63,953.26, or an average of a little less than $37 per rifle.[7]

Government purchases of Henry ammunition amounted to 4,610,400 cartridges and cost $107,352.05, or an average of something over $23 per thousand.[8] This amount was much larger than the Government orders of Henry rifles would warrant. It is accounted for chiefly by the fact that so many of the Henry rifles were bought by individuals in the services, who were supplied with ammunition by the Ordnance Department.

His failure to obtain a Government contract forced Winchester to seek other outlets for the Company's products. While he was successful in selling the Company's guns and ammunition to customers outside the U.S. Government, directly and indirectly the demand was closely related to the war. A number of sales were made directly to individual officers and men of the Volunteer and State Militia forces which made up such an important part of the Union armies. Some rifles were purchased by officers attached to the Regular Army and Navy, but the bulk went to civilians living principally in Kentucky and the neighboring states of Ohio, Indiana, Illinois, and Missouri. On one occasion Winchester wrote, "There are few in this neighborhood who have tested the rifle or know of its existence. Yet the border states give us more than we can do."

The Company depended chiefly on dealers for distribution. In general, the arrangements were similar to those developed prior to 1861. Discounts were scaled according to the amount of the orders and an extra commission was given to wholesalers. The list price of the rifle in October 1862 was $42, and ammunition was quoted at $10 per thousand. The discounts on the rifle were set so as to return the Company a minimum of $34, while the ammunition returned $8. In spite of rising costs, the list price of the rifle did not change, and discounts remained practically the same. On ammunition, however, there were several price increases, and by the latter part of 1863 the figure quoted was $17.50 per thousand, although it should be noted that this was the improved ammunition using compressed powder.

Contacts with dealers came from inquiries directed to the Company and from the personal efforts of Winchester, who wrote to likely prospects and made frequent trips into the Kentucky area as did Stanton, who continued as the organization's travelling representative.

In general, Winchester took care to give his dealers equal terms and to protect them against price cuts and unfair competition. This was not always easy. There was the case of George D. Prentice, of Louisville, Kentucky, who ordered some $10,000 worth of rifles and ammunition in September 1862. Soon after this shipment arrived a sudden scare that the city might be attacked caused Prentice to sell his order to individuals at prices less than what it had cost him. This action produced a strong protest from the other dealers in the region, which caused Winchester considerable embarrassment. Under the extenuating circumstances he kept

# SIXTY SHOTS PER MINUTE

# HENRY'S PATENT

## REPEATING

# RIFLE

**The Most Effective Weapon in the World.**

This Rifle can be discharged 16 times without loading or taking down from the shoulder, or even loosing aim. It is also slung in such a manner, that either on horse or on foot, it can be **Instantly Used**, without taking the strap from the shoulder.

**For a House or Sporting Arm, it has no Equal;**

**IT IS ALWAYS LOADED AND ALWAYS READY.**

The size now made is 44-100 inch bore, 24 inch barrel, and carries a conical ball 32 to the pound. The penetration at 100 yards is 8 inches; at 400 yards 5 inches; and it carries with force sufficient to kill at 1,000 yards.

**A resolute man, armed with one of these Rifles, particularly if on horseback, CANNOT BE CAPTURED.**

"We particularly commend it for ARMY USES, as the most effective arm for picket and vidette duty, and to all our citizens in secluded places, as a protection against guerilla attacks and robberies. A man armed with one of these Rifles, can load and discharge one shot every second, so that he is equal to a company every minute, a regiment every ten minutes, a brigade every half hour, and a division every hour."—*Louisville Journal.*

**Address** **JNO. W. BROWN,**
Gen'l Ag't., Columbus, Ohio,
**At Rail Road Building, near the Depot.**

R. NEVINS' Steam Printing Establishment, No.'s 36, 38 and 40 North High Street, Columbus, Ohio.

*Advertisement for Henry Rifles*

*Cover of 1863 New Haven Arms Company Catalogue*

Prentice on as a dealer, but in the letters written subsequently, Winchester was careful to admonish Prentice not to sell below the established price.

In another instance rifles were sold to Messrs. B. Kittredge & Company of Cincinnati, Ohio, who, according to reports received by the New Haven Arms Company, not only resold the guns below the established prices, but made disparaging remarks about their performance as well. Winchester attempted to stop this practice by refusing to sell to Kittredge & Company. He was not immediately successful and a few months later he asked one of his dealers to go around to the latter's place of business, buy up the stock of Henry rifles, and find who was supplying them. Kittredge & Company was pushing the Frank Wesson rifle at this time, and during the course of correspondence insisted that it was a better gun than the Henry. Winchester offered to wager "not less than $5,000 nor more than $10,000" that in a competition between the two guns, the Henry would prove the better performer, a challenge that seems to have ended this episode.

Winchester aided his dealers by doing a certain amount of advertising in newspapers in the chief marketing areas.[9] Early in 1863 he began gathering material for the first catalog to be published by the company. He asked A. A. Vanwormer, a dealer in St. Louis, to make tests of the accuracy of the Henry rifle at various distances from the target, explaining: "We have no expert nor anyone in this vicinity who has tested the rifle as you have. In fact few in this vicinity know even of the existence of the weapon. While the demands from the border states have been and still are beyond our means to supply and used so far away from us that we have no means of getting exact results, as we desire to publish."

He also solicited personal accounts of combat performances of the rifle, explaining that the "Romance of War as a matter of history should be preserved."

Late in 1863 the Company issued a small catalog which included a number of testimonials concerning the effectiveness of the Henry rifle as a combat weapon, in addition to a description of the gun and ammunition. This catalog appears to have been distributed quite widely. It was translated and sent to prospective dealers in France and Germany. Shortly thereafter some orders began to come in from Prussia, which were especially welcome because exchange rates happened to be favorable.

One of the most exciting of the personal experiences published in the 1863 catalog concerned James M. Wilson, later to become a captain in the Kentucky Cavalry. The account of his adventure, which was reproduced in Cleveland's well known book, *Hints to Riflemen,* tells how Wilson, "an unconditional Union man, living in a strongly disloyal section of Kentucky," had been threatened by his neighbors.

In consequence of this, Capt. Wilson had fitted up a log crib across the road from his front door as a sort of arsenal, where he had his Henry Rifle, Colt's Revolver, etc. One day, while at home dining with his family, seven mounted guerillas rode up, dismounted and burst into his dining room and commenced firing upon him with revolvers. The attack was so sudden that the first shot struck a glass of water his wife was raising to her lips, breaking the glass. Several other shots were fired without effect, when Capt. Wilson sprang to his feet, exclaiming, "For God's sake, gentlemen, if you wish to murder me, do not do it at my own table in the presence of my family."

This caused a parley, resulting in their consent that he might go out doors to be shot. The moment he reached his front door he sprang for his cover, and his assailants commenced firing at him. Several shots passed through his hat, and more through his clothing, but none took effect upon his person. He thus reached his cover and seized his Henry Rifle, turned upon his foes, and in five shots killed five of them; the other two sprung for their horses. As the sixth man threw his hand over the pommel of his saddle, the sixth shot took off four of his fingers; notwithstanding this he got into his saddle, but the seventh shot killed him; then starting out, Capt. Wilson killed the seventh man with the eighth shot.

In consequence of this feat the State of Kentucky armed his Company with the Henry Rifle.

One of the most colorful tributes to the effectiveness of the Henry rifle came from the Southern soldiers themselves. Sawyer tells how "Major Claudman of the 1st D.C. Cavalry, in a letter to Mr. Winchester, said that when he was held in Libby Prison he often heard the enemy discuss the merits of the Henry rifles and he heard one of them say, 'Give us anything but that damned Yankee rifle that can be loaded on Sunday and fired all the week.' "[10]

In *Letters from Lee's Army* there is the sober comment: "We never did secure the Winchester [Henry] whose repeating qualities made the enemy's cavalry so formidable towards the end of the war."[11]

*Operations during the War Period*

In the absence of large Government contracts, Winchester was unable or unwilling to take the risk of expanding the Company's facilities beyond the physical limit imposed by the location of the plant, which remained at 9 Artizan Street, until after 1865.[12] To John W. Brown, of Columbus, Ohio, who had suggested that the organization might move into larger quarters, Winchester replied on May 4, 1863: "We shall go into an Armory, as you have in your eye, but we must creep a little longer. By and by we hope to walk and then we shall soon be in a position to drive." Eventually he was able to make good his prediction, but not until after the war was over.



Operations as a result remained on a relatively small scale. The average

*Plant of New Haven Arms Company in 1859*

number of 53 employees during the last half of 1863 was below the figure of 68 reported to the Census of 1860. Employment reached a peak of 72 during the third quarter of 1864, but after the end of the war, which came in April 1865, employment declined abruptly to around 25 workers.

It is possible to make a fairly accurate estimate of the output of rifles during the period. By January 31, 1863, seven months after the first Henry rifles were ready for delivery, about 1,500 had been made and sold. After 1863 production was stepped up approximately twenty-five per cent. Output figures are not available for 1864, but in 1865 some 3,011 rifles were produced and sold. This rate of around 250 per month is consistent with the fact that the Company's total sales between 1862 and the end of 1865 amounted to a little over ten thousand rifles.[13]

Information on ammunition capacity is more scanty. In September 1863 there is a notation in a letter to Messrs. Potter, Gay & Tollman that the Company was using forty to fifty pounds of powder per day. On the assumption that these were avoirdupois pounds, containing 7,000 grains, the 25-grain load in the Henry cartridge would have given a daily output of between 11,000 and 14,000.

Some months before, Winchester had already begun laying plans for expanding the Company's ammunition production. On April 20, 1863, he wrote Smith & Wesson: "Mr. Leete has been here and hired the man we employed to make tools for our cartridges and I am desirous of securing a competent man to take entire charge of that department, which I propose to perfect and extend to a scale sufficient to meet all demands, for all sizes, and if we succeed in making a perfect article we should be pleased to furnish you at about cost. My purpose is to inquire of you if you know such a man. If Mr. Warner or Mr. Wade are either or both of them calculated to fill this position, if so which is the best, and is he so situated as to make an engagement desirable. By giving these questions your careful consideration and an early reply you will much oblige [me]."

The following October, there is mention made of an order for cartridge machinery that would enable the Company to make twenty thousand cartridges per day.

A few production problems were encountered in ammunition manufacture. One correspondent wrote in complaining about misfires and suggesting the difficulties came from overheating. Winchester's response gives a good example of his interest in suggestions of this sort and the empirical approach that was used to analyze this sort of problem. He reported: "We took fresh made ammunition, 15 cartridges, and set them on end in a hot place for two hours, until all the grease had melted down onto the powder. Of these three misfired and the penetration (of the rest) was less by about one inch than that of 15 others taken from the same box but not warmed. None of the last misfired. This, of course, would indicate some force in your suggestion that the melting of the tallow affects the powder and certainty of firing. We will experiment further in this direction; and if the results confirm this view, we will make the necessary alterations." He concluded by requesting that "you will aid by so far as is in your power, to discover the cause of any defects in the ammunition."

Winchester was able to fix the blame for the difficulty with the lot of ammunition about which the complaint was originally made. "It is due," he wrote, "to the faithlessness of our man employed to put the cartridges together, as he must have put the grease in hot, instead of cold, to save time."

The Company made other experiments with ammunition, and in January 1863 reported "an improved cartridge with the powder compressed, by which the power is much increased."

Rising costs of labor and materials also contributed to management problems. As early as October 1862, Winchester explained an increase in prices: "Lead, copper, and steel have advanced 50% within a short time. Our ammunition *costs* us $12 per 1,000. We shall stand this for awhile in hopes of a decline; but if costs advance more, or continue on at the present high prices for any considerable length of time, we shall have to advance the price of ammunition. It is very annoying to us, as it must be to others, to be constantly changing prices; but with the state of the market we have no choice, as we are not safe in guaranteeing the price today to be the price tomorrow." The following month he noted ". . . the immense increase in the costs (gunsmiths to whom we used to pay $2 per day, are now getting $4.50), has made it imperative on us to sustain our prices firmly to save us from loss, if not ruin."

Winchester was especially interested in the performance of the Company's products and in correcting any faults that users experienced. The Henry rifle did, in fact, develop two weaknesses. One was a tendency for the firing pin to break, attributed by Winchester to pulling the trigger without ammunition in the chamber; the other defect arose when the magazine became dented. To one captain he wrote: "I regret that the metal in the breech pin should have failed in so many of the guns furnished your company. We have used the greatest care to have them perfect and of the best material. It is the weak point in the rifle, the most important we have yet discovered, but it is easily [corrected] and shall be remedied in the next lot, which we are now commencing." In the same letter he cautioned against pushing up the plunger in the magazine and letting it fly back against the cartridges, as this damaged the magazine and prevented the ammunition from feeding back into the breech.

While Winchester was receptive to suggestions about improving the Company's products, there were limits to the amount of changes that could be undertaken. As he noted to one correspondent, all the improvements the latter had suggested could be made, for example: ". . . increasing the length of the barrel and breech, and adding globe, telescopic or other sights; but all or any of these alterations would require time and expense, which, in the present scarcity of hands, and the hurried demand for our rifle, we can not possibly give in to at present."

*Position of the Company in 1866*

In spite of being forced to sell largely to non-Government markets, the New Haven Arms Company emerged from the war period with a greatly improved financial position and prepared to adapt its operations to meet the contingencies of postwar adjustments. Virtually bankrupt in 1860, the net worth of the concern was approximately $354,000 at the end of 1866 (*see Appendix G-1*). The dealer contacts made during these years gave the Company the nucleus of an established marketing organization to carry on its postwar commercial business. Furthermore, certain of the features of the rifle, such as the smaller caliber and the rapid fire, which had only limited attractions for the military authorities, became increasingly popular among hunters and frontiersmen.

These were important considerations for an arms and ammunition manufacturer during the postwar years. With the end of hostilities, the industry as a whole was greatly overexpanded. Foreign purchases took up some of the slack in military demand for a few years, until those countries built up their own small-arms production facilities. But this demand was not sufficient to support the entire industry and a large number of firms went into receivership. Those that survived did so by adapting and diversifying their production.[14]

The New Haven Arms Company was not immune to the sudden slackening of business that followed the end of the Civil War. Partial sales figures indicate that only 470 guns were sold during the last quarter of 1865 and the first half of 1866. During the same period only 672,000 cartridges were marketed. A continuation of these conditions could have been embarrassing to the Company, for the balance sheet indicates that a considerable portion of the assets was made up of inventory and the cash position was low.

Winchester, however, was not discouraged by the outlook for the future. Over the preceding nine years he had learned a great deal about guns and ammunition and their manufacture. Early in 1865 he began laying plans for expanding operations by applying to the Connecticut Legislature for a new corporate charter. In July of that year the State Assembly granted a charter for the Henry Repeating Arms Company with permission to carry on business either in New Haven or Bridgeport. Capital stock was set at $500,000 (par value $100 per share) with a provision that this figure might be increased to $1,000,000. No attempt was made during 1865 to re-form the organization under the new charter, but in 1866 Winchester sold his share of the shirt business to his partner, John M. Davies, which freed him to devote full attention to firearms production.[15] He also moved to identify the organization with his own name, by getting the Legislature in 1866 to change the title of the new corporation to the Winchester Repeating Arms Company.[16]

Meanwhile Winchester's growing stature in the community was reflected in the fact that he served as Lieutenant Governor of Connecticut for the term 1866-1867. Thereafter he was commonly addressed as "Governor Winchester" by his friends and business associates.

### *The Henry Rifle in the West*

Two incidents, involving the use of the Henry rifle in 1865 and 1866, offer a prologue to the subsequent tremendous popularity of the Winchester repeaters in the West.

The first of these came late in 1865 and marked one of the earliest experiences of the Indians of the Rocky Mountains area with the deadly effect of a repeating firearm. For nearly two hundred and fifty years there had been more or less continuous conflict between red and white men armed with single-shot guns. The chief and most effective tactic of the Indians was to maneuver within charging distance of an opponent and tempt him to fire by offering one of their number as a target. The brave involved, unless he was disabled, and his companions would then rush in and overwhelm their white adversary before he could reload his firearm.

How the Blackfoot Indians of Montana tried this same maneuver against two prospectors armed with Henry rifles was told by one of the white participants to Paul B. Jenkins many years later. The two white men were former Union soldiers who had kept the Henry rifles issued to them just before being mustered out. They began mining borax in the heart of the Blackfoot Indian country, knowing it was only a matter of time before the Indians would attempt to wipe them out. As retold by Jenkins,

One morning the two young ex-soldiers had hardly begun the day's operations when they saw the enemy approaching in force and knew that they were in for it. Some forty warriors dismounted at a distance, approached to nearly gun range, lay down in the grass and began deliberately to creep in, spreading out to surround their supposedly doomed victims. Once in range, some began to expose themselves for an instant, bobbing up in the hope of drawing a desperate bullet, but always doing so two at a time in the hope of getting the guns of both whites empty simultaneously. One of the youths caught the idea from the fact that two Indians always showed themselves at the same instant, and said to his companion: "As soon as they get near enough, we'll fire together. They'll rush us the moment we both fire; and then'll be the time for you and me to do some shooting!"

It happened precisely as he foresaw. With full magazines they agreed to bring on the decisive charge. At the word of one, both fired as two warriors showed themselves above the grass for an instant; and the moment that the two flashes and puffs of smoke were seen simultaneously the whole band of Blackfeet sprang to their feet and dashed yelling in on their supposed temporarily unarmed and helpless victims. But those two guns kept on firing! Shot after shot kept pouring from the guns over the low log breastwork, and to the indescribable horror of the warriors who considered themselves already victorious, man after man of their number fell shrieking or silent in the prairie grass as the deadly and unheard-of continuous firing blazed steadily at them; and that at a range so short, chosen for the final dash to close quarters, that few if any of the young riflemen's bullets missed. To halt, to wheel and dash madly away in any direction to escape the ceaseless fire, were moves of but an instant; but as they fled the guns kept at them, and only a few escaped unhit. Reloading their magazines the youths sprang from their rude barbette and ended the desperate work by leaving alive no wounded victims. Indeed, for the effect of the thing, they riddled every corpse with innumerable bullets and dragged the whole number to a heap at a distance beyond rifle range of their fort, that the survivors might return and contemplate the fatal results of their terrible encounter with weapons that obviously appeared never to need to be reloaded at all.

From that day no other attack was ever made upon that pair. Not only were they thereafter immune, but the one of them I later knew told me that passing Indian bands would make wide detours to avoid even the neighborhood of their cabin; or, on meeting one of them, would rush off to a distance for fear of coming into any proximity with the awful magic of death that they had so terribly exhibited. Once, he told me, meeting an Indian whom he had reason to believe to have been one of the survivors of the fight, the brave, with a face of horror exclaimed, "Spirit guns! Spirit guns!" and was off as fast as his pony could gallop.[17]

The second incident involved a brush between "the law" and some stagecoach robbers. Neill C. Wilson, in his book, *Treasure Express: Epic Days of the Wells Fargo,* tells how the stagecoach carrying a large shipment of cash was held up and robbed by three armed bandits near Nevada City one May day in 1866. Steve Venard, the former town marshal of Nevada City, did not join the posse that set out after the robbers but, armed with his Henry rifle, picked up the trail at the point of the robbery and followed it into a steep and rocky canyon to a point where his way was barred by a waterfall. To let Wilson continue the story:

Climbing doggedly with feet, knees, and one hand, Steve Venard reached the top of this fall. A half-shattered log led to the base of the islet. The man-tracker advanced over the bridge, stepped ashore around a granite block, and came full on Jack Williams' ghost. The ghost was cocking and leveling a long .44 revolver.

Williams and Venard sighted each other at the same instant. And at the instant, Venard's rifle leaped to his shoulder. Also, at the instant, Venard saw Finn, alias Kerrigan, drawing bead on him from the summit of the islet.

No time to change targets. Venard drilled Jack Williams' ghost directly and speedily through the heart. A flip of trigger-guard and another half-ounce cone of lead was in firing position, just where Tyler Henry had once pledged Mr. Winchester it would be. The second shot, dispatched before echo of the first had caromed off the cliffs, sped upward and spattered on the canyon wall, having entered Finn's skull below the right eye and toured his skull en route. A scramble for the top of the islet proved the third bandit vanished. Venard kicked leaves over the Wells Fargo buckskin bag which lay beside Finn's body, took new bearings on the ravine that still mounted by big, wet terraces in front of him, and set up its eastern face.

Bandit Number Three was doubling and twisting like a hare along the steep brush-covered hillside. Venard's rapid shot all but nipped him. The quarry turned at bay, full of fight, as its dust spurted in his face. The next shot out of the pursuing Henry explored his heart, sent his spirit winging and his person crashing downhill into the canyon.

The rest of the posse found Venard sitting on the buckskin bag, communing with his plain old, well oiled rifle. The odds had been three to one and the three had been under cover while he had advanced in the open; each adversary in that one high-blazing instant had held fair bead on him; yet here they were. Three dead men, two of them still clutching cocked revolvers, and one live deputy. But—four expended bullets. The Henry must be getting old. Steve Venard was regretful.

The stage had been robbed at 4:30 a.m. It now was noon. The treasure was back in express company keeping by two p.m.

The governor of California commissioned Venard a lieutenant colonel of militia "for meritorious services in the field," and the express company made over to him its $3,000 reward money and, with considerable celerity, a brand new, suitably inscribed sixteen-shot Henry. It had become fixed policy with the express management, when a man showed himself adept at gunning bandits, to present him with a fine rifle and its hearty compliments.[18]

# PART 3

# THE STRUGGLE FOR LEADERSHIP

CHAPTER FIVE

# POSTWAR ADJUSTMENT

*Organization of the Winchester Repeating Arms Company*

The first step toward formal organization of the Winchester Repeating Arms Company came on December 30, 1866, when the books were opened for subscription to the stock. On February 7, 1867, the incorporators, O. F. Winchester, E. A. Mitchell, Morris Tyler, and Henry Hooker, met at the office of the New Haven Arms Company, and sent out a notice of the first stockholders' meeting to be held thirteen days later. On February 20, the stockholders met at the same place and adopted a set of bylaws and elected O. F. Winchester, E. A. Mitchell, Nathaniel Wheeler, and John M. Davies to be directors. At the directors' meeting which immediately followed, James Wilson was added to the group, and Winchester was elected president and treasurer, Mitchell vice president, and Oliver T. Davis secretary.

This group of officers and directors, none of whom, with the exception of Winchester, had been connected with the New Haven Arms Company, was distinguished by the business achievements and associations of its members. Davies was Winchester's former partner in the shirt business. Wheeler and Wilson were well-known Bridgeport sewing-machine manufacturers. Mitchell, Postmaster of New Haven during President Tyler's administration, was prominently associated with a number of Connecticut firms including the Roger Smith Company, the Meriden Britannia Company, Benedict & Burnham, and the Willimantic Linen Company.

The liquidation of the former concern and the formation of the new corporation resulted in certain changes in the personnel of the stockholders. An arrangement was made with the shareholders of the New Haven Arms Company, giving them the option of exchanging their holdings for stock in the Winchester Repeating Arms Company, or receiving cash at a rate which was apparently fixed at $182 per share, the approximate book value of the New Haven Arms Company stock. As nearly as can be determined, the owners of some 750 shares of the old stock chose the second offer and received $136,500. The holders of the remaining 1,190 shares exchanged them for 2,170 of Winchester Repeating Arms Company stock valued at par of $100.

New subscribers purchased some 830 shares and an additional 1,500 shares were turned over to Winchester "as trustee for patent rights." [1] He appears to have distributed some four hundred of these shares to certain of the new stockholders as a bonus.

The new company began operation with an estimated net worth of around $450,000 (*see Appendix G-2*). Working capital, however, was quite small, amounting to $71,000. This could have made the financing of early operations rather difficult, but the personal credit ratings of Winchester and the directors were undoubtedly high enough to enable the organization to borrow on paper, backed by their endorsement. The management followed a conservative policy in respect to allocation of earnings and increased the amount invested in the Company substantially over the succeeding half-dozen years.

*Management and Control*

Although Winchester had associated a strong group of directors with the Company there was no perceptible weakening of his control over operations. The stockholder list of February 1, 1869, shows that out of the 4,500 shares that had been issued, he personally held 2,040 and his immediate family owned an additional 450.

How far Winchester consulted with his directors on policy is impossible to determine, but insofar as the minutes of the directors' meetings give any clue, discussion was limited and action confined largely to matters that required their official sanction. It is quite likely that policy matters were discussed informally and decisions made which were later confirmed at the periodic formal directors' meetings.

The first six years of the new Company's history were to be the crucial test of how well the management could adapt its policies to meet conditions in the postwar market. More specifically, success would depend upon finding substitutes for the American military demand, which had directly and indirectly aided the New Haven Arms Company.

*Shift of Plant to Bridgeport*

The end of the Civil War gave Winchester a chance to move out of the quarters in which he had felt so crowded after 1862. The shift was begun late in 1866, even prior to the formal organization of the Winchester concern, into a building in Bridgeport which was leased from Wheeler & Wilson, and the last of the equipment was transferred in March 1867.

Little information is available from which to judge the size of the plant after it was first installed in the new location. Within two years, however, operations had been expanded considerably beyond the size of the New Haven Arms Company plant. In 1869, the size of the labor force at Bridgeport was 260, some two and a half times the peak of 101 reached by the older company in September 1864. The annual output of guns was estimated at 12,000, valued at $240,000, and the production of ammunition at 4.5 million cartridges, worth $40,000.[2] Actually net sales for 1869 came to the sizable figure of over $323,000 (*see Appendix F*).

Measured by the number of employees devoted to gun and ammunition manufacture, the Winchester Repeating Arms Company was, by 1869, among the leaders in the firearms industry. (*See Appendix H.*) Actually the Company was probably in first place in the repeating-rifle field, because Colt's was largely manufacturing revolvers and neither Remington nor Sharps was producing repeating rifles. Even though production of ammunition was chiefly confined to supplying cartridges for its own guns, the Company ranked about third in a field of eight, being narrowly removed from second place by one other plant (probably C. D. Leete, of Springfield, Massachusetts). The newly formed Union Metallic Cartridge Company of Bridgeport, Connecticut, was by far the largest producer of ammunition.

## *The Model 66 Rifle*

Even prior to the organization of the new company Oliver Winchester had his organization working on an improvement of the Henry rifle. The chief faults of that arm, it will be recalled, had developed in the cartridge extractor, which frequently broke off, and the slotted magazine, which was easily bent and was liable to pick up foreign material when the weapon was dropped. During the latter part of 1865 and continuing into the following year a number of patents were taken out and others acquired which covered various extracting devices and types of magazines.

After several experimental guns had been made up the Company announced a new rifle to the trade in 1866. This was the Model 1866, more commonly referred to as the Model 66, and the first gun to bear the name of the Winchester Repeating Arms Company.

According to the Company's catalog for 1867, ". . . The Winchester Rifle remains in the mechanism for loading and firing precisely the same as the Henry, except the cartridge extractor. The latest improvements consist of an entire change in the magazine and the arrangements for filling it. By these changes, the gun is made stronger yet lighter; the magazine is closed and strongly protected; it is more simple in operation, requiring fewer motions in the one case and fewer pieces in the other. Not only can this gun be fired thirty times a minute continuously as a repeater, but it can be used as a single loader without any attachment to be changed for the purpose, retaining the magazine full of cartridges to be used in an emergency, when the whole fifteen cartridges can be fired in fifteen seconds, or at the rate of sixty shots a minute, or in double-quick time, in seven and a half seconds, or at a rate of one hundred and twenty shots per minute, or two shots per second, loading from the magazines—an effectiveness far beyond that of any other arm." [3]

The gun was produced in several styles, including two sporting rifles, and a military musket. (*See Appendix A-1.*) The rifle carried 17 cartridges and the carbine 12. The ammunition was essentially the same as the original Henry cartridge, being produced with both a 200-grain pointed and a flat-nosed bullet and a standard load of 28 grains of black powder.

With the advent of the Model 66, the production of the Henry rifle was dropped. A few of the new guns were made during 1866, but manufacture really began the following year, after the move to Bridgeport had been completed. For six years the Company concentrated on this one model and during that period approximately a hundred thousand were manufactured and sold.

## *Promotion of Markets: Attempt to Obtain Government Adoption*

As far as Oliver Winchester was concerned the Civil War had demonstrated conclusively the superiority of the repeating rifle over the single-shot. With an improved model, he began an immediate campaign to get the United States military authorities to adopt the Winchester rifle for the services. The attractions of such an adoption were twofold: there would be large and presumably regular purchases, and the prestige would help sales in other markets.

In a long memorandum, entitled "Winchester's Patent Repeating Fire Arm the Coming Gun," which was printed in the Company's catalogs from 1867 to 1875, he reviewed the development of the single-shot breech-loader and the repeating guns and stressed the popularity of the latter among troops during the Civil War. On logical grounds he could see no reason why the Government did not adopt the repeating rifle as the official arm for the services. This failure he attributed to the "immobility of prejudice." He scoffed at the objections that soldiers would waste ammunition and that the gun was too delicate for military use, and ended with the query, ". . . where is the military genius that is to grasp this whole subject and so modify the science of war as to best develop the capacity of this terrible engine—the exclusive control of which would enable any government (with resources sufficient to keep half a million men in the field) to rule the world?"

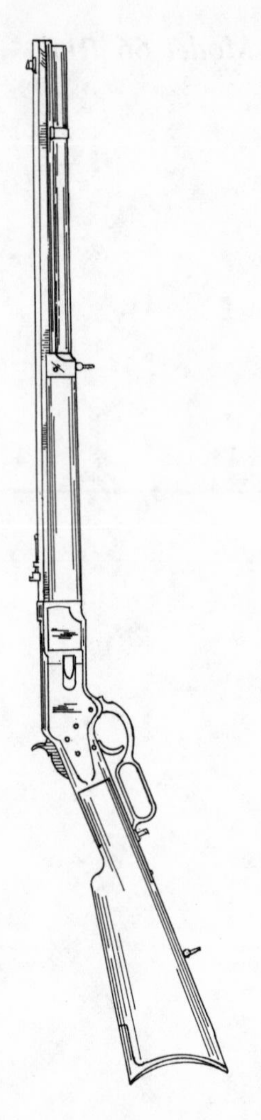

*Winchester Model 1866 Rifle*

Based upon experiences during the Civil War, the military authorities were convinced of the value of the single-shot breech-loader, and they were not willing to adopt a repeating rifle. This was in part because of a somewhat characteristic unwillingness to accept innovations and because of genuine doubts about the ruggedness and reliability of the repeating rifle in service. To these was added the fact that the Government had on hand a large quantity of muzzle-loading guns which could be converted to breech-loaders and for some five years after 1865, the Ordnance Department confined its attention to having these arms remodeled.[4]

In 1872 the Department did request $150,000 for manufacturing an improved breech-loader at Springfield Armory. This money was appropriated on the condition that trials be held of models submitted by inventors and manufacturers and that a competent military board choose the gun best suited for military adoption. Under this legislation a board was convened and tests began in September which continued throughout a part of the following year. The tests which these guns had to pass were severe, and were made up of the following:

*I. Rapidity with aim.* The number of shots which, fired in one minute, strike a target 6 feet by 2 feet at a distance of 100 feet. Any cartridges missing fire in this or other tests to be tried with a prick-punch, or opened to ascertain the cause of failure. The test to be begun with an empty chamber or magazine, the cartridges to be disposed at will on a table.

*II. Rapidity at will.* The number of shots that can be fired in one minute, irrespective of aim.

*III. Endurance.* Each gun to be fired 500 continuous rounds, without cleaning. The state of breech-mechanism to be examined at the end of every 50 rounds.

*IV. Defective Cartridges.* Each gun to be fired once with each of the following defective cartridges: 1. Cross-filed on head to nearly the thickness of the metal. 2. Cut at intervals around the rim. 3. With a longitudinal cut the whole length of the cartridge from the rim up. A fresh piece of white paper marked with the number of the gun being laid over the breech to observe the escape of gas, if any occurs.

*V. Dust.* The piece to be exposed in a box prepared for that purpose to a blast of fine sand-dust for several minutes; to be removed, fired 50 rounds, replaced for 5 minutes, removed and fired 50 rounds more.

*VI. Rust.* The breech mechanism and receiver to be cleansed of grease and the chamber of the barrel greased and plugged, the butt of the gun to be inserted to the height of the chamber in brine for 10 minutes, exposed for two days to the open air standing in a rack, and then fired 50 rounds.

*VII. Excessive Charges.* To be fired once with 86 grains of powder and one ball of 450 grains of lead; once with 90 grains and one ball; and once with 90 grains and two balls. The piece to be closely examined after each discharge.[5]

The Company made up a special model rifle (now on display in the Company's museum at New Haven) which was entered in this competition. This gun was basically the Model 66, but was designed to fire a much heavier, centerfire cartridge loaded with 70 grains of powder and a bullet weighing 360 grains. On February 2, 1873, it passed the first tests satisfactorily although the stock was split for a distance of some twelve inches. But after the gun had been subjected to a blast of fine sand-dust the Board reported: "After the first exposure the utmost exertion in working the lever and other parts failed to clear the piece of dust sufficiently for the movement of the carrier and the arm was dropped from further consideration." [6]

In fact, none of the half-dozen repeating rifles submitted at this time was acceptable, and the Army picked the single-shot Springfield Model 73 carbine, developed at Springfield Armory, for official adoption. At the same time the famous .45-70 Government centerfire cartridge was chosen as the ammunition for the arm. This cartridge, with 70 grains of black powder and a bullet weighing either 405 or 500 grains, became a standard by which the performance of all rifles was subsequently measured. No rifle would be acceptable for military adoption which could not handle ammunition of this size and caliber.

While adopting the single-shot Springfield breech-loader, the Board did express an opinion that: ". . . the adoption of magazine guns for military service, by all nations, is only a question of time; that whenever an arm shall be devised which shall be as effective, as a single breech-loader, as the best of the existing single breech-loading arms, and at the same time, shall possess a safe and easily manipulated magazine every consideration of public policy will require its adoption."

Within three years the Battle of the Little Bighorn was to offer a dramatic if inconclusive test of the combat merits of the Army single-shot Springfield and the Winchester repeater. In this battle which occurred on June 25, 1876, General Custer and his 220 troops were annihilated by a group of Sioux warriors numbering between two and three thousand. The soldiers were armed ". . . with single shot 45-70 caliber Springfield carbines, an accurate and deadly weapon up to 600 yards. But when fired rapidly the breech became foul and the greasy cartridges often jammed and could not be removed by the extractor. This meant that the empty shell had to be forced out by the blade of a hunting knife. This very fact was responsible for the death of many a trooper this hot Sunday, and may actually have been the indirect cause of the great disaster. Each trooper also carried the latest model six-shot, single-action Colt army pistol. All the soldiers had been ordered to carry 100 rounds of rifle ammunition and twenty-four rounds of pistol ammunition, either on their person or in their saddlebags. As the troopers dismounted and each fourth man became a horse holder, many of the horse mounts were stampeded and thus thousands of rounds of much needed ammunition were lost, especially to the men with Custer." [7]

There has been considerable controversy over the type and quantity of firearms used by the Indians. One reliable source states "It has been generally accepted that all the red warriors were armed with the latest model repeating Winchester rifles and that they had a plentiful supply of ammunition. For my part, I believe that fully half of all the warriors carried only bows and arrows and lances, and that possibly half of the remainder carried odds and ends of old muzzle-loaders and single-shot rifles of various vintages. Probably not more than 25 or 30 per cent of the warriors carried modern repeating rifles." [8]

Accepting this estimate, the number of Indians armed with Winchesters would have numbered between 500 and 900 against some 220 soldiers, not to mention the number of Indians armed with other weapons. For this reason the Battle of the Little Bighorn was not a definitive test of relative combat effectiveness of the firearms used.

*Swiss and British Trials of Breech-Loaders*

Meanwhile, Winchester had not neglected the possibility of getting foreign governments to adopt his firearms. In 1866, just prior to the formation of the Winchester Repeating Arms Company, he made a special trip to Europe to enter a Henry rifle in a Swiss ordnance trial. The gun was awarded first place and the committee strongly recommended that it be officially adopted. This recommendation was not followed, however, and the total business with the Swiss Government was confined to a small sale of rifle-making machinery valued at about $2,000.[9]

In 1867 Winchester entered a Henry rifle in a British trial which ". . . stood the test very well and worked satisfactorily." [10] Hearing of an improvement in the Henry, the committee asked Winchester to submit two models of the new gun for further testing. These guns were the Model 66 and after trying them out, the committee decided that the Winchester model was the best repeating rifle submitted for military use but it was unwilling to recommend a repeating rifle for general use in the service. The chief objections listed were the complicated mechanism and the weight of the arm when loaded. The committee did, however, conclude its report with the following statement: "There may, however, be occasions when a repeating arm might be useful, and, if such should be the opinion of the military authorities, the Committee recommends that the Winchester arm should be taken as being the best that has been brought before their notice, and that it be strengthened and otherwise modified to render it more suitable as a military arm."

The failure to obtain an adoption by either the Swiss or British was a keen disappointment. Winchester capitalized on the enthusiasm of the Swiss commission by reproducing in full the results of the trial and the commission's recommendation in the Company's catalog for several years beginning in 1867.

*Thomas Emmett Addis and Sales to Mexico*

Notwithstanding the failure to get an adoption by the Swiss and British, sales to foreign governments proved to be the most important outlet for the Company's products for over a decade after 1866. Mention has already been made of a few guns being sold in 1863 to Prussia by the New Haven Arms Company. The first sizable foreign sale, however, was made to Mexico in 1866, and marked the initiation of "Colonel" Thomas Emmett Addis as the chief foreign-sales representative for the Company.

Conditions were unusually turbulent in Mexico at this time. Through the influence of Napoleon III of France, whose armies had overthrown the Mexican Republic of 1863, Maximilian had been made Emperor of Mexico the following year, in spite of strong protests by the United States Government. With the end of the American Civil War, the collapse of Napoleon's scheme became inevitable. Encouraged by the knowledge that the American government was now in a position to force Napoleon's hand, the forces opposing the Emperor, under Benito

*Thomas Emmett Addis*

Juárez, grew stronger within Mexico during 1866, and unrest began to spread rapidly.

Sometime in late 1866, Winchester received an order from Juárez for 1,000 rifles and 500,000 rounds of ammunition to be delivered at Brownsville, Texas. Winchester chose Addis to see that the merchandise was delivered and to collect the money. Addis waited a month at Brownsville without hearing further from the Juárez forces. Finally he received word that if he would deliver the guns and ammunition to Monterrey, he would be paid.

Contrary to orders from Winchester not to leave American territory, Addis took his goods across the Rio Grande and made his way to Monterrey. There he hired an empty store in which he put the cases of guns and ammunition along with a cot to sleep on, where he remained on guard until the deal was completed. The Juárez government was at first unwilling to make a payment upon delivery but when Addis threatened to sell to the Maximilian forces, he got action and was paid some $57,000 in silver coin for the order.

Having received the money, the next problem was to get it out of the bandit-infested country. There was no railroad, so Addis hired a coach and driver and several guards and started out over a little-used road. He sat at the rear of the coach with the guards and driver in front. Once through the dangerous mountains, he forced the guards to put aside their guns and get down from the coach. He had placed double the amount of money agreed on for their services in a bag which he dropped as he ordered the driver to proceed. Not trusting the driver, he forced himself to keep awake by sticking a scarf pin from time to time into his thigh during the three days it is said to have taken to reach the American border. (Addis took great pride in this scarf pin and used it to show to his friends when relating this story.) Safely back in the United States he sent a wire to the Company announcing the successful culmination of his venture. Considering the cash position of the Company, the receipt of this money must have been unusually welcome.

Addis was a colorful and somewhat mysterious figure. He is thought to have been an O'Connor, but because of some family trouble changed his name. He came to the New Haven Arms Company from Remington and was working in the shop at the time Winchester sent him on the Mexican venture. He served as the Company's principal foreign-sales agent for the succeeding thirty-five years. During these years he traveled extensively in those parts of the world where there was a possible market for firearms and ammunition.

Addis seems to have looked his part. Above average in height, he usually wore a black cutaway coat, dark trousers, dark shoes, and a high-crowned derby, and carried a cane. He claimed to have received his title as a colonel during his Mexican trip, although he never produced any documentary evidence of having received such a commission.[11]

### *The First Turkish Contracts*

Just how much other business was done with foreign governments between 1867 and 1870 is not known. There is record of an order for a hundred carbines at $33 each and two rifles at $40 each, plus an undisclosed amount of ammunition at $18 per thousand, sold through a Paris agent in 1867. This order may have gone to the French Government or it may have been distributed to the non-military market. The Chilean-Peruvian assets, valued at $57,000, included in the balance sheet for April 1, 1867 (*see Appendix G-2*), were undoubtedly a result of sales of arms and ammunition to those two countries. In 1868, the firm of V. Azarian Company in Constantinople ordered 70 rifles, 53 carbines and 16,000 cartridges for distribution to the Turkish market.

The year 1870, however, marked the beginning of extensive sales in the foreign markets. There was an order totaling $36,000 from the Peruvian Government. Through Remington, whose entire output had been contracted by the French Government at the outbreak of the Franco-Prussian war, Winchester received an order for 3,000 Winchester muskets, 3,000 Winchester carbines, and 4.5 million cartridges to be delivered to the French.

But the biggest prizes of all were the first Turkish contracts which came the same year. During the late 1860s, the Turkish Government began preparing for an anticipated war with Russia. In May 1869, Rustan Bey, a Turkish Army officer, was sent to the United States to purchase military supplies. Rustan did not speak English and he relied upon his old friend, Christophus Oscanyan, the Turkish Consul General in New York, to act as his guide and interpreter.

Oscanyan, a naturalized citizen of the United States, was an interesting character. An Armenian Turk by birth, he had been educated in the United States and had acquired quite a reputation as a speaker and author on Turkish life and customs. According to testimony brought out in court, his job as Consul General was an honorary position and he made his living by receiving brokerage fees for clearing shipments from the United States to Turkey.[12]

Oscanyan claimed that he was asked by Winchester to use his influence with Rustan to persuade the latter to recommend the Winchester arm. Upon being informed by Oscanyan that he was receiving a commission from other arms manufacturers for this service, Winchester agreed in writing to pay a ten per cent commission on all sales made by Oscanyan of Winchester or Spencer arms.

Meanwhile, Winchester had not neglected the possibility of securing a contract directly from the Turkish Government. Early in 1870, Caleb Huse, representing the Company, made an agreement with Azarian Pére et Fils, of Constantinople, the successor to V. Azarian Company noted above, to act as the Company's official representative in all transactions with the Ottoman government. Sixteen Winchester guns, including one gold-plated and five silver-plated models, were sent to Azarian Pére et Fils to be distributed to Turkish officials.

About the same time, Rustan received instructions from his government to examine the Spencer repeating rifle with a view of possible purchase. Oscanyan claimed that he persuaded Rustan to condemn the Spencer and recommend the Winchester guns, which the latter did out of regard for Oscanyan although he objected to the Winchester rifle on the ground that it was too complicated for the Turkish soldier to use.

When Winchester heard of this he was not pleased, because the Company now owned a large inventory of Spencer arms. Oscanyan explained that the Ottoman government was planning to purchase surplus Spencer guns from the United States Government and he had taken this way of insuring consideration of Winchester rifles.

In any event, a number of Winchester guns were sent to Turkey in 1870 on Rustan Bey's orders for inspection by the officials of the government. This shipment arrived safely some time in April but it was found that no ammunition was available to try them out. An attempt to get some cartridges from Switzerland was unsuccessful and as ammunition shipment by steamer was illegal, a lot was sent by sailing ship, which arrived early in July.

The Winchester Repeating Arms Company was now in a position where it might have to pay a double commission on any business with the Turkish Government, one to Azarian Pére et Fils, and the other to Oscanyan. In April 1870, soon after the guns had arrived but before the ammunition was received, the Company received a telegram from the Turkish Government requesting prices on guns and ammunition. The Company wired back its terms promptly but no further word was received from the Turkish Government for some two months.

On July 15, Winchester wrote to Oscanyan reminding him that in March the Company had submitted terms to him under which it would supply arms to the Turkish Government. Having received no answer from Oscanyan and because the Company's business had picked up sharply, Winchester announced that he was withdrawing this offer.

Oscanyan claimed the reason for this withdrawal was that Winchester had heard through Azarian Pére et Fils that the Ottoman government had decided to give an order to the Company. He also accused Azarian Pére et Fils of using their influence at the Court of the Sultan to have the contract signed by them as official representatives of Winchester instead of letting it come through him. Even though he had not handled the contract, he claimed a commission for his services in influencing Rustan to recommend the Winchester instead of the Spencer without which the Winchester arms would not have been sent.

Azarian Pére et Fils had another story. In a sworn deposition made in connection with the case, Azarian told of the long association of his firm with Winchester which extended back to the days of the New Haven Arms Company. He reviewed the efforts made by Azarian Pére et Fils to interest the Turkish officials in the repeating rifle, including a gift to the Sultan in 1866. In 1869, various officials of the Ministry of War requested some Winchester rifles, and the sixteen guns, already noted above, had been distributed to the members of the *Darichaura* (Supreme Council for War). As far as Azarian knew, Oscanyan took no part, directly or indirectly, in the transaction.[13]

The first contract was signed November 9, 1870, and, according to Oscanyan, called for 15,000 muskets at $28 each, and 5,000 carbines at $20 each. Actually Oscanyan was a thousand short on the number of muskets ordered. The second contract was made on August 19, 1871, for an additional 30,000 muskets at the same price. The total amount of both contracts came to $1,360,000, upon which he claimed his commission of ten per cent under his agreement with Winchester.

Winchester refused to pay the commission and Oscanyan brought suit in the United States Court in New York in October 1875, to recover $136,000. After a preliminary hearing the court ordered postponement until depositions could be taken from various Turkish officials in Constantinople. On December 3, 1877, the case was reopened. The Company rested its case on the agreement being in violation of public morals and laws in the United States and made no attempt to refute Oscanyan's claim that he was responsible for the adoption of the Company's arms by the Turkish Government. The following March 7, 1878, the Court, Judge Nathaniel Shipman presiding, directed the jury to find for the defendant, the Winchester Repeating Arms Company.[14] The case was appealed on a writ of error to the United States Supreme Court, where in 1880, a decision was handed down sustaining the lower court.

Including ammunition, these Turkish contracts brought the Company an estimated gross income of over $1.46 million.[15] They were followed by others from the same government a few years later.

*Nonmilitary Sales*

While sales for military uses formed the most important outlet during these years, probably a third or more of the Company's output went into the nonmilitary or sporting-goods market.[16] For this side of the business the marketing connections built up before and during the Civil War were undoubtedly a great aid. As is shown below, the Company had some nineteen domestic jobbers and dealers handling its products in 1869. Of this group the first seven had been customers of the New Haven Arms Company:

COOPER & POND OF NEW YORK
SCHUYLER, HARTLEY & GRAHAM OF NEW YORK
JOHN P. MOORE & SONS OF NEW YORK
J. C. GRUBB & COMPANY OF PHILADELPHIA
LIDDLE & KAEDING OF SAN FRANCISCO
WILLIAM GOLCHER OF SAN FRANCISCO
WILLIAM READ & SONS OF BOSTON
HENRY FOLSOM & COMPANY OF NEW YORK AND NEW ORLEANS
FREUND & BROTHER
E. P. ALEXANDER
BARTON, ALEXANDER & WALLER
J. D. & D. C. SUTPHEN
SPIES, KISSAM, & COMPANY OF NEW YORK
A. D. MCAUSLAND
MERWIN & SIMPKINS OF NEW YORK
R. J. ALBRIGHT & SON
NORTON & DEUTZ
CHARLES FOLSOM
E. K. TRYON OF PHILADELPHIA

Sales agents were appointed to represent the Company in various foreign areas. Henry S. Chapin, a resident of London, was appointed European representative in 1867. Wexall & de Grees acted in a similar capacity in Mexico. Addis acted as a roving representative and trouble-shooter.

While sales to nonmilitary outlets were thus maintained and expanded, Winchester was personally still chiefly occupied with military adoptions of his products. For example, the Company's catalogs prior to 1875 were devoted almost exclusively to the advantages of the Winchester rifle as a military arm. Aside from the promotion done by jobbers and dealers, the Winchester Model 66 repeating rifle largely sold itself on its merits to the nonmilitary market.

*Purchase of Competitors*

The Winchester Repeating Arms Company not only improved its own repeating firearm but it strengthened its position in the field by absorbing the Spencer Repeating Rifle Company in 1868 and the American Repeating Rifle Company, formerly the Fogarty Arms Company, the year following.

The purchase of the Spencer concern must have given Oliver Winchester a great deal of personal satisfaction. Unlike the Henry rifle, Spencer arms were purchased in large quantities by the United States Government during the Civil War. Now, a little over three years later, the Winchester Repeating Arms Company was in a position to buy up the Spencer Company.

The Spencer repeating rifle was the invention of Christopher M. Spencer, who was born in Connecticut in 1833. While employed at the Cheney Silk Mills at South Manchester, Connecticut, he began experimenting on a repeating firearm with a rolling block action operated by the trigger guard and with a tubular magazine contained in the butt. This action was patented in 1860, and with the backing of the Cheney brothers, the Spencer Repeating Rifle Company began manufacture of military rifles and carbines in a plant in the Chickering Pianoforte Building in Boston. Of various calibers and models (*see Appendix A-3*), these arms were all chambered to use metallic rimfire cartridges, manufactured by the Spencer Company. During the Civil War a number of Spencer firearms were produced under a subcontract by the Burnside Rifle Company of Providence, Rhode Island.

With the end of the Civil War, Christopher Spencer left the organization to join with Sylvester Roper in the production of the Roper repeating rifle and shotgun at Amherst, Massachusetts. This venture failed, and in 1868 he joined with C. E. Billings to form the Billings & Spencer Manufacturing Company of Hartford.

Meanwhile, after trying for three years to carry on under peacetime conditions, the owners of the Spencer Repeating Rifle Company decided to liquidate the concern. Apparently they approached the Winchester Repeating Arms Company with a proposal to sell out the business. At a stockholders' meeting of the latter company, held on November 16, 1868, the secretary recorded that the purpose of the meeting ". . . was to consider the proposition to purchase the stock of the Spencer Repeating Rifle Company." A committee consisting of Bishop, Wheeler and Winchester was appointed ". . . to proceed to Boston and examine into the affairs of the Spencer Repeating Rifle Company, with the power to purchase the assets or capital stock of the said company."

Beyond the facts that the Winchester Repeating Arms Company acquired the Spencer patents and a considerable inventory of finished arms, the subsequent details of the transaction are not clear.[17]

The American Repeating Rifle Company was a newcomer in the field, having started production in Boston as the Fogarty Arms Company sometime during 1866 or 1867. Its products were made under US Patents 59,126 and 82,819, issued to Valentine Fogarty. The guns used a lever-action repeating mechanism with the magazine contained in the butt, and in general appearance resembled the Spencer. (*See Appendix A-3.*) The repeating action differed from both the Spencer and the Henry in that the cartridges were fed up from the side of the carrier block by the action of a trigger-guard operating lever. Production apparently never amounted to more than a few thousand guns before the concern decided to go out of business.

On August 6, 1869, the directors of the Winchester Repeating Arms Company authorized the president to purchase the entire assets and all the patent rights of the American Repeating Rifle Company of Boston, ". . . provided on examination they prove to be not less favorable than the statement sent to this company and at the best terms as to cash and credit that can be met by this company for a sum not exceeding One Hundred and Fifty Thousand Dollars ($150,000). In paying for the same he is authorized to sell such number of shares of the stock of the Winchester Repeating Arms Company as may be decided by sellers at not less than Ninety Dollars per share." [18]

The purchase of the American Repeating Rifle Company turned out exceptionally well. As reported to the directors of the Winchester Repeating Arms Company, the total cost of the machinery, patents, and expenses of moving came to slightly over $118,000. By February 1870, the sale of machinery had returned more than $127,000 and there still remained tools and equipment on hand valued at approximately $23,000. Thus in addition to securing possession of the patents, the Winchester Repeating Arms Company netted around $32,000 on the deal.

The purchase of these concerns was obviously to decrease competition in the repeating-rifle field. No attempt was made by Winchester to manufacture arms under these patents. There must have been some temptation to capitalize on the fame of the Spencer; but the Company had agreed to pay Spencer one dollar per gun manufactured under his patent. This, plus the necessity of operating a separate plant or enlarging facilities at Bridgeport, were sufficient deterrents to such a procedure.

With the elimination of the Spencer concern, Winchester was in a dominant position in the field. There were, to be sure, other producers of such arms, but they were small. Rivals subsequently entered the field but, for nearly a decade, the Company had a chance to get a head start and establish its reputation firmly as a producer of repeating rifles.

*Shift of Plant Back to New Haven*

In 1870 the management began to consider the advisability of moving the plant from Bridgeport back to New Haven into a new building to be constructed. For some three years manufacturing had been carried on in Bridgeport, while the business office and a warehouse had been maintained in New Haven. The attractions of a new structure located in New Haven especially designed for gun and ammunition production and in an area where facilities could be readily expanded, were strong. A further consideration was that Winchester personally owned land in New Haven which could be used for the site of a new building.[19]

At the annual stockholders' meeting held in February 1870, the secretary reported that "... after a discussion of the building of a new armory in New Haven, without any definite action, the meeting was adjourned." During the next few months this question must have been discussed at some length, with Wheeler and Wilson, who owned the building being used at Bridgeport, objecting. The decision went against them, with the result that they sold their stock and resigned from the board of directors. The decision was formalized at the directors' meeting in August 1870, at which time authorization was given for the purchase of a tract of land from Winchester for $12,000 and the construction of a building not to cost over $80,000.

The new armory, a two-story brick building with a basement, was constructed at the corner of Munson Street and Canal Street (later changed to Winchester Avenue) and became the nucleus of the large expanse of buildings that was subsequently built for the Company. Its floor space of nearly 103,000 square feet was sufficient to take care of expanding operations for over a decade. Ready for occupancy early in 1871, the equipment and machinery were moved from Bridgeport in April of the same year. This shift came at a time when the Company was engaged in filling the Turkish contracts. The shops were running a double shift, twenty-four hours a day and, in order to avoid delay, work was continued on the machines at Bridgeport until the horse-drawn drays were at the door to take them to the railroad station.

### *Financial Results and Summary*

By the end of 1872 it was evident that the management of the Winchester Repeating Arms Company had been successful in conducting the business through the immediate post-Civil War period. Since April 1, 1867, the net worth of the Company had been increased by some $727,105, and now stood at $1,177,105.35. (*See Appendix G-3.*) Of this increase, all but $50,000, which represented new capital, came from profits.[20]

There had been some changes among personnel of the board of directors. Wheeler and Wilson had been replaced during 1870-71 by Cornelius Bushnell who, according to Veader and Earle ". . . will be remembered as one of those interested in the development of the *Monitor* of Civil War fame, which was designed by Ericsson," and Jeremiah Bishop who was president of the Yale National Bank of New Haven. In 1872, R. K. Davies was elected to replace his father who had died the year before.

Meanwhile the officers of the corporation had taken on a family complexion. William Wirt Winchester, Oliver Winchester's son, was elected secretary in 1869 and held that position until 1871, when he was made vice president. He was succeeded as secretary in 1871 by Thomas Gray Bennett, who married Hannah Jane Winchester, William Wirt's younger sister, in 1872. Oliver Winchester continued to hold the combined office of president and treasurer during this period. These moves put the immediate direction of the Company under the control of the family with Oliver Winchester remaining the dominant personality.

At their annual meeting held April 4, 1871, the stockholders of the Winchester Repeating Arms Company adopted the following resolution:

> *Whereas:* O. F. Winchester, President and Founder of the company has for fifteen years displayed the most untiring perseverance and under every discouraging circumstance imaginable, by consummate financial skill and inventive genius has succeeded in perfecting the most perfect arm in the world, which the last war in Europe has so favorably tested, and the very handsome financial returns to the stockholders enables us fully to appreciate, therefore
>
> *Resolved* that the thanks of the stockholders are most heartily tendered Mr. Winchester with the hope that he may live long to enjoy the fruits of his well earned success.

At the directors' meeting held in March 1872, a more tangible recognition of Winchester's services was made when his salary as president and treasurer was increased from $5,000 to $10,000.

This tribute and the increased salary were on the whole well deserved. Because of Winchester's tight control over the management of the Company during these years, it was appropriate that he should receive credit for bringing the concern through the immediate post-Civil War adjustment. Not only had the

Company survived a period when the casualty rate among arms producers was high but its competitive and financial position had been strengthened as well. It was well prepared to continue its drive toward leadership in the arms and ammunition industry. According to Felicia Deyrup in *Gunmakers of the Connecticut Valley,* some twenty-five New England firms manufacturing firearms had disappeared between 1865 and 1870. It may be noted, however, that eight newcomers started during the same period.[21]

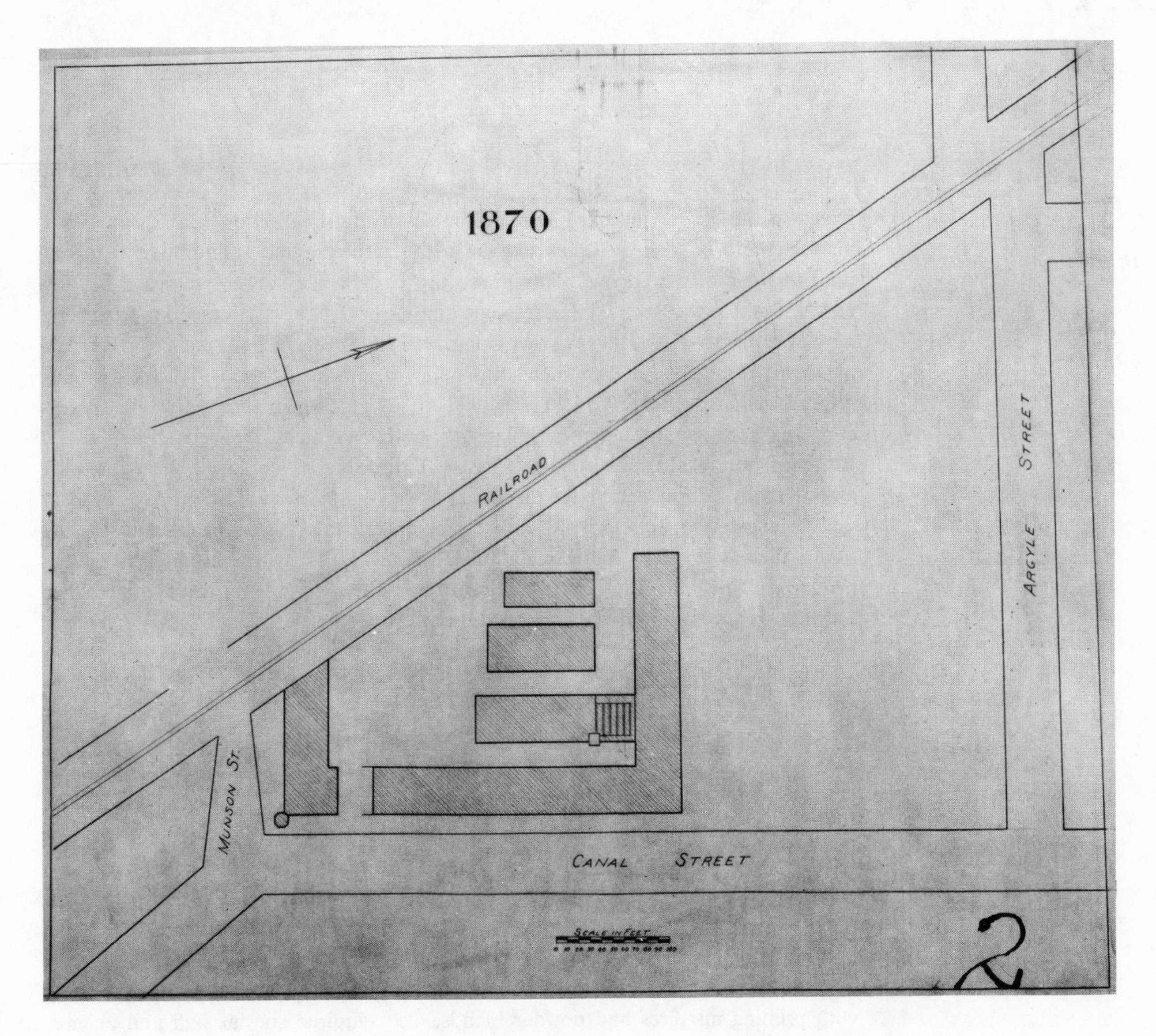


*Plant of Winchester Repeating Arms Company in 1870*

CHAPTER SIX

# DIVERSIFICATION AND EXPANSION

*Specialization in Ammunition Production*

Down to the end of the Civil War a number of the firearms producers had either manufactured or closely supervised the manufacture of the ammunition that was used in their own weapons. This procedure had been followed, for example, by Colt's, Smith & Wesson, Spencer Repeating Rifle Company, Volcanic Repeating Arms Company, New Haven Arms Company, and others. The Winchester Repeating Arms Company had continued this policy in producing the caliber .44 ammunition used in the Henry and the Model 66. Beginning in the late 1850s, a few concerns, such as Crittenden & Tibbals of South Coventry, Connecticut, and C. D. Leete of Springfield, Massachusetts, were established solely to produce metallic ammunition, although the latter firm was closely associated with Smith & Wesson.

The growing popularity of breech-loading pistols and rifles after 1865 led to an increased demand for metallic ammunition. Many of the breech-loaders produced during the Civil War had been manufactured by companies that either did not produce ammunition or had subsequently gone out of business. There had been an extensive conversion of muzzle-loading arms to breech-loaders using metallic cartridges. This combination of circumstances presented an opportunity for ammunition manufacturers to expand their line to include a sufficient variety of cartridges to meet the needs of the owners of these many kinds of weapons.

Several forces subsequently tended to concentrate ammunition manufacture in the hands of a few companies. The mechanical processes involved in making ammunition were comparatively simple, but the machines which performed the various steps were expensive and complex to construct. In contrast to the equipment used in gun production which was generally standardized and usually supplied by machine-tool concerns, the ammunition companies ordinarily designed and built their own special-purpose machines.

To maintain production control and improve the product by experimenting with priming mixtures and powder blends, also required special skill and eventually led to the establishment of chemical and ballistics laboratories. Another factor that favored the larger concerns was the necessity for special facilities to handle the dangerous fulminate and powder and to store the ammunition after it was manufactured.

Once installed, the machinery and equipment could be tended by relatively unskilled workers and were capable of turning out enormous quantities of cartridges and shells.[1] Indeed, in order to cover the capital investment it was necessary

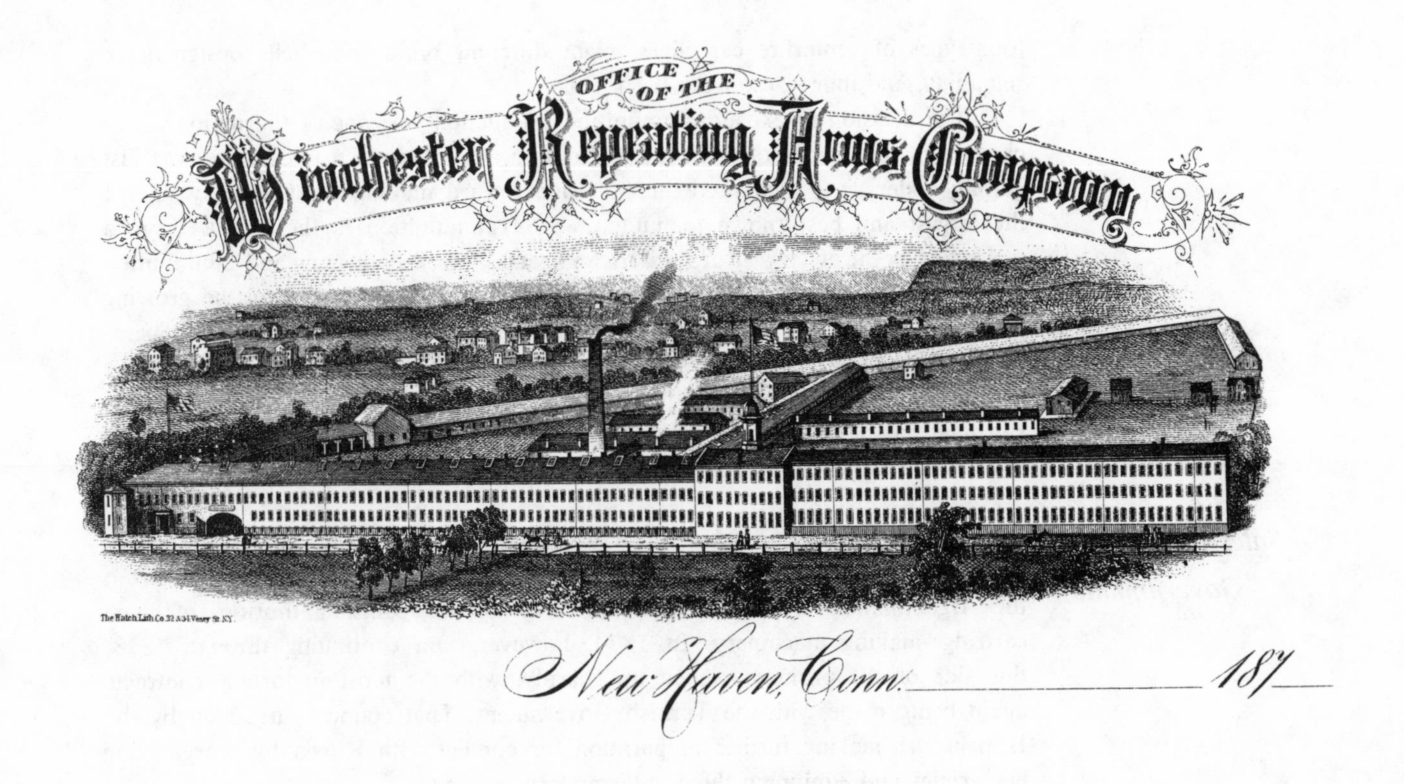


*Letterhead of Winchester Repeating Arms Company in 1870s*

to turn out large amounts. At the same time the demand for ammunition was fairly inelastic and price cuts were likely to lead to ruinous competition. For this reason the leading companies in the industry, rather early, agreed to insure a more orderly marketing of ammunition.

*Expansion of Ammunition Manufacture*

The Winchester Repeating Arms Company announced in its catalog for 1873 that it was ". . . prepared to manufacture 250,000 cartridges per day, embracing every size and description of a quality superior to anything heretofore offered."

This announcement coincided with the introduction of a new rifle (the Model 73) using centerfire ammunition. The new gun forced the management to decide whether to let outsiders supply the ammunition for it or to add the manufacture of centerfire cartridges to the rimfire cartridges already being produced for the Model 66. The decision to manufacture would involve an additional investment in equipment that could be expanded fairly easily to produce ammunition for other types of breech-loading weapons as well.

Having had considerable experience already in manufacturing metallic ammunition and attracted by the financial opportunities in the field, it was decided to expand. By 1875, two years after its original announcement, cartridge capacity had been stepped up to a million a day. (As stated in the catalog for 1875; this capacity was built up in part, at least, to take care of the large ammunition contracts filled for the Turkish Government beginning in 1874.) By this date the Company carried in stock some twenty-five varieties of rimfire cartridges, twenty-four types of centerfire cartridges, eight different brass shot-shells designed for reloading, and four sizes of paper shot-shells.

The decision to expand ammunition production was one of the major policy changes in the history of Winchester. Coming at a time when integration was just getting under way, it marked the first step toward making the Company one of the largest and best-known manufacturers of ammunition in the world. From a marketing point of view it proved advantageous to sell both guns and ammunition under the same trade mark and Winchester was able to capitalize on the growing popularity of its repeating rifles. Finally the decision served to diversify operations, making the Company less dependent upon gun sales for its principal source of income. This not only proved to be an important element in the concern's long-run financial success, but paid immediate dividends in connection with the revival of contracts with foreign governments.

*Sales to Foreign Governments*

The lull in foreign sales which had come in 1872 continued during 1873, although there is a record in the latter year of an order for 500,000 shells from the Argentine Government and the delivery to the Spanish authorities of some cartridge-making machinery. In 1874, however, and continuing through 1878, this side of the business picked up sharply, with the most important contracts again being made with the Turkish Government. That country, urged on by the British, was making further preparation for conflict with Russia by reorganizing her armies and equipping them with modern weapons.

At the outbreak of war in 1879 it was reported: ". . . In the [Turkish] arsenals and in the hands of the troops there were 334,000 Martini (Peabody) rifles; 323,000 Snider rifles; and 39,000 Winchester Repeating rifles." [2]

The inventory of the Snider and Martini-Peabody rifles shows clearly the British influence. The American Civil War and the Prussian-Danish conflict of 1864 had demonstrated the superiority of the breech-loader over the muzzle-loader. As a consequence, the British in 1866 began to convert the Enfield muzzle-loading rifles into single-shot breech-loaders using the Snider mechanism.

Some five years later the British, after extensive tests, made an official adoption of the single-shot, breech-loading Martini-Henry as a military weapon. The basic action was the same as that used in the Peabody rifle, invented by Henry L. Peabody, of Boston, in July 1862. Frederick Martini, a Swiss inventor, modified the action by substituting a spiral spring to operate the firing pin, in place of an ordinary side lock, and gave the arm the name Martini-Peabody. Alexander Henry, a Scottish gunsmith, combined this action with a barrel rifled according to a theory he had developed and received a British patent for the Martini-Henry in 1865. The Peabody action was unusually strong and could handle heavy military loads effectively. It also stood up well in the field and could stand rough usage and abuse without loss of efficiency.

After the British adopted the Martini-Henry, they apparently sold a large number of their Snider rifles to the Turks, at the same time recommending that the Turks also adopt the Martini-Henry or Martini-Peabody rifle, which recommendation was followed.

Winchester played an important, if indirect, role in supplying these firearms to the Turks. In 1872, Oliver Winchester, who had been in Constantinople in connection with the contracts earlier mentioned, brought back an agreement to supply the Ottoman government with 200,000 Martini-Henry rifles. The contract was sold, in August 1872, to the Providence Tool Company, of Providence, Rhode Island, which had purchased the original Peabody patent in 1864, and had been engaged in producing rifles under it since that date.[3]

It is noteworthy that Oliver Winchester should have brought back a contract for Martini-Peabody rifles instead of Winchester repeating arms, for it may be assumed that he made a vigorous attempt to sell more of his own company's rifles. How much influence the British had on the choice of arms and how much the experience of the Turks with the Winchester repeaters was an influence, is difficult to say.

Whatever may have been Oliver Winchester's disappointment at not receiving an arms contract, it must have been largely assuaged by the contracts received from the Turks for ammunition. The first of these, signed in May 1874, called for 87.5 million Martini shells (primed, empty cartridge cases) and bullets. In April 1875, this order was followed by an additional 112.5 million. During 1876 and 1877, the Company also supplied the Ottoman government with 80.1 million loaded Snider cartridges.

There were two major reasons for the order of Martini cartridge components instead of completed cartridges; one was that the Turks were short of funds to make extensive foreign purchases, the other was they had a powder plant and cartridge-loading equipment but no machinery to make cartridge cases and were low on supplies of lead. They therefore bought the empty cases and bullets and loaded them with their own powder. Just why the exception was made in the case of the Snider cartridges is not clear.

There are no details in regard to prices and total amounts involved in these ammunition contracts, but it has been stated that the profits from this group of contracts came to about $1.5 million. Nor was this all; sometime during 1878 and 1879 there were "large sales" of the Model 73 musket to the Chinese Government plus "millions of cartridges," but there are no records which could be found of the totals involved.

These profits, added to those already realized on the earlier Turkish contracts, were sufficient to put the Company in a strong financial position. Winchester now had ample resources to push ahead with its program of further diversification and its drive toward leadership in both the arms and ammunition fields.

From this time on, however, expansion was to be in the nonmilitary field, because the year 1878 marked the end of an era. For the next thirty-six years, except for a brief interval during the Spanish-American War, governmental purchases were to play a relatively minor part in the Company's business. While the implications for the future were probably not fully realized at the time, this change was recorded in the treasurer's report to the board of directors on January 22, 1879. According to this report, total sales for 1878 were $1,319,828, a decrease of $1,482,736 over the eleven months ending December 31, 1877. This, it was explained, was attributable ". . . to the fact that all our foreign contracts were completed during the first part of the year 1878, since which time we have depended on our domestic trade which is constantly increasing against a strong and growing competition." Oliver Winchester did not give up his attempts to get an official adoption by the United States Government, but more and more attention was directed toward the promotion of the nonmilitary markets.

## *Centerfire Cartridges and the Model 73*

The Company's position in the nonmilitary market was considerably strengthened by the development of a new-model rifle, the Winchester 73, designed to use a centerfire cartridge.

The rimfire cartridge, which was used so successfully in the Henry and the Model 66, was limited to relatively weak loads of powder and comparatively lightweight bullets. These limitations, which still apply, came from the construction of the rimfire cartridge and from the action of the priming mixture. Rimfire cartridges must be made of thin metal or the firing pin cannot indent the head and explode the primer. This thin-walled cartridge case limits the pressure developed by the powder charge and consequently the weight of the bullet. If too much powder is used, there is a danger that the cartridge case will burst at the folded rim when it is fired, and that the primer flash, passing laterally across the rear of the powder charge, will not ignite a large load sufficiently to consume all of the powder before the bullet leaves the cartridge case.

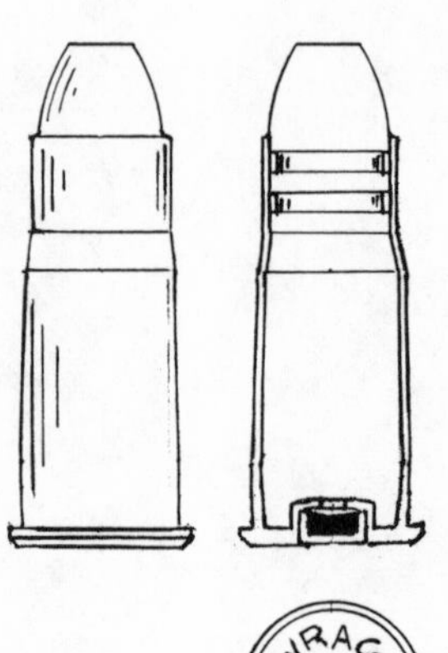

*.44-40 (.44 WCF) Centerfire Cartridge*

These limitations were overcome with the development of the centerfire cartridge, made with a solid or reinforced head and with a separate primer cap inserted, which is exploded by the action of the hammer striking the center of the cartridge head. In this type of shell only the primer cup needs to be of copper, and the case can be made of brass which is much stronger and can be loaded with a much larger charge of powder and heavier bullet. The stronger head also makes it possible to use more powerful priming mixtures, which, because the flame shoots forward parallel with the length of the cartridge case, insures a more complete burning of the powder. Misfires are less likely than with the rimfire variety. Finally, the fact that the centerfire cartridges, unlike rimfire, can be reloaded, has always been of special interest to shooters.

The idea of a centerfire cartridge was as old if not older than the rimfire, but the design of the head and primer caps presented more difficult problems of construction and manufacture than were involved in the rimfire. For these reasons, their development was delayed until after the rimfire had become rather widely used, but by 1870 the centerfire cartridge had been perfected sufficiently to be used increasingly both in rifles and pistols.

Because the rimfire cartridges are less expensive to manufacture they have continued to be popular for short-range shooting, especially in the caliber .22, but for long-range, high-velocity purposes, they have been completely superseded by the centerfire type.

The advent of centerfire ammunition threatened to make the Model 66 obsolete. The caliber .44 cartridge used in this gun carried a powder charge of 28 grains and a bullet weighing 200 grains. It had been a great advance over the Volcanic firearm it had replaced, but there was an obvious need for a gun that could handle a more powerful centerfire cartridge.

After considerable experimentation with various loads and adaptations of the repeating mechanism, the Winchester Repeating Arms Company introduced a new model rifle in 1873. First announced as the "New Model of 1873" the gun became more commonly known as the Model 73. In general appearance this rifle was quite similar to the Model 66. The toggle-link repeating action was the same, except that the firing pin was changed to handle a centerfire cartridge. The gun also had a slide cover over the carrier block, which protected the mechanism from dirt and moisture. The frame, butt plate, and certain other parts of the Model 73 were made of iron instead of gun metal or brass. This reduced the weight (and probably the cost) and increased the strength of the arm. Finally, the firing pin was carried back by a positive action instead of by a spring, which reduced the danger of accidental firing.

The ammunition brought out by the Company to use in the Model 73 rifle was the famous "forty-four-forty cartridge," so named because of the .44-caliber bullet and the 40-grain powder charge of the cartridge. The weight of the bullet, 200 grains, was the same as the caliber .44 rimfire used in the Model 66, but the larger powder charge (the older cartridge having 28 grains) made the Model 73 a more powerful and longer-ranged weapon than the Model 66.

The Model 73 (and its ammunition) was ". . . the rifle that put the name Winchester on the map of the West, trotting along with the equally formidable Colt gun at the belt of the frontiersman. It killed more game and more Indians, and more United States soldiers when the Indians awoke to its virtues, than any other type rifle." [4]

The reasons for this popularity came from the rapidity of fire, the rugged construction, and reliability in all kinds of weather. These qualities made it an ideal arm for short-range hunting and the kind of mobile warfare that was typical of Indian-white man fighting. The construction of the gun with no protuberances, such as a bolt, made the Model 73 carbine with its short barrel an ideal saddle gun, and paired with the Colt's revolver, it became one of the two favorite weapons of the Western pioneers. This association was strengthened when Colt's, in 1878, brought out its famous single-action Frontier Model caliber .44 revolver, chambered for the same ammunition used in the Model 73. A frontiersman could now carry one or more revolvers and a rifle that would all take identical cartridges. The Winchester 73 and Colt's revolvers were later produced in calibers .38 and .32 using interchangeable ammunition.

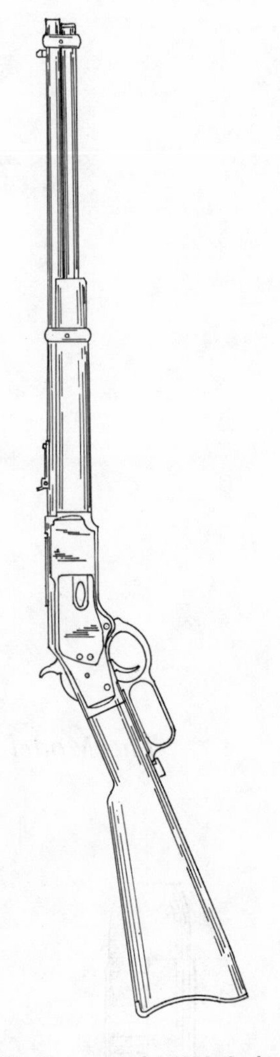
*Winchester Model 1873 Carbine*

Among those who were prompted to write to the Company regarding the Model 73 was Colonel W. F. (Buffalo Bill) Cody, whose letter, written from Fort McPherson, Nebraska, appeared in the Company's catalog for 1875:

> I have been using and have thoroughly tested your latest improved rifle. Allow me to say that I have tried and used nearly every kind of a gun made in the United States, and for general hunting, or Indian fighting, I pronounce your improved Winchester *the boss.*
>
> An Indian will give more for one of your guns than any other gun he can get.
>
> While in the Black Hills this last summer I crippled a bear, and Mr. Bear made for me, and I am certain had I not been armed with one of your repeating rifles I would now be in the happy hunting grounds. The bear was not thirty feet from me when he charged, but before he could reach me I had eleven bullets in him, which was a little more lead than he could comfortably digest.
>
> Believe me, that you have the *most complete* rifle now made.

Even some of the British authors, who in general tended to favor the products of their own gunmakers, were impressed by the Winchester rifle. An English writer, John Mortimer Murphy, in his *Sporting Adventures in the Far West,* published in 1879, stated: ". . . A capital weapon for general shooting on horseback is the latest model of the Winchester or the Sharps rifle, the former being especially convenient owing to its magazine and the rapidity with which it can be fired."

The same author, in discussing the hunting of bighorn or mountain sheep, said: "The best weapon that I ever used against them was a Winchester magazine rifle, as it enabled me to fire in rapid succession and its charge of powder, which might be considered too small for larger game was strong enough to send a bullet crashing through the body of a bighorn at a distance of three or more hundred yards."

The popularity of the Model 73 was not confined to the American West. Major Ned H. Roberts speaks of a trip to the Hudson Bay country in the late 1880s where ". . . I found the great majority of hunters and trappers—whites, Indians, and half breeds—using the 44-40 Winchester Model 1873, with which they killed all kinds of big game. The 44-40 cartridges were then practically the only ones you could be sure of finding at every Hudson Bay trading post in that country." [5]

Until 1879, when a caliber .38 was put on the market, the Model 73 was produced in caliber .44 only. It was available in several styles, however, including sporting rifle, special sporting rifle, carbine and musket, the last being fitted with an angular or saber bayonet. Barrel lengths ranged from 20 inches on the carbine to 30 inches on the musket. These came in round, octagon and half-octagon shapes.

*The Model 76*

The principal appeal of the Model 73 came from its repeating action which, in the case of the sporting rifle, enabled a shooter to fire sixteen cartridges in rapid succession without reloading. But it was a short-range weapon and was not effective against big game or for combat beyond a distance of 150 to 200 yards.

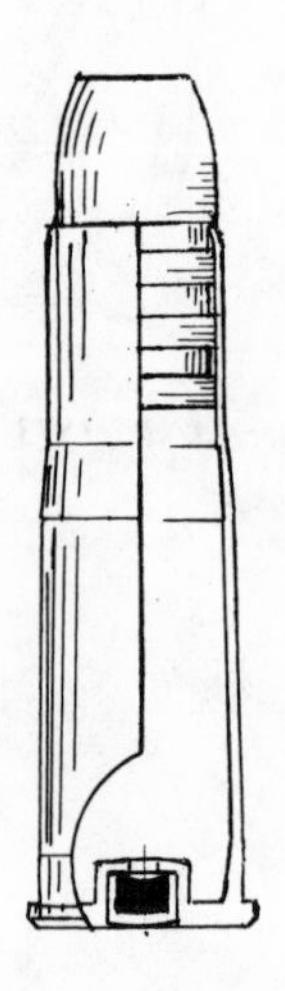

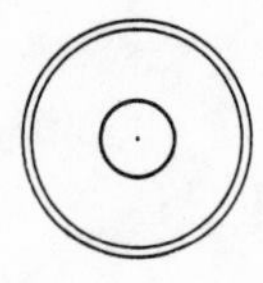

*.45-75 Centerfire Cartridge*

Meanwhile, centerfire cartridges were being manufactured which, used in single-shot breech-loaders, were effective over ranges of a thousand yards or more. Of these new loads, the United States Government cartridge, the .45-70 centerfire, introduced in 1873, became especially popular. This cartridge, with a powder charge of 70 grains and a bullet weighing 405 grains, was effective up to distances in excess of 600 yards, and became a yardstick by which the performance of rifles was judged. For example, the editors of *Field and Stream,* in June 1875, advised a correspondent who lived in Grass Valley, California: "For your country the improved Winchester, the Model 73, is an excellent arm. Where long range shooting is desired, say up to 1,000 yards, we would suggest the single shot Remington, Sharps, or Whitney."

For two reasons Winchester was eager to produce a repeating rifle that used this higher-powered Government ammunition. First, it might be possible to obtain a Government adoption. Secondly, it was most desirable to put out a gun that would appeal to shooters who were interested in longer-range performance than the Model 73 provided.

The difficulty faced by the Company lay in adapting the repeating mechanism of the Model 73 to handle heavier and longer ammunition. The .45-70 Government cartridge was almost two and three-quarters inches long, about twice the length of the .44-40 cartridge used in the Model 73. To have made the receiver and the other parts large enough and strong enough for this improved ammunition would have made the arm too heavy to carry conveniently. Furthermore, the toggle-link action was not rugged enough to stand the strain of firing the 405-grain bullet.

Within these limitations, the Company brought out the Model 76, sometimes referred to as the "Winchester Centennial Model," because it was first exhibited at the Philadelphia Centennial Exposition held in the summer of 1876. Basically the same as the Model 73, the various parts were made heavier and stronger to use a heavier ammunition. In announcing this gun to the trade the Company made the following statement in its catalog for 1878: "The constant calls from many sources, and particularly from the regions in which the grizzly bear and other large game are found, as well as the plains where the absence of cover and shyness of some require the hunter to make his shots at long range, made it desirable for the Company to build a still more powerful gun than the Model 73."

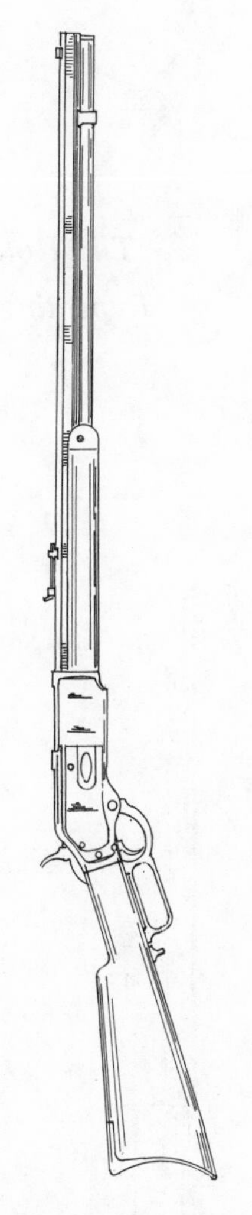

*Winchester Model 1876 Rifle*

The ammunition used in this gun was the .45-75 Winchester centerfire cartridge which had a powder charge of 75 grains and a bullet weighing 350 grains. This was as close to the Government .45-70 cartridge as it was possible to come and still be used in the rifle. The powder load was in fact five grains larger than the Government cartridge although the bullet was not as heavy.

The Model 76 won a considerable number of enthusiastic users, and was an early favorite of Teddy Roosevelt. (*See Chapter Sixteen.*) It was adopted in the carbine style by the Royal Canadian Northwest Mounted Police and remained their official weapon until 1914. Ned Roberts, in the article previously quoted, tells of borrowing one of these carbines from the Mounties, ". . . and with it I shot caribou, wolves, and several moose. It had good killing power at moderate ranges, especially with the hollow point bullet. The accuracy was fair, averaging about 5-inch groups at 100 yards and 10-inch at 200. The gun was very reliable, functioned properly in the extreme cold, and I never knew of one to freeze or jam if correctly handled."

While the Model 76 had some measure of success it never became a popular gun. The basic difficulty was the limitations of the toggle-link repeating action invented by Smith & Wesson over twenty years before.

With one exception, since the formation of the Winchester Repeating Arms Company in 1867, the organization had not had in its employ a gun designer of the stature of Daniel Wesson or B. Tyler Henry. If the Company was to maintain its position as the leader in the production of repeating rifles, it would be necessary to obtain the services of someone capable of developing an improved type of repeating action. The situation was by no means critical, as both gun and ammunition sales were large and profitable, but the management was alert to the desirability of getting an improved repeating mechanism.

## *The Borchardt Revolvers*

The one gun designer employed by the Company during this period who might have replaced Henry or Wesson was Hugo Borchardt. Borchardt, a German immigrant, apparently started to work for Winchester during the early 1870s. He was principally interested in revolvers and by 1876 had developed some five different models. (These models are now in the Winchester Museum.) These caliber .44 revolvers, in contrast to the solid frame or break-open type generally used at the time, were similar in design to the modern swing-out cylinder revolvers.

The Company was interested enough in their possibilities to submit samples to the Bureau of Ordnance of the U. S. Navy and to the Russian Ordnance Department. No orders were received from either source and the revolver was not put into production. Borchardt, possibly discouraged by this turn of events, left Winchester for the Sharps Rifle Company, which brought out the famous Sharps-Borchardt model in 1877. Some ten years later he returned to Germany, where, working in Loewe's factory, he produced the well-known Borchardt automatic pistol, the forerunner of the later German Luger.

*The Hotchkiss Repeating Rifle*

One of the rifles displayed at the Philadelphia Centennial Exposition in 1876 appeared to offer an answer to Winchester's problem of producing a firearm that would be acceptable both as a long-range sporting rifle and for military use. This rifle was the invention of B. B. Hotchkiss, an American who was living in Paris. It was a repeating rifle with a tubular magazine in the butt stock and used a bolt action that was much stronger than the toggle-link system. Noting the favorable attention this gun received from the military men who attended the Exposition, Winchester bought the rights to manufacture the arm in 1877.

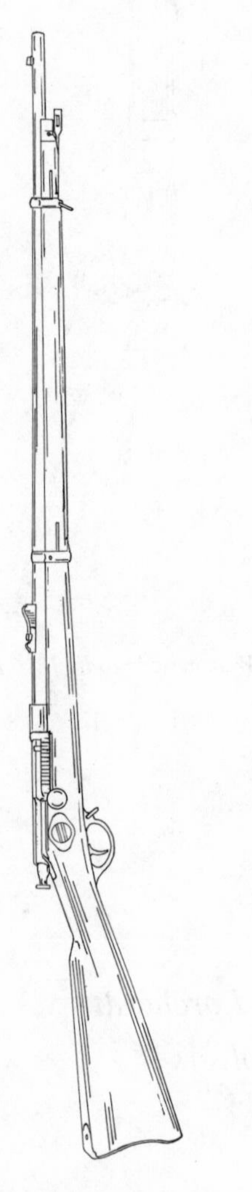

*Hotchkiss Rifle, First Type*

Almost immediately the Company had an opportunity to submit the Hotchkiss for consideration by the Government. In 1877 Congress appropriated $20,000 for testing a repeating rifle. Trials began in April 1878, and Winchester made up several Hotchkiss rifles which were entered in competition with some twenty-eight repeating firearms.[6] The Hotchkiss was awarded first place and the Board recommended that the $20,000 appropriated by Congress be expended on one hundred Hotchkiss rifles which were to be tried out in the field in the hands of troops.

Oliver Winchester's long-sought goal of official adoption by the U. S. military authorities seemed about to be realized. The order was made up by the Company in cooperation with Springfield Armory in 1879 and the guns delivered for use by the troops.

The results were disappointing. As reported by Brigadier General S. V. Benét, in 1880: "The Hotchkiss has met with reverses, due to hasty manufacture and imperfect design in some of its minor parts, which can hardly be charged to the invention. It is believed that these defects, in which the mechanical principles of the invention were not involved, have been corrected in the new model, and more favorable results may now be anticipated. The manufacturer's experience with this gun proves that difficulties are ever to be met and overcome in perfecting a new invention that has to stand the severe test of field service. As a rule, a first-rate military arm must be of gradual growth; and be finally made up of successive improvements rendered necessary to correct defects developed in the hands of the soldier. The principle of the Hotchkiss is a good one, but there seems to be some prejudice existing in our service against the bolt system and its awkward handle that time and custom may overcome." [7]

The Company still faced the problem of developing acceptable firearms that could handle heavier ammunition than its current models. This episode marked the final attempt by Oliver Winchester, personally, to secure a Government adoption. The Hotchkiss was again considered for military use by the United States authorities, but subsequent tests of the arm came after Winchester's death in 1880.

Winchester's interest in a military adoption had grown out of his observations during the Civil War which had convinced him of the superiority of a repeating rifle over the single-shot as a military weapon. While he undoubtedly aroused interest in the repeating military rifle, it is quite possible that his preoccupation with obtaining a military adoption prevented an early appreciation of the possibilities of promoting the nonmilitary market.

## *Promotion of Domestic and Nonmilitary Markets*

The belated recognition of the importance of the domestic and nonmilitary demand and the extent to which its guns had sold themselves, is contained in a statement in the Company's catalog for 1875:

> One hundred and fifty thousand have been sold without advertising or puffing, and they have everywhere given unqualified satisfaction, having earned their position solely by their merits.
>
> It has become a household word, and a household necessity on our western plains and mountains.
>
> The pioneer, the hunter and trapper, believe in the Winchester, and its possession is a passion with every Indian.
>
> They have found their way to every country in the world. In the armament of the explorer in the wilds of Africa, and other countries, they are sure to have a place.

This catalog for 1875 gives further evidence of a change in policy. The extensive material on the Swiss tests of the Model 66 and Winchester's various memoranda to United States Government officials were dropped. A number of testimonials regarding the effectiveness of the Henry during the Civil War were retained but for the first time the nonmilitary advantages of the Winchester rifles were stressed. Some twenty pages were devoted to letters from the users of the Model 66 and the Model 73, who told of their satisfaction with these arms for hunting and Indian-fighting.

For the many shooters who, for reasons of economy or a liking for a particular combination of powder and bullet, preferred to load or reload their own cartridges, the Company listed a handloading tool. According to the catalog description, the device ". . . removes the exploded primer, inserts the new primer, and fastens the ball in the shell, at the same time swaging and shaping the entire cartridge to exact form and with absolute safety." The Company also sold primers to be used for reloading and machine-swaged bullets to those who preferred them over the hand-molded type.

The catalog for 1875 also listed "Extras" for the Model 73 rifle, including set triggers, special sights, fancy stocks, engraving, nickel, silver or gold trimming and the like, which could be had by paying an additional price.

During the succeeding six-year period, the Company expanded its offerings to the domestic and nonmilitary markets. Interestingly enough, the use of testimonials in the catalog was dropped in 1876, but more information was included of special interest to shooters. Specific recommendations as to the correct powders to use in reloading cartridges appeared in the catalog for 1878. The lists of ammunition carried in stock were expanded and increasing attention called to the desirability of using Winchester ammunition with Winchester guns.

## *"One of One Thousand"*

A most interesting sales promotion plan, introduced in 1875, made a special appeal to the shooters who wanted a premium gun. The Company explained the offer as follows:

> It is the purpose of the manufacturers of these arms to introduce a greater variety than has heretofore been made, to meet the different purposes and uses to which they are applicable, whether for sporting or war. Among these, the demands of the amateur sportsman are the most exacting, for an arm that will shoot with unerring accuracy.
>
> With the perfect machinery and great skill of the men we employ in boring, rifling, straightening, polishing and finishing our barrels, we can always count with confidence

upon any barrel shooting with accuracy; but in this as in all other cases, the degree of accuracy will vary. The barrel of every sporting rifle we make will be proved and shot at a target, and the target will be numbered to correspond with the barrel and be attached to it.

All of those barrels that are found to make targets of extra merit will be made up into guns with set-triggers and extra finish, and marked as a designating name 'one of one thousand', and sold at $100. The next grade of barrels not quite so fine, will be marked 'one in a hundred', and set up to order and style at $20 advance over the list price of the corresponding style of gun as shown in price-list.

In practice their rifles were first marked "1 of 1000" or "1 of 100" and later in script "One of One Thousand" or "One of One Hundred."

Company records show that 136 "One of One Thousand" Model 73 rifles and 47 Model 76 rifles were distributed between 1877 and 1900. During the same period 7 "One of One Hundred" Model 76 rifles were sold. The offer was dropped from the Company's catalog in 1878. This was probably because the management decided that it was not good sales policy to suggest that the Company produced different grades of guns.

The "One of One Thousand" variety of the Model 1873 is more famous today than it was when it was introduced, and to collectors of antique firearms is probably the most valuable of all American shoulder arms. Many are valued by their owners up to $5,000 and individual rifles have been sold for $2,500. The "One of One Thousand" owes its current fame to a nationwide search conducted in 1950 by W. H. Depperman to determine how many of the rare variety were still in existence. At that time factory records disclosed that out of 720,610 Model 1873s manufactured, 124 were of the "One of One Thousand" variety. By 1952 it was established that 136 rifles had been manufactured and owners of 36 were located. The rifle's sudden leap from obscurity to fame was due to its rarity and Winchester's historic association with the early West. With 100 of these rare rifles still to be found, collectors have the lure of a windfall if they locate one of them. So well established has the "One of One Thousand" now become that, as a result of requests from school children, the Wells Fargo Bank and Trust Company of San Francisco felt obliged to add one to its famous collection of historical items relating to the early West in which it played such a significant part.

*Marketing and Price Policies*

The number of Winchester dealers and jobbers was sharply expanded after 1873, and the Company had over 150 domestic and Canadian jobbers on its list by 1880. Such an expansion was consistent with the increased emphasis on the domestic and nonmilitary markets.

There are no data on the nature of trade discounts given to jobbers and dealers during these years beyond a statement in the 1875 catalog that dealers who ordered in case lots, ten guns or 2,000 cartridges, would receive a discount of fifteen per cent. Special terms and prices, not specified, were offered to purchasers of large quantities.

It seems most likely that jobber and dealer relationships during the late 1870s were in a state of flux. The Company was meeting stronger competition and a more complex pattern of jobber and dealer relationships was beginning to emerge.



The period 1873-1881 was marked by a sharp reduction in the list prices

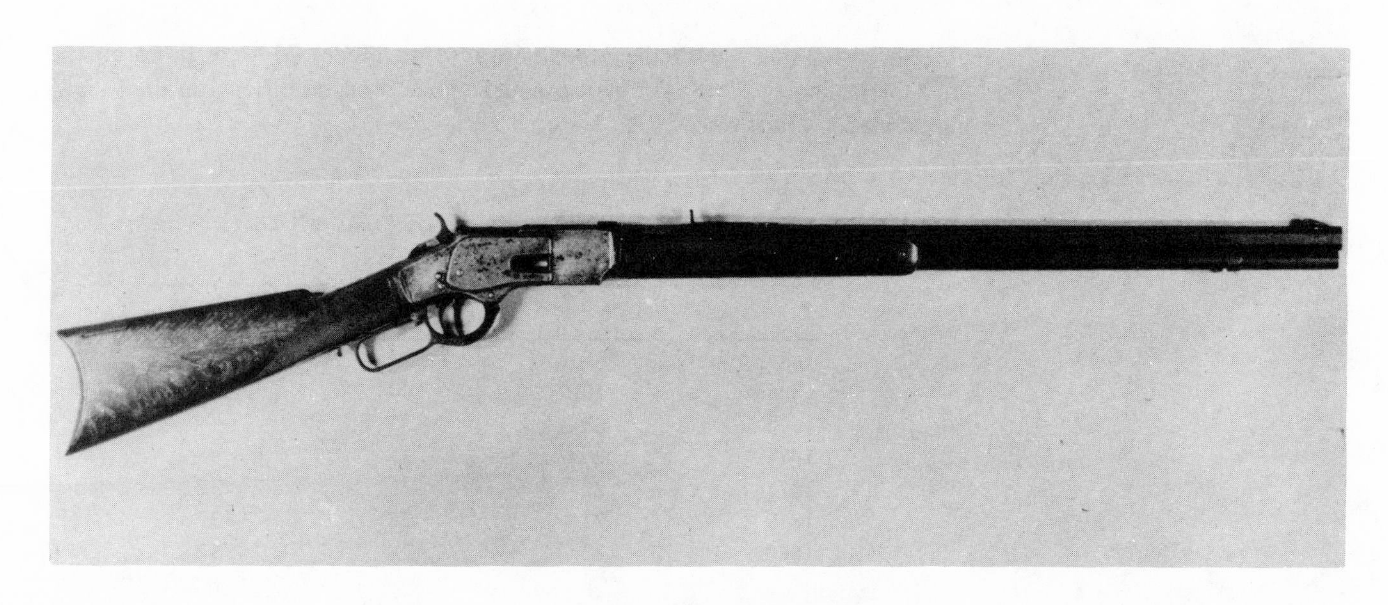

*Winchester Model 1873 Rifle*
*One of One Thousand*

*Engraving on Model 1873 Rifle*
*One of One Thousand*

of Winchester rifles. Both the Model 66 and the Model 73 were listed at $50 until the beginning of 1874. The subsequent price drops are shown in the following tabulation of list prices:

RIFLES (ROUND BARREL, SPORTING MODEL)

| *Year* | *Model 66* | *Model 73* | *Model 76* |
|---|---|---|---|
| 1874 | $45 | $50 | $— |
| 1875 | 28 | 40 | — |
| 1876 | 28 | 35 | — |
| 1877 | 28 | 35 | 40 |
| 1878 | 22 | 25 | 32 |
| 1879 | 22 | 25 | 32 |
| 1880 | 24 | 28 | 32 |

These price reductions were associated with influences affecting the Company and with general conditions of business in the United States. The years 1868 through 1872 had been reasonably prosperous, but 1873 marked the beginning of one of the major depressions in American history which continued until late in 1879.

Sales to the Turkish Government had kept gun sales at fairly high levels between 1870 and 1872. The completion of these contracts, coupled with the onset of the depression, cut gun sales sixty per cent in 1873, and they remained relatively low for the following three years. It was during this period that the first price reductions were made.

In 1877 there was a sudden spurt in gun sales, probably the result of the sales to China mentioned before, but the year following the market began to lag again and on March 18, 1878, minutes of the board of directors note that they met ". . . to consider the advisability of making a large reduction in the prices of arms. After discussing the matter it was voted to leave the whole matter to the board of officers to take such action as in their opinion would be for the best interests of the Company."

The management chose to introduce the second round of price reductions at this point. The Company was apparently able to meet these lowered prices through lowered manufacturing costs.

It is not possible to check on ammunition prices during this period. List prices remained practically unchanged, but there is some evidence that discounts to jobbers and dealers may not only have been increased, but varied considerably from time to time. The first available record is for January 22, 1880, at which time the jobbers' trade discounts from list prices on various types were: rimfire, 60 per cent; centerfire pistol, 20 per cent plus 5 per cent; centerfire sporting, 15 per cent; and .45-60, .45-70, .50-95 Winchester, 20 per cent plus 5 per cent. These discounts, however, should not be taken as typical. The competition among the ammunition manufacturers had led to cut-throat price wars which, by 1881, had brought prices down to the point where the producers were giving serious thought to the formation of a joint marketing association.

*The Adirondack Arms Company*

Winchester purchased one small competitor in 1874, the Adirondack Arms Company of Plattsburg, New York. This concern had been organized sometime in the early 1870s to manufacture repeating rifles. These arms employed a modified bolt action and utilized a tubular magazine under the barrel. (*See Appendix A-3.*) The magazine and trigger guard, shaped like a finger level, gave these rifles a superficial resemblance to the Winchester lever-action guns. The purchase was not important enough to be recorded in the minutes of the board of directors, but must have been in line with a policy of acquiring actual or potential competitors when a favorable opportunity presented itself.[8]

*Relationships with Union Metallic Cartridge Company*

One especially important event that came during the period under consideration was the beginning of a "community of interests" between the Winchester Repeating Arms Company and the Union Metallic Cartridge Company. Their association, which began in connection with the Turkish ammunition contracts, was in many respects a "marriage of convenience" and relationships were not always peaceful, but the association lasted for many years and had a considerable influence on the operations of both concerns.

The leading personality in the Union Metallic Cartridge Company was Marcellus Hartley.[9] By various combines and purchases he had by 1870 made the Union Metallic Cartridge Company the largest firm in the industry.

By its policy adopted in 1873, of supplying the market with all types of ammunition, Winchester came into active competition with the Union Metallic Company. The situation was further complicated by controversies over patent rights covering the design and manufacture of ammunition. The result was a series of claims and counterclaims by both concerns of patent infringements.

These controversies continued until 1873 when, in return for an arrangement entitling it to a share in future Turkish orders, the Union Metallic Cartridge Company entered into an agreement with the Winchester Repeating Arms Company, of which the following were the most important points:

> . . . all claims that either of the said parties for the use of patents in manufacture of metallic cartridges have against each other up to this date are hereby cancelled, and set off one against the other.
>
> . . . each of the parties to this agreement shall in the future be entitled to use the patents of the other so far as they may elect to do so. The royalty or compensation to be paid by each party to the other shall be fixed and determined by a Board of Arbitration.
>
> In case of either party suing or being sued in suits regarding their patents, the expense of such suits is to be borne by the party owning the patent paying two-thirds of said expense, and the other party paying the other third.
>
> This agreement refers only to patent rights now in general use in the manufacture of cartridges, and does not refer to any radically new mode of depositing metal by galvanic process.

According to Veader and Earle this contract was modified in September 1874, by restricting the patent-pooling privileges only to contracts mutually undertaken for the Turkish Government. Even with this modification the contract offered an effective means by which differences between the two companies could be kept out of the courts and a united front could be presented against third-party violators of patents used jointly.

*Picture at Plant Entrance Taken about 1875*

While these objectives were apparently realized, it is doubtful if Marcellus Hartley and Oliver Winchester could have anticipated how difficult it would be to arbitrate the differences that arose over the patents that were used jointly. The sessions, often marked by acrimonious debate, were conducted over a period of ten years until 1883, when the problems were resolved by the formation of a closer association between the two companies.

*Growth of the Company*

Judged by available standards the Company's operation showed a noteworthy expansion during the 1873 1880 period. Employment of the latter date numbered 688 which was nearly three and a half times the figure seven years earlier. (*See Appendix J-1.*) Annual net sales which had averaged approximately $619,000 for the years 1869-1873, were nearly twice that amount in 1880. (*See Appendix F.*)

This expansion had also improved the position of the Company relative to the arms and ammunition industry. (*See Appendix H.*) In 1879, Winchester employed 10 per cent of the industry's total labor force, compared to 8 per cent ten years earlier. The Company's sales had expanded from 4 per cent of the industry total to around 12 per cent during the same period. It is of interest to note that these increased activities were carried on within the factory building that had been constructed in 1870.

The general prosperity of the Company during the period January 1, 1873, through December 31, 1880, is evidenced by a further improvement in its financial strength. Net worth had been increased by $1,767,571, to bring the total over $3,000,000. (*See Appendix G-4.*) [10] More than a million dollars had been invested in real estate, plant, equipment, and patents.

The management continued its earlier policy of distributing a conservative proportion of the total profit in dividends, approximately twenty-seven per cent of the total income being paid out throughout the period. This was equivalent to an average yearly dividend of eight and three-quarters per cent on the capital stock of one million dollars. There was no deflection from a conservative dividend policy even during "good times," a profit of $668,000 in 1878 leading to a dividend of a mere $100,000. (*See Appendix F.*) There is, indeed, evidence that the management was taking a long view of the possibilities for future development. It commenced, in 1878, to invest in outside securities of a "gilt-edged" character, the first security purchased being $200,000 of U. S. Government 4 per cent bonds.

*End of Oliver Winchester's Regime*

Sixty-two years of age in 1873, Oliver Winchester had kept most of his earlier vigor and drive, and remained active in the business during the succeeding seven years. He had given some thought to the training of his successors by bringing his son, William Wirt Winchester, into the management as vice president and by appointing his son-in-law, T. G. Bennett, as secretary. The family character of the management was strengthened in 1878, when William W. Converse, who was married to the sister of Mrs. William Wirt Winchester, was elected treasurer. Converse had been a member of the board of directors since 1875, and had apparently impressed Oliver Winchester sufficiently for the latter to resign as treasurer so that Converse could be given the position. In this connection it may be noted that during 1878 and 1879 Converse received an annual salary of $5,000, whereas William Wirt Winchester was paid $3,500 and T. G. Bennett, $2,500. Early in 1880 all three salaries were raised: Converse's to $7,500, W. W. Winchester's to $4,500 and T. G. Bennett's to $3,500.

In April 1880, Oliver Winchester requested the board of directors, "in view of the present condition of my health and incapacity for taking an active part in the business," to reduce his salary from $10,000 to $5,000 a year. On December 10, 1880, a month after he reached his seventieth birthday, he died at his home on Prospect Street in New Haven.

Winchester's death marked the end of a career in the gun and ammunition business that had extended over a quarter of a century. From virtual bankruptcy in 1860 he had directed the organization through the succeeding years with a firm hand and left to his successors a corporation valued at over three million dollars.

Winchester's career was in the best American tradition. His success was achieved as a business man, and starting with little or no capital he died, leaving a personal fortune amounting to nearly one and a half million dollars.[11]

Probably the most important single quality that contributed to Winchester's success as a business man was his ability to foresee and take advantage of long-run opportunities. His venture with shirt production apparently came at a time when the demand for men's dress shirts was expanding. His early experience with the Volcanic Repeating Arms Company convinced him of the future possibilities of a repeating firearm to the point where he finally gave up his connection with

*William White Converse*

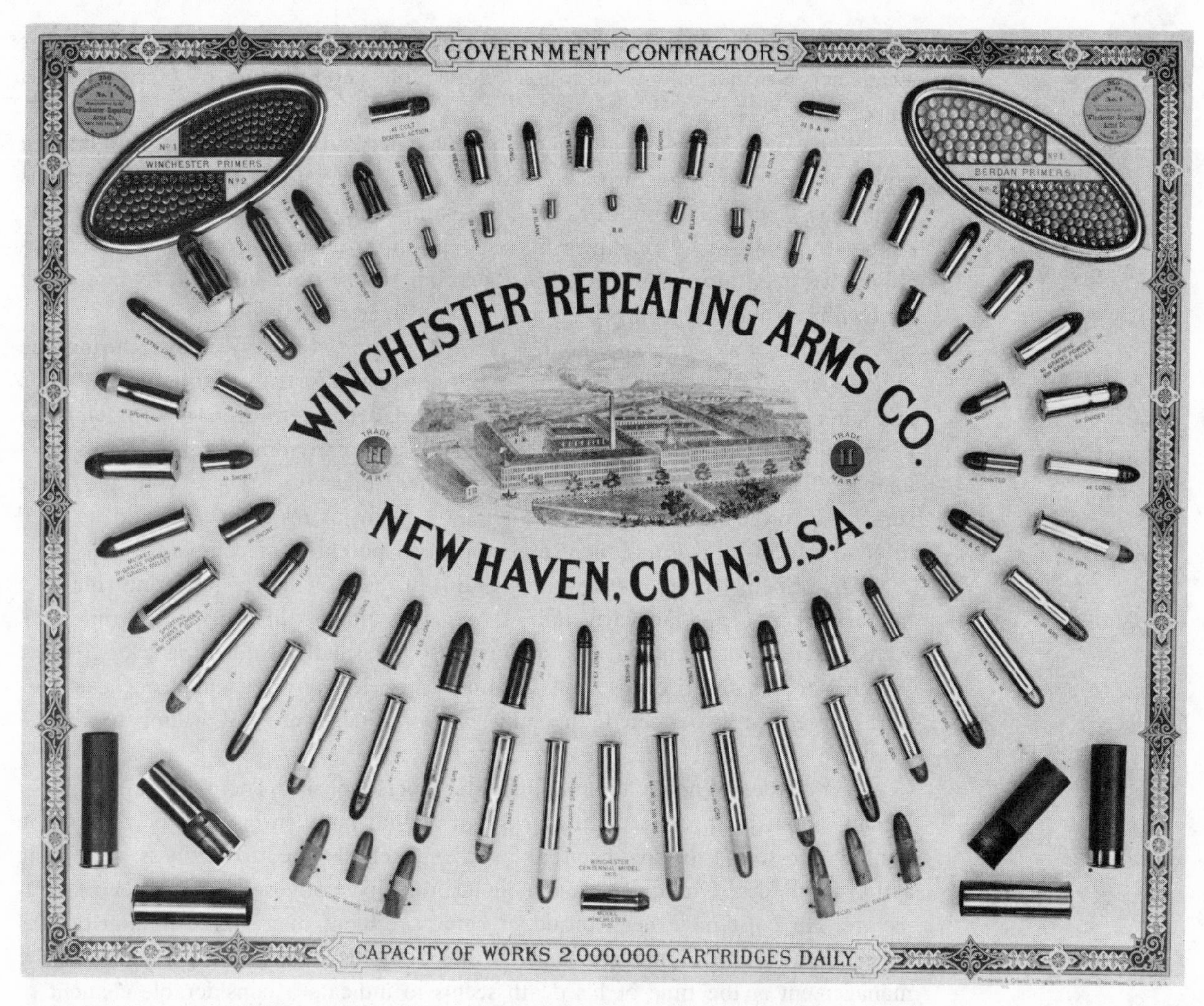


*Winchester Cartridge Board Issued in 1879*

the shirt business and devoted his full time to the promotion of firearms. The decision to expand into ammunition manufacture was an especially significant one that contributed much to the Company's financial success.

Many of Winchester's major policies were undertaken during the depression phases of the business cycle. He set up his retail shop in Baltimore in 1837; the New Haven Arms Company was launched in 1857; the move to Bridgeport was undertaken in 1867, during the post-Civil War doldrums; and the expansion of ammunition production came in 1873; all depression years. Once having decided upon a policy, it appears that he was not deterred by existing economic uncertainties from pushing it through.

Along with imagination Winchester had considerable ability as an administrator and particular talents in the fields of finance and marketing. He first demonstrated his organizing ability in the production of shirts and was apparently able to shift from the putting-out system to the factory organization without difficulty and to operate a large-sized establishment with marked financial success. He was able to apply his experience to the production of firearms, utilizing the principle of interchangeable-parts manufacture. Not particularly gifted as a technician or mechanic, Winchester on the whole chose able subordinates to take over this function.

Winchester's financial administration was marked by a policy of building up capital out of earnings through a conservative dividend policy. As his actions during the Civil War demonstrated, he was unwilling to expand operations at the risk of straining the Company's financial position. Once convinced of the desirability of such a move, however, he was willing to back his judgment by increasing his own investment and in getting others to advance capital.

Winchester's marketing ability showed to particular advantage during the critical period following the Civil War. His personal efforts in negotiating the arms and ammunition contracts with the Turkish Government were instrumental in keeping up the Company's business at a time when many other firearms firms were unable to find enough customers to keep them operating. These contracts were sufficiently profitable to give the Company a financial reserve that could be used to good advantage in subsequent expansion and purchase of competitors.

His principal blind spots were his faith in the Winchester repeating rifle as a military weapon and an early failure to see its potentialities as a sporting arm. Actually in recommending the military use of smaller-caliber repeating rifles, Winchester was ahead of his time, but until smokeless powder and stronger actions were subsequently perfected, the military authorities were not willing to change from the single-shot type.

Very little is known about Winchester's personal life. There are no stories or legends about his prowess as a marksman or that he even enjoyed or engaged in hunting. He seems to have been almost completely devoted to business, remaining active until forced to quit through ill health. His motives are a matter of conjecture. He must have been proud of being president of a "three million dollar" concern and of the fame of the rifles that bore his name. The personnel of the management at the time of his death seems to indicate a considerable element of family pride and a desire to see its members take over after he had passed away.

# PART 4

# CONSOLIDATION OF POSITION: 1881-1889

CHAPTER SEVEN

# MANAGEMENT, LABOR, AND INSIDE CONTRACTING

*Management and Control*

As has already been indicated, Oliver Winchester had groomed his son, William Wirt Winchester, to take over the presidency of the Company. The latter, unfortunately, was already suffering from advanced stages of tuberculosis and outlived his father only a few months, dying late in March 1881. William Wirt's obvious incapacity to take an active part in the management at the time of the election of new officers on March 2, 1881, left the choice of a successor to Oliver Winchester between William Converse, W. W. Winchester's brother-in-law, and T. G. Bennett, Oliver Winchester's son-in-law. Bennett, who was secretary, in reporting on the meeting of the board of directors held on that date, stated laconically that ". . . as a result of several ballots the following were declared elected unanimously: for president, William W. Converse; for vice-president, William W. Winchester; for treasurer, William W. Converse; for secretary, Thomas G. Bennett." The notation of "several ballots" suggests that there were some differences of opinion regarding the exact slate of officers.

This decision was essentially a family matter because the majority control of the 10,000 shares of stock outstanding was in the hands of Mrs. Oliver F. Winchester (4,440 shares), Mrs. William Wirt Winchester (777 shares), and Mrs. T. G. Bennett (400 shares). The choice of Converse, who was forty-six at this time, for these offices was probably because of his maturity and his experiences as treasurer. Bennett, to be sure, had been with the Company over ten years and had already demonstrated his ability in technical matters, but he had not reached his thirty-seventh birthday.

Even so, it is a little astonishing that Bennett should have been selected for the relatively minor position of secretary. The advisability of giving him a more important title was apparently recognized, because during the following month, after the death of William Wirt, Converse resigned as treasurer and Bennett was elected to that office. At the next general election of officers, held in March 1882, Bennett was made vice president to fill the office left vacant by the death of William Wirt the year before and he held that position for the succeeding eight years.

At this same election, A. W. Hooper was made treasurer, and George E. Hodson secretary. Hooper had been employed to take charge of the Company's New York store in 1878, and in 1880 had been brought to New Haven to work in the front office. Hodson had joined the Company in 1872 and worked up from the payroll department. Both men were to be connected with the management for many years.

Few presidents of large companies have been cloaked with greater anonymity than William White Converse. His marriage to the sister of Mrs. William Wirt Winchester and his election as treasurer in 1878 have been noted. His file in the Company's archives reveals that he was born in Ware, Massachusetts, June 23, 1834, and that he had worked at one time for the firm of Arnold & Company, lumber dealers in Albany, New York. Beyond this scanty information, nothing is known of his background and education. His election as treasurer to succeed Oliver Winchester suggests that he had demonstrated some ability because of the significance that office had assumed during the early history of the Company. Arthur Earle, who was with the Company at the time Converse was president, recalled that Converse was a very keen and energetic man. He came to the office early and had usually finished for the day by noontime. He took great pleasure in fishing and if the "little blues" were running he sometimes would be able to get away from the office much earlier than noon. Several days of each week were spent by him in New York. Converse and Marcellus Hartley of UMC were the prominent figures in the ammunition business at that time and the former delighted, as he expressed it, "to cross swords" with Hartley, saying that Mr. Hartley would find he had met "a foeman worthy of his steel."

Converse appears to have been more dependent upon the advice of his associate officers and directors than Winchester. The best evidence of this is the greater detail recorded in the minutes of the directors' meetings and in the more comprehensive information given in the financial statements. It is true that these changes may be the result of the activity of the new secretary, but they more likely represent the desirability for more precise definition of decisions. There is some evidence that the functions of management were more clearly defined under his administration, with Bennett in general charge of the development of guns and ammunition, Hooper devoting his major efforts to marketing and costs, Hodson to financial matters, and Converse exercising general supervision. This division of functions should not be exaggerated as all the officers shared the same office space which made for easy, informal communication.

In general, the management was concerned during the decade ending in 1890 with strengthening and consolidating the position of the Company in the arms and ammunition industry. More specifically, attention was directed toward achieving the following objectives: first, tightening up on the control system which affected the costs of manufacture; second, the introduction of improved firearms and ammunition; and third, strengthening the Company's marketing organization and in the case of ammunition securing the cooperation of other manufacturers in matters of output and prices. Because of the greater complexity of operations each of these major subjects will be treated in a separate chapter.

*The Labor Force*

By 1881 the Winchester Repeating Arms Company was operating on a scale that made the supervision of labor-management relations a problem of considerable significance. As shown in Appendix J-1, the number of employees was more than doubled between 1880 and 1890. In contrast with the 1870-1880 period, which has been marked by wide fluctuations, this growth was quite steady.



Between twenty and twenty-five per cent of the total labor force were women.

Except for a few operations in the gun shop, they were employed exclusively on ammunition production, where they made up approximately fifty per cent of the workers. This high proportion of women in the ammunition shop reflects the general character of many of the jobs in that department where an extensive use of automatic machinery made it possible to use relatively unskilled and cheaper labor. The manufacture of ammunition was subject to more seasonal variation than was the case with guns, and many women were willing to accept temporary employment to supplement family incomes. It is estimated that annual wages for ammunition workers averaged around sixty per cent of the pay for gun-shop employees.

The working hours and the work week were typical of American manufacturing for the period. Monday through Friday the plant operated from 7:00 until 6:00 with an hour for lunch. Occasionally a second ten-hour shift was used. On Saturday, work stopped at 5:00.

Payments were biweekly until 1887, after which they were put on a weekly basis. Payday was on Saturday. Although the plant was closed at 5:00 on Saturday, making it only a nine-hour shift, any worker who had a perfect attendance record on the job for the preceding period would receive payment for ten hours. This incentive pay for cutting down on absenteeism and tardiness was continued until 1915.

An examination of the names on the Company's payroll books between 1875 and 1890 shows that workers of British origin dominated, chiefly because that country supplied skilled workers.

*Inside Contracting: Background*

The principal features of the Winchester labor-management relationships during this period were connected with the system of inside contracting employed by the Company. Although the system was quite widely used in New England industrial plants, it has been largely ignored by students of labor history. For this reason it will be discussed in more detail than is strictly warranted by its importance in the development of the Winchester Repeating Arms Company.

Historians of industrial development have noted that the rise of modern industry was marked not only by increasing specialization of labor and machinery, but by an increasing specialization and division in managerial activities as well.

This trend is well illustrated by New England's industrial development. As long as manufacturing was carried on in small establishments catering to a local demand, all the functions of management (and often times that of labor as well) were carried on by the proprietors. Many factors contributed to the economic success or failure of these shops, but among the clockmakers, gunsmiths, and early tool builders, technical skill was especially important.

As transportation improved and communication became easier and cheaper, the establishments of the small tool builders and armorers of New England grew, along with the reputation of their owners. The increased demand for fabricated metal products made it increasingly difficult to fill orders without substantial additions of capital and labor. Much larger plants were necessary to exploit the principle of interchangeable-parts manufacture. This expansion led to increasing division of labor within the plants and to a separation of management functions. Under this situation, the master armorer, mechanic, or tool builder ran the risk of losing his independence and becoming an employee in a large plant. On the other hand, the capitalist frequently had neither the training nor the ability to organize the production of such articles as precision tools or guns, nor did he have the inventiveness which was an integral part of manufacturing at this time.

This situation led to the system of inside contracting which offered advantages to both parties. By taking a contract to secure and supervise a labor force and to manufacture products within the factory of the capitalist, using his machinery and equipment, the works supervisor or master mechanic could maintain considerable independence, yet avoid the problems of salesmanship and financing. At the same time the capitalist was freed from most, if not all, of the more technical problems connected with production, process improvement, and labor supervision.

In an article which appeared in *Scribner's Monthly* in 1880, it was pointed out:

> The contractor is a man of special ability and experience in the particular line of production which he undertakes. Receiving so much per piece, and being held to a strict accountability for quality, he gives his whole thought to the direction of his work, to the employment of the best artisans and to the invention and application of new machinery, processes, and tools—in a word, conducting the department with as much economy and skill as if it were his own. Thus, on executing a large order, one device after another for economizing work, reducing the number of "cuts" or imparting a better finish, discovers itself. Though the contractor receives a given sum for his work, he is required to render an account of his expenditures, and the factory gains ultimately the advantage of any reduction in the cost of production. Not a few of the marvelous labor saving processes that distinguish American mechanical production are the result of the contract system in our large workshops. In contrasting this system with that which prevails, even in this country, in manufactories of textile fabrics, it should be borne in mind that the manufacture of guns, and other machinery, consists in the fabrication of a multitude of distinct parts, each of which had its individual character and cost to be considered. The government arm, the Springfield, has sixty-eight separate parts, sixteen of which parts are screws of one sort or another, and nine of them springs. The constant change and improvements in the manufacturing of these parts is shown by the fact that, of them all, only four remain as they were in the original model of 1855, so as to be interchangeable with the corresponding parts of the present arm.
>
> An essential part of the system we have suggested is the use of gauges to test the accuracy of the work as it progresses. The mechanical definition of the gauge is "any instrument used to measure". It may be a pattern from which the manufactured part has taken its shape; a plug to fit exactly a tube and determine the correctness of its dimensions; a cunningly precise instrument to determine the alignment of sights, or a combination of screw work, Vernier scale, and expanding profile, to indicate the slightest variation from the true form for a breech-chamber.[1]

The contract system was an important source of skilled mechanics. A contractor would ordinarily employ several apprentices on the job. This provided an opportunity for inexperienced boys to acquire a technical education under the direct tutelage of a master craftsman. A distinguished list of New England mechanics received their early training in this fashion. Furthermore, the contractors not infrequently became owners and managers.

The use of inside contractors dates back in the United States at least to 1798. In that year Nathan Starr, who had received a Government contract for swords, made subcontracts with individuals working within his plant at Middletown, Connecticut, to supply him with forgings, finished scabbards, and the like.[2] From this early beginning the system spread, and during the nineteenth century the system of inside contracting became widely used in the northeastern manufacturing belt of the United States especially among the machine-tool builders and metal fabricators, being employed in such well-known plants as Eli Whitney, Robbins & Lawrence, Brown & Sharpe, Colt's, Remington, Singer Sewing Machine, and the U. S. Cartridge Company. Several of the brass mills up and down the Naugatuck Valley, occasionally a textile mill, and the United States armories at Harpers Ferry and Springfield, and even the state prisons in Connecticut also made use of inside contractors. There is evidence that in Great Britain, as well, the contract system was used in some plants.[3]

*Inside Contracting at Winchester*

There is little doubt that the system played an important role in Winchester labor-management relations during the Company's early history and made it easier for Oliver Winchester to devote his attention to financial and marketing problems. Its use may well have prevented serious bottlenecks from developing during the sharp expansion of the labor force that occurred at the time of the Turkish contracts.

Prior to 1876 the data are too sketchy to make any analysis of the operation of the system within the Company. Beginning around 1873, however, the Company began to feel the pressure of lowering prices and increasing competition. The management became more cost-conscious and the changes in personnel that occurred in 1881 brought a further tightening of the control exercised over their contractors. J. M. Clough, who had previously gained experience with the contract system at the Remington plant at Ilion, New York, was installed as works superintendent and Arthur Hooper came in as treasurer. For the first time, relatively complete and careful records were kept and the prices which the Company agreed to pay the contractors for finished work were formally written down.

The discussion which follows is based upon the records for the gun shop which have been preserved. Statements by older employees and scattered data indicate, however, that there was little difference in the contract system as it operated in the ammunition shop.

As it had been developed within the Winchester Repeating Arms Company by the late 1870s, the system of inside contracting had the following characteristics. The operations involved in manufacturing gun components and ammunition were delegated to super-foremen who hired and fired their own workers, set their wages, managed the job, and turned over the finished parts to the Company for assembly. The Company supplied raw materials, the use of floor space and machinery, light, heat, and power, special tools, and patterns for the job. The management credited the account of the contractor so much for every hundred pieces of finished work which passed inspection, and debited his account for the wages paid to his men and the cost of oil, files, waste, and so on, used in production. Anything left over was paid to the contractor as a profit. In addition, the Company paid him day wages at a foreman's rate as a guarantee of a minimum income. If the contractor incurred a loss which could not be traced to his own mismanagement, this was subtracted from his future profits but left his day pay unaffected.

A typical account, that of John B. Harris, who had a gun-stocking contract, showed the following entries for the year 1886:

| | | |
|---|---|---|
| Total Credits | | $16,613.35 |
| Less: | | |
| Payroll of Men | $14,148.23 | |
| Stores | 685.14 | 14,833.37 |
| Profit | | 1,779.98 |
| Day Pay | | 1,110.40 |
| Total income for year | | $ 2,890.38 |

*Number of Contract Employees*

Only about half the workers employed in the gun shop during this period were covered by the inside contracting system. In general the Company used its own employees for maintenance, inspection, and assembling. The Company also operated the rolling mill, steam plant, the forge shop, and the drafting and model room under its own foremen. The contract system was used in the processes more directly concerned with production such as gun components, finishing work, and ammunition. The machine shop, which made most of the special machinery and jigs and fixtures used for both gun and ammunition production, was under a variation of the contract system.

The number of contractors, contract employees, and Company employees in the gun shop for this period are shown in Appendix J-2. These data indicate that as total employment increased there was a marked trend toward putting more of the employees under the contract system. The number of contractors remained fairly well stabilized after 1881, increasing slightly toward the end of the period.

*Contract Rates*

In discussing the operation of the system at Winchester, the prices paid to contractors offer a real starting point. From the Company's vantage point they represented a large part of the costs of production, whereas from the contractor's point of view they governed the size of his income. These arrangements were thus the focal point in the bargaining relationship; they were also the basis for the secondary bargains which existed between the contractors and those who were employed by them.

The procedure followed in drawing up a contract depended upon whether a new component was to be produced which meant the formulation of a new contract, or whether an old agreement was up for renewal. In the case of the former, the Company drew up the appropriate specifications and then called in the prospective contractor to discuss operations and to reach an agreement for remuneration. By the 1880s, the discussion was culminated by a formal agreement made for a specific job. With the establishment of the new contract, the contractor proceeded to hire workers and start production to fulfill the obligations.

The major conflicts arose when contracts came up for renewal, as it was at this time that management attempted to bring about a proper alignment of contract rates. The core of this trouble lay in the fact that the front office had relatively little information on which to base the prices paid to contractors. For the sake of illustration, assume that the agreement with Richard Russell, who ran the screw-machine shop, came up for readjustment. The management knew that during the previous contract Russell turned out certain quantities of screws of various sorts to fit parts of the different gun models and that he made what seemed to be a substantial profit after paying his workers. Although the Company had a record of the monthly incomes of all his workers, it did not know what piece rate he had set, nor whether his rate of profit was the same for each variety of screw. Since the Company's control of raw materials was inadequate at this time, the changes which had occurred in Russell's inventory position during the year were also unknown. Therefore, the estimation of his profit could not, at best, be very accurate.

Furthermore, this general setup gave the contractors considerable opportunity and inducement to withhold information from the front office. For example, Russell's original agreement might have called for six operations, but he may have discovered that the screws would pass inspection after only five operations. In such a case, he could hardly be expected to inform the Company that his contract price should be reduced. Most of the contractors were excellent and ingenious mechanics, who operated their own machine shops and had enough time to experiment. Any discovery of how to speed up operations or to substitute unskilled labor for skilled labor by the use of some new jig or fixture would be carefully guarded from the management. Furthermore, Russell might have some improvements in mind which, if installed, could save him both time and money. These innovations, however, would entail considerable trouble; they might cause some dissatisfaction among his own workers, and he was not completely sure of the results. Therefore, he would not plan to change the current arrangement of production unless the Company reduced his prices. Thus the Company was often unaware of improvements in production already put in practice and of potential economies that could be introduced.

If, for any reason, the management was under compulsion to lower the costs of gun manufacture, it would move to cut contract rates all along the line. But because Russell had made more profits than the other medium-sized contractors during the previous year, and because he was an ingenious mechanic and probably could introduce some cost-saving processes if pressed, his contract would be cut eight per cent while the others would receive five per cent reduction.

The bargaining situation just outlined presented certain obvious difficulties in determining contract rates. About one-third of all price adjustments took place at the beginning of the year just prior to the usual increase in gun production during the second and the third quarters, and whenever a change occurred, all of a contractor's prices were reduced by the same amount. To return to the example, as there was no way of knowing which screws Russell was making an excessive profit on and which screws he might be losing money on, rates were reduced the same percentage on all. The prices paid for the parts of a model which had been in production for a considerable length of time, such as the Model 66 or the Model 73, would have already been reduced many times, whereas those for a more recent model would have been cut but a few times. Thus, a contractor who received an order to make parts for the Model 73 would almost certainly operate on a low margin of profit. Similarly, the prices paid for some parts or operations on any model would yield a larger profit than others which were customarily made by the same contractor.

The element of "unfairness" involved was a constant source of dissatisfaction to the contractors and the Company officials. It was something about which the front office could do little, since it did not have access to the records kept by the contractors nor the staff to handle more complicated price adjustments. The general problem was particularly evident whenever a contract was split up, as happened several times during the period under consideration.

Another source of discontent arose because the Company had incomplete control over the wage structure of the entire plant. Discrepancies must have occurred from time to time between the pay scales of the Company and of the various contractors for work of the same general skill, difficulty, and status. Dissatisfaction on the part of the work force which arose from this cause could not easily be corrected, although changes in the prices paid to contractors would perhaps result in some adjustment of the wages paid to their workers.

*Reduction of Contract Rates*

The general average of contract rates in the gun shop dropped approximately twenty-five per cent during the nine-year period ending 1889. (*See Appendix J-5.*) It is doubtful if the management used any exact formula to set these rates. As has been noted, the Company was under strong competitive pressure in the marketing of guns during these years, which would be sufficient to account for the move to reduce manufacturing costs which in turn would permit lower selling prices.

It is reasonable to assume that a contractor who had received a cut in his rate would consider the possibility of passing the reduction on, in part at least, to his employees. These workers were paid on a piece-rate basis, but none of the contractors' own wage-rate books has been preserved. The contractors did, however, turn in the amounts owed to laborers to the Company, which paid the laborers directly. From these records it has been possible to derive average annual incomes for the contract workers, presented in index form in Appendix J-3.

A comparison of contract rates and average annual incomes of the contract workers indicates a high correlation between 1881 and 1885, but after that date the workers' incomes dropped relatively slower. This suggests that the contractors during the latter period either absorbed a part of the cuts themselves or were able to introduce methods that increased the productivity of the workers.

There is only a slight correlation, at best, between the contract rates and the income of the contractors. This is partly explainable by variations in the output of guns.

*Other Aspects of the Inside Contract System*

The use of inside contractors had an influence beyond the formal economic relationships between them and the management and the formal organization of a part of the labor force within the factory. The system affected the social structure, the interpersonal grouping, and the status of the hierarchy in the organization. No complete analysis is possible, but a few general statements can be made about the relationships between the contractors and their employees, and between the contractors and the management.

Recollections of older employees indicate that the labor force was reasonably content and stable; the low annual turnover figures in the gun shop of around twenty-three per cent and the absence of labor strife give confirmation to this picture. The homogeneity of the work force and the fact that the hiring and firing prerogative was in the hands of the contractors also helped make for a stable work force. A contractor would hire those who lived near his own home, and in many cases the names of half a dozen of his own relatives were on the payroll. For this reason, a large contractor was an important figure in his neighborhood. It was not at all unusual for a youngster who wished to become an apprentice to a contractor, to mow the latter's lawn and do all sorts of odd jobs for the privilege. Those who worked in a given department were thus more than a work group; they were also bound together by the social life of the community.

Since the prestige and position of the contractor depended to a large extent on the attitude of his workers who were oftentimes also his neighbors, he could not act in a totally irresponsible manner. The incomes of the workers were not reduced proportionately to cuts in the contract rates, but this does not mean that a contractor would not try to pass on any reduction in his own rates to his workers. Whenever this could be done, he could lay the principal blame on the management which had forced this action. It is not unlikely that the workers under the contractor had an unfavorable view of the management, an attitude that was fostered by the unpopular inspection trips of Company officials through the plants.

The contractor also gained respect because he was himself highly skilled in a trade which was considered important by his workers. Bonuses at Christmas, the gift of a bicycle to an exceptional apprentice, and a departmental baseball team or brass band undoubtedly contributed to his position. Any envy of the contractor's position must have been tempered by the possibility that a worker had a chance of becoming a contractor himself.

The very fact that the contractor, rather than the Company, was the real "boss" of his men tended to decrease the possibility of unionization. It would have been more difficult to organize the various groups of workers who were hired by different contractors or by Winchester, than under a more centralized setup where all the workers were directly employed by the one firm.

The relationships between the management and the contractors were probably less harmonious. The bargaining procedure, with its strategy of secrecy, depended upon incomplete knowledge on both sides. From the contractor's point of view any steps taken by the Company to obtain greater knowledge and control by expanding accounting procedures, greater inspection, and the introduction of rate cuts, represented a threat to his position and status.

From the point of view of the management, which otherwise controlled operations with a strong hand, it must have been somewhat unsatisfactory to have a substantial part of the Company's activities outside its immediate control.

Insofar as money incomes were a measure of status and position both within the organization and in the community, the large contractors occupied an enviable position. The information in Table I shows that the largest contractor received an average income second only to the president of the Company and above that of the average official. (*See also Appendix J-4.*) This situation could have further increased the dissatisfaction of the management with the contract system and may well have been a factor in the introduction of a bonus system for the benefit of the officers in 1887. What effect this may have had on the morale of the officers and their attitudes toward their jobs is not known. Their position within the management hierarchy may have carried sufficient prestige to have offset any lack of income differentiation.

TABLE I

COMPARATIVE AVERAGE ANNUAL INCOMES OF VARIOUS INDIVIDUALS: 1881-1889

| | |
|---|---|
| President of Company | $14,200 |
| Average official | 7,600 |
| Most important contractor | 10,800 [a] |
| Average large contractor | 4,860 |
| Largest stockholder | 86,670 [b] |
| Average stockholder | 3,090 [c] |

[a] In all but two years the most important contractor was Albert Tilton who had the receiver contract.

[b] The largest stockholder was the Winchester estate, with a holding of 4,000 shares. The income from this holding was divided between Oliver Winchester's daughter, Mrs. T. G. Bennett, and his daughter-in-law, Mrs. William Wirt Winchester.

[c] The average holding per stockholder was 154 shares.

*Noncontract Employees*

Those workers not employed by the contractors were under the supervision of the shop superintendents and foremen and their relationships with the management followed a more conventional pattern. On the whole the Company employees included a larger percentage of unskilled workers than the workers of the contractors. Company workers averaged $590 a year between 1880 and 1889 as against $690 for contract workers. (*See Appendix J-3.*)

By the end of the 1880s the system of inside contracting had been fully developed within the Winchester plant. It was only as circumstances changed both within and outside the Company that increasing difficulty was experienced with the system and the disadvantages began to outweigh the advantages.

CHAPTER EIGHT

# ERA OF DEVELOPMENT

By the end of 1880, the success of the Model 73 had made the name of Winchester practically synonymous with the term "repeating rifle." In ammunition production the Company had made a good start especially in the manufacture of metallic cartridges and components.

The Company's position did not remain unchallenged. Remington, Colt's, Whitney, and the Marlin Arms Company of New Haven, were alert to capitalize on the increasing popularity of repeating rifles, and the last three concerns had or were about to bring out finger-lever action rifles that were directly competitive with the type associated with Winchester. The Company was also meeting stronger competition in the ammunition field, the Union Metallic Cartridge Company being the principal rival.

*Gun Development: The Hotchkiss-Winchester Model 83*

One way to meet the challenge was to improve and enlarge the Company's gun line. The immediate problem still facing the management was to get a satisfactory weapon that would handle the .45-70 Government ammunition. Beyond this immediate objective was the desirability of improving and expanding the Company's general line of firearms. For both purposes it proved necessary to obtain the services of an able gun designer. Some three years were to elapse before the services of a qualified individual were obtained and in the interval the Company put its main efforts into making the Hotchkiss rifle an acceptable firearm both for the United States Government and for the sporting market.

In 1880, Congress again made an appropriation, this time $50,000, to be spent on the development of a repeating rifle to be adopted by the services. By this time the Company had eliminated the mechanical weaknesses in the Hotchkiss which had shown up previously and an improved model was entered in the new trials which began in July 1881 and continued through October of the year following.

Competition was somewhat keener than it had been in 1879; some fifty-three repeating rifles, both foreign and domestic, being submitted. Of this number the Board recommended that the Lee, the Chaffee-Reese, and the Hotchkiss, all bolt-action guns, be manufactured and put in the hands of the troops for the field trials. This recommendation was accepted by Robert T. Lincoln, Secretary of War, and the Winchester Repeating Arms Company entered into a contract with the Ordnance Department on February 16, 1883, to produce 750 Hotchkiss rifles at a price of $15.00 per gun. The Lee rifle was manufactured by Remington and a similar contract was made with that concern. The Chaffee-Reese guns were made by Springfield Armory.

But the military authorities were still not ready to adopt a repeating rifle for the services. After field trials extending over a year, General Benét reported to the Secretary of War on December 15, 1885:

> After a careful consideration . . . I am satisfied that neither [*sic*] of these rifles should be adopted and substituted for the single shot Springfield rifle as an arm for the service.
>
> I have been and am an advocate for the magazine gun, but it would seem the part of wisdom to postpone for the present day further efforts toward the adoption of a suitable magazine arm for the service. The Springfield rifle gives such general satisfaction to the Army that we can safely wait a reasonable time for further developments of magazine systems.[1]

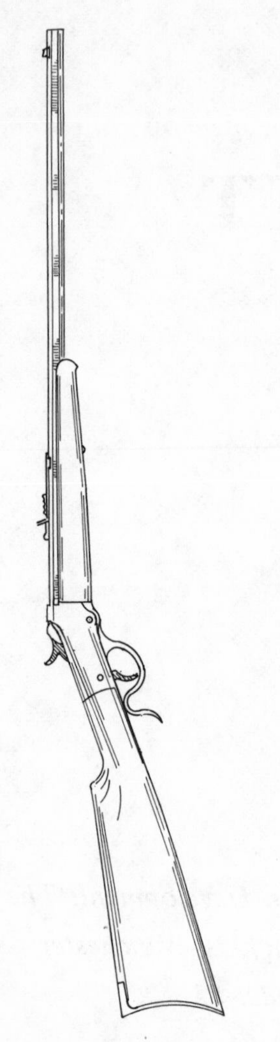

*Winchester Model 1885 Single-Shot Low-Wall Action*

After this experience, the Winchester Repeating Arms Company lost much of its enthusiasm for a Government adoption. The Company, for example, did not even enter a gun in the competition held by the Ordnance Department in 1890, which resulted in the adoption of the first repeating rifle for the service, the Krag-Jörgensen.

Meanwhile some attempt was made to popularize the Hotchkiss as a sporting rifle. First listed in the Company's catalog for 1879, the improved model was introduced in 1883 as the Winchester Model 83, with the notation that: "It embodies the experience of six years of manufacturing and the valuable suggestions of many experienced officers who have used it in the field. It is a most simple and solid repeating gun, capable of doing good service under the most disadvantageous circumstances."

This statement could hardly be taken as a highly enthusiastic endorsement of the Model 83, but it appears to have been justified by the reception the gun received from the sporting trade. There were several reasons for its lack of popularity. The magazine of the Model 73 carbine held twelve cartridges and the sporting rifle held fifteen. In contrast the butt-stock magazine of the Model 83 carried only six cartridges. The bolt action was new in this country and there was resistance to accepting it. The bolt itself formed a protuberance that made the gun more difficult to carry in a saddle holster.

Actually the Winchester Repeating Arms Company, in its attempt to promote the Hotchkiss, was to some extent a victim of its own success in popularizing the finger-lever action rifle. The bolt action was well adapted to handle high-powered ammunition and, prior to World War I, this type of action was incorporated in practically all military small arms, including those of the United States. After World War I, the bolt-action rifle became widely acceptable as a sporting weapon, but to the potential users in the 1880s the bolt-action Hotchkiss did not look or handle like the type of repeating rifle that the Winchester organization had promoted so successfully.

## *The Winchester Single-Shot Rifle*

Notwithstanding the increased popularity of the repeating rifles there was still a large number of boosters for the single-shot during the 1880s. None of the repeating arms of the day would handle the extra-heavy ammunition that many shooters preferred because of its long range and effectiveness against big game. The relative merits of the single-shot versus the repeating rifle were argued at great length around many a camp fire and wherever shooters gathered in frontier settlements.

This controversy even got into the fiction dealing with the period. Clarence

E. Mulford's famous character, Hopalong Cassidy, belonged to the school that favored the Sharps rifle. He was scornful of the affection which his best friend, Red Connors, had for his Winchester. Hopalong called it a sawed-off carbine and at one point said, "You're like the Indians—want a lot of shots to waste without reloading." Red Connors' most effective answer was to use his Winchester with deadly effect against the rustlers and desperadoes who made life exciting, if hazardous, for the heroes of the story.[2]

In 1885, the Winchester Repeating Arms Company, after a quarter century devoted exclusively to the production of repeating rifles, announced the production of a single-shot model, designed by John Moses Browning of Ogden, Utah. He and his brother, Jonathan Edmund, better known as Ed, had developed the gun in their little shop located in that city and were granted a patent in October 1879. Working largely with hand tools, the two brothers made up about six hundred rifles over the next couple of years and began selling them in the area.

Sometime in 1882 or early 1883, the rifle came to the attention of Andrew McAusland, a Winchester salesman, who brought it before the management at New Haven. There is no question that the Company was interested and it is said that T. G. Bennett immediately took a train to Ogden for the purpose of investigating the rifle with a view of purchasing the patent. As the story goes, when Bennett arrived at this destination, he was directed to the Browning shop and told that Browning was working upstairs. He returned to the ground floor almost at once and stated that there was no one upstairs but a couple of workmen. Upon being reassured that the two workmen were John Browning and his brother Ed, Bennett made himself known. On behalf of the Company, he purchased the patent for the single-shot rifle and the supply of guns on hand for $8,000.[3] He also saw and brought back to New Haven a wooden model of a gun that later became the Model 86.

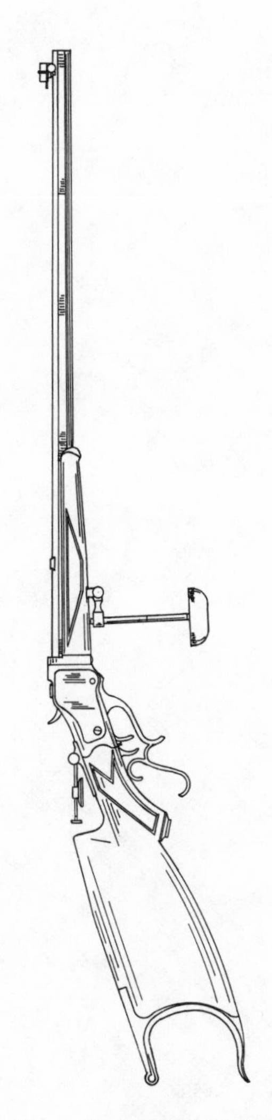

*Winchester Model 1885 Single-Shot, High-Wall Action—Schuetzen Rifle Type*

The reasons for adopting the Browning single-shot were not recorded, but several circumstances seem to have influenced the management. The single-shot would add a gun to the line capable of handling the .45-70 Government cartridge as well as both heavier and lighter loads. The single-shot would contribute to the diversity of the Company's firearms without being directly competitive with the repeating rifles. Finally the failure of the Sharps Rifle Company in 1881 had eliminated an important producer that Winchester might replace.[4]

The new catalog for 1885 carried the following description of the new model:

> This gun has the old Sharps' breech-block and is as safe and solid as that arm. The firing pin is automatically withdrawn at the first opening movement of the gun and held back until the gun is closed.
>
> The hammer is centrally hung, but drops down with the breech-block when the gun is opened and is cocked by the closing movement. It can also be cocked by hand. This arrangement allows the barrel to be wiped and examined from the breech.
>
> In outline, everything has been done to make the gun pleasing to the eye. It can be furnished either with or without set triggers, with barrels of all ordinary lengths and weights and for all standard cartridges also with rifle and shotgun butt, plain or fancy wood, or with pistol grip.

This catalog description hardly does justice to the new gun. Lucian Cary has pointed out in a letter to the author: "The Sharps had a sound breech—a block sliding in a mortise. It had been used by many designers for a hundred years, including designers of light artillery. But the Sharps' action was merely an adaptation of a percussion design with as little change as possible. It had a big and heavy outside hammer, which, according to H. M. Pope, made it a hard gun to shoot. The jar of that heavy hammer was too great. Browning's original hammer was much heavier than necessary and Winchester eventually lightened it. Pope in adapting the gun for accurate shooting regularly lightened it further by drilling the largest possible hole through the web and a smaller hole through the hammer spur, the objective being to reduce the jar although he also gained something in speed of ignition. The Sharps had a mechanical monstrosity of a firing pin—a round-the-corner affair. Browning used a pin relatively light working in the axis of the bore, as well as being mechanically retracted."

T. G. Bennett, who was responsible for the Company's gun development at the time and could have probably purchased the Sharps patents and good will at a low figure, showed good judgment in adopting the improved Browning action incorporated into the Winchester model.

By producing four different sizes of receivers, five different weights of barrels and several different calibers for each weight barrel, the Company was able to furnish its customers with a rifle that could handle any one of the seventeen standard sizes of metallic cartridges currently manufactured. Eventually the rifle was produced in more than thirty-three different loads, ranging from the .22 short rimfire to the .50-90 Sharps cartridge with a powder charge of 90 grains and a bullet weighing 473 grains.

The Winchester single-shot took its place among the more famous guns in the Company's line. In the small bores it became widely used as a target rifle and varmint killer; in the larger calibers it made a place as a big-game rifle. William H. Wright, an experienced hunter, writing in 1909 in his book, *The Grizzly Bear,* speaks of ". . . my single-shot rifle, made to order for me by the Winchester people; the .45-100, in which I shot one hundred grains of powder and six hundred grains of lead. It was one of the guns that killed at both ends, but I liked it better than any I have ever carried. I used it for years, and I discarded it for a lighter .30-30 only when I gave up hunting with a gun and took to hunting with a camera. Personally, I could depend on this old rifle for a sure three shots in twelve seconds, by holding two spare cartridges between the fingers of my right hand, and I have always thought that a hunter is apt to be much more careful if he knows that every shot must tell. I always got as close to the game as I could before shooting, and whatever I shot, it generally dropped, if hit, and I was usually near enough to be sure of hitting."

While the single-shot served to round out the Company's gun line, there was still need for a repeating rifle that could be used for longer-range shooting. Indirectly the adoption of the single-shot rifle contributed significantly to the solution of this latter problem because it brought John Browning into association with the Company.

*John Moses Browning*

John Browning's inventive talent and interest in firearms came naturally from his father, Jonathan Browning. The latter, born in 1805 in Tennessee, had moved to Kentucky as a youngster and while yet in his teens learned the art of gunsmithing and set up his own shop. He was attracted to the Mormon Church and joined the westward movement of that organization, setting up a gunshop in Nauvoo, Illinois, some time before 1846. Forced out of Nauvoo, the Mormons moved across the Mississippi River to Kanesville, near Council Bluffs, Iowa, where Browning again set up his gun shop. It was here that he produced the two repeating rifles, one a slide repeater with a five-shot magazine and the other with a revolving cylinder. It was here also that, with a rare sense of humor, he ran the following advertisement in the September 19, 1849, issue of the *Frontier Guardian* in Kanesville, Iowa:

GUNSMITHING

The Subscriber is prepared to manufacture, to order, improved *Fire-arms,* viz: revolving rifles and pistols; also slide guns, from 5 to 25 shooters. All on an improved plan, and he thinks not equalled this far East. (Farther west they might be.) The emigrating and sporting community are invited to call and examine Browning's improved fire-arms before purchasing elsewhere. Shop eight miles south of Kanesville on Mosquito Creek, half a mile south of TRADING POINT.

JONATHAN BROWNING [5]

In 1851, Jonathan Browning moved on to the newly formed Mormon colony near Salt Lake and once more established a gunshop in Ogden. It was in Ogden that John Moses Browning was born in 1855, one of twenty-two children, eleven boys and eleven girls, that his father had by his three wives.

Young John Browning was encouraged by his father to follow an early displayed interest and flair for mechanics and invention. The boy worked in his father's shop and when the latter died in 1879, took over the general responsibility for the family, along with his half-brother Ed, and his brother Matthew Sandefur, the latter more frequently addressed as "Matt."

No small part of the Browning success was due to the teamwork of these brothers. All three had considerable mechanical talent, but John was the most able original thinker and confined his attention largely to inventions. Ed, sometimes described by John as his "right arm," was an unusually able mechanic and translated his brother's ideas into working models. Matthew more and more came to handle the financial and commercial matters connected with the business.

The Browning brothers during the early days by no means confined their attention to guns. They repaired farm equipment, bicycles, and machinery of all sorts. Experiments were made in the improvement of such diverse objects as farm implements and surgical instruments. But their main interest became increasingly concentrated on firearms.

The shop in which repairs and experiments were made, in addition to the production of firearms, was crude, even judged by contemporary standards. The machinery consisted principally of a lathe, drill press, and milling machine all operated by hand. According to Frank Browning, power-driven machinery was not used in the shop until around 1900. John Browning used to draw up his plans on brown butcher paper and Ed, often times using bar iron picked up at the local railroad yard, would turn out the parts on the machines or with the aid of hand tools.

Working under these conditions was not without certain advantages from the standpoint of gun design. The components, of necessity, had to be designed in such a way that they could be made on the simple machines which in turn made their fabrication and fitting easier on a larger scale. The brothers were excellent target and game shooters and lived in an area that enabled them to try out their products under good hunting conditions.

In 1879, at the time the patent for the single-shot rifle was taken out, the brothers had opened a sporting-goods store in connection with their shop. It was on the second floor of this building that T. G. Bennett is said to have made his first acquaintance with John Browning.

It is doubtful if the management of the Winchester Repeating Arms Company could have realized the significance of the connection made with the Browning brothers as a result of the purchase of the single-shot patent. John Browning was only twenty-eight years old in 1883 when the purchase was made and on the threshold of his distinguished career. This apparently was the first sale of any of his inventions to a major firearms producer, and it marked the beginning of an association that lasted for some seventeen years. During that time John Browning sold his gun patents exclusively to the Winchester Repeating Arms Company. These covered some forty-one inventions and included some of the most famous of the products of the Winchester Repeating Arms Company. Browning also took out a large number of inventions during this period covering pistols. These were purchased principally by the Colt's Patent Firearms Manufacturing Company of Hartford, Connecticut, and the Fabrique Nationale d'Armes de Guerre, Liége, Belgium.

*William Mason*

While the Winchester Repeating Arms Company came to depend upon Browning's inventive talent for the leading developments in its gun line, the management also acquired the services of an able inventor and skilled mechanic, William Mason, to work in the New Haven plant. Mason has been described by J. W. Roe as a ". . . modest, kindly man, little known outside his immediate associates, but of singular fertility in invention and almost unerring in mechanical judgment." He had learned his trade with the Remington Arms Company, at Ilion, New York. After a number of years with that Company he went to Colt's around 1869, where he was superintendent and made several notable contributions to the revolvers manufactured by that concern. In 1882, he came to Winchester and three years later was appointed master mechanic and served in that capacity until his retirement in 1910.

Evidence of Mason's ability as an inventor are some 125 patents granted him during his lifetime. These included appliances for looms, steam pumps, bridges and the like, although most of them were connected with guns and ammunition and the machinery and tools for their manufacture. While with Winchester he made many improvements in the manufacturing methods employed by the Company, being credited, for example, with the introduction of a vertical barrel-drilling machine that gave greater output and accuracy to that process.

Mason was not only an inventor in his own right but he had that rare talent of "almost unerring mechanical judgment" that enabled him to suggest the modifications and improvements that are so often necessary before an original idea or invention can be converted into a usable product. This was an especially important function for him to perform for the Winchester Repeating Arms Company in view of their relationship with Browning. Whatever may have been the exact merits of the improvements that were made in the models submitted by the Ogden

William Mason

inventor, it was necessary to make certain additions and changes before they could meet the requirements of manufacturing or marketing. Few of the Browning inventions, which were incorporated into the Winchester firearms, were without modifications suggested by Mason, many of which were important enough to be patentable.

*The Model 86*

The management of the Winchester Repeating Arms Company appears to have put Browning to work on redesigning the repeating action of the Models 73 and 76 almost immediately following the purchase of the single-shot patent. In October 1884, he was granted a patent for a new action (US 306,577) which was incorporated in the Model 86, introduced to the trade two years later.

Browning's improvement not only utilized the finger lever, which was the earmark of the Winchester guns, but he successfully overcame the weakness of the toggle-link mechanism by attaching the lever to two flat bolts which moved vertically in the receiver and which were locked into slots in the frame when the action was closed. The result was an exceptionally smooth operating action and a rifle that could easily handle the heavier, more powerful ammunition loads. The feeding mechanism on this model, it should be noted, was patented by William Mason in January 1885.

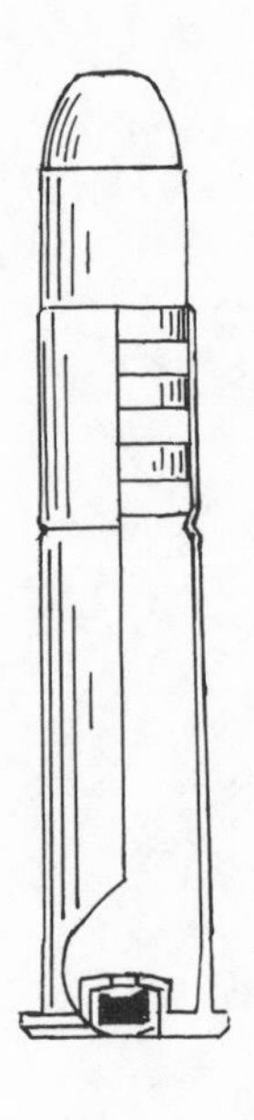

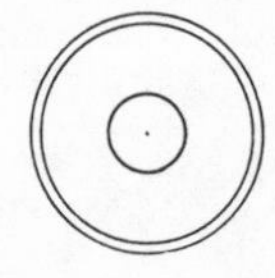

*.45-70-500 Centerfire Cartridge*

The importance attached by the management to the rugged construction of the Model 86, is illustrated by the following extracts taken from the catalog for 1886, first announcing the new model: "This gun is adapted to the .45-70 Government cartridges with 405 or 500 grain bullet, and to the .45-90-300 or .40-82-260 Cartridges especially made for it. The magazine . . . is provided with a stop which permits the use of cartridges having the same shell, of varying lengths less than standard. Thus, the same gun will use .45-70-405 or .45-70-500 Government cartridges." Additional calibers of the Model 86 were subsequently added; the .40-65, the .38-56, and the .50-110 Express in 1887, the .40-70 and the .38-70 in 1894, the .50-110-450 in 1895, and the .33 in 1903.

In the Model 86, the Company had the answer to the problem that the Model 76 and the Hotchkiss Model 83 had failed to solve. The production of the latter two models was dropped, the Model 76 in 1886 and the Hotchkiss in 1894.

The Model 86 had an especial appeal for the big-game hunter. A number of these tell of their experience with the gun in the volume *Hunting in Many Lands,* edited by Theodore Roosevelt and George Bird Grinnell and published in 1895. Under the chapter heading "Dog Sledding in the North," D. M. Barringer described the shooting exploit of a companion: "He carefully steadied himself, raised his .45-90 Winchester, aiming at the caribou lying down and fired. When he went up to look at it, to his amazement, he came across another caribou between the spot where he had fired and the one he had aimed at. And going farther, he found the other caribou shot exactly where he had aimed at it, some twenty yards distant from the first one."

Roosevelt noted that "Mr. H. L. Stimson has had built a special .577 Winchester which he tells me he finds excellent for grizzly bears." He goes on to relate how an English friend, "Mr. William Chandler, after trying English double barrel rifles, finally threw them aside in favor of the .45-90 Winchester for use even against such thick-hided beasts as rhinoceros. In a letter to the London *Field* he happened to mention his preference for the .45-90 Winchester. His letter was followed by a perfect chorus of protests in the shape of other letters by men who preferred the double-barrel . . . and who seemed to think that Mr. Chandler's preference for the .45-90 repeater showed some kind of moral delinquency on his part."

Another volume entitled *The Big Game of North America,* edited by G. O. Shields and published in 1890, gives further evidence of the popularity of the Model 86. W. A. Perry, in telling of "Elk Hunting in the Olympic Mountains" said:

> In my opinion, the best arm for hunting the Elk is the Winchester, Model 86, in the larger bores—.40-82, .45-90, or, best of all, the new .110-300 Express. I have given this gun an exhaustive trial on large game, and do not hesitate to pronounce it the best rifle for big game hunting that human ingenuity has yet produced. Light, strong and rapid of manipulation, terrific in killing power, there is no animal on this continent that can escape from a cool, nervy man armed with one of these superb weapons. Some sportsmen object to the heavy recoil of this rifle, but a recoil that is uncomfortable when shooting at a target is never felt in the excitement of game-shooting, and it is evident, from my own experience, that a wound from one of these bullets leaves such a trail of blood that it can be followed over bare ground by the veriest novice.
>
> The .40-82 is a good substitute, when the Express bullet is used. So is the .45-90; but while they will do the work, I do not consider them as sure as the .110-300. One of my hunting companions, a man who has killed more Deer and Elk than any man of my acquaintance, uses a .44-caliber Winchester Model '73. With him that gun was the only gun worth owning until he tried my Express. Since then, when a difficult shot is to be made, when we are hunting together, he stands back, and calls me to use the 'thunderbolt'.
>
> One disadvantage in using a common small-bore rifle is that, in moments of excitement, the novice frequently forgets to elevate his sights, and so frequently undershoots his quarry. With the Express, I find that it is almost point-blank up to two hundred yards, so that no changing of elevation is necessary.

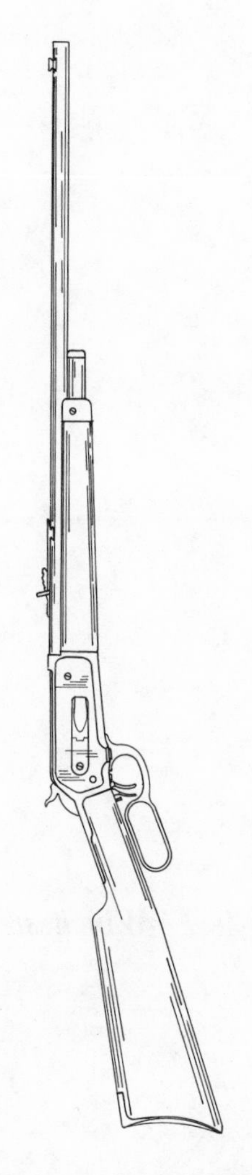

*Winchester Model 1886 Rifle*

"The Grizzly Bear" was the subject of an article by W. S. Rainsford. He wrote: "Good weapons in great variety are now to be had, and had cheaply. The improved Winchester, Model 86, .50-100, is an excellent 'saddle gun'. Personally, I prefer the Bullard; the action is so silent, and the shooting of such weapons as I have used can not be surpassed. But I am ready to admit that the Winchester, though not so silent in its action, is a stronger rifle, and more convenient on horseback. It is somewhat lighter, too; and since all who are determined to follow their game up and kill it in sportsmanlike manner must be prepared to leave their ponies at the foot of the mountain—not on the side—every extra ounce to be carried is a burden."

The most glowing tribute to Winchester firearms was made by Arthur W. du Bray in an article on "Still Hunting the Antelope." He wrote:

> For Antelope shooting, or, in fact, for any kind of big game shooting, I prefer the Winchester, Model 86, my choice being the repeater of large bore, say fifty caliber, with its 110-grain powder charge and hollow-pointed, 300-grain bullet. Those preferring the single-shot need not swerve to any other make, as this company makes the best single-shot rifles, of all calibers from twenty-two to fifty; and were I using a single-shot rifle for Deer, Elk, Bears, or Antelope, my choice would be the forty-five caliber, shooting one

hundred and twenty-five grains of powder and three hundred grains of lead-hollow-pointed ball. I must frankly admit, however, that I never could see where any single or double barreled rifle could, in any way, compare with a repeater—every advantage clearly going to the many-shot rifle.

I am partial to the Winchester rifles, for these reasons: They are safe, accurate, and durable; they are made in all calibers; they are sold at prices within the reach of all; as repeaters, they are more reliable than any other kind with which I am familiar; as single-shot, they are quicker to load, less liable to get out of order, and, in my judgment, just a little better than any other single-loader made. The Winchester Company has proved itself imbued with a progressive spirit, and has catered to the ever-changing and manifold wants of men of many minds and diverse experiences. It is, furthermore, an essentially American concern, and I believe that Americans should patronize American manufacturers. And, to cap the climax, the Winchester is about the only sporting rifle that has come up to the hypercritical and fastidious scrutiny of the English sportsmen, than whom none are better judges, owing to their early education and vast experience. These men shoot wild and dangerous game all over the globe, and know a good rifle when they see it. Moreover, as none but the wealthy among them can indulge in such sport, the price paid for their weapons is a matter of no concern whatever, its absolute reliability and accuracy being the *sine qua non* of the arm. When, therefore, the plain but thoroughly sound and serviceable Winchester, costing say £4, supplants the elaborate double rifle of twenty times its value, something inherent to the Yankee rifle must be there to back it up.

*Winchester, Idaho*

One of the most unusual tributes to the popularity of Winchester firearms arose when a town, Winchester, Idaho, was named in honor of the rifle. As told by Jessie L. Kelly, Postmistress of the town in 1941, it happened in the following manner: "In 1888 or 89 a group of men met in a little store four and one half miles from the present Winchester to decide on a name for a Post Office. At that time everybody carried guns wherever they went. Someone suggested that they name the office or town after the gun with the largest representation. Winchester was largest so that is how our town was named." [The author is indebted to Edwin T. Hyde, Jr. of the Winchester Repeating Arms Company, whose interest in the subject prompted the inquiry leading to the letter quoted.]

*Development of Shotguns*

Compared with the development of rifles and pistols, the history of shotguns has been relatively prosaic. Descendant of the old blunderbuss, which scattered a handful of missiles over a range of about a hundred feet, the modern gun delivers pellets effectively between fifty and seventy-five yards in a closer group than the ancient weapon, and is a lighter and stronger firearm. Quick shooting at short range, without the necessity of taking accurate aim, however, remains its distinctive qualities. In ignition, breech-loading, and in the adoption of repeating actions, the shotgun has generally followed the ideas brought out in connection with the rifle.

Down to about the middle of the nineteenth century the barrel of the shotgun remained simply a smooth-bore cylinder. Some time after the breech-loading principle was applied to shotguns around 1850, it was discovered that by choking or narrowing the barrel slightly at the muzzle the missiles or pellets would stay bunched together.

One of the first American patents covering a choke barrel was granted to Sylvester Roper of Roxbury, Massachusetts, in July 1868 (US 79,861). In his application he noted: "It is well known that some shotguns will scatter the shot much more than others of the same caliber. I have discovered, by repeated experiments, that the scatter of the gun depends mainly upon the shape of the extreme end of the barrel or muzzle." Roper did not claim a patent covering this principle but was granted a patent on a detachable muzzle which could be applied to any shotgun which would convert it into a choke-bore.

Probably the construction of barrels has presented the greatest problem in connection with shotgun development. To handle the heavy charge of lead the bore must be large and the barrel must be long enough to point well and to avoid the unpleasantness of having the muzzle blast too close to the shooter's face. Because of the low pressure developed compared with the rifle, however, the barrels may be thin, which has the advantage of keeping the weight of the arm down.

A great deal of time and attention has gone into the problem of barrel-making. One type of barrel that proved especially suitable was the Damascus or "twisted" barrel, made by twisting and welding alternate strands of wrought iron and steel into a cylinder which was then reamed to proper size. Until quite recent times this type of barrel was the mark of an expensive gun. Only as control over the quality of metal was improved and better steel was produced was it possible to drill satisfactory shotgun barrels out of a solid rod.

English gunmakers took the lead in the production of shotguns. Beginning around the middle of the nineteenth century, they became increasingly popular in the United States, especially for birds and small game. Most of the early guns used appear to have been imported from Britain and Belgium. A few American manufacturers, including Sylvester Roper, who combined forces with Spencer around 1865, began production in the late 1860s. Soon after, the larger gun companies began considering adding shotguns to their line.

## *Winchester Shotguns*

Winchester's first venture into the shotgun market came in 1880, when the Company announced a line of double-barrel, breech-loading guns. These were advertised as the Winchester Match Gun, listed at $85, and Winchester classes A, B, C, and D, which were priced at $70, $60, $50, and $40, respectively. Also available were lower-grade shotguns at $20 and up.

These shotguns were not manufactured by the Winchester Repeating Arms Company, but were imported from British makers and distributed through the New York office of the concern. Apparently unwilling to market a gun under the Winchester brand name that was not produced by the Company, the name Winchester was removed from these guns in 1881 and they were simply listed as Match and classes A, B, C, and D.

In 1884 the Company dropped its line of imported shotguns. One of the reasons for this decision was that the marketing of these guns put the Company into competition with the jobbers who were also handling imports. It is also possible that this decision was influenced by the Tariff Act of March 3, 1883, under which, "all sporting breech-loading guns" had to pay an *ad valorem* duty of thirty-five per cent. As these guns had previously come in duty free, it is not unreasonable to assume that the effect of the tariff was to cut profits margin to the point where there was no longer any advantage in handling the imported articles.

## *The Winchester Lever-Action Shotgun*

The Company did not remain long out of the shotgun business. The imposition of the tariff and the demand of the American market were a combination that appealed to the management that was following a policy of diversifying production.

The demand in the American market was based upon an abundance of wild life that the modern shooter finds hard even to imagine. Paul Jenkins, speaking of the 1870s, describes how "Every forest swarmed with partridge, Virginia to the 'Indian Territory' with quail, the Middle West with prairie chickens (I know of sixty being shot over dogs in one Illinois stubble in one afternoon.) Ducks and geese in every variety were everywhere in numbers as incredible today as they were then supposedly to be inexhaustible. At the junction of the Vermillion and the Missouri in the 'Territory of Dakota'—the site as it chanced, of Audubon's camp of 1843 for his studies of American water fowl—I saw certainly 10,000 awing at one time and not anyone considered it extraordinary. Mississippi sandbars were often solid with acres of snow geese, and Chesapeake Bay with rafts of swans. As for jack snipe, I once shot 98 in two half-days on one Missouri marsh and there were hundreds left when I ran out of ammunition." [6]

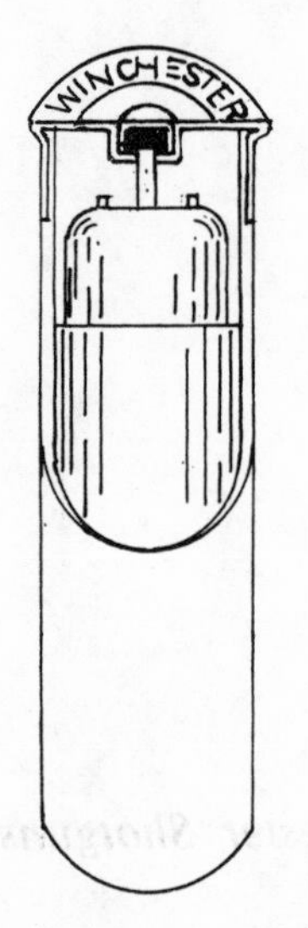

10-Gauge Sectioned Shot Shell

While the most widely used guns of the time were single-barrel or double-barrel models, it is not astonishing that Winchester should be interested in producing a lever-action repeating shotgun. Browning showed his versatility by inventing such an action in February 1886. This was not the first repeating shotgun made in the United States; Colt's had put out one using the revolver action; Roper made one with a revolving magazine in 1866, and Spencer a slide-action model in 1882. While Browning's gun was then the fourth American repeating shotgun, it was the first successful one. The action was simple and rugged and held up well in the hands of the shooters. The gun carried four shells in the magazine under the barrel, and one in the carrier.

Even before the gun was announced in the Company's catalog for May 1888 it had tied for first place with a double gun in a trap shooting contest at Plainfield, New Jersey, held in February 1887. Until it was superseded by the "trombone" form of repeater, the Winchester lever-action shotgun enjoyed a considerable popularity. Approximately 79,000 were sold up to the time its manufacture was discontinued in 1919. Made in both 10- and 12-gauge, the standard gun, with a rolled steel barrel, was priced at $25, which put it into competition with the lower-priced imported guns. For those who wished, the Company offered a three-blade or four-blade Damascus barrel at an extra cost of $15 and $25, respectively.

## *Production of Individual Gun Models*

Because the records of the annual sales of individual models produced by the Company have not been preserved, it is not possible to measure accurately their popularity in the market. There are available figures on annual production for each model during this period, which indicate the estimate of the management as to how well the various guns would sell. A comparison of these figures with total yearly sales indicates some production for inventory, but over the period, the production and sales show a fairly close correlation.

The production figures given here confirm the comments about the relative popularity of the various models. As might be expected, the Model 66 was produced in small quantities and 1884 marked the end of its manufacture. But the last one was sold in 1898. The production of the Model 76 and the Model 83 made up approximately ten per cent and twelve per cent of the total production for the period. The single-shot was moderately popular, while the Model 86 and the lever-action shotgun had not been in production long enough to show any trend.

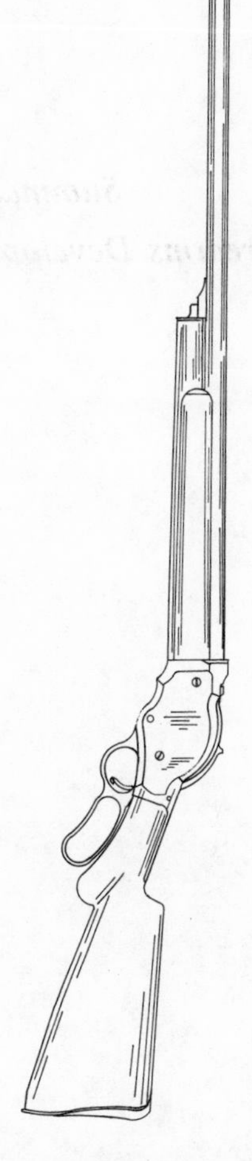

*Winchester Model 1887 Lever-Action Shotgun*

PRODUCTION OF INDIVIDUAL MODELS
AND TOTAL SALES: 1881-1889
(in thousands)

| *Year* | *Model 66* | *Model 73* | *Model 76* | *Improved Hotchkiss Model 83* |
|---|---|---|---|---|
| 1881 | 5.0 | 20.5 | 10.0 | 10.0 |
| 1882 | — | 24.1 | 10.7 | 3.0 |
| 1883 | 5.5 | 36.9 | 12.3 | 1.8 |
| 1884 | 5.1 | 34.1 | — | 20.9 |
| 1885 | — | 25.3 | 10.4 | 14.1 |
| 1886 | — | 20.4 | — | 8.3 |
| 1887 | — | 28.8 | 8.0 | — |
| 1888 | — | 37.1 | — | — |
| 1889 | — | 37.1 | — | — |
| TOTAL | 15.6 | 264.3 | 51.4 | 58.1 |

| *Year* | *Single Shot* | *Model 86* | *Lever Action Shotgun Model 87* |
|---|---|---|---|
| 1881 | | | |
| 1882 | — | — | — |
| 1883 | | | |
| 1884 | — | — | — |
| 1885 | 4.8 | | |
| 1886 | 5.6 | — | — |
| 1887 | 12.5 | 5.2 | 7.3 |
| 1888 | 21.5 | 14.5 | 18.4 |
| 1889 | .5 | 9.9 | 5.1 |
| TOTAL | 44.9 | 29.6 | 30.8 |

| *Year* | *Rifles Produced* | *Rifles and Shotguns Produced* | *Total Sales Rifles and Shotguns* |
|---|---|---|---|
| 1881 | 45.5 | 45.5 | 41.5 |
| 1882 | 37.8 | 37.8 | 44.8 |
| 1883 | 56.5 | 56.5 | 41.4 |
| 1884 | 60.1 | 60.1 | 49.0 |
| 1885 | 54.6 | 54.6 | 51.1 |
| 1886 | 34.3 | 34.3 | 46.4 |
| 1887 | 54.5 | 61.8 | 61.4 |
| 1888 | 73.1 | 91.5 | 64.4 |
| 1889 | 47.5 | 52.6 | 72.0 |
| TOTAL | 463.9 | 494.7 | 472.0 |

The most striking feature of the table is the continued large production of the Model 73, which, except for the single year 1884, was manufactured in larger numbers than all the rest combined. It is quite apparent that the Company continued to be dependent upon this model for the bulk of its gun sales and that the other models were supplementing rather than replacing it in the market.

### *Summary of Firearms Development*

Browning was the answer to the Company's need for an exceptional designer who could help maintain the concern's position as the leading producer of repeating firearms. Including those already mentioned, Winchester had, by the end of 1889, acquired some thirteen patents from the Ogden inventor. Several of these, as has been indicated, were incorporated in the new models brought out during the period. In some cases, they were used in later models, while others were never developed beyond the experimental stage. Thanks largely to this working arrangement with Browning the Company not only had in the Model 86 a rifle that could handle high-powered ammunition, but it had expanded its line to include the single-shot and the repeating shotguns, and had laid the foundation for further expansion in subsequent years.

There were certain minor irritations which accompanied dealings between the Company and Browning. These were due in part to the geographical separation of Ogden and New Haven, and in part to differences of opinion on the merits of the modifications made by the Company in the models submitted by Browning before they were put into manufacture.

On the latter point the Company took the position that the models, made as they were under the limited shop conditions of the inventor, were too crude to be put into production without rather extensive modifications. Browning took a somewhat natural pride in his handiwork and felt that many of the changes were unnecessary. Working at a distance meant that problems had to be handled largely by correspondence although Browning would visit New Haven from time to time. But on the whole, the relationships between Browning and the Company were amicable and based upon mutual respect and trust.

Apparently the arrangement between Browning and the Winchester Repeating Arms Company was never formalized in a general contract. Winchester stood ready to purchase all of his patents having to do with shotguns and rifles and Browning would send his working models to New Haven as soon as he developed them. The Company made the necessary patent search and arrangements for application to the Patent Office. The patents were taken out in Browning's name and assigned to Winchester at a price that was agreed on for each invention.

It should be noted that the Company always made an outright purchase and never entered into a royalty agreement with Browning. An absence of records makes it impossible to state how much the latter received for his inventions sold to the Company. It is believed that he was paid $50,000 for the patent covering the Model 86 rifle.[7] This was undoubtedly a top price and paid because of the importance of the repeating action involved. The best estimate is that he averaged around $16,000 for patents covering each gun.

Considering the small scale of their operations during the early 1880s, these sums must have added considerably to the income of John Browning and his brothers. Until they were firmly established financially it is doubtful whether they would have been interested in a royalty arrangement.

During the decade following 1880, the production of metallic ammunition was not marked by any outstanding innovation comparable with the introduction of the centerfire cartridge, or the use of smokeless powder which came later. Except for comparatively minor changes, cartridge design was relatively stabilized. There was, however, a great expansion in the variety of centerfire cartridges which reflected the growing number and increasing popularity of rifles using this type of ammunition.

There was almost a fourfold increase in types of centerfire cartridges from 39 in 1881 to 140 in 1889. In this expansion, the Company was following the policy begun in 1873 of manufacturing ammunition for every type of small arms currently used.

Noting that "As a matter of economy, many sportsmen desire to have cartridges that will reload," the Company called attention to the fact that all of its centerfire rifle cartridges "are made of extra thickness for this purpose." Two handloading tools were advertised in the 1889 catalog: one for small and medium calibers and one for large sizes. "Where the powder is compressed, and where it is desired to resize the shell throughout the greater part of its length." Recommendations regarding the best brands of powders to use for various types of cartridges were also given.

Winchester was able to capitalize to a considerable extent on its position as both a gun and ammunition producer by introducing new types of cartridges simultaneously with its new model firearms. In 1882, the Company brought out a .32-20 centerfire cartridge to be used in the Model 73 rifle which was made available in that caliber the same year. The Model 86 was chambered for the U. S. Government .45-70-405 and the .45-70-500 cartridges, but the Company also announced two especially developed cartridges the same year which could be used with the arm; the WCF (Winchester Center Fire) .45-90-300 and the WCF .40-82-260. The following year the WCF .40-65-260 and WCF .38-56-255 were added for the same gun. These cartridges were developed to get higher velocities and a flatter trajectory desired by hunters although with black powder the greater velocity usually resulted in some loss of accuracy. The WCF .45-90-300 was probably the most successful of the group and enjoyed considerable popularity among shooters.

The cartridges developed by the ammunition companies were not patentable insofar as the specifications regarding caliber, powder load, and weight of the bullet were concerned. Certain components, such as primers, could be patented but there was nothing to prevent any company from duplicating as far as possible a cartridge originally issued by another concern. Indeed it was only a matter of time before any new type that promised to be popular, would be issued by rival concerns. Winchester, for example, manufactured "Remington" cartridges for the firearms produced by that concern, and other ammunition producers put out "Winchester" cartridges with the same specifications as those manufactured by Winchester. These, however, carried the individual firm's solution of particular problems and while the cartridges would chamber they were generally different in detailed design. To some extent these differences would catch the consumers' fancy, but these preferences were not strong enough to stand up under any considerable price difference between brands of either metallic ammunition or shot shells.

While the general design of metallic cartridges remained stabilized, there appears to have been considerable improvement made in the manufacturing processes. A number of William Mason's patents were taken out covering ammunition-making machinery during these years, although a lack of data makes it impossible to trace their effect.

One notable technical improvement in primers can be credited to the Winchester organization. The primer used for centerfire cartridges and shot shells consists of a cup or cap containing a priming mixture which is inserted in a pocket in the center of the head of the cartridge. It is placed in position against a small piece of metal, called the anvil. When the firing pin strikes the priming cap and pushes it against the anvil, the priming mixture explodes and ignites the powder in the cartridge of the shot shell. Primers measure about one-fifth of an inch in diameter and as they have to fit snugly into the pocket in the cartridge head, their manufacture requires a high degree of accuracy.

In 1878, John Gardner, Winchester's cartridge superintendent, took out a patent for an improved primer [8] which was assigned to the company. Instead of the older solid and rigid types of anvil Gardner's patent covered a novel type of folded anvil with sufficient spring to the metal to grip tightly against the inside of the primer cup. It was a clever and practical solution of many of the previous primer difficulties and it was immediately adopted in 1879 and contributed to the high reputation of the Company's ammunition during the succeeding decade. It also made for a somewhat simpler problem of manufacture and assembly. Winchester later found that primers constructed in this way would be used with smokeless loads and the Company continued their use down to recent times.

*Shot Shells*

For the first few years following 1880 there was little change in the Winchester line of shot shells. Production was confined to primed and unprimed brass and paper shot shells, wads, and primers, which were sold to users who loaded them according to their own preference in respect to powder and shot combinations.

Handloading was quite an operation. Paul B. Jenkins recalls the time when, "We all 'rolled our own' and paper or brass shells, decappers, recappers, red and green canisters of powder, canvas bags of shot, powder and shot measures, green and pink cardboard rolls of felt and card wads, the loading block, the rammer, and the crimping tool—all were indispensables of every hunter's equipment." [9]

It was during this period that the ammunition companies began loading shot shells in the factory. Despite the hours saved in preparing shells for hunting, not all shooters were convinced of their acceptability. On this point Jenkins notes, "About 1885 machine loaded shells were fairly widely purchasable, and a subject of debate at every gathering of shooters was whether or not it was possible to load them by machinery with the reliability of one's own product."

The loading of paper shot shells in the factory was made possible by the development of mechanical loading machines which cut the costs of manufacture so that the loaded shells could be sold at an attractive price. This machinery appears to have been developed and constructed by the various ammunition producers. As the processes were usually well guarded, it is not possible to trace their evolution. It seems reasonably clear that no spectacular innovations or inventions were involved. Improvements appear to have resulted from continual experimentation with the details of the processes.

*Plant in 1889*

*Summary of Ammunition Development*

Despite real progress in the development and manufacture of ammunition, the problems facing the Company in this department were still formidable in 1889. The metallography of brass and copper was unknown and no one knew how to prevent neck-cracking in centerfire reduced shells. The priming mixtures were fairly stable as long as the chlorate fulminate mixtures were maintained, but the residue caused trouble from amalgamation on reloading. The rimfire caliber .22 cartridges loaded with black powder were so dirty that unless the barrel was cleaned frequently, it was impossible to shoot a box of shells without a bullet sticking in the barrel. Shot shells cut off in spite of reinforcements such as steel liners and the like, and not until the accordion-pleated base was hit upon was there a satisfactory solution to this problem. Waterproofing and fireproofing of paper shot shells presented further difficulties. Even under normal storage conditions shells would often swell so they would not chamber. Misfires and hangfires were quite common. The inadequacy of rule-of-thumb and empirical methods was becoming increasingly apparent. Sooner or later the manufacturers would have to enlist the aid of scientifically trained personnel to work out solutions to these problems.

*The Brass Mill*

Until the early 1880s Winchester purchased its sheet brass and gilding metal used in the manufacture of metallic ammunition and shot shells from outside suppliers, chiefly in Waterbury, Connecticut. In 1881 the directors, as a part of a general expansion program authorized the construction of a brass-rolling mill. The completion of this mill in 1883 marked an important step in further integrating the production of ammunition in the Winchester plant and was a part of a general movement to make the Company relatively independent of outside suppliers. The immediate incentive for the construction of the mill was apparently connected with a movement among the brass manufacturers to stabilize their competitive relationships through the formation of pooling agreements designed to control prices and production.[10]

CHAPTER NINE

# COMPETITION IN MARKETING FIREARMS

By continuing to acquire competing firms when the opportunity presented itself, and by elaborating its marketing procedure, Winchester was able to strengthen and consolidate its position between 1880 and 1890. These two policies paralleled the expansion of the types of firearms the Company manufactured.

In 1880 the best-known firms in the firearms industry (including pistols and revolvers) were, in addition to the Winchester Repeating Arms Company, Colt's Patent Firearms Manufacturing Company, of Hartford, Connecticut; Smith & Wesson, of Springfield, Massachusetts; Whitney Arms Company and Marlin Firearms Company of New Haven, Connecticut; and E. Remington & Sons of Ilion, New York.

Of these firms the only one that did not produce firearms that were more or less competitive with the Winchester line was Smith & Wesson which confined its attention to revolvers, but the others including Colt's had or were about to manufacture repeating rifles.

*"Gentlemen's Agreement" with Colt's*

In the museum of the Winchester Repeating Arms Company there is a collection of five revolvers, other than the Borchardt group mentioned before, which appear to have been made up sometime around 1883. As the Company has never manufactured pistols or revolvers for sale, this collection has raised some interesting speculations.

It seems reasonably clear that these arms played an important role in an informal agreement made around 1883 between Colt's Patent Firearms Manufacturing Company of Hartford and the Winchester Repeating Arms Company. Winchester was especially sensitive to the competition of any repeating rifle that employed a finger-lever action. In July 1883, Colt brought out the Burgess-Colt repeating rifle, chambered for the Winchester .44-40 centerfire cartridge, which used a finger-lever action developed by Burgess. In external appearance this gun was almost identical to the Winchester Model 73 and its action was equal if not superior to that arm.

The Winchester management was fully aware of the threat this rifle held for their own models. Many years later T. G. Bennett told Edwin Pugsley that, at this point, the Company made up several revolver models and took them up to Hartford ostensibly to get the advice of the pistol experts regarding their mechanical features and marketability. In this move, Winchester revealed an "ace in the hole" because their models had certain desirable features that had not been incorporated by Colt's in its own line.[1]

No formal agreement was made, but in November 1884, Colt's discontinued the manufacture and sale of its lever-action rifle. Winchester in turn put the revolvers into its collection of experimental models and continued its policy of not manufacturing pistols or revolvers. It should be noted, however, that this tacit agreement applied only to the lever-action guns. In 1885, Colt's brought out the Colt Lightning magazine rifle, a slide- or pump-action gun that was competitive with the Winchester in the general repeating-rifle field in 1885 and a direct competitor with the slide-action rifles brought out by Winchester in 1890 and later.

*Purchase of Whitney Arms Company*

In 1887, Winchester was asked to consider the purchase of the Whitney Arms Company of Whitneyville, Connecticut, just outside of New Haven. Eli Whitney, the founder of the business, had carried on the production of firearms at this location from 1798 until his death in 1826. His son Eli Whitney, Jr., was only six years old at the time of his father's death and the organization was put in the hands of two uncles, Eli Whitney Blake and Philos Blake until 1842, when Eli Whitney, Jr., assumed control. The Company continued to produce firearms and was especially active during the Civil War.

In 1864, the business was incorporated as the Whitney Arms Company, and after the end of the war expanded its offerings of firearms for the sporting market. By the middle of the 1880s the Company was featuring two single-shot models, the Whitney and the Phoenix, and two repeating rifles, the Burgess and the Kennedy.[2] (*See Appendix A-3.*)

The single-shot models were, of course, competitive with Winchester's newly adopted model, but the repeating rifles were a more serious threat. Both of these were lever-action guns with the magazine under the barrel. The Whitney version of the Burgess which had been brought out in 1879 was almost a duplicate of the Burgess-Colt, already noted, and like that model was chambered for the .45-70 Government cartridge, but could also handle the same list of cartridges as the Winchester Models 73 and 76, and was a direct competitor with those guns.

At the meeting of the board of directors of the Winchester Repeating Arms Company on December 22, 1887, "It was voted that the Executive officers of the Company be authorized to purchase the business of the Whitney Arms Company for a sum not to exceed $65,000 and further to lease their property and water privileges at a sum not exceeding $35,000 per year for a term of twenty (20) years."

On the following February 8, the officers reported to the board that ". . . they had concluded the purchase of the business and machinery of the Whitney Arms Company, of New Haven, Connecticut, and the lease of their property and water power for a term of ten (10) years with the option of renewal."

Following this purchase the Winchester Repeating Arms Company withdrew the Whitney line of firearms from the market. It is not known whether the purchase included the Burgess and Kennedy patents, but in any event, Winchester made no attempt to manufacture a rifle utilizing these actions. By this time, of course, the Winchester Model 86, handling the heavier cartridges, was already in production.



The Whitney plant, called the Water Shop, was operated under lease by Winchester until 1903, the land and buildings were sold by the Whitney interests to the New Haven Water Company and Winchester moved the machinery and tools to its main plant.

*The Remington Arms Company*

In 1888, the Winchester Repeating Arms Company joined with Marcellus Hartley of the Union Metallic Cartridge Company to purchase the Remington Arms Company of Ilion, New York. This was a real prize. Started in 1816 by Eliphalet Remington, the business had grown during succeeding decades into one of the largest and best-known firms in the industry. Remington firearms were used extensively in the Mexican War but it was during the Civil War that the company, now the partnership of E. Remington & Sons, expanded sharply and emerged in 1865 with a plant employing around a thousand workers.

Incorporated in 1865, under the same name as the partnership, two years later the company advertised an extensive line of ". . . revolvers, rifles, muskets, carbines, shotguns, pocket, belt and repeating pistols, rifle canes, revolving rifles, rifle and shotgun and accessories." [3] Early in the 1870s the Remington Company began production of cartridges and cartridge-making machinery.

Beginning around 1867, Remington began to sell extensively in foreign markets. An estimated one million arms were sold to the governments of Denmark, Spain, Egypt, Puerto Rico, Cuba, Chile, Mexico and China. The decline in foreign business which came in the late 1870s found the company overexpanded. Meanwhile, a number of other lines had been started, including the manufacture of typewriters, agricultural machinery, cotton gins, and sewing machines. The financial position of the company steadily deteriorated and sometime in 1886 it went into the hands of receivers.

At a meeting of the board of directors of the Winchester Repeating Arms Company on January 24, 1888, Converse referred to the forthcoming receiver's sale at public auction of the Remington armory at Ilion, New York, to be held the first day of the following month. According to the minutes, "Messrs. Hartley and Graham in a recent conversation with him asked if our Company would consider entering a syndicate with him for the purchase of a 3/5 or controlling interest in the Remington business and property which would probably require as our share $75,000. Mr. Converse said he would like to have the board authorize the executive officers of the Company to invest sufficient money to get such controlling interest in the Remington Company, providing after a thorough investigation it was thought advisable. On Motion it was voted that the executive officers of the Company be authorized to go into the Remington transaction to the extent of $75,000 if it was thought advisable."

At the meeting of the directors, held January 30, 1888, Converse and Bennett were authorized to bid up to $300,000, in behalf of the Winchester Repeating Arms Company, subject to a one-half interest in the purchase by Marcellus Hartley, for the land, plant, and machinery of the estate of E. Remington & Sons. They were also authorized to bid on sole account of the Winchester Repeating Arms Company to such amount as in their discretion the property was worth to the Company, it being understood that if purchase was effected on these terms Hartley should have the option of buying a half interest at the purchase price. A sale made February 1, 1888, was set aside by the court on a technicality and another sale ordered for March 7. On this latter date the property was bought by

Hartley and Graham for $200,000. The Winchester Repeating Arms Company paid $100,000 for one-half of the purchase. The plant was operated jointly with Marcellus Hartley as president and Thomas G. Bennett as vice president, manufacturing arms and bicycles until the Winchester Repeating Arms Company disposed of its interest to Mr. Hartley in September 1896. During this ownership there was a small migration of mechanics from Ilion to New Haven. This group was the source of a number of inside contractors for Winchester.

None of the repeating rifles produced by Remington utilized a lever action, but by this move Winchester now shared the control of what had been a major competitor in the industry, both in guns and ammunition. By agreement with Hartley, the Remington company did not put out a lever-action gun.

### *Company-Jobber Relations*

When Oliver Winchester was trying to build up a market for the products of the New Haven Arms Company and the Winchester Repeating Arms Company, it will be recalled that he sold both to jobbers and dealers. In fact many of his big customers combined both jobbing and retailing functions. As late as 1869 the total number of jobbing houses that were customers of the Company was less than two dozen. This number of outlets was no doubt sufficient at the time, but as production expanded and became more diversified it became necessary to increase the number of jobbing houses in order to insure adequate distribution.

Because of a lack of records it is not possible to trace the intermediate changes, but sometime after 1869, sales directly to dealers seem to have been abandoned. By 1887 Winchester had on its list of customers some 141 domestic and around 18 Canadian houses. The increased number of jobber outlets undoubtedly served to provide a wider distribution of Winchester products. It also meant that relationships between the jobbers and the Company became more formalized.

In selling through jobbers or wholesalers who in turn supplied the retail outlets, Winchester followed the practice that was almost universal at the time. The spectacular rise of the mail-order houses, chain stores, and revival of direct selling to retailers or consumers, were still largely in the future. The jobbing houses, therefore, occupied a key position in the marketing structure. Each had its own group of retail dealers who customarily depended on it to supply them with merchandise in amounts and at times that were convenient, and on satisfactory price and credit terms. In some instances this dependence was strengthened by direct financial control of retailers by the jobbing houses. Within limits dealers would purchase the brands of merchandise handled or recommended by their own jobbers.

The bargaining relationships between jobbers and manufacturers varied considerably. In some instances the producers were owned in part or entirely by the jobber. Not infrequently financially independent manufacturers supplied jobbers with merchandise carrying the latter's own trade mark. The E. C. Simmons Hardware Company of St. Louis, for example, had already made its Keen Kutter trade mark famous by the late 1880s, under which it sold a large number of purchased articles. In other cases where manufacturers maintained financial independence and were producing their own trade-marked articles, the jobbers might handle several competing brands. Finally there were concerns whose products were so well known that the jobbers were willing to agree to handle them exclusively or at least give them preferential treatment. The Winchester Repeating Arms Company was in this last category, especially in respect to repeating rifles.[4] The popularity among users was such that dealers and jobbers found it desirable to carry them.

The preference for Winchester products should not be exaggerated. The Company by no means had a monopoly in the field, and could not be sure that jobbers and dealers wouldn't push the sale of competing lines. Several steps were taken to insure the continuance of Winchester's position in the market.

To keep up dealer and retail customer interest the Company advertised in sporting and hardware journals; it developed a group of "missionaries" who called on dealers, not to take orders, but to be sure they were kept informed about Winchester products and were pushing the Winchester line, and it made sure that the Company's guns and ammunition in the hands of expert shooters were represented at leading shooting matches. This last activity was especially important. Handloading by individual shooters was still widely practiced and special loading companies were beginning to increase their output. If shooters, using factory-loaded cartridges and shot shells, were successful in shooting matches it would help build up a demand for this type ammunition. These types of promotion became more important after 1890, and will be described in more detail in a succeeding chapter.

The Company's policies were: first, to maintain uniform prices at which all jobbers would sell to dealers; second, to have jobbers handle Winchester firearms exclusively or at least give them preferential treatment; and third, to keep the large jobbers as customers. Of particular interest is the system of rebates worked out by the Company to secure adherence to the agreements reached between it and the jobber.

*Rebate and Discount Pattern*

By the early 1880s the following rebate and discount pattern had emerged. All jobbers were given the same trade discounts, which remained at 25 per cent, 10 per cent, and 10 per cent off list prices for the period. For rebate purposes the jobbers were divided into three groups, depending upon the amount of business they did with the Company. The amount of the rebates, which varied from time to time, was scaled according to the amount of business done, and payment was made contingent upon satisfying the terms of the agreements with the Company.

This arrangement of differential rebates gave the preferred jobbers a substantially larger mark-up on guns than that received by the smaller houses. In part this was the price Winchester was willing to pay in order to keep the big jobbers as customers. To some extent, however, these differentials were justified by the size of the individuals' orders which cut handling costs to the Company. It was also a part of a policy to enable the big houses who distributed their products over a wide geographic area, to compete with smaller jobbers supplying a more restricted market, where transport costs from the jobber to the retailers were less.

*Price Policies*

An interesting feature of the price policies followed by the Company was that they were applied at two levels. There were changes in list prices, which because dealer discounts remained the same, probably resulted in proportionate changes in retail prices.[5] More important, from the point of view of securing and retaining the jobbers' interest in Winchester products, were variations in the effective price paid by the jobbers through changes in the amount of rebates. While these were not reflected in prices to dealers, they did affect the net return to the Company.

The changes in the list prices on the Company's firearms during the years 1880 to 1890 are shown in the following tabulation:

| | *1880* | *1881-1884* | *1885-1890* |
|---|---|---|---|
| Model 1866 | $24.00 | $22.00 | $16.00 |
| Model 1873 | 28.00 | 25.00 | 18.00 |
| Model 1876 | 32.00 | 27.00 | 19.50 |
| Hotchkiss | 25.00 | 25.00 | 19.50 |
| Single Shot | .... | .... | 14.50 |
| Model 1886 | .... | .... | 19.50 |
| 1887 Shotgun | .... | .... | 25.00 |

[*Note.* The price of the lever action shotgun is for the standard steel barrel model. All rifle prices are for the standard round barrel type. The prices of guns with octagon and half-octagon barrels ran somewhat higher and the carbine lower. In all cases of changes in list prices the same differentials were maintained among the various types.]

Until the agreement with Colt's and the purchase of Whitney and Remington, the Winchester organization was undoubtedly under competitive pressure on prices at the retail level. It was about this time that foreign imports of low-priced guns, largely single-shot rifles and shotguns, many being converted foreign army muskets, began to come in to the United States in increasing quantities. It was probably no coincidence, therefore, that the second and larger round of price reduction came in 1885, before these purchases and agreements were made and before the Model 86, handling the Government .45-70 cartridge had been put on the market.

The Company was also meeting increased competition at the jobber level. During the same period (1880 to 1890) there was a considerable increase in the amount of discounts from list prices and rebates given to the jobbing houses, as shown in the following tabulation:

| | *1880-84* | *1885 to June 1886* | *June 1886 through 1888* | *1889 through 1890* |
|---|---|---|---|---|
| Dealer Discount | 25+10 | 25+10 | 25+10 | 25+10 |
| Jobber C Discount | 25+10+10 | 25+10+10 | 25+10+10 | 25+10+10 |
| Jobber C Rebate | (*) | (*) | (*) | (*) |
| Jobber B Discount | 25+10+10 | 25+10+10 | 25+10+10 | 25+10+10 |
| Jobber B Rebate | (*) | 5 | 10+5 | 10+5 |
| Jobber A Discount | 25+10+10 | 25+10+10 | 25+10+10 | 25+10+10 |
| Jobber A Rebate | 5 | 10+10 | 10+10 | 15+5 |

(*) Determined by the Winchester Repeating Arms Company at end of contract period.

[*Note.* The categories A, B, and C have been applied arbitrarily to the jobbers based on their preferential position in respect to rebates.]

The combined effects of the reduction in list prices and the increase in rebates are shown in the following summary price index (1880-100) and dealer and jobber mark-ups: [6]

| Year | List Price | Net Price Dealers | Net Price A Jobbers | Dealers' Mark-up | A Jobbers' Mark-up |
|---|---|---|---|---|---|
| 1880 | 100.0 | 100.0 | 100.0 | 48.2% | 14.0% |
| 1881-84 | 90.0 | 90.0 | 90.0 | 48.2% | 14.0% |
| 1885-86 | 64.8 | 64.8 | 60.7 | 48.2% | 23.5% |
| 1886-87 | 64.8 | 64.8 | 54.6 | 48.2% | 37.1% |
| 1888-89 | 64.8 | 64.8 | 54.6 | 48.2% | 37.6% |

[*Note.* The price index is weighted to account for the high proportion of Model 73 sales to total, estimated to be approximately fifty per cent.]

*Foreign Marketing*

About the same time the Company was expanding and elaborating its domestic and Canadian marketing organization it took steps to strengthen its position in the foreign field. Prior to the 1880s, Winchester's chief contacts with foreign outlets was through sales representatives and indirectly through large export houses in New York. In 1875, James Kerr & Company of London, later to become the London Armoury Company, had been appointed to handle Winchester's products in Britain and in the British colonies.[7]

About 1885 it was decided that the Company's business would be stimulated and developed by direct representation and Thomas Emmett Addis was selected to act as a combination "missionary" salesman and direct Company representative. His immediate objectives were to see that Winchester had adequate representation in the principal trading centers, to be sure that the dealers handling the Company's products were in a favorable competitive position, and to take care of special orders that would not be handled through regular channels. Addis appears to have had wide discretionary power to make whatever arrangements were necessary to achieve these objectives. This is reflected in the discount and rebate policies followed in the foreign field.

The details are not clear, but foreign purchasers buying directly from the Company regularly received trade discounts somewhat higher than domestic dealers. This was probably because competition was somewhat keener in the foreign markets and because all prices were made f.o.b. New York. In addition to the regular trade discounts, Addis extended a rebate privilege to certain dealers who bought directly from the Company. The extension of rebates followed no uniform pattern but was apparently given whenever Addis thought they were desirable.

Full details are not available on the price policies followed in the foreign market but scattered quotations indicate that prices were reduced at about the same time and in about the same percentages as they were domestically. On occasion Addis would quote a special price to meet competition.

Addis sent a steady stream of letters to the Company about the prospects for business in various areas, the credit rating of merchants, shipping instructions, the nature of competition, trade restrictions, and the like. These letters have not been preserved but extracts and paraphrases covering 1887 and 1888 were entered into a foreign contract book which has been kept.[8] The datelines on Addis's letters clearly indicate the basis of his claim to the title of "World Traveler."

Addis's comments during this period give an impression of his own activities and the way the business was carried on in foreign markets at the time. The following, for example, give his opinion about the prospects for selling merchandise in various areas:

*Japan:* There is very little demand for sporting arms of any sort in Japan.

*Saurebaya, Java:* Dealing in arms is attended with some difficulties. Authorities will not permit more than ten guns of any description to enter the city in a month.

*Singapore, Straits Settlement:* This would be a grand market for arms were it not for the fact that their exportation is absolutely prohibited to all of those countries whose inhabitants desire to purchase them; the natives of Java, Borneo, and Sumatra desire arms, but no arms of any sort are openly allowed to leave this port for those places. However, it being a "free port" considerable smuggling is done; the penalty in case of detection is a fine of $5,000 and imprisonment.

*Bangkok, Siam:* Siam would be a grand market for our goods were free importation permitted but the regulations are practically prohibitive as a permit must be obtained from the King himself who will only grant a permit where he is satisfied the arms will not be used against him. Nevertheless arms are arriving from time to time without permits, but it is extremely risky business and the profit on our arms is not large enough to warrant any risks. The present regulations have been in force about a year. A good many of our guns were imported before these regulations went into effect, and they are much liked. The King's Body Guard were at one time armed with them, but now use Martini-Henrys of Belgian make which cost $13.50 Mexican each—every arm was furnished with a sword bayonet and an iron scabbard all *delivered in Bangkok,* the sale was made through Jucker, Bigg and Co. Therefore there is very little prospect of the Government purchasing our single shot muskets with bayonets and scabbards as we could not come near this price delivered.

T.E.A. had interviews with the Chiefs of Bureaus and the Commander-in-Chief of the Army and learned that they desire to purchase 5,000 muskets but they will have nothing but the Lee using the new cartridge which is being adopted by the Powers of Europe, cal. not exceeding 8 mm.

*Western Australia:* T.E.A. does not think it advisable to visit there—no town of 5,000 inhabitants, and would require months time to make the trip.

The Company had some trouble with producers of imitation Winchester firearms. There was a comment on Anton Bertrand et Fils of Liége, Belgium: "These parties have been buying counterfeit Winchesters from Pirlot and Fresart, but promise in future to push the genuine article because they can buy them for less. They gave the names of the parties engaged in the manufacture of imitation Winchesters, Pirlot and Fresart."

A subsequent arrangement with Pirlot and Fresart also located in Liége is of special interest because it shows Winchester's competitive position in respect to these imitation guns. Addis reported:

These parties are engaged quite extensively in the manufacture of imitation Winchesters; have an agent at Shanghai; have furnished quotations for lots of 1,000. They quote for 500 Winchester Model '73, 12 Shot Carbines: 70 francs each—our price $17.50 less 25 x 10% would be 53 16/100, a difference in our favor of 16 84/100 francs.

For Winchester Model '73, 16 shot muskets, they quote 79 50/100 francs. Bayonets 2 50/100 francs.

Mr. Pirlot promises in future to buy from us.

In view of the outbreak of the South African or Boer War that occurred some years later (in 1899) there is an interesting notation from Port Elizabeth,

Cape of Good Hope, "Only Winchester cartridges are used in Winchester guns by the Boers."

In some cases Addis dealt directly with government officials or agents. In Bangkok, Siam, for example, Ramsay & Company had an inside track with the Government. Addis reported on this firm: "Army Contractors, Commission Agents and General Warehousemen. They are good solid people—supply the army with clothing and other articles, but have not been able to place an arms contract although they have tried. Have many samples of military guns, among them a Hotchkiss musket old model and a Hotchkiss musket new model with sabre bayonet and scabbard. Mr. O. H. Ramsay, the manager, introduced T.E.A. to the army officials. Sent an order for very finely finished carbines and shot guns intended for the King and Princes occupying high places and some for Mr. O. H. Ramsay."

Jardine, Matheson & Company in Shanghai, China, held a similar position: "*The* merchants of the place—Do large shipping and insurance business. Negotiate loans for the Government. Take contracts for the supply of 'materials' of war. Mr. Macgregor, Manager. Mr. Spencer, Manager of the Arms Department."

There was one dealer in Sydney, New South Wales, W. S. Friend & Company, with whom Addis had no success: "Will have nothing to do with us and feel very sore on account of our making no allowance for the rifles which were stolen and replaced by New York papers and bricks several years ago. They bought through W. H. Crossman & Brothers."

There were a few complaints about the Company's firearms. James W. Rosier, a large dealer in Melbourne, Australia, thought Winchester guns too heavy and preferred Colt's Lightning. He and other dealers wished that Winchester would get out a lighter gun for the Australian market. Addis noted that this same comment was made in Mexico.

Colt's and Marlin appear to have been the principal competitors in the foreign market. Addis noted with satisfaction that, "Mr. Bullard of H. W. Peabody and Company is pushing the Marlin rifle but not very successfully in Sydney." But he also noted that Sayle & Company in Singapore were handling Colt's "trombone" rifles which were finding a ready sale.

There is no way of determining how much the foreign sales contributed to Winchester's total business. The best guess, made by individuals long associated with the Company, is that probably they did not make more than ten or fifteen per cent of the total. This amount was significant enough to keep Addis on the road for many years.

*Gun Sales and Profits*

Winchester's gun sales increased nearly threefold during 1880-1890. (*See Appendix D-1.*) It is not possible to measure how much this increase was attributable to the policies followed by the Company. The period, however, was one during which the arms and ammunition industry as a whole grew relatively slowly. (*See Appendix H.*) For this reason, it is probable that Winchester's diversification of models, the agreement with Colt's and the purchase of Whitney and Remington, the strong relations with jobbers, and the drop in prices, were important factors in the expansion of sales.

In spite of the increase in the number of guns sold, it is doubtful, because of the sharp reduction of prices, whether the Company's total profits from this side of the business were any greater in 1889 than they had been in 1880, and in fact they may have been lower.

It is unfortunate that the remaining records of the Company are inadequate to provide a basis for estimating the effect of this fall in net price of guns upon the profits. As will be shown in the discussion of ammunition marketing in the next chapter, the information available concerning profits from that source is also not sufficient to provide a reliable starting point for proper analysis of the profits. Some generalizations can be attempted, however, from the data that are available.

While the index of the selling price to the jobbers on guns fell from 100 in 1880 to 54.6 in 1888-1889 (*see p. 116*), the index of sales of guns rose from 100 in 1880 to 273 in 1889. At the same time, there is good reason for assuming that the labor cost per gun also fell, the index of payments to labor contractors dropping from 100 to 73.3 over the same period. Labor costs, however, probably represented no more than a third of total costs (including overhead) and it would appear that if the costs of raw materials and overhead had remained the same, the fall in the net prices to the Company was great enough to absorb almost the whole of the effects of the increase in the number of guns sold.[9]

The substantial increase, during this period, of the Company's investment in productive assets in the shape of buildings and machinery suggests that the overhead costs of the Company increased, if only because of added responsibilities for repair and maintenance, insurance and real-estate taxes.[10] It may be fairly assumed, therefore, that the gun department's contribution to the total profit may have decreased *absolutely* during the nine years and that the growth in the profits through 1889 was, in fact, provided by the ammunition department.

By the end of 1889, the Winchester Repeating Arms Company had met the challenge to its position in the firearms field, on the technical side, by the introduction of new guns. It had faced the challenge of the competition situation, both on the technical and on the price side by two methods of approach. It made agreements with potential competitors, as with Colt's, or secured more or less control of their policies as in the cases of the outright purchase of the Whitney Arms Company and the securing of an interest in Remington (with Hartley and Graham). Prices were adjusted downward by lowering the list prices and by increasing the jobber and dealer margins. While these changes were at the cost of a reduction in the proportion of the Company's income derived from guns, they were more than offset by the increasing profitability of ammunition.[11]

CHAPTER TEN

# COMPETITION IN MARKETING AMMUNITION

## *Integration, Agreements, and Combination in American Industry*

The decade of the 1870s marked the beginning of a widespread movement among industrialists in the United States to avoid or soften the impact of competition. Several factors contributed to this movement. First, the standardization of products and the technical advances in methods of mass production involved large capital investment and increased the size of individual establishments. Second, improved transportation, brought about chiefly through the expansion of the railroad network, made competition keener over a wider area. Finally, there was a downward trend in prices that began about 1870 and continued to the middle 1890s.

The scope of this movement over the succeeding three decades can hardly be exaggerated. Among the better publicized industries that tried, in one way or another, to soften or avoid competition were salt, petroleum, steel, rubber, tobacco, cordage, wall paper, window glass, plate glass, nails, thread, baking powder, starch, smelting, leather, bicycles, photographic supplies, and coal. For every example that attracted public attention there were many others that lived and died in obscurity. Charles M. Schwab testified in 1901 to the ubiquity of cooperation among producers. Asked if there had been agreements in the steel industry prior to the formation of the United States Steel Company, he replied, "Yes; in all lines of business, not only in steel but everything else. There were similar agreements, known as joint agreements, to maintain prices. They have existed in all lines of business as long as I can remember." [1]

One of the most popular forms and the one most relevant to the history of Winchester was the pool. In some instances the pools took the form of simple agreements to divide markets or to maintain uniform prices; in other cases they were formalized by committees with power to allocate markets, set prices, and to administer marketing policies in general, including the distribution of the sales income to members according to agreed-upon quotas or percentages. The main advantage of the pool, from the standpoint of the members, was that each individual firm maintained its independence in respect to all matters except those covered by the pooling agreement. The main disadvantage was its relative instability and, after 1890, its questionable legal status under the American antitrust legislation.

As far as Federal statutes were concerned, there was no question about the legality of pooling agreements among business men prior to 1890.[2] The contracts involved were not enforceable in court if adjudged contrary to public interest, but if all parties to an agreement abided by it the law simply could do nothing about it. After the passage of the Sherman Anti-Trust Act in 1890, the situation changed, but as will be noted later, there was considerable uncertainty for many years as to whether that legislation applied to manufacturing establishments.

It is not astonishing that Winchester should become a member of a combination to control the marketing of ammunition. The nature of the business was such as to lead to cut-throat price competition. The product, despite the attempts of firms to build up consumer preference, was fairly standardized, so that relatively small price changes would attract customers to the lower-priced product. At any particular time the total demand was inelastic so that the aggregate amount of ammunition purchased would not be increased or decreased proportionately to changes in price. Finally, the investment cost of equipment was fairly high, but once installed the machinery was capable of turning out enormous quantities of product.

By the early 1880s the market, from the standpoint of the members of the industry, had become quite unsatisfactory. As explained by Arthur Earle, a former officer of the Winchester Repeating Arms Company, "There had been very serious competition among the larger ammunition manufacturers . . . and they thought it would be much better for all hands to get together and make some money rather than spend their time and money and energy cutting each other's throats." The result was the formation of a pooling arrangement operated through a corporation established for the purpose, and called the Ammunition Manufacturers' Association. This association was only one of a large number of similar organizations that lived and died in relative obscurity. Yet it played an important role in the history of its members and its organization and operation, in themselves, give an interesting case example.

### *Ammunition Manufacturers' Association*

The Winchester Repeating Arms Company joined the Union Metallic Cartridge Company, the U. S. Cartridge Company of Boston, Massachusetts, and the Phoenix Metallic Cartridge Company of South Coventry, Connecticut, and on September 27, 1883, the Ammunition Manufacturers' Association was incorporated under the laws of the State of New Jersey. The U. S. Cartridge Company had been started in 1864 by General Benjamin F. Butler to manufacture metallic ammunition. The Phoenix concern had been organized in 1872 and occupied the buildings vacated by Crittenden & Tibbals when that company's equipment was moved to Bridgeport by the Union Metallic Cartridge Company. It had been financed by the New York firm of Merwin, Hulbert & Company, which was the chief owner in 1883.[3] Neither company was as large as the Winchester Repeating Arms Company or the Union Metallic Cartridge Company, but both had been successful in the production and marketing of metallic ammunition.

The Association began business with one thousand dollars paid in capital and an issue of one thousand shares of stock with a par value of one dollar per share. William W. Converse held 374 shares for the Winchester Repeating Arms Company and an identical number were issued to the Union Metallic Cartridge Company. The U. S. Cartridge Company held 179 shares, Phoenix 79 shares, and Horace Fowler, a lawyer in New York City, the remaining 4 shares. The percentage of stock held by each company determined the share in general of the sales and profits. Precise division was effected through a series of agreements made by members of the Association.

According to the certificate of incorporation, the three main objectives of the Association were ". . . to buy and sell ammunition of all kinds and act as agent for others in the purchase and sale thereof; to make contracts with Manufacturers and Dealers in Ammunition for the purpose of producing and securing uniformity and certainty in their customs and usages and preventing serious competition between them; to settle differences between those engaged in the manufacture of or in dealing in ammunition, and to devise and take measures to foster and protect their trade and business."

To establish prices at which ammunition was to be sold, each member furnished its cost of manufacture on different items to the Association. From these figures an average cost was established on each product to which a shop profit of ten per cent was added. The resulting amount was called the Association cost, which was used as a base to fix list prices and the discounts available to jobbers and dealers. The Association profits were the difference between the net prices and the Association cost.

Each month the members reported their production of various lines and sent impression copies of all sales invoices to the Commissioner. The sales were tabulated and the total Association profits estimated, which were reported back to the membership.

At first glance, it appears that there would seem to be little incentive for any one company to push its sales. This, however, was not the case. In the first place, apportionment of the profits was subject to periodic adjustment based to a considerable extent on actual sales during the preceding period. Secondly, none of the members, especially the Winchester Repeating Arms Company and the Union Metallic Cartridge Company, could afford to let any one company get such a high percentage of total sales that it would be tempted to withdraw from the organization because it possessed a near monopoly of the business. The result was that, while competition was no longer on a price basis, it remained quite strong and active in terms of quality, brand, dealer preferences, and the like.

The principal classes of purchasers with which the Association was concerned included the dealers, the jobbers, and a special group of large jobbing houses and foreign commission houses. The commission houses or agents representing the Association in foreign countries were allowed the same discounts and rebates as the domestic special jobbing houses.

At the same time the Association was engaged in establishing stable relationships among the membership, it purchased several outside ammunition concerns. In 1884, for example, the Winchester Repeating Arms Company, the Union Metallic Cartridge Company and the U. S. Cartridge Company bought the Strong Cartridge Company of New Haven and distributed its machinery among themselves. In 1889 the business of the American Buckle and Cartridge Company of West Haven, Connecticut, was purchased and the machinery distributed in the same manner.

The members of the Association either collectively or individually also took steps to strengthen their ties with suppliers, and agreements or contracts were made with the principal producers of powder, lead and paper used in shot shells. The Winchester Repeating Arms Company on its own account purchased two hundred shares of the American Powder Company of Boston in 1883.

Cooperation among the members of the Association included a certain amount of pooling or sharing of patents on ammunition-making machinery. This sharing of patents did not extend to those that were developed independently by the members. In at least one instance, the Winchester Repeating Arms Company brought suit against the Union Metallic Cartridge Company for infringement on a patent covering the construction of shot shells.

List prices and discount rates remained unchanged from 1884 through 1889, indicating that whatever schedule was decided upon at the beginning was maintained through the period. Once stable prices had been established, the returns to the Association members seem to have been attributable more to the increase in the total demand for ammunition than to the degree of control over the industry achieved by the Association. According to the Bureau of the Census, the total value of ammunition produced in the United States in 1879 was $1.9 million; ten years later it was reported at $6.54 million. Even after making full allowance for any increase in unit prices, this must have represented between a two- and threefold expansion in output.

Information is lacking to measure with any accuracy the percentage of the 1889 figure contributed by Association members. If the rate of Association sales of around $1.5 million established for the ten-month period, January 3 to October 1, 1888, is assumed to apply to 1889, the figure for the latter year would have come to approximately $1.8 million. This would have amounted to about twenty-seven per cent of the industry's total of $6.54 million. Because the industry figure includes the value of the product of loading companies, which bought their components from others, including the Association members, some double counting was involved, which would mean that the Association's percentage of the total would actually be higher. At most, however, it is doubtful if the Association controlled over fifty per cent of the industry total.

The contribution of the ammunition department to the total sales and profits of Winchester Repeating Arms Company during the period covered by the Association agreements, can only be estimated. The reports of the Association show that from September 3, 1883 to October 1, 1888, Winchester's total sales of ammunition amounted to some $4.9 million which returned an "Association profit" of a little over $1.2 million. The Company's total net sales of firearms and ammunition for the nearest equivalent period, January 1, 1884, to December 31, 1888, came to $9.5 million on which the net profit was $2.2 million. On this basis something over one half of the sales were made by the ammunition department from which came a little more than one half of the net profit.

CHAPTER ELEVEN

# SUMMARY OF CONVERSE'S ADMINISTRATION

No separate information is available for the value of guns and ammunition produced by the Company, but combined sales of $2.5 million were over two and a half times larger in 1899 than they had been ten years before. (*See Appendix F.*) Winchester's share of the total industry value (taken from Census figures) for guns and ammunition rose from 12 per cent to 27 per cent, in part because of the drop in the value of firearms for industry. (*See Appendix H.*)

Employment for the Company in both guns and ammunition approximately doubled. Here again the drop on industry employment in firearms was a factor in increasing Winchester's proportion of the total, in this case from 7 per cent to 27 per cent. In ammunition, the Company held its own in the face of a general expansion; its share of the total industrial employment being 27 per cent in 1890. Taking the combined employment figures as a measure, Winchester's position as a firearms and ammunition producer moved from 10 per cent of the total to 27 per cent. (*See Appendix H.*)

Both in absolute and relative terms the Company's growth was impressive. Even after due allowance is made for the difficulties of comparison and the uncertainties of Census data, it indicates that the management was successful in strengthening and consolidating the Company's position as a producer of firearms and ammunition during these years.

*Financial Results*

The financial results were equally impressive, the net worth of the Company having increased some $2,519,152 to $5,563,253 by December 31, 1889. (*See Appendix G-5.*) This increase had been built up almost entirely out of earnings as the following statement shows:

| | |
|---|---|
| Profit from operations 1881–1889 | $3,988,355 |
| Other receipts | 10,797 |
| TOTAL | 3,999,152 |
| Less: dividends distributed | 1,480,000 |
| Surplus invested in business | $2,519,152 [1] |

Beginning in 1882, the Company began a building program that continued with varying degrees of activity over the succeeding thirty years. During 1881-1889 some $259,923 was spent on buildings, the floor area of the plant being more than tripled by the addition of some 230,000 square feet to the original 102,000 square feet developed on Tract B in 1870. At the same time, expenditures on machinery and equipment continued at a high rate, $873,176 being invested in this way, mostly during the years 1885-1888.

A continued increase in the dollar volume of sales (the annual average for the nine years was nearly $1.9 million, compared with an annual average of $1.4 million for 1873-1880), and suggests the need for additional working capital. (*See Appendix F.*) While the total net working capital did, in fact, increase by $1,108,520 the inventories show an increase of only $287,507, the rest of the growth being reflected in cash balances and outside investments. This situation was probably due in part, at least, to the sudden growth of sales in 1889. While the average for 1881-1888 was $1.8 million, sales in 1889 amounted to $2.5 million, so that it would not be unreasonable to expect a fall in inventories and an increase in cash for that year. That the Company was experiencing no difficulty in financing its outside activities is clear from the fact that it was able to increase its outside investments by $431,000 during the period.

This was in addition to the investment in Remington Arms Company which appeared on the balance sheet of December 31, 1899, at $175,075. The original cost was probably more but no information is available as to the details of the transaction or its impact on the Company's finances. This investment was probably regarded as different in nature from those made for the purpose of earmarking funds for future needs.

There was considerable relaxation of the earlier policy with regard to the rate of dividends. As shown in Appendix F, a little more than 37 per cent of the income was distributed as dividends over the nine years. This was equivalent to 16.4 per cent per annum on the issued capital at $1 million. It represented, from the stockholders' point of view, a substantial increase over their income in the period 1867-1880. This change in policy seems to have been progressive during the "Converse" period, for in the years 1887-1889 over 48 per cent of the profits was paid out to the stockholders.

With an increasingly liberal dividend policy there came, also, a first approach to giving the officers a direct interest in the profitability of the Company. At the board meeting of February 1, 1887, the officers voted the sum of $10,000 "to be distributed *Pro rata* to their present salaries." This was probably treated as an addition to their 1886 remuneration and represented an increase of 37 per cent. In the following April, the directors approved of the payment to the "executive officers," (presumably, the president, vice president, treasurer, and secretary) of additional salaries determined by the amount of dividend paid to the stockholders. The formula adopted for 1887 provided, "$1,375 for each (1) per cent of dividend declared and paid to stockholders above the customary regular dividend of (12) per cent." For 1888 the sum was increased from $1,375 to $1,575, the latter figure being applied, apparently, also in 1889.

The "customary regular dividend" of 12 per cent, referred to in the minutes, seems to have been adopted first in 1884, when quarterly dividends of 3 per cent were paid. After that year, the practice was followed of declaring the same quarterly dividends, with an extra amount added at the meeting of the board of directors held in January or February, just before the annual stockholders' meeting. On this basis the following dividends were declared: 1884, 12 per cent; 1885,

## WINCHESTER

# SINGLE SHOT RIFLE.

**THE BEST.**

ASK YOUR DEALER TO SHOW THEM.

**Send for 76 Page Illustrated Catalogue of Arms and Ammunition.**

# Winchester Repeating Arms Co.,

Stores, { 312 BROADWAY. NEW YORK
418 and 420 MARKET STREET, SAN FRANCISCO, CAL.

**NEW HAVEN, CONN.**

# WINCHESTER - Model 1886

## .50-100-450.

# A New Cartridge.

**.50 Caliber, 100 Grains Powder.**

**450 Grain Solid Bullet.**

LIST PRICE, $48 PER 1000.

To meet the demands of our friends for a .50 caliber carrying a heavy bullet, we are now prepared to furnish the above. The bullet has a penetration of about 16 pine boards ⅞ inch thick, and a trajectory of about 12 inches at 200 yards. This cartridge cannot be fired with good results out of the .50-110-300 rifle, but requires a barrel especially rifled for it.

# Winchester Repeating Arms Company,

## NEW HAVEN, CONN.

*Send for our 112 page catalogue-free.*

*Typical Advertisements of This Era*

17 per cent; 1886, 17 per cent; 1887, 22 per cent; 1888, 25 per cent; 1889, 50 per cent.[2]

These dividends provided substantial sums for the officers, as the following table shows:

| *Year* | *Additional Payment to Officers* | *Regular Salaries* | *Total* | *Additional Payment as % of Regular* |
|---|---|---|---|---|
| 1887 | $13,750 | $27,500 | $41,250 | 50% |
| 1888 | 20,475 | 31,500 | 51,975 | 65% |
| 1889 | 59,850 | 31,500 | 91,350 | 190% |

The "bonus" scheme seems to have been primarily devised to give Converse, who was a small stockholder during the period, some share in the expanding profits of the Company.[3] His regular salary had been raised from $10,000 to $16,000 in 1888 but the majority stockholders, who were represented by T. G. Bennett, apparently felt it would be appropriate to increase his income further through the bonus.[4]

These arrangements also offer an explanation for the increased generosity to the shareholders and demonstrate unequivocally the liquidity of the Company's affairs during this period. Considering the building and development program undertaken at this time, the officers would not have increased the dividend so as to secure a bonus of the size indicated, without due regard to the Company's commitments and other foreseeable needs.

W. W. Converse died on November 19, 1889, at the age of fifty-five. A review of the concern's development over the period during which he was president indicates that Converse was a worthy successor to Oliver F. Winchester. In fact, his grasp of the general problems that affected the Company during these years shows that Converse had many of the same abilities possessed by his predecessor.

Because Converse shared the management responsibility to a greater extent with his fellow officers, especially T. G. Bennett, than Winchester had, it is more difficult to credit him with specific policy decisions. It is unlikely that he had much to do with the development of ammunition or new model firearms or took much interest in the system of inside contracting. His activities were more concerned with the external relations of the Company. He seems to have played the principal role in negotiating the purchase of the Whitney Arms Company and Remington, in the formation of the Ammunition Manufacturers' Association, and in working out relationships with the jobbers. In terms of their significance for the fortunes of the Company, these policies compare favorably with any of the major decisions made by Oliver Winchester.

# PART 5

# REWARDS OF LEADERSHIP: 1890-1914

CHAPTER TWELVE

# END OF THE CONTRACT SYSTEM

*Management*

There was no question about selecting Thomas Gray Bennett, son-in-law of Oliver F. Winchester, to succeed William Converse as president of the Winchester Repeating Arms Company. The Winchester family still held a clear majority of the stock and the tradition had been established that a member of the family should be the active head of the business. Even without this backing, Bennett would have been a logical choice for the position. Not yet forty-five, he had been with the Company nearly twenty years and had served variously as secretary, treasurer, and vice president.

Those who knew Bennett remember a large man, erect in carriage, with a build that reflected his interest and participation in wrestling as a young man. His high-pitched voice and quiet, austere manner did not give an impression of power and drive unless he turned a pair of piercing, steel-gray eyes on someone who had failed to do his job. Generally kind and patient in his relations with associates, he took matters seriously and there was little joking in his presence. While he was frequently referred to as "T. G.," everyone called him "Mr. Bennett" except Hooper, who was his cousin and called him "Tom." Bennett's time and energies were almost completely devoted to the business, although he liked to get away occasionally to sail, fish, and hunt.

Born in New Haven, Connecticut, on March 22, 1845, Bennett attended Russell School in the same city until 1861, when at sixteen, he enlisted for service in the Civil War with the 28th Connecticut Volunteers. After serving as a lieutenant with that regiment for a time, he was transferred to the 29th Connecticut Volunteers. On September 20, 1864, he was wounded in the Battle of Chapins Farm and on the same day received a captain's commission.

After being honorably discharged from the Army in November 1865, Bennett entered Yale Sheffield Scientific School, graduating with the class of 1870. For a few months he was engaged in railroad construction, after which he entered the employ of the Winchester Repeating Arms Company where his first job was to survey the site and stake out the buildings for the Company's armory which was built in New Haven during 1870-71. He was then put to work in the gun shop following which he served in the model room, where new gun designs were worked out. With his election as secretary in 1871, he became increasingly active in the management of the Company.

While T. G. Bennett was not without considerable experience in various aspects of administration, his selection as president marked a change in the type of chief executive. Neither Oliver F. Winchester nor William Converse had received any formal scientific education or worked as a mechanic, nor was either a gun man in the strict meaning of the term. Their capacities had been more in the fields of finance and marketing, and both had largely delegated the responsibility for technical development to others. T. G. Bennett reversed this relationship. Four years of Army service had given him first-hand experience with firearms; to this had been added engineering training in one of the country's leading scientific schools, followed by an apprenticeship in the Company's machine shops and model room. Thus by training and experience he continued, after becoming president, to be primarily interested in this side of the business.

In many respects, these qualities made T. G. Bennett a sound choice to head the Winchester Repeating Arms Company during the greater part of the succeeding twenty-five-year period. Under the two preceding administrations the organization had been brought into a leading position in both gun and ammunition manufacture. Marketing relationships with jobbers and dealers were strong in both guns and ammunition, and finances had long since ceased to be a major problem. Success during the succeeding years was to be achieved by following the broad lines of policy already established. The principal innovation during this period was the introduction of smokeless powder which affected both firearms and ammunition in their design and manufacture; raising problems which the new president was especially well equipped to handle.

*Management Personnel*

Bennett shared the management with George Hodson and Arthur Hooper, who had been active during the preceding administration. At the meeting of the directors on February 12, 1890, at which Bennett was elected president, Hooper, who had been treasurer, was made vice president and Hodson was elected treasurer. Aro Ward replaced Hodson as secretary, but his duties appear to have been somewhat nominal.

At this meeting the bonus system of paying the officers was dropped and the following salary scale was adopted: president $10,000, vice president $9,000, treasurer $8,000, secretary $2,000.

This represented an increase in the base salaries of the vice president and treasurer to compensate them for the loss of the bonus. The president's salary reverted to the figure that had been paid Oliver Winchester during the latter part of his administration and Converse's until 1888. Bennett evidently considered it appropriate to follow Oliver Winchester's tradition of depending upon his stock for supplementary remuneration.

The top management administered the Company with a firm hand and under conditions of greatest secrecy. Bennett appears to have formally consulted his board of directors even less than did Oliver Winchester. This is not so astonishing as Bennett, Hodson, Hooper, and Daniel Veader, who was at that time an employee in the front office, were members of the seven-man board of directors. (The remaining directors were Morris Tyler, Frank Hooker and Wilber F. Day.) The other directors may have been consulted unofficially on matters of policy, but the minutes of the board meetings during Bennett's term of office were perfunctory to an extreme and only the briefest of financial reports were submitted orally to the group. (It is said that the directors were not allowed to carry any

*Thomas Gray Bennett*

written memoranda on these reports from the meetings.) Even less revealing financial statements were read at the annual stockholders' meetings.

This was all in the tradition of operating a closely held concern administered by a strong personality, but as the board customarily met for the pleasant task of declaring dividends, its members and the stockholders had little reason to object.

The executive group took its responsibilities seriously and worked hard on the job. Peter L. Smith, a former employee who came with the Company around 1900, recalls that "Mr. T. G. Bennett usually rode to work but the rest walked and were in the office before 7 a.m. The shop hours were 7 a.m. to 6 p.m. with one hour for dinner and Saturday from 7 to 5 p.m. The office hours were 7:35 a.m. to 11:50 a.m. and 1:20 to 5:35 p.m., but regardless of this, the chief executives worked shop hours and were very conscientious about not being late."

As operations became more complex and as Bennett in turn began to give some thought to his successor, the number of officers was increased and T. G. Bennett's son, Winchester Bennett, was brought into the management. T. G. Bennett even resigned as president in 1911, in favor of Hodson, and became consulting director. Despite these changes, which will be noted in more detail below, the 1890-1914 period was dominated by the leadership of T. G. Bennett, with the assistance of Hooper and Hodson.

*Management Functions*

It is doubtful if any of the top executives ever thought in terms of an organization chart. The three principal officers continued to share one large office which made it easy for them to operate more or less continuously as an informal executive committee. Although T. G. Bennett exercised the final authority, all important policy matters were apparently decided on a basis of group discussion.

If it had occurred to anyone to draw up an organization chart at the time, it would have shown the following general outline: Bennett, in addition to exercising general supervision, was directly responsible for technical matters concerned with developmental work and production; Hodson was in charge of finances, costs and purchases and had a small accounting staff working under him; Hooper personally took care of all sales, acting for a number of years as his own sales manager.

Directly in charge of manufacturing, and reporting to the front office, was the general superintendent. Under him were the superintendents of the gun and cartridge departments who were in turn responsible for the inside contractors and the foremen under their direction.

One feature of the organization which would not have been apparent from any organization chart was the jealousy with which each subordinate official ran his own department. "In those days a person was not allowed to wander where his business didn't take him." A cartridge employee would be as summarily ejected from the gun shop as a worker from the latter would be if he were discovered in the cartridge shop without permission.

One of the most important managerial problems affecting the internal operation of the Company during the 1890-1914 period involved labor-management relations. This problem was brought on principally because of the necessity of absorbing a rapidly increasing labor force and by a growing dissatisfaction with the system of inside contractors.

The expansion of the labor force, recorded for the decade of the 1880s, continued at a somewhat accelerated rate throughout the period 1890-1914. (*See Appendix J-1.*) From 1,430, the number had approximately doubled by 1900 and had doubled again by 1914, making the total employed over 6,000. A lack of records makes it impossible to indicate a division of employment between guns and ammunition, but it appears most likely that from 50 to 60 per cent continued to be employed in gun manufacture. Nor is it possible for the same reason to determine how many women workers were utilized. The best guess is that the approximate rate of 25 per cent established between 1880 and 1890 continued to apply after the latter date.

*Labor Force*

The plant continued to operate on the basis of a ten-hour day and six-day week and as far as can be determined there was no pressure on the management to change this schedule.

Probably the greatest attraction offered to workers at the Winchester Repeating Arms Company was the relative steadiness of employment. Only once between 1860 and 1915 did the plant shut down other than for Sundays, holidays, and occasional repairs. This occurred during the economic uncertainty brought on by the outbreak of World War I.

The management's reasons for keeping as many of its skilled workers employed as possible stemmed from a desire to keep its organization intact. Despite the extensive use of power-driven machine tools, gun manufacture and certain processes in ammunition production required the services of experienced hands. Both foremen and inside contractors were anxious to keep help which had demonstrated its ability to perform particular types of jobs. The net result was that once a worker had established a reputation with a foreman or a contractor he was reasonably sure of steady employment with the Company.

*Maintaining an Open Shop*

The Winchester concern was apparently unaffected by the early labor-union movements. The Knights of Labor waxed and waned during the 1880s and early 1890 without making any attempt to organize the workers in the plant. Between 1897 and 1904 the American Federation of Labor, organized along craft-union lines, expanded its membership from some 272,000 to nearly 1.7 million. It was during this drive for increased membership that the question of a labor union among the employees of the Company first presented itself, coming in 1901 in connection with an attempt by the International Association of Machinists to organize a group in the Winchester plant.

It is doubtful if there was any strong sentiment for unions in the Winchester plant at this time. Nevertheless, this limited attempt at organization seems to have greatly disturbed the management. Factory workers had up to this time been hired by the inside contractors or foremen. Feeling that the Company ought to exercise closer control over the employees who came into the plant, the management directed Albert Tilton, the superintendent, to give closer supervision to hiring. He began on an informal basis to screen all new employees. At first he exercised only a veto power, but his small office near the gate of the factory soon began to serve as an informal hiring hall. His assistant began keeping a record of all likely candidates for employment. Soon the foremen and contractors began to call upon the office when they needed new workers. Around 1903 these practices were formalized and all hiring was ordered done through this office. Personnel records were kept of all employees and applicants, including any information which would militate against their being hired or rehired. From the management's point, union activity was considered to be in this category.

### *Decline of Inside Contracting*

The advantages and disadvantages of the system of inside contracting to the Company have already been pointed out. Until 1905, fifteen years after T. G. Bennett came into office, the advantages of the system continued to outweigh the disadvantages in the eyes of the management. The number of contractors remained virtually unchanged during the same period, which meant that on the average each contractor had a larger labor group working under his direction. (*See Appendix J-2.*) It was not until about 1904 that the scale began to tip in the other direction. From that date on, the Company moved to reduce the number of contractors, and by 1914 the system had been virtually eliminated in both gun and ammunition production.

The reasons for this shift in policy were complex. They arose in part from certain weaknesses inherent in the contract system itself, in part from changes in administration personnel within the Company, and in part from external pressure.

To a considerable extent the growing dissatisfaction with the contract system, which came to a head in 1905, was a result of the management's own policy over the preceding period. In general terms, this policy was to lower contract rates by tightening up controls over the contractor, since the reduction in prices and discount policies adopted during the decade of the 1880s had apparently brought the margin of profits on firearms to a low level.

This policy may have been colored by a feeling that the large contractors enjoyed an economic and social position in the community that made it more difficult to secure the loyalty and cooperation of the Company's own administrative staff. There are stories of several contractors who came to work in fancy horse-drawn carriages, wearing frock coats, and sporting diamond stickpins, spats, and gloves. These individuals not uncommonly had subforemen under them and supervised their departments at arm's length.

One of the first steps in strengthening the management's control over the contract system was the appointment of Albert Tilton as general superintendent in 1892. Tilton had been one of the most successful of the Winchester contractors and knew all the intricacies involved in contract negotiation from first-hand experience. It was no small advantage to the Company to have the determination of contracts in his hands.

After 1890, the position of some of the large contractors was weakened by dividing the jobs among two or more individuals. The renewal of all contracts became more regular and formalized and each agreement was scrutinized carefully at the beginning of each year. This marked a change from the irregularity of such negotiation during the previous period. Beginning about 1903, the Company apparently began making a charge against the contractors for spoiled work and an expanded list of items was debited against the latter's account under the heading of "stores." There seems to be little question that contractor incomes had been sharply reduced by 1904. This is confirmed by the recollection of older employees now with the Company who recall the complaints and the reluctance to bid on certain jobs.



As the mechanical processes of manufacture became more fully developed and stabilized the importance of the contractors' role as innovators was lessened. Empirical methods, based on long experience and inherent mechanical aptitude were replaced by scientific principles and knowledge. During the earlier period the contractors had been able to cushion the impact of the rate reductions by introducing new methods. Because the contractors were beginning to reach the limits of mechanical improvements after 1890, it is probable that the reduction in contract rates fell more heavily on wages than previously. Indeed one of the principal reasons advanced by the management for abandoning the system was that the contractors were paying wages that were too low, which was contributing to labor unrest.

One important element in the growing discontent with the system appears to have come from the influx of younger, college-trained executives during the 1890s and early 1900s. T. G. Bennett, having this type of background himself, encouraged a number of engineering-school graduates, including his own son, Winchester Bennett, to enter the firm. Relationships at best must have been strained between this group and the older, less well educated, but more experienced contractors. In addition, many of the newcomers were familiar with the principles of scientific management being currently popularized by Frederick W. Taylor and his associates. No formal attempt was made to introduce the "Taylor system" until World War I, but the contrast between the loose control over labor and production under the contract system and the rigid direction of workers and supervision of manufacturing methods envisioned by Taylor was obvious and led to agitation to take control out of the hands of the contractors.

The actual shift from contractors to foremen raised a number of administrative problems. The details of production in affected departments had to be understood by the individuals taking over responsibility. In arranging the shift from contractors to Company foremen, the management showed a considerable skill in minimizing disturbance. At first the foremen operated under a bonus system which was quite similar to the profits earned by contractors. The foremen also had considerable discretion over the workers employed directly under them. Although hiring was done by the personnel office, the foremen did not have to accept all workers sent over, and their recommendations were usually enough to put an applicant on the Winchester payroll.

Even under the most favorable circumstances it was no easy task to absorb the former contractors into the hierarchy of the Company's executives. There was no escaping the fact that in terms of past prestige the contractors stood above the foremen. Moreover their previous bargaining relationships with the management made it difficult for them to accept the attitude expected of an executive employee. In this connection, the appearance of a semisecret club around 1900 may have helped to build morale. Named Abdul-Tu, this organization was formed by some of the key men engaged in production. Annual clam bakes, monthly dinners, and regular meetings made it possible for executives and salesmen to become better acquainted with the new foremen, to exchange ideas, and in general develop an *esprit de corps*. This club was later discouraged because after a time it began to operate on a restricted or exclusive basis which contributed to discontent among those not invited to become members.

In 1913 the Company made another move in the direction of building good will among its employees by awarding gold medals to those who had been with

Winchester for twenty-five years or more. In all some 160 medals were given out.

One unexpected result of the change-over from the contract system was a rise in costs of production, at least in the cartridge division. Henry Brewer, one of the college-trained executives who had come with the Company, was superintendent of the cartridge shop. He kept a careful record of costs on all jobs during the two or three years after they were taken off contracts and compared it with similar costs under the contract system. According to his account which also summarized the attitude of the management:

> I had expected that we would produce the goods cheaper . . . but to my surprise I found that in practically every instance where we changed from the contract to the non-contract system the costs were increased.
>
> An analysis of the conditions showed a number of causes for this. In the first place, some contractors were keeping the wages down below the wage which was established by the Company; were paying too low a piece rate to the workers and too low an hourly rate to the adjusters and workers, and under the non-contract system, where the Company set the rate, these rates were increased to be on a par with the other non-contract jobs in the Cartridge Department. However, in spite of the increased cost, which in most cases was not very great, we felt that the jobs were much better under the non-contract system than under the contract system, because the Company had better control of the job. One of the difficulties which had arisen under the contract job was that the contractor would push that class of work on which he was making the largest profit and would hold back on the work on which the profit was low and it frequently became impossible for us to get the work which we needed the most to fill our orders. Under the non-contract system, this difficulty was entirely eliminated. Also, there were some instances in the contract system where the contractor was using methods which we felt were not entirely satisfactory but which the contractor held to and insisted on maintaining. Under the non-contract system we could operate this as we saw fit. I do not know what the Gun Department experience was but I think it was somewhat similar.[1]

CHAPTER THIRTEEN

# ADVENT OF SMOKELESS POWDER

*Black Powder*

Black powder had been known for centuries in China before it was introduced into the Western world and put to use in warfare. It is a matter of conjecture who was the first European to discover that a combination of charcoal, sulphur and saltpeter would burn violently. In any event, for more than five hundred years after its first use in firearms around the middle of the fourteenth century, black powder continued to be made of these ingredients. (In this combination charcoal produces gas volume, sulphur the temperature, and saltpeter supplies oxygen to cause fast burning.) Over the years the importance of using pure ingredients had been recognized and a moderate control over the rate of burning had been achieved by varying the grain size; otherwise a combination of 75 parts (weight) of saltpeter, 10 parts of sulphur, and 15 parts of charcoal, remained the basic formula for gunpowder.

The lethal qualities of the first weapons using black powder were less important against an enemy than the unnerving effect of the flame and smoke they produced. Gradually firearms were improved and their superiority over the armored knight, the longbow, and the crossbow, became firmly established and the art of war revolutionized.

Over the course of the nineteenth century the increase in the efficiency of firearms, especially the rifle, had been rapid. The best of the Kentucky riflemen might have held his own in a shooting contest up to a range of 150 yards, but beyond that distance he would have stood no chance against an opponent using almost any rifle above a caliber .22 being manufactured in 1890.

By 1890, however, technical developments both in guns and ammunition had just about reached the limits imposed by the use of black powder. Little more could be done to improve the balance between the weight of the gun, the length of the barrel and the twist of the rifling of firearms using this type propellant. To obtain greater velocities and flatter trajectories, with the same calibers and weights of bullets, the powder loads and cartridge cases had been lengthened to the extent that such high-powered, black-powder cartridges as the Sharps .40-90 and the Winchester .40-110-260 Express measured nearly four inches long. These dimensions precluded their use in repeating arms and even the single-shot weapons capable of handling them were about as large and heavy as could be made and still be used as a shoulder arm.

The principal limitations of black powder as a propellant are its incomplete combustion which fouls the barrel of a firearm, the heavy smoke it gives off when fired which reveals the position of the shooter to an enemy or game, and the fast rate at which it burns after ignition. This last quality is of especial significance. The sudden explosion in the gun means that the breech has to be heavy to withstand the impact, and the projectile is ejected from the end of the barrel without the full force of the gas pressure being applied to it. This results in a rate of velocity that is comparatively low and a trajectory that is comparatively high. The road to the arms maker's goal of higher velocity, flatter trajectory, and better accuracy and range of shooting, could only be unblocked by the development of a propellant superior to black powder.

### *Smokeless Powder*

Two discoveries in the explosives field made during the 1840s were the beginning of a development that led to an improvement in the propellant used in firearms. In 1845 Schoenbein, in Basel, Switzerland, first produced guncotton by nitrating cellulose. A year later an Italian chemist, Asconio Sobero, discovered nitroglycerin, formed by the action of nitric and sulphuric acids on glycerin. Guncotton and nitroglycerin are powerful explosives. They contain carbon and hydrogen in combination with available oxygen to support combustion; both are unstable and capable of rearranging themselves with extreme rapidity into more stable compounds in the form of gases and with a concomitant great increase in volume.

In their original form, neither guncotton nor nitroglycerin was usable for small arms. Both explosives are too violent and some way had to be found to prevent detonation and slow down their conversion rate. In 1885 a French Government chemist named Vieille discovered that dissolving guncotton in ether or alcohol produced a colloid which could be dried and used safely as a substitute for black powder. It proved impossible to adapt nitroglycerin directly but within a few years Alfred Nobel and Sir Frederick Able combined guncotton with nitroglycerin to produce a similar product. In both processes the resulting pasty colloid was easy to handle and could be formed into grains, flakes, or cylinders of various sizes. Because these nitrocellulose mixtures rearranged themselves into gases without producing smoke they came to be known as smokeless powders.

Powder made by the Vieille process became known as single-base or bulk smokeless. The methods of its manufacture were sufficiently advanced by the late 1880s for the powder companies to begin supplying the market. The powder made by the use of nitroglycerin was called double-base or dense smokeless. More powerful, and originally somewhat more difficult to control, this latter powder was made available during the early 1890s.

In addition to the characteristic the name suggests, smokeless powder burns cleaner than black powder and is by weight and volume many more times as powerful. Even more important is the control which can be exercised over the rate at which it is changed into gas. This is done by manufacturing the powder in different shapes and sizes and by coating the grains with graphite. Slowing down the rate of combustion makes it possible to overcome the inertia of the projectile and start it on its way before the full pressure of the gas is developed. This "slow" build-up of pressure reduces the impact of gas pressure on the breech, lessens the recoil, and gives greater velocity to the projectile through an accelerated push. Increased velocity gives flatter trajectories to bullets and improves the accuracy of shooting. Coupled with the greater power of smokeless powder, the higher velocity makes possible the use of smaller cartridges and lighter-weight bullets which have a satisfactory striking power on impact with the target.

These qualities made the adoption of smokeless powder for ammunition one of the major innovations affecting the entire history of firearms, starting a new phase in the development of guns and ammunition that has not yet run its course. Among the more immediate consequences was the birth of the modern rifle and the subsequent evolution of guns with higher velocities, flatter trajectories, and greater accuracy.

While the superior qualities of smokeless powder insured its adoption, the introduction of smokeless powder added to the complexity of design and manufacture of both guns and ammunition. A whole host of chemical, metallurgical, and ballistical problems had to be solved before satisfactory results could be obtained. Its use hastened the substitution of scientific methods and laboratory techniques for rule-of-thumb and empirical procedures in the manufacture of guns and ammunition.

*Ammunition Development*

One of the major problems affecting all ammunition companies using the early smokeless powder came from the increase in the number of powder mixtures. Black powder had long been standardized and limited to a few brands. Because of the different methods used in manufacture and the processes used to control burning speed, and because the powder companies were constantly experimenting, smokeless powder became available in dozens of varieties, each with its own particular characteristics. It was several years before the performance of these various powders could be controlled and standardized in ammunition use. To add to the problem, the powder companies for some time had great difficulty controlling the quality of smokeless powder. Variations in different batches of the same brands made it even more difficult for the ammunition producers to maintain uniform performance of their product.

The greater pressures developed by the new propellant made the balance more delicate between the kind of powder used, the weight of the bullet, and the design of the case in order to get normal performance. The dangers from overloading were increased, especially after the double-base or dense smokeless powder became available. As one authority had pointed out: "If we load an abnormal amount of smokeless powder into a cartridge, or use a heavier or tighter, or harder bullet, or crowd a lot of powder into a small powder chamber, the pressure curve rises very rapidly. For example, if a maximum safe charge in a certain cartridge gives 50,000 pounds pressure, one grain by weight additional may give 60,000 pounds and cause the brass cartridge case to expand so much that it sticks tightly in the chamber and is difficult to extract, and 3 grains of powder above the maximum charge may give about 75,000 pounds and blow out the primer, and allow gas to get back into the gun's mechanism, and 5 grains above the normal maximum charge may disrupt the case entirely, and the powerful gas escaping to the rear may completely demolish the breech action of the weapon." [1]

Often the solution of one problem led to another. This is illustrated in connection with bullet design and construction. The greater pressure and higher velocity generated by smokeless powder permitted the use of smaller-caliber bullets with the same or a better impact on the target. Decreasing the caliber, however, reduced the diameter of bullets relative to their length. In order to keep them from "keyholing" or rotating laterally in flight, it became necessary to increase their rate of spin, which was done by increasing the twist of the rifling in the gun barrels. This brought a further complication: when the lead or lead-alloy bullets were forced at the greater speed through the rifling, they tended to disintegrate or become deformed.

By "patching," or inclosing bullets with a thin layer of gilding metal or cupro-nickel, the ammunition companies largely were able to overcome this tendency of the soft-lead bullets to disintegrate. Furthermore, the hard surface gave the projectile a better hold on the rifling of the gun barrel, increasing its spin and accuracy in flight and resulting in greater penetration of the target. It was then discovered that completely patched or coated bullets would penetrate or go through a target without necessarily inflicting any serious damage. The final solution came through leaving the nose of patched bullets uncovered, which caused them to mushroom upon impact. (The difference in the penetration of a soft-nose and a full-patched bullet is illustrated by tests made of the WCF caliber .30 smokeless cartridge. From a distance of fifteen feet, the soft-nose bullet went through twelve dry pine boards, each seven-eighths of an inch thick. The full-patched bullet penetrated through thirty-five boards from the same distance.)

These and other difficulties made the adoption of smokeless ammunition a slow process. Not for some ten years after the new propellant was first introduced were smokeless loads sufficiently perfected to meet the approval of any large number of shooters.

### *Winchester Smokeless Powder Ammunition*

The Company began experimenting with smokeless powder as early as 1888. Indicative of the difficulties encountered is the fact that the first announcement of smokeless loads did not come until five years later, the catalog for 1893 carrying the statement that the Company would load, on order, its paper Rival shot shells with nitro (smokeless) powder. The following year the Company announced that it was carrying one brand of loaded smokeless paper shot shell in stock. (This was the Winchester Leader, the Rival being changed to black powder.) This policy was continued until 1905 when a second smokeless load was added. At the same time the number of empty-primed shells to be used with smokeless powder was increased from two to four during the same period.

While the use of smokeless powder in shot shells presented some problems, to be noted, it proved much more difficult to use the new propellant in metallic cartridges. It was to the solution of this latter problem that the Winchester management devoted most of its attention during the succeeding years.

The first smokeless cartridge produced by the Company, the .30 U.S. Army for use in the Winchester single-shot and the newly adopted United States service rifle, the Krag-Jörgensen, was announced in the catalog for April 1894.

With the statement that "new smokeless cartridges will be added as fast as experimental work permits," the list of smokeless loads was increased to seventeen the following year. Actually, in all but four of these cartridges smokeless powder was substituted for black powder without any attempt to get higher velocities.

This was explained in the following head note to the list: "The smokeless cartridges enumerated below may be divided into two classes. In the one class are those cartridges in which black powder has been replaced with smokeless powder. In these, to meet the requirements of the guns for which black cartridges were intended, no attempt has been made to get additional velocity. The name of the black powder has been retained, and the word 'Smokeless' added. The smokeless cartridge in point of excellence differs from the black powder cartridge only in smokelessness and cleanliness. Velocity and penetration remain the same. In the other class of cartridges may be numbered the .236 Navy, .25-35 Winchester, .30 U.S. Army, and .30 Winchester Smokeless. These are purely smokeless cartridges. The velocities obtained cannot be gotten with black powder, nor have we been successfully able to use lead or alloys without metal patches. These are cartridges belonging entirely to the smokeless powder class, and cannot be used with black powder. Their excellence is in high velocity and consequent flat trajectory. The full metal patch gives great penetration. The soft nose bullet will expand to give effects upon animal tissues very much greater than the small caliber would otherwise enable."

*The Winchester Laboratories*

To produce this rather modest list of smokeless loads by 1895 had taxed the ingenuity and facilities of the management, and T. G. Bennett had already taken steps to put the work on a more scientific basis by establishing a laboratory. This laboratory had its beginning about 1886 when Addis, who was in Europe at the time, purchased a Schultz chronoscope for the Company, a device which measured bullet velocities. Within a short time, Addis acquired, also in Europe, a Boulenge chronoscope, a superior instrument used for the same purpose. Addis, at such times as he was in New Haven, and T. G. Bennett did considerable testing with these machines. These experiments appear to have continued on an intermittent basis, largely by the two men when they could spare time from other duties. (In February 1889 the Company catalog first included a small ballistics table, which was expanded in later editions.)

With the advent of smokeless powder, laboratory testing took on a new significance. After early experiments had demonstrated some of the difficulties involved in its use and after it was clear that the new powder had come to stay, T. G. Bennett moved to put the laboratory on a more formal basis and, in 1894, he employed E. L. Uhl, a recent graduate of the Yale Sheffield Scientific School, to take charge.

This laboratory represented a major step in the direction of scientific control over developmental work and manufacturing processes. This is well illustrated in the case of priming mixtures. Prior to the introduction of the laboratory, their development and production were entrusted to the primer-shop foreman, who had long experience in the work. New mixtures were tried out empirically without any very clear understanding of why certain combinations worked better than others. The foreman had a "little black book" into which he entered the various formulas. This information was available only to the foreman who kept it a closely guarded secret. It is said that the Company did not dare fire the primer-shop foreman because without his little black book the primer shop would shut down. There was also the possibility that he would be hired by a competitor.

The demands for smokeless-powder primers made this method of development inadequate. The new propellant required much more powerful primers. Hundreds of mixtures were tried and the construction of the primer was changed many times before satisfactory results could be obtained. With the application of chemical analysis it was not only possible to compound more accurate and satisfactory mixtures, but in the laboratory, the existing formulas lost their mystery and the little black book lost its significance.

Essentially the same condition applied in the case of metal working, the method used to anneal brass, harden steel and the like, had been evolved over many years of empirical observation. The men in charge of these operations were master craftsmen who had a "feel" for their work. With the advent of smokeless powders, the pressure put upon guns and cartridge cases, the greater heat generated, and the action of the gas on metal, all required a more careful analysis of the structure of metals which only a trained metallurgist could make.

The importance of more accurate analysis of metals is illustrated by the experience of Winchester in 1898, even after the laboratory was in operation. Working on a Government order for caliber .30 smokeless ammunition for use in the Spanish-American War, the Company had lot after lot of ammunition rejected by the Government inspector because of defects. These took the form of "cut-offs" on separation of the cartridges about a half-inch from the head, of splits in the neck of the cartridge cases, and of swelling to the point that they could not be ejected after being fired.

The trouble, according to Henry Brewer, who was brought in to help solve the difficulty, ". . . lay entirely with our lack of knowledge of the molecular structure of brass and the effect of heat treatment on the molecular structure. It led to a long series of studies and investigations, first with the Brinnell test and later with micro photographic sections and eventually we were able to determine in advance the crystal structure required for the various parts of the cartridge."

As the application of smokeless powder to ammunition was pushed ahead, the activities of the laboratory grew. By 1901 the work had become extensive enough to warrant the establishment of a chemical division and Joseph Wild, a graduate of the Yale Sheffield Scientific School, was put in charge. In 1904 he was succeeded by William Buell, a graduate of the same school, with several years experience in the laboratories of the Pennsylvania Railroad. Buell was an exceptionally able chemical engineer and under his direction the work of the laboratory assumed increasing significance over succeeding years.

*Increase in Smokeless Cartridges*

Winchester kept its promise made in 1895 to add new smokeless cartridges as fast as they could be developed. By 1905 the list had grown to 100 and in 1914 the total came to 175. Many of these were available in both full-patch and soft-point bullets, so the actual number of individual loads was probably at least twenty per cent greater than indicated.

A considerable number of these new cartridges were still black-powder types with smokeless powder substituted but with no attempt to get greater pressures. These were designed to be used in firearms manufactured before smokeless powders were introduced, in which it was dangerous to use high-pressure ammunition. A second group, including a line of Winchester high-velocity cartridges, was described as giving higher velocity and increased muzzle energy, with only a moderate increase in initial pressure. Many of these could be used safely in the Company's Models 86 and 92 rifles, originally designed for black-powder ammunition, but users were cautioned against using high-velocity cartridges in the Model 73. The third class of smokeless cartridges were high-power loads, such as the 6mm

Navy, the U.S. Army .30, the British .303, and the Winchester .30-30, .33, .35, and .405, and could be used safely only in guns designed especially to handle high pressures.

Not all of the smokeless loads offered in 1914 had been originally developed by Winchester. In line with its policy of producing a full line of ammunition for all types of firearms, the Company expanded its manufacture to include practically all the new cartridges brought out by the U.S. Government and the other arms and ammunition companies.

At least twenty-five of the group can be definitely credited to Winchester, of which a considerable number became very popular with shooters. (*See Appendix B.*) As the best-known of these were usually developed in connection with a particular model firearm, they will be described along with the guns with which they were most prominently associated. (*See Chapter Fourteen.*)

### *Black-Powder Cartridges*

While adding smokeless loads to its ammunition line, Winchester did not reduce the manufacture of black-powder metallic cartridges and components. Including loaded and empty primed cartridge cases, bullets, blanks, and other components, the catalog for 1914 listed approximately the same 375 items that had appeared in 1890. This is not astonishing considering the hundreds of thousands of guns in use which were designed for black-powder ammunition.

Beginning in 1911 the Company offered to load rimfire and centerfire pistol-size, black-powder cartridges with Lesmok at no extra cost. Lesmok was a semi-smokeless powder developed by Du Pont. This powder gave a high degree of accuracy to small-caliber ammunition. While it gave off more smoke and fouling than smokeless, the fouling was of such a nature that it did not cake and harden in the barrel and firing did not have to be interrupted for cleaning.

### *Handloading*

While sales of factory-loaded ammunition had grown enormously over the preceding quarter century a large number of shooters during the early 1890s still preferred to load or reload their own metallic cartridges. The reasons for this preference are well stated by A. C. Gould in his *Modern American Rifles,* published in 1892: "Every person who shoots a rifle, will be likely to sometime prepare ammunition. One rarely finds an expert rifleman who uses factory cartridges, especially if he shoots at target, or where extreme accuracy is desired. Factory made cartridges are expensive, and, however excellent when leaving the factories may rapidly deteriorate by being stored in an unfavorable place. Tyros usually shoot factory cartridges; the old and skillful marksman rarely does. But, besides the questions of economy and more reliability in properly reloaded cartridges, is the necessity of reloading when one is located away from the large cities, where it is impossible to procure the products of the factories. If residing in a section where gun dealers are numerous, the great variety of cartridges make a very large stock necessary, if the dealer would keep a full line, and as many of the cartridges would be seldom called for, the stock would become old and deteriorate in quality; therefore, only the most called for rim and centerfire cartridges are found in the average gun store. Thus it seems necessary for a rifleman, if he desires to economize, to have reliable ammunition and be able to supply himself with such at will, to possess a knowledge of how to reload rifle cartridges."

Winchester had long supplied the demands of the handloaders. It continued

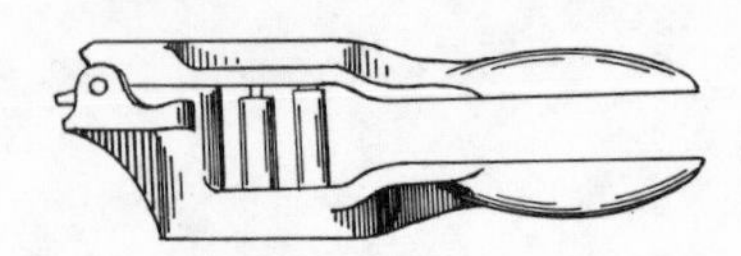

*Winchester Reloading Tool, First Type—1874–1875*

to advertise the fact that "shells of all our centerfire rifle cartridges are made of extra thickness for this purpose." A considerable part of the Company's sales was made up of ammunition components, including primed empty cartridge cases, wads, bullets, and primers. In 1890 the Company listed in its catalog two types of reloading tools, in addition to bullet molds and charge cups for measuring powder. Also included were directions for reloading and recommendations of the best types of powders. Between 1890 and 1915 there was no change in policy and the Company continued to cater to the handloaders using black powder.

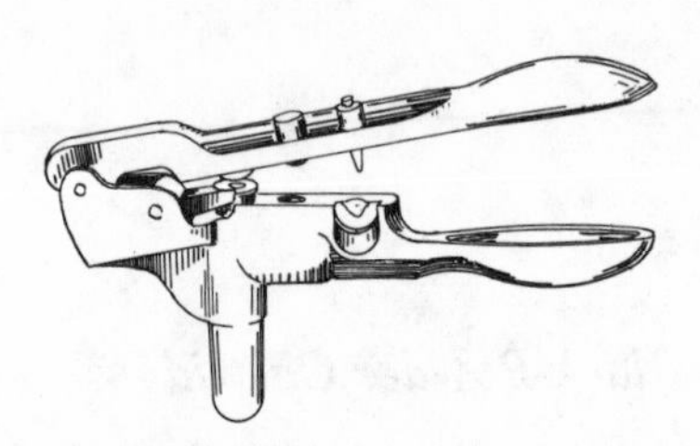

*Winchester Reloading Tool, Second Type. First Listed in 1875*

The handloading of smokeless powders was a different proposition and beginning in 1898 the Company made every effort to discourage the practice. While this attitude may have been colored by a desire to increase the sale of factory-made ammunition, the main reason was based upon the increasing number of accidents suffered by shooters using handloaded smokeless cartridges. As a large number of these accidents involved Winchester firearms, the management was especially interested in taking steps to eliminate them. In the catalog for 1898 the Company, under the heading, "Reloading Smokeless Powder Cartridges Impractical," explained its attitude:

> We are constantly in receipt of letters of inquiry regarding the reloading of smokeless powder rifle ammunition, and we, therefore, make the following general statement:
>
> It has been the common experience of persons using reloaded smokeless powder cartridges to have a large number of shells so reloaded rupture in the gun. Extensive experiments carried on by the Winchester Repeating Arms Company, and by the Ordnance Department of the United States Army, with shells, guns, and smokeless powders of nearly every known manufacture, have alike failed to find a remedy for this difficulty. Experiments show that after the first firing with smokeless powder, the metal of the shell undergoes a slow but decided change, the exact nature of which the best experts have as yet failed to determine. No immediate deterioration attends the shooting of smokeless powder: for, by reloading and shooting immediately, the shells may be shot many times with no sign of rupture. If, however, the fired shells are not allowed to stand for two or three days, no matter whether they are cleaned or uncleaned, wet or dry, loaded or unloaded, the result is always the same, namely, the metal becomes brittle, and rupture of the shells at the next discharge is probable . . . For this reason the Winchester Repeating Arms Company cautions its patrons against the reloading of smokeless powder rifle ammunition, and wishes to do its utmost to discourage this practice.

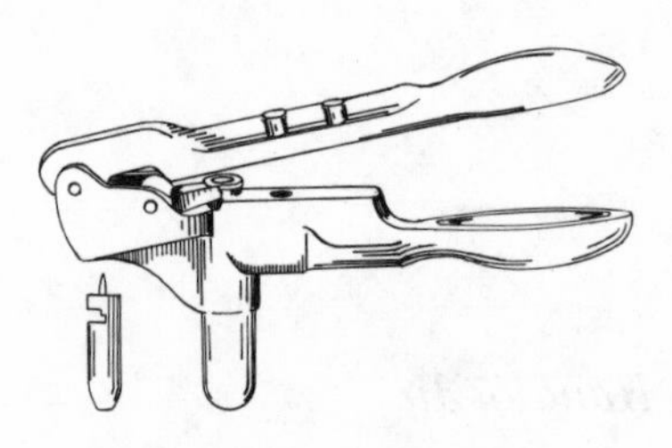

*Winchester Reloading Tool, Third Type. First Listed in 1879*

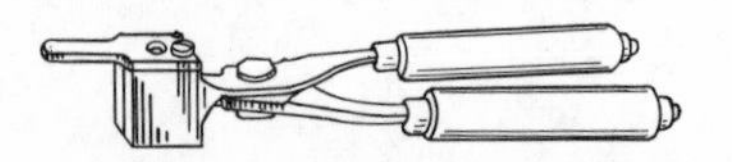

*Winchester Bullet Mold for .44-40 Cartridge*

Within two years more careful analysis of the effects of the amalgamation of the primer residue removed the principal danger from ruptured cartridges due to defective metal. Meantime the use of the double-base smokeless powder had become more prevalent. This brought a new danger from overloading. Winchester, therefore, continued to warn against handloading of smokeless cartridges by pointing out in the catalog for 1900:

> The many smokeless powders on the market differ so greatly in their various qualities and characteristics that their use may be attended with very great danger through improper loading. Many smokeless powders, excellent powders in themselves and perfectly safe and satisfactory if used in the proper amounts and in the cartridges for which they are designed, may become very dangerous when used in other cartridges, or in the wrong amounts.

Smokeless powders vary greatly in bulk, density, rapidity of combustion chamber pressure and charge required, and for this reason it is very unsafe to load smokeless powder, unless the means of determining the chamber pressures are at hand . . . Thirty grains of one powder might be a perfectly safe and satisfactory load, while thirty grains of another powder in the same cartridge might burst the strongest nickel steel barrel. Many things tend to increase the chamber pressure to an extent little to be expected by the novice. An increase of but a few grains in powder charge will sometimes produce the most astonishing results, and what was previously a perfectly safe load, may thus be rendered a very dangerous one indeed.

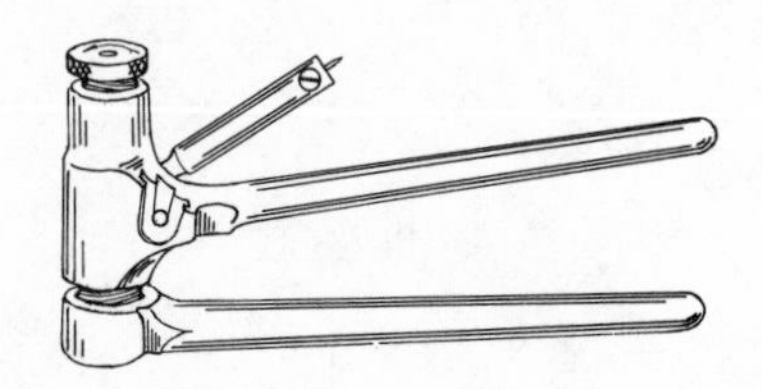

*Winchester Model 1891 Reloading Tool*

Winchester was joined in this campaign by the other ammunition manufacturers and by the powder companies. How effective these warnings were in minimizing handloading of metallics is impossible to determine, but it is interesting that Whelen, writing in 1918, observed, "An acquaintance with thousands of riflemen throughout our country enables me to assert that very few of them load their own ammunition." [2] There is no question that these warnings helped to educate shooters in the necessity of using greater care in the selection of powder, the amounts used in particular loads and the weight of the bullet.

## *Shot Shells and Smokeless Powder*

While the advantages of smokeless over black powder were not as striking in shot shells as in rifle ammunition, the absence of smoke, the greater pressures developed, and the lower recoil were sufficient to bring about its growing use in shotgun ammunition. The smooth bore and larger diameter of shotgun barrels, compared to the rifles, simplified the problems of adaptation somewhat; but even so, the difficulties encountered were formidable enough.

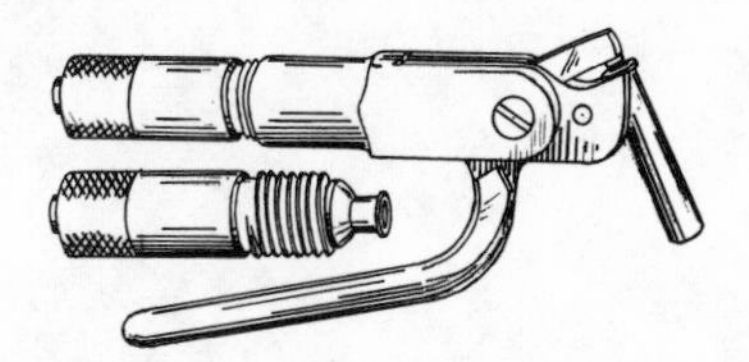

*Winchester Model 1894 Reloading Tool*

As in the case of the metallic cartridges, the varieties of smokeless powder and the subsequent introduction of the stronger, double-base types, necessitated continual changes in the composition of priming mixtures, the construction of the primer, and the balance between powder charges and the weight of the shot. Among other things the greater heat generated tended to melt shot made of pure lead and chilled shot, made by adding antimony as a hardening agent, had to be used. The higher pressure necessitated special wads that were more elastic and a number of changes were made in the design of the head and brass portions of the paper shot shells in order to increase their strength.

There was one early major contribution to the design of shot shells made by the Winchester organization that deserves special mention. Because of the higher pressures developed by smokeless loads all the ammunition companies had trouble with their paper shot shells "cutting off" or separating at the junction of the paper body with the brass head of the shell.

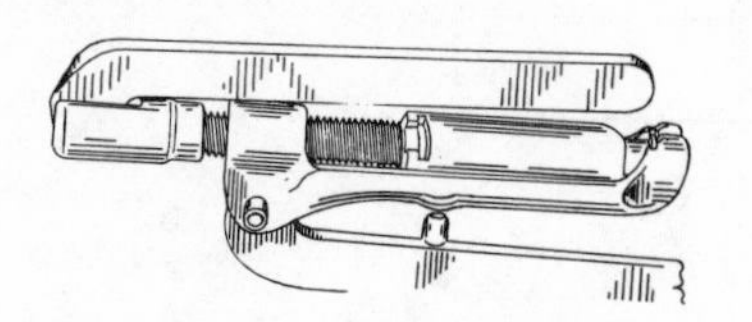

*New Model Reloading Tool*

On June 9, 1896, John Gardner, superintendent of Winchester's cartridge shop, was granted U. S. Patent 25611 which he assigned to the Company, on a method of construction designed to overcome this difficulty. The essential feature of his patent was the use of circumferential grooves around the body of the brass head of the shell. These circumferential grooves not only held the paper cartridge more firmly in place, but also acted as a shock absorber by flattening against the walls of the chamber when the shell was discharged and at the same time stretching lengthwise.

The advantages of this type of construction were so obvious that it was quickly adopted by other ammunition companies. Winchester brought suit against these concerns, including the Union Metallic Cartridge Company, and forced them to abandon its use.

Gardner's patent, however, covered only the use of grooves around the entire circumference of the brass heads. Other ammunition companies found that they could get the same effects by indenting their name in the same position, and in this way were able to get the same effect without infringing on his patent.

Gardner's patent solved but one of the many problems connected with adapting shot-shell ammunition to smokeless powders, many of which responded only to the same laboratory techniques applied in the case of metallic ammunition.

*Black-Powder Shot Shells*

Winchester did not reduce its offerings of black-powder shot shells because, as was the case with metallic ammunition, smokeless powder did not eliminate the demand for black-powder loads. Many shotguns were still in use which were not strong enough to handle the more powerful ammunition. Also, the smokeless loads cost more. In 1914, for example, the list price of loaded Nublack 12-gauge black-powder shells was $25 per thousand; while the corresponding smokeless loads in the Repeater and Leader brands were quoted at, respectively, $37.50 and $48.

In respect to the handloading of smokeless-powder shot shells Winchester, beyond cautioning against overloading, issued no warnings. On the contrary, beginning in 1895 and continuing thereafter, the Company included tables in its catalog giving the comparative strength of the various smokeless powders and their equivalents in black powders for the benefit of handloaders. The advantages of the Company's empty shot shells designed for smokeless loads were featured and special wads and primers made for their use were added to the line of ammunition components.

Nevertheless the advent of smokeless powders did have an effect on handloading and contributed to a subsequent decline in the practice. This has been explained by Henry Brewer:

> Black powder loading was a pretty simple affair but when smokeless powder came on the market, shot shell loading became very different and much greater knowledge, skill, and experience was required. There were a good many accidents (burst guns, etc.) resulting from overloading by inexperienced handloaders. As a result, quite a business was built up in various localities where game shooting was prevalent, by local handloaders who bought the empty shells, powder, wads, and shot, and loaded the shells to meet the requirements and whims of their particular customers.
>
> These handloaders were usually themselves sportsmen and knew the requirements of the local sportsmen, and they also knew from personal experience good loads from poor loads. The local sportsmen came to rely on their advice as to loads and many of them built up a big reputation for their product and correspondingly large sales. This was especially true in the Chesapeake Bay region, noted for its duck and goose shooting.
>
> As a matter of fact, these handloaders were doing a better job than the factory loaders, for they were in closer touch with the shooters and were themselves shooters and sportsmen and constantly testing the results of their loads in the field.

From the foregoing it is apparent that the initial effect of smokeless powder was not to reduce handloading but to put it more into the hands of specialists. It was only after the ammunition companies noted the popularity of these special loads and decided to expand their own offerings that handloading of smokeless shot shells as well as black-powder loads began to decline.

*Increase in Factory Loading*

Until around 1895 neither Winchester nor the Union Metallic Cartridge Company seems to have made any particular effort to push their sales of factory-loaded shells. Winchester did not even list loaded shells in its catalog until 1894 and during the early 1890s there is evidence that both companies were willing to sign an agreement not to load shot shells as long as they and the U. S. Cartridge Company could continue to control the supply of components.

Several considerations apparently led to this lack of enthusiasm; the sale of components was highly profitable, the early loading machines were relatively inefficient so that the costs of factory-loaded shells were too high to compete vigorously with the handloaded products, and there was no reason to think that the demand for loaded shells would be very great.

Between 1890 and 1895 the general situation changed. The rise of competing firms not only threatened the control over the manufacture of components but specialized loading companies were beginning to build up large markets. Machinery had been improved sufficiently to make the margin between costs and selling prices more attractive. The growing use of smokeless powder had cut down on individual handloading. Finally, the sales of factory loaded shells had shown a remarkable increase. (Winchester's annual production of loaded shells, for example, grew from 23.2 million in 1890 to 67.5 in 1895. (*See Appendix K.*) It may be assumed that the production of loaded shells by UMC and the U.S. Cartridge Company increased in approximately the same proportion.)

Noting the success of the special handloaders, the management decided in 1896 to expand its offerings of individual shot-shell loads and Bert Claridge was hired to take charge of shot-shell loading. This was an excellent choice. Claridge had been in charge of the shot-shell loading department of a large sporting-goods house in Baltimore. He was an expert shooter, famous among the hunters and sportsmen of the Chesapeake Bay region for the quality of his loaded shot shells, and he knew from personal experience which powder-and-shot combination gave the best results.

Under Claridge's direction Winchester's list of shot-shell loads began to multiply. He not only increased the number of standard loads but paid particular attention to "special orders" which in many cases developed into considerable volume. It was Brewer's judgment that "No other one feature of our Loaded Shell job played such an important part in building our sales as did Bert Claridge. Under his guidance we led all the loading companies in Smokeless Shells in spite of the fact U. M. C. had always led in Black Powder Loads. Smokeless loads sold on *quality* to the more particular shooters and it was Claridge who put our smokeless loads ahead of all others as to quality."

This move by Winchester to cater more to the individual demands of shooters, was followed in general by the other ammunition companies and marked the decline of handloading. Even with black powder one of the chief attractions had been to get special performance which was now supplied, except for the very particular shooters, in factory loads. Nor could handloading specialists, using smokeless powder, compete with the improved machinery and the laboratory techniques available to the large concerns.

The demand for factory-loaded shot shells continued to expand. Data for the industry are lacking, but Winchester's annual output grew from 67.5 million in 1895 to 243.4 million in 1907.

*Multiplication of Individual Shot-Shell Loads*

The use of smokeless powder, plus more catering to the demands of individual shooters, multiplied the variety of loads in shot shells. In 1885, just prior to its first sale of loaded shells, Winchester carried only four brands of paper shot shells and two brass shells. In 1914, the catalog listed two types of brass shells, four empty paper shot shells, and six brands of loaded paper shot shells.

This small number of brands completely obscures an almost fantastic increase in individual loads that were being manufactured by the latter date; an expansion which was closely related to the relationships among the powder companies, the loading companies, and the users of shot shells.

Prior to the advent of factory-loaded shells, the powder companies had concentrated their sales efforts on the demand of the handloaders. Dealer and jobber connections were carefully built up, and the powder companies employed expert shooters as "missionary salesmen" whose function was to build up a preference for particular brands of powder.

When the manufacturers started loading shells at the factory they not unnaturally stressed the qualities of their ammunition and did not feature the powder brands. This move threatened to upset or destroy the whole pattern of consumer-dealer-jobber relationships built up by the powder companies. Not wishing to fight the powder companies in their efforts to expand the sales of factory loads, the ammunition concerns began quite early to furnish shot shells loaded with the brand of powder specified by the buyers. This, in itself, added to the multiplicity of different loads; but, because shooters also had preference for different combinations of powder and shot sizes, the companies also extended this option to purchasers.

Even before smokeless powders became widely adopted the variety of individual shot-shell loads had mushroomed. In 1895, just a year after it had first listed loaded shells in its catalog, Winchester was prepared to furnish its customers at no extra cost with a choice among twenty-three combinations of shot-and-powder weights, sixteen sizes of shot, and at least twelve brands of powder. The result was between four and five thousand individual loads.

After the introduction of smokeless powder the list grew steadily, largely because of the increase in powder brands. It has been estimated that, by 1907, Winchester's total allowable loads came to 14,383.

The increased variety of shot-shell loads added seriously to the manufacturing problem in this part of the business. The shooting season began in the fall and continued through the winter. Orders began to come in during the late spring and early summer, but until these orders were received and the particular loads were known production could not begin. The result was intense activity during the summer months involving the use of night shifts, followed by a comparative lull in activity in the off season.

Assembling the finished product for shipment was a complex task. Each case had to be carefully labeled. Not infrequently an individual order would call for several varieties of powder. The Company also had to be careful not to have excessive stocks on hand at the end of the season. This was in part because particular loads might not be popular the following season and in part because shot shells loaded with smokeless powder were subject to serious deterioration unless very carefully stored.

Beginning around 1901, the ammunition companies moved to spread their production over a longer period by giving jobbers a predating privilege on carload lots. Under this arrangement, if a jobber would order shells on or before March 15, he would be allowed to pay for the shipment the following September and still receive a discount. These arrangements, which were carefully worked out under the Ammunition Manufacturers' Association, were effective in lengthening the production period.

About 1907 the Company began to restrict the variety of loads by listing definite shot sizes for each of the smokeless loads which would be furnished at standard prices. Orders for shot sizes not on the standard list were accepted only at an increased price. About the same time the Company began to restrict the powder loads to specific brands. While these moves helped somewhat to reduce the variety of loads and spread manufacture over a longer period, no determined attempt was made to cut the list until after World War I. In 1921 the various loading companies moved to eliminate some 5,200 loads from their shot-shell lists. These 5,200 loads eliminated comprised but ten per cent of all the business.

With the cooperation of the Department of Commerce, the manufacturers moved to simplify shot shells still further after 1921. In 1924 a committee consisting of George R. Watrous of the Winchester Repeating Arms Company and H. J. Strugnell of the Remington Arms Company was appointed by the ammunition manufacturers to study the possibility of a further reduction in number of loads. On January 1, 1925, the manufacturers further reduced load combinations to 1,747. Further elimination brought the list down to 137 by 1947.

*Improvements in Machinery*

Mention has already been made of the importance of improved machinery in loading shot shells. There is scattered evidence of a considerable improvement in these machines and in the general methods of manufacture during the 1890-1914 period. Available information is lacking for any discussion of these beyond noting a general trend toward increasing labor productivity. It is of interest that of some 77 patents taken out by Winchester during this period, 51 covered metallic ammunition and shot-shell design, 11 applied to primers, and 15 to machinery used in the manufacture of both metallic ammunition and shot shells. Not all the ideas contained in these patents were utilized, of course, but at the same time a number of improvements were introduced which were either not patentable or which the Company felt could be kept secret without being patented.

The importance attached to certain of these "secret" manufacturing processes is illustrated by the following experience of Henry Brewer. While no date is specified, it must have been around 1900 when he was called into the office by T. G. Bennett and told that the Union Metallic Cartridge Company was being sued by a workman who had been injured in their loading room. They had asked Bennett to send someone familiar with loading machines to examine their machines, so he could testify as a loading expert that they were designed and operated with a reasonable degree of safety. According to Brewer: "Mr. Bennett directed that I go to the U. M. C. Company and do whatever I could to help them in the matter. I was greatly elated because this gave me an opportunity of seeing the U. M. C. loading room—so far as I know, no Winchester representative had ever been in their loading room and it seemed to me a great opportunity to see how they did things and possibly pick up some good ideas. I, therefore, said to Mr. Bennett, 'There is no objection I suppose to my keeping my eyes open and seeing what I can see?' Mr. Bennett replied, 'Now Brewer, you are going there at their request, do what they ask you to do, but don't go prying into things that are none of our business.' Mr. Arthur Hooper, Vice President, who was sitting at the adjoining desk spoke up, 'Why, Tom, there is no objection, is there, to the young man keeping his eyes open?' So I went determined to learn all that I could, that might be of help to Winchester."

Brewer made the most of his opportunity and when he returned to New Haven he informed T. G. Bennett that Union Metallic Cartridge Company had Winchester "licked a mile in the matter of the cost of loading." This he explained was because

The U. M. C. loading machines were operated by one operator whereas the Winchester loading machines required four operators. The U. M. C. Machine had automatic devices for feeding wads and shells, whereas on the Winchester machine, we had one girl to feed shells and two girls to feed wads, and a boy to tend the machine. The speed of the Winchester machine was limited to the speed of the girl feeder and our daily output was generally a little less than 25,000 shells per day, whereas the U. M. C. loading machines on similar loads were turning out over 30,000 per day. This with one operator as compared with four operators.

I suggested to Mr. Bennett that we immediately design automatic wad feeds and automatic shell feeds for our loading room, so that we could reduce the number of operators and increase the output to equal that of U. M. C. loaders, and I told him that I thought if we could accomplish this we could save $50,000 per year. Mr. Bennett turned to Mr. Hooper and said to him, "Hooper, what would you give to be a young man again? Listen to this young man, saving $50,000 a year," and they both had a good hearty laugh over it. However, Mr. Bennett with his usual confidence in the men under him approved the plan, authorized our designing automatic feeds and after several years of experimental work and very costly building of the automatic feeds, all of our shot shell machines were so equipped.

This development of automatic feeds again brought attention to automatic shell feeds, and we continued to develop automatic feeds for our various machines, notably in the Paper Shot Shell Department, and in time we developed automatic paper shot shell feeds, which were used in our shot shell headers, our shot shell primers and our other machines.

When we were saving an amount which I estimated at $200,000 a year, I had great pleasure in going to Mr. Bennett and calling his attention to the fact that he had laughed at me when I said we could save $50,000 a year, and that I now estimated we were saving in excess of $200,000 a year as a result of my two hour visit to the U. M. C. loading room.

*The Winchester Shot Tower*

One problem connected with shot-shell manufacture involved the purchase and storage of shot. Prior to 1912 Winchester purchased its shot from outside concerns. Shot was shipped in cloth bags weighing twenty-five pounds each, which had to be carefully stored and handled to prevent the bags from bursting. During the course of production the Company had to handle a large variety of shot sizes. Because the demand for particular sizes varied from season to season it was not possible to purchase the required amounts until orders began to come in without

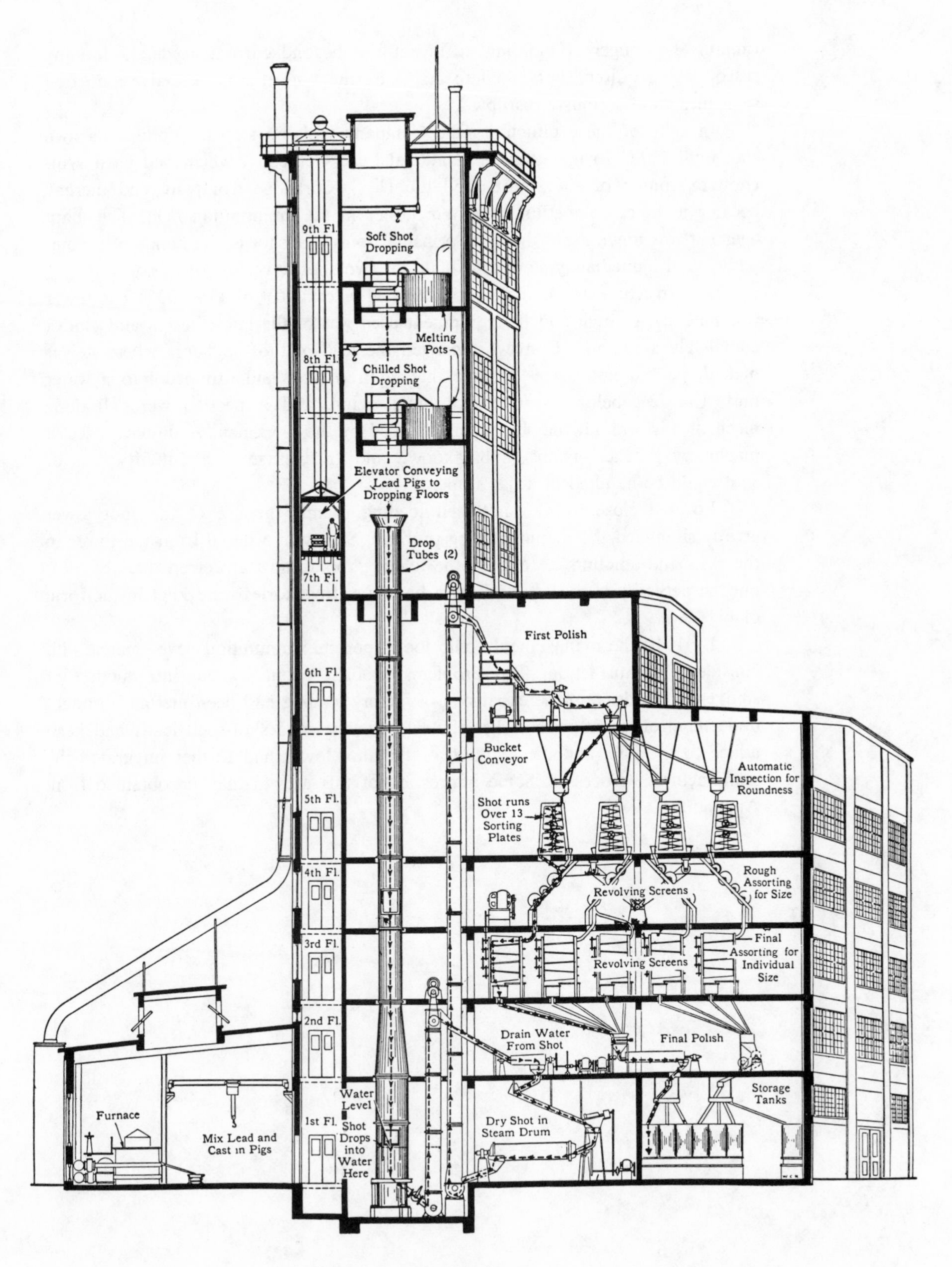


*Winchester's Shot Tower*

running the danger of building up inventories beyond current needs. If, for any reason, the required shot failed to arrive by the time it was needed, production schedules were seriously disrupted.

In spite of these difficulties the Company took no step to produce its own shot until 1911. In that year the National Lead Company, which had been Winchester's source of shot, purchased the U. S. Cartridge Company and thereby became a direct competitor with Winchester in the ammunition field. The management was unwilling to have its principal source of shot in the hands of a competitor and immediately started to build its own shot tower in New Haven.

The structure was completed in 1912 at a total cost of $190,000. The tower was nine stories high and the equipment used was of the latest design and almost completely automatic. Conveyors carried the lead to the top floors where it was melted, poured into sieves to give the required sizes and dropped into a water tank 154 feet below. Sorting, polishing, sizing, and inspection were all done mechanically without the shot being handled by the workman. A duplicate set of machinery guarded against a breakdown and an average of about fifty tons of shot could be handled in a day's operations.

Located close to the shot-shell loading rooms, the use of the shot tower greatly simplified the manufacturing problem. Shot was ordered from the tower in the sizes and amounts needed by the loading room and transferred directly without the necessity of storage and extra handling. Inventories were kept in the form of pig lead.

By 1914 the management could look upon its ammunition development with considerable satisfaction. The problems brought about by the introduction of smokeless powder and the expansion of factory loading had been met and brought under control, an impressive list of new cartridges and shot-shell loads had been added to the line, and the addition of the shot tower had further integrated the manufacturing processes. Some impression of this growth may be obtained from Appendix K.

CHAPTER FOURTEEN

# STRUGGLE FOR SUPREMACY

Winchester's position in 1890 as leader in the gun field rested largely on the popularity of the Company's lever-action repeating rifles, especially the Model 73 and the Model 86. The bolt-action Hotchkiss had not caught on and it was reasonably clear that the lever-action shotgun introduced in 1887 would never become widely accepted.

Although shooters were not yet willing to accept a bolt-action firearm with any enthusiasm it was evident that they were interested in other types of repeating actions. Colt's success with its line of Lightning rifles had already demonstrated the potential demand for a pump- or slide-action repeater and the Spencer Arms Company of Windsor, Connecticut, had put out a pump-action repeating shotgun around 1884, which had attracted favorable attention. Inventors had been working on the semiautomatic or self-loading principle, which represented a second major line of development. Finally, the advent of smokeless powder was to bring about radical changes in rifle and shotgun design.

The Winchester management fully recognized that if the Company was to maintain its position in the industry its gun line would have to be improved and expanded. The twenty-five-year period beginning in 1890 was marked by a sharp increase in the number of models offered for sale. In 1890 the list of offerings stood at seven; in 1914 the total had reached twenty. Actually this represented a net increase of sixteen new guns because several, including the Model 66, the Model 76, the Hotchkiss Model 83, and the Model 87 lever-action shotgun, had been dropped during the intervening years. Some of these new models represented improvements on older guns; in other instances they were newly designed firearms.

This was the part of the business that was close to the heart of T. G. Bennett. He not only made the final decision in respect to the adoption or rejection of new models and improvements, but took time to work on gun design. Like William Mason, Bennett's talent lay principally in making improvements in basic designs which would increase their operating efficiency or simplify their manufacture. He made significant contributions to the firearms that were added to the Company's list during the period.

For more than ten years, however, the Company continued to depend chiefly on John Browning for new gun designs. Each year he brought on to New Haven one or more new model firearms or suggestions for improving those already in production. With the exception of his original machine gun which did not appeal to T. G. Bennett, these were all purchased by the Company. Such models or improvements that appeared to be suited for manufacture and commercially acceptable were put into production. There are, at the present time, some thirty model guns in the Winchester Museum which were submitted by Browning that were never manufactured.

*The Model 90*

The first new model brought out during the Bennett regime was based on U.S. Patent 385,238 granted to John M. and Matthew Browning in 1888. This was the Model 90, the first pump- or sliding-action gun manufactured by Winchester. The Model 90 was chambered (not interchangeably) for the .22 short, the .22 long, the .22 long rifle and the .22 Winchester rimfire cartridge. This last cartridge was developed especially for use in the gun. It was nearly an inch and a half long and was a popular load.

While the Model 90 was not effective or accurate beyond relatively short ranges, it became ". . . the most popular .22 caliber pump action rifle ever made." [1] Frequently it was the first gun given to boys after they had graduated from the BB-rifle class; it was widely used for small-game and target shooting. Its most extensive demand came from shooting galleries in the United States and in foreign countries, becoming so popular in Great Britain, for example, that the shooting galleries in that country are generally called "Winchester rifle ranges." [2] Listed at $16, over a half million Model 90 guns had been sold by the Company by the end of 1914.

*The Model 93 Shotgun*

The pump-action Model 90 rifle was followed by the Model 93 shotgun which used the same type action.[3] The gun was listed in the Company's catalog for April 1894 with the following description: "This gun is operated by a sliding forearm below the barrel. It is locked by the closing motion and can be unlocked only by pushing forward the firing-pin, which may be done by the hammer or by the finger. When the hammer is down, the backward and forward motion of the sliding forearm unlocks and opens the breech block, ejects the cartridge or fired shell and replaces it with a fresh cartridge."

Listed at $25, the Model 93 shotgun was fairly popular and around 35,000 were sold between 1893 and 1897, when it was succeeded by the greatly improved Model 97 shotgun.

*Bannerman v. Sanford*

The Model 93 shotgun had scarcely been introduced to the trade when the Company became involved in a patent infringement suit involving the slide action used in it and the Model 90 rifle. In a circular letter dated October 2, 1894, Francis Bannerman of New York, well-known dealer in firearms, announced that he had filed suit against Philip G. Sanford, the New York agent of the Winchester Repeating Arms Company. Noting that he was the owner of U.S. Patent 316,401, which was being infringed, Bannerman warned: "The suit is brought for the sale by such agent of *Winchester Shotgun, Model 1893, and the Target Rifle, Model 1890,* manufactured by said company. All persons, firms, or corporations, using or selling the said shotguns or rifles are infringers of the said Patent and will be held responsible for such infringements."

The patent for the production of slide-action shotguns, referred to by Bannerman, had been originally issued on April 21, 1885, to Sylvester H. Roper, a former partner of Christopher M. Spencer (inventor of the famous Civil War Spencer rifle) soon after Spencer had started the Spencer Arms Company of

Windsor, Connecticut. Spencer had been forced to mortgage his property to Pratt & Whitney in 1889 and, when the latter concern foreclosed on the mortgage, Bannerman purchased the rights to the patent and an inventory of some three thousand guns.

Winchester decided that its best defense was to prove that a prior patent had been issued covering the same invention. A search was made of the American patent records and George D. Seymour, of Seymour & Earl, was sent to Europe to examine the European patent records. Thomas E. Addis was dispatched to interview Spencer in an attempt to show that the patent under dispute had been antedated by U.S. Patent 255,894, which had been issued to Spencer and Roper in April 1882.

Somewhat to their astonishment, the officials of Winchester discovered that several patents for slide-action guns had been taken out in France and Great Britain. Immediate steps were taken to obtain copies of these patents and a sample gun of any that had been manufactured. At the trial copies of four foreign patents were submitted as evidence by the Company. These included three British patents which had been issued to Alexander Bain in 1854, to Joseph Curtis in 1866, and to William Krutzsch in 1866, plus one French patent taken out by M. M. Magot in 1880.

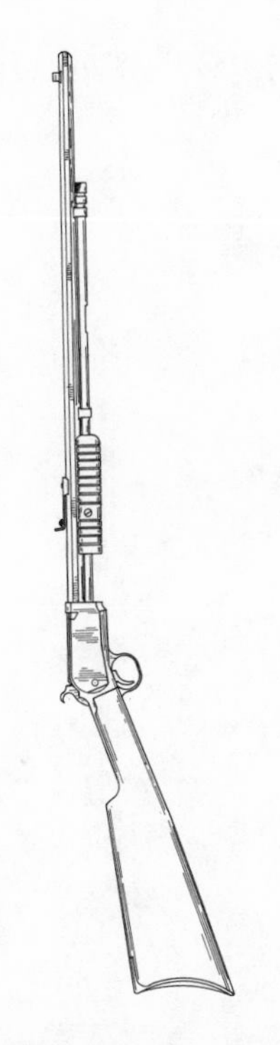

*Winchester Model 1890 Rifle*

In the course of the trial, which was held in the United States Circuit Court of the Southern District of New York, the Winchester lawyers put the prosecution on record as saying that these foreign patents covered arms that were unworkable. This admission set the stage for the most dramatic episode in connection with the trial. Winchester had been able to procure one of the Magot guns which had been manufactured and from the other patent specifications the Company had constructed working models of the Curtis and Krutzsch inventions which apparently had never been produced. These guns were then submitted to the court as evidence to prove that workable guns involving the sliding action under dispute had been invented prior to the Roper patent of 1885 which was allegedly being infringed.

On June 5, 1897, the court, Judge Wheeler presiding, rendered a decision in favor of the Winchester Repeating Arms Company. Actually the Court's decision was based on the fact that the Roper patent under dispute had been preceded by the Spencer and Roper patent noted above, and therefore no infringement was involved.[4]

Now it was Winchester's turn to get out a circular letter, which it did, announcing: "The attention of all our customers is invited to the following matter: Under date of October 2nd, 1894, one Francis Bannerman, notified the trade and general public that he had commenced suit against the Winchester Repeating Arms Company for infringement of certain letters patent, advising all selling the Model 1893 shotgun, and the Model 1890 rifle, that they were infringers of his patents. Under date of November 5th, 1894, we notified our customers that there was no infringement, and guaranteed any user or seller against any loss whatsoever incurred by reason of this alleged infringement. *Judge Wheeler of the United States Circuit Court for the Southern District of New York has rendered decision in favor of the Winchester Repeating Arms Company, and is dismissing the bill of Francis Bannerman.*" [5]

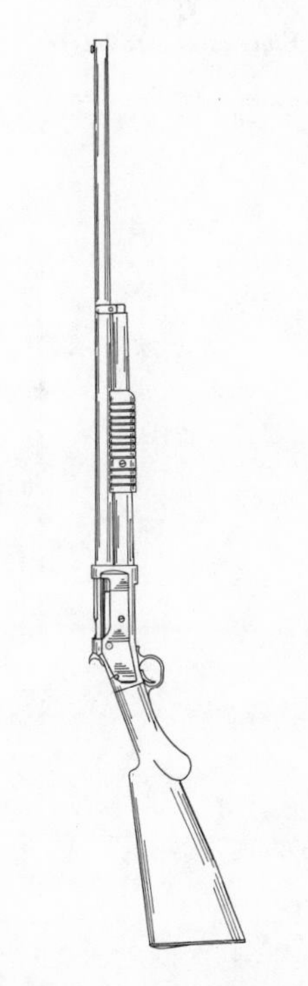

*Winchester Model 1893 Shotgun*

*The Model 1897 Shotgun*

The Winchester management was confident enough of a favorable decision in the *Bannerman* v. *Sanford* case to develop an improved version of the slide-action Model 93 shotgun and a new gun, the Model 97, was brought out in November 1897. In the Model 97 a number of weaknesses that had shown up in the Model 93 were remedied. Of these the most important was an improved slide lock which kept the gun locked until actual firing occurred and prevented the gun from jamming in case of a misfire.[6]

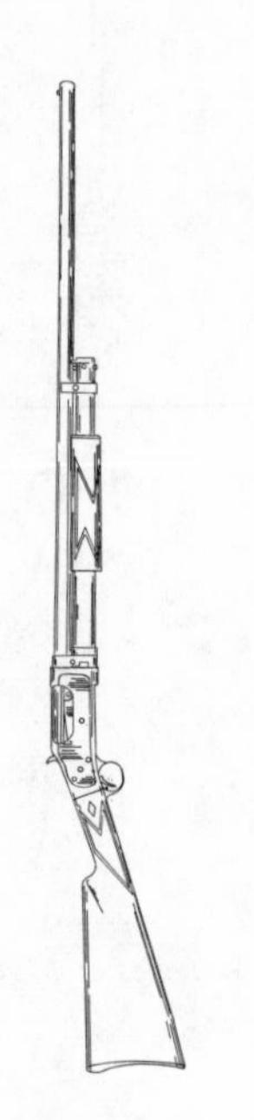
Vinchester Model 1897 Shotgun

Made in various styles, the Model 97 became the most popular shotgun on the American market and established a standard of performance by which other kinds and makes of shotguns were judged, including the most expensive imported articles. The gun became noted for its simple, rugged construction and unfailing reliability. According to one enthusiast, "It would stand any sort of minor abuse such as being run over by the old farm wagon or being dropped in the creek and rescued a few days later and never even stutter when called on to speak." [7]

The list prices—$25, for the standard gun and $27 for the take-down type—put the cost well below the hand-made, imported shotguns and by the end of 1914 nearly 623,000 had been sold.

The Model 97 was immediately adopted by the professional "market-hunters" because of its effectiveness. Acceptance by this group proved to be something of a boomerang to the Company because the gun began to be associated with the so-called "game hogs" who were a threat to the preservation of wild life in the country. Beginning around 1900, the various states began to restrict the use of repeating and automatic shotguns.

A short-barrel version of the Model 97, using buckshot loads, became widely used as a "riot gun." The American Express Company armed its messengers with this type of weapon and it was also adopted by various police departments throughout the country,

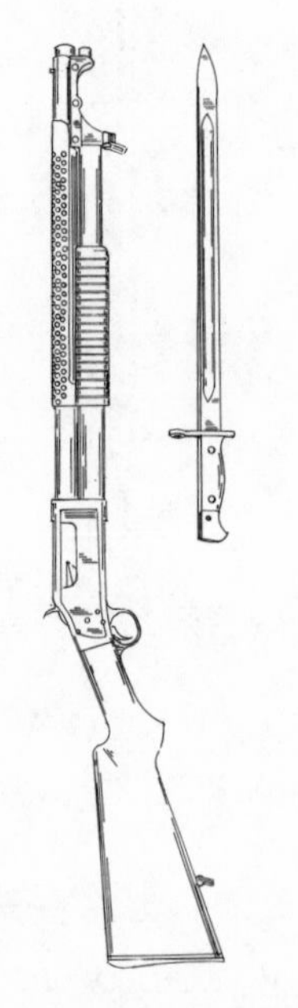
Winchester Model 1897 Trench Gun

During World War I a considerable number were used by American troops as trench guns. A group of American soldiers especially skilled at trap shooting were armed with these guns and stationed where they could fire at enemy hand grenades in midair and deflect them from falling into the American trenches.

The gun was especially effective on night patrols and in protecting outposts against attack by superior numbers. Paul Jenkins tells of their devastating effect on a German infantry attack on an American position. The Germans were allowed to come on until within range of the shotguns:

> . . . and when those shotguns got going—with nine .34 caliber buck shot per load, 6 loads in a gun, 200-odd men firing, plenty more shells at hand—the front ranks of the assault simply piled up on top of one another in one awful heap of buck shot-drilled men.
>
> . . . Perhaps it was this fight that resulted in the historic cablegram of September 14, 1918, to Secretary of State Lansing:
>
> "The German Government protests against the use of shotguns by the American Army and calls attention to the fact that, according to the laws of war, every prisoner found to have in his possession such guns or ammunition belonging thereto forfeits his life."

The passage in the Hague decrees alluded to in the German protest reads: "It is especially forbidden to employ arms, projections or materials calculated to cause unnecessary suffering." The American reply, too long to be quoted here, remarked pointedly that shotguns did *not* come under the Hague ban, and that if the Germans carried out their death-threat "in a single instance" the United States Government knew what to do in the way of reprisals, "and notice is hereby given of the intention to make such reprisals!" Uncle Sam did not intend to have his trench-shot-gunners massacred simply because he had given them a weapon which even the pick of the Prussian "shock troops" dreaded more than anything that four years of war had called on them to face. The shotguns went right on at their business—so terrible a success that message after message from G.H.Q. to America begged: "Give us more shotguns!" and by November 1918 two more models (the Winchester hammerless and the Remington) were about to be brought into production; when the Germans cried "Enough!" [8]

*The Model 92*

During the same period that the Company was bringing the slide-action firearm into production the management took steps to improve and expand its line of lever-action repeaters. The first addition to this line was the Model 92 rifle, which was essentially a simplified, lighter version of the Model 86. Using the same locking principle as that arm, a number of the other parts were eliminated, which made the Model 92 a lighter gun and somewhat cheaper to manufacture. It was chambered for the smaller-sized black-powder cartridges that had been so popular in the Model 73, but proved adaptable to these cartridges when they were later loaded with low-pressure smokeless powder.

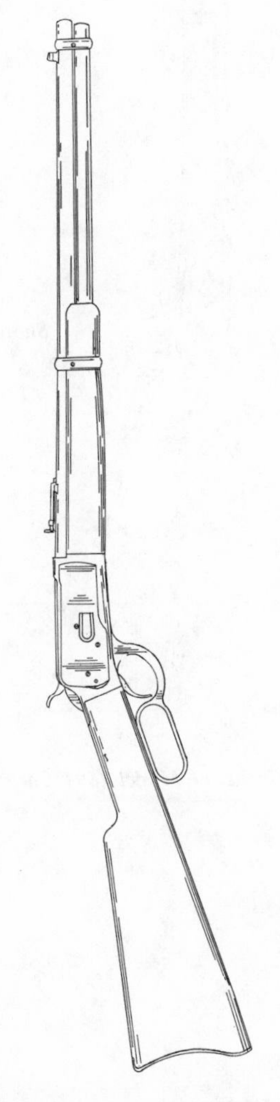

*Winchester Model 1892 Carbine*

First listed in the Company's catalog for 1892 and priced at $18, the Model 92 gradually took over a portion of the market that had formerly demanded the Model 73. One interesting use of this gun was among the trappers in northern United States and in Canada. In running a line of traps for smaller animals these men would not infrequently catch a wolf or a bear, and a Model 92 with a fourteen-inch barrel was effective in dealing with these animals. The short-barreled Model 92 also proved to be popular in the jungles of Brazil for use on the rubber plantations.

A most interesting testimonial regarding the use of the Model 92 came from Admiral Peary and was circulated by the Company in 1909 under the heading, "The Rifle That Helped Peary Reach the North Pole." Peary's statement read: "Personally I always carry a Winchester rifle. On my last expedition I had a Model 1892, .44 caliber Carbine and Winchester cartridges, which I carried with me right to the North Pole. After I left the ship I depended upon it to bring down the fresh meat that we needed. Since 1888, both in Nicaragua and in the Arctic regions, I have always used the Winchester Repeaters. Each of my Arctic expeditions since '91 has been fitted with these arms. The last expedition carried the .44-40 Carbine, for use on deer, seals, hare, and the like, and the .40-82 for use on musk-oxen, walrus and polar bears. In facing the polar bears, in gathering a herd of musk-oxen with the least expenditure of time and priceless ammunition, and in securing the greatest number of walrus out of an infuriated herd in the least time, I desire nothing better than a Winchester Repeater."

Some measure of the demand for the Model 92 is shown by the fact that approximately 735,000 had been sold by the end of 1914. In December 1932 the Company presented a beautifully engraved Model 92 rifle bearing the serial number 1,000,000 to Patrick J. Hurley, who was then Secretary of War.

## *The Model 94 (Winchester .30-30)*

If any one rifle can be designated as the "most famous of the Winchester line," it is the lever-action Model 94, more popularly known as the "Winchester .30-30." Based on a patent granted to the Browning brothers (U.S. 524702) in August 1894, this gun was in external appearance quite similar to the Model 92. It differed from all previous models, however, in being the first sporting repeating-action rifle adapted to handle smokeless cartridges.

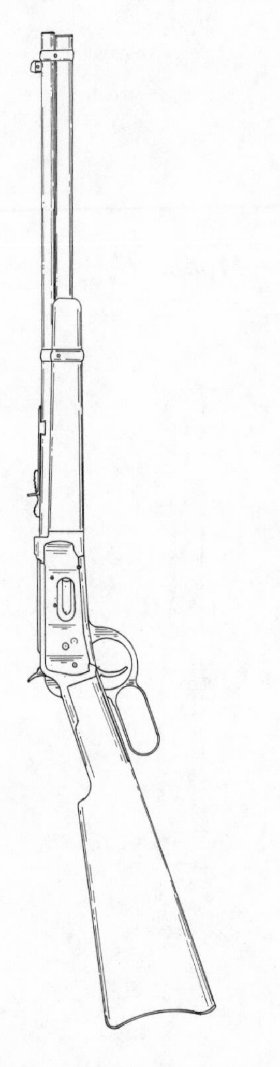

*Winchester Model 1894 Carbine*

The Model 94 is a good illustration of the changes that had to be made in rifles to adapt them to the greater pressures developed by smokeless powder. The maximum breech pressure generated by black-powder cartridges probably did not exceed 25,000 pounds to the square inch. Mild or ordinary steels composed of approximately ninety-nine per cent iron and one per cent carbon, were strong enough to withstand this pressure.[9]

With the introduction of smokeless powder it was soon discovered that the metal used for black-powder rifles was inadequate. Even the early smokeless cartridge loads stepped up the pressure on the breech to around 38,000 pounds to the square inch while later cartridges raised the figure to over 50,000.

Fortunately by this time enough progress had been made in the manufacture of alloy steels to give a metal that could withstand the increased pressure although the qualities of hardness, toughness, and the tensile strength of the new steels made it a difficult task to find the right combination for small arms.

When the Model 94 was first announced in the Company's catalog for November 1894, no mention was made of any special steel going into its construction and only two standard black-powder cartridges, the .32-40 and the .38-55, were listed to be used with the gun. Browning's repeating action used in the Model 94 proved strong enough for smokeless cartridges, but the barrels had to be made of stronger material.[10] Proof of the Company's activity in adapting the gun to smokeless loads came in August 1895, when the catalog stated that the barrels of the gun were made of nickel steel and two new especially developed smokeless cartridges, the Winchester .25-35 and the Winchester .30 (.30-30) were available for use in the weapon.

The use of nickel steel for this purpose was high tribute to the ingenuity and ability of the Winchester organization. In tensile strength, wearing qualities and resistance to corrosion it was somewhat superior to ordnance steel adopted by most manufacturers of high-powered rifles but these qualities made it much more difficult to machine. By developing new rifle-barrel drilling equipment, William Mason enabled the Company to process the nickel steel satisfactorily and for some thirty-five years the Company used this material for all of its high-powered rifle barrels.[11]

The Winchester caliber .30 cartridge was a singular triumph in ammunition development. Loaded with 30 grains of smokeless powder and a bullet weighing 170 grains, this cartridge, better known as the .30-30, soon became the most popular game cartridge in the country, and is today more popular for deer-hunting than any other type of ammunition. Because of its association with the cartridge, that rifle was commonly referred to as the Winchester .30-30.

Between them the Model 94 and the .30-30 cartridge practically revolutionized everyone's idea of what could be expected of a sporting rifle. The Model 94 was the first popular gun using the smaller-caliber smokeless cartridges which had the striking energy of the larger-sized, black-powder loads.[12] Even when more powerful smokeless cartridges became available, the .30-30 retained its popularity. Powerful enough to kill game such as deer at ordinary ranges, it could be used in the lightweight Model 94 (the sporting rifle weighed about eight pounds, the carbine six and a half pounds) without developing a kick or recoil that was unpleasant to the user.

*Winchester .30-30 Cartridge*

The Model 94 became especially popular in the West where by this time game was becoming more scarce and more wary of hunters and there was a demand for a longer-ranged, more accurate rifle. Priced at $18, the Model 94 began to replace the Model 73 and the Model 86 as a part of the standard equipment of the Western pioneers, hunters, and ranchers.

F. F. Chatfield-Taylor, writing in 1934, commented on the popularity of the Winchester .30-30 in the American Southwest. Pointing out that the revolver and the rifle are among the important tools on a ranch, he stated that when the rancher goes out on the range, "He packs the rifle in the scabbard on his saddle, in any one of different positions. Sometimes it is hung on the left side, with the stock to the front; sometimes on the right side with the stock to the rear. What the rancher desires is a position from which he can readily grasp the rifle, whether he be mounted or afoot; a position from which the rifle will not drop out accidentally, and also one which will not interfere if he should have to chase and rope a cow. Furthermore, the rifle must be so hung that the brush will not get caught or tangled up on the stock, or between the stock and the horse. Considering all these things, most ranchers prefer to have the stock of the gun toward the rear. A rifle to be packed in this manner, however, *must* be short, and it *must* be flat. Twenty inches of barrel is the very outside limit. Likewise, rifles with protuberances on the sides cannot qualify. This includes the bolt handle of a bolt-action rifle, and the cocking piece on a Remington Model 8 autoloader. Anything of this nature that makes the rifle stick out, seriously slows up the draw. Finally, one other thing that these saddle guns possess is a set of rugged sights which will withstand knocking around without being damaged or losing their adjustment. There are only a few rifles which can meet all these requirements. They are the lever actions—Winchester, Marlin, or Savage—the slide-action Remington, and the single-shots of various makes. Of these the Winchester is far and away the most popular, principally in .30-30 caliber, though often in .32 Special. The other calibers adapted to the 1894 action are to be seen from time to time, but in nowhere near the numbers as the first two. But while the 1894 Winchester is by far the most popular rifle, other models of Winchesters are also used. There are a good many 1895 carbines, for example, usually in .30-40 caliber. Then there is the famous Model 1886, in .45-70, and, .40-82 calibers, etc. These latter models, however, have the disadvantage of being rather heavy. They all weigh around eight pounds, while the 1894 carbines run just over six, and this makes a difference to the cattle man who is anxious to spare his horse as much as possible." [13]

Still being produced, the Model 94 has outsold any other rifle ever manufactured by the Company. By the end of 1914 more than 707,000 had been distributed, and in 1927 a specially engraved Model 94 bearing the serial number 1,000,000 was presented to President Calvin Coolidge. On May 8, 1948, the Company presented President Harry Truman the Model 94 bearing the serial number 1,500,000.

With the Model 94 the Company had a rifle in which smokeless cartridges of medium caliber could be used. To meet the demand for a big-game weapon, the Company in 1895 brought out the lever-action Model 95. Also based on a Browning patent (U.S. 549,345) the gun was quite similar to the Model 94, except that it was stronger in the breech and utilized a box magazine instead of the tubular magazine under the barrel. The box magazine had the chief advantage of avoiding accidental explosions of the pointed ammunition in the magazine. This rifle would handle the heaviest military type small-caliber smokeless cartridges which were increasingly used for big-game shooting.

Among the military cartridges for which this gun was chambered were the .303 British, the U.S. Government .30 M1902, and .30 M1906, and the .30-40 Krag. In addition, the Company developed several new cartridges of its own to be used with the gun, including the .35 WCF, the .38-72 WCF, .40-72 WCF, and the best known of all for big game hunting, the .405 WCF. These were all long cartridges measuring from three and an eighth to three and a quarter inches in length. Their greater striking force over the WCF .30-30, used in the Model 94 is shown by the following tabulation:

| *Cartridge* | *Weight of Bullet* (grains) | *Energy at 50 feet* (foot pounds) | *Mid-range Trajectory for 300 Yards* (in inches) |
|---|---|---|---|
| .30-30 WCF | 170 | 1449 | 15.23 |
| .303 British | 215 | 1833 | 14.08 |
| .30-40 Krag | 220 | 1880 | 13.55 |
| .35 WCF | 250 | 2150 | 12.24 |
| .405 WCF | 300 | 3077 | 12.82 |

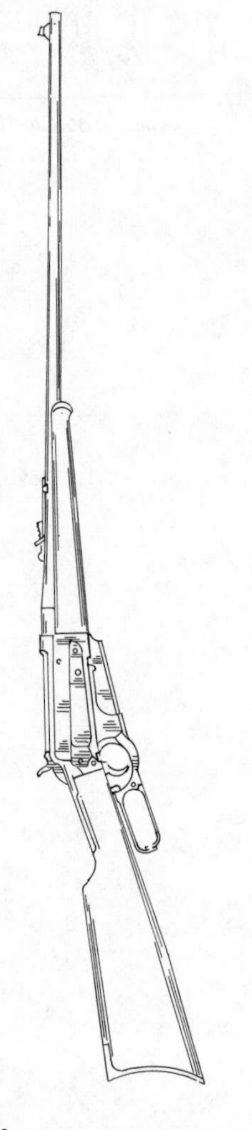
*Winchester Model 1895 Rifle*

The Model 95 was a more expensive gun than the Model 94. The standard round-barrel type was first listed at $25, at which price it remained until 1902, when it was raised to $30. This higher price and the more specialized uses to which the gun was put limited sales to around 67,000 down to the end of 1914.

The Model 95 had a considerable vogue among big-game hunters. It was especially popular for shooting moose, elk, caribou, bear, and walrus on the North American continent, being a favorite of such well-known hunters as Colonel Townsend Whelen, Edward M. House, John A. McQuire, Malcolm McKay, and Major Charles Askins.

Even in Africa against elephants, rhinos, lions, and buffalo the Model 95 had its advocates. Stewart Edward White, famous big-game hunter and author, used the .405 Model 95 Winchester with singular success in shooting lions, killing fourteen of the animals with thirty-three shots, of which four were misses. Leslie Simpson and Arthur Young, well-known African hunters, between them killed sixty-five lions with a .30-06 Winchester.[14]

There were some complaints about the cartridge jamming in the .30-40 Model 95, yet Stewart Edward White in his *Camp and Trail,* published in 1915, wrote: "My rifle is a .30-40 box magazine Winchester, with Lyman sights. This I have heard is not a particularly accurate gun. Also it is stated that after a few hundred shots it becomes still more inaccurate because of a residue which only special process can remove from the rifling. This may be. I only know that my own rifle today, after ten years' service, will still shoot as closely as I know how to hold it, although it has sixty-four notches on its stock and has probably been fired first and last—at big game, small game, and targets—upward of a thousand times. I use the Lyman aperture sight except in the dusk of evening, when a folding bar sight takes its place. At the time I bought this rifle the .33 and .35 had not been issued, and I thought, and still think, the .30-30 too light for sure work on any animal larger than a deer. I have never used the .35, but like the .33 very much. The old low-power guns I used to shoot a great deal, but have not for some years." [15]

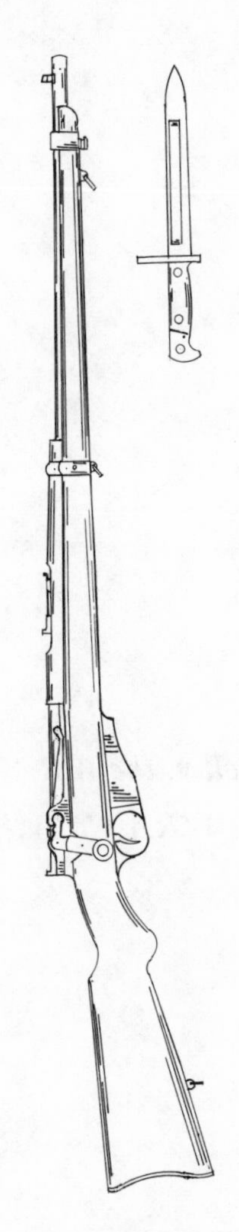

Lee Straight-Pull Rifle

A relatively small group, big-game hunters have always been especially careful in their choice of weapons, and inclined to be quite strong in their likes and dislikes of particular types and makes of guns. Africa more than any other area in the world was the testing ground of big-game rifles. Winchester's strongest champion in this area was Theodore Roosevelt, whose exploits as a big-game hunter will be described in Chapter Sixteen.

The Model 95 was also used as a military weapon. During the Spanish-American War the Company received an order for ten thousand musket-type chambered for the caliber .30 Army ammunition, and with a bayonet attached. (Some 300,000 were sold to the Russians during World War I.) (*See Chapter Nineteen.*) The Regular Army was equipped with the Krag-Jörgensen but there were not enough of these to supply the Volunteers and State Militia, who were armed with the single-shot Springfield black-powder rifles. Neither of these guns, especially the Springfield, was as good as the latest Mauser rifle in the hands of the Spanish troops and the Model 95S promised to be a welcome addition.

Colonel Addis was sent by the Company to interview Secretary of War Alger who approved the order. The Army officials were apparently not so enthusiastic about having an additional type of firearm in the service. As soon as the rifles came off the production line the Company began to have great difficulty in getting them passed by the Government inspector. T. G. Bennett asked Addis to take care of the problem. The latter went to the Government inspecting room and had the officer in charge write out the reasons for the failure of some ten rifles to pass inspection. Addis then informed the inspector that he was taking these guns personally to the Secretary of War, because he had promised the Secretary that he would do everything possible to speed their delivery. This got an immediate reaction from the inspector's superiors without the guns being taken to Washington and there was no further difficulty getting the guns accepted.

## *The Lee Straight-Pull Rifle*

Three years before the Army contract for the Model 95, the Company had obtained a contract to supply the United States Navy with 15,000 bolt-action repeating rifles. These were manufactured under patents granted to James Paris Lee who sold the rights to manufacture the rifle to the Company.

Winchester hoped that this gun might prove acceptable to the sporting trade that had not been enthusiastic about the bolt-action Hotchkiss. In November 1897 after the Navy order had been completed, the Company introduced the gun to the sporting trade with the following catalog announcement: "This gun is known as the Lee Straight-Pull Rifle, and has been adopted as the small arm for use in the United States Navy. The caliber of the gun is .236 in. (6mm) and it shoots a smokeless powder cartridge with a hardened lead bullet, having a copper jacket plated with tin, and giving an initial velocity of 2,550 feet (777.24 meters) per second. The magazine holds five cartridges, which may be inserted separately or at one time, in which latter case they are placed in the magazine in a pack, held together by a steel clip. The superiority of this rifle over all other types of bolt guns lies in the fact that the operation of opening and closing is by a 'straight pull,' instead of the customary 'up turn' and 'pull back.' "

Attempts to popularize the Lee straight-pull rifle as a sporting arm were unsuccessful. Listed at $32, it was the most expensive rifle in the Winchester line. This relatively high price may have discouraged purchasers but the main reason for its limited sales, which amounted to slightly under two thousand (not including the Navy contract) for the period, was the continued resistance of shooters to a bolt-action gun. As one authority has put it: "This was a box-magazine, high velocity, small caliber rifle and died an early death simply because it was forty years ahead of its day. Today we are just commencing to appreciate the possibilities of the high velocity, small caliber arms and if the 6mm. were revived it undoubtedly could be developed to a high accuracy and velocity far ahead of the 1895 era." [16]

*Russell v. the WRA Co.; WRA Co. v. U.S.*

In taking on the manufacture of the Lee straight-pull rifle, the Company became involved in an extended legal controversy. At the time the original contract with the Navy was under consideration, Winchester's patent experts warned that the Lee patents might be subject to a suit for infringement, but as the Government authorities agreed to compensate the Company for any damages which it might be forced to pay as a result of a suit, the management decided to accept the contract.

The prediction of the Company's patent experts proved correct. On November 11, 1899, Captain Andrew H. Russell, U.S. Army, brought suit alleging infringement by Winchester on a number of patents owned by him. He claimed damages of $100,000 and asked for a permanent injunction against the Company. After an extended and tedious suit, marked by complicated legal and technical considerations, the court decided, on November 21, 1906, in favor of the Winchester Repeating Arms Company and the suit was dismissed.[17]

At the conclusion of this long and expensive suit the Company applied to the Government for reimbursement for legal expenses, amounting to over twelve thousand dollars. But the Government authorities took the position that since the suit had been dismissed and no damages had been incurred by the Company, no payment would be made by the United States Government to Winchester for defending the suit.

This was an unexpected interpretation of the Government's original guarantee to hold Winchester ". . . harmless from any and all suits which may be brought against it for and on account of the rifles required." In effect the Winchester management was being penalized for its success in winning a suit that saved the Government from paying out a large amount for damages.

After attempting for several years to get a reversal of the interpretation by the Government authorities, Winchester in 1915 brought suit in the U.S. Court of Claims to recover the amount involved. On April 10, 1916, the court in a strongly worded decision criticized the Government's handling of the matter, upheld the Winchester Repeating Arms Company, and ordered the Government to pay the Company the sum of $12,446.20.[18]

*The Model 1900 and the Model 1902*

The defense and prosecution of legal cases did not interfere with the Company's development of its gun line, and in 1900 Winchester made its first entry into the low-priced field with a single-shot, bolt-action rifle, based on a patent purchased from Browning (U.S. 632,094). This rifle was chambered for .22 short or .22 long rimfire cartridges and weighed only two and three-quarter pounds. Listed at five dollars, during the two years this Model 1900 was produced 105,000 were sold.

In 1902 the Company replaced the Model 1900 with an improved version of the same gun called the Model 1902. Differing from its predecessor only in relatively minor details, the Model 02, also listed at five dollars, continued to be a popular gun in the low-priced field. Between 1902 and the end of 1914 over 355,000 had been purchased by shooters who wanted an inexpensive rifle.

*Browning-Winchester Contract*

Only three copies of the contracts made between the Company and the Browning brothers have been preserved, all three relating to models purchased by Winchester in 1894 and 1895. The agreement which covered the patent on the Winchester Model 92 as well as a gun which was not put into production, was affected by the following exchange of letters:

*New Haven, Conn.*
*April 6th, 1894*

MESSRS. BROWNING BROTHERS,
OGDEN, UTAH

*Gentlemen:*

The Winchester Repeating Arms Company will purchase all your rights, title and interest to the invention shown by the two models presented by you on the date of this letter, being two lever guns, one with box magazine, and one with tubular magazine for the sum of Twenty Thousand Dollars ($20,000); payment to be made in goods to the extent of Seventeen Thousand and Five Hundred Dollars ($17,500.00), and in money to the extent of Two Thousand and Five Hundred Dollars ($2,500.00).

It is understood that, if the patents obtained on these two guns do not convey to the Winchester Repeating Arms Co. the complete right to make the guns shown by the two models; or, if the models infringe other patents, so that the Winchester Company is unable to use them, then the Winchester Company may assign to the Messrs. Browning Brothers, the patent rights which may be obtained for the two guns, and need not make any payment for such patent rights and understood that the Browning Brothers will return any payment which may have been made therefor.

Yours truly,
WINCHESTER REPEATING ARMS CO.
T. G. Bennett, President

WINCHESTER REPEATING ARMS CO.
CITY

*New Haven, Conn. 6th Apr. '94*

*Dear Sirs:*

Replying to your favor of this date would say that we accept the $20,000 for the two guns, also accept the conditions named and hereby acknowledge receipt of the $2,500 cash payment.

Yours very truly,
BROWNING BROTHERS

*John Moses Browning*
*(After a Medal Struck by Fabrique Nationale d'Armes de Guerre)*

It will be noted that under this agreement the Browning brothers conveyed all rights, title, and interest in their patent to the Winchester Repeating Arms Company. The provision that only $2,500 was payable in cash and the remainder in merchandise is noteworthy. Not only did this provision reduce the cash outlay of the Company, but permitted it to make a profit on the goods delivered to the Browning brothers. The latter were willing to accept this arrangement because they were operating a store in Ogden handling sporting goods and ammunition.

The other two contracts covered firearms which were not manufactured by the Company. Both conveyed all rights to Winchester but they varied in respect to payments. The first, dated February 9, 1895, called for a total payment of $15,000 in cash. The second, made on December 9 of the same year, provided for a payment of $8,000, all ". . . to be taken in goods of the manufacture of the Winchester Repeating Arms Co."

Some time during the latter part of 1901 or early 1902 the long association between the Browning brothers and the Winchester Repeating Arms Company came to an end. The cause of this break was the failure to come to a mutually satisfactory agreement on the automatic shotgun invented by John Browning.

*Disagreement with Browning*

As Browning's earlier invention of the machine gun indicates, he had been interested for several years in the development of automatic firearms. Along in March 1899 he wrote to New Haven that he had a model of a semiautomatic shotgun to show T. G. Bennett. The following month he brought the new gun, which utilized a recoil-operated action, to New Haven. As had been the practice with all Browning models, the gun was analyzed to check possible patent infringement and was tested for its mechanical performance.

Apparently the patent department of Winchester found that Browning's original model was an infringement on an existing patent. The following letter indicates the nature of this infringement and the extent to which the Company was prepared to go to avoid any patent difficulty:

*October 11, 1899*

MR. JOHN BROWNING,
BROWNING BROTHERS CO.,
OGDEN, UTAH.

*Dear Sir:*

In the matter of the automatic shotgun, we find ourselves squarely up against the following issue.

The second claim of the Borchardt patent is held by our best advice to cover the link lifting arrangement in your gun. We have worked with our attorneys in every way, but do not see a good defense in anything which we have been able to present. You probably have Borchardt's patent #571,260, November 10th, 1896. Please look at the second claim.

We tried to buy the Borchardt patent, going to the extent of sending Mr. Addis to Berlin for that purpose, and have not succeeded in getting a price which would enable us to touch it. The negotiation with the concern owning the Borchardt patents on the other side is not yet concluded, but it seemed best to write you and let you know exactly how we were fixed. Some device other than that now used, say, a cam on the rear or on the front link, should be devised which will lift the links out of the straight line.

Please consider the matter and write as soon as possible. We are sorry to have to come up with this difficulty. No patents of Maxim, nor any foreign patents which we are able to produce, exactly hit the matter, in the opinion of our attorneys, and I can see how their position is taken from their experience in the courts. The whole system looks like Borchardt's and unless we can show different operation, it does seem to me that a court might be very liable to hold that the models which we have infringe Borchardt.

Just at present we see no good way out of this of our own devising. We are working at it nevertheless.

Yours respectfully,
WINCHESTER REPEATING ARMS COMPANY.
T. G. Bennett, President.

Browning was able to work out a different lifting arrangement for his gun, which was not in violation of the Borchardt patent. There were, however, certain mechanical troubles which developed during the testing period and the gun was returned to Browning for examination and changes. Browning sent the gun back to New Haven on August 1, 1900 with the following letter:

WINCHESTER REPEATING ARMS CO.,
NEW HAVEN, CONN.

*Gentlemen:*

We are in receipt of yours of the 23rd, and the gun which I have put in good order and return today by express. Have made a few changes which experiments in auto. guns since that was made, have shown to be for the better. I see the gun has been worked with considerably by parties who did not understand the system. The reason it jarred off was on account of the sear having been bent. You will see I have made an easier and shorter pull than it was before, yet, it will not jar off. We have had no mis-fires and think this fault is with the cartridges. By the way, this is a fault that bobs up with the Winchester cartridge more frequent than with any other cartridge we have had any experience with. The changes I have made are in the carrier latch, the ejector and ejector lever and the end of the sear. Have also straightened the trigger which was bent. Think the way the trigger and sear got bent was by jerking the trigger plate out, unhooking the trigger from the sear; before pulling the trigger plate out, the links should be drawn back. Our experience has been that a gun gets worse treatment in a draughtsman's office than in a duck hunter's camp. Another thing the gun requires no oil at all and if you should oil it, it is not necessary to fill it full. Did you ever put oil on the end of a Winchester breech block and snap it; if not just try it. We have fired a lot of cartridges in the shop and in the field at doves and have no failures whatever and we hope you will have better luck with it. We have always considered the standard load for the gun is 31 grs. of du Pont, 1 oz. shot, 2⁹⁄₁₆ in. shell which is what we generally use, but the gun will work alright with 31 grs. ⅞ oz. 34 grs. ⅞ or 1 oz., 3½ or 2¾ drs. black powder, ⅞ or 1 oz. shot. The gun will operate with smaller loads than above if held reasonably firm against the shoulder, but 31 grs. du Pont smokeless, 1 oz. in Repeater or Leader shells is a good load in our regular 16 gauge cartridge.

Speaking of cartridges will here say, that we got some .303 British cartridges from your San Francisco house which were loaded with Laflin and Rand powder and primed with black powder primers and in taking them out of a case that had never been opened, we found a .30 Government cartridge mixed with them. This would be a nice thing in a machine gun and a hot corner.

Yours very truly,
JOHN M. BROWNING

Browning's impatience with some of the attempts to improve his gun are clearly demonstrated in the foregoing letter as well as his opinion of Winchester ammunition.[19] These various mechanical difficulties were remedied during 1901, and by the end of the year the automatic shotgun was sufficiently perfected to be put into production.

Meanwhile the Company had made arrangements to patent the automatic shotgun for Browning. Three patents covering the arm were filed by Seymour & Earl, the Company's patent lawyers, between February 8, 1900, and January 11, 1902.[20] It was just prior to this last date that the question of purchase of the patent rights came up. Negotiations were apparently carried on personally between T. G. Bennett and John M. and Matthew Browning, and no record was kept of proceedings, but it seems clear that the break came over a request by Browning that Winchester enter into a royalty agreement with him covering the new gun. This point has been confirmed by Edwin Pugsley on a basis of subsequent conversations with both John M. Browning and T. G. Bennett.

Winchester, as has been noted, had always followed the policy of acquiring exclusive rights to patents and had never entered into a royalty agreement with a patent holder. The Company had been willing to purchase all the Browning patents, including those which in its judgment were not marketable. While this policy may have been to keep such patents from going to rivals, it did insure Browning of a certain market for his gun inventions.

In the automatic shotgun Browning believed, with reason, that he had a gun of unusual design and one which would sell in large quantities. Other companies had been willing to enter into royalty arrangements with him on his pistol patents. His fame as an inventor had become widespread by this date and he must have felt that his bargaining position was stronger than it had been when he first began selling his patents to the Company.

T. G. Bennett faced a difficult decision. To grant Browning's request meant a change in a long-established policy and the setting of a precedent which might have to be followed with other inventors. To refuse meant the loss of the services of a man who contributed much to Winchester gun development. The established policy won out and Bennett refused to make such an agreement even to continue the association with Browning.

When the negotiations with T. G. Bennett broke down John Browning is said to have made an immediate appointment with Marcellus Hartley in New York, who was now in full control of the Remington Arms Company. He was waiting in the latter's office when word came that Marcellus Hartley had died suddenly while at a luncheon meeting. Browning then took a ship for Europe where he made arrangements with the Fabrique Nationale d'Armes de Guerre, of Liége, Belgium, to produce the gun. At a later date a similar arrangement was made with the Remington Arms Company which brought out the gun in the American market in 1905.

The Winchester Repeating Arms Company soon regretted the thoroughness with which it had written out the patent specifications for the Browning automatic shotgun. The gun proved to be enormously popular and T. C. Johnson, who had been in charge of the patent application, often remarked to his associates that it took him nearly ten years to design an automatic shotgun (the Winchester 1911) which would not be an infringement on the Browning gun.

How much the Company had depended upon the Ogden inventor for its new model guns has already been illustrated, and the failure to secure the Browning automatic shotgun and the break with Browning represented a serious loss. But the loss was not irreparable because by this time the Company had within its own organization a gifted inventor in the person of T. C. Johnson, who helped maintain the high quality of the Winchester gun line.

*Thomas Crossly Johnson*

Thomas Crossly Johnson, more familiarly known as "Tommy," was born on May 12, 1862, the son of Samuel C. Johnson, president of the Yale Safe and Iron Company of West Haven, Connecticut. He attended grade school and preparatory school in New Haven, and entered the Yale Sheffield Scientific School in 1881, graduating with the class of 1884. After a year spent in his father's com-

*Thomas Crossly Johnson*

pany Johnson came to Winchester in November 1885 where he remained until the time of his death in 1934.

In 1902 Johnson already had nearly eighteen years' experience in gun design. During most of that time he had worked with William Mason and T. G. Bennett on improving new and older model guns. While he shared the talent of those two men in being able to make the modifications necessary to achieve better operation or manufacturing of firearms, Johnson was also an original thinker, as his later contributions to the Company's gun line demonstrated. During his service with the Winchester Company he took out some 124 patents which were assigned to the Company.

*Self-Loading Rifles: Models 03, 05, 07, and 10*

The first addition to the Winchester line credited to T. C. Johnson was a series of self-loading or semiautomatic rifles, all modifications of the same basic design. The action used by Johnson utilized the gas pressure developed in the breech to push or "blow back" the mechanism which automatically reloaded the weapon each time the trigger was pulled and released. They were all delicately balanced and could be used only with the special smokeless cartridges which the Company introduced with each new model.

The Model 03 came with a tubular magazine in the butt stock, holding ten cartridges. It was chambered only for the Company's new smokeless .22 automatic rimfire cartridge. These cartridges were of comparatively low velocity, which tended to limit the demand for the new gun.

The Model 05 was an enlarged version of the Model 03, chambered for caliber .32 and .35 Winchester centerfire cartridges, designed specially for this gun. The magazine on this model was a box type holding five cartridges later increased to ten. Even with the increased calibers the velocities developed by this gun were too low to appeal widely to shooters and the gun never sold in large quantities.

In 1907 a third self-loading rifle was added to the line. This was the Model 07, which was identical to the Model 05, except that it was heavier and chambered for the higher-velocity cartridge, the Winchester .351 centerfire developed for its use. This model was more popular than its immediate predecessor and was widely used in police work where a rapid-fire, medium-velocity rifle was desired.

Three years later the Model 1910 was introduced. This was in turn an enlarged version of the Model 07, chambered for the special Winchester .401 centerfire cartridge. This cartridge developed sufficient velocity to be used in deer hunting but was not especially effective over longer ranges.

*Single-Shot Rifles: Thumb-Trigger Model and Model 04*

At the same time T. C. Johnson was working on semiautomatic arms, T. G. Bennett took over the improvement of the Company's line of single-shot rifles. These were essentially modifications of the bolt-action Model 1900, originally designed by Browning and modified in the Model 02 by T. G. Bennett.

The first of these was a thumb-trigger gun which was first described in the Company's catalog for July 1904: "The Winchester Thumb Trigger Model is a novelty in .22 caliber rifles. It has the same simple and reliable bolt action which made the Winchester Model 1902 such a popular gun and caused it to be so widely imitated. It will handle either a .22 Short or .22 Long Rim Fire cartridges. As its name indicates, the trigger which is located on the upper side of the grip at the rear of the bolt is operated by pressing down with the thumb. Simplicity and quickness of action are features of the thumb trigger. It is also claimed that it is an aid to accurate shooting, as the shooter is not so apt to throw the gun off the object aimed at in pressing down the trigger as when pulling it in the old way."

The thumb-trigger model was simple to manufacture and was produced to compete with the cheap, foreign rifles. It was the lowest-priced gun in the Winchester line, being listed at $3.50. While it never became very widely used in the United States, it was especially popular in Australia, where most of the 59,000 sold between 1904 and 1915 appear to have been shipped.

The catalog for July 1904 also listed the Model 04, a larger version of the more conventional Model 02. The gun was chambered interchangeably for the .22 short and .22 long rimfire cartridges. Its listed price was $6 and during the succeeding ten years over 121,000 were sold.

*The Model 06*

The Model 06 was a revision of the Model 90 pump-action repeating rifle. When it was first introduced in January 1906 it was chambered only for the .22 short rimfire cartridges. Two years later it was brought out to handle interchangeably the .22 short, the .22 long, and .22 long rifle cartridges.

The circumstances that led to the introduction of the Model 06 illustrate Winchester's sensitivity to actual or potential competition. Shortly before 1906 T. C. Johnson learned that the Stevens Arms Company, of Chicopee Falls, Massachusetts, was planning to bring out a new line of "Visible Loading" repeating rifles, chambered for caliber .22 cartridges. These guns would compete with the Winchester Model 90, especially if they were listed at a lower price. By working intensively Johnson was able to put the Model 06 on the market a year before the Stevens concern introduced its own new model to the trade.

Listed at $10.50 compared with the $16 of the Model 90, this gun was immediately popular in the medium-price market for repeating rifles. In the first eight years it was on the market nearly 423,000 were sold.

*The Model 1911 Shotgun*

After the break with Browning, T. G. Bennett put Johnson to work designing a self-loading shotgun to be added to the Winchester line. Johnson experienced considerable difficulty in trying to work around the patent specifications he had personally drawn up for Browning. Described as a "recoil operated, hammerless, take-down, five shot repeater," the gun was introduced in the Company's catalog for October 1911 as the Model 11 "Winchester Self-Loading Shotgun."

Though a tribute to Johnson's ingenuity, the Model 11 was only moderately popular. At a list price of $38, it was the most expensive gun in the Winchester line.

*The Model 12 Shotgun*

The last model brought out by the Company prior to 1915 was the Model 12 shotgun, first listed in January 1913. In developing this model T. C. Johnson showed his real capacity as a gun designer when he was not forced to work around an existing patent situation.

The Model 12 was a slide-action, hammerless, repeating shotgun with a tubular magazine under the barrel which held five shells. Made initially in a 20-gauge take-down style, the gun was later produced in a wide variety of styles suitable for all kinds of game shooting and for skeet. Priced at $20, the gun became

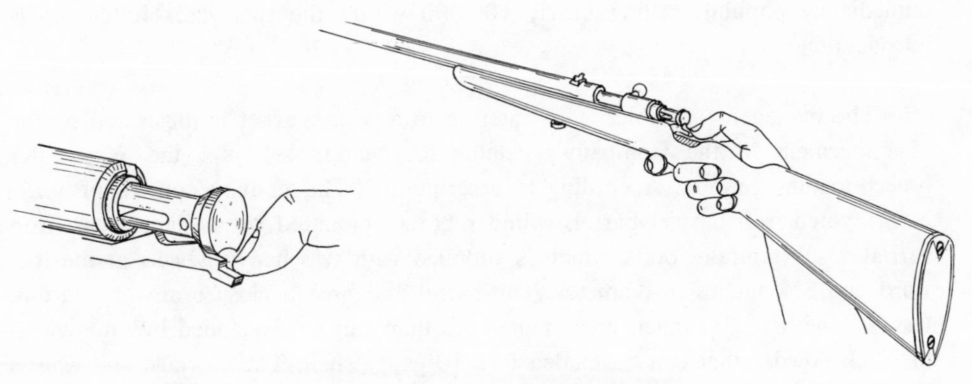

*Winchester Thumb-Trigger Rifle*

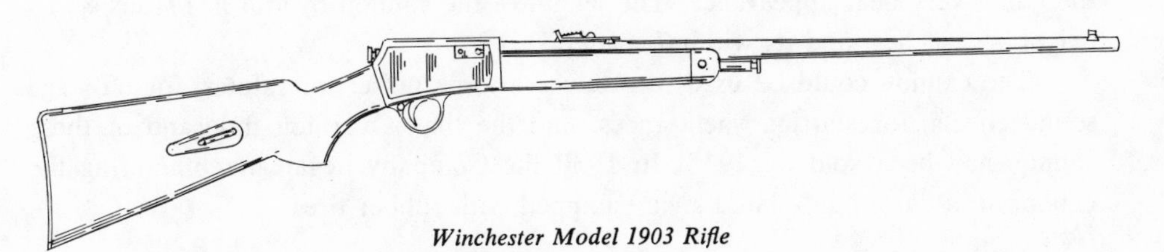

*Winchester Model 1903 Rifle*

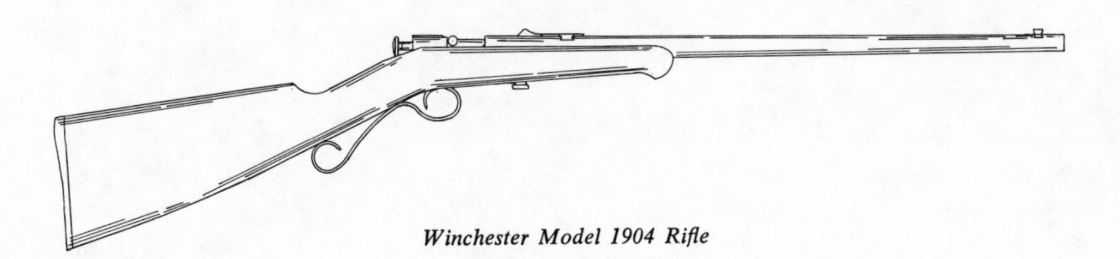

*Winchester Model 1904 Rifle*

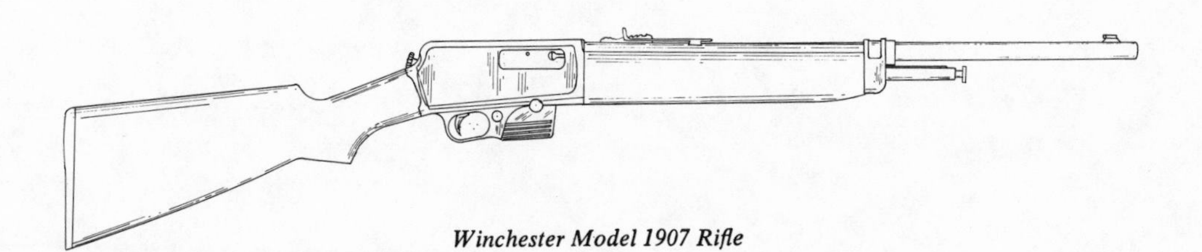

*Winchester Model 1907 Rifle*

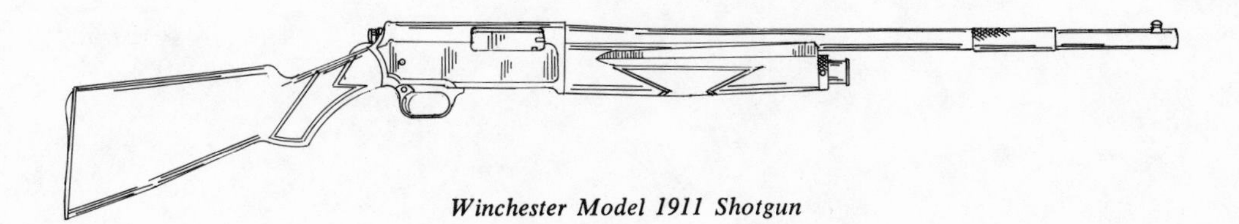

*Winchester Model 1911 Shotgun*

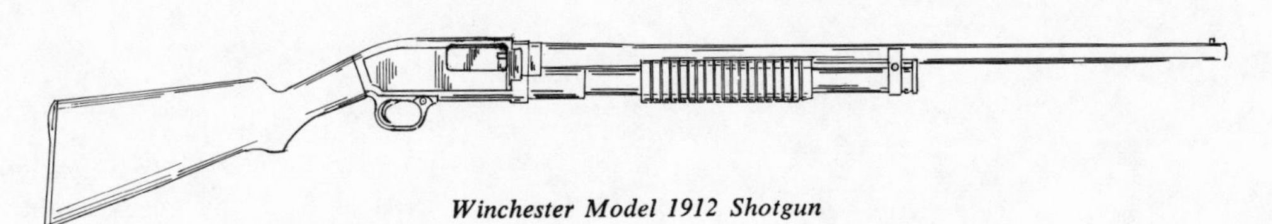

*Winchester Model 1912 Shotgun*

immediately popular, selling nearly 100,000 within the two years following its introduction.

### *Breech-Loading Cannon*

The management's interest in catering to a wide market is illustrated by the announcement in the Company's catalog for March 1903, of the Winchester breech-loading cannon. According to description: "This cannon consists of a 12-inch tapered, rolled steel barrel, cylinder bored, mounted on a shapely cast iron carriage, substantially built, which is supplied with two heavy wheels at the forward end 3⅝ inches in diameter. The barrel and breech closure are proved and tested to withstand a much greater pressure than can be developed by any charge of black powder that can be loaded in a 10 gauge shell. The carriage and wheels are nicely japanned, the barrel blued, and breech closure hardened black giving the gun a very neat appearance. The length of the cannon overall is 17 inches, its height 7¼ inches, and its width 7 inches."

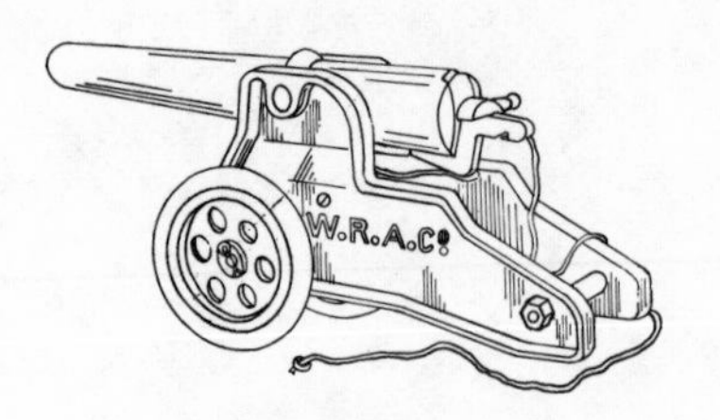


*Winchester Model 98 Cannon*

The cannon could be used to produce a large noise; for salutes, for off-stage sound effects, for starting yacht races, and the like. Over ten thousand of these cannon had been sold by 1915. In 1930 the Company began manufacturing the cannon in a chromium-plated style equipped with rubber tires.

CHAPTER FIFTEEN

# SALES PROBLEMS OF THE EARLY 1900s

*Competition*

Aside from Winchester, the principal firms producing rifles and shotguns during the 1890s were Remington (jointly owned and operated by Winchester and the Union Metallic Cartridge Company), Colt's, Marlin, and Stevens. All these firms were marketing rifles and shotguns which were more or less competitive with the various guns in the Winchester line. There was also a number of concerns specializing in the production of shotguns during the early 1890s, including Parker Brothers of Meriden, Connecticut; Ithaca Gun Company of Ithaca, New York; Burgess Gun Company of Buffalo, New York; and L. C. Smith Gun Company, of Fulton, New York.

Colt's ceased to be a factor in the rifle field when its Lightning magazine rifle was dropped from production in 1903. The reasons for this action are not apparent, but it may have been based on a decision to concentrate on the manufacture of revolvers for which that company was so famed.

The most important newcomer into the industry during this period was the Savage Repeating Arms Company (later the Savage Arms Company) with its factory at Utica, New York. First incorporated in 1894, this concern began the manufacture of arms around 1897. One interesting feature of this company is that it began just as smokeless powders were coming into use. Its rifle line, as a consequence, featured the high-powered, smaller-calibered models from the start.

From Winchester's point of view, however, the most significant change in the competitive situation involved the Remington plant. Unfortunately, the records covering the administration of this concern by Winchester and UMC have not been preserved, but it is clear that the production of guns and pistols was continued along with certain other products including bicycles and sewing machines.

The Remington guns were more or less competitive with Winchester's products.[1] Of particular importance to Winchester was the absence in the Remington line of any lever- or pump-action guns that would have been in direct competition with its own repeating rifles and shotguns.

The combined ownership of Remington was continued until September 1896, when Winchester sold its share to Marcellus Hartley and his associates for an undisclosed sum. What immediately led to this decision is not known. To judge from the limited information available, the joint operation of the Remington plant did not go too smoothly, or profitably.

For some nine years following the sale there was no basic change in the Remington gun line. Meanwhile, in September 1899, Winchester purchased the machines, tools, fixtures and patents of the Burgess Gun Company, which had been active in the manufacture of repeating shotguns. (*See Appendix A-3.*) The Burgess shotguns were withdrawn from the market and, as far as is known, Winchester made no use of the patents acquired in its own guns.

In 1905, three years after the death of Marcellus Hartley, Remington's policy changed in respect to the production of repeating firearms. In that year it brought out the Remington auto-loading shotgun, Model 11, based upon the patents issued to John M. Browning, which Bennett had declined to buy on a royalty arrangement. As T. C. Johnson was still working on the design of a semiautomatic shotgun which was to be the Winchester Model 11, Remington's gun was not directly in competition with any gun in the Winchester line. In 1906, however, Remington began manufacturing an auto-loading rifle, also based on a Browning patent, which competed with Winchester's self-loading rifles, first brought out in 1903, and in 1909, Remington began selling a slide-action repeating rifle which appealed to the same market as the Winchester Model 90, and its recently introduced Model 06.

The reaction of the Winchester management to these moves has been related by Veader and Earle: "At the time the Company sold its interest in the Remington Company to Marcellus Hartley, it was understood by Mr. Bennett of the Winchester Repeating Arms Company that the Remington would not place upon the market a repeating arm in competition with the Winchester guns. When the Remington Company, after Mr. Hartley's death, did place upon the market a repeating arm in competition with the Winchester gun, the Winchester Repeating Arms Company desired to protest. A careful search was made for some agreement in writing between Mr. Hartley and Mr. Bennett, which would sustain the Winchester Repeating Arms Company's position, but no such document could be found."

These moves by Remington brought a competitor into the repeating arms field backed by strong financial interests and an able management, which was willing to acquire rights to John Browning's patents on his own terms.

There is little doubt that Winchester was still the leading producer of firearms during the decade preceding 1915. The variety of models offered for sale, the Company's long history in the industry, the fact that Winchester and repeating rifle were synonymous terms in the minds of most users, all combined to make a Winchester gun the standard of comparison for other firearms. Nevertheless, the emergence of Savage and the changed policy on the part of Remington had weakened the predominance of the Company just prior to World War I.

*Gun Sales*

Whatever may have been its competitive position, Winchester (as shown in Appendix D-2) experienced a remarkable increase in annual gun sales over the 1890-1914 period; the average of over 300,000 being nearly four times as large during the last five years as during the first five. Within this trend there was a considerable cyclical fluctuation. The panic of 1893 was reflected in a drop of fifteen per cent in the number of guns sold for that year compared to 1892. Sales did not again rise to the 1890 level until 1898, actually reaching the low point for the entire period during the depression of 1896. The impact of the Spanish-American War is visible in the rise of sales for 1898, and while the war lasted only a few months, it marked the beginning of an upward movement that reached a peak for the entire period in 1906. The panic of 1907 was accompanied by a reduction in sales that carried through the following year, but beginning in 1909 and continuing through 1914, the yearly total of guns sold averaged over 290,000.

To a very considerable extent this expansion of Winchester's sales paralleled the growth of the entire firearms industry. No exact comparisons can be made as the Census did not report physical production, and combined pistols and revolvers in reporting the value of the industry's products during these years. The combined figure reported for 1889 was $2.92 million, for 1899 $5.45 million, for 1909 $8.06 million, and for 1914 $10.54 million.

Judged by these and other data, Winchester was in about the same relative position in the firearms industry in 1914 as it had been in 1890. Even so, it would be a mistake to assume that the growth necessary to maintain this position would have come without any attempt on the part of the Company to push sales. According to Emerson's well-known observation, the world will beat a path to the door of the most skillful manufacturer. Experience seems to show, however, that quality alone may be insufficient to build and maintain customer interest. The well-worn paths are much more likely to lead to establishments whose products are brought frequently and forcibly to the attention of the public.

In any event, there was no tendency on the part of the Winchester management to test the validity of Emerson's generalization after 1890, even though by that date the reputation of the Company's products was based solidly upon their performance. An increasing amount of attention was given to keeping the "paths" to the New Haven establishment clear and in good repair. The Company's emissaries were sent out, charged with the responsibility of seeing that the public was well acquainted with the virtues and qualities of Winchester guns and ammunition.

### *Marketing Organization*

With the increased emphasis on selling, the principal marketing channels were undisturbed; merchandise being sold to jobbers or wholesalers who in turn distributed to retailers, but the marketing organization was gradually elaborated and expanded during the succeeding twenty-five years.

This expansion was reflected in the personnel of the management and an expansion of the group. From 1890 to 1900, Hooper continued to be responsible for sales. Sometime during this period the general supervision of the sales force was put under the direction of Irby Bennett (no relation to T. G. Bennett), general agent for the Company in Memphis, Tennessee. In 1897 William R. Clark was made advertising manager.

Hooper resigned in 1900 and Hodson was elected vice president and treasurer. To take over Hooper's work on sales, Harrie S. Leonard was appointed assistant treasurer. Shortly thereafter, the supervision of salesmen was transferred to New Haven, and around 1907 a sales manager, Seneca G. Lewis, was appointed.

### *Raising the Profit Margin on Guns*

For a number of years after 1890 the Company seems to have been concerned with raising the low-profit margins on guns that had come about during the 1881-89 period. There were several alternatives open to the management. The situation might have been remedied simply by raising list prices, without changing the rebate and discount pattern. Such a move would have no doubt increased prices to the final purchasers. On this point the officials were apparently convinced that many of their customers would either be unwilling or unable to pay higher prices, or that other concerns would not raise their prices correspondingly and would take away a considerable amount of business. With two exceptions, therefore, list prices were unchanged during the twenty-five years beginning in 1890.

A greater amount of sales at the same price would, of course, increase total profits even with a low margin per gun. As already noted, sales did in fact increase remarkably during the period, but not until after 1897. With or without increased sales, profit margins could also be increased by cutting manufacturing costs. Insofar as contract rates are an index, production costs were lowered, the index falling about 31 per cent between 1890 and 1904. (*See Appendix J-5.*)

Finally profits could be raised by cutting trade discounts and rebates to jobbers. This the Company was able to do. The jobbers' mark-ups were cut approximately in half during the period; an indication, in part at least, of how desirable the jobbers and retailers felt it was to handle the Winchester gun line. (In the absence of general information on jobbers' discounts and rebates in other fields during the period it is not possible to determine whether the margins on Winchester products were out of line.)

This lowering of jobbers' margins involved the risk that the big jobbing houses, which the Company was especially anxious to keep, would withdraw their business. The jobbers were presumably compensated to some extent after 1897 by an increased volume of business, but there were complaints that mark-ups were too narrow to be profitable. Winchester apparently lost a few of its accounts, but seems to have been able to replace them without serious difficulty without changing the jobbers' margins.

*Price-Cutting*

While Winchester was interested in keeping prices to the dealers and customers reasonably low, it was insistent that prices should not go below established or conventional levels. For this reason the management moved vigorously to prevent price-cutting that began on a serious scale after 1900. By this date jobber margins had been substantially reduced and while the Company believed that these discounts and rebates gave both the jobbers and dealers a reasonable profit margin, it realized that such margins had to be protected if jobber and dealer loyalty were to be maintained. The Company also wished to avoid giving the public the idea that its products could be bought at cut prices.

One source of price-cutting came from firms which, because of the prestige of Winchester firearms and ammunition, used them as "loss leaders" to attract customers. The other source of price-cutting came from the mail-order houses, especially Sears Roebuck & Company, which followed a policy of selling merchandise whenever possible at prices that were generally below those quoted by retail dealers.

Prior to about 1904 Sears Roebuck had observed Winchester's price policies on guns, merely challenging price competition, and in the case of the Model 86 rifle, offering a cleaning rod free with every purchase. In 1901, referring to the Winchester firearms, the mail-order house stated in its catalog: "We would be glad and perfectly willing to sell this line at lower prices, but the manufacturer restricts the selling prices and would not supply us with goods if we were to sell below these printed prices. These prices are guaranteed to be as low as offered by any reliable dealers in the United States, and should you be offered these goods lower by any dealer you would confer a great favor by advising us, in order to give us an opportunity of adjusting the prices."

In 1904 Sears Roebuck took the first step toward cutting prices by offering a Winchester take-down shotgun as a premium for every $300 worth of goods purchased from the mail-order house. T. G. Bennett took quick action and on November 26 of that year wrote the Company's sales force and the trade stating that because of this plan, all quotations on guns had been withdrawn from Sears Roebuck and that the Company had cancelled all orders.

This action by Winchester evidently affected the Sears Roebuck stock quite promptly because the latter concern wrote to one customer on November 23, explaining: "The reason our stock is exhausted and that we are unable to state definitely when we can again furnish the firearms ordered by you is partly due to the fact that the Winchester Repeating Arms Co., has deemed it advisable to discontinue selling us owing to the fact that they consider our profit sharing plan . . . as being a cut on their line of goods. . . . Our profit sharing plan has created so much disturbance and agitation among dealers that the Winchester Repeating Arms Co. . . . has considered it advisable to sacrifice our business to further the interests of the other dealers who are almost universally in favor of large profits and opposed to a profit sharing plan similar to ours . . . Understand, it is not our intention to cease selling Winchester goods . . . We will continue to sell them but . . . we are compelled to receive our supplies from sources other than direct from the factory." [2]

Sears Roebuck accepted Winchester's challenge by quoting the Company's guns in its catalog for 1905 at prices below the restricted retail levels set by the Company. For example, the Winchester standard Model 1897 repeating shotgun, restricted to a minimum retail price of $18 by the Company, was offered for $15.50. At the same time Sears Roebuck stated in its catalog: "While we will gladly furnish this Winchester Repeater for only $15.50, since we can furnish you the celebrated Take Down Model Marlin Repeating Shotgun, a gun we consider worth $10.00 more, for only 55 cents additional, only $16.05, if you want a repeating shotgun we would advise by all means you order the Take Down Marlin Repeater."

Sears Roebuck resorted to various devices in order to obtain Winchester guns. Fred Biffar, manager of the Sears gun department, who appears to have taken the chief responsibility in the contest, established at least two dummy concerns, the Clinton Hardware Company of Chicago, and the Model Sporting Goods Company of Evansville, Indiana, and through them purchased guns.

Biffar was able to get some of his suppliers of other merchandise to order guns for him and in some instances, European houses received orders which were reshipped unopened to Sears Roebuck. Certain retail dealers were offered a five per cent premium for Winchester guns, being instructed to be sure to display Winchester guns in their windows and appear to be doing an over-the-counter business for the benefit of the local jobbing houses. To conceal the identity of suppliers, the serial numbers on guns were filed off.

Winchester was able to cut off supplies to the mail-order house in various ways. Dealers who were discovered selling to Sears Roebuck were prohibited from purchasing Winchester goods. The Company formalized and increased the rebates to the jobbers and obtained a signed statement from them that they would not sell below established minimum prices. The Company also advertised that it would assume no responsibility for guaranteeing the quality of any guns sold at cut prices or with the serial numbers erased. Special retail price lists were sent to all dealers which could be shown to customers, stating that goods were not shipped to anyone who sold below these prices, and that for the sake of their own protection, Winchester products should be purchased only through authorized dealers.

This struggle between Winchester and Sears was a part of a larger movement against the mail-order or catalog houses that had been launched by the hardware industry in 1904. Instigated by the jobbers and retailers, a Wholesale and Retail Hardware Joint Committee was appointed in that year by the National Hardware Association, the National Retail Hardware Dealers Association, and the Southern Jobbers Association. The Joint Committee took the position that although many well-known brands of hardware were being sold through the mail-order houses, only a small percentage of any one manufacturer's business went through these channels, and their price-cutting practices served to demoralize prices on a whole and caused discontent among the trade. A resolution was passed that the manufacturers should refuse to supply the mail-order houses.[3]

There is no evidence that Winchester took an active part in the initial negotiations of the hardware trade, but after the Company decided later in November to cut off supplies to Sears Roebuck it kept in touch with the National Retail Hardware Dealers and National Hardware associations. These associations took the matter up with their members and advised them not to sell to any houses supplying Sears Roebuck. Winchester on its part sent numerous letters to the trade concerning Sears Roebuck's tactics and published lists of houses which had been discovered selling guns to the mail-order house. On December 30, 1905, a letter was sent to the trade as well as to representatives of hardware associations containing the names of 55 companies which Winchester believed to be dealing with Sears Roebuck and requesting that no orders for guns from any of these houses be filled. By August 1906 this list was expanded to include over a hundred names.

Relationships between Winchester and Sears Roebuck continued to be strained for several years. Sometime in 1906 Sears established a gun manufacturing plant in Meriden, Connecticut, and thereafter pushed the sale of its own firearms, especially the Aubrey brand. It continued to list Winchester firearms in its catalog at prices below established levels set by the Company.

Meanwhile Winchester was having trouble with other members of the trade who were selling at cut-rate prices. In October 1908 it put the Baltimore Bargain House, of Baltimore, Maryland, on its public blacklist.

Early in 1910 Winchester inaugurated a new marketing plan designed to strengthen the maintenance of minimum prices. This was done by making its patented products subject to license conditions. Printed notices of these license conditions were placed in the catalogs and attached to invoices, price lists, guns, and other patented articles, and were included in boxes of shells. The act of purchase was enough to signify acceptance and assent of the conditions. According to the terms: "Any violation of the license condition revokes and terminates all rights and license as to the patented article sold and to all other patented articles made by the Company in the violator's possession, and subjects the violator to suit for the title to all of its patented products in the possession of the violator and upon demand and tender of purchase price thereof entitles the Company to immediate possession of all such patented products." The conditions imposed were:

(1) Jobbers may sell at wholesale only to retail dealers regularly handling this line of goods; may not sell to anyone designated by the Company as a violator of license conditions; may not mutilate or remove any license notice; may not sell without the license notice of the Company upon or with the articles sold; and may sell only at the rates specified in the current schedules of prices issued by the Company.

(2) Retailers may not mutilate or remove any license notice nor expose for sale nor sell without such license notice; and may sell only at the retail prices established by the Company and printed in its current schedules and instructions.

(3) All sales must be made with the article and its serial number (if any), and accompanying instructions, directions and identifying marks unchanged and unmutilated.

Between 1907 and 1912 the right of the manufacturer to control the selling prices of his products began to be challenged in the courts. Two leading cases, one in 1911 and one in 1912, held such practices to be illegal because they interfered with the right of distributors to set prices as low as they might wish.[4] The manufacturer was free to select his customers and suggest resale prices but could not coerce purchasers or make such prices a matter of contract.

Winchester was thus under compulsion to change its price-maintenance policy and on June 14, 1913, the Company wrote the trade: "All license notices and limitations on sale or prices of our goods for dealers are withdrawn and should be ignored. Prices indicated in discount sheets and price lists for the retail trade and consumers are suggestive only. Our past extended experience has demonstrated these suggested prices to be fair and just to both trade and public and we trust they will be observed in the future."

About a week later the Company, evidently fearing that the change might be misunderstood, sent out a notice to the jobbers stating in part: "You can readily see that if no regard is paid to our suggestions and any jobber shall cut prices and enter into unfair competition with others, thus demoralizing the trade through an endeavor to monopolize the business, we should not be inclined to continue our special discounts to such jobber."

The broad issues of price maintenance were by no means settled by 1914. The controversy began again after World War I, resulting in 1937 in the passage of the Miller-Tydings Act which legalized resale price maintenance on a national level. As far as Winchester and Sears Roebuck were concerned, the truce achieved around 1912 lasted into the 1920s. By that time Winchester was engaged in a marketing experiment of its own involving a chain of retail stores which was as disturbing to the jobbers and most of the retailers as sales by the mail-order houses had been during the earlier period.

### *Foreign Marketing*

There was little change in the foreign marketing procedure until near the close of the 1890-1914 period. Addis continued to serve as a missionary salesman until 1901, when he resigned. He was succeeded by Adolph Mueller and later by William Scherer, who continued to travel in South America, South Africa, Australia, and the Far East. Competition in Europe from the British, especially on ammunition, and from the Germans on both guns and ammunition, in addition to tariff restrictions, made it impractical to send a traveling representative to that area, and the London Armoury Company handled most of the business for the Company that was done with Europe and some of the British colonies.

Probably not over ten per cent of the total foreign business was handled on direct order. Addis and his successors worked largely through New York commission houses. These houses handled both imports and exports for customers, especially in the South American and Far Eastern markets. The Company's New York store maintained contact with the commission houses and took care of the details of shipment and financing. These houses were billed generally at the lowest domestic jobbing price and charged a commission of around five per cent to their foreign customers for handling the merchandise.

Just prior to 1914 some of the other American gun and ammunition manufacturers decided to push their foreign sales more vigorously. Finding that most of the New York houses were closely tied to Winchester, these companies began sending out salesmen and selling direct to foreign importers at domestic jobbing rates. This saving of commission plus the direct contact with customers began to eat into Winchester business and in 1915 H. F. Beebe was put in direct charge of foreign sales. The number of traveling representatives was increased and the Company began to move over to more direct selling to foreign customers. By the 1920s most of the exports were sold in this fashion and a marketing pattern established which has persisted pretty much down to date.

### *Domestic Sales Promotion*

Like every producer of trade-marked commodities, Winchester was especially concerned with maintaining and strengthening interest in its products among the final users of firearms and ammunition. Its bargaining strength *vis-à-vis* the jobbers depended largely upon the degree to which retail customers would accept no substitute for the Winchester brand. Because of their immediate contact with purchasers it was also highly important to have the good will of the retail dealers. These considerations explain the main features of the sales-promotion program which was continued and elaborated after 1890.

The Company's sales organization as it had evolved around 1900 included three separate groups of field representatives: the salesmen, the missionaries, and the shooters.

The salesmen called on the jobbers. Their principal function seems to have been to maintain strong personal contacts with the buyers of such houses and to report back to the Company any complaint or demands for changes in rebates or discounts. It is doubtful if there were ever more than eight or nine salesmen employed at any one time by the Company.

Some twenty to twenty-five missionaries called on the dealers. Their chief job was to distribute advertising matter, display Winchester arms and ammunition, and in general advocate the Winchester brand over all others. Winchester put out a number of posters and hangers to be placed in store windows and show cases, and a large variety of fancy envelopes, stationery, stickers, and order blanks which might be requisitioned by the missionaries for the use of sympathetic dealers. This material was also distributed by missionaries at tournaments and club shoots where they invariably set up a tent or booth for the purpose and sold Winchester ammunition. At these tournaments the missionaries were supposed to get in touch with captains and coaches of teams as well as shooters and receive pledges from them, if possible, to use Winchester ammunition. They were instructed to get to the tournament grounds early, although not to overdo the entertainment feature. County fairs were also attended by the missionaries; there they made arrangements to exhibit Winchester products with the local hardware dealers who had displays at the fair.

Neither the term "missionaries" nor their employment in sales promotion was original with Winchester. No one has traced this evolution but the emergence of missionaries was probably associated with the distribution through jobbers of branded products which the manufacturers wanted to identify with themselves and not with the jobbers.

Around 1900 Winchester began employing "missionary salesmen." These men would accept orders from retail dealers which they would turn over or credit to the appropriate jobbing house in the territory.

All of the principal gun and ammunition concerns took steps to see that their products were well represented in shooting matches and tournaments. These events were closely followed by sportsmen and gun users generally, and it was considered a distinct advantage for a company to be able to advertise that its guns or ammunition had been used by the winners of an important shooting contest.

Not infrequently the missionaries were themselves expert shots and took part in tournaments. Companies might also have some one on the payroll who did nothing but represent it as a shooter. One of the best known of the early shooters was James E. Stetson, who represented Winchester. Stetson began working for Winchester in the 1870s as a barrel-maker. His skill as a marksman was such that the Company soon had him traveling full time representing it throughout the country. On these trips he competed against such marksmen as Doc Carver and Buffalo Bill and on one occasion won a diamond belt symbolic of the championship of the country.[5]

Until about 1900, however, the shooters were generally amateurs who regularly took part in various contests. As already noted, it was the duty of the Winchester missionaries to see that the best of these used Winchester guns and were supplied with Winchester ammunition. Apparently there was no payment involved beyond possibly furnishing a gun at a reduced price and contributing free ammunition for use in matches. After 1900 the competition for the services of capable marksmen became keener and Winchester found it desirable to maintain a group of experts to whom it paid salaries. It was about this time that the Company also employed Ad Topperwein and his wife full time to travel about the country giving exhibition shooting under its auspices.

### *The Topperweins*

Individually, the Topperweins take their place among the world's finest marksmen; together they formed a husband-and-wife combination unique in sporting annals. The son of a gunsmith of German descent, Adolph Topperwein was born near San Antonio, Texas, in 1869. He began shooting at the age of six and as a young man traveled with a circus doing trick shooting. In 1901 he was employed by Winchester as a missionary, and for a time represented the Company in that capacity in the Southwest. Around 1903 it was decided to send him on the road representing the Company as an exhibition shooter.

On one of his visits to New Haven he met Elizabeth Servaty who was at the time working in the ammunition-loading room in the Winchester plant, and they

*Elizabeth Servaty ("Plinky") Topperwein*

*Adolph Topperwein*

were married in 1903. Until she was married Mrs. Topperwein's acquaintance with shooting had not extended beyond the loading of ammunition. It turned out that she had an exceptional talent as a marksman. The late combat correspondent, Ernie Pyle, who was proud to include the Topperweins among his friends, told how she first became interested in shooting:

> Things were pretty tough for her at first. She either had to stay home or else go on those exhibition trips and just twiddle her thumbs. She didn't like it. So she made Ad teach her to shoot. It wasn't long before she was as good a shot as her husband. And then Winchester hired her too. For twenty-nine years the world's greatest shooting couple traveled the North American continent together. But always, the home they came back to between-times was San Antonio.
>
> They called her "Plinky" because when she was first learning to shoot, she'd keep saying, "Throw up another one and I'll plink it." [6]

Plinky made her first world's record in 1904 at the World's Fair in St. Louis by breaking 967 clay targets out of a possible 1,000 at trap shooting. Following this performance, Winchester arranged to have the Topperweins travel as a team.

Between them the couple set some remarkable shooting records. Pyle tells of how, in 1907:

Ad shot steadily eight hours a day, for ten days in a row. He was firing a .22 rifle at 2½-inch wooden blocks tossed into the air. He shot at 72,500 blocks, and missed only nine. Out of the first 50,000 he missed four. He had a number of runs of more than 10,000 without a miss, and one run of 14,540. But the strain of it, day after day, almost drove him insane. His muscles and nerves were in painful knots. At night he had horrible dreams: the blocks would be a mile away; the bullets wouldn't come out of the end of the gun. As for Plinky, her trapshooting record of 1,952 hits out of 2,000 targets was a world's record for anyone, man or woman. She shot for a total time of five hours, using a pump gun. It raised such a blister that a few days later the skin came off the whole palm of her hand.[7]

Included among the fancy position shots with a rifle in Ad Topperwein's repertoire were shooting backward while lying down and using a mirror to sight the target, hitting a playing card held edgeways, and extinguishing a lighted match held between the thumb and forefinger of an assistant. He had a number of wing-shooting stunts, such as hitting a potato thrown directly toward him, breaking balls thrown over his head from behind, and hitting targets thrown directly across in front of him. One feat which was advertised as having never been accomplished by any other shooter in the world, was to ride a bicycle at full speed and to throw up balls which he broke using a rifle and solid bullets.

The Topperweins continued to travel for Winchester until their retirement in 1940. At that time Ad Topperwein was seventy years of age, and his wife but a few years younger, but apparently both had retained their skill as marksmen. For more than thirty-six years they had represented the Company and during that time had done much to keep the name of Winchester before the public as a sign of high quality.

*Buffalo Bill*

To thousands of Americans and Europeans, William Frederick Cody, popularly known as Buffalo Bill, was the epitome of the American frontiersmen, entitled by his experiences to be associated with such illustrious and romantic figures as Daniel Boone, Kit Carson, Jim Bridger, California Joe, and Wild Bill Hickok. No hero ever looked his part more adequately. A striking figure, tall, wearing long curly hair (for the benefit of any Indian who might be successful in claiming his scalp), a mustache and goatee, he was a superb rider and marksman. Between 1872 and 1916, first on the stage, then with his own Wild West Show, he re-created the atmosphere of the American West before audiences throughout the United States and western Europe.

Buffalo Bill was never employed as a shooter by Winchester to publicize the Company's products, but directly and indirectly he did much to spread their fame. As the hero of fictionalized Western dime novels, he was often armed by the authors with a Winchester rifle in his fights with the Indians and the bad men. In the famous Wild West Show, he and his fellow marksmen, including Annie Oakley, used Winchester rifles and ammunition.

Buffalo Bill's debut as a hero of Western stories began around 1880. Various authors adopted him as the chief figure in their fictionalized version of frontier life, although Colonel Prentiss Ingraham was the most prolific. In many of his 211 stories the type of rifle used by the hero was not named, but in a considerable percentage, the bad men or Indians were neatly dispatched with a Winchester. Typical references are shown on the covers of two "nickel novels"

*Covers of Nickel Novels*

published by Street & Smith. On one, *Buffalo Bill's Mascot, or, The Mystery of Death Valley* (no publication date given), under a picture of two men riding away from a group of Indians, there appears the statement: "Buffalo Bill turned in his saddle and sent a dozen shots from his Winchester rattling back up the hill at the savages."

On the second, bearing the title, *Buffalo Bill's Desperate Mission, or, The Round-Up in Hidden Valley* (dated September 15, 1906) the hero is shown rescuing a girl from the Indians. The caption reads: "Crack! Crack! went Buffalo Bill's Winchester, and howls and yells followed the reports."

These predecessors of later-day "comic books" were read eagerly by a large audience of youngsters, who were undoubtedly impressed by the effectiveness of a Winchester in the hands of their hero, and determined some day to own such a gun themselves.

Whatever may have been Cody's choice of rifles for fighting and hunting, there was no question that he and his troupe used Winchesters in the famous Wild West Show. Older employees at the Winchester plant recall his frequent visits to New Haven where he arranged for supplies of rifles and ammunition. Cody in his autobiography tells of introducing one of his girl shooters to Queen Victoria, who had witnessed the show: "I had the pleasure of presenting Miss Lillian Smith,

*Buffalo Bill*

the mechanism of whose Winchester was explained to Her Majesty, who takes a remarkable interest in firearms."

Finally, Richard J. Walsh, in his *The Making of Buffalo Bill: A Study in Heroics,* states: "On the authority of Johnny Baker (long associated with Cody) we know that he used a Winchester repeating rifle, smooth bored, 73 model, .44 caliber and shells of .44 caliber, 1⅛ inches long, loaded with about twenty grains of black powder and ½ Oz. No. 7½ chilled shot."

The use of shotted shells was necessary. During the first year of the show, Cody and Carver used rifle bullets, as Walsh explains: "After they got bills for broken glass from green houses eight or ten blocks away, they decided for safety they must use shot, which would drop harmlessly within the grounds."

Walsh also cites Johnny Baker as authority for the fact that the pellets of these shells made a pattern about the same size as a glass ball at the usual range of twenty yards. It was just about as hard to hit an object at that distance with shot as it would have been with a rifle bullet. Nor was there any question about Cody's marksmanship. In his prime he could split the edge of a playing card with a rifle bullet. Mrs. Cody is said to have been terrified when her husband shot coins from between the fingers of their own children who had complete confidence in the accuracy of their father's shooting.

No part of the Wild West Show was more enthusiastically received than the shooting exhibitions by Cody, Annie Oakley, Johnny Baker, and others. Straight marksmanship and fancy shots were both featured. The Winchester Repeating Arms Company did not fail to publicize the fact that its products were the choice of these star performers.

CHAPTER SIXTEEN

# THEODORE ROOSEVELT AND WINCHESTER

Of all users of Winchester firearms, Theodore Roosevelt was among the most enthusiastic and certainly the most famous. His prominence as a public figure and sportsman and his unsolicited endorsements of the Company's products were both a tribute to the quality of Winchester's firearms and invaluable publicity.

Born in New York on October 27, 1858, Roosevelt was a frail child and early set about to build up his physical strength. By the time he had graduated from Harvard College, in 1880, he had become an excellent boxer and had developed a love for outdoor life. Immediately after graduating he went into politics, but in 1884, after a disagreement over the nomination of Blaine as the Republican candidate for President, Roosevelt decided to spend some time in the West. During the next two years he led the life of a rancher in North Dakota, rounding up steers, serving as a deputy sheriff, showing drunken bullies the advantage of a college course in boxing, and hunting the game which abounded in the neighborhood.

Roosevelt's experiences during these years formed the background for his book, *Hunting Trips of a Ranchman,* published in 1885. It was in this volume that he first expressed his enthusiasm for Winchester rifles. When he first came to the plains, Roosevelt states: "I had a heavy Sharps rifle, .45-120, shooting an ounce and a quarter of lead, and a .50-caliber, double-barreled English Express. Both of these, especially the latter, had a vicious recoil; the former was very clumsy; and above all they were neither of them repeaters; for a repeater or magazine gun is as much superior to a single or double barreled breech-loader as the latter is to a muzzle-loader."

At the time he wrote his book Roosevelt had given up both of these guns and was using instead: ". . . a .40-90 Sharps for very long range work; a .50-115 6-shot Bullard express and better than either, a .45-75 half magazine Winchester [Model 76]. The Winchester . . . is by all odds the best weapon I ever had, and I now use it almost exclusively, having killed every kind of game with it, from a grizzly bear to a big-horn. It is as handy to carry, whether on foot or on horseback, and comes up to the shoulder as readily as a shot-gun; it is absolutely sure, and there is no recoil to jar and disturb the aim, while it carries accurately quite as far as a man can aim with any degree of certainty; and the bullet, weighing three quarters of an ounce, is plenty large enough for anything on this continent. For shooting the very large game (buffalo, elephants, etc.) of India and South

*Theodore Roosevelt with Model 1876 Winchester Rifle*

Africa, much heavier rifles are undoubtedly necessary; but the Winchester is the best gun for any game to be found in the United States, for it is deadly, accurate, and handy as any, stands very rough usage, and is unapproachable for the rapidity of its fire and the facility with which it is loaded."

Further information on Roosevelt's choice of firearms during this period has been made available by Charles Edward Chapel in his article, "The Guns of Teddy Roosevelt." [1] Noting the latter's preference for Winchester rifles and Colt revolvers, Chapel states: "At one time or another Teddy used the Winchester Repeating Rifle, Model 73, cal. .44 W.C.F. . . . He fired the Winchester Repeating Carbine, Model 73, cal. .44 W.C.F.; the Winchester Repeating Rifle, Model 76, cal. .45-75 W.C.F. (necked), and the Winchester Repeating Carbine Model 1876, cal. .45-75 W.C.F. In 1884 he acquired a Winchester Hammerless Top Lever Breech-Loading Double Shotgun." [2]

The same author also tells how Roosevelt took a Winchester Model 95, caliber .30, U. S. Army carbine, with him to Cuba during the Spanish-American War. One of Roosevelt's Rough Riders, Bob Wrenn, arrived too late to get a Government-issued Krag carbine and Roosevelt gave him the Winchester. When the troops were mustered out at the end of the war Wrenn ". . . carried it home in triumph, to the envy of his fellows who themselves had to surrender their beloved rifles."

Roosevelt had left his position as Assistant Secretary of the Navy to serve in the Spanish-American War. His exploits as Colonel of the Rough Riders added greatly to his popularity and, returning to politics after 1898, he was elected Governor of New York. The Republican leaders attempted to remove him from active politics by making him Vice President under McKinley in 1901 but this plan went awry when the latter was assassinated, and Roosevelt became the twenty-sixth President of the United States. After serving the remainder of the term, he was returned to the Presidency in 1904 by a large majority, but declined to run for reelection in 1908.

During his last year in office Roosevelt began to plan an African hunting trip with his son Kermit to gather specimens for the Smithsonian Institution. When it came to a choice of firearms for the trip, he decided, on the basis of his past experience, to consider Winchester rifles and, on June 16, 1908, he had his secretary, William Loeb, Jr., write to the Winchester Repeating Arms Company: "The President is going to Africa with his son a year hence. He probably has all the rifles he needs, but his son has not. Before deciding what he will buy, the President would like to see your catalog, his idea being to give his son—one a high-power small caliber rifle of the .30-40 type, or one approaching it; and the other a very much more powerful rifle, such as he could use for buffalo, rhinoceros and even elephant. Will you send your catalog to the President at Oyster Bay where he will arrive Saturday next?"

This letter was the beginning of an extensive correspondence between the White House and the Company arranging for the details in connection with the guns and ammunition Roosevelt was to take on the trip. The attention given this matter by the President is shown by the number of letters he personally dictated between June 1908 and March 1909 when the party sailed for Africa.

One feature of this correspondence worth noting was the impersonality of the salutations of the letters received from the President. Winchester Bennett, son of

WHITE HOUSE,
WASHINGTON.

Personal

November 17, 1903.

Dear General Crozier:

I have sent you over my Winchester rifle, so that you may have one of the new Springfield carbines made like it for me. I want the sights reproduced exactly. If necessary they can be obtained from the Winchester Company. I want the butt just like my present butt, only one inch shorter.

With great regard,

Sincerely yours,

Theodore Roosevelt

Brig. Gen. William Crozier, U.S.A.,
Chief of Ordnance,
War Department.

*A Roosevelt Letter*

T. G. Bennett, was vice president of the Company and took personal charge of supplying Roosevelt's needs. Most of the letters from New Haven went out over his signature but not once was any letter received from Roosevelt or his secretaries addressed other than, "The Winchester Repeating Arms Company, Gentlemen:"

Nor was Roosevelt easy to please. He became very upset, as will be presently shown, over the way the guns were first made even though he was himself chiefly responsible for the confusion. Nevertheless the management of the Company handled the whole matter with tact and diplomacy. It was practically the American equivalent of the British "By Appointment to His Majesty" and no effort was spared to get the guns and ammunition exactly as Roosevelt wanted them.

Roosevelt's tentative choice of weapons was outlined in a letter sent to the Company on June 29, 1908: "What I think I would like would be a .30-40 [Model 95] shooting the same ammunition I use in my Springfield, and two .405 caliber rifles [Model 95]. . . . My son will bring in his .30-30 Winchester

[Model 94] to have the sights and stock duplicated unless we decide to have the front sight with a gold bead. In addition I shall take my .45-70 take-down Winchester [Model 86] which certainly ought to be good for lion, zebra, and the smaller antelopes in the bush; and probably a double-barreled .450 cordite English rifle. Your rifles will be shooting in competition with the latter so I want to be sure they are good ones."

The President was especially fond of his .45-70 Winchester, Model 86. In a subsequent letter, July 9, 1908, he expanded on his reasons for wishing to take it with him: "This is the rifle I used in Louisiana last year, and which both son Ted and Dr. Lambert used in killing moose in Canada. We all of us used soft-nosed bullets, and certainly for moose and black bear it is so efficient that I am going to take it to Africa to use, altho I have been warned that the gun is not right for African game. I am rather inclined to doubt this. How will the penetration of the full metal covered bullet for this .45-70 rifle compare with the penetration of the similar full-jacketed bullet for the .405? Have you any data which would show how this .45-70 would do on African buffalo and rhino, for instance. I should use the soft-nosed bullet for lion, for I do not believe that a lion is a tougher animal than a moose or a bear. As I have said to you, I do not want to use any one of our American guns for any game for which it is unsuited, because there will be a good deal of attention attracted to my trip and I want to be sure that it comes out all right."

The Company doubted the advisability of the use of the .45-70, writing on July 16: "As to the use of this arm in Africa, we are inclined to believe that it is amply powerful if the bullet is placed in the right spot, but it is not as powerful as arms generally used in that country. It does not, in fact, even compare favorably in power with the .30-40 but 1486 foot-pounds muzzle energy, against 1880 foot-pounds developed by the .30-40. Nevertheless, quite a few have been used, and quite successfully with soft point bullet, for lion. For larger animals, such as rhinoceros where the full metal patched ball would be desired, we certainly could not recommend it while we have the .405 to offer, for this arm (the .405) develops muzzle energy of 3077 foot-pounds, almost twice that of the .45-70-405."

It was decided after some discussion that the Company should supply two Model 95 rifles, caliber .405, and one Model 95, caliber .30, chambered for the U. S. Government ammunition. The Company was also to furnish the ammunition for the trip.

Roosevelt was anxious that the rifles perform well. He wrote on August 10, 1908: "As you know, I have always used your rifles and I am using them now instead of the English rifles which my English friends are giving to me, because it is a matter of pride with me to use an American rifle. Now I don't want to have any slip-up. A friend of mine, young Forbes of Boston, was in to see me the other day. He has been using your .405 in Africa for elephant, rhinoceros, buffalo and lion. He found it worked well except that twice the cartridges jammed (once with a lion). Now do try these guns you are to send me for my son and myself so as to be sure that they will not jam. Ought we not to carry spare sights, and perhaps spare pieces? As we will have five rifles, of course we could get along even if one or two of the rifles went wrong; but again I don't want to run any chances."

Winchester replied on August 11: "We wish to express to you our thorough appreciation of the fact that you are using our rifles and to assure you that we will take every precaution to see that your arms are turned out in such shape that no criticism can be found with them. On the other hand, in the instance you bring to our attention, the user may not have taken proper care of the arms. The Model 95 is generally in use throughout this country and complaint is almost unheard of."

The Company in the same letter took occasion to inform the President of the successful performance of its rifles in Africa:

It might be of interest to you to know that we have been advised by a Dr. Davies, of Brussels, who recently made a trip as medical advisor for a hunt under the auspices of Mr. Solvay, the Belgian inventor of the Solvay sodium carbonate process, that he is forwarding us 49 photographs of their trophies. Mr. Solvay took steamer at Khartoum and proceeded by the White Nile to the neighborhood of Darbo, not far distant from Albert Nyanza, being gone from Paris 70 days, 50 of which were spent in hunting country, during which time the party (three guns) took 11 elephant, 6 rhinoceros, 8 buffalo, 1 lion, 7 roan antelope, 5 white eared cob, 10 reed buck, 6 bush buck, 3 aiaing, 3 hippopotamus, 3 wart hog and a considerable quantity of other smaller game which he refers to but does not mention as to number.

All of their work was done with the .32 Winchester Special Model 94 rifles and .405 caliber Model 95 rifles. Of the .32, it is with enthusiasm that he writes:

"The .32 Special does very well and kills in a perfect manner although I should be afraid to tackle buffalo with it. It killed one elephant with one head shot—the animal was struck [as] by lightning. That arm is adapted for all game except buffalo and rhinoceros. For elephant with body shots, aiaing, antelope, and even elephant if you shoot at the head, the .32 is correct.

"The .405 with soft point makes a hole as big as the head of a man. Out of curiosity I once shot into the flesh of a dead hippo's shoulder. The muscles are about 2 ft. thick, and the skin 2 in. I opened it with my knife. The bullet had made no expansion in the skin, in which a clean round hole was cut, but I plunged my hand and forearm, my elbow, my arm, in the smashed flesh and found a well expanded 300 grain bullet in the rib."

In closing his nineteen-page letter he says:

"If people ask me what arms for Africa, I answer two .405s, but if you do not wish elephant, buffalo, or rhino, take the .32 Special. It is handy and light. I myself should not be afraid to tackle everything with a .32. I must say that the .405 is good for all game. As to ammunition, take 80% soft point and 20% full metal patched."

As the doctor on his own confession is not much of a hunter and has had but little experience, the above must be taken with a considerable grain of salt. Certainly we would not advise the .32 Winchester Special in place of the '95 .30 Government Model 1903 cartridge, but about the best that could be said for it is that it compares favorably with the .30-.30. From the doctor's observation we are inclined to believe you will find the .30-.30 a very handy gun.

Roosevelt was especially concerned over the sights and the stocks that he wanted the Company to furnish. In his letter of July 9, he wrote: "I sent you the .30-30 as a model for the two .405s which I desire to have from you. Please have the top of the barrels roughened as in the case of the .30-30. Have the sights like those of the .30-30, and the stocks excepting, of course, the pistol grip. For the last inch and a half of the stock have put on each gun (I think it is called) Silver's gun pad."

In his reply of July 16, Winchester Bennett wrote: "We note your specifications as to the .405 caliber rifles which we can readily comply with, furnishing them with special stocks, oil finish, with cheek piece, matted barrels, Flat Top Sporting Rear and Lyman Gold Bead Front Sights, sling straps and swivels. Silver's recoil pads over ¾ in. thick can not be had in this country. The 1¼ in. pads which you specify we have ordered from abroad and should obtain in from four to six weeks time. As we have no matted barrels in stock, as this matting should be done before the barrel is rifled, we should probably receive them so that this special thickness of recoil pad will not delay delivery of guns."

Toward the end of August Roosevelt became impatient to try the guns. His secretary wrote from Oyster Bay on August 31 that "He is very anxious to get at the earliest practicable moment the rifles he has ordered as he will want to test them and he will only be here three weeks longer. May I ask you to advise me, therefore, when he may expect them?"

As the special pads had not arrived the Company could not finish the guns but because of the President's eagerness to try them out, temporary stocks were fitted and the two Model 95s chambered for the .405 cartridges were sent on to Oyster Bay on September 9. Stating that the stocks were temporary, Winchester Bennett wrote on the same day: "They are not exactly the same as we will furnish when the guns are finished and he [Roosevelt] may rest assured that with the regular stocks on, such as we are intending to equip the guns with, the fit and other particulars will be much more satisfactory."

About a week later the Company received the following blast from Roosevelt dated September 16:

I am really annoyed at the shape in which you sent out those rifles. I return them to you, together with my Government rifle, so that you may have before you the stock and sights I use. I had already sent you, as you of course remember, rifles showing my sights; yet you sent out these rifles with a rear sight which does not pretend to be like that I use, and which taken with a front bead, I regard as the poorest rear sight ever used for game, the one with the sharp, narrow notch.

It was entirely useless to send them out to me in such shape. Moreover, while the two .405s were sighted accurately, the .30 caliber shoots about twelve inches high and six inches to the left; and moreover, extraordinary to relate, its rear sight is actually different from the rear sight of the two .405s, and if possible, worse. I cannot see what excuse there was, when I had already sent you the rifles as models, for you to send me rear sights such as there are on the three guns you sent me. Please be sure to copy exactly the rear sight of the Government weapon which I sent you, and then have it sent on to Washington with your three rifles when they are ready.

There are two other matters to which I desire to call attention with these rifles. By comparing the stocks you will find that at present the stocks of the Winchester are shorter than the stock of my Government rifle. When you get the thick rubber pads put on, will this difference be equalized and will the stocks be of exactly the same length as my Government rifle? This you must surely see to, as I want them exactly and precisely in every respect like the stock of the Government rifle. Moreover, I find that the magazine mechanism is totally different in the two .405s from what it is in your .30 caliber. In the last, the .30 caliber, I can put all five cartridges into the magazine, and then by working the magazine the top one goes into the breech. But in the .405s I put only four cartridges in the magazine. If I try to put a fifth in it jams when I attempt to work the lever and get it into the breech. In other words, I can put four in the magazine and then one in the breech, whereas in the .30 caliber I put all five in the magazine and work the lever to get one of them into the breech. Now is this the proper and normal as I am naturally a little unsettled by the extraordinary failure in the matter of the rear sights.

In replying to the President's criticisms, on September 21 the Company apologized for the sights explaining that they were only temporary and that the ones Roosevelt wanted were being made to order and were not ready when the guns were sent. The letter continued:

As regards the stocks, these, as we wrote you, are temporary and when the guns are furnished with extra thick pads, they will be of the exact dimensions which you wish. We are, however, a little in doubt as to how to proceed in the matter of the stocks. In your original order for the M'95 .405 rifles dated July 9th, you stated you were sending us the .30-30 as a model for the two .405s and that the sights were to be like those on that gun "and the stocks, excepting, of course the pistol grip." We have had your .30 caliber gun here while we have been making up the guns, and have followed carefully the dimensions, style of cheek piece, etc. of this rifle in making up the .405s. We also are following this gun as a pattern in making up the M'95 as you told us in your letter of July 23 that you wished this exactly similar in style to the .405 which we were then making for you. You now say in your letter of the 16th instant in referring to the stocks that they must be exactly the same length as your Government rifle; that you want them exactly and precisely in every respect like the stock of the Government rifle. We find upon taking measurements that there is a difference between the stocks of the .30 Winchester, which we have been using here as a pattern, and the Springfield gun which you now send us. The measurements of the two guns are as follows:

| *.30 Winchester* | | |
|---|---|---|
| Pull or length of stock | 13-13/16 | in. |
| Drop at comb...... | 1-1/2 | in. |
| Drop at heel....... | 1-7/8 | in. |
| *Springfield Rifle* | | |
| Pull or length of stock | 14-1/8 | in. |
| Drop at comb...... | 1-7/8 | in. |
| Drop at heel....... | 2-5/16 | in. |

There is also a difference in the style of the combs and the cheek pieces of the two guns. Now, we have the stocks practically made up according to the dimensions of the .30-30 but if you desire, we will start all over again and copy the stock on the Springfield gun."

William Loeb, Jr., Roosevelt's secretary, wrote back on September 24, 1908:

The President has received your letter of the 21st instant. He is puzzled about the stocks. He sent you not only the .30-30 but the .45-70 which has a stock which he does not like. The stocks of the rifles you sent him are exactly like the .45-70 and he thinks you must have gotten mixed, and therefore he will ask you to have the stocks made just like the Government rifle which he sent you.

Have you got the inch and a half pad now? If not, do not wait for it, but simply put on the type of pad you had on the rifles sent to Oyster Bay for trial, but be careful that, whichever pad is used, the stock *when fitted with it* is exactly like that of the Government rifle.



Winchester accepted the changes in the specifications of the stocks and on

October 9, wrote the President that they were forwarding one of the rifles for his inspection and criticism, noting:

> We believe that we have carried out your instructions to the letter, and we have as far as possible copied the dimensions of the stock on the Springfield rifle, form of sight thereon, etc. We trust you will find the arm entirely satisfactory. If it is not we shall be pleased to have you return it to us with any criticism which you may have to make.
>
> Should you find, as we fear you may, that the stock is rather too long to permit of the free operation of the finger lever from the shoulder, we shall be pleased to provide a stock as much shorter as you may desire. We trust you will give us an opportunity to do anything which we can to make the arm more satisfactory for your service.

As had been anticipated, Roosevelt did not like the feel of the new stock on the Model 95, even though it was made exactly according to the dimensions of the Springfield. The difficulty lay in the fact that the Springfield used a bolt action while the Winchester used a lever action. The latter required a longer reach to operate which made the stock seem too long. The President accepted the Company's suggestion that the stock be shortened a quarter of an inch and that a facing be put on the rubber pads to make them fit the shoulder more smoothly.

Late in November the two Model 95 .405s and the Model 95 '06 were finished and after a thorough testing sent off to the White House. This time the reception was different. On December 5 the President wrote saying, "The rifles have come. They are beautiful weapons and I am confident will do well." About a week later he again wrote: "I cannot say how much I like those two .405 rifles you sent me. Now, my belief is that in Africa those will be the two rifles my son and I will habitually carry in our own hands; the rifles upon which we will most depend. As this is so, I think I should like to have you make me a third rifle, a duplicate of these two. If you have any difficulty about the Silver pad of the full thickness for this you might make it a little thinner. Could you make me a duplicate of these two rifles in time for me to take it out to Africa next March? I would probably leave it at some central point, say Nairobi, where I will make many preliminary hunts; but it would be a good thing to have it as a kind of insurance against accidents. If I cabled you from Nairobi how long would it take you to get me out extra cartridges for the rifles? Have you heard if those cartridges that you sent have arrived in Mombasa yet?"

The Winchester management was conscious of the prestige attached to having its arms and ammunition used by Roosevelt on his forthcoming African trip. At the same time it could not in good faith use the President's name in advertising the fact. On December 14, 1908, the following letter was sent to William Loeb, Jr.:

> We have been overwhelmed of late by requests from representatives of the press and individuals for descriptions of the Winchester rifles and ballistic data of the cartridges which it is understood that the President is to use on his coming African trip. Not knowing whether the President would care to have his equipment exploited, we have refrained from admitting that we have made any guns especially for his prospective African trip, the tenor of our reply to all inquiries being that President Roosevelt has used Winchester rifles to a certain extent for a good many years and that we presume some of them would be included in his complement of arms. Notwithstanding our reticence in the matter, considerable information more or less inaccurate has been published in different sections,

which seems to have tended to whet the appetite of the press and sportsmen in general for accurate data, with the result that we are placed in a rather embarrassing position with many of our friends. Naturally we would like very much to be in a position to state frankly that the President is planning to use our product and, if agreeable to him, we would appreciate the courtesy deeply if we may be permitted without objection upon his part to state in effect that the President will use Winchester Repeating Rifles and Winchester Ammunition on his forthcoming African Hunting and Collecting Trip and that the President's complement of arms includes the following:

Model 1895 rifle, .405 Caliber
Model 1895 rifle, .30 Government Model 1903 Caliber
Model 1886 rifle, .45/70 Caliber
Model 1894 rifle, .30 W.C.F. Caliber

The above phraseology is purely a suggestion and we would be glad to change it to conform with the President's ideas.

Loeb replied the following day: "I am in receipt of your letter of the 14th instant in reference to the requests you are receiving as to the guns the President will take with him, and in reply would say that the President would not want the matter used in any way as an advertisement, but there is no objection whatever to your stating in answer to queries that the President will have your guns on the trip."

Strict orders were given to William Clark, Winchester's advertising manager, to observe these instructions. Brewer relates how

This was a great disappointment to Clark who felt this was one of our great opportunities for advertisement and it almost broke his heart not to be able to use the President's name in connection with it. However, just about the time the President sailed for Africa, the monthly magazines and other papers which usually carried Winchester advertisements, all appeared with a full page advertisement showing a picture of the map of South Africa with a hand thrust thru the map from the rear holding a Winchester rifle, the shadow of which fell directly across the central part of Africa—beneath the picture was a caption in large letters, "COMING EVENTS CAST THEIR SHADOWS." When Mr. T. G. Bennett saw this advertisement, he was terribly upset as he felt that we had broken faith with the President. He called Clark in immediately but Clark tried to hedge by saying that the advertisement did not mention Roosevelt's name in any way, which had been his instructions. Mr. Bennett replied that tho Clark might have followed the letter of the instructions, he certainly had not followed the spirit of them, and Mr. Bennett wrote to the President a most apologetic letter explaining that he personally had given instructions that the President's name should be used in no way in connection with the sale of the guns or in our advertising material, but that evidently the pressure had been greater than our Advertising Manager could stand, and that while he had adhered to the letter of his instructions, he had certainly violated the spirit of them and Mr. Bennett expressed his regret and made apology for same.

The President did not seem to be a bit annoyed—in fact loving publicity as he did, he seemed to be rather amused and rather tickled with the situation, and his letter to Mr. Bennett was in no way critical. He was, of course, a great admirer of the Winchester Company and of the Winchester rifles, and I have no doubt that this feeling toward the Company tempered his reply.

Theodore Roosevelt, his son Kermit, and a group of naturalists sailed from New York for Mombasa, British East Africa, on March 23, 1909. Landing in

*The Ammunition for Roosevelt's African Hunting Trip*

April, the party spent nearly eleven months hunting wild animals. The party sent back to the United States ". . . 4,897 specimens of mammals, more than 4,000 birds, about 2,000 reptiles and batrachians, and approximately 500 fishes, besides a vast multitude of other specimens that defy a brief description." [3]

Accounts of the trip written by Roosevelt ran in *Scribner's Magazine* during 1909 and 1910. They were later incorporated in his book entitled *African Game Trails*. Winchester received frequent mention in these accounts. For example, commenting on the relative merits of his rifles, Roosevelt stated: "The Winchester and the Springfield were the weapons one of which I always carried in my own hand, and for any ordinary game I much prefer them to any other rifles. The Winchester did admirably with lions, giraffes, elands, and smaller game, and, as will be seen, with hippos. For heavy game like rhinoceros and buffalos, I found that for me personally the heavy Holland was unquestionably the proper weapon. But in writing this I wish most distinctly to assert my full knowledge of the fact that the choice of a rifle is almost as much a matter of personal idiosyncrasy as the choice of a friend. The above must be taken as merely the expression of my personal preferences."

The descriptions of actual use are more graphic, as one or two excerpts will illustrate. Hunting lions on the Kapiti Plains, the party flushed two of the animals: "Right in front of me, thirty yards off, there appeared, from behind the bushes which had first screened him from my eyes, the tawny, galloping form of a big maneless lion. Crack! the Winchester spoke; and as the soft-nosed bullet ploughed forward through his flank the lion swerved so that I missed him with the second shot; but my third bullet went through the spine and forward into his chest, down he came, sixty yards off, his hind quarters dragging, his head up, his ears back, his jaws open and lips drawn up in a prodigious snarl, as he endeavored to turn to face us. His back was broken; but of this we could not at the moment be sure and if it had merely been grazed, he might have recovered, and then, even though dying, his charge might have done mischief. So Kermit, Sir Alfred, and I fired, almost together, into his chest. His head sank, and he died."

On another occasion in the same region, Roosevelt faced a charging lion: "The first few steps he took at a trot, and before he could start into a gallop I put the soft-nosed Winchester bullet in between the neck and shoulder. Down he went with a roar; the wound was fatal, but I was taking no chances, and I put two more bullets in him."

The advantages to the Company of this publicity are self-evident. Brewer noted: "His book . . . was full of reference and praises of the Winchester rifles, so that we got a very large amount of favorable free advertising from it, which of course was much more valuable to the Company than [any] paid advertisement."

CHAPTER SEVENTEEN

# END OF THE ASSOCIATION

The growth of industrial combinations during the 1880s was viewed with great concern by many persons in the United States. There was an increasing pressure put upon Congress to pass legislation which would deal with the problem and both the Republicans and the Democrats had planks in their platforms in 1888 declaring their opposition to trusts and monopolies.

Congress took up the question in 1889 and the following year the bill known as the Sherman Anti-Trust Act was passed and signed by President Harrison. The legislation was broad in scope with the principal objectives stated in the first two sections of the Act. Under section one every contract, combination, in the form of a trust or otherwise, or conspiracy in restraint of trade or of commerce among the several states or with foreign nations was declared illegal. Section two was directed against monopolizing or attempting to monopolize any part of the trade or commerce among the states or with foreign countries.

Under this broad wording it was conceivable that almost any kind of agreement or combination might be considered in restraint of trade or as an attempt to monopolize trade, depending upon what interpretation was put on those terms. The failure to define more clearly just what constituted a violation of the Act was a reflection of the uncertainty both in and out of Congress of what particular evils were to be corrected. Pending court interpretation business men and industrialists generally had no way of telling whether their particular activities were in violation of the statute.

Because of the uncertainty of the interpretation of the Sherman Act it is unlikely that the sponsors of the Ammunition Manufacturers' Association had any doubts about the legality of the organization or its activities. There was no reason to assume *a priori,* especially after 1895, that the Association was in any way in violation of antitrust legislation. In any case, for some seventeen years after 1890 the Ammunition Manufacturers' Assocation continued to serve as the marketing agency through which its members sold their ammunition.

There was little apparent change in the relationships between the Association and the trade during the period under consideration. Price quotations, discounts, and arrangements for rebates were all handled directly between the commissioner of the Association and the jobbers.

The earlier practice of giving a basic percentage rebate to all houses on the Association list appears to have been modified during the 1890s. Under the new arrangement a "salary" based in general on an average volume of orders was paid the dealer instead of giving him a basic percentage rebate. By offering a "salary" instead of a basic rebate the Association could treat each jobber individually and make such modifications as were necessary to keep him loyal to the organization.

In addition the Association had a list of big houses which were often given special discounts and privileges principally in connection with large orders.

Mention has already been made of the attempts by the manufacturers to reduce the effects of the seasonal demand by offering buyers dating privileges on loaded shot shells. This practice was exercised by the members of the Association through that organization. The first record of the use of the dating privilege is contained in a letter sent by the commissioner of the Association to a selected list of jobbers on January 31, 1901. According to that offer, if the houses would place their orders on or before March 15, they would be allowed to pay their bills on September 10, and would still be given a discount of two per cent, just as if they had paid for their shells within ten days after delivery. Each jobbing house was given an allotment of shells on which it could exercise the dating privilege. In this general form dating privileges continued to be granted to the trade on large orders during the remaining life of the Association.

In the final analysis the success of the Association depended upon the continued demand of the consumer for the products of its members. Retail dealers placed their orders with the jobbers for the kinds and amounts of ammunition which they estimated would be taken by their customers. Just as in the case of firearms, if the dealer was "sold" on one particular brand he could in turn exercise some influence over the choice of his customers. Similarly the jobber was able within limits to persuade his dealers to handle one type of ammunition in preference to another.

It was to push the sales of their products among customers and dealers and to strengthen their ties with the jobbing houses that the ammunition companies, both in and out of the Association, appear to have expanded and elaborated their sales forces during the 1890s.

The list prices on ammunition remained virtually unchanged between 1890 and 1907, and as far as Winchester was concerned, through 1914. In 1889, trade discounts typically ranged between 25 and 55 per cent. While discounts varied for the different classes of ammunition the pattern as a whole was stable throughout the 1890-1907 period, the only changes being a reduction of 5 per cent in the discounts on shot shells in 1902.

It is noteworthy that the jobbers received no extra trade discounts on their purchases compared with the dealers, and that the rebates or "salaries" represented their entire margin. Only the rebates on shot shells were formalized during this period being set at 10-2½ per cent in 1902.

Without definite information on "salaries" it is not possible to determine the net price of ammunition to jobbers, but in 1907, after the dissolution of the Association, Winchester, without changing trade discounts, formalized its rebates on metallic ammunition to the jobbers at 12½-2½ per cent, maintaining the 10-2½ per cent on shot shells.

The only available data on Association sales between 1887 and 1907 are for the years 1900 and 1901. These are presented along with similar information for the earlier year, in the tabulation of total sales (in thousands) on the following page.

Ammunition sales, as shown by these figures, were more than two and a half times as large during 1900-1901 as they had been during the earlier years.

| *Year* | *Metallic Ammunition* | *Shot Shells* | *Wads* | *Total* |
|---|---|---|---|---|
| 1887 | $1,872 | $ 330 | $211 | $2,413 |
| 1900 | 3,504 | 1,552 | 442 | 5,498 |
| 1901 | 4,209 | 2,211 | 611 | 7,031 |

Because of the relative stability of prices during this period, this figure measures the approximate increase in physical output. The nearly sevenfold increase in shot-shell sales is especially noteworthy and helps account for the trouble encountered by the Association in equating sales and quotas in this line. The sales of wads were closely tied with the demand of hand loaders and loading companies which bought wads and other supplies from the members of the Association. Metallic ammunition showed a more moderate expansion although the income from its sale was almost double the amount received from shot shells in 1900 and 1901.

During this period the members of the Association produced a considerable volume of ammunition components which were loaded or "assembled" by others. These items were purchased by two groups—the first being made up of shooters who preferred to load or reload their own ammunition, the second consisting of the so-called "loading" companies. From a competitive standpoint the most important of the loading companies were those sponsored by the powder manufacturers who were attracted by the opportunity of developing a controlled or assured market for a portion of their output. The companies promoted in this fashion generally used loading machinery and were operated on a more substantial scale than the hand loading outfits.

A loading company might handle metallic cartridges or shot shells, but most of them appear to have concentrated on the latter. The principal reason for this was the comparative simplicity of operations; the machines for loading shot shells being less complicated and easier to operate than the equipment needed for metallic ammunition; because 10- and 12-gauge shot guns were the most widely used, production could be concentrated on one or two sizes of shot shells, whereas metallic ammunition involved a large number of different calibers. There was also the attraction to the powder companies of a larger use of powder in a given number of shot shells than in the equivalent amount of ordinary calibered metallic ammunition.

Until the early 1900s the policy of the Association was to encourage the loading companies, as the latter were an important outlet for empty shot shells, wads, and primers. While the Association members were willing to sell ammunition components, they were highly sensitive to any move by other concerns to engage in the manufacture of such components. This is shown by the activities of Winchester and UMC during the 1890s. In 1892 the Creedmore Cartridge Company, of Barberton, Ohio, a concern which had been established by the Diamond Match Company interests to produce metallic ammunition in competition with the Association, was acquired. The factory was operated for a time by the Association, after which it was dismantled and the machinery distributed among the members.

Winchester and UMC also bought the cap department of the Waterbury Brass Company in 1899, and discontinued its production of caps and primers. This department, it may be noted, had been a member of the Percussion Cap Association, an organization to which both UMC and Winchester belonged and which down to 1907 sold through the same trade channels as the Ammunition Manufacturers' Association.

In 1894, Winchester purchased the Wehle factory in Brooklyn, makers of Gold Mark percussion caps, and moved the machinery to New Haven. Thereafter the Company used the Gold Mark label on its own percussion caps.

Two factors caused a change in policy about 1900 toward the loading companies by the members of the Association. One was the experience of having one such company develop into a full-fledged ammunition concern and the other a decision to push the sale of their own factory-loaded ammunition, especially shot shells. This change in policy may be illustrated by tracing the early history of the principal concerns which were more able to establish themselves as integrated ammunition manufacturers during this period.

*Peters Cartridge Company*

The Peters Cartridge Company of Kings Point, near Cincinnati, Ohio, owed its beginning to a close association with the King Powder Company of the same city. Started in 1887 for the purpose of loading empty shot shells for the trade, Peters received its powder supply from the King Powder Company and, during the first few years of its operations, purchased its empty shells from the members of the Ammunition Manufacturers' Association. By agreement with the Association these loaded shells were not to be sold below Association prices and Peters was not to purchase empty shells from any other source.[1]

In 1889, just before it sold its cartridge business to Winchester, the American Buckle and Cartridge Company of New Haven had begun negotiations with Peters to have shot shells loaded by machines recently designed and built by American Buckle. Immediately following the sale of its cartridge business, American Buckle, on June 14, 1889, wrote Peters: ". . . We have just . . . sold out our paper shell machinery and stock of shells to the Winchester Repeating Arms Company. . . . Our patents are still our own property. . . . It will not be possible for any one to successfully enter the paper shell business unless they come into the possession of the patent or invent entirely new processes and machinery, and it is certain that the last named alternative would be very difficult, if not altogether impossible." [2]

The following month Peters purchased the patent rights and two sets of machinery and tools for the manufacture of paper shot shells from the American Buckle and Cartridge Company.

On March 18, 1892, Winchester brought suit against the Peters Cartridge Company alleging patent infringement on one of the machines sold to Peters by the American Buckle and Cartridge Company. The case which dragged on for a number of years was bitterly fought. Winchester finally won the case in March, 1900, and was subsequently paid damages of $1,000. By this time, the patent under controversy had run out and there was no question about Peters' right to use the machinery under dispute.

While this suit was being carried on Peters had been able to continue its manufacture of shot shells using machinery which did not infringe any existing patents. The Company had an exclusive agreement with its paper supplier, made its own shot, and developed its own facilities for the manufacture of primers and wads.



Peters seems to have built up its sales outlets during the period when it was loading empty shells purchased from the Association. These outlets remained with the concern after its break with that organization.

*Western Cartridge Company*

The second company to develop as an integrated ammunition concern during this period, the Western Cartridge Company, was also sponsored by a powder manufacturer. In 1892, F. W. Olin and his associates organized The Equitable Powder Manufacturing Company at East Alton, Illinois, to manufacture black powder which was sold chiefly to the mines in the area.

The sale of blasting powder to the mines was subject to seasonal fluctuations and for three or four months of the year manufacturing operations were slow. Olin, who was the active head of the business, became interested in loading shot shells. In February 1898, he persuaded his associates to join him in forming the Western Cartridge Company, also located in East Alton, the principal purpose being to provide a market for powder which could be produced by The Equitable Powder Company in the off season.[3]

Olin, anticipating difficulty in securing loading equipment, and unknown to the Association had developed a machine which did not infringe on any of the patents held by the members.

For a short time the Association made no efforts to stop Western from continuing in business. Indeed, Olin, who was dependent, except for powder, upon outside suppliers for all of the components of shot shells, was able to contract through 1899 and part of 1900 with the Association members for empty shot shells and wads.[4]

But this inaction was short-lived. By their purchase of the cap department of the Waterbury Brass Company in 1899, Winchester and UMC cut off Western's supply of primers. The following year the Association informed Olin that its members would no longer sell him empty shot shells and wads.

These moves were a serious threat to the continuation of operation by Western. Fortunately for Olin he was able to import primers from Eley Brothers in England until he could promote the Union Cap and Chemical Company a few years later which gave him his own supply of primers. On wads and shot shells the problem was more difficult. The Association controlled the existing suppliers of paper suitable for shot shells and the felt used in wads. Before he could even begin the manufacture of shot-shell cases and wads, which in themselves involved the designing and building of special machinery, Olin had to start the production of paper and felt, which was accomplished only after much experimentation and expense.

Western was forced into a further integration of its operations some time during 1903 and 1904, when it had to build its own shot tower. The occasion was the purchase of its former supplier by the United Lead Company which refused to make any further deliveries.

Olin not only had to solve his manufacturing problems but had to make arrangements for the distribution of his products as well. This he was able to do by an agreement with the Simmons Hardware Company of St. Louis to distribute his loaded shells to its retail dealers. Simmons was attracted by the quality of the Western shot shells and by a better discount compared with its former Association "salary" which was described by Simmons as ". . . but a small part of the expense of doing business."[5]

It is a tribute to the skill and ability of F. W. Olin that he was able to keep the Western Cartridge Company in operation in the face of the obstacles put in his path. By 1905 he had become self-sufficient in respect to the supplies of all the components of his ammunition. Two years later he was confident enough of his position in the industry to add the manufacture of metallic ammunition to his operations.

### *Savage Arms Company*

Mention should be made of the Savage Arms Company of Utica, New York, which began the manufacture of metallic ammunition during this period. This concern had started as a rifle manufacturer in 1894. For some six years it purchased primed empty cartridge cases and bullets from the members of the Ammunition Manufacturers' Association, which it loaded and sold under the Savage trade mark. In 1900, Savage, like Western, was cut off from its supplies. Within a year the management had been able to establish its own cartridge department. Operations were apparently not on a large scale but were sufficient to supply ammunition to those customers who wanted Savage cartridges to use with Savage rifles.

As the foregoing examples of the Peters, Western, and Savage concerns illustrate, the Association members were unable to keep integrated companies from developing within the industry. For this reason the competitive position of the members was not as strong in the early 1900s as it had been in 1890.

### *Dissolution of the Association*

On September 23, 1903, the trustees of the Ammunition Manufacturers' Association, at a special session passed the following resolution: "Resolved, that the corporate existence of this association be extended for twenty years from and after the said 27th day of September." [6] An application for the extension of the corporate existence was filed with the Secretary of the State of New Jersey on the following day which was favorably acted upon.

From this action it appears that there was no question in 1903 about the advisability of continuing the existence of the Association. Yet, on November 7, 1907, the same group filed an application for dissolution, stating that they deemed ". . . it advisable and—for the benefit of the said corporation that the same should be forthwith dissolved." During the interval there was a strong move to bring about a formal merger of the members of the Association. According to Veader and Earle: "In 1906 and 1907 the consolidation of the interests of the Winchester Repeating Arms Company, the Union Metallic Cartridge Company, the United States Cartridge Company . . . and of the Remington Arms Company was seriously considered." Some five months were spent by New York accountants going over the books of these corporations for the years 1902-1906, but negotiations broke down when the officers of the Winchester Repeating Arms Company ". . . were not willing on a basis of these reports to continue."

It is possible that the failure to agree on a merger generated enough differences among the members of the Association to cause its dissolution. But it was probably motivated by external considerations, chiefly connected with the enforcement of antitrust legislation against manufacturers.

Apparently the relative position of the three firms in the industry was not materially changed during the seven years following 1907. Peters and Western had established themselves prior to the break-up of the Association and these two companies maintained their proportion of industry sales to 1914.

In spite of the failure to keep out competitors, Winchester and UMC in particular continued to be the dominant firms in the industry. In addition to the prestige of their products, acquired over a long period, they were able to maintain strong relationships with the principal jobbing outlets supplying both the domestic and foreign markets. In the case of these two concerns, they were able to use their position as gun producers to help control their sale outlets for ammunition.

While competitive conditions within the industry remained virtually unchanged from 1907 through 1914, the dissolution of the Association was an important event in changing the relationships after World War I. Had there been a formal organization in existence it would probably have been easier to maintain a continuity in the competitive behavior pattern. In the absence of such an organization the impact of World War I, plus changes in management personnel of the chief concerns, brought about much more vigorous competition at all levels in the marketing of ammunition.

CHAPTER EIGHTEEN

# SUMMARY OF BENNETT'S ADMINISTRATION

*Changes in Management Personnel*

In March 1910 T. G. Bennett reached his sixty-fifth birthday and was about to complete forty years of service with the Company. The urge to retire as active head was strong and at the meeting of the directors held in December he submitted his resignation as president. The board accepted his decision with reluctance but stated that: ". . . because of the high estimation in which Mr. Bennett is held by the trade throughout the country it is of utmost importance to the Company that Mr. Bennett retain before the public some more important position than director." Accordingly, a new office was created, that of consulting director, to which he was elected. Thus while T. G. Bennett gave up the active direction of the Company, he kept a close contact with the management, and as will be noted below, was again called back to be president in 1918.

The member of the family in line to succeed T. G. Bennett was his son, Winchester Bennett. The latter, born in New Haven on August 22, 1877, had followed his father's example by attending Yale Sheffield Scientific School, from which he was graduated in 1897. He entered the employment of the Company in January 1899 and spent the next several years in the shops learning the production side of the business. In 1905 he became director and was appointed to a newly created position of second vice president. Like his father at the time of the election of Converse to the presidency in 1881, Winchester Bennett in 1911 was still in his thirties and it was decided not to make him president but to elevate him to the position of first vice president and make George E. Hodson the successor to T. G. Bennett.

While Hodson, who also held the office of treasurer, was more than a figurehead, there is little question that the final policy decisions between 1911 and 1915 were made by Winchester Bennett with the advice and counsel of his father. With the election of Hodson, Harrie S. Leonard was made second vice president to succeed Winchester Bennett, while Aro Ward continued as secretary.

The reconstructed slate of officers which took office in 1911 and their salaries were: president and treasurer, George E. Hodson, $20,000; first vice president, Winchester Bennett, $10,000; second vice president, Harrie S. Leonard, $10,000; secretary, Aro F. Ward, $5,000; consulting director, T. G. Bennett, $1,000.

## General Growth of the Company

If at any time between 1911 and 1915 T. G. Bennett paused on his way to his office and looked out over the expanse of the Winchester plant he must have felt a real sense of pride in the establishment he had turned over to his successors. With a total floor space of over a million square feet, it was a far cry from the modest building that he had helped lay out in 1870. That structure had accommodated some 222 workers at the time the Company moved back from Bridgeport; the average employment between 1910 and 1914 was over 5,500. Thanks to the first Turkish contracts, annual gun sales during 1870-1872 came to around 25,000 but dropped to less than 10,000 for several years thereafter; for the 1911-1914 period sales averaged around 300,000 guns per year. The great bulk of the industry's increased production was sold in the domestic market.

While Bennett had played an important role in the Company's growth prior to 1890, it was the expansion after that date that came under his direct administration. This was impressive. As already noted, employment in 1914 was over four times the number in 1890 and gun sales had grown over three and a half times during the same period. (*See Appendices J-1 and D-1.*) To accommodate this larger number of employees and the machinery and equipment needed for their use, no less than 1,092,000 square feet of floor space had been added to the approximately 330,000 square feet in use at the end of 1899. No breakdown of the total is available, but the aggregate expenditures on real estate, plant, machinery, and patents amounted to over $9.8 million while working capital was increased by an estimated $5.7 million. Income from all sales, shown in Appendix F, was approximately four times as large during 1910-1914 as it had been during 1890-1894.

The balance sheet for December 31, 1914 (*Appendix G-6*), reveals that the net worth of the Company had grown to around $16.8 million, after provision for depreciation, which had been introduced into the Company's accounting system in 1912. On a basis comparable with the earlier periods, when no allowance was made for depreciation, this represented an addition of over $15.52 million since 1889.

As had been true of the earlier period, the Company financed its expansion out of its own resources, mainly derived from operating profits. The following summarizes the operation for the 1890-1914 period (in millions):

| | | |
|---|---|---|
| Profits from operations (before depreciation) | | $30.94 |
| Less: | | |
| Distributed as dividends | $15.28 | |
| Write down of securities | .13 | 15.41 |
| Surplus invested in business | | 15.53 |

Of this surplus, some $4.25 million had been used by the end of 1914 to write down the physical assets of the Company; $1.62 million being set up as a "reserve for depreciation" and the remainder absorbed by valuing the assets at less than their original cost.

## Comparative Growth of the Company

Impressive as the Company's general growth was between 1889 and 1915, it apparently occurred without any substantial change in the relative position of the concern in the firearms and ammunition industries. As indicated in Appendix H, total industry sales (including pistols) measured in dollars, expanded over four-fold during the period, while employment increased about in the same proportions. Because of the relative stability of prices, at least of guns and ammunition, this expansion of dollar-sales probably correlated fairly closely with an increased physical output.

This general growth of gun and ammunition sales is remarkable because population during the same period expanded much less rapidly. Moreover, as the "frontier" yielded to settlement it might be assumed that the demand for firearms would have declined rather than increased.

A number of factors apparently account for the growth which actually occurred. Improved transportation made it possible for hunters to seek big game in the remote areas. Within the more settled regions there was a growing interest in small-game shooting. This interest was quickened by the Spanish-American War when thousands of young men, who had never handled a gun, learned to shoot and brought their new interest back with them into civilian life. The enthusiastic accounts of Theodore Roosevelt and others of their hunting experiences were an inspiration to their readers to engage in the sport. Even when live-game hunting was impractical many enjoyed target shooting with rifles and glass balls and later clay pigeons with shotguns.

The gun and ammunition companies through their exhibits, the employment of missionaries, and expert shooters gave further stimulus to the demand for their products. Finally, and by no means least in importance, were the policies followed in keeping prices relatively low which made it possible for the average would-be shooter to purchase firearms and ammunition.

A lack of information on the respective incomes from guns and ammunition or employment in those two divisions, makes it impossible to determine what changes, if any, occurred in Winchester's position as a gun manufacturer, distinguished from an ammunition producer. Judged by the aggregate value of the combined products and the total numbers of employees (*Appendix H*) the Company was approximately in the same relative position in 1909 as it had been twenty years earlier.

By sharing in the expanding demand for firearms and ammunition and by the reduction in production costs and the margins allowed to jobbers already indicated, the Winchester Repeating Arms Company was able to show an impressive earnings record.

### *Dividends and Dividend Policy*

The dividend policy of the board was not consistently the same during the whole period. (*See Appendix F.*) From 1890 through 1903, when the stockholders at the annual meetings were given a reasonably adequate review of operations for the preceding year, dividends were generous, over 69 per cent of the reported income being paid out. This amounted to an average annual dividend of nearly 65 per cent on the par value of the stock which remained at the nominal figure of $1 million. From 1904 through 1914, while nearly $6.4 million was invested in plant and equipment compared to $3.4 million during the preceding fourteen years, there was a resumption of the earlier trend to reduce dividends as well as the information made available at the annual stockholders' meetings and somewhat less than 35 per cent of the income was distributed. Because of the increased sales this still represented a substantial dividend to the stockholders, averaging over 56 per cent on the par value of the stock. It is clear that during these later years the Bennett regime continued to give precedence to the Company's capital needs.

There was little necessity for a "dividend policy" designed to attract outside investment as long as all capital requirements could be met internally.

*Stock Ownership and Control*

The dividends from the Company's operations went largely to the same group or their heirs who had held stock in the Company since the 1870s. Largely through the distribution of stock in settling estates, the recorded number of shareholders had increased over the years. In 1875 the number was 29; in 1887 it had grown to 65; by 1903 to 111; and by 1914 to 136.

Considering the earning and dividend record of the concern it is not astonishing that the stock should be highly prized. It is said that many an heir was given a strong recommendation that the two securities which should not be sold under any circumstances were the stock of the Winchester Repeating Arms Company and the New York, New Haven & Hartford Railroad.

The expansion of the number of stockholders did not affect the control of the Company by the Winchester and Bennett families. Oliver F. Winchester at the time of his death in 1880 had left 4,000 shares in trust for the benefit of his wife, who had 475 shares of her own. At this time Mrs. Winchester's daughter, Mrs. T. G. Bennett, owned 406 shares, and her daughter-in-law, Sarah Winchester (Mrs. William Wirt Winchester) 777 shares. After the death of Mrs. Oliver F. Winchester in 1897, the trust was divided equally between her daughter-in-law and daughter, her own personal stock going to the latter. As of 1904 the family holdings were: Mrs. T. G. Bennett 2,875 shares; Mrs. William Wirt Winchester 2,777 shares; T. G. Bennett 32 shares; Winchester Bennett 6 shares; total 5,690 shares.

*The Winchester Purchasing Company*

These holdings gave the family a working majority of the ten thousand shares of common stock outstanding. Until 1905 T. G. Bennett voted the stock of his wife and sister-in-law at the annual meetings of the stockholders. Some time prior to that date there were rumors that a group of New York capitalists was interested in buying control of the Company. While it would have been impossible to accomplish this without the stock owned by either Mrs. Bennett or Mrs. William Wirt Winchester, it was decided to insure control by forming a holding company, and a Connecticut charter for the Winchester Purchasing Company was acquired in May 1905. This corporation, capitalized at $2,000 was empowered among other things, ". . . to buy, hold, sell and deal in, the notes, bonds and other obligations, and the shares of the capital stock of corporations and persons engaged in the manufacture or sale of firearms or ammunition." The members of the family and a small group of minority stockholders deposited 5,025 shares of stock with the Winchester Purchasing Company which T. G. Bennett proceeded to vote at succeeding annual stockholders meetings.[1]

The formation of the Winchester Purchasing Company made it certain that no one could gain control over the Winchester Repeating Arms Company by any secret purchase of stock. While it was legally possible for depositors to withdraw their stock from the holding company, this could not be done without the knowledge of the officers. Nor would it have been possible to gain control of the Winchester Purchasing Company as the entire $2,000 capital stock was owned by Mrs. T. G. Bennett; the earnings of the deposited stock apparently being divided according to a separate agreement.

*Educational Interests of the Winchester and Bennett Families*

The Winchester and Bennett families showed an interest in educational philanthropy, their principal gifts being made to Yale University. Oliver Winchester had donated a site on Prospect Street for an observatory in 1871. In 1879 he gave the present Observatory building and in 1909 a part of the original land was sold for around $120,000 which was added to the Observatory endowment. In 1891, Mrs. Oliver Winchester, in memory of her husband, gave Winchester Hall, costing over $150,000, to the University. In 1895 she also established the William Wirt Winchester Fund, amounting to $15,000, in the Yale Art School. Another $5,000 was added to this fund in 1899 by Mrs. T. G. Bennett. In 1910 an anonymous donor, presumably a member of the family, established the Jane Ellen Winchester (Mrs. Oliver Winchester) Fund in the Medical School. Originally $25,000 of this amount was subsequently increased to $125,000 by 1913.

There is no record that T. G. Bennett personally gave any funds to the University, but he served as a member of the Fellows from 1884 through 1904 and he was a trustee of the Yale Sheffield Scientific School from 1887 to 1923, being president of the board during the last ten years of his term of office. In addition he was a member of the board of managers of the Observatory from 1881 until his death in 1930.

*Sarah Winchester and the Mystery House*

The only member of the family who attracted unusual attention by her expenditures was Sarah Winchester, who had become well known by 1914 as a wealthy eccentric.

Soon after the death of her husband in 1881, she lost her only child. This, added to the loss of her husband, affected her health and she was advised by her doctor to move to a different climate and to pursue a vigorous hobby. Around 1892 she bought a house near San Jose, California, where she established her home. The house which she originally purchased had eight rooms but soon after she moved in she began adding to the structure and at the time of her death some thirty years later, it had grown to 160 rooms and into the strangest patchwork ever put into one building. All during these years a crew of sixteen or more carpenters were very busy building, tearing down, and reconstructing.

There is no apparent design to the structure. Spread over six acres, within an estate of 160 acres, the house is a hodge-podge. In one room inside windows are barred, outside ones are not. There are screens on blank walls; exterior water faucets extend beneath second-story windows; a balcony or skylight may be found in the middle of a room. Narrow passages and stairs with steps one or two inches high lead from one room and one level to another. Some stairways lead to blank walls, others open out into space. There is a gas light operated by an electric push button and one room has four tiled fireplaces and four hot-air registers. Parts of the house are furnished with beautiful Tiffany cut-glass doors and windows, rich paneling and fine furniture.

There is no adequate explanation of Mrs. Winchester's actions. The legend grew that she was a "spiritualist" and that she was told by the "spirits" that she would live as long as her house was not completed. An alternate version is that she was afraid of being haunted by the ghosts of individuals shot by Winchester guns and ammunition and only by building activity would these spirits be pacified.

Much, but not all, the mystery disappears under an alternative explanation. Weldon Melich, writing in *Holiday* (February 1947), after interviewing her lawyer, doctor, and servants, advances the theory that the construction of the house was a hobby. Many times additions were made without changing the original structure which would account for screened and barred windows. The second-story faucets may have originally supplied water for window boxes. The slow-rising stairways were built after she was so stricken with arthritis that climbing was a task. Later an elevator was installed to accommodate her wheel chair.

The foregoing helps explain certain features of the house, but as Melich notes, there is no easy interpretation of two stained glass windows bearing the inscription, "Wide unclasp the table of their thoughts" and "These same thoughts people this little world." Nor does it explain why the number 13 should have been featured in a number of rooms, some having thirteen windows, candelabra with thirteen lights, and thirteen wall panels; nor the inlaid mahogany newel post that is upside down.

In any event it was a strange and extravagant hobby; the structure as a whole having been built at an estimated cost of between three and five million dollars.

Aside from a niece and a small group of servants, Mrs. Winchester lived alone. She was sensitive to the gossip that her activity occasioned and no visitors were ever allowed in the house during her lifetime. After Mrs. Winchester's death in 1922, the house was sold and, known as "The Winchester Mystery House," has since been open to sightseers.

Despite her eccentricity Mrs. Winchester had a reputation for shrewdness in business affairs. In addition to her returns from Winchester stock she is said to have invested in California real estate that added substantially to her income. In 1911 she contributed a sum of $300,000 to a group of New Haven people for the establishment of a memorial to her husband in the form of a sanatorium for tuberculosis victims. Additional sums were added by her until a total of $1.2 million was accumulated. The William Wirt Winchester Memorial Sanatorium was opened in 1916. She continued throughout her life to give financial support to a large number of charities and at her death provided generously for the New Haven Hospital.

*Summary of Bennett's Administration*

T. G. Bennett's administration of the Winchester Repeating Arms Company offers an interesting contrast to those of his two predecessors. Under the guidance of Oliver Winchester and Converse, the Company moved from a small concern to a leading producer of both arms and ammunition. Oliver Winchester's original decisions to produce a repeating firearm and to engage in ammunition manufacture were bold innovations that set the pattern for the Company's subsequent history. The part played by Converse in forming the Ammunition Manufacturers' Association was in the same category.

None of the policies adopted during T. G. Bennett's regime changed the character of the business to the same degree as those initiated by his predecessors. This is understandable. Combined with the expansion in demand that was affecting guns and ammunition as a whole, steady prices and the lowering of manufacturing costs and jobber margins made operations highly profitable. There was little point in initiating any basic changes in the line of products, marketing procedures, or intercompany relationships established by 1889.

For these reasons it is difficult to compare the management qualities of T. G.

Bennett with the first two presidents of the concern. In many respects it is probable that he had the more difficult task. Business history amply demonstrates that an organization does not maintain a leading position in an industry without able management. This is especially true when a firm grows as much as the Company did during the period under consideration. While this growth was spread over twenty-five years it was sufficient to challenge the management's ability to handle problems of internal reorganization and adaptation.

Able to command the respect and loyalty of his associates and subordinates, T. G. Bennett was at his best in handling problems of this kind. His engineering background was especially noticeable in the important encouragement given to the introduction of scientific principles in the manufacturing processes which helped solve the technical problems brought on by the advent of smokeless powder. He was especially interested in costs and through improved machinery and lower contract rates, these were lowered markedly during his term in office. This interest extended into the marketing field and seems to have been one of the considerations behind the lowering of jobbers' margins.

Bennett did not let his concern with costs affect the quality of the Company's products. He had an extraordinary pride in the reputation of Winchester and insisted on rigid inspection. He had no hesitancy in scrapping gun and ammunition components costing thousands of dollars if they failed to measure up to Winchester standards. He was also interested in increasing the variety of guns and ammunition which would appeal to various classes of shooters and these expanded sharply during his administration. He appears to have been convinced that sales would be stimulated by maintaining stable prices at the retail level. These, plus a conservative financial program, were the policies that enabled T. G. Bennett to maintain the Company's position among the leaders in the manufacture of arms and ammunition and make it one of the outstanding industrial establishments in the country.

# PART 6

# WINCHESTER AND WORLD WAR I: 1914-1918

CHAPTER NINETEEN

# WINCHESTER AIDS THE ALLIES

According to the proposition advanced by the Nye Committee, American arms and ammunition manufacturers experienced "a very positive increase in the market for armament during [the] years before the war," arising out of the general political unsettlement.[1] Actually the gathering clouds of World War I had no noticeable effect on Winchester. Sales which had reached a volume of approximately $9.4 million in 1908 fluctuated between that figure and $11.8 million during the succeeding six years. Henry Brewer, testifying in 1925, stated that the Company's business had "reached about a stationary period for a period of five years previous to the world war and our yearly increase in sales had averaged only about two per cent. We felt that the sporting arms and ammunition business . . . was perhaps likely to go into a retrogression from then on." [2]

*The Winchester Plant in 1914*

With the outbreak of war in August 1914, interest in negotiating contracts for arms and ammunition picked up sharply. Winchester wrote the London

Armoury Company in October 1914 pointing out that there had been formed, "a ring of export merchants who are claiming, without any foundations [of] fact, that they control the output of the American gun and ammunition factories. These parties have somehow or other been posted on the arrival of foreign representatives who are looking for munitions and have made it a practice to meet them, take them on tours, and demand all sorts of concessions and commissions for their services."

In view of the official neutrality of the United States, there was no reason why firms such as Winchester could not legitimately accept orders from any of the belligerents. There was no question, however, about the sentiments of the Winchester management. Winchester Bennett, writing on September 14, 1914, stated that he found it "difficult to maintain in person the neutrality which our national position demands and one is inclined to feel from all one sees and hears, that the neutrality is of the nation and of the federal government only, for certainly much sympathy [for Great Britain] is evident."

In any event the whole of Winchester's war work prior to 1917 was done for the Allies and there is no evidence that the Company was ever called upon to consider any business for the Central Powers.

### *Negotiating War Contracts*

The Company wrote the London Armoury Company on September 19, 1914, calling attention to the fact that its Model 95 rifle was chambered to handle the British .303 Mark VII cartridge, and could if desired, be made up in musket form with bayonet. The London Armoury Company was also asked to convey to the British authorities in confidence, the information that, "we are now working on a Mauser type rifle, bolt action, which will be chambered for the .303 cartridge. This new military arm will be without question far superior to any other military arm now on the market or furnished by government arsenals to the troops . . . If any sort of rearmament idea were in view or a sufficiently large contract could be given, we would erect a new factory and install machinery to take care of a contract of any size . . . [but] it will be several months before our preliminary work on this arm will be completed."

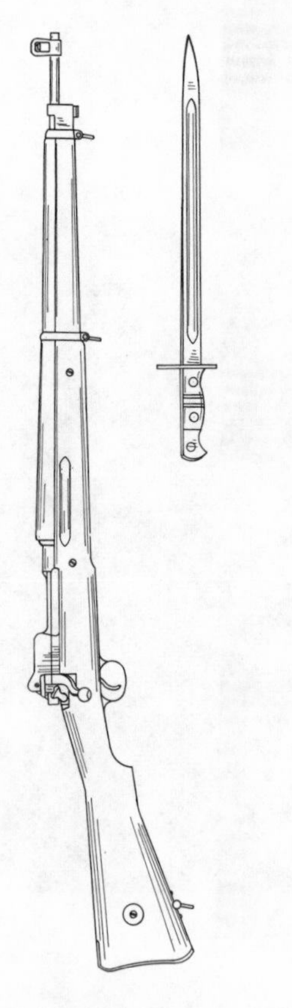

*British Enfield Rifle, Pattern of 1914*

The Company was also prepared to supply military ammunition and in the same letter it was stated that on cartridges, ". . . just at the present time we would only be able to deliver comparatively small quantities weekly, say five hundred thousand possibly a little more, but, after our present obligations are completed in the course of a few months, we could deliver very greatly increased quantities, say up to two or perhaps over three million per week."

The British were interested in the production capabilities of the Winchester plant and on November 11, 1914, two representatives of the British Army Council for War, who had managed to avoid the "welcoming committee" at the New York docks, visited New Haven. Within a week the Company received an order for 50 million long rifle caliber .22 rimfire cartridges from the British and negotiations had begun on a rifle contract.

Meanwhile Remington-UMC had received large orders for ammunition from the British and Belgians, a part of which were subcontracted to Winchester. Baldwin Locomotive Works, which had close contacts with the Russian Government, contracted with the Company for 100,000 Model 95 rifles, to be delivered to the Russians. On November 24, 1914, the British Consul signed an order for 200,000

*Winchester Bennett*

British Enfield rifles, and negotiations were started on an order for a large cartridge contract.

These various contracts brought the Company's war orders to a figure of over $16.7 million by the end of November 1914. Between that date and the end of 1915 additional orders, all negotiated by J. P. Morgan & Company, had increased the amount nearly $31 million to a total of approximately $47.5 million. Included were a second contract for 200,000 Enfield rifles; a second contract for 200,000 Model 95 7.62mm. rifles for the Russians; ammunition contracts for 300 million Russian 7.62mm. cartridges; 1.5 million French 7mm. cartridges; 44 million British .303 Mark VI cartridges; 9 million .44 Winchester centerfire cartridges (for use by the British Home Guard to whom a considerable number of Model 92 rifles had been sold); plus miscellaneous orders for 18-pound cannon cases and primers, and military supplies. On these various orders under contract at the end of 1915 the Company expected to make a gross profit of around $5 million.

### *The Problem of Plant Expansion*

As the Company expected to maintain a high percentage of its normal sporting arms and ammunition sales, which had been running around $10 million a year, the acceptance of these war contracts was the rough equivalent, measured in dollars, of adding five years' production to existing plant facilities. No one knew, of course, how long the war would last, but the contracts, which contained cancellation clauses, generally called for a completion of deliveries by the end of 1916, which would spread production over approximately two years. Tooling-up would absorb a part of this time, but once ready, long runs of the same products promised to insure a volume large enough to meet delivery dates. Taking the most conservative estimate, the Company was committed by the war contracts to a total output, including normal business, that was the equivalent of at least twice the prewar figure.

In late 1914 the management, on the assumption that commercial business might decline somewhat, figured that by using night shifts, it could handle the ammunition contracts, then undertaken, and the Russian order for the Model 95 with existing facilities. The British order for 200,000 Enfields was a different proposition and would require additional space and equipment; but as shown by its letter to the London Armoury Company on September 19, the Company was willing to extend the factory to take care of a substantial rifle contract.

The involvement of the United States in the war was not considered probable, and the American arms and ammunition makers were rather pessimistic of the opportunities for any increased sales to our military establishment. The decision to invest in new facilities seems in no way motivated by the expectation of orders from that direction.[3] Yet by the end of 1915, the cost of plant expansion had reached $13.3 million, an amount sufficient to absorb the bulk of the expected profits from the war contracts.

Testifying in 1925, Henry Brewer stated that the management, as of 1914, anticipated no postwar use for any additional buildings erected, but expected to "amortize" the capital expenditures out of profits from war business.[4] Because of the importance of the "surplus" buildings in Winchester postwar history it is worthwhile examining this statement in view of actual building construction.



Had it been the purpose to scrap the new construction at the end of the war, it would have been logical to erect temporary structures. The Company owned property near the New Haven harbor which could have been used for this purpose and the management gave serious consideration to the possibility. It was decided, however, not to erect temporary structures, but to build new, permanent-type buildings.

This policy, in addition to the magnitude of the program, suggests an alternative explanation to the one advanced by Brewer for the plant construction which began in 1914. At that date most of the buildings had been constructed prior to 1900. If these structures had been more or less fully depreciated they could, aside from technical considerations, have been scrapped without financial burden to the Company. There were in fact extensive plans laid for plant construction prior to the outbreak of the war. On this assumption, it appears that the management contemplated an extensive "rehousing" program in the fall of 1914. The possibility of large war profits offered an opportunity for a thorough reconstruction of the plant, the intention being to scrap some of the older buildings at the end of hostilities. This explanation would also account for the fact that the new buildings were placed in among existing structures in such a way as to keep the general plant layout approximately the same. The rationality of the plant layout should not be exaggerated. Under the pressure of military orders, apparently little attention was given at the time to locating and equipping the new buildings in such a way that the old structures could be conveniently scrapped following the war period.

The success of this policy depended upon realizing the estimated profits on the war contracts. These, it should be noted, were fixed-price contracts. There was no provision for any rise in manufacturing costs which might come from increased prices of raw materials or higher wage rates. The allowance for overhead which was included in the cost estimate was not based upon any careful estimating of the effects of the war contracts upon the general operating costs of the Company. The management followed its experience with "civilian" business in which there was generally an ample cushion out of which any excess overhead could be met. That cushion had also to bear somewhat arbitrary charge for depreciation which, like other business concerns of the time, Winchester regarded as a matter to be dealt with out of realized profits. In planning to spend anticipated profits on a building-expansion program, the management was, therefore, planning also to rely on the profits of other business to provide any real additions to depreciation funds; it was also running a risk that if costs were greater than expected, the Company would find itself drawing upon working capital to finance the building program. Taking the total war business together, however, the prospective profits seem to have offered a reasonable justification for the decision which was made. With its skill and experience in the field the management probably assumed that it could overcome production problems and secure the required returns from the war commitments.

### *Financing the Expansion Program*

As of December 31, 1914, the Company's net working capital was approximately $8 million, of which over $7.25 million was invested in inventories. Finances for capital expansions, as well as for increased inventories to cover work in progress, had of necessity to come from outside. The source immediately available was the deposit of a portion of the contract price by the Allied governments or other buyers of war material. The usual amount was twenty-five per cent of the value of the contract, roughly equivalent to the expected profit. This source of funds was sufficient to carry the Company through the first year of the war, but by November 1915, it had become increasingly clear that outside financial assistance would be necessary. This was a new experience for the current management. Since the 1880s the Company had been completely independent of outside financial institutions other than banks providing short-term finance. The prospect of asking for such aid, with the disclosure of the financial and business data that such an application would entail, was repugnant.

In this emergency the Company turned to J. P. Morgan & Company, which by this time was handling all Allied war contracts in the United States and with which Winchester had already negotiated in connection with several contracts. There was another tie with J. P. Morgan & Company. In 1907, during the panic, Winchester had needed more cash than it had on hand or could borrow from local sources. In this emergency J. P. Morgan & Company had made a temporary loan of $200,000. The cordiality with which the application had been received was still remembered in 1914. Accordingly on November 1, 1915, the directors authorized the borrowing of not over $1.5 million from J. P. Morgan & Company; on November 29 this amount was raised to $3 million. Under this authorization $2 million was borrowed on promissory notes.

By early December it was apparent that this amount would be insufficient and arrangements were made to borrow a total of $8.25 million from the same source, $2 million of which was used to repay the loans already contracted.

The need for these funds was shown with unusual clarity to the stockholders at the annual meeting held February 9, 1916. During the preceding thirteen months the following amounts had been allocated or expended (in millions):

| | |
|---|---|
| Land, building, building equipment | $5.238 |
| Machinery, equipment, tools, gauges, etc. | 3.676 |
| Increase in inventories | 6.617 |
| Increase in accounts receivable | .441 |
| Deferred charges to operations | .383 |
| Dividends | .250 |
| TOTAL | $16.605 |

Part of these requirements were met from the following sources (in millions):

| | |
|---|---|
| Advances on special (war) contracts | $8.678 |
| Net profits for 1915 | 3.298 |
| Additions to depreciation reserves | 1.029 |
| TOTAL | $13.005 |

The proceeds of the $8.25 million loan from J. P. Morgan & Company, less the $2 million repaid, left the Company with $6.25 million with which to meet the deficit of $3.6 million and increase its cash resources.

Even with the Morgan loan it seemed doubtful whether the Company could carry on without additional assistance. As of February 1916, only $12.7 million of the $47.5 million total contracts had been delivered, leaving unfilled orders amounting to approximately $35 million, while working capital at this time was around $20 million, some $13.5 million of this was in inventories, the remainder being in the form of advances, accounts receivable, and cash. The advances on these contracts had already been made and further income would be received only upon delivery. Because of difficulties in meeting production schedules, there was a need for further working capital, which was supplied in this case by Kidder, Peabody & Company, of Boston.

The reasons for the shift from J. P. Morgan & Company to Kidder, Peabody & Company are obscure. The latter concern, to be sure, had a long and respected history as a banking house, but there was no apparent connection between it and Winchester. It has been suggested that by this time, J. P. Morgan & Company was heavily committed and decided to turn over some of the New England business to the Boston firm.

In any event, the Winchester directors on February 17, 1916, voted to accept the offer of Kidder, Peabody & Company to lend the Company $16 million. Of this amount, $8.25 million was used to repay the Morgan loans, the remainder being put into working capital. By the terms of the agreement, no further plant expansion beyond that already contemplated should be undertaken during the term of the loan. The loan was made on notes of the Winchester Repeating Arms Company, under a provision that no mortgage should be placed on the property during their life without the consent of the bankers. This new money gave the Company a sufficient financial margin to carry on through the remainder of the war. It remained to be seen, however, whether the profits from operations would yield enough to repay the borrowing.

*Plant Expansion*

Construction of the new buildings was begun with a minimum of formality. The Aberthaw Construction Company of Boston, which had built the shot tower, undertook the principal construction work for the new program, on a cost-plus-ten-per-cent basis.

It was especially important to provide immediate space for the manufacture of Enfield rifle parts and construction was started along Munson Street in late November 1914. By working around the clock seven days a week, this five-story reinforced concrete building was completed in the record time of five weeks from the time the foundation was laid. Meanwhile construction was started on others and all through the winter, which was fortunately mild, and continuing on through the succeeding twelve months, the contractors were busy. By the middle of 1916, the plant had been expanded to 3.25 million square feet, approximately double the size at the beginning of 1914.

Getting the buildings erected was only a part of the general rehousing and expansion program. To make way for the new structures, several old buildings had to be torn down. As the Company was under pressure to start production on the war contracts as soon as possible, the equipment had to be moved out of these and set up for operation in temporary quarters, and then moved back into the new buildings as soon as the latter were completed. This "checker game" which applied especially to cartridge manufacture, made it difficult to maintain production schedules.

Most of the new space, however, represented an addition to existing facilities and had to be equipped. Contracts were made with suppliers and while the bulk of these met their obligations on time, a number of bottlenecks developed on particular equipment.

Plant expansion also called for a larger labor force. The average number of workers during the third quarter of 1914 was 5,608; a year later it had grown to over 12,700, and during the last two quarters of 1916 was averaging around 17,000. (*See Appendix J-1.*)

The impact of this group, drawn as they were from different parts of the country and divergent ethnic backgrounds, disturbed the established pattern of management-labor relationships. It was almost inevitable that the new workers should include a number of union sympathizers. During November and early December 1915, there was a wave of small strikes affecting various operations. These were not organized on a plant-wide basis and apparently the rank and file was not behind them for they subsided rather quickly. A year later there was another strike, this time called by the Machinists International Union, which claimed a plant membership of 2,500. The Company, in line with its long-established policy, refused to deal with any union organization. Not over two hundred workers went out on November 18, 1916, the day for which the strike was called, and the next day the strike was over, with most of the workers returning to their jobs.

These labor disturbances had little effect on production but they were partly symptomatic of the difficulties the Company was having in adapting its labor force.

*The Russian Rifle Contracts*

Under the terms of the first Russian contract, negotiated through the Baldwin Locomotive Works, Winchester was to supply 100,000 Model 95 rifles, modified to handle the standard 7.62mm. Russian service cartridge. The original contract price of $21.50 net to Winchester was increased to $22.90 for 26,000 rifles and $23.40 for 74,000, giving a total net contract of $2.327 million.

This contract, signed on November 4, 1914, was most welcome. The initial impact of the declaration of war the preceding August had resulted in considerable business uncertainty. Orders for the Model 95 had dropped and production of receivers for the gun, which had been in continuous operation since 1895, had stopped. There was little question that the Russian order could be cared for with existing plant facilities. It was estimated that about six weeks would be required to make the necessary changes in equipment and deliveries were scheduled to start about the middle of December 1914. Final delivery was to be made by November 15, 1915.

Preparing for this operation proved more time-consuming than anticipated and no deliveries had been made by February 1915. At this point the Russians announced that the rifle must be altered to load from a different clip. Research and tooling for this alteration required a further eight-week delay, suggesting the commencement of deliveries by the middle of April. Actual assembly did not begin in earnest until the end of May. This was caused in part by the failure of the Russians to supply gauges for inspection and their refusal to accept Winchester gauges. It was also caused by a bottleneck developed within the Winchester organization at the assembling stage of production.

Deliveries after assembly were also held up by the Russian inspectors who refused to let Winchester test the rifles with ammunition currently being made by the Company on the Russian cartridge contract and which was being passed by the Russian cartridge inspectors. The first shipment of cartridges from Russia via Vladivostok had been blown up en route and inspection was delayed until another shipment was made. The Company also experienced minor difficulties with subcontractors over dismounting and assembling kits to be packed with the rifles. Despite these obstacles deliveries finally commenced in June 1915 and the entire order for 100,000 rifles was completed by November 30, 1915, just two weeks beyond the scheduled date.

Meanwhile, on August 27, 1915, a second order for 200,000 of the Model 95 had been received for delivery to the Russians. This contract was placed by the British Government on behalf of their ally through J. P. Morgan & Company which had become the American agent of the Allies. The price per rifle was $27.15 and final delivery was to be made by December 31, 1916.

Despite difficulties typical of those delaying the first order, production on the second Russian contract went ahead on schedule. Nearly 140,000 guns had been accepted by September 1916. The remainder of the order was completed by the end of the year.

In view of the pressure on the plant in connection with the Enfield contract, it is of interest to note that in September 1916 the management was worried about further employment of the facilities being devoted to the Model 95. The following month it was decided that Harrie S. Leonard should be sent to Russia to negotiate directly with the Russian Government for further business.

### *The Russian Cartridge Contracts*

The largest single order received from the Allies was for 300 million 7.62mm. Russian service cartridges. A preliminary agreement was reached between Winchester and J. P. Morgan & Company on May 17, 1915, setting the purchase price at $36.50 per thousand, or a total contract price of $10.95 million. Deliveries were to begin in October, the same year, at 500,000 cartridges per week, increasing to 8 million per week at the end of April 1916. At these rates completion of the order should have come by the end of December 1916.

At the same time, the British Government took an option to purchase, at the same price, the entire surplus capacity of the Winchester plant in 1916, surplus being defined as the "excess of the quantities of cartridges required by your regular trade and by contracts heretofore made," and to purchase a further 200 million for 1917 delivery.

It is not without interest that this order was placed a few days after the sinking of the *Lusitania* on May 7, 1915. The British War Cabinet feared that this event would lead to the prohibition of arms export by United States manufacturers, so much so that Lord Kitchener, then Secretary of State for War, determined to prevent interruption to the flow of arms from the United States, having conceived the "grandiose idea of transplanting to Canada three or four big works which are now making guns and shells for us in the States." [5] No inkling of this plan, which would have seriously affected the Winchester Company, seems to have come to the management.

In setting delivery dates, the management had undoubtedly planned for the completion of existing commitments, then occupying the plant; yet, by November 1915, a month after deliveries were supposed to commence, no cartridges had been accepted. The reason for this inordinate delay was, again, in the relations of the Company with the Russian inspection staff.

The dispute concentrated around the major point: should Winchester produce a cartridge, under American methods of testing, which could be effectively used in the Model 95 under service conditions, or must its product comply precisely with the Russian specifications in every respect? Putting the matter in another way: should the product be an American one or a Russian one?

The matter was finally arbitrated by Major W. Farmer of the British Army inspection staff; his decision was in favor of Winchester, the Russians being, in effect, charged with overconcentration on trivialities which were of no detriment to the serviceability of the cartridges.

By the end of September 1916, only 30.6 million cartridges—slightly over ten per cent of the contract—had been accepted by the Russians. At this point (September 29) the British Government, acting as agent for the Russians, decided to exercise its option to cancel all future deliveries as of December 31, 1916.[6] Upon petition by the Company this date was extended to May 1, 1917, by which time total deliveries had amounted to around 174 million cartridges.

### *The British Enfield Contracts*

While the management was having its troubles with the Russian orders, it was experiencing even greater difficulties of the same sort with the British Enfield contracts. The contract for 200,000 Enfield rifles, dated November 24, 1914, had been followed by a second for an additional 200,000 dated March 16, 1915, made between the Company and J. P. Morgan & Company, in behalf of the British Government. The contract price on the first order was $32.50 per rifle; on the second, this was reduced to $30. The two contracts together came to $12.5 million.

No final delivery date was set but both agreements contained the provision that the contracts could be cancelled by the purchaser "on reasonable notice," later interpreted by agreement to mean "on 90 days' notice." Notice could be given any time after May 31, 1916, by which date, it was implied, deliveries should be completed.

The British Army had been using what was known as the Lee-Enfield rifle; but during the period immediately preceding the war, the Royal Arsenal had developed a new type of Enfield, called the Pattern of 1914, to take a new rimless caliber .276 cartridge. At the outbreak of war, production of the new gun had not been started, and, in making a decision to produce in quantity, the British were faced with two choices: using two types of ammunition in the field, or modifying the new Enfield to take what had been the standard ammunition—the British .303 rimmed cartridge.

The British chose the second, so that when their representatives arrived in the United States in November 1914 they had a model of a gun which had not been produced in volume and which was still not in its final form.

Although the British also had American contracts for the Enfield rifle with Remington and Eddystone, Winchester was chosen to work out the final model of the rifle to be put into production. (The Eddystone plant, located at Eddystone, Pennsylvania, near Philadelphia, was owned by the Baldwin Locomotive Works. It was operated during the war by the Remington Arms Company.) This was not accomplished without difficulty. It was soon discovered that there were discrepancies between the dimensions of the model and those on the detailed drawings received from England. Winchester gun experts were concerned over the tendency of the British rimmed .303 to jam, and recommended the use of a rimless cartridge instead, a recommendation that was not accepted.

A considerable part of the Company's difficulties both at this stage and later with inspection arose from the personality of the British representative assigned to the plant, Captain Smyth-Piggott. Not a gun expert, Captain Smyth-Piggott's job was to get guns delivered and to follow the specifications laid down by the Royal Arsenal. He took his instructions very literally which made it difficult to get approval of such changes in design and inspection methods that were necessary to get the rifle ready for production.

On January 7, 1915, Winchester submitted the modified Enfield which was accepted by A. E. Reavill, Captain Smyth-Piggott's assistant, subject to "some additional alterations to the sight which depended on shooting trials now being carried on in England." "Final approval" was given to the new model on March 22, 1915, by Captain Smyth-Piggott and the Company was authorized to put the gun into production.

An office memorandum dated July 8, 1915, shows that already the Company was worried about its capacity to complete deliveries on the first contract by May 31, 1916. By the beginning of August 87½ per cent of the tools, fixtures and gauges were completed but the Company was vexed by machinery problems and by the delay between the initial acceptance of the model by Reavill in January and its formal acceptance by Smyth-Piggott on March 22, 1915.

In spite of the favorable start on the building program, Winchester Bennett was complaining, in September 1915, of the "slowness of the contractors in completing buildings we have counted upon." There were continued disappointments about the delivery of machinery and on October 27, 1915, out of 1,053 operations scheduled, complete equipment had been received for 967, or 91.5 per cent; but only 587 (55.6 per cent) were ready for manufacturing, and 415 (39.4 per cent) actually in production.

The expectations at this point, however, were not completely pessimistic. In October 1915 W. H. Tilton, the gun superintendent, was able to schedule deliveries to start in January 1916 at 1,000 a day which would have completed the contracts for 400,000 rifles by January 1917. (It is of interest to compare this report with a similar one dated March 15, 1916, when an output of 80 a day was expected by March 22!) At the same time the Company was quoting J. P. Morgan & Company on 1917 deliveries at the rate of 1,300 a day.

As of October 1915, the management had made only a modest revision of the estimates of costs of the Enfield. The cost had originally been set at $19.46 which would have given a profit of $13.19 on each gun under the first contract (priced at $33.65) and $10.54 per gun (priced at $30) on the second contract. On October 20, 1915, the costs were estimated at $22.78 per gun. By that date steel had risen 10 per cent in price, wood 20 per cent, and labor approximately 15 per cent. At this time the management had nothing to say about the possibility of a further rise in the cost of raw materials or labor, nor is there any evidence that consideration was given to the effects on costs from the delays experienced in getting production under way.

There is no reference to any "labor problem" until January 1916 when the Company complained to the British Government representatives that a former employee, on behalf of the Ross Rifle Company of Canada, had been attempting to lure away Winchester Repeating Arms Company workers by offering them higher rates of pay.

By the end of January 1916, the Company was ready to begin assembling the Enfield rifles. This was four months before the date (May 31, 1916) after which the British could, under contract, cancel orders on all undelivered rifles. A tentative production schedule was prepared calling for a rate of production of 1,000 per day by the beginning of May. If this rate could be achieved, the first 200,000 rifles would have been completed by December 1916.

This production schedule proved much too optimistic and on April 19, 1916, a new schedule was drawn up which, if kept, would have insured the delivery of the first 200,000 rifles by the following December 4, and the second 200,000 by April 17, 1917. Production, however, continued to fall behind the revised schedule. By September 15, 1916, the number of assembled guns was short by some 46,000; by December 2, the gap was almost 97,000.

A major factor in the failure of Winchester to keep up deliveries as planned arose from inspection difficulties. As early as March 10, 1916, the Company had written J. P. Morgan & Company that the British inspectors were ". . . under the most rigid instruction. [They are] not inclined to grant us any concession [and their attitude] is likely to be a serious handicap to our production." This proved to be only too true and the Company found it increasingly difficult to get assembled rifles accepted.

The substance of the dispute over inspection was the insistence by the British on minor technical details in contrast with the initial understanding by the Company that what was wanted was quantities of guns that "would function and shoot properly."

An obvious contributory cause of the trouble was the fact that the Winchester modification of the Enfield had been developed from a model. In the process of development to secure proper functioning there had been a departure from the original British specifications, which became, by definition, faults which were serious enough to cause rejection.

Difficulty with British inspection methods was not unique with Winchester, but affected the other American manufacturers supplying the British with arms. Fundamentally the problem was based upon a different attitude toward production methods in the two countries. Colonel W. G. Lyddon, one of the chief officers of the British inspection staff stationed in the United States during World War I, has pointed out: "Prior to the war the aim of American manufacture generally had been the production of quantity; except in the case of a few firms carrying out a high grade of work, comparatively little attention had been paid to quality. Very little consideration had, therefore, been given to the development of inspection staffs within the firms' own organizations." [7]

The inspection standards imposed by the British affected the fulfillment of Winchester's Enfield contracts in two ways. The initial effect, as early as June 1916, was to bring about the reorganization of several shops and to rework several parts. The second result was a widening gap between the number of guns assembled by the Company and the number accepted by the British inspectors. By the end of June 1916, this divergence amounted to over 10,000; by the end of September it had increased to nearly 15,000.

This was the situation when, on September 21, 1916, the British gave formal notice, under the second contract, of cancellation of the Enfield contracts, not only to Winchester but to Remington and Eddystone as well.

*Cancellation and Revision of Enfield Contract*

According to the British Ministry of Munitions it had been decided in August 1916 to cancel a "considerable portion" of the Enfield contracts because "the failure of delivery . . . according to contract has caused us great inconvenience. We have had to remedy this out of our own resources as best we can."

In June 1916 the Winchester management had arranged with the officials of Remington and Eddystone to hold periodic conferences as a countermove to any British attempt to set one manufacturer off against another. When the notice of cancellation was received, all three concerns immediately stopped deliveries on the Enfields.[8]

J. P. Morgan & Company had warned the British Government prior to the cancellation notice that the manufacturers would probably stand on their legal rights, especially as they could bring in strong testimony that "failure in deliveries were the direct outcome of interference in construction on the part of representatives of the buyer." Any unfair and arbitrary action by the British Government would have serious repercussions on its financial operations in the U.S.[9]

It appears from the J. P. Morgan & Company records that the final crisis was precipitated by the bankers of Remington Arms-UMC and Winchester, who ". . . have taken a very firm position in insisting that the companies shall immediately discontinue manufacture, as they contend that otherwise the W.R.A. will be seriously embarrassed and it will become all the more difficult, if not impossible, to work out an adjustment of the complicated affairs of R.A.-U.M.C. Company." Winchester claimed, according to J. P. Morgan & Company, to have invested $4,300,000 of its own capital in addition to the $2,700,000 advanced by the British Government.[10]

Winchester and Remington had retained the services of a lawyer, Thomas L. Chadbourne, to propose, in their behalf, that the British Government assume responsibility for the whole cost of the rifles, other than the cost of buildings and fixed equipment used in their production.[11]

The cancellation brought about certain political repercussions, the problem being of sufficient importance to merit discussion by the British War Council in the private room of the Prime Minister on October 18, 1916.[12]

The change in Britain's demand for American products—from rifles to wheat, copper, and steel—reflected the extent of her own development of war industries, as well as the change in war conditions which had made the wastage less than anticipated.

After extended negotiations the parties finally came to an agreement the effect of which was: (1) To obtain immediately weekly cash allowances for wages; (2) To provide for the reimbursement of the manufacturers for "actual expenses . . . in carrying out of their rifle contracts" other than the cost of buildings and fixed machinery; (3) To reduce the total number of rifles to be delivered to 2,000,000, of which Winchester's proportionate share was 235,528; (4) To enable the companies to go ahead with production, all their expenditures on the completion of the manufacture to be paid by the British Government.

The intention was that the companies should "derive no profit nor [should] they suffer any loss in the manufacture of the . . . 2,000,000 rifles. Expenditures were to be audited by accountants representing the companies and the British Government." [13] A supplementary contract giving effect to these arrangements was signed on December 30, 1916.

*Effect of Enfield Revised Contract*

Under the original Enfield contracts Winchester had expected to make a profit of $13.19 per rifle on the first 200,000 priced at $32.50 each, and $10.54 per rifle on the second 200,000 priced at $30 each; or a total profit of $4.746 million. Subsequent cost calculations reduced the expected profit $4.46 per rifle, bringing the total anticipated return to the Company down to a figure of $2.962 million.

At the termination of deliveries during the last week in December 1916, Winchester had completed the first order of 200,000 rifles and 35,528 on the second contract. The achieved costs on this number of guns would have given the Company a substantial loss in the absence of the revised settlement. Based on the prices specified in the original contracts this would have been made up of the following:

| | |
|---|---|
| Loss on the first 200,000 rifles @ 40¢ | $ 80,000 |
| Loss on 35,528 @ 3.05 | 108,360 |
| Loss on tools, jigs, gauges, etc. not included in original cost estimate | 2,994,065 |
| TOTAL | $3,182,425 |

Under the settlement with the British the Company received approximately $10.778 million, $7.784 million of which was for "production costs" and $2.994 million was for "movable plant." This was the equivalent of $45.76 a rifle on the number actually delivered. "Pure production costs" amounted to $33.05 and "capital costs" to $12.71 per rifle. This latter item would have been reduced, and possibly recovered, if the original (second) contract had been completed, or if additional orders had been secured. (There was a considerable correspondence between the Company and J. P. Morgan & Company during 1915-1916, with reference to the possibility of acquiring options for the use of Winchester's entire 1917 capacity.)

It is clear, however, that the minimum costs (i.e., labor, raw material, and overhead, including a proportionate share of jigs, fixtures and gauges) exceeded the management's original calculations by an amount that would have turned profits into losses. (Part of the miscalculation was undoubtedly attributable to the prolongation of the time originally planned for the contract work. While there is no evidence that the management was very sophisticated in the approach to the problem of overhead, it would probably have reconsidered its quotations if it had reason to expect an abnormal production period.) For this reason the settlement with the British, although yielding no "profit" no doubt kept the Company from suffering a considerable loss, if the contracts had been completed according to the original terms.

*War Materials Delivered to the Allies*

The following is a summary of the principal items of war material actually delivered to the Allied governments:

| | |
|---|---|
| Enfield rifles | 235,528 |
| British .303 cartridges | 99,285,500 |
| 18-pounder cannon cases | 1,965,000 |
| 18-pounder primers | 7,604,600 |
| Russian Model 95 rifles | 293.818 |
| Russian 7.62mm. cartridges | 174,198,000 |

*Nonmilitary Sales*

The volume of nonmilitary sales between 1914 and April 30, 1917, shows that Winchester, in addition to adding military orders to its production, was able to follow a policy of maintaining production and distribution of its regular line of guns and ammunition. The annual dollar volumes of $9.17 million for 1915 and $10.12 million for 1916 were, in fact, very close to the average sales of the Company during the immediate prewar years, and contributed over two thirds as much to the income as the war contracts. Moreover, the gross margins on this business were considerably higher than the amounts obtained from military contracts, being $7.388 million compared with $5.47 million for the latter.

It is not astonishing that domestic and nonmilitary sales should have been maintained during this period. The country generally was enjoying economic prosperity and the European war may have stimulated an interest in shooting. From the standpoint of production the principal limitation would have been labor. While there was considerable demand for general-purpose machinery, the special tools and fixtures used for regular lines, especially guns, could not be used for military orders. (The principal exception involved the Model 95 produced for the Russians. This was not a large seller in normal times, however.)

During the relatively inactive period between the completion of the British and Russian contracts and the entrance of the United States into the war, the Company built up its inventories of regular line products in order to keep as large a labor force as possible employed.

While the dollar volume of nonmilitary sales was roughly equivalent to prewar figures, the physical volume was less. This is explainable by the fact that by 1917 there had been a considerable rise in the prices of both guns and ammunition. Prices at this time were some 38 per cent above 1914 levels on rifles and from 23 to 30 per cent higher on shot guns. On ammunition, the rise for the same period was about 60 per cent. These prices generally reflected a rise in costs of labor and raw materials, ammunitions being particularly affected by the increased prices of copper and lead. While there are no available data on the physical output of nonmilitary ammunition, the figures for guns sold during 1915 and 1916 confirm the drop in the number of guns distributed. Compared with a total of 293,113 for 1914, the number of guns distributed in 1915 came to 265,681, and in 1916 to 184,449. (*See Appendix D-1.*)

*Management Personnel*

With the exception of Aro Ward, who died in May 1914 and who was replaced by Arthur Earle as secretary, the top officials—Hodson, Winchester Bennett, and Leonard—carried through until the end of 1915. On December 31 of that year, Hodson put in his resignation "for reasons of health" and Winchester Bennett was elected president and treasurer to succeed him. The following February Henry Brewer was appointed to a newly created office of third vice president, his position as cartridge superintendent being taken over by Edward Uhl. Further changes were made in February 1916 when Leonard, Brewer, and Frank Drew (from the sales department) were all made vice presidents. The following September John E. Otterson—of whom more later—was added to their number.

This increase in the number of officials was a reflection of the growing complexity of management problems brought on by the war business—problems that were aggravated by changes in some of the key personnel in the production departments. Albert Tilton, long superintendent of the gun shop, had resigned in

May 1914. He had been succeeded by his son, Walter H. Tilton, who was an able mechanic, but who lacked the force and vigor of his father as an executive. T. C. Johnson, the Company's chief gun designer, was taken ill in December 1914 and was out until the following September. This put the chief responsibility for modifying the Enfield upon Roy Crockett, his assistant, who rose to the occasion, but found it a considerable burden.

Until the middle of 1915, the plant operated without a general manager in charge of production. By that time the problems connected with tooling up and scheduling the war work were serious enough to demand the attention of a strong hand. Winchester Bennett, who had assumed this responsibility, was already feeling the strain and he began looking for some one who could take over this burden. Upon recommendation of officials of the Aberthaw Construction Company, for whom he had done consulting work, John Edward Otterson was appointed general superintendent on July 1, 1915.

*John Edward Otterson*

Otterson's appointment brought a new personality into the management which was to play an important role in the subsequent history of the Company. Born in Allegheny (now part of Pittsburgh), Pennsylvania, in March 1881, he had attended the U. S. Naval Academy, graduating high in the class of 1904. After a tour of duty Otterson was sent to the Massachusetts Institute of Technology, receiving an M.S. in naval architecture in 1909. He was then assigned to duty as a naval architect, serving for a period in the Brooklyn Navy Yard and the Charlestown Navy Yard near Boston, Massachusetts.

Otterson was much interested in scientific management being popularized at the time by Frederick W. Taylor and he attempted to apply these principles to naval construction and repair. He ran into strong opposition from labor and he resigned from the Navy in 1915, just prior to accepting the position with Winchester.

Almost immediately Otterson introduced time study analysis into the Winchester plant. Carl A. Barth, already famous in the field, was hired as consultant, and Dwight V. Merrick, later to become an authority in the field, was employed full-time.[14] From this period on time studies became an accepted procedure in Winchester production. By the time the United States entered the war, many changes had been made in rates and worker efficiency had been substantially increased.

Within two months after Otterson's appointment Winchester Bennett contracted typhoid fever, followed by pneumonia, which was complicated by an appendectomy. He spent from September 1915 until the following April in Florida, attempting to recover his health. This put an extra burden on Hodson, and brought about his resignation at the end of December 1915. This event, coupled with serious doubts concerning Winchester Bennett's ability to resume responsibility, raised a question as to who should be the real head of the organization. T. G. Bennett attended the meetings of the board of directors during this period, and in fact acted as president and treasurer *pro tem* from January 1 until his son's return, but he had neither the inclination nor the strength to assume heavy responsibility.

T. G. Bennett was greatly upset by the failure of his son's health and undecided about the best future policy. He was in fact willing, as of February 1916, to turn the control of the Company over to outside interests. At the time of the Kidder, Peabody & Company loan he gave the bankers an option to buy a controlling interest in the stock of the Company. Kidder, Peabody & Company interested E. I. du Pont de Nemours & Company in the possibility of acquiring the stock. The Du Pont concern required, as a condition of taking over control of Winchester, an extension of existing contracts and additional orders. When these were not forthcoming the matter was dropped.

This decision by Du Pont narrowed the problem down to a choice between Harrie S. Leonard and Otterson as the active head of the Company. In the subsequent contest with the "Old Guard" Otterson won out largely through sheer ability. T. G. Bennett was at first torn by indecision, but he soon made up his mind for Otterson who showed an unusual capacity to handle complex problems. The latter's position was strengthened by being elected a director in February 1916 and a vice president the following September. Continuing as general superintendent he took an increasingly active part in top management decisions during 1916. In October 1916 Leonard, who was also a director and vice president, was sent to Russia to negotiate an arms contract. On January 31, 1917, Otterson was elected to the office of first vice president and general manager. Leonard returned the following March, without having had any luck on a contract and after traveling across Siberia and the Pacific Ocean to avoid the submarine menace. At the directors meeting on June 25, 1917, his resignation as vice president, effective December 31, was accepted and he was given a leave of absence with pay until that date.

Otterson's election as first vice president in January 1917 was in recognition of his *de facto* position as head of the Company. By the time Winchester Bennett had returned, in April 1916, conditions at the plant had changed so much that he was completely out of touch. This, coupled with continued poor health, kept him from resuming an active role, although he held the office of president and treasurer until the end of the war.

*Financial Summary*

As far as can be ascertained from surviving records, the war contracts with the Allies, which had been expected to total $47.5 million and yield a manufacturing profit of $15.5 million, actually totaled $30.7 million and returned a manufacturing profit of $5.47 million. Since the expansion of the plant was based on the original estimate, the Company's financial position as of April 1917 was quite different from what had been visualized two and a half years earlier.

The gap between expectation and realization was immediately attributable to the cancellation of contracts and the rise in manufacturing costs. It has not been possible to analyze their relative influence in detail, but the loss from cancellations amounted to approximately $2.10 million, while the rise in costs absorbed $7.93 million.

Henry Brewer stated in 1925 that "out of all the foreign contracts taken we made practically little or nothing." [15] According to the management, ". . . Owing to the failure of [Winchester] to provide in its agreements for the contingency of extraordinary costs resulting from increase in labor rates and in costs of materials, etc., or for inefficiencies in production owing to the great lack of skilled labor, these fixed price [with the Allies] contracts proved to be unprofitable, and the advances herein referred to were by plaintiff in its accounting finally applied to costs of manufacture and no part allocated to the amortization of the cost of the special plant and special facilities."

These statements were essentially correct. If depreciation and amortization of special war facilities, not included in manufacturing costs and amounting to some $4.46 million, are subtracted from the realized manufacturing profit of $5.47 million, that "profit" is reduced to approximately $1 million. Even this is not a "true" profit because no allowance has been made for any allocation of general overhead costs to the war business. Any decision regarding such allocation must be somewhat arbitrary, but if the war business were charged with one fifth of the general overhead of nearly $5 million (*see Table II*) incurred during these years the net profit on the Allied contracts would be reduced to nothing.

The effect of the failure to realize the expected income from the war contracts can be shown by an analysis of the allocation and sources of funds for the period December 31, 1914, to April 30, 1917. During that period the fixed plant and equipment, inventories and working capital had been increased some $24.706 million. The principal individual items were (in millions):

| | |
|---|---|
| Expansion of fixed plant and equipment | $11.254 |
| Increase in inventories | 7.284 |
| Increase in working capital other than inventories | 6.168 |
| TOTAL | $24.706 |

TABLE II

DISPOSABLE INCOME FROM OPERATIONS
DECEMBER 31, 1914-APRIL 30, 1917
(in millions)

| *Net Sales* | *Military* | *Nonmilitary* |
|---|---|---|
| 1915 | $10.267 | $ 9.170 |
| 1916 | 16.315 | 10.126 |
| 1917 (four months) | 4.083 | 3.697 |
| | $30.665 | $22.993 |
| Estimated cost of goods sold | 25.195 | 15.605 |
| Gross Margins | 5.470 | 7.388 |
| Costs of operations [a] | | 4.742 |
| Net profit on nonmilitary business | | 2.646 |
| Add gross margin on military business | | 5.470 |
| Total disposal income [b] | | 8.116 |
| Less Dividend paid for 1915 | | 250 |
| Reinvested in business | | 7.866 |

[a] Assumed to be all chargeable to nonmilitary business.

[b] Not a net profit because no deduction has been made for depreciation and amortization in connection with the war business amounting to $4.457 million. Net profits, after depreciation were $3.659 million.

Returns from the Company's military and nonmilitary business during this period (shown in Table II) came to $8.116 million, of which $7.866 million was reinvested in the business. This left a difference of some $16.840 million to obtain from outside sources. Short-term borrowing took care of $840,000 and the Kidder, Peabody & Company loan of $16 million made up the remainder.

It was not unreasonable to assume that eventual liquidation of the increased inventories might yield enough to pay back half of the $16 million borrowed from Kidder, Peabody & Company. By April 30, 1917, the United States had become an active belligerent and the Company was sure of getting large orders from the U. S. Government, but had the war ended at that date, the Company would have found itself with an added permanent investment of which $8 million was owed to the banking house. On annual net sales of around $11.5 million during 1913 and 1914, the Company had averaged a net profit of $1.3 million. Interest charges at seven per cent on this $8 million would have been a heavy drain on net income, if the prewar pattern had resumed. Variations of this pattern during the postwar period would, of course, ease or accentuate this burden depending on their direction.[16]

CHAPTER TWENTY

# WINCHESTER AND THE U.S. GOVERNMENT

Winchester's position just prior to the American declaration of war was succinctly described by Edwin Pugsley (in 1925): "At the end of 1916 and the early months of 1917 we had either completed or had cancelled practically all the work we had for foreign governments . . . so that the first part of 1917 found us with a plant entirely equipped for making small arms and ammunition and an organization completely trained and nothing to do. Great portions [of the plant] were idle."

This statement is graphically borne out by the figures on employment. The total number of workers (excluding salaried personnel), which had reached the peak of 17,549 in October 1916 had dropped to 14,980 by January 1917; by April the number stood at 10,635.

Financially, too, the Company was in a position to undertake large commitments. The equity of the stockholders (in millions) was represented as of April 30, 1917 by:

| | |
|---|---|
| Working capital, other than inventories | $ 7.05 |
| Inventories | 14.54 |
| Fixed assets (book value) | 14.76 |
| TOTAL | 36.35 |
| *Less:* Debt to Kidder, Peabody & Co. (Due March 1, 1918) and banks | 16.84 |
| Net Worth | 19.51 |

These resources provided reasonable working capital with which to undertake large orders. While the debt of $16 million owed to Kidder, Peabody & Company would have to be met on March 1, 1918, it was possible that contracts with the United States Government would provide sufficient income to repay this loan. If so, the management might bring to a successful completion the plans laid during the latter part of 1914 and early 1915, and emerge in the postwar period with a new plant free from debt.

As late as January 1917, it looked as if the United States might maintain its neutrality, but the attempts of the Germans during 1916 to stir up trouble in Mexico, coupled with their announcement of unlimited submarine warfare on February 1, set the stage for an American declaration of war on April 6, 1917. On

February 3, in anticipation of such a declaration Winchester had sent telegrams to the War and Navy Departments offering to place the Company's facilities at their disposal, and two days later Henry Brewer was sent to Washington to make this offer in person. On March 6, Otterson was made a member of the newly established Munitions Standards Board, and shortly thereafter he was appointed chairman of the Board's subcommittee on small arms and ammunition.

*Adoption of the Modified Enfield*

The subcommittee on small arms and ammunitions met in New Haven on March 27 and two days later Otterson made a report in its behalf regarding facilities available for the production of service rifles and recommendations as to how the Government could best use these facilities. The manufacturers unanimously recommended that, to avoid the delay which would ensue if the extension of production were concentrated on the Springfield rifle, the United States adopt the British Enfield rifle as the standard small arm. The rifle could be modified, if this were preferred by the Government, to take U. S. Government .30-06 rimless cartridges. The use of this ammunition would overcome one of the principal difficulties experienced with the British model—namely, the tendency to jam inherent in the rimmed cartridge. The proposed modification would, in fact, put the Enfield rifle back into the form in which it was originally planned.

The American service rifle at this time was the Springfield Model 1903. It was an excellent firearm, superior in accuracy, range, and firepower to any military rifle currently in use, including the German Mauser. The Springfield had been manufactured in the two Government plants, Springfield Armory, and Rock Island Arsenal, at Rock Island, Illinois. But for several years prior to 1917, the Government had cut production and Rock Island Arsenal had ceased manufacturing the rifle altogether. The skilled workers involved had scattered and found jobs elsewhere.

As of March 1917, the military authorities had three broad choices. One was to try and recruit a new labor force for the two arsenals. This would have taken some time and even if successful their combined output would have been inadequate. A second was to have the Springfield manufactured in private plants. This choice would have also been time-consuming because of the necessity of providing thousands of gauges, jigs, dies and other small tools, as well as special machinery. The third alternative was to accept the recommendations made by Otterson's committee.

This recommendation had the obvious virtues of permitting the three plants —Winchester, Remington, and Eddystone—which had been producing Enfields, to use the equipment installed for that purpose and to continue the production of rifles with minimum dislocation. The tools, machinery, and equipment which had been sold back to the British were available in the respective plants and apparently little disturbed.

Up to the time war was declared no decision had been made by the Ordnance Department on the choice of a rifle. In the meantime, the manufacturers had, by April 4, 1917, agreed on a modified Enfield with limited interchangeability of some seven basic parts most likely to be lost or damaged in the field.

Sample Enfield rifles, modified to handle the Government .30-06 cartridge, were tested at Springfield Armory on May 9. The results showed that, while the gun was not as good as the Springfield, it was the equal or superior of any of the military rifles being used by the belligerents. The Ordnance Department decided therefore on May 11 to accept the modified Enfield as the rifle for American troops, a decision described by competent authorities as ". . . one of the great executive choices of the war." [1]

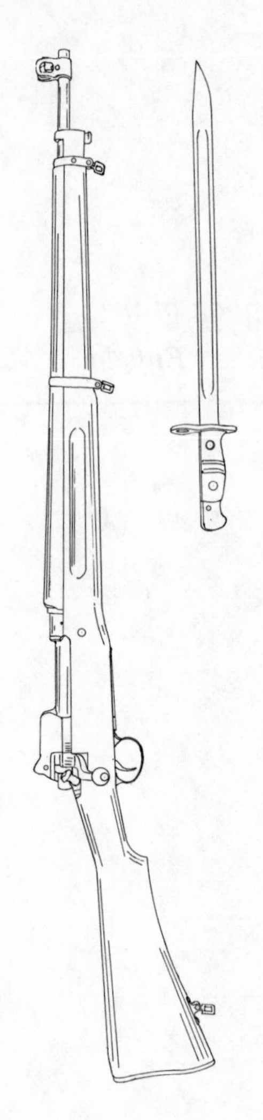

*U. S. Enfield, Model 1917*

It was of utmost importance that the parts of the modified Enfields made in the three plants should be interchangeable. The rifles tested in May were not standardized in this respect, being all hand-fitted. Official approval of specifications was therefore held up until July 12, when a second group of rifles was submitted. These were much improved but still short of the desired standards of interchangeability. Nevertheless, the Ordnance Department authorized the companies to start manufacture with the understanding that standardization would be improved as work progressed. Remington and Eddystone were understandably not willing to proceed under the circumstances and preferred to wait until final specifications were adopted, which was not until August 18, ". . . after thousands of dimensions had been carefully checked and finally approved by the ordnance officers." [2]

Otterson took a different position. He did not wait either for official action or a contract before starting production of the modified Enfield. On April 23, 1917, he ordered the start of the manufacture of 10,000, ". . . on the theory that if we got those rifles made and it developed that they were not satisfactory . . . we would be able to sell them commercially or perhaps sell them to some other government."

Following the preliminary decision of the Ordnance Department on May 11 to accept the new model, orders went forth within the Winchester organization to build up to maximum capacity as rapidly as possible. Only on June 1 did a formal order for 225,000 rifles come from the Secretary of War. By this time the Company had production well started.

By not waiting for final specifications Otterson drew criticism from some American military authorities. Crowell and Wilson note that "word came from Europe not to send rifles of Winchester manufacture of that period." [3] From other branches of the service, especially from officers in charge of training, he was congratulated, because the scarcity of rifles was such that many recruits were drilling with broomsticks.

Actually it was not until December 1917 that the standard of interchangeability satisfactory to the U.S. Government inspectors was finally achieved by all three manufacturers. (It is not without interest that the American inspection standards were apparently more exacting than the British. In a memorandum, dated December 20, 1917, to the War Department, Henry Brewer stated, ". . . up to Saturday, December 15, we had delivered to the Government 83,000 rifles but . . . we could have delivered in that time 170,000 rifles . . . made to the British degree of interchangeability.")

Thanks to an early start, Winchester was able to deliver its first rifles on August 13, a little over two months after the formal contract had been signed. By the middle of December, the Company had delivered over 80,000 compared to "something over 100,000" delivered by the Eddystone Company, which had three times the Winchester capacity.[4] By this date Winchester was two months ahead of contract requirements.

The Ordnance Department faced essentially the same problem with ammunition as it did with rifles. The principal, in fact the only large, source of Government .30-06 cartridges was Frankford Arsenal. The capacity of that plant was around 100 million annually, which was far short of expected needs. Rather than expand the capacity of the arsenal, or build new plants, the Ordnance Department decided to place orders with existing ammunition plants and let them expand facilities to take care of orders. This meant a certain relaxation of rigid Government standards for the sake of speed.[5]

*Beginning of Ammunition Production*

Here again the Winchester management accepted several Government orders before the decisions regarding specifications were finally made, taking a chance on an ultimate reconciliation of commercial specifications with Government standards. In fact the gauges used by the Government inspectors to test the ammunition produced in the plant were made by the Company and approved by the Ordnance Department. This approval came on August 22, a week after deliveries of cartridges had begun on August 14. These deliveries were made, however, on a Navy order, rather than an Army contract, because the Company was "a little troubled about our getting these cartridges accepted under these revised specifications" and had bid on a Navy contract for 40 million, receiving the award on a competitive basis.

Even with this Navy order the Company was able to start Army deliveries on September 15, the agreed date, and therefore effectively increased war production by the gamble on the acceptance of its own standards for ammunition production.

*Rifle Contract Negotiations: Cost-Plus Contracts*

The relationships between the rifle manufacturers and the United States Government were undoubtedly influenced by the experiences prior to 1917. The companies had been caught between the anvil of a fixed price and the hammer of a cost factor that was affected not only by problems of internal organization and management, but by two uncontrollable external pressures. One of these was the unpredictable rise in the price of raw materials and labor, the other the arbitrariness of a Government buyer whose insistence on a standard of performance cantrary to commercial experience interrupted the smooth plan of production.

Winchester had not hesitated to place its manufacturing capacity at the disposal of the United States Government and it went ahead on production without the benefit of contracts or procurement orders: but there was a noticeable restraint in quoting specific prices or in agreeing on the form of the contract.[6]

In cooperation with the other manufacturers the management seems to have made it clear to the Chief of Ordnance of the Army (Brigadier General William Crozier) that it would, in effect, have to be guaranteed against losses on Government work.

It was agreed on in principle that a payment of cost-plus-ten-per-cent would be a fair basis for participation in the "partnership." (In this connection it may be noted that something of a precedent had been established in the settlement of the British Enfield contracts on a "cost" basis with Winchester, Eddystone, and Remington. Winchester also had the experience of its cost-plus contracts in connection with its wartime building program.)

It was easy to enunciate the principle but it was not easy to put this unprecedented conception into workable form. The inclusion of such items as wages, costs of raw materials, depreciation of special tools and equipment, and other expenses directly attributable to production offered no problems. The difficulty came over such elements as depreciation of buildings and interest on the investment in the plant used for the war production.

Apparently it was the hope of the Winchester management that the Company would be able to amortize cost of the plant especially erected prior to 1917 for the war business.[7] Otterson pushed this concept vigorously during negotiations but was unable to get a complete or final acceptance.[8]

In one important respect the rifle companies were able to obtain a concession from the Government that increased their total profits from an accounting point of view. This concession was an allowance of interest on that part of the plant which the contractors were going to use in connection with the rifle contracts; and it was made with considerable misgiving on the part of General Crozier and Colonel Frank A. Scott, a negotiator on behalf of the U.S. Government. A Congressional committee afterward criticized the arrangement and Colonel Scott thought that they did so with some justice, in view of its unusualness. This was, however, according to Colonel Scott, ". . . the only concession . . . that [was] made to Mr. Otterson, who representing the Company in the best way he could, contended for a good many things." [9]

Even this concession was not made without a considerable amount of argument, the accountants called in to testify being very much divided in their attitude, those opposing the inclusion of interest being as strenuous as those who favored it. The position of the proponents of the concept was that the nonallowance of interest would bear unfavorably on contractors who owned their plants. Those who rented their facilities could charge rent as a cost, while those who purchased a large proportion of the parts used in assembly were, in fact, including in their costs a substantial element of profit paid to their suppliers. The first part of their argument had especial reference to the equities as between Winchester and the Eddystone plant of Remington. The latter plant was rented from Baldwin Locomotive Works, so that if the opponents of the interest concept had their way, "Winchester . . . would get no allowance for the use of their capital which is invested . . . in good brick and stone buildings which, of course, would result in manifest inequality." [10]

This provision of the contracts had been fairly well agreed upon by July 1917, when a Congressional committee threatened to throw out the whole concept.[11] General Crozier and Colonel Scott, who appeared before the Committee, were particularly hard-pressed on their agreement with the rifle manufacturers to allow six per cent interest on their capital investment, especially as this was to be treated as a cost and, therefore, would qualify for inclusion into total cost for the ten per cent profit allowance to be given under the cost-plus contracts.

The committee, too, found it very difficult to appreciate the desirability of allowing a ten per cent profit on the turnover. They were inclined to take a position in favor of ten per cent of authorized capital, disregarding the factor of reinvested profits, which was particularly important in the case of Winchester. Even where the committee members understood the problem, there was dissatisfaction with the principle of paying ten per cent profit on turnover irrespective of the size of the capital investment in a situation in which the dollar volume of business done was large, because high (if not unreasonable) profits as a percentage of that capital might be paid to the contractors.

When the Appropriations Bill came before the House, the chairman of the Appropriations Committee justified the whole arrangement on the grounds of expediency. The scheme for the cost-plus contracts had been evolved by the executive power, acting under competent advice and unless it could be shown that there was incapacity, inefficiency, incompetency or corruption, ". . . we must rest content in the exercise of the executive power in the discretion exercised by the executive." [12]

*Cost of Rifles*

Information is lacking on the exact prices paid by the Government to Winchester for the rifles. Crowell and Wilson state that the modified Enfields cost the Government approximately $26 each, a price which evidently did not include the bayonet.[13] This price was somewhat below the cost to the British of their American-built rifle, not including any charge for equipment. (This price paid by the U.S. Government to the manufacturer did not include any allowance for the use of the special Enfield machinery used by the manufacturer which was purchased by the Government—at a figure around $9.5 million—and put at the disposal of the manufacturers.)

Considering the fact that wage rates and raw material costs were further increased during American participation in the war, the delivered price to the Government seems to have been reasonable and was a tribute to the greater manufacturing efficiency that had been achieved by 1917.

*Ammunition Contracts*

The cost-plus contracts on the rifles set the pattern for ammunition with the added feature of a bonus and penalty clause which took the following form. The contractor was guaranteed his cost, plus 10 per cent on the cost. The estimated "fair cost of production" was predicated on "base prices" for essential raw materials, including copper, zinc, lead, and powder. For each 1 per cent variation in the actual cost of these materials, the contractor's price was increased or decreased by a defined amount. If the contractor's cost, as actually achieved, was below "normal cost," he was given, in addition to his 10 per cent profit, a bonus equal to 20 per cent of the "saving"; if above, there was a deduction of 20 per cent of the excess above normal cost. This bonus and penalty clause served as an effective incentive for the various manufacturers to keep their expenditures at a minimum.

Some grievance was felt by the Winchester management from the omission in these contracts of any means of adjusting "normal costs" for variations on the labor cost involved. The contractor received, of course, his ten per cent on the expenditure but any increase in that labor cost meant an automatic deduction in the bonus through no fault on the part of the contractor. The effect of this would appear to have been to increase the resistance of the contractors to demands for wage increases. Since all war contracts (under legislation passed in 1912) contained a clause requiring the limitation of the working day to eight hours, the contractor's costs were probably affected, adversely, by any overtime payment necessary to get production on to the ten-hour-day basis which the factory had long maintained. Average weekly wages rose in the cartridge department from $16.22 in September 1917 to around $19.50 by November 1918, or approximately twenty per cent. So far as can be determined the Company was unable to get the normal cost figures increased.

## *Winchester Primer Mixture*

One particular triumph for Winchester standards of ammunition production came when the Company's primer mixture was made the standard for all ammunition produced for Government orders. The situation arose out of the tendency of early shipments of American ammunition to France to hangfire or misfire. The cartridges in question were traced to Frankford Arsenal and there was an immediate suspicion of sabotage. It was found, upon investigation, however, that the primers long used in ammunition manufacture by the Arsenal were at fault. Containing sulphur, potassium chlorate, and antimony sulphide, these primers work well as long as the materials are thoroughly dried, but sulphur, when oxidized, changes into an acid extremely corrosive to metal and oxidized primers are liable to function badly. Heat and moisture change sulphur into acid rapidly and when the ammunition using this mixture was shipped overseas in nonmoisture-proof containers, the primers deteriorated.

When the trouble was recognized, the various private ammunition companies were asked by the Government to submit priming mixtures for adoption. Winchester at this time was using its patented 35 NF primer mixture, consisting of a small amount of TNT (trinitrotoluol), antimony sulphide, potassium chlorate, and lead sulfocyanid. Misfires or hangfires in ammunition using this mixture were virtually nonexistent.

After testing the various formulas, the Government asked the Company to make its mixture available to the other ammunition concerns to be used as the standard for all ammunition produced for the Government, which the Company did. The Company also supplied Frankford Arsenal and the Peters Cartridge Company with completed primers for Government ammunition during the remainder of the war period.

Because of the excellent functioning of its ammunition, Winchester was also called upon to help in setting up the standards for the cartridges used in the machine guns mounted on American airplanes. These guns were designed to fire between the blades of the propeller as it revolved and any tendency to hangfire through faulty primer action or cartridge construction would have destroyed the propeller. The machines for testing this ammunition were worked out at the Winchester factory in cooperation with Ordnance Department experts.

In addition to the production of service ammunition, the Company also manufactured large amounts of other types of ammunition and ammunition components, including caliber .50 cartridge cases for antisubmarine guns for the Navy.

Winchester was especially proud of its record on ammunition production; of the millions of rounds manufactured not one lot was rejected by Government inspectors.

## *Expansion of Production*

All during the period of negotiations over contract terms Winchester pushed ahead on its war production. By the end of 1917, the Company had delivered over $16 million in orders to the Government; during 1918, the total was over $50 million. In contrast to the situation during 1915 and 1916, manufacturing schedules were established and maintained and in some instances exceeded during 1917 and 1918 without serious interruptions.

The labor force was built up gradually during the six months immediately following the declaration of war and by December 1917 the total number of nonsalaried employees was 15,416. In February 1918, employment reached 17,975, higher than the peak during 1916, and in July 1918 stood at 19,806, the highest point during the entire war period. Some difficulty had been met in getting a sufficient labor supply, but the training programs proved quite effective. Labor-management relations were on the whole peaceful and there were no strikes in the plant.

To a considerable extent, the success of the management during this period was attributable to the fact that the plant expansion program had been largely completed by the end of 1916. It was also a tribute to the organizing ability and leadership of Otterson. Above all he had established himself as the active and aggressive head of the concern. During 1916 and early 1917, he had greatly improved and strengthened the internal administration of the Company. He set up a functional organization which gave a considerable amount of authority to heads of departments and at the same time made clear the lines of communication and authority. (For Otterson's theory of management, see Chapter Twenty-one.)

Several changes had occurred among key personnel in the production departments. William Thiel took over as gun superintendent in July 1917, George Watrous was made cartridge superintendent in November 1915 and about the same time Edwin Pugsley was appointed to a newly created post of manufacturing engineer, which brought under one head all the engineering work connected with the operation of the plant.

While it was the specter of idle plant facilities that prompted the management to take the risk in anticipating formal orders and contracts from the Government, the speed with which Winchester moved into production, in spite of the apparent lack of preparedness of the War Department, is a tribute to the drive of Otterson and his staff. As it turned out Otterson guessed well; the problem of interchangeability on the modified Enfield was solved without inordinate delay and the production of cartridges was resumed at a high rate with a minimum waste of effort.

*Browning Automatic Rifle*

The most dramatic test of the ability of the Winchester organization came in connection with the manufacture of the Browning automatic rifle. When the United States entered the war, the facilities for the production of automatic guns of the machine-gun type were embryonic. The French and British had placed small orders but were mainly dependent upon their own facilities. The Savage Arms Company was completing an order for 12,500 Lewis guns for the British; Marlin-Rockwell had been producing a large number of lever-type Colt machine guns for the Russians, and Colt's was tooling up in the spring of 1917 for the manufacture of Vickers guns.

A special board appointed by the Secretary of War was to select an automatic rifle. On May 1, 1917, it commenced testing the various types available. Among the guns submitted were models of "two newly developed weapons produced by the inventive genius of that veteran of small arms manufacture, John M. Browning." The simplicity of their design and their performance led the investigating board to describe them as "the most effective guns of their type known to the members." [14]

The decision of the board to adopt the Browning heavy machine gun and the Browning automatic rifle (as well as the Servis and Vickers guns) was complicated by the fact that neither of the Browning arms was yet ready for quantity production. The exclusive rights to the inventions were held by Colt's Patent Fire-

*Picture Taken in Chief Engineer's Office in 1918. Gun on Table Is First Model of BAR. Persons in Picture Reading from Left to Right Are: Kenneth Browning, Edwin Pugsley, Fred Werme (Standing) John Browning, Frank Burton, W. C. Roemer.*

arms Manufacturing Company, which was already heavily engaged in the production of the Vickers gun, whose output could not be interrupted. Colt's had, therefore, to plan to produce the Brownings at a new factory at Meriden, Connecticut. To prevent a restriction in the output, inevitable if one firm only were to undertake production, the U.S. Government acquired, in effect, Colt's rights for the duration of the emergency and then undertook a survey of available productive facilities. When this survey was completed in September 1917, orders were placed for various types of the Browning automatic gun, the Marlin-Rockwell Corporation getting an order for 20,000 automatic rifles. At the same time, Winchester was instructed "to begin its preliminary work" on the automatic rifle and in October 1917 received an order for 25,000.[15]

The instructions to proceed with the BAR were received on September 10, 1917, and on that date a group representing the Company, headed by Edwin Pugsley, went to Colt's to see the gun. It was discovered that there was only one model in existence, which Colt's could not spare during working hours, there were no drawings or models of that sample gun, nor was it exactly what the Government wanted.

Arrangements were made to borrow the gun over the following week-end and it was brought to New Haven from Hartford Saturday afternoon. By working until late Saturday night and all day Sunday the drafting department was able to start work on detailed drawings and the manufacturing engineers had their estimates of the needed special equipment and materials. The model was returned to Colt's early Monday morning and the Winchester staff went to work.

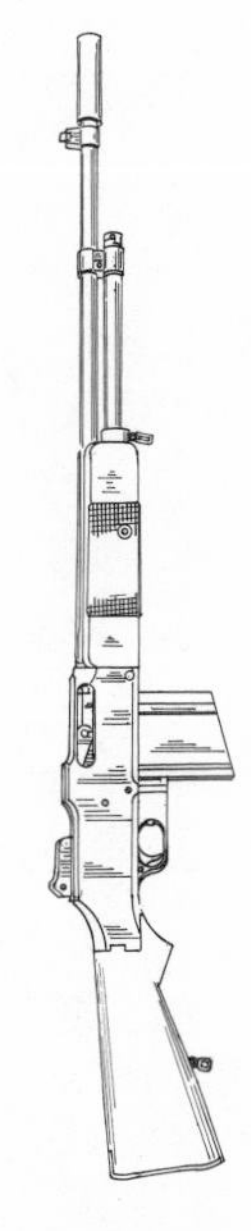

*The BAR*

On December 29, 1917, just three months and nineteen days from the date when the Company was instructed to proceed, the first gun, "produced eighty per cent on permanent equipment and twenty per cent on temporary equipment," was assembled. Two months later the Company was completely tooled up and began turning out guns for delivery to the War Department. By the first of May Winchester had turned out 1,200 Browning rifles a month ahead of Marlin-Rockwell whose first production came in June, and nearly two months ahead of Colt's. By the end of November 1918 some 52,238 guns had been produced, of which Winchester's share was around 27,000. (Winchester made an even better record in getting out the Browning caliber .50 machine gun. Getting the sample gun on Labor Day in 1918, a working model was assembled, tested, and sent to Aberdeen Proving Ground on November 11, the day the Armistice was signed. There the gun passed the Army tests, but as the war was over, it was not put into production by the Company.)

## *The Community Plan*

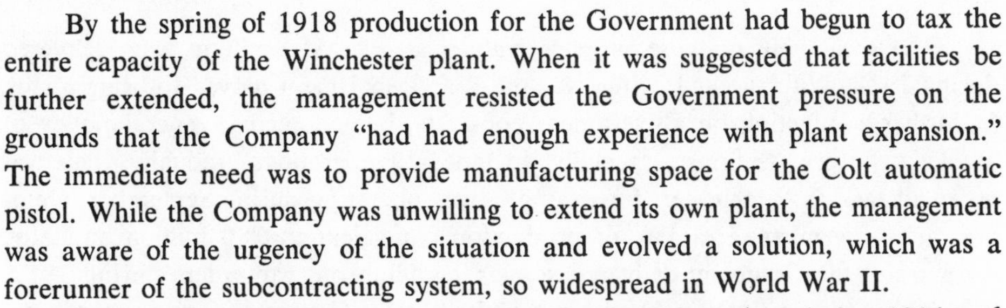

By the spring of 1918 production for the Government had begun to tax the entire capacity of the Winchester plant. When it was suggested that facilities be further extended, the management resisted the Government pressure on the grounds that the Company "had had enough experience with plant expansion." The immediate need was to provide manufacturing space for the Colt automatic pistol. While the Company was unwilling to extend its own plant, the management was aware of the urgency of the situation and evolved a solution, which was a forerunner of the subcontracting system, so widespread in World War II.

Winchester had itself been a subcontractor, in effect, when during 1914 and 1915 it undertook the production of shell cases and primers for the Bethlehem Steel Company and other producers of heavy ammunition for the Allied governments. It now proposed to apply this same principle to gun and ammunition production. According to Brewer: "We suggested to them another means by which we could get still further production . . . by using the facilities of other plants in our immediate neighborhood; . . . we would do part of the work in our own plant, that being generally the assembly work . . . the components [to be] made by other plants in New Haven that were then available and which had been previously engaged in war work, they to manufacture the components but under our supervision, we giving them our engineering assistance and experience in their construction and manufacture."

In the case of cartridges, the work was to have been subdivided, the outside plant manufacturing the cartridge shells and bullets, furnishing labor, materials, and buildings for this purpose, while Winchester would make the primers, perform the loading operation, assemble, test, and pack. As to pistols, Winchester would keep "the rather technical work" of barrel-making and would assemble the barrel with pistol parts made outside, and then would test the arms and pack them for delivery.

Five plants in New Haven were included in the plan, and supplementary contracts recognizing the increased cost involved were signed; but the coming of the Armistice prevented the testing of the efficiency of the plan by actual experience.

*Summary of Military Production*

Winchester's principal contributions to the American war effort during World War I, are shown in the following tabulations:

| | |
|---|---|
| Rifles, model 1917 (modified Enfield) | 545,511 |
| Bayonets, model 1917 | 458,689 |
| Browning automatic rifles (includes postwar production) | 47,123 |
| Riot guns (Models 97 and 12 shotguns) | 19,196 |
| Howitzer cartridge cases, 4.7-inch | 40,000 |
| Gun cartridge cases, 4.7-inch | 81,000 |
| Cartridge cases for antisubmarine guns, 4-inch, caliber .50 | 395,000 |
| Cannon primers, Mark X | 4,500,000 |
| Stokes 3-inch trench mortar shells | 3,062,000 |
| Tracer cartridges, caliber .30 | 840,000 |
| Tracer and incendiary cartridge components 4 items (sets) | 6,187,500 |
| High-pressure cartridges (for testing caliber .30) | 1,075,000 |
| Blanks, dummies, and primed shells, caliber .30 | 26,995,000 |
| Service cartridges, caliber .03-06 | 525,000,000 |
| Pistol cartridges, caliber .45 | 58,000,000 |
| Primers and caps | 344,151,000 |

The great bulk of these supplies, valued at over $50 million, was delivered during 1918. With the end of the war the War Department moved to bring a stop to further production on Government contracts, but adopted a general policy of allowing the private firms, especially, to taper off operations gradually. This was no small task as Winchester, for example, was operating during September, October, and November, at a rate of production equivalent to $80 million annually. As a result the Company delivered some $9 million on war orders during 1919, bringing its total war business with the United States Government to approximately $76 million.

*Nonmilitary Sales*

Beginning about the middle of 1917 and continuing until the fall of 1918, the Company had devoted nearly its entire effort to military production. The dollar volume of nonmilitary sales was maintained at quite high levels during 1917 and 1918, the total for the two years amounting to some $18 million. This was made possible in part by drawing on the accumulated inventories built up in the previous period and in part by a further rise in prices.

No data are available on the physical volume of cartridge sales, but the number of guns distributed during 1917 was 221,861, and 182,528 during 1918, compared with 293,113 in 1914. (*See Appendix D-1.*) Meanwhile, the prices on both guns and ammunition were further advanced. On guns the advance was around thirty-five per cent.

With the signing of the Armistice the Company was able to resume production of its regular line of guns and ammunition. These items found a ready market in late 1918 and 1919. Sales during the latter year totaled over $15.9 million, the largest dollar volume in the history of the Company. The total number of guns distributed in 1919 was 304,646, a figure which exceeded 1914 by some 11,-000. This record was achieved despite some further price increases on guns of around twenty per cent and twelve per cent on ammunition. By 1920 these increases, added to those already made brought the average prices of the Company's line of guns and ammunition to approximately double the 1914 figures.

*Financial Summary*

It was pointed out at the conclusion of the preceding chapter that, in April 1917, the Company was faced with the necessity of raising $16.84 million from outside sources; this being the measure of the financial problem attributable to the disappointing results from the Allied war business. In broad terms the expectation that the new plant expansion could be financed out of profits from that business had not been realized.

How far the Company was able to retrieve its position out of the contracts with the U.S. Government was impossible to determine as of November 11, 1918, because deliveries on those contracts continued for more than a year after that date. It is only by including the business done during 1919 with the war period that an approximate answer can be given to the question as to how near the goal was reached of financing a new plant out of war profits.

Up to the end of 1918 approximately $12.6 million had been expended on new buildings and equipment. An additional $1.40 million was spent in connection with the new products program introduced in 1919, discussed in Chapter Twenty-one. Originally the intention had been to pay for their expenditure out of the gross margin from the war contracts; the assumption was that the nonmilitary business could carry all other expenses. Judged by this standard alone, the plant expansion costs were more than covered from this source. As shown in Table III, total gross margin on the military business from January 1915 through April 1917 came to some $21.85 million.

TABLE III

PROFITS FROM OPERATIONS
(in millions)

| JANUARY 1, 1915 – APRIL 30, 1917 | | | |
|---|---|---|---|
| | *Government* | *Nonmilitary* | *Total* |
| Sales | $30.67 | $22.99 | $53.66 |
| Less: Estimated Cost of goods sold | 25.20 | 15.60 | 40.80 |
| Gross Margins | 5.47 | 7.39 | 12.86 |
| Less: Operating Costs [a] | 5.06 | 3.38 | 8.44 |
| Net Profits | .41 | 4.01 | 4.42 |
| **MAY 30, 1917 – DECEMBER 31, 1919** | | | |
| Sales | 75.34 | 34.00 | 109.34 |
| Less: Estimated Cost of goods sold | 58.96 | 24.08 | 83.04 |
| Gross Margins | 16.38 | 9.92 | 26.30 |
| Less: Operating Costs [a] | 10.29 | 4.40 | 14.69 |
| Net Profits: Before Taxes | 6.09 | 5.52 | 11.61 |

[a] Operating costs include selling and general expense, plant rearrangements, idle plant expense, depreciation and interest on borrowed funds.

In reality this approach is quite misleading as it ignores the effect on the financial position of the Company of the increases in operating costs more or less directly attributable to the war business; costs that should be deducted before any accurate measure of the profitability of the war business can be obtained.

If operating costs, apportioned according to sales to military and nonmilitary outlets, are charged against the gross margins, the net profits derived from the war business amounted to approximately $6.5 million. (*See Table IV.*) According to this calculation the Company failed by $6.1 million to recoup the costs of its plant expansion.

This approach, however, is probably misleading in the other direction. There is a question as to what percentage of operating costs should be charged against the war business. It is doubtful, for example, if the selling costs were as high for military orders as for nonmilitary business. Similarly, decisions regarding the proper allocation of depreciation and interest charges are not easy to make in a plant that is supplying two markets. For these reasons any specific figure on the correct amount of "war profits" would be arbitrary, although it would probably be considerably larger than the $6.5 million just noted.

Actually a much clearer picture of the general effects of the war upon the financial status of the Company can be obtained by an examination of the data on disposable funds and disbursements during the entire war period (shown in Table IV). While total net profits came to only $16.03 million, the accumulation of depreciation reserves amounted to $9.67 million, bringing the total disposable funds to $25.70 million. After providing for a write-down of inventories, total plant expansion (including $1.40 million in 1919), income taxes, dividends and other expenses, amounting to $18.97 million, there remained a net increase in funds in the business of $6.73 million. Furthermore, the Company had, as of December 31, 1919, some $4 million in working capital (other than inventories) in addition to the funds borrowed during 1919. This amount was probably sufficient to finance a volume of business equal, in physical terms, to that of prewar. This record suggests that the management had, in fact, been able to retrieve the Company's financial position between May 1, 1917, and December 31, 1919.

TABLE IV

DISPOSABLE FUNDS AND DISBURSEMENTS: 1915-19
(in millions)

| | | |
|---|---|---|
| Disposable Funds | | |
| Net Profits | $16.03 | |
| Accumulation of depreciation reserves | 9.67 | $25.70 |
| Application of Funds | | |
| Write-down of inventories | 1.25 | |
| Expansion of plant | 14.07 | |
| Income Taxes (1918-1919) | 3.14 | |
| Dividends | .51 | 18.97 |
| Net Increase of Funds in Business from Operations During War | | 6.73 |
| Net new money from Kidder, Peabody & Company (1919) [a] | 2.98 | |
| Less: Expenditures on new products (1919) | 1.40 | 1.58 |
| Net Addition to Work Capital | | 8.31 |

[a] Amount borrowed for new products program initiated during 1919.

It might be assumed that the officials were proud of this achievement and were looking forward with confidence to the postwar period. Actually, at the time of the Armistice, the attitude of the management regarding the future operations was distinctly pessimistic. A report from the Company's accountants, dated November 19, 1918, based on the September 30 balance sheet, indicated an immediate need for an additional $4 million, and a future need for an amount that could not be estimated "though it may run into a very large sum, probably many millions of dollars." These statements were largely based upon an assumption regarding peacetime operations, to be considered in the following chapter, and may have been made to obtain a serious consideration of a plan for reorganization. In any event, the implication regarding the immediate financial position of the Company was obvious. (One of the principal reasons for concern over Winchester's finances during late 1918 arose from uncertainty over the amount of federal income taxes the company might be called upon to pay. For the basis of this uncertainty, see p. 270.)

The balance sheet of December 31, 1918, as published, reflected this situation by showing a reserve of $8.9 million for taxes and contingencies and for meeting expenses arising out of the termination of the war. As a result of their allowance, the net unappropriated surplus was stated as $16.4 million, only $600,000 more than at January 1, 1915, and over $2 million less than the free surplus at April 30, 1917.

Another reason for pessimism arose from the full realization of the inadequacy of the initial planning in connection with the Company's wartime building program. Placing the new structures in among the old had made it easier to carry on expanded war production, but this arrangement made it exceedingly difficult to segregate the latter for sale or lease to new potential users. Nor was it possible, except in a few instances, to raze the old buildings, because a number of these structures contained special equipment, as in the case of the shot-shell loading room, which could not be changed without an inordinate expense. Thus, while the older buildings had been "written off" in respect to depreciation, they loomed as a potential financial drain because of taxes and upkeep, unless some way could be found to put them to use in the postwar period.

These considerations formed an important part of the background which affected the management's plans for a return to peacetime operations.

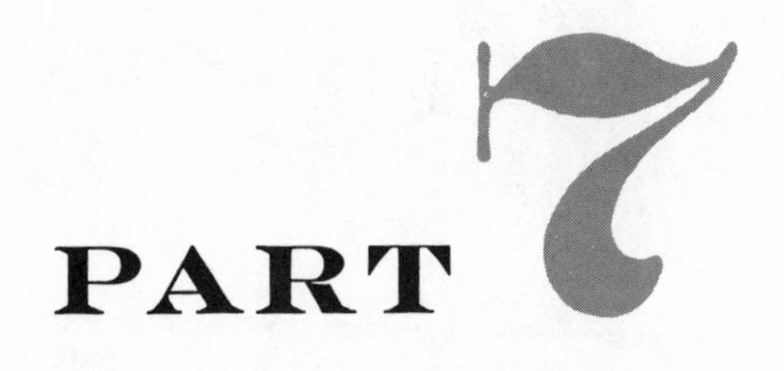


# POSTWAR EXPERIMENT: 1919-1924

CHAPTER TWENTY-ONE

# POSTWAR REORGANIZATION

*Planning for Peace*

Apparently the Winchester management, prior to 1918, had given a little thought to the future of the organization. According to Henry Brewer, who was vice president at the time: "Quite early during the first World War, Otterson remarked to me that when the war was over, our problems would be entirely changed. At the present moment our problem was one of production—we could sell everything that we could manufacture. However, as soon as the war was over, our problems would become one of sales and distribution, that we could produce more than we had distribution channels to get proof. Although Otterson foresaw this change and condition long before others in the Company, nothing was done seriously in the way of preparing for this change until the war was practically at its close."

Some further consideration may have been given to future operations early in 1918. The Company's notes, covering $16 million which had been borrowed in 1916 to provide funds for plant expansion, were due in March 1918. In January, T. G. Bennett and Otterson were appointed by the board of directors to make arrangements with Kidder, Peabody & Company for meeting this obligation. An agreement was made with the bankers to pay off half the loan out of current assets of the Company and to refinance the remaining $8 million by sale of one-year notes to Kidder, Peabody & Company. It is more than likely that prudent banking practice would cause Kidder, Peabody & Company to make some inquiry at this time about the Company's postwar plans. Even so, there was no particular pressure to develop an explicit program, Winchester having Government contracts that promised to realize highly satisfactory profits.

During the summer of 1918, the situation changed quite abruptly. On July 15 the Germans launched the last phase of their final offensive, known as the Second Battle of the Marne. Three days later the attack was played out and Foch launched a counteroffensive that marked the turning point of the war. Late in the same month, Otterson made a trip to Washington, in connection with the Company's war contracts. While in Washington, he sensed a change in the attitude of Government procurement officers which led him to believe that the end of the war was imminent. (R. E. Anderson, who accompanied Otterson on this trip, recalls that when he and Otterson boarded the train to return to New Haven, Otterson said, "Anderson, the war is over.")

This possibility completely changed the outlook for the future and made it necessary promptly to develop a more definite plan for the operation of the Com-

*The Winchester Plant in 1919*

pany in the postwar period. Immediately on his return from Washington, Otterson arranged for an informal meeting of the board of directors and told them of the impression he had gained in Washington.

During the next few weeks there followed what T. G. Bennett later described as: ". . . protracted negotiations which were initiated by himself and the officers of the . . . corporation in anticipation of the termination of the war contracts, which it was recognized would create a new situation in the Company's affairs."

This preliminary discussion of the postwar program was carried on unofficially and under conditions of great secrecy, but from the character of the plans which emerged and from later testimony it is clear that T. G. Bennett, John E. Otterson, Louis K. Liggett, and Charles E. Sargent were the principal participants.

The general outline was worked out with considerable speed, for at a special meeting of the board of directors, held on August 7, 1918, the secretary reported:

"The President announced the purpose of the meeting was to consider a plan for the refinancing of the company. The tentative plan submitted was approved and a committee composed of Thomas G. Bennett, John E. Otterson and James T. Moran was appointed to formulate and submit the same to the stockholders. Messrs. Sargent, Liggett, and Otterson, because of their interest in the plan, requested that they be recorded as not voting."

*Reorganization Plan*

By September 23, the committee was ready to submit its recommendations to the stockholders. Actual circulation of the plan was delayed until clearance was obtained from the capital issues committee. This was obtained, and on October 26, 1918, the following letter was mailed to the stockholders:

*To the Stockholders of the Winchester Repeating Arms Company:*

In the early days of the European War the Company entered into large contracts for arms and ammunition with certain foreign governments, notably the British Government, and greatly expanded its plant facilities for the purpose of these contracts. It became necessary to obtain loans upon the Company's notes to the extent of some $16,000,000. These loans have been reduced by repayments from time to time, so that at present the Company has outstanding notes payable of about $8,000,000. In addition the Company has other current liabilities aggregating over $9,000,000, of which $4,000,000 is an advance from the United States Government against Government contracts.

The Company's earnings prior to the war may be taken as an indication of the earning power of its commercial business. There seems little likelihood that the Company's normal commercial business can be materially increased after the war. The Company will, therefore, find itself with a large investment in plant facilities subject to taxation, insurance, depreciation, and interest, upon money invested therein, without existing business sufficient to carry these charges, and at the same time pay adequate dividends to the present stockholders.

It becomes necessary, therefore, to divert the plant facilities in substantial degree to the manufacture of articles other than those previously manufactured, involving the rearrangement of the existing machinery, and the purchase and installation of machinery suited to the new purposes.

In addition to making provision for the manufacture of new products, it will be necessary to make arrangements for their sale and distribution involving expenditures for sales promotion and advertising. It will require time and money to develop these new manufacturing and sales facilities. The present stockholders who have not received dividends for some time face a further deferring of their dividends by reason of the necessity of devoting the Company's earnings to the purpose of this new development. This seems inevitable unless additional funds are obtained.

The Company has heretofore borrowed on short-term notes, and still has $8,000,000 of these notes outstanding. These notes mature March, 1919, and it is expected that a portion of them will be retired out of the Company's earnings and surplus; but to insure the payment of the remainder of the notes, and at the same time provide working capital for the development outlined above, it is desirable that there should be invested in the business a large additional sum in cash, and that there be associated with the Company's management a strong financial interest.

In order to insure a development of the Company's business in the broad and extended sense necessary for its success, it is necessary to provide an aggressive executive management, and to have associated with that management business and commercial connections that make available to it the counsel and experience of other large business developments.

It will be appreciated that this undertaking on the development side is of necessity somewhat speculative, and the profits accruing therefrom depend entirely upon its successful conduct. It is desirable to find a method for accomplishing these things that will relieve the present stockholders of the hazards of this undertaking, and at the same time offer them the opportunity of a restoration of dividends indicated by the Company's previous experience.

To this end the management has conferred with Messrs. Kidder, Peabody and Company, who have heretofore arranged the Company's loans, and otherwise assisted in the Company's financial arrangements in connection with this matter, and to form such syndicate as may be necessary for its proper handling, provided Mr. J. E. Otterson, 1st Vice-President and General Manager for the Company, will continue in active management of the Company's business, and Mr. Louis K. Liggett, President of the United Drug Company, will associate himself with the undertaking and provided the present stockholders indicated their approval by deposit of their stock. These things Mr. Otterson and Mr. Liggett have on their part consented to do, and Messrs. Kidder, Peabody and Company, Otterson and Liggett will become, therefore, associately interested in the Company's future development.

The Board of Directors of the Company has given consideration to these matters, and on August 7, 1918, appointed a committee to formulate and perfect a plan for making these developments possible, and to submit the same to the stockholders. The committee has prepared such a plan, and presents it for your approval.

THE PLAN IS AS FOLLOWS:

It is proposed to organize a new company of substantially the same name as the present company to take over the property and business of the latter through the medium of a purchasing intermediary or otherwise; the original issue of capital stock of this new company to be $10,000,000 of seven per cent cumulative first preferred stock, $2,000,000 of six per cent non-cumulative second preferred stock, and $1,000,000 of common stock; all of this stock to be issued as fully paid for the assets of the present company, subject to its liabilities, and the sum of $3,500,000, in cash, which is to be contributed as new capital.

The first preferred stock will be preferred both as to assets and cumulative dividends, and will be redeemable in whole or in part at $115 per share. The Company will agree that no mortgage or other indebtedness maturing later than one year after being incurred shall be created by it without the consent of two-thirds in amount of the outstanding first preferred stock. Dividends on the first preferred stock will be made payable in equal semi-annual installments.

The original issue of common stock alone will have voting powers, except that if the full cumulative dividends on the first preferred stock be unpaid and shall have at any time accumulated in excess of seven per cent, the first preferred stock shall have full voting powers except as to the redemption of the said first preferred stock. Under the plan, $7,500,000 par value of the first preferred stock of the new company will be delivered to the stockholders of the present company in exchange for their stock in the latter. That is, each stockholder of the present company will be entitled to receive for each share of stock now held by him seven and one half (7½) shares of the new first preferred stock of the par value of $100 each.

The balance of the original issue of stock of the new company, namely, $2,500,000 of first preferred stock, $2,000,000 of non-cumulative 6% second preferred stock, and $1,000,000 of common stock will be delivered to Kidder, Peabody and Company and their associates upon completion of the arrangements for the contribution of $3,500,000 of new capital in cash as above stated.



The committee appointed by the directors has been informed by Kidder, Peabody and Company that it is expected that the annual 7% dividend on the first preferred stock will be paid regularly to the plan, and has been deposited.

In order to put the plan into effect provision has been made for the deposit of the stock of the present stockholders of the Winchester Repeating Arms Company with The Union and New Haven Trust Company of New Haven, Conn. on or before the 15th of November, 1918, under a deposit agreement, copies of which may be obtained from the Trust Company. A majority of the outstanding stock has already assented.

We believe that if the plan is adopted the outstanding indebtedness will be taken care of and better provision made for future prospects, and that the stockholders will begin at once to receive regular dividends from the payment of the contemplated dividends on the new first preferred stock; whereas, in the absence of some such plan the financial situation of the Company will be exceedingly unsatisfactory, and for a long time to come it is doubtful if the stockholders would receive any dividends as the earnings of the Company should be used in the business.

On behalf of the Board of Directors, therefore, we strongly recommend the deposit of stock under the proposed plan.

In view of the fact that Mr. Sargent is a member of the firm of Kidder, Peabody & Company, and that Mr. Liggett and Mr. Otterson will be associated with Kidder, Peabody & Company in this plan, these gentlemen although Directors of your Company, have taken no part in the above recommendation.

The consummation of this plan is subject to the approval of the Capital Issues Committee.

THOMAS G. BENNETT JAMES T. MORAN
GEORGE E. HODSON *Committee.*

To the stockholders who had no part in the preliminary discussion, this plan must have come as a bomb shell. It is true that they had been without dividends since 1915, a circumstance which could be justified by the uncertainties of war financing and especially by the need for enormous inventories. They had, however, at their last annual meeting in February 1918, been assured of the Board's concern for improving the liquid position of the Company and, indeed, were given evidence of a successful program in this direction. They had received no warning that a year which promised a higher turnover of business would include a proposition for refinancing the Company as drastic as that now contemplated. They were now faced with an ultimatum: First, it was suggested that the Company had a necessity to expand its peacetime production into lines other than guns and ammunition, although the specific products were not indicated. Second, the implication was clear that Winchester did not have resources to meet the liability of $8 million due in March 1919, to say nothing of paying the expenses of reconversion and the development of new products. Third, it was proposed to turn the financial control of the organization over to Kidder, Peabody & Company at a rate of $750 per share in new preferred stock for each share of old stock in return for the investment of additional capital of $3.5 million and an arrangement under which Otterson and Liggett would take over the management. Finally the stockholders were presented with a very limited choice: they could accept, with the possibility of getting immediate and regular dividends on their preferred stock; they could refuse, and face the possibility of deferred dividends and the necessity of raising additional capital.

The financial status of the Company implied in the letter was particularly astonishing. The balance sheet as of December 31, 1917, which was circulated to the stockholders, had shown the book value of the concern to be $18 million, or

$1,800 per share. According to the same statement the Company, in addition to its regular commercial business, held United States Government contracts to the value of over $50 million largely on a cost-and-percentage basis. It is a small wonder that a number of the stockholders were unwilling to accept the statement that the Company could not finance its postwar needs and in order to raise the needed capital it was necessary to turn over the stock to Kidder, Peabody & Company at a rate of $750 per share.

The reorganization plan emerged as a consequence of the wartime introduction into the Winchester organization of a number of new interests. That it was designed, apparently, to satisfy their claims upon the future of the Company will be apparent from an examination of the personalities involved, their relations with the Company and the circumstances surrounding the discussions.

*Otterson*

Otterson, the logical candidate to carry on the management of the Winchester organization, was naturally interested in a plan which would provide an expanding outlet for his capacity. Since 1916, he had been the active head of the organization. His contribution to the success of the Company during the latter part of the war had placed him high in the esteem of T. G. Bennett and had given him a considerable reputation as a business executive. By 1918, at the age of thirty-seven, he was vice president and general manager and a member of the board of directors. Greater opportunities were opened up to him, however, with the proposed reorganization. Under this plan, he was scheduled to take over the presidency of a well-known company which was about to embark on an expansion program that promised him wide chances for financial reward and enhanced prestige.

*Liggett*

Louis K. Liggett was a newcomer to the Winchester organization, having been elected to the board of directors in January 1918. His election seems to have been originally sponsored by Robert Winsor, president of Kidder, Peabody & Company. Liggett had been associated with Winsor in several projects prior to 1918. The latter was apparently impressed with Liggett's success in the drug field and suggested his name as someone who could strengthen the merchandising side of the business. This suggestion appealed to Otterson who also felt that the marketing organization of the Company needed strengthening.

The reasons for Liggett's interest in the reorganization plan are somewhat obscure. In 1918 his success in establishing the United Drug Company and the Liggett chain of drug stores had already placed him in the top bracket of American merchandisers. At no time during his subsequent association with the Winchester organization, however, did he have any substantial financial interest in the concern.

The best explanation of Liggett's role appears to be that he enjoyed being associated with a well-known concern and liked to collect directorships. According to his own account he was, in 1918, "President and a director of the United Drug Company, Chairman of the Board of Directors of the Louis K. Liggett Company, a director of the John Hancock Mutual Life Insurance Company, President of the United Mutual Fire Insurance Company, Chairman of the Board of Directors of the United Jewelers, Inc., a director of the National Shawmut Bank of Boston, and was at one time President of the Boston Chamber of Commerce. . . . [he] is

*John Edward Otterson*

also a director in sundry other companies. For many years . . . [he] has had extensive experience in manufacturing and financial matters."

This propensity of Liggett is demonstrated by the condition he is said to have laid down at the time he became a member of the Winchester board. His agreement, in essence, was that he would give the management a six-month trial. If during that time he became convinced that it was a live, progressive organization he would remain; otherwise he would withdraw his association.

Once elected to the board of directors, Liggett entered into the job with characteristic enthusiasm. He afterward reviewed his own activities during this period: "Since deponent [Liggett] became a director he had attended practically all of the meetings of the Board of Directors. He had given special study to the business and affairs of the defendant company and in connection therewith has inspected the factory and manufacturing facilities, and has met and conferred with the officers of the Company, and with many of the executive heads. Deponent has also spent considerable time in studying, discussing and conferring upon the various plans and policies of the Company, both in the meeting of the Board of Directors and in conferences with the executives." (The records show that Liggett attended eight of the ten board meetings held between February and October 1918.)

Liggett was a consummate salesman with great ability to persuade his associates of the merits of his proposals. That part of the reorganization plan which emphasized the necessity of a postwar expansion and a new marketing program show most clearly the Liggett influence. It was the prospect of such an expansion that seems to have convinced him that Winchester would be a live, progressive concern, the kind with which he liked to be prominently associated.

*Kidder, Peabody & Company*

(It should be explained here that, except for the name, the Kidder, Peabody & Company of today has no connection with the banking house which was operating during the 1920s. The older organization failed in 1931, and a group of men, none of whom had been associated with the former company, organized the present firm.)

Kidder, Peabody & Company's representative in the formulation of the reorganization plan was Charles E. Sargent, Jr., a member of the firm who had been a director of the Winchester Repeating Arms Company since 1916. His election had come at the time when the Company borrowed $16 million through Kidder, Peabody & Company for financing its wartime expansion, and he had acted as financial counsel during the succeeding years.

In 1918 Kidder, Peabody & Company ranked among the top investment banking houses in the United States. Its long-established reputation was based on conservative investment-banking practices which had been carried on for several generations of management. After the end of World War I, Kidder, Peabody & Company apparently became interested in acquiring ownership interests in various organizations that offered attractive earning possibilities.

The only available account of the way Kidder, Peabody & Company became interested in the reorganization plan was brought out by Liggett when the program was being defended in court by the officials of the Company. According to his statement he learned, sometime in the spring of 1918, ". . . that the management had from time to time conferred with Messrs. Kidder, Peabody & Company, as regards possible future financing and development, but conditions were such at the time that Kidder, Peabody and Company, had not yet committed themselves to participation in any plan. In the meantime deponent [Liggett] had frequent discussions with the management in an effort to form his own ideas as to the proper future development of the business, and finally discussed the matter with Mr. Sargent, representing Kidder, Peabody & Company, following a directors' meeting pointing out to Mr. Sargent that future success in the undertaking depended upon development of the management and organization, and of products and business outside of those at present being manufactured by the Company. Mr. Sargent was somewhat in doubt as to whether the firm of Kidder, Peabody & Company was interested in the future development of the Company, and said in effect that they would not be interested unless they could be assured of a competent and adequate management capable of developing and putting through a sound plan. He asked deponent if he would be willing to associate himself with the future undertaking and deponent told him that he would upon the assumption the Company should continue its present active management, and he then told deponent that he would take it up with his firm upon that understanding. In the course of a few days he reported that his firm was ready to go forward accordingly. It was further understood that Mr. Sargent in the name of his firm and their associates would then take the matter up with Mr. Bennett and inform him that they were prepared to go forward in accordance with the suggestions theretofore made by Mr. Bennett to Kidder, Peabody & Company."

This sequence of events is confirmed by T. G. Bennett, who told of ". . . informal conferences between the directors and officers of [Winchester] which led to the suggestion that this matter be taken up with Messrs. Kidder, Peabody & Company. The initial step in this matter was taken by Winchester and not by Kidder, Peabody & Company, and it was only after considerable negotiations and numerous conferences that Kidder, Peabody & Company agreed to look into the matter to take it up on their own account."

When it seemed necessary to secure extra capital, the Company, according to Bennett ". . . turned naturally to Kidder, Peabody & Company . . . in view of their past services and the relations between Kidder, Peabody & Company and Winchester." Referring to the war period he continued: "At all times Kidder, Peabody & Company have been most helpful and co-operative in their support, financial or otherwise, and [Winchester] in large measure owes its present favorable condition thereto, and without such support it is highly probable that [the Company] would have suffered serious financial difficulties."

The attraction of the reorganization plan for Kidder, Peabody & Company lay in the fact that in exchange for \$3.5 million, they would receive \$2.5 million par value first preferred stock, \$2 million par value second preferred stock, and all of the voting common stock with a par value of \$1 million. This gave the bankers an attractive set of securities for marketing purposes. The first preferred stock was marketable at least at par, which should return \$2.5 million, and a second preferred stock could be expected to yield a minimum of fifty per cent of the par value as a speculation, which would make up the rest of the sum to be advanced under the reorganization plan. All or a majority of the common stock could, under this procedure, remain in the hands of Kidder, Peabody & Company, which would ensure its financial control of Winchester and a management of its own choosing. The principal risk was that the future earnings of the Company would not be sufficient to pay dividends on the preferred securities. Such a failure could discredit the banking house with its customers and weaken its general reputation.

*Majority Stockholders: The Winchester and Bennett Families*

No plan for reorganization could have been carried through without the consent of the principal stockholders—Mrs. T. G. Bennett and Mrs. William Wirt Winchester—who between them still held over fifty per cent of the stock. In general they followed the advice of T. G. Bennett who was convinced of the necessity of the changes proposed by the reorganization plan.

One important consideration involved management. A member of the family had been the active head of the business since Oliver F. Winchester formed the New Haven Arms Company in 1856; now, in 1918, there was no one of this group who appeared capable of bearing this responsibility in the future. T. G. Bennett had reached his seventy-third birthday on March 22, 1918. Since 1916, he had been trying to give up his share in the management. His son, Winchester Bennett, was still in ill health brought on by his exertion during the war. Furthermore, the latter's training had been largely technical and confined to the production side of the business. It was doubtful if he could assume the responsibility for carrying out the type of program which was contemplated for the postwar period.

T. G. Bennett had been willing to sell the business during 1915 or 1916, but as he explained in a letter to a stockholder: "During the time of the speculation at the beginning of the war, I attempted to get a price which could be offered to all the stockholders, but found nobody who could offer as much as $700.00 a share. I would say that having been with the concern since 1870, I shall be obliged to quit. My son has lost his health carrying on this business and will, therefore, not be able to work for a considerable period."

T. G. Bennett's attitude toward the reorganization plan and the arguments he used to convince the other members of the families of its merits are best brought out in the correspondence between him and Mrs. William Wirt [Sarah] Winchester through her lawyer, S. F. Leib, of San Jose, California, where she was then living. Her decision followed Mr. Leib's advice.

Sometime about the middle of September, T. G. Bennett addressed a letter to Leib, outlining the proposed reorganization plan. (Unfortunately no copy of this letter has been preserved in the Company's records.) The latter replied on September 23, 1918:

Mr. Hooper submitted to me the last annual statements of the assets and liabilities of the Company. From that statement it appears, that, even after leaving out of view the value of good will of the Company, the actual net assets after the payment of all liabilities, would be something over twenty million dollars. The present owners would, by this new arrangement, receive paid up stock for only seven and one-half million dollars; but, after considering all the matter connected with it, including your statement that you did not think it wise for the family longer to keep control of the Company, owing to the fact of the advancing age of yourself and if the old stockholders and their rights as to the new preferred stock to be issued to them could be, and would be fully protected against any possible misadventure, and also considering the peace of mind and quiet which those who are part of the Winchester family are entitled to enjoy during the latter part of their lives, it would be best to advise, and have advised my client to consent to the proposed arrangement.

The question still remains as to whether the old stockholders, who are parting with their property at so much less than its value, can be absolutely protected against any future loss or trouble; in other words, whether they will be protected in receiving what they do receive without the danger of possible future diminution of the value thereof, and without future trouble to themselves after having entered into the contemplated transaction; and it is to this one question I am giving my attention.

On October 2, Bennett answered Leib:

I wish to say, first, that I feel it is very fortunate for Mrs. Winchester that she has your advice in this matter, as I hesitate to commit her property, under the circumstances in which she finds herself, without counsel other than her own.

In the matter of the suggestion that the consideration for the old stock is not as great as it should be, I desire to say that in addition to the stock consideration we get new stockholders of great ability financially and in business matters, and they are tied to the interests by the investment of money as related. I could have obtained in paper a much larger sum, but I could not have got the other engagements, which are the real compensation, a large part of it, for the change in ownership. You will realize, as in the case of an irrigation ditch, with deep banks and high fillings with cement and steel, while the water runs and the land is irrigated, the building is of value, but as soon as the water stops and there remains only the cement and embankments and fillings, the ditch is of no value to its owners, and is a target only to the tax-gatherer. A good deal of the property concerned in this transaction is in that condition. It will be valuable if business is found for it and skillful management goes along with this. I believe that in addition to the new money put into the business we shall have men qualified and interested by reason of that money. It is repetition to say that the immense buildings which have been forced by this present business will be a burden to the Company and the stockholders, unless by active management we can put them into paying operation. Since the first of the year I have seen immense sums of money flow through our particular ditch. Very little of it has been gathered to us, and so much as we hope to obtain is liable to the excessive taxation now existing and soon coming in additional severity.

Leib continued to be somewhat concerned as to the adequacy of the protection which the plan gave to his client's interests. In a subsequent letter on February 3, 1919, he again raised the question of ". . . the wisdom of making this contemplated sale [to Kidder-Peabody] at all; especially is this so in view of the fact that there is being sold what the books show to be twenty million dollars after all indebtedness is paid, for the sum of $7,500,000 of stock in other words for only three-eighths of its apparent value. It seems to me, that it is possibly worth considering whether *after all* it might not be the best plan to run the business ourselves; or if we cannot go on running the plant profitably, then to go into voluntary liquidation."

To these suggestions Bennett replied on February 10:

The book value is not the selling value of the assets shown and it seems to me that the bargain is a good one, even in case of dissolution. The larger part of the $20,000,000 of which you speak is in buildings, unusable at the present time for any purpose of our own and so intermingled with our own plant that it will be difficult to sell them except to our disadvantage. We would actually be better off today if we did not have them. Each year they must pay the local taxes of 2%. They are largely a burden rather than an asset. Probably, there are in the State of Connecticut, aside from what we have, 100 acres of such floor space which will be vacant. It is useless to think that this company is rich by reason of this real estate.

Generally, I feel that the bargain is a good one and all of us here who are knowing to the matter are of the same opinion.

When you speak of running the plant by ourselves, if the "ourselves" includes myself I would say that it is impossible in my opinion. We must have adequate management to take hold of a corporation without funds—that the management would be obliged to begin borrowing forthwith. Under the plan which I have advocated we get a strong management.

I think I have written you before that Messrs. Kidder, Peabody & Company have been with us now for years, have attended all our directors meetings through their representative, Mr. Sargent, and are a mainstay.

Bennett's letters to Leib show the importance he attached to expanding postwar production into new lines to utilize the Company's excess facilities and to procure new management and the investment of additional capital.

One feature of the reorganization plan that especially appealed to the principal stockholders was the provisions whereby the holders of the old common stock could retain a financial interest in the new concern without having to make any further investment. Bennett insisted on this latter requirement on a number of occasions; he testified in March 1919, for example, that he "and the interests he represents were unwilling [in 1918] to furnish any additional capital for the operation of [Winchester]." This position is confirmed by correspondence with Mrs. William Wirt Winchester, who stated through Leib that, "Whatever happens she absolutely cannot put any more money into the concern."

Furthermore, the return on the preferred stock of the new company to be exchanged for Winchester Repeating Arms Company common promised to restore the prewar dividend rate. During the period immediately preceding 1914, dividends had averaged around $50 per share. If things went according to plan, the $750 par value, seven per cent preferred stock of the new concern exchangeable for each share of old stock would return $52.50 per annum. In addition the holders of this new stock would be placed in a preferential position in respect to earnings, and should dividends amounting to 7 per cent accumulate and not be paid, voting control would revert to the preferred stockholders.

*Minority Stockholders*

While the majority group had an opportunity to weigh the merits of the reorganization plan in the light of detailed information available only to the officers, the minority stockholders, not represented in the discussions that went on among the officials prior to October 1918, were not. They were called upon to accept or reject a plan that could be evaluated only on a basis of the information laid before them in the letter recommending the reorganization program. Whether the plan involved a large or small financial sacrifice by the stockholders depended upon the validity of several of the statements and implications contained in the letter. More specifically, the issues may be stated as follows. First, how imperative was it for the Company to expand its peacetime production beyond the gun and ammunition lines? Second, what would be the result of applying an unknown sum to the development of undefined products? Third, what was the real financial status of Winchester in 1918, and what were its future earning prospects? Fourth, was the business so unprofitable in 1918 that the Company was in a worse financial position than it appeared to be at the end of 1917? And finally, was it possible for the Company to finance the immediate postwar needs out of its own resources or by temporary borrowing without bringing in outside capital and control?

The information in the letter to the stockholders was much too vague and general to give a basis for any analysis of these questions. It was not until the officials of the Company were faced with an injunction proceeding that more detailed information was made available. Before considering this material it is necessary to trace the events that occurred between the submission of the plan to the stockholders and the initiation of injunction proceedings.

Prior to the circulation of the letter to the stockholders in October, some effort had been made quietly to persuade various minority holders to agree to the plan. By the middle of October, owners of over 6,000 shares of stock, including approximately 5,800 shares owned by the Winchester and Bennett families, had agreed to deposit their stock with the committee. The rest of the shares were held by some 350 stockholders. To carry out the original idea of having one hundred per cent of the stock of the Winchester Repeating Arms Company exchanged for preferred stock in the new concern, all of this group would have to be persuaded of the merits of the reorganization plan.

The initial reaction on the part of the minority stockholders to the announcement of the plan varied widely. A fairly high percentage was willing to accept the judgment of the officials; but a considerable number registered protest against the plan. The following letter from George W. Gale to T. G. Bennett, dated October 27, 1918, indicates the general feeling of this latter group:

It is with a great shock I learn from the columns of the "New York Tribune," of the proposed financial plans of our Company, and that a majority of the holders of the stock now outstanding has already assented to the plan. The details of the plan, of which this announcement is the first intimation I have received, are iniquitous in the extreme if the newspaper is correctly informed and I hereby serve formal notice that I shall at once instruct my attorney to apply for an injunction restraining the "Committee" from presuming to further represent the stockholders, until I shall have had opportunity to communicate with the minority stockholders and call their attention to the wretched manner in which their interests are being sacrificed in the proposed "Reorganization."

I respectfully request that you at once send me a list, complete, of our present stockholders, and the number of shares standing in the name of each.

Let me remind you that the plan, as outlined in the "Tribune," proposes to turn over to a syndicate, headed by a banking firm of which one of the members is a director in our Company, assets having a book value of $20,000,000, and a good will worth as much more, for $7,500,000 of seven per cent "First Preferred Stock," with the implied threat if this is not effected "stockholders will have to face a further deferring of dividends."

The fact that this serious action on the part of a small "Committee" has been taken without communication with each and every stockholder is an indication of the nature of the deal.

Your prompt response to my request for a list of all stockholders is respectfully asked.

Probably the most vigorous objections came from stockholders who had bought stock at high prices between 1914 and 1917. For example, Samuel Weil wrote to Bennett on October 29, 1918:

> I am the holder of 10 shares of stock in your company which I bought in 1915, at considerably over $2000 per share. I was told at that time, upon good authority, that the book value of this stock was $3700 per share.
>
> I am in receipt of stockholders' agreement, which if consummated on the terms as proposed in the agreement, will realize about one-fifth of the book value at that time. In order that I may be able to judge what is best for me to do, I kindly request you to forward me a balance sheet as to the financial standing of this company at this time, to which I think I am entitled.

Bennett's answer to Weil, dated October 30, 1918, indicates his general response to such letters:

> Your favor of the 29th instant is received and contents noted. We regret that you paid so much for your stock and are sorry that you did not look further for information when you were told that the stock had a book value of $3700.00. It never had this book value.
>
> Earning capacity considered, the bargain which is offered by our proposed reorganization is a good one. Book values do not always represent earning capacity and that is the trouble in this case. We have assets which, after the war, will have little value unless we can find business which will occupy their facilities.
>
> I will send you a balance sheet shortly. If you could come up here we would be glad to talk this matter over with you and we feel sure that we could convince you and that you would deposit your stock with the rest.

Several stockholders expressed a wish to share in the common-stock holdings of the new company. To meet this type of request a revision of the original plan was presented on December 3, 1918, by Kidder, Peabody & Company, offering two proposals. Under the first, a depositing stockholder could exchange one and a half shares of new first preferred stock with Kidder, Peabody & Company for one share of new common stock. Under the alternative option, for each share of old common stock deposited, a stockholder was entitled to a right to purchase from Kidder, Peabody & Company two and a half shares of new first preferred stock, one share of new second preferred stock, and one share of new common stock at a total cost of $350.

The foregoing offer, plus the continued efforts by the officials of the Company, brought most of the remaining stockholders into the plan and by the early part of 1919, approximately ninety-seven per cent of the stock had been deposited.

*Threat of Injunction*

There still remained a few stockholders who refused to accept the proposed reorganization. This group was headed by Elmer W. Demarest, a lawyer of Jersey City, New Jersey, and represented an interest of 38 shares. Beginning in October 1918, he entered into a prolonged discussion of the plan in letters and in conferences with officials of Winchester. It became increasingly apparent that he was not going to be satisfied with the original proposal and that he might bring the matter to court.



The officials of the Company did not underestimate the seriousness of the threat that Demarest represented to the completion of the reorganization plans. The original agreement with the stockholders terminated automatically on July 1, 1919, if reorganization had not been accomplished by that date. There was an understandable anxiety to get matters settled especially after the end of the war on November 11, 1918. Failure to quiet Demarest's demands might also cause other stockholders to reconsider their decision.

Out of the correspondence with Demarest and the testimony taken in connection with the legal case, parts of which have already been cited, the officials gave somewhat more explicit information as to why they favored the proposed reorganization. Even so, much of the material deals in quite general terms with certain aspects of the program. This was especially true when it came to proving that the Company did not have the resources to meet the expenses which would have to be met immediately at the end of the war, and therefore capital had to be borrowed from outside sources.

Two documents submitted to the court by the Winchester officials contain the principal arguments used in this connection. One was a memorandum, a copy of which had been sent to Demarest on November 5, 1918, and the balance sheet as of June 30, 1918. (*See Appendix G-7.*) The memorandum reviewed the general financial needs and future earning possibilities of the Company and gave particular attention to an interpretation of the items in the balance sheet. According to the memorandum:

> The financial problem confronting the Company is twofold: It involves first, the provision of funds to care for its immediate financial needs as represented by the notes maturing March 1, 1919, for which purpose it is estimated that there will be required from $3,000,000 to $4,000,000 beyond existing resources.
>
> It involves, further, the provision of funds for future business developments necessary for the utilization of excessive plant and requiring expenditures for the rearrangement of existing facilities, the provision of additional facilities to supplement and balance those existing, and the development of a manufacturing and sales organization and the conduct of extensive sales and advertising campaigns.

No attempt was made to estimate the financial outlay necessary to expand the Company's postwar business. The main impression was that expenses would be large. The costs of rearranging old machinery and purchasing new equipment were estimated at a figure between $3 million and $6 million. Beyond this, according to the memorandum there would be ". . . expense and time necessary for the development of these new products, requiring experimentation, research and the development of an organization for their manufacture. In addition, good will must be created or purchased in connection with these products and a sales organization and channels of distribution developed for their disposal, involving expenditures on account of advertising and sales effort. Under the highly competitive conditions that will probably obtain after the war, the difficulties and expense incident to this undertaking will be appreciated."

Securing these funds was to be left to the future: "It seems undesirable to make financial provision for these future expenditures and developments at present and they are accordingly not provided for in the immediate plans, but are contemplated as obligations which will require to be met as they develop. The new financial management has this fact in mind and realizes that before the present plant can be profitable, additional funds will require to be provided and an operating plan having reasonable promise of success must be developed."

The balance sheet that accompanied the memorandum (*see Appendix G-7*) at first glance did not appear to support the arguments just noted. In fact a cursory examination seems to confirm the allegations of those who were protesting that Kidder, Peabody & Company was getting a bargain. The net worth of the Winchester Repeating Arms Company according to the statement was about $22 million. Even more significant for the immediate financial needs was the fact that current assets exceeded current liabilities by almost $15 million. If the notes payable of $8 million are deducted from this figure, which would be reasonable, there would be almost $7 million to meet expenses that might arise in the near future.

According to the memorandum, however, the balance sheet was not an accurate picture of the Company's financial condition. The reasons may be summarized as follows: (1) Heavy borrowing had been undertaken during the war because of total absorption of the current assets into the war-contract business. (2) Because of increasingly heavy Government taxes on profits, the operations under the United States contracts would not provide funds adequate to liquidate the balance of the Company's notes. (3) Over $8 million (at depreciated values) of the Company's building and plant had no usefulness in the "normal" business of the Company and could only be "valorized" as the result of an expansion program. (4) About $10 million of the inventory was of such character as to be realizable only over considerable time and as the result of further expenditure of funds to complete their manufacture.

The memorandum thus indicated that the actual position of the Company was less favorable than that shown in the June 30, 1918, balance sheet to the extent of $10 million of working capital and $8 million of fixed assets: an apparent net worth of $2,100 a share, disclosed in the balance sheet became a mere $300 a share at current liquidation values. At the same time and more urgently, an apparent deficit in working capital account meant that the Company could not expect to meet its liabilities as they fell due unless it obtained an immediate infusion of $3.5 million of new money; and notice was given of a program of expansion which would require an unspecified amount of new capital to procure the rights to new processes, to install them, to develop and, finally, to market the output.

The defense in the Demarest action was drawn for the purpose of pressing the plan for reorganization to its consummation rather than fully to disclose the Company's position to the minority stockholders. This is evident from a comparison of the June balance sheet, as modified by the memorandum, with three subsequent balance sheets which are on the record and of which two were available to some or all of the parties to the action during the proceedings. The first balance sheet, dated September 30, 1918, was prepared by Arthur Young & Company at the request of the directors as the basis for an appraisal of the probable postwar position submitted to the board in November 1918. The second balance sheet, that for December 31, 1918, was included in the annual report to the stockholders laid before the annual meeting held on February 18, 1919. In this full advantage was taken of the uncertainties in the tax situation discussed more fully below, although some closer estimate of the true liability was probably already available at that time.

The third balance sheet, also dated December 31, 1918, was prepared on May 31, 1918, and incorporated recommendations made by Arthur Young & Company in their report in November 1918, and represented fair-going concern values which were subsequently used by the Company for comparative purposes. This final revision of the December 1918 balance sheet also reflected the tax liability as determined, at least provisionally, by the return filed in March 1919. (It should be noted that for some years there was the possibility of a further liability arising out of the disallowance of certain tax deductions claimed by the Company. This, however, was held to be covered by a contingency reserve established on the revision of the balance sheet.)

A comparison of these balance sheets is presented in the following tabulation:

COMPARATIVE BALANCE SHEETS, 1918
(in millions of dollars)

| | June 30 [a] | Sept. 30 [b] | Dec. 31 [c] | Dec. 31 [d] (revised) |
|---|---|---|---|---|
| Current Assets | | | | |
| less | | | | |
| Current Liabilities | 4.8 | 14.3 | 15.3 | 18.1 |
| Less | | | | |
| Notes due Mar. 1, 1919 | 8.0 | 8.0 | 6.6 | 6.6 |
| Net Working Capital | 3.2 (deficit) | 6.3 | 8.7 | 11.5 |
| Net Worth (including appropriated surplus) | $3.7 | $19.5 | $20.3 | $21.1 |

[a] As modified by memorandum dated in Demarest Action.
[b] Incorporating Arthur Young & Company recommendations for revision of values.
[c] As submitted to stockholders, February 18, 1919.
[d] As revised to incorporate Arthur Young & Company's recommendation of November 1918, and tax liability for 1918 as determined by tax return.

There is a striking difference between the net worth of $3.7 million indicated by the memorandum in June and the $19.5 million reported by Arthur Young & Company three months later. This divergence in valuation is a reflection of the uses to which the two estimates were put. The memorandum was used to defend the reorganization against a threatened attack in the courts by a minority stockholder group. It understandably presented as unfavorable an outlook regarding the future as could be derived from the figures.

The subsequent revision by Arthur Young & Company was for the benefit of the majority stockholders and the bankers. If it be assumed that the accountants were objective in their review of the balance sheet values and that their suggested reductions were adequate to put the figures on a postwar going-concern basis, the position of Winchester was evidently far less desperate than alleged by the memorandum. There would seem, in fact, to have been a basis for instituting an expansion program on terms that were financially more favorable to the existing stockholders than those offered by Kidder, Peabody & Company. (It may be noted that in spite of the alleged financial stringency, $1.4 million of the Company's notes had been purchased between September and December 1918.)

There were, to be sure, some large elements of uncertainty in the situation as it faced the Winchester management in the middle of 1918. The end of hostilities would bring an end to the war contracts upon which a good profit was being realized. Furthermore, the current discussion about taxes was disturbing to concerns engaged in war production. In May 1918 President Wilson had urged the passage of a revenue bill of $8 million, the bulk of which should come from war profits. During the following months, when the bill was being considered in Congress, the tax rates suggested ranged from eighteen to eighty per cent of such profits. This discussion in Congress, coming as it did during the period when the future plans of the Company were being considered, caused a downward revision in the estimate of expected earnings after taxation; but by the end of the year, it became clear that the rates would be considerably below the extreme that had been suggested. The revenue bill as finally passed in February 1919 included rates which when applied to Winchester amounted to about twenty-two per cent of its profits. (This figure is arrived at on the basis of the tax found to be payable when the return for 1918 was filed.) By this time, however, the major decisions regarding the financial needs of the Company had been made and the arrangements for reorganization completed.

All things considered, it seems clear that the majority stockholders, at least, were willing to give up considerable of their financial interest in Winchester in return for avoiding the burden of management and being required to put up more capital in the future. T. G. Bennett's satisfaction with the arrangement is shown by his comment to S. F. Leib in May 1919 that "Without [our arrangement with Kidder-Peabody] we should, today be in bankruptcy or so near it as to be helpless—drifting into bankruptcy because we had no working capital to go ahead. Now all our debts are paid and we have plenty of money to take care of current expenses and go ahead."

*Injunction Proceedings*

Demarest, however, was unwilling to accept the arguments advanced by the officials of Winchester. Having failed to obtain what he considered a fair settlement from the Company, he filed a bill of complaint on February 18, 1919, in the U. S. District Court of Connecticut in which he asked the court to enjoin the Company from going through with the reorganization plan and to require the officials to answer specific questions contained in the complaint.

In his bill, Demarest took the general line that the equities of the Winchester stockholders were not being protected under the proposed plan. He pointed out that the stock had sold for over $3,000 per share during the war; that the financial statement of the Company had indicated a strong position as a result of war work. To this he added the accusation that Otterson and Sargent were conspiring to defraud the minority stockholders who would not agree to the plan.

In their answer to the bill of complaint and in the affidavits that accompanied it, the officials of Winchester defended their position along the lines already indicated. On April 13, 1919, Judge Thomas handed down his decision that, in his opinion, the record presented too many elements of doubt to warrant issuing a preliminary injunction. To protect Demarest and his associates, however, the court ordered Winchester to file a bond of $83,000, pending a settlement of an amount that should be adjudged a fair value of the stock.

Meanwhile the promoters of the reorganization were anxious to get on with their plans. When it became clear, late in 1918, that it was going to be difficult to get one hundred per cent deposit of stock, it was decided to modify the original proposal, maintaining the corporate existence of the Winchester Repeating Arms Company and establishing a new corporation to be called the Winchester Company to act as a holding company. This arrangement did not change the essential features of the original plan respecting deposit of stock and financing, but did permit the reorganization to be carried through in the absence of one hundred per cent adherence. These modifications were approved by the depositing stockholders, and, on April 16, 1919, five days after the District Court's refusal to grant Demarest's request for an injunction, the Winchester Company was incorporated under the laws of the State of Connecticut.

Demarest still proved troublesome. On May 2, 1919, he filed an appeal calling for a review of the case in the U. S. Circuit Court of Appeals in New York. But before the matter could come up in this court, the following agreement dated July 2, 1919 was made between Winchester Repeating Arms Company and Demarest: "The above case is settled and disposed of by the sale of thirty-eight (38) shares of the stock of the Winchester Repeating Arms Company for the sum of $75,000, which sum is to include all Complainant's costs, counsel fees, expenses and other charges. The action is to be discontinued and the bill dismissed without costs to either party. It is understood that the Complainant in this case will not purchase or otherwise acquire any additional stock in said Winchester Repeating Arms Company, and that he will not, directly or indirectly, bring or instigate the bringing of, any suits, actions, or proceedings against said Company, its directors or stockholders, or against the Winchester Company, or its directors or stockholders."

Under this settlement Demarest received for himself and his clients a little less than $1,974 per share, which, it is interesting to note, was slightly above the net worth per share as indicated by the September 30, 1918, balance sheet. On July 3, Sargent wrote Otterson: "I enclose herewith copy of a memorandum signed by Mr. Demarest. I am sorry that we couldn't get the stock any cheaper but I think in this case it was wise to get rid of him while we could rather than run the risk of trying to make a trade."

With the formation of the Winchester Company and the settlement of the Demarest case, the reorganization of the Winchester Repeating Arms Company was completed, substantially in the manner originally proposed. For all practical purposes, the Winchester Company and the Winchester Repeating Arms Company were operated as one concern although they had separate legal identities. Kidder, Peabody & Company exercised the final control by virtue of the ownership of the majority of the $1 million par value voting common stock of the Winchester Company, which in turn held some ninety-seven and a half per cent of the common stock of the Winchester Repeating Arms Company. (The remaining two and a half per cent represented shares whose owners had not been reached during the negotiations or cases where the title to the stock was not clear. It is interesting to note that Bennett, Otterson, and Liggett held only one share each of the common stock of the Winchester Company during the latter part of 1919. Sargent, however, had 502 shares in his own name during the same period. Robert Winsor, president of Kidder, Peabody & Company, held some 600 shares.)

Otterson was elected president of both companies and was directly responsible for the operation of the combined organization. T. G. Bennett lent his prestige to the venture by serving as chairman of the board of the Winchester Company while Liggett continued as a director of the Winchester Repeating Arms Company.

CHAPTER TWENTY-TWO

# POSTWAR PLANNING AND MANAGEMENT

*Planning*

By the terms of the agreement reached with the stockholders of the Winchester Repeating Arms Company, the new management was committed to a broad expansionist program which involved manufacturing new products in addition to guns and ammunition and the development of extensive marketing facilities. As was noted in the letter of October 1918 to the stockholders, it would ". . . take time and money to develop these new manufacturing and sales facilities." Furthermore, according to the same letter, for this venture to be successful it would be necessary to have ". . . an aggressive executive management, and to have associated with that management, business and commercial connections that will make available to it the counsel and experience of other large business developments [plus] a strong financial interest."

At first glance these requirements for success as set forth by the promoters of the plan seem to have been met. Financially the concern was in a strong position. After retiring, on March 1, 1919, the balance of the $8 million that was owed on the loan made during the war, there remained about $13.5 million of net working capital of which nearly $4 million was in cash or receivables. Kidder, Peabody & Company because of its equity interest and according to the agreement implicit in the reorganization plan, was committed to supply both additional funds and financial advice as they might be needed.

In Otterson, the organization had a president who stood high in the estimation of his associates and the new owners. While it remained to be seen how aggressive his management would be, during the war he had demonstrated his capacity to develop an effective production organization. He had also shown great skill in negotiations as is indicated by the terms of the agreements with the United States Government. To be sure, Otterson lacked experience in marketing and financial matters, but this deficiency was apparently met by the "business and commercial connections" and the "strong financial interest" associated with the Company; associations which were represented on the board of directors chiefly in the persons of Liggett and Sargent.

Much weight was attached to the importance of Liggett's experience and counsel, which were to be drawn upon in establishing a marketing policy and in setting up a marketing organization. Furthermore, according to Otterson, Liggett had promised to lend a number of his key merchandising men from the United Drug Company for this purpose. With the broad background and experience of these men to draw upon, in addition to Liggett's advice, the establishment of a marketing program promised to present no major difficulties.

Sargent, as the New York partner of Kidder, Peabody & Company, could not only utilize his own knowledge and experience, but could call on his associates in the firm for any needed advice concerning the financial operation of the Winchester organization.

While Sargent and Liggett were key figures in the management, there is no question that Otterson was the real head of the organization, subject only to ultimate control by Kidder, Peabody & Company. For some five years, beginning in 1919, he had what amounted to a *carte blanche* to work out the details and implement the broad expansionist program laid out in the reorganization agreement. In the early phases, at least, no specific time or financial limitations were imposed. The principal job was to get the program under way as rapidly as possible, without giving too much initial attention to the costs involved, so long as the organization was eventually put on an earning basis.

The most urgent matter that faced the new management was to work out the details of the postwar program. Aside from the general statements that the Company was going to expand its production into lines other than guns and ammunition and develop a new marketing system, little was done toward making these plans more definite prior to the middle of 1919. But as soon as it was clear that the reorganization plan was going through the management began to develop its program more explicitly.

*New Products*

The choice and development of new products presented a major task. The goal was to expand the production of new lines by an amount that would absorb the factory space left idle by the ending of the war. To do this meant virtually doubling the prewar manufacturing output.

A detailed study was undertaken to determine the general types of products and the individual items that might be undertaken for manufacture. In setting up standards for choice, the Company's reputation in the gun and ammunition business was taken into account, as well as its experience in the fabrication of metal products. As a result, it was decided that the following qualifications should be met in the selection of new products: first, they should be articles of personal use in order to capitalize upon the "Winchester" trade mark; second, they should be items that would utilize the same general kinds of labor and equipment used in the manufacture of guns and ammunition; third, they should be of high quality; finally, they should be products that were customarily sold through the same trade channels as guns and ammunition.

It was decided that the types of products that most closely met these requirements were sporting goods and certain kinds of hardware that were bought for personal use. Among the items that seemed to be most appropriate were pocket and kitchen cutlery, skates, fishing equipment, flashlights and batteries, tools, shears, and the like. It was thought that the purchasers of such articles would be interested in selecting well-known brands of merchandise, in which case the Winchester reputation and trade mark could be used to attract customers.

Not only did Winchester plan to fill its idle plant with the manufacture of new products, but it anticipated making major improvements in production methods as well. To do this, the Company expected to take advantage of its long experience in the manufacture of metal products and of the techniques, which it had developed by means of chemical analysis, to control the quality of the raw materials. A preliminary examination of the processes currently used in sporting-goods and hardware manufacture convinced the management that it could develop better methods for the production of a number of the contemplated lines. In the case of cutlery, for example, the processes currently used had not progressed much beyond those that had been developed in Sheffield, England, in the nineteenth century and subsequently adopted in this country. Blades were hand-forged to give high cutting and finishing qualities; other components were made in such a way that each individual knife required a large amount of expensive hand-fitting while being assembled.

The analysis of the effects of heat treatment had been developed by Winchester to the point where high-quality blades could be stamped out, eliminating hand-forging. By using precision methods in machining of individual parts, worked out in the production of guns, it seemed possible to reduce hand-fitting to a minimum. The result would be both a better and cheaper product.

*Marketing*

The second major feature of the new program was establishing a marketing organization. From the beginning the Company had sold its products principally through jobbing or wholesale houses which in turn had distributed the merchandise to the retail dealers. It was conceivable that this practice might have been followed in respect to the new products, but the idea was vetoed for a number of reasons. It was argued that Winchester's new lines would be competing, as far as the jobbers and the retailers were concerned, with established brands, some of which were owned by the jobbing houses. At best, it would probably take a long time to build up the desired volume of distribution; meanwhile the idle plant would be a heavy financial burden. Something that would promise quicker results was needed and Liggett supplied the answer by suggesting that Winchester follow the plan that he had used so successfully in the drug business.

*The Liggett Organization*

The Liggett organization, which served as a model for Winchester in 1919, was an impressive business institution that had started on a small scale some sixteen years before. In the fall of 1902 a group of individual druggists attended a convention of the Vinol Company agents in Boston. Liggett, who was twenty-five years old at the time and general manager of the Vinol Company, suggested to the members of the group that they form a company to manufacture various drug items under one trade name. This, he pointed out, would permit economies in buying and make feasible an extensive advertising campaign to publicize a trade mark that would be the property of the proposed organization. Under the plan proposed by Liggett, each dealer who subscribed to the stock was to have the exclusive right to sell the branded articles in his respective city or town.

The United Drug Company was formed with Liggett as president and early in 1903 began operations in Boston. "Rexall" was the trade name adopted for the Company's products and stores were known as Rexall Stores. Some forty druggists subscribed $4,000 each to the plan. Each agent who operated his own establishment was required to purchase a certain amount of United Drug Company stock and to enter a contract to distribute the manufactured articles of the company and its subsidiaries. Provision was made for additional drug-store operators to join the organization by subscribing to stock and signing a contract providing they did not infringe on the sales territory of an existing member.

One of the features of the organization was the personal contact that Liggett maintained with the agents. Annual conventions of Rexall dealers were held until 1910. By that time the number had grown so large that regional and then state clubs were formed, which met annually. At these conventions Liggett and the other officials of the company met with the dealers and discussed questions of mutual interest. Liggett supplemented these contracts by his series of "Dear Pardner" letters, which began in 1903. These were informal, chatty epistles that discussed new products, company problems, future plans, and the like.

The United Drug Company acquired its first retail store in 1903, but the movement really gathered momentum in 1909 with the purchase of Jaynes Drug Company of Boston and its consolidation with William B. Ryker & Sons Company of New York City. These stores formed the basis of the United-owned Liggett Drug Stores and in 1909, the Louis B. Liggett Company, a subsidiary of United Drug Company, was formed to operate these establishments and to extend the chain into the larger cities, where the Rexall plan had not taken hold.

The business mushroomed during the decade ending in 1920. Manufacturing facilities were greatly expanded, subsidiary plants producing rubber goods, grape juice, fountain syrups, and the like were acquired and warehouses established; business was extended to Canada and to Great Britain. All financing was done within the Company by the Rexall agents until 1916, when a small amount of preferred stock was offered to the general public.

All through this development Liggett remained the leading personality. He was a dynamic figure with an extraordinary flair for selling. He brought into his organization men to handle the manufacturing and financial affairs, as he was not especially interested in these matters. His chief concern was to expand the organization and to seek new merchandising worlds to conquer. His biographer says of the formative period of the organization: ". . . and the money went faster. Faster and faster it went. Liggett simply couldn't think in terms of niggardly economy. He must lay his foundations deep and wide." [1]

In Liggett's philosophy there were no problems connected with the business that volumes of sales couldn't cure: "[Sales] figures were the marks to shoot at. The accounting department could keep track of the costs. They'd remind him fast enough. As a matter of fact they would and did pester him day by day. But that was all right, too. He'd find a way to meet those costs. Invent a way if he had to . . . They all believed in him." [2]

By 1919 Liggett had ridden out his early financial difficulties and his organization and his methods of selling were both admired and feared in merchandising fields.

The Winchester management (which, of course, included Liggett himself) showed its faith in the possibility of applying Liggett's methods to the hardware and sporting-goods field by copying his marketing organization almost intact. This resulted in two main features: one the dealer-agency plan and the other the Company-owned retail stores.

Under the dealer-agency plan the Company proposed to bypass the jobber and sell directly to a selected group of hardware merchants throughout the United States. The plan was to apply to towns with 50,000 population or less where the ablest and best equipped hardware merchant was to be offered an exclusive Winchester agency. Further details of the proposal were given in an article which appeared in *Printers' Ink* for March 18, 1920:

> Each store will be a model of its kind. Its construction, arrangement, merchandising methods and accounting system will be the best that the Winchester system, based on experience and research, has been able to devise.
>
> Even the color scheme of the store plans will be standardized. The basic color of each front will be a uniform gray; the name of the owner will appear in red; other lettering will be in gold against blue. The purpose of the gray basic color is to form a neutral framework for the standardized window displays, which will be in bright and glowing colors.
>
> It may be thus seen that the plan has overlooked not even the smallest detail that is related, however remotely, to the Company's purpose.
>
> It is expected that about 8,000 dealers in the various parts of the United States will accept the plan. Each of them will purchase a block of Winchester stock and agree to lend his full cooperation. For the services to be rendered him he will pay a nominal fee of from $3 to $8 a month, with an average charge of about $60 a year.

For the privilege of becoming exclusive agents, each dealer was required to buy from three to eight shares of Winchester Company seven per cent preferred stock in the open market, the number of shares depending upon the size of the town in which his store was located. Each dealer was expected to promote the sales of the Company's products and sell those products at retail within the territory assigned to him. As the Winchester organization did not plan to manufacture a complete line of hardware and sporting goods, the members would continue to buy merchandise through established sources of supply. They were also permitted to handle brands that were competitive with Winchester products, but it was felt that it would be to their advantage to push the sale of the Winchester-branded goods whenever possible.[3]

It was anticipated that the dealer-agency plan would change the methods of the retail hardware stores. The average hardware store in 1919 was still being operated in much the same way that such stores had been run a half-century earlier. Many of them were a counterpart of the general country store with its hodge-podge of merchandise and with the same informal way of doing business. Winchester expected, of course, to choose only the more progressive hardware dealers to represent them. By further improving the merchandising methods of this group, the Company hoped to make them the outstanding hardware merchants in each locality, which, if successful would insure a wide market for Winchester products. The ultimate goal of 8,000 would bring almost one-third of the approximately 26,000 retail hardware dealers in the United States into the dealer-agency plan.[4]

Anyone acquainted with the marketing of hardware as it was carried on at the time will appreciate the revolutionary aspects of the dealer-agency plan. Hardware distribution had for generations been handled by wholesale or jobbing houses that bought merchandise in large quantities and in turn supplied local retailers. These jobbing houses performed several important economic functions. From the manufacturer's point of view they simplified the selling and handling of large quantities of merchandise. Not infrequently they contracted for delivery several months ahead which aided in production plans by the manufacturer. By buying and holding goods in their warehouses for subsequent delivery they assumed an important financing burden. They took on the responsibility for the physical distribution of merchandise from the manufacturer through the principal marketing centers. To the retail outlets, the jobber also gave significant help. The retailer was able to order merchandise in amounts and variety and in time to meet his needs. Jobber salesmen called on the trade and acquainted it with new products, prices, and other information that might be useful. Not infrequently the jobbers extended credit to the retail merchants.

The Winchester officials were, of course, not unaware of the functions performed by the jobbers, but on the assumption that a market had to be developed quickly for the new products and that jobbers would be reluctant to push its new lines, the management felt that it had no choice but to sell direct to dealers. By direct selling it was possible that any extra cost to the Company of performing these services itself would be offset by greater manufacturing profits from larger volume of sales. If the jobbing functions could be carried at no extra cost, so much the better. A third possibility was that the Company could cut the costs of distribution and in this way improve its own and the dealer's position.

Just how much, if any, the management expected to save by performing the jobbing function itself is not clear. For the purpose of selling prospective merchants on the dealer-agency plan, the Company made a study of hardware distribution in 1919, which indicated that of approximately $570 million spent annually at retail for hardware items, manufacturing costs amounted to about forty per cent, the remaining sixty per cent or around $342 million, being absorbed in distribution.

| | *Sales through Jobbers* | *Sales through Dealer-Agency Plan* |
|---|---|---|
| Production cost | $ 40,000 | $ 40,000 |
| Manufacturer's selling cost | 3,000 | 2,000 |
| Manufacturer's advertising cost | 2,000 | 2,000 |
| Manufacturer's profit | 5,000 | 5,000 |
| Freight from factory to warehouse | 1,000 | 750 |
| Warehousing cost | 6,000 | 5,000 |
| Traveling salesmen cost | 5,000 | 2,000 |
| Jobber's advertising cost | 1,000 | 0 |
| Jobber's profit | 6,000 | 0 |
| Cartage cost warehouse to store | 1,000 | 1,250 |
| Retailer's advertising and selling cost | 20,000 | 20,000 |
| Retailer's profit | 10,000 | 10,000 |
| TOTAL | $100,000 | $ 88,000 |
| Price to the consumer | $100,000 | $100,000 |
| Margin available for additional profits, etc. | | $ 12,000 |

Much was made of this "high cost of distribution" in subsequent talks to dealer groups and the foregoing tabular comparison was made to show how much could be saved by Winchester's proposed methods of distribution, based on sales of $100,000 at retail prices.

Taken at their face value the "savings" indicated in the foregoing table are impressive. But even a superficial analysis indicates a considerable degree of rationalization and the acceptance of the most optimistic estimates of how economically direct selling could be carried on. Furthermore, even accepting the validity of the $12,000 margin shown, such an amount would be available only if the dealer in question bought all of his merchandise direct from the manufacturer. To the extent that Winchester was prepared to supply only a part of the needs of its dealers, this margin would be reduced.

*Retail Stores*

The second main feature of the Company's new marketing system involved the establishment of its own retail stores. This plan of marketing in general was to be limited to cities of 50,000 population or more, although the Company was prepared to modify the basis of selection where conditions warranted. A number of considerations entered into the decision to establish these retail outlets which were to be owned and operated by the Company. Brewer noted, for example, that while the local hardware store was usually one of the leading stores in town, ". . . in the large cities the hardware store occupied a relatively unimportant position in the cities' trade. It seemed, therefore, that while the village and small town hardware store would form suitable basis for the agency-plan, the city hardware store would not be satisfactory as a distributing medium for our new products and that it might become necessary for the Company to open its own stores in the larger cities. This followed along the practice of the United Drug Company which operated its own drug stores in the larger cities."

While these retail stores would handle other brands of merchandise, they were primarily designed to insure a market for Winchester's products in the larger cities. It was further suggested that these stores could serve as laboratories and models for the merchants under the dealer-agency plan. Merchandising experiments could be made and successful store arrangements and selling methods demonstrated more easily in this manner than would be possible to secure through the agency dealers. There seems no doubt the success of the Liggett stores was an important consideration in the decision to follow this type of marketing.

*Distribution through Jobbers*

The marketing system just described was to apply chiefly to the new lines of products. While guns and ammunition were to be sold through the dealer-agent and the Company's retail stores, it was decided also to continue their distribution through jobbing houses. In some respects this was the most remarkable feature of the Company's postwar marketing program. To be sure, the Winchester brand was well established in the gun and ammunition fields but otherwise the same arguments concerning the savings which could be made by direct selling would seem to apply.

The decision was based on the realization that to cut the jobbers off before the dealer-agency plan and the retail stores were established would result in a sharp drop in sales. It was assumed that the demand for Winchester guns and ammunition was so strong that both jobbers and retailers outside the Company's own marketing organization would and could continue to do business with the Company.

*Summary of New Plans*

The general plans proposed by Winchester in 1919 called for an extraordinary change in the Company's previous way of doing business. It was a bold program which was designed to capture a substantial share of the hardware and sporting-goods market from companies that had long been established in the field. Implicit in the decision to follow this policy were several major assumptions. One was that the Company had the financial resources to carry the program through the developmental period and to provide for any unforeseen contingencies. Second, that the engineering practices and knowledge worked out in guns and ammunition could be applied successfully to the new products in such a way as to bring costs of manufacture to competitive levels. Third, that the Liggett marketing example could be used as a basis for the development of sales outlets that would absorb an amount of production of new items somewhat arbitrarily set by available factory space. Finally, it was assumed that the jobbers would continue to purchase the bulk of the Company's output of guns and ammunition.

Success or failure would also depend upon how well the management was able to coordinate these various activities. The arguments advanced for each phase of the new program stressed the importance of getting sufficient volume of production to utilize the idle plant's capacity. While profits might be realized from the operations of the Company-owned stores and from performing the jobbing functions, the chief source of income would have to come from manufacturing profits. Skillful operation of the manufacturing end of the business might be offset by a failure to build sufficient sales volume or through losses sustained from performing the jobbing functions or operating the retail stores.

The stakes involved were high. Failure would mean the collapse of a business institution that had been operating with increasing distinction for over fifty years. Full success would result in a smoothly functioning organization with 8,000 dealers, plus 150 or more retail stores, and a fully occupied plant which would go far toward achieving the goal set forth by Otterson for making "Winchester the largest single manufacturing institution in the world manufacturing sporting goods, cutlery, tools, and hardware specialties."

*Management Personnel*

The plan for extending the scope of Winchester's activities presented a challenge to the management staff which could hardly have been met in the absence of a leadership with a clear idea of the means by which the objective was to be attained. So far as the human element was concerned, Otterson had a well-developed concept of management organization which had during the war attracted the attention of the trade press.[5] He had applied his theories, already developed in his work at the Boston Navy Yard, to the problem of organizing the greatly expanded war output; and their success in this direction no doubt encouraged him to believe that the infinite complexities of the organization of the plant could now be resolved by application of the same principles.

All management operations, according to Otterson, could be subdivided into the five functions of planning, preparation, scheduling, production, and inspection. To the extent that this analysis is applied ". . . it is much less important to pay attention merely to the details surrounding a particular task than it is to select the proper type of man for any particular function applied to this task. It is more important to get the right type of man than it is to determine whether he has the highest degree of knowledge for the particular thing he is to do. A man may know very little of the particular set of activities he is to supervise if he has the right set of characteristics and the right temperament for the job to which he is assigned." [6]

This fivefold job analysis was applied not only to the major divisions of organization, but within each operating division of the Company including the shops. (Apparently even such a department as personnel was supposed to follow this pattern in carrying out its duties.)

A part of Otterson's purpose in setting up this form of organization seems to have been educational. Believing that all or most processes connected with business operations could be analyzed and executed more effectively by following this procedure of planning, preparation, scheduling, production, and inspection, he expected to get his staff to think habitually along these lines. To the extent that operational problems could be more easily solved by application of this type of analysis, the job of the top administrators would be made easier.

This was an important consideration in view of the other principal features of the organizational set-up. The lines of communication were directly between heads of departments and the president. Otterson followed military procedure by delegating authority to the person in charge of each major division of the Company, who in turn gave his own subordinates the responsibility for carrying out duties. No provision was made for any individual or executive committee to coordinate the activities assigned under the various major functions. Only to the extent that each department functioned well within this framework would Otterson have time to coordinate the major activities of the Company and to consider general policy matters.

By May 1920 the organization had been developed into the pattern shown on page 282. The key men in the framework had been obtained from three sources: employees who had served the Company in the prewar period; those who had been brought in to assist in the wartime expansion; and, finally, new men brought in to fill specialist functions in the expanded range of activities.

The bulk of the top positions was distributed among the old-line employees, who had antedated Otterson's coming with the Company. Longest in point of service was Daniel Veader, cashier, who had gone to work for Oliver F. Winchester in 1869. Second longest with Winchester was H. F. Beebe, in charge of export sales, who came to the Company in 1891 and who had been in the foreign-sales department during most of the time since that date.

Henry Brewer, vice president, was a graduate of the Yale Sheffield Scientific School and had come to Winchester in 1894 upon graduation. He had been superintendent of the cartridge shop from 1906 to 1915, when he was elevated to vice president.

Frank Drew, the other vice president of the Winchester Repeating Arms Company, had been active in the Company's sales department since 1903. He had risen to be sales manager when he was promoted to vice president in 1916. While he had no specific function assigned on the organization chart, his principal job was to maintain good relationships with the jobbers and other members of the trade, whom he knew well from his long experience on the road. (D. W. Weeks, one of the two vice presidents of the Winchester Company, was appointed by

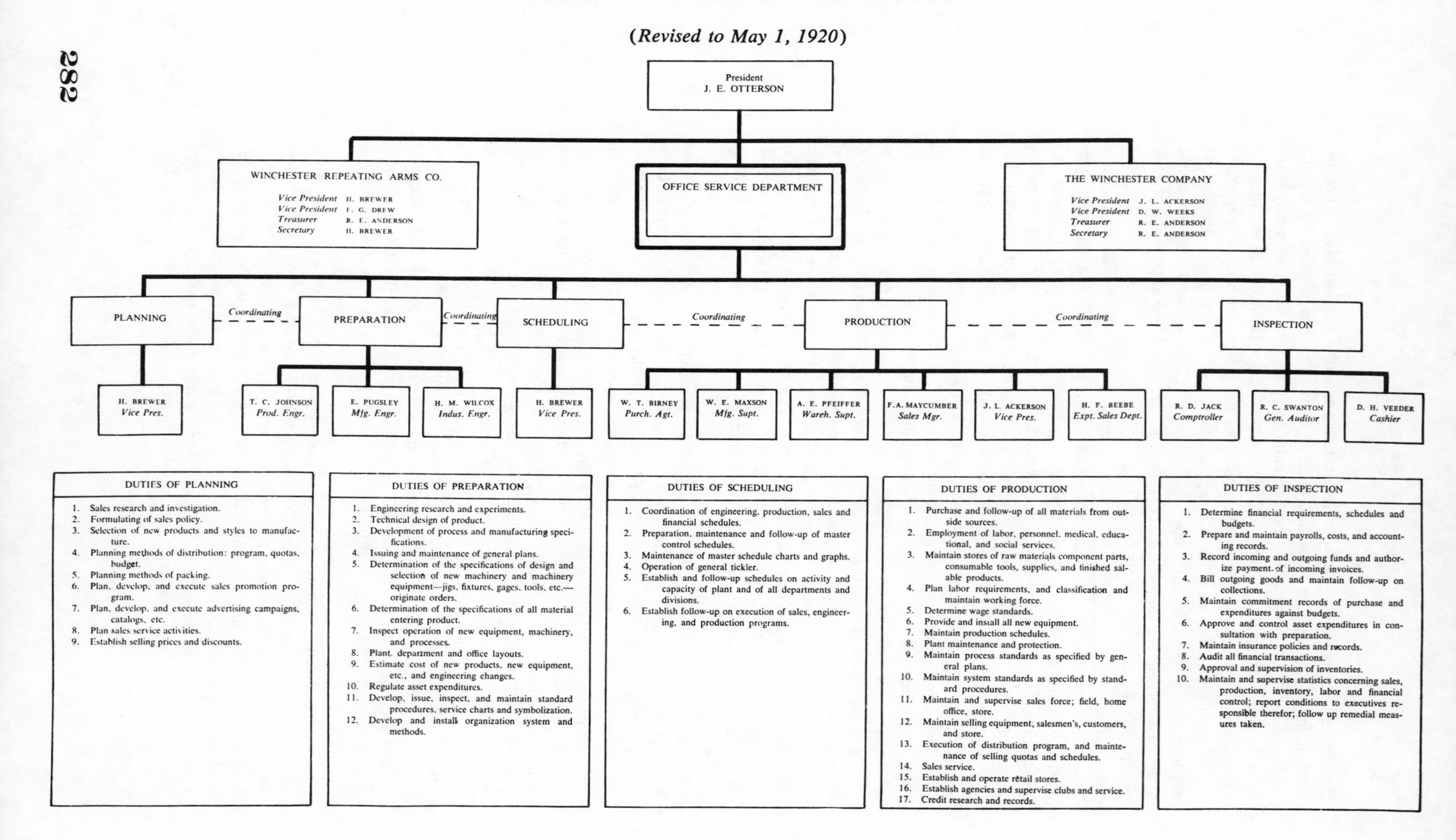
GENERAL ORGANIZATION SERVICE CHART
WINCHESTER REPEATING ARMS COMPANY
(Revised to May 1, 1920)
President
J. E. OTTERSON
WINCHESTER REPEATING ARMS CO.
Vice President H. BREWER
Vice President F. G. DREW
Treasurer R. E. ANDERSON
Secretary H. BREWER
OFFICE SERVICE DEPARTMENT
THE WINCHESTER COMPANY
Vice President J. L. ACKERSON
Vice President D. W. WEEKS
Treasurer R. E. ANDERSON
Secretary R. E. ANDERSON
PLANNING
Coordinating
PREPARATION
Coordinating
SCHEDULING
Coordinating
PRODUCTION
Coordinating
INSPECTION
H. BREWER Vice Pres.
T. C. JOHNSON Prod. Engr.
E. PUGSLEY Mfg. Engr.
H. M. WILCOX Indus. Engr.
H. BREWER Vice Pres.
W. T. BIRNEY Purch. Agt.
W. E. MAXSON Mfg. Supt.
A. E. PFEIFFER Wareh. Supt.
F.A. MAYCUMBER Sales Mgr.
J. L. ACKERSON Vice Pres.
H. F. BEEBE Expt. Sales Dept.
R. D. JACK Comptroller
R. C. SWANTON Gen. Auditor
D. H. VEEDER Cashier
DUTIES OF PLANNING
1. Sales research and investigation.
2. Formulating of sales policy.
3. Selection of new products and styles to manufacture.
4. Planning methods of distribution: program, quotas, budget.
5. Planning methods of packing.
6. Plan, develop, and execute sales promotion program.
7. Plan, develop, and execute advertising campaigns, catalogs, etc.
8. Plan sales service activities.
9. Establish selling prices and discounts.
DUTIES OF PREPARATION
1. Engineering research and experiments.
2. Technical design of product.
3. Development of process and manufacturing specifications.
4. Issuing and maintenance of general plans.
5. Determination of the specifications of design and selection of new machinery and machinery equipment—jigs, fixtures, gages, tools, etc.—originate orders.
6. Determination of the specifications of all material entering product.
7. Inspect operation of new equipment, machinery, and processes.
8. Plant, department and office layouts.
9. Estimate cost of new products, new equipment, etc., and engineering changes.
10. Regulate asset expenditures.
11. Develop, issue, inspect, and maintain standard procedures, service charts and symbolization.
12. Develop and install organization system and methods.
DUTIES OF SCHEDULING
1. Coordination of engineering, production, sales and financial schedules.
2. Preparation, maintenance and follow-up of master control schedules.
3. Maintenance of master schedule charts and graphs.
4. Operation of general tickler.
5. Establish and follow-up schedules on activity and capacity of plant and of all departments and divisions.
6. Establish follow-up on execution of sales, engineering, and production programs.
DUTIES OF PRODUCTION
1. Purchase and follow-up of all materials from outside sources.
2. Employment of labor, personnel, medical, educational, and social services.
3. Maintain stores of raw materials component parts, consumable tools, supplies, and finished salable products.
4. Plan labor requirements, and classification and maintain working force.
5. Determine wage standards.
6. Provide and install all new equipment.
7. Maintain production schedules.
8. Plant maintenance and protection.
9. Maintain process standards as specified by general plans.
10. Maintain system standards as specified by standard procedures.
11. Maintain and supervise sales force; field, home office, store.
12. Maintain selling equipment; salesmen's, customers, and store.
13. Execution of distribution program, and maintenance of selling quotas and schedules.
14. Sales service.
15. Establish and operate retail stores.
16. Establish agencies and supervise clubs and service.
17. Credit research and records.
DUTIES OF INSPECTION
1. Determine financial requirements, schedules and budgets.
2. Prepare and maintain payrolls, costs, and accounting records.
3. Record incoming and outgoing funds and authorize payment of incoming invoices.
4. Bill outgoing goods and maintain follow-up on collections.
5. Maintain commitment records of purchase and expenditures against budgets.
6. Approve and control asset expenditures in consultation with preparation.
7. Maintain insurance policies and records.
8. Audit all financial transactions.
9. Approval and supervision of inventories.
10. Maintain and supervise statistics concerning sales, production, inventory, labor and financial control; report conditions to executives responsible therefor; follow up remedial measures taken.

Kidder, Peabody & Company to represent it on the board. He seems to have had no active duties.)

The background and qualifications of Thomas C. Johnson, production engineer, have already been noted. Since 1895 he had been a leading figure in the Company's development work in guns and ammunition.

W. T. Birney's employment dated from 1897. He had worked for a number of concerns, including the Binghamton Oil Company and the U.S. Rubber Company, in purchasing and sales. He continued this type of work for Winchester prior to becoming purchasing agent.

Edwin Pugsley, manufacturing engineer, a graduate of Yale (1908) and Massachusetts Institute of Technology (1911), had come to Winchester in 1911. He was put through what was known unofficially as "Winchester's Apprentice Course for College Grads" which involved learning the business from the bottom up. Upon completion of this training, he was assigned to the gun department, where he had served in various production and engineering capacities.

Herbert M. Wilcox, industrial engineer, was a graduate of Princeton (1902), after which he attended Massachusetts Institute of Technology, finishing his work there in 1905. Between 1905 and 1914, he was engaged in industrial engineering work of various types, principally for engineering firms, including the Miller-Franklyn Company. In 1914, he came to Winchester, where he was assigned to industrial engineering in the gun department.

Strategic positions in the new organization were filled by men who had been recruited during the war period. Of these, R. E. Anderson, had the most important place. A close friend of Otterson, Anderson was first employed in 1915 as the former's assistant. He had been successively production engineer and comptroller, prior to his appointment as treasurer. He was a graduate in engineering from Princeton, and his previous experience had been in ship construction for the U. S. Navy and for the Lake Torpedo Boat Company.

To head up the manufacturing operations, Otterson appointed William Maxson who had served a number of years in building and dam construction and engineering, prior to coming to Winchester in 1915.

R. C. Swanton's employment with Winchester also dated from 1915. Previously he had worked for the Star Electric Company in Binghamton, New York, where he had specialized in cost-accounting work. Upon coming to Winchester, he had established a cost system in connection with the British contracts and, when the U. S. Government cost-plus contracts were made, he was put in charge of the accounting involved. In 1919 he became general auditor.

R. D. Jack, comptroller, was employed first in 1916. He was originally trained in mechanical engineering but had turned to accounting and had worked in this capacity for a number of years with the American Locomotive Company and with Scovell, Wellington & Company, certified public accountants.

A few positions were assigned to new employees. Of those who came with the Company after 1918, F. A. Maycumber had the most important post as sales manager. Employed in 1919 to manage the sales to the dealer-agents, his previous experience had been in selling and sales promotion with Yale & Towne and the General Fire Extinguisher Company.

Two other men, whose names appear on the chart, were new to the organization. The first of these was J. L. Ackerson, vice president of the Winchester Company and directly in charge of retail stores. A graduate of the Naval Academy, Ackerson had occupied a responsible position in the Hog Island shipyards during the war. His stay with the Company was brief. Hired in February 1920, he resigned the following September, to be succeeded by Edwin Pugsley. A. E. Pfeiffer had also been in Government service, in connection with the U. S. Shipping Board's activities, before being employed by Winchester in 1919.

A considerable number of subordinate positions in industrial engineering and market analysis were filled by newly hired employees.

The organization of personnel was designed to provide effective supervision of a greatly increased range of production activities and, at the same time, to weld into the successful arms and ammunition business a new approach to the marketing problem. It is clear that Otterson was taking some risks in putting innate qualities before experience in his selection of his men.

Probably the most striking feature of the plan is the lack, on the part of several of the key men, of experience with the sort of work they were called upon to perform. This lack of experience is especially noticeable in respect to the marketing functions. There was no one in a top position who had any first-hand knowledge of the United Drug Company or with the other chain-store operations either in the form of dealer-agent or company-owned retail stores. Maycumber, to be sure, was an experienced sales executive, but not in these particular fields. Ackerson's background was quite foreign to the retail-stores field, and, as has been noted, his stay with the Company was brief. Edwin Pugsley, who succeeded him, had no first-hand experience with retail merchandising.

The absence of capable executives from the United Drug Company indicated that Liggett had not fulfilled his promise to lend experienced personnel to Winchester from that organization. The reason for this failure apparently stemmed from the fact that the United Drug Company executives saw little to be gained from devoting their time and energy to working out the details of the Winchester marketing program, especially as they were rather fully occupied with keeping their own organization functioning under a rapidly expanding program.

Otterson found himself unable, in the absence of Liggett's aid, to attract able marketing personnel to Winchester. Furthermore, Liggett himself was in England during the greater part of 1920, when he was negotiating for the purchase of the stock control of Boots Cash Chemists, Ltd., the famous British drug chain. Liggett was too occupied with his own affairs to be of any extensive aid to Winchester during the critical phases of the marketing development.

In financial matters, Otterson's chief liaison with Sargent of Kidder, Peabody & Company was through R. D. Anderson. Anderson was a trusted lieutenant, whose loyalty to Otterson was unquestioned. By his own account, he was not experienced in financial matters especially as they related to borrowing operations. In any case, it was Sargent's counsel that would be a major determinant in respect to financial policies. But whereas Sargent was familiar with investment banking practices, he had little experience in obtaining short-term working capital. It remained to be seen how effective his advice would be in these matters.

W. E. Maxson, in charge of manufacturing, had made his reputation in the field of construction. He had shown considerable ability in handling men on massive construction jobs. Winchester's new production program, however, called for a different type of engineering skill with which he was not familiar.

It is noteworthy that a number of the executives were former Navy men or had been closely associated with naval work. W. E. Freeland, one of the sales engineers remarked on this point at a meeting of the National Association of Winchester Clubs in June 1920: "Naturally we found but few men fully trained for this new task so we went out into the highways and by-ways of the industry and selling field, and brought into us men of all shades of training so that in our group we are prepared to meet almost any problem that may arise. We were fortunate in getting hold of a number of the younger engineers who had matured with great rapidity as officers in the Army and Navy and who came to us keen to play a large part in this development and were unhampered by the traditions and precedents of those older in the hardware business. That we have been able to approach our complex problems with open minds is unquestionably one of the secrets of the success of which we are now assured."

There was undoubtedly some resentment among the older employees of the Company against the "Navy" influence, but there is no evidence that it seriously affected the working relations among the group.

Here, then, was the team organized to compete with firms which had had long experience in their respective fields. Otterson's suggestions respecting the selection and use of personnel came at a time when managements were still largely dependent on empirical processes of selection, usually influenced by accumulated personal experiences or prejudices. He was attempting to demonstrate that scientific methods would aid substantially in the more effective use of human resources. While his thesis might be applicable in those areas where individuals were to be trained to the organization's needs, its effectiveness had still to be shown in the case of top management men. The higher executives, however highly qualified in respect to innate or acquired characteristics, had to demonstrate that they could handle situations for which their experience provided no precedents.

Otterson had made his organization work effectively during the war. Then he was concerned with the production of a large volume in a limited range of products and was working for an assured market. Now he was faced not only with a wider range of products, for most of which he had yet to organize the details of production methods, but also with a complex marketing organization and a market of a size yet to be developed and sold.

CHAPTER TWENTY-THREE

# LAUNCHING THE POSTWAR PROGRAM

For a few months after the armistice in November 1918, there was a period of economic uncertainty, caused by the expectation that the end of the war would bring about a price deflation and a depression. By the spring of 1919, these immediate postwar fears had been dissipated, and industry began to push ahead rapidly with the job of reconverting to peacetime activities and to supplying accumulated demands. Only a few dissonant notes were sounded. The price level was high and there were numerous complaints about the cost of living. Labor was somewhat troublesome. Union activity had increased during the war and management reported a decline in worker efficiency. But these elements were largely ignored in the general feeling of confidence that did not or could not anticipate the sharp period of economic adjustment that was still in the future.

It was in this general atmosphere that Winchester's postwar program was launched. Every effort was made to get the new plans into operation as soon as possible. By spending money the Company expected to gain time and experience, and to accomplish, in a matter of a few years, what had taken most of their competitors in the hardware and sporting-goods fields a much longer period to achieve. While the various phases of the new program were developed simultaneously, for purposes of analysis it is necessary to consider each part separately.

*Development of New Products*

The goal set for this part of Winchester's program was rapidly to expand the manufacture of new products in order to fill the factory space previously used for military production and to supply the dealer-agents and the retail stores. Beyond the immediate goal was the objective of achieving costs that would put Winchester in a favorable competitive position.

This was a formidable undertaking. Under the most favorable circumstances it could not be accomplished in a few weeks or months. Even if the management had planned to follow production methods already developed by competitors or in the businesses that were subsequently purchased, time was needed to acquire, install or rearrange equipment and to familiarize both the management and the workers with the new products or methods. The experiments in production methods which were proposed for almost every line would make for further delay in getting production under way.

Beginning in the latter part of 1919 and continuing through 1920, surveys were made of a large number of products by various departments within the organization to determine which would be suitable for manufacture. In this process, the sales engineers occupied a strategic position. This group would pass on the advisability of adopting new lines after making in most cases an elaborate marketing and production analysis. (The cutlery survey, for example, involved an extensive sampling of the retail hardware dealers and jobbers on total sales, seasonal fluctuations, the amounts of business done by stores in different localities, the quality of merchandise demanded by various buying groups, the nature of competition, and the like.)

If the decision were favorable, this department would also suggest output

BUSINESSES ACQUIRED BY WINCHESTER

| *Name* | *Location* | *Products* | *Date Acquired* | *Price Paid* |
|---|---|---|---|---|
| Eagle Pocket Knife Co. | New Haven, Conn. | Pocket knives | June 1919 | $174,500 |
| Napanoch Knife Co. | Napanoch, N.Y. | Pocket knives | Aug. 1919 | 40,000 |
| Andrew B. Hendrix Co. | New Haven, Conn. | Fishing reels, Artificial bait | Sept. 1919 | 99,257 |
| Morrill Target Co. | Omaha, Nebraska | Clay targets | Sept. 1919 | 17,000 |
| E. W. Edwards | Bangor, Me. | Fishing rods | Oct. 1919 | 10,000 |
| Barney & Berry | Springfield, Mass. | Skates | Nov. 1919 | 165,000 (less loans) |
| Lebanon Machine Co. | Lebanon, N.H. | Auger bits | Dec. 1919 | 30,000 |
| Page-Storm Drop Forge Co. | Chicopee, Mass. | Flat wrenches | Dec. 1919 | 59,000 |
| Mack Axe Co. | Beaver Falls, Pa. | Axes | May 1920 | 200,000 |
| | | | | $695,027 |

quotas and sales prices. On a basis of these recommendations, the manufacturing engineers would estimate the costs of manufacture, based upon the output quotas established by the sales department, and the methods of manufacture that could be applied. If the estimated manufacturing cost was within the limits of the sales prices set by the sales engineers, the product or products under consideration would be adopted and manufacturing facilities built up or acquired. (Apparently there were some differences between departments. The sales department usually demanded as complete a line as possible of any product. The manufacturing engineers would argue for more limited production or fewer lines that would utilize space more effectively or simplify production methods.)

Once a decision had been made to manufacture the new lines, Winchester followed two procedures in building up its production facilities. One was to develop and begin the production of items that seemed especially adapted to the methods and equipment already being used in gun and ammunition manufacture. The second was to acquire going concerns from which one or more of the following advantages might be gained: equipment that could be immediately used or easily adapted, technical or manufacturing experience including the employment of key personnel, patents, trade marks, and access to marketing channels.

Under this second procedure, some nine companies were acquired between June 1919 and May of the following year. In some instances, as will be noted, these plants were immediately absorbed into the factory at New Haven. In other cases, the companies were operated, for a time at least, at existing locations. In addition to these purchases, a licensing and royalty agreement was made with a battery company whereby the licensor set Winchester up in the battery business.

*Cutlery*

Cutlery was one of the first lines to be considered. As has been noted, the manufacture of flatware and knives seemed to fall into the group of products which could be easily adapted to the methods of the gun and ammunition business. (It is of interest to note that Remington also went into cutlery manufacture in 1921 because of their experience with treating blade steel in bayonet manufacture during the war.)

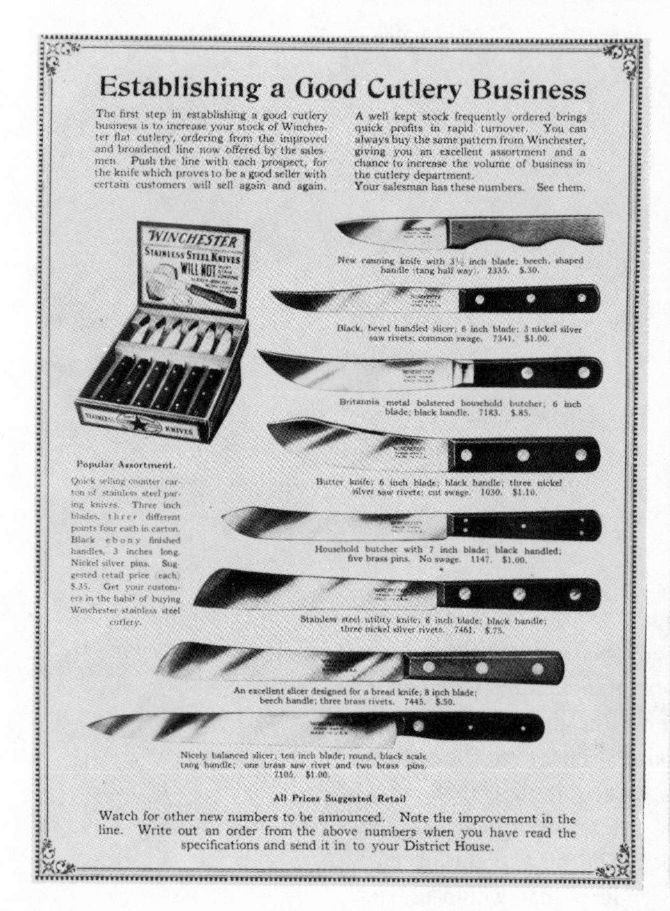

*Typical Examples of the Cutlery Line*

These items could be processed with minor adaptations of existing equipment and the production of kitchen knives, scissors and shears was begun within the New Haven plant. More specialized machinery and manufacturing experience were needed for pocket knives. For this reason two companies engaged in this line were purchased in 1919 and their equipment moved into the New Haven plant.

The first of these was the Eagle Pocket Knife Company of New Haven, which had grown considerably during the war period, supplying low-priced knives to the trade that had formerly imported this type of merchandise from Germany. The chief customer of the concern was George Borgefeldt & Company, of New York, which had specialized in handling German imports. Otto Hemming, the president of the Eagle Company, and his brothers had invented and developed machinery that produced interchangeable components in large quantities at low cost. Blades, for example, were blanked out by presses and semiautomatic grinding machines were used to give a cutting edge.

These methods of production appealed to Winchester because of their similarity to gun manufacture. In addition to moving the equipment of the Eagle concern into its plant, Winchester employed practically the entire labor force. Otto Hemming was put in charge of the operation and given responsibility for the development of special machinery.

Some of the equipment developed by Hemming proved adaptable to other lines of production. The grinding machines, for example, were used in the manufacture of ice skates.

For a time knives were sold through the Borgefeldt Company, branded with that organization's trade mark. As this method of distribution was contrary to the marketing policies being developed by Winchester, this channel of distribution was given up when existing contracts ran out.

The second concern, Napanoch Knife Company, produced a better-quality product using older methods of manufacture that involved a good deal of hand-fitting. From this purchase the chief asset acquired by Winchester was the technique involved in producing a high-grade line. The foreman of Napanoch and a small number of skilled workers came to New Haven with the purchase. Winchester set its production engineers to work on the methods used by Napanoch in order to adapt them as far as possible to mass-production techniques, and at the same time retain a high-quality product.

It was soon discovered that there was more to the production and marketing of cutlery than first appeared. For example, the Company initially stamped out knife blades of chrome-vanadium steel which gave a good cutting edge and was technically superior to the forged product currently used in high-quality knives. But the chrome-vanadium blades would not take a mirror-like polish which was accepted in the trade as an indication of a high-grade product. As a result Winchester was forced to use the forging process even though it gave an inferior product and was more expensive.

Problems also arose in connection with marketing. The Company's hardware and sporting-goods salesmen were not experts in the highly specialized field of cutlery. It was necessary for the Company to prepare a manual, both for the benefit of salesmen and the manufacturing engineers, which contained a glossary of terms and a description of the different types of knives, which ran into the hundreds. Also, the renewal of imports of low-grade German cutlery, which began in the early 1920s, made the competitive situation more difficult.

*Tools*

In addition to cutlery, tools were the most popular line for the hardware trade and it was especially important that Winchester have an extensive range of this type of product. Manufacture was begun promptly on a few items such as screw drivers, chisels, punches, hammers, hatchets and pliers, using methods developed within the Company.

*The Tool Line Was as Varied as It Was Complete*

To round out this line, the Lebanon Auger Bit Company, of Lebanon, New Hampshire, and the Page-Storm Drop Forge Company, of Chicopee, Massachusetts, were purchased in late 1919 and their machinery and equipment moved to New Haven. A third concern, the Mack Axe Company, of Beaver Falls, Pennsylvania, was acquired the following year. Winchester continued producing large axes at Beaver Falls but concentrated the manufacture of the other items at its main plant in New Haven.

From the Lebanon purchase came important technical information and skills. The Page-Storm purchase was valuable chiefly for the acquisition of a large number of drop dies used in the production of open-end wrenches. The Mack Axe Company gave Winchester a going concern and immediate production of this line of tools. An important added advantage was the knowledge of trade preferences for different types of axes.

To supply its dealers and the retail stores with tools not produced in its own factory or subsidiaries, Winchester bought articles such as saws, squares, and planes from other manufacturers, chiefly Sargent & Company of New Haven, which it distributed under its own trade mark.

*Batteries and Flashlights*

The Company was also attracted by the possibilities of the battery and flashlight business. The leading figure in the battery field at the time was Dr. C. F.

*Examples of Batteries and Flashlights*

Burgess of the University of Wisconsin, whose organization, Burgess Laboratories, of Madison, Wisconsin, had produced high-grade batteries for the United States Government during the war. As Burgess Laboratories was in need of financial assistance in 1919, it was willing to enter into an agreement to put Winchester into the battery business in return for the payment of $26,000. The agreement also provided for the use of the Burgess patents by Winchester on a royalty basis.

This proved to be a good arrangement, as Dr. Burgess had developed a chemical control of his batteries far ahead of his rivals and was able to specify raw materials that insured a product that would not deteriorate in storage and would give long life.

Experience in the production of flashlight cases was less happy. While the cases could be drawn out with no great trouble, the Company ran into patent difficulties. Eveready had just been purchased by National Carbon Company and had patented a large number of case and switch combinations. Winchester succeeded in working around these patents but only after considerable cost and delay.

*Fishing Equipment*

Fishing equipment was one of the most important lines developed in the sporting-goods field. Steel rods were quickly put into production. Using familiar

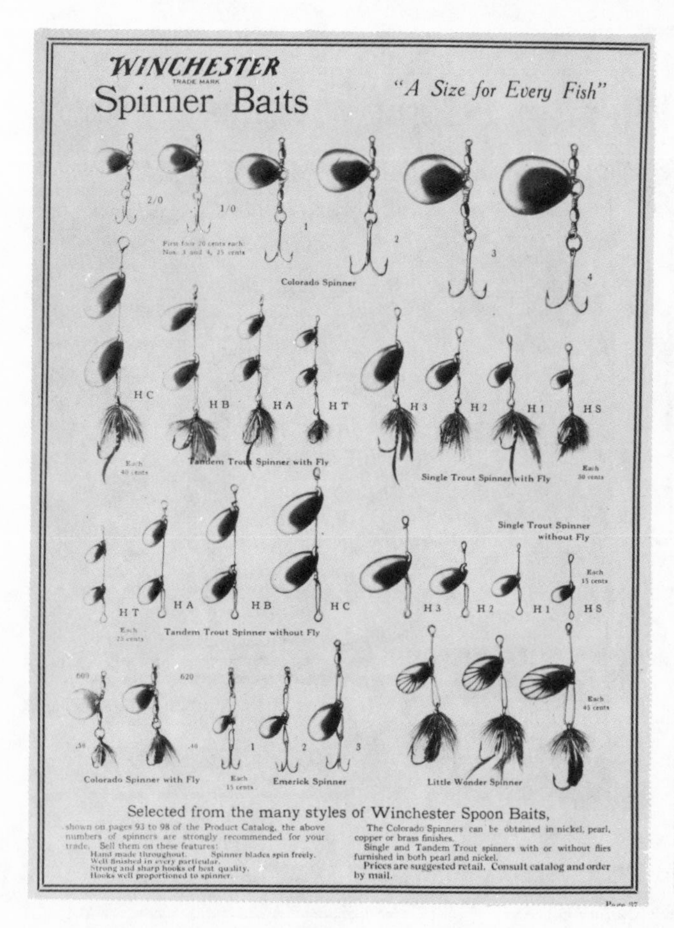

*Lines and Baits Supplemented Fishing Poles*

manufacturing methods, the Company was able to produce a high-quality product, especially in obtaining an accurate fit between the components of the jointed rods.

To manufacture a high-grade line of split-bamboo rods, Winchester purchased the business of E. W. Edwards, of Bangor, Maine, and employed him to supervise this branch of production at New Haven. Edwards was an excellent craftsman who had been trained by the famous rodmaker, H. L. Leonard, and his rods had a very high reputation among fishermen.

Winchester studied the methods followed by Edwards very carefully and was able to apply quantity methods of production to the manufacture of bamboo rods. While the quality of these rods was acceptable, it proved difficult to get manufacturing costs down to satisfactory levels.

Reels and baits were produced after the purchase of the A. G. Hendryx Company, of New Haven, which was manufacturing an extensive line of these items. The plant was bought apparently through the friendship between Frank Drew, vice president of Winchester, and Robert Oliver, president of A. B. Hendryx Company. After the equipment had been moved into the Winchester plant, it was discovered that the tools and machinery were largely worthless and they had to be almost completely rebuilt, at a high developmental expense.

*Skates*

Another line that looked promising was skates. Probably the best-known manufacturer in this field was the Barney & Berry Company, of Springfield, Massachusetts. Under the will of Mr. Barney, the city of Springfield had been given the controlling interest in the concern. In 1919 the financial position of Barney & Berry was weak and after some maneuvering, during which the disposal of the property became a partisan issue in local Springfield politics, Winchester bought the company. Until 1923 the plant was operated in Springfield, after which time the facilities were shifted to New Haven.

Much had to be done to bring the equipment of Barney & Berry up to modern standards. In addition Winchester added tubular ice skates and skate outfits to the regular line of ice and roller skates which had been produced by Barney & Berry. These introductions brought about certain manufacturing and marketing problems. Skate outfits, especially as they involved women's shoes to which the skates were attached, brought the management up against a style problem. Experience with accumulated inventories of shoe-skates which would not sell because they were no longer fashionable, plus continued manufacturing difficulty, prompted the management to drop ice skates from production.

Winchester capitalized to some extent on the good will and reputation of Barney & Berry. Skates, for example, were branded with a Barney & Berry-Winchester trade mark in the Company's catalog for 1920, although in subsequent issues all reference to Barney & Berry was dropped and the products bore only the Winchester trade mark.

*Clay Targets*

The most unfortunate purchase of outside companies during these years involved the production of clay targets. The Morrill Target Company, of Omaha, Nebraska, had apparently worked out a continuous target-casting machine. After a somewhat superficial investigation, the plant was purchased and the equipment brought to New Haven. It was then discovered that the machinery was defective and a new design was worked out that functioned well. Two machines were built

*Roller Skates and Ice Skates Promised To Be Highly Profitable*

incorporating the new features and production was begun during the summer of 1920 in New Haven and in a newly opened plant in Chicago. It was subsequently found that the apparatus was too expensive to operate and in January 1921, the machinery was scrapped and the Chicago plant closed.

The foregoing summary indicates something of the nature of the problems that were met in getting the new-products program under way. The examples of the target company and the bait business show that careless or inadequate investigations caused some of the difficulties. Considering the magnitude of the venture and the speed with which it was pushed, it is not astonishing that some errors were made. As Otterson reported to the stockholders at the end of 1920, the new-products program had involved up to that time ". . . the removal of the war machinery; the rearrangement of the machinery remaining; the purchase of new machinery suited for the manufacture of these new products; the installations of such machinery; the selection and design of the new products; the invention of improvements in such design; patenting of such inventions; the design and manufacture of tools, fixtures and gauges; the selection and employment of qualified experts in the several lines; the selection, employment and training of operators in the new processes; the creation of inventories of raw materials, work in process and finished goods of these new articles so as to make them available for sale in sufficient quantity and variety. . . ."

At this time Winchester had the following lines of new products including about 750 individual items either in production or under development: fishing rods, fishing reels, fishing lines and bait, roller skates, ice skates, flashlights, batteries, butcher knives, kitchen cutlery, pocket cutlery, carving sets, scissors, razors, axes, hammers, hatchets, chisels, screw drivers, wrenches, pliers, auger bits, planes, saws, files, and shears.

While these represented a considerable advance, the development of the new-products program was far from being completed. Only a few lines had been brought into full production and many problems of manufacture were still to be worked out. This general situation was reflected in the net sales of the new products which amounted to approximately $1.85 million. The business depression which swept the country during the latter part of 1920 and early 1921 caught Winchester at a bad time. In view of the general uncertainties brought on by the decline in prices, costs of raw materials, and the drop in general demand, the management decided not to introduce any new lines during that year, concentrating its attention on the full development of those already started. At the end of 1921 Otterson reported that: "The development of some twenty-five lines of new products previously started is practically complete, and sales of these new products have steadily increased. . . . During the year further large manufacturing economies have been effected. Labor and overhead costs have been substantially reduced."

Sales of the new products for 1921 were reported at $2.5 million, an increase of nearly thirty per cent over the figure for the previous year. This was encouraging, but the total was considerably below the amount needed to utilize the manufacturing capacity allocated to the new products. It remained to be determined whether the new lines under production at this time could be manufactured in sufficient volume and at costs which could achieve the desired objective.

### *Dealer-Agencies*

After a quiet survey of prospective candidates, Winchester formally launched its program to sign up dealers in October 1919 with a series of meetings held in twenty-six principal cities in the United States to which prospective agents were invited. Three top officials of the Company—Otterson, Brewer, and Anderson—divided the territory and gave a set speech at each of the meetings after which there was an opportunity for questions. They gave a brief outline of the Winchester Repeating Arms Company's history and discussed the reasons for branching out into new lines and adopting a new marketing method. They then described the dealer-agency plan and the advantages to be gained by becoming members. In announcing the condition that each dealer should purchase an amount of preferred stock of the Winchester Company, determined by the size of the town in which he did business, they explained that the intention was to bring him into closer relationship with the Company and insure his loyalty to the objectives of the dealer-agency plan.

These general meetings were followed by personal calls on dealers by Company representatives. Under the direction of Maycumber a staff of men familiar with hardware distribution was assigned to this job. A manual prepared for the use of these representatives gave the principal arguments that were to be used to persuade dealers to join. Particular emphasis was put upon the exclusive features of the plan. It was pointed out that by concentrating on one brand, repeat sales would be encouraged. The fact that a dealer would be the sole Winchester representative in his town would mean that much could be gained at meetings of Winchester dealers through an exchange of merchandising ideas without fear of competition. Considerable emphasis was given to the services to be offered to the dealers in laying out their stores, giving them merchandising ideas, supporting them with national advertising, and the like.

Apparently some difficulty was expected in explaining the stock-purchase requirement. The Company's representatives, who were carefully briefed on this phase of the program, were told:

> The psychological effect on a dealer purchasing this stock is something wonderful and we only have to take our own case as we have purchased a small amount of stock in a large corporation, and the hardware dealers are not different from ourselves. We should approach the dealer to buy stock in our Company very much along the same lines as his own local banker would do when he has some bank stock to sell which is very much in demand by the stockholders of that particular bank. As a matter of policy, the banker prefers to obtain a subscriber who has a personal following and influence and also one who would use that influence to bring more business to the bank because of that particular subscriber's connection with it.
>
> We do not want any hardware dealer as the Exclusive Winchester Dealer who has not a financial interest in us and furthermore, to make it equitable we must insist that all dealers in a town of comparative size would purchase the same amount of stock and that is why we have put the minimum amount noted above and this also is the maximum as we do not care to have the dealer purchase more than this amount, although we cannot control them if they purchase such stock on the open market.

There was a definite attempt made to build up the loyalty of dealers to the Company in other ways. Considerable stress was laid upon the prestige of the Winchester Company and the ability of Otterson. According to the manual:

> There is one man in our organization who is the driving power and personality back of the whole idea, who has pledged himself to see that the reputation of Winchester and the Winchester dealer does not suffer. On the other hand his whole effort is put forth to assure all concerned that cooperation between the Company and the dealer will attain results gratifying to both. This one man is a modern engineer of industry who has been successful by his unselfish efforts in upholding the honor of the interests he represented and not an effort toward an individual goal. By always working for this end his own advancement has been remarkable.
>
> This man is John E. Otterson, our president, and it is needless to say that the dynamic force which he has put into his efforts in the past will now be directed towards making the Winchester plan something to be desired rather than something to be sold.

Winchester's plan to develop the dealer-agency method of distribution created a tremendous stir in hardware circles. Even prior to formal announcement numerous rumors were being circulated about the future plans of the Company.[1]

The formal announcement by the Company of its plans was even more disquieting to the trade. Hardware jobbers and those retailers who had not been invited to join the dealer-agency plan, or who objected on principle were especially critical. A considerable number of articles, editorials, and "letters to the editor" appeared in various trade journals throughout the latter part of 1919 and during

1920. Probably the most interesting comments appeared in *Hardware Age.* The discussion began with an editorial in the December 18, 1919, issue entitled "Winchester Chain Stores Promise Fireworks," in which it was announced that the magazine would run a series of articles that would consider the subject from the point of view of all the interested parties. Indicating that it would maintain a neutral position, *Hardware Age,* through its editor, Roy F. Soule, stated in the December 18, 1919, issue:

In all, five distinct groups of hardware people have already been developed by the activities of the New Haven concern. They are the Winchester Company, other hardware manufacturers, the hardware jobbers, the selected Winchester dealers and all other hardware dealers. And already these forces are antagonistically arrayed in lines of battle that threaten to everlastingly rip peace and quiet from the trade.

In the succeeding issue of December 22, Soule presented "The Manufacturer's Side of the Winchester Plan." After reviewing the reasons given by Winchester for its plans, he continued:

Louis K. Liggett, the man responsible for the success of the Liggett Drug Stores, is prominently identified with the Winchester Company, and this gives rise to repeated statements in hardware circles that the methods used to build up the chain of drug stores that bear Mr. Liggett's name will be largely duplicated in the Winchester endeavor.

The Winchester Company has gathered about it a very large staff of skilled hardware men and is most energetically pushing its plans. These plans naturally affect other hardware manufacturers. If the Winchester chain stores succeed it will be a great thing for the Winchester Company. In like proportion it will be a blow at a lot of other American hardware factories. Naturally these other factories are not sitting still while Winchester romps home with the commercial bacon. If the Winchester Stores take over and vigorously push all the new Winchester products, what is to become of the carefully developed business of the old manufacturers of such hardware? This question alone is enough to put every competitive manufacturer right up on his toes.

The Winchester Company hopes that ten per cent of the hardware stores in the country will become Winchester dealers. That would mean a frightful jolt to a lot of manufacturers whose names are watchwords in the hardware trade.

The editor predicted that other manufacturers would not submit meekly to the new competition:

The facts are that most of the hardware manufacturers in the United States feel that the Winchester plans are a menace to their business and they are going to fight to the finish, and they cannot be blamed.

These other manufacturers looking upon a Winchester store are frequently seeing in that store a carefully developed distributor, a merchant whose business has been courted with courtesy, co-operation and good merchandise for many years. They say that to see that merchant's business go to another factory on a strictly competitive basis of price and quality would not arouse their ire, but to see it go as the result of a plan is a keen disappointment. Feeling that way they are vigorously presenting the merits of their goods as never before. They believe that many merchants are going to make the grave errors of giving up accounts for well-known lines of hardware, and that the Winchester line will not be accepted with the same public favor. This side of the question is being most emphatically impressed upon the retail trade by the sales forces of hundreds of factories who propose to hold the business they have built. Then too scores of hardware manufacturers are going on record saying that they will not manufacture private brand goods for the Winchester Company, as it is their belief that as soon as sufficient business has been developed by Winchester they will begin to manufacture it themselves. They feel that such action would also jeopardize a large number of their wholesale accounts.

Under the title "The Wholesalers' Side of the Winchester Plan" the editor prefaced his comments in the January 1, 1920, issue with the following:

In [manufacturing] circles considerable heat has developed, but when compared to the conflagration the Winchester system has started among wholesalers of hardware the manufacturer's blaze seems but a bonfire.

The main fears of the wholesalers were summarized as follows: first, the number of Winchester dealers would be greatly expanded which would result in a substantial loss of business to wholesalers; second, Winchester would take over the jobbing functions through its own warehouses, and finally, the exclusive dealers would be able to undersell the jobber's customers even on guns and ammunition. This last possibility touched an especially sore spot.

The jobbers were so aroused that the executive committee of the National Hardware Association called a conference with Otterson in New York in December 1919. A stenographic report of a part of this conference was reprinted by Soule at the end of his editorial. Otterson was not inclined to placate the jobbers as the following extract indicates:

*Mr. Decatur:* I would like to be informed by you if we are to be in a position to sell the retailer loaded shells, ammunition and arms at the same price as you sell the Winchester stores.

*Mr. Otterson:* Probably not—what our price will be to the selected dealers is, of course, a matter of determination. When we have our new plan in force, we will be able to determine it—it may be that we can distribute at a lower cost than you do, in which event our exclusive dealers will have a lower price than some dealer in the same town would have to pay.

*Mr. Decatur:* We have come in contact with many of the men whom you have signed up. They have been impressed with what your solicitors have said to them that your policy in the very near future is to eliminate the jobber.

*Mr. Otterson:* It is not our policy to eliminate the jobbers on Winchester guns and ammunition. Whether we do or not, I think it depends more on you than ourselves. If our present plan is successful, it is our plan to continue it—if it is unsuccessful, it will probably be modified. Whether it is successful depends largely on your attitude toward us. I think there is still an incentive on the part of the jobbers to continue to sell Winchester guns and ammunition. The fact that we have gone into competition with you in this one particular does not warrant the suggestion in our mind that you go out of the business.

*A Member:* What is the incentive?

*Mr. Otterson:* That there will still be a profit to be made and your customers will be served. We do not expect to eliminate the profit any more than we have in the past. We are not going to reduce your profits. We are going to sell you as we have sold you and as favorably as our competitors have sold you.

In discussing "The Retailer's Side of the Winchester Plan," in the January 1 issue Soule became almost lyrical. Speaking of the dealers who had already signed up he commented:

No effort has been spared to woo them into the Winchester family, and then to march them right up the altar where mutual promises changed the name over the store door.

The love song of the Winchester swain has been vibrant with the advantages of co-operative merchandising, plaintive with the pulling power of wonderful window trims and serious with the services of numerous specialists on the pay roll. These notes intermingling with the attractive trills of exclusive territory on new Winchester products brought the adored dealer to the balcony. Then the Red "W" Romeo strummed and tenored his temptations with renewed vigor, singing stanzas of wealth-wedded drug brides in palatial domiciles of commercial happiness, and under the spell of that weird well-directed music the dealer wavered.

Quick to note and profit by ecah changing emotion, the ardent gallant in the new garden of distribution threw full lung power into the high notes of final appeal, and as the words pregnant with price preference on guns and ammunition tumbled from his trembling lips the triumph of conquest came to crown his effort. The dealer succumbed and slipped down the winding stairs. There in the garden of hope he gladly pledged love, loyalty, and merchandising devotion.

Soule doubted seriously that Winchester would or could eliminate the hardware jobbers. In his judgment, some ten per cent of the hardware dealers at most could be included in the plan, which would leave the rest to be supplied through regular jobbing channels.

The concluding paragraph is of unusual interest:

Already this innovation in merchandising has stimulated the hardware merchants of this country to most unusual efforts, and it is a safe prediction that 1920 will be marked by selling effort that will make the whole nation sit up and wonder at the splendid initiative of men who merchandise under the name of hardware.

In view of subsequent events, one of the most interesting attacks on the Winchester plans was made by Major George W. Simmons, vice president of the Simmons Hardware Company and reported in the February 19, 1920, *Hardware Age*. Major Simmons was no mean opponent. The Associated Simmons Hardware Company, located in St. Louis, was unquestionably the best known and probably the largest wholesale jobbing house in the country. Major Simmons launched a full-scale offensive. Speaking before the Philadelphia convention of the Pennsylvania and Atlantic Seaboard Association in February, 1920, he announced that he was going to give ". . . such information as has come to us from our 600 salesmen, who cover every county in the United States, regarding the new Winchester plan."

His remarks reveal clearly the strategy employed to discredit the Winchester program. "Do we," he asked, "desire a centralized control by financial interests in Wall Street of the retail hardware businesses throughout this country?" He warned the retail dealers that this was a move to have them build up a demand for the Winchester brands, after which the Company would move to open its own stores even in small towns. Drawing a doubtful analogy from the methods used in financing by the "tobacco crowd," he said that the Winchester plan was "primarily a stock-promotion scheme." Liggett's connection with the Company was regarded as ominous. He also intimated that Winchester was connected with

Montgomery Ward & Company. He stressed the fact that the dealers were expected to push an unknown brand of hardware in competition with well-established names, and noted the possible loss of identity by the individual storekeepers. He emphasized the problems of production faced by the Company, ending his remarks by announcing that Simmons had dropped the Winchester guns and ammunition from its catalog and was no longer taking orders for these goods.

Other opponents of the Winchester plan also took positive action. A number of the jobbers followed Simmons's example by dropping the Winchester line of guns and ammunition. Some jobbers continued to purchase guns and ammunition but used them to undermine Winchester dealers by cutting prices. A field representative of the Company reported that one dealer was giving up the plan in part because ". . . he can get the same or better discounts on Winchester guns and ammunition from his jobber as are given by us to our dealers." Many salesmen of jobbing houses were given arguments that could be used to undermine the confidence of Winchester dealers or those who thought of joining.

Several manufacturers of products that might be bought by Winchester to fill out its line of hardware to its own dealers announced their unwillingness to make such supplies available. The principal reason advanced was that Winchester's policy was to expand its own production capacity as rapidly as possible which would eventually deprive these manufacturers of a part of their market.

The retailers also showed their antagonism in various ways. The subject of the Winchester plan was argued violently in several regional hardware dealers associations. While in most instances no action appears to have been taken, the Pacific Northwest Hardware and Implement Association, meeting in January 1920, resolved that "The sentiment seemed unanimously opposed to the Winchester plan as being demoralizing to the trade and tending to subvert the existing system of distribution, believed to be, on the whole, more efficient."

Winchester was not without its supporters. A number of letters indicated the dissatisfaction of many dealers with the jobbers and showed an appreciation of the possibility of the Winchester plan. Typical of this attitude was a communication addressed to *Hardware Age,* January 22, 1920, which stated in part:

> I have just read with interest and smiles the jobbers' position on the Winchester plan. What a difference it makes when the shoe fits your own feet instead of someone else's. I am pleased to find they have so much interest in the ninety per cent of the retailers—how we retailers have been trying in years gone by to interest them in that same ninety per cent.
>
> I am glad the Winchester Company has dropped a bomb in their midst, and if I lose the large amount of money I have put in Winchester stock, as has been suggested by some jobbers, it would greatly embarrass me and other retailers financially. I cannot help but feel that it is money well spent and that we poor devils who have sacrificed ourselves on the Winchester altar will be remembered as martyrs in the cause of the retailers, and that at some future date they will erect a monument in our memory for having been the cause of waking up the jobber and interesting him in the retailer.

In several hardware-dealer conventions the supporters of Winchester were able to force an official expression of neutrality toward the dealer-agency plan against rather violent opposition. Meanwhile the Company gave wide publicity to the nature of its plans through announcements and articles in the trade journals.

The controversy aroused in hardware circles over the Winchester plan for dealer-agents seems somewhat out of proportion to the threat that Winchester itself offered to the trade. To be sure, success of the Company's manufacturing and distribution plans would be disturbing to existing producers and distributors; but a considerable part of the reaction seems to have come from a fear that the success of the Winchester plan would cause other similar ventures. Prices were high during 1919 and 1920 and distributors were on the defensive. This was the first major experiment in chain-store type distribution in hardware, and Liggett's association with the Company and his success in the drug-store business showed what might happen to distribution in this field as well.

On the whole the Winchester management welcomed the publicity. It was not unflattering to be the subject of long articles and editorials in the trade journals and to be included on the agenda for discussion at trade association meetings, especially when the opponents appeared to be so much on the defensive.

The Company's most effective answer to criticism and attack was to proceed with its campaign. By February 1920, almost 2,400 dealers, scattered throughout the United States, had signed contracts. These dealers were organized into some twenty-nine district associations or clubs which met periodically to discuss matters of mutual interest. The officers of these district associations were elected from the membership of the respective areas.

These district associations were popular among the retailers, and they provided a convenient means through which officials of the Company could meet with dealers. The management was also able to turn over certain problems to the association for solution. For example, several hardware merchants signed up who were unsympathetic with the organization or who were closely allied with jobbers who were bitter opponents of the Winchester plan. By giving each district club power to pass on the eligibility of members from its area, this problem was solved.

On the whole, the dealer-agents were highly enthusiastic about the plan. This enthusiasm was based upon tangible evidence of the Company's ability and willingness to be of real aid in improving merchandising practices. Advertising displays were supplied by Winchester at an average cost of five dollars per month to each dealer and were well conceived and of substantial help in attracting customer attention. National advertising by Winchester in such periodicals as the *Saturday Evening Post* and the *Literary Digest* was tied in with advertising copy that could be run by the dealer in his local newspaper. The Company published and sent out to the dealers each month the *Winchester Herald,* containing numerous suggestions for improving merchandising methods, pictures of prize-winning window displays, announcements of new products, and the like. Members could get at a nominal cost plans for modernizing store layouts and installation could be supervised by a Company representative where desired. Advice was also furnished on matters of proper store accounting, methods of finance, and analysis of credit risks.

In June 1920 Winchester took a further step to build up the enthusiasm of the dealer-agents for the plan by inviting them to a five-day convention in New Haven. Some one thousand dealers, many with their families, attended.

A great deal of time and effort went into making the convention a success. The general purposes were to increase the loyalty of the dealers and to give them a first-hand acquaintance with the organization and its personnel. The program

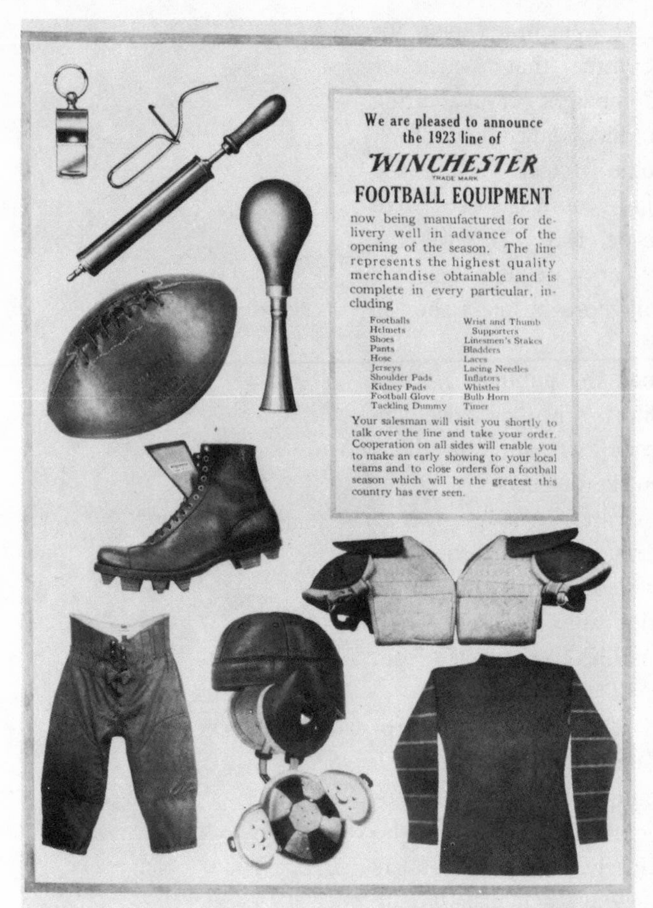


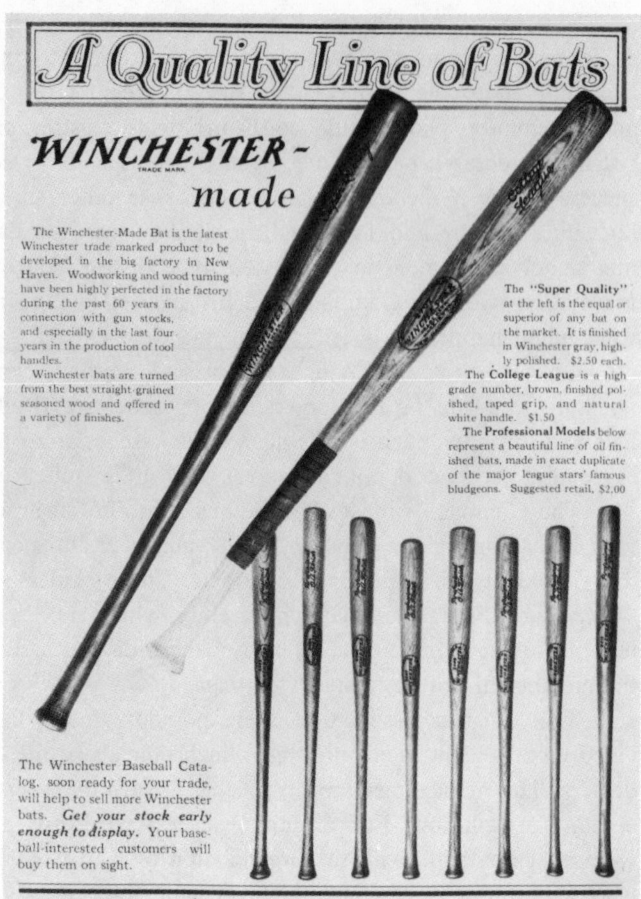


*Football Equipment and Baseball Bats Were Included in the Sporting-Goods Line*

combined business and pleasure. Most of the delegates passed through New York where they embarked on a steamer, the *Highlander,* for the overnight trip to New Haven. Arrangements had been made with Yale University to house a considerable number of delegates, to supply meals at the college dining hall, and to hold meetings in the Yale buildings.

The entertainment was fairly elaborate and included a moonlight trip on Long Island Sound aboard the *Highlander,* a musical show at the Schubert Theater, a clambake at a nearby beach, topped off by a banquet. A special supplementary program of musical recitals, sightseeing trips, and teas was provided for the ladies.

The more serious side of the convention included tours of the factory, "classroom" instruction on various aspects of the hardware and sporting-goods business, speeches by the principal figures in the Company, and a meeting at which the delegates were asked to raise questions and problems. At this convention a National Association of Winchester Clubs was formed and officers were elected from the membership.

The convention was undoubtedly successful in arousing the attending members to increased enthusiasm for the Winchester plan and for the organization behind it.

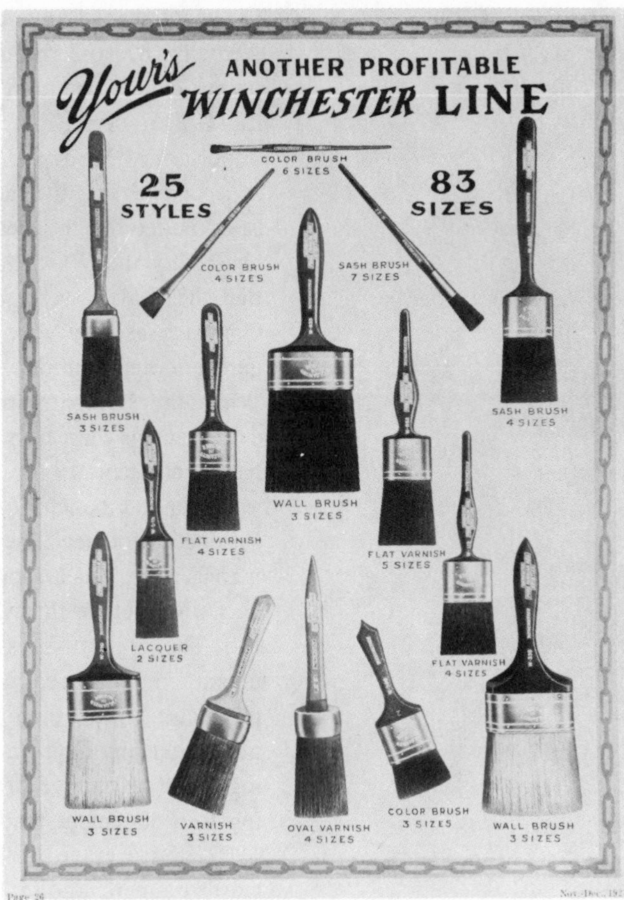


*Paints and Brushes Supplemented the Hardware Line*

The original intention had been to hold a second annual convention in 1921, but the unsettled business conditions of that year forced a postponement until 1922. Meanwhile, the Company pushed its campaign to sign up additional dealers. By the end of 1920, the total was just under 3,400. A year later, in spite of the depression, almost 4,000 dealers were enrolled. While this figure was considerably below the original goal of approximately 8,000, under the circumstances it was a creditable record, and was a tribute to the appeal that the Winchester plan had for hardware dealers and the effectiveness of the Company's promotional activities.

By this time it was possible to make some estimate of success of the dealer-agency program, although it was still too soon to make any adequate judgment concerning the future role these outlets would play in the marketing of the Company's products.

The relative place that the dealer-agents had come to occupy in Winchester's marketing structure is shown by the fact that this group absorbed some 24 per cent of the Company's total net sales of $17.2 million in 1920, and 45 per cent of the total of $11.5 million in 1921. (*See Appendix I-2.*) A breakdown between new and old lines indicates that the Winchester dealers took 20 per cent of the total gun and ammunition production in 1920 and 38 per cent the year following.

On new lines the amounts ran 55 per cent and 70 per cent for the same two years. Actually, because the new lines made up such a relatively small part of the total output of the Company during three years (11 per cent for 1920 and 23 per cent for 1921), dealer purchases of guns and ammunition were still about twice as important as hardware and other sporting goods in 1921.

Considering the fact that the dealer-agencies were established as the principal sales outlet for the new products, the trend and percentage of these lines purchased by the Winchester dealers was encouraging. On the other hand, the fact that the dealers were spending twice as much on guns and ammunition from the Company as they were on new lines was not so impressive, if it is assumed that guns and ammunition would probably have been sold anyway through the jobbers. While the Company received a slightly higher price for its old lines from the dealer-agents than from the jobbers, as will be noted below, this differential would hardly compensate for the cost in developing the agency plan.

But this conclusion would not be justified by the situation existing in 1921. Production of new lines, as has been noted, was just getting under way, and the management had reason to be confident that a much larger volume of these products would move through the dealer-agents as soon as they became available.

The opportunities for future sales through this channel are perhaps better illustrated by a breakdown showing average sales per dealer-agent of Winchester products. These amounted to about $1,400 for both years. As the Company did not gather any data on total sales of its dealers, there is no accurate way of figuring what percentage of the total requirements Winchester was supplying. According to a statement made by William T. Birney, assistant sales manager, in April 1922, the average hardware store sold annually between $35,000 and $75,000 worth of merchandise. If an arbitrary figure of $50,000 be taken as representing the total purchases of an average Winchester dealer, then the Company was supplying less than three per cent of his requirements. For hardware and sporting goods other than guns and ammunition the percentage was but a little over one per cent. Considering the effect of the depression and the probability that the new lines would be available in greater variety and volume, it required no unusual optimism to believe that these percentages could be substantially increased.

One reason for the amount of the gun and ammunition sales to the dealers was the price advantage given them by the Company over the jobber outlets. For example, in early 1922, a Winchester dealer could buy a Model 94 rifle, which cost the jobber $25.19, direct from the factory at $26.95. The jobber would ordinarily sell this same gun to a non-Winchester dealer for $30.05. Thus while the dealer-agent paid $1.76 more than the jobber, he had an advantage of $3.10 over rival retailers, unless the jobber wished to cut his margin. Somewhat comparable advantages were given the dealer-agents on ammunition. These prices and the prestige of the Company's old-line products put this part of the sales to the dealer-agents on a reasonably firm basis.

To sell its new lines of products to the dealers the Company relied more upon the exclusive features of the dealer-agency plan and the quality of products than it did upon price. This situation put the sales of its new lines to dealer-agents by Winchester on a fairly narrow margin. While the Company set resale prices for the retailers, these were not mandatory. Only by making Winchester's reputation for quality firm in the minds of the customers, could the higher resale price of the Company be maintained against the prices of competitors' merchandise. Thus the retailer was under more or less constant pressure to take advantage of any better prices offered to him by jobber representatives.

While the loyalty of the dealers and the reputation for quality might prove to be sufficient to expand the sales of new products to this group, it is clear that a reduction of manufacturing costs, that could be passed on in part to the dealers, was necessary to put this part of the marketing organization on a firm basis.

*Retail Stores*

Originally, the management's plan was to build up the Winchester retail stores, as Liggett had initially done, by acquiring existing hardware and sporting-goods outlets in the larger cities, and in April 1919, the board of directors authorized the purchase of the Thomas E. Wilson concern of Chicago. This particular negotiation not only fell through, but the Company was generally unsuccessful in buying going concerns except in Boston, where the United Hardware Company and William Read & Company were acquired and converted into Winchester stores.

These difficulties brought a shift to a policy of building up a chain of newly organized stores. Beginning in November 1919, a number of surveys were made of possible sites and, early in 1920, a campaign to obtain a rapid expansion of a retail chain was launched. J. Paul Foster, who was in charge of the development, adopted a slogan of "A Store a Week," which if carried out would have given a group of some fifty stores by the end of the year. A staff of some 195 persons was assigned to the program. Elaborate surveys were made of some ninety-two locations in seventy-five cities. These surveys were conducted in the grand manner and at considerable expense, and with as much publicity as could be obtained. At the same time, studies were made of what promised to be the most effective ways of displaying and merchandising hardware and sporting goods. A large inventory of store fixtures and merchandise was acquired during 1920 in anticipation of the needs of the contemplated chain.

Providence, Rhode Island, was in April 1920, the scene of the opening of the first Winchester store. It was an auspicious affair, attended by members of various fishing, gun, rifle, and fly-casting clubs, as well as public officials and representatives of social and political organizations. These groups were entertained at a special evening opening attended by the principal officials of the Company. The next day the general public was invited and some 3,500 people are said to have visited the store.

The general arrangement of this store and its appearance, which was typical of all the Winchester retail stores, indicated the great amount of work that had gone into the plan. The Winchester name appeared on the front in vivid red against a background of gray. Interior fixtures and lighting were of the latest design. Merchandise was displayed so that everything was within reach for inspection by the customer. Stock was carried in numbered drawers which made it possible "to secure the article without taking the sample away from the sight of the customer." There was also a ladies' reception room for the benefit of feminine shoppers.

It proved physically impossible to keep up the proposed schedule of opening a store each week. The speed with which this program was initially launched led to carelessness in the negotiation of leases and some embarrassing legal controversies resulted. The most serious obstacle to building up a large chain of stores, however, was the advent of the depression of late 1920 and early 1921. A period of rapidly falling prices was not one during which it was desirable to sign long-term leases and build up further inventories.

Under the circumstances, the management decided in October 1920 to hold up further expansion until business conditions improved and to consolidate the gains already made. By this time seventeen leases had been signed and some six stores were being operated. Five more were opened by the following July, bringing the total to eleven (shown in the following tabulation) which marked the peak of expansion of the retail stores.

| *Location* | *Opening Date* |
|---|---|
| Providence | May 1, 1920 |
| Boston (Tremont) | June 12, 1920 |
| New Haven | June 26, 1920 |
| Troy | August 7, 1920 |
| Pawtucket | September 4, 1920 |
| Springfield | September 11, 1920 |
| Lawrence | October 23, 1920 |
| Boston (Summer) | November 13, 1920 |
| Worcester | November 27, 1920 |
| New York | July 1, 1920 |
| Boston (Read) | July 1, 1921 |

Net sales of the stores during 1920 came to about $683,000. An operating loss of approximately $59,000 was incurred during the same period. The loss was not unexpected, considering the fact that the stores had not been operating long and the effect of the depression.

In 1921 Otterson expressed his optimism concerning the future of the stores. Reporting to the board of directors in March of that year he stated that sales quotas had originally been established for the retail stores based upon the expectations that they would make good in six months. He went on to say that he thought a one-year or possibly a two-year period was more reasonable. He also pointed out that while developmental cost had been higher than was justified by the small chain, the original intention to establish a much larger group of stores could be regarded as merely postponed because of the depression. These costs could, on a resumption of the program, be spread over a larger number of units. He concluded: "I have not the slightest doubt in my mind that these stores will immediately return to a profitable basis when business conditions improve and that they will fully meet our expectations in comparison with any reasonable quotas that we may set."

During the succeeding twelve months the organization and operation of the stores underwent considerable modification. The difficulties which led to this reorganization resulted largely from the initial assumption that the Liggett model was applicable. One obvious difference between the two organizations was, of course, the number of stores in the respective chains. In contrast to Winchester's eleven retail outlets, the Louis K. Liggett Company was operating some 226 Liggett drug stores in the United States in 1921.



The differences between operating a retail drug chain and a group of hard-

Labels in Red, Gold, Gray and Black

Red letters on a gray panel with a background of red, gold, and black stripes make up a very smart label. The red and gold seal is placed on the ferrule

*Examples of Winchester Garden-Tool Labels*

ware and sporting-goods stores were, moreover, basic and serious. For example, one of the fundamental features of Liggett's organization was the highly centralized control exercised over individual store operations. This was accomplished in part by having the stores as nearly identical as possible in respect to layout, types of merchandise handled, and so on. All decisions concerning marketing policies, advertising, special sales, dates of sales, and the promotion of particular products, were made at the central office. The clerks were largely order-takers who were not required to have any special knowledge of the products they handled. The cost of this central control when spread over a large number of stores and over a large volume of business would, of course, be small for each dollar of sales. Winchester attempted to follow this pattern faithfully. According to Pugsley: "The Home Office was to do everything for the stores and the Manager was to have no leeway, but was to work under instructions from the Home Office, as to what to sell, how to sell it, and when to sell it. Advertisements were handled from the Home Office."

A large staff was built up in New Haven to handle purchasing, selling policies, and the like. At its peak in 1920, the central office staff of 240 outnumbered the employees in the stores.

By the middle of 1921, Winchester was finding it increasingly difficult to maintain this high degree of centralization. Unlike drugs and allied items, for which the demand was apparently quite uniform in different urban centers, the Company found that the market for sporting goods and hardware varied noticeably in the various cities in which its stores were located. Springfield, Lawrence and Worcester, for example, offered a fair market for hardware in addition to sporting goods. In New York and Boston hardware moved slowly, but sporting goods, camping equipment, and men's and women's sportswear were quite popular.

As a result, Winchester found it was impractical to maintain a highly centralized management control even for its relatively small chain. More responsibility for buying and merchandising policy had to be given to the local managers. In early 1922, Otterson reported the shift in policy, which had been initiated some months before: "The idea is that we take the best men we have now, and put them into the stores as district managers. They will turn the organization into better men. At some future time we can take these men and draw them together in a central office and put the men that they have trained in charge of the stores. We have two or three very good men in the central organization, and by making them District Managers, it puts them in competition with each other. Their future will depend upon the success of their work in their own store."

The change in the character of the different stores represented a necessary adaptation to the circumstances. Winchester now owned, and was operating, a small group of stores, each with its peculiar problems. The absence of uniformity took away one of the main features of successful chain-store operations, and lessened still further the chances for financial success.

Attempts to operate the Winchester stores according to the Liggett model also broke down in another, though less serious, respect. As has been noted, the Liggett clerks, like most chain-store sales employees, were not required to have any special familiarity with the product sold. To some extent in the case of hardware, and especially in respect to sporting goods, this did not hold. As Pugsley noted on one occasion: "The successful sporting goods salesman must be a specialist in his particular line; in other words, it is desirable that he know as much about his line as the prospective customer." This meant that Winchester needed more experienced and presumably higher-paid store salesmen than did the Liggett organization.

A further change in the original conception and position of the retail stores in the Company's general marketing program came in 1921. This shift in policy is indicated by a drive which began in the summer of that year to extend the dealer-agency plan to cities of over 50,000 population. Reporting to Otterson in September, Maycumber stated, "We have been very successful in establishing agencies in the larger cities." He noted that some 121 contracts had already been signed, including twenty-one in Boston, where the Company already had three stores of its own.

At first glance, this policy suggests a complete abandonment of the Company's original idea to reserve the larger urban centers for its own stores. In fact, however, this move represented a change in the character of the retail-store operations which was prompted by Winchester's further experience in retail selling.

In choosing its store locations Winchester had followed Liggett's practice of a high-rent district as the area in which to locate. Anderson explained this policy before the Winchester dealers on one occasion: "I think that in some instances the dealer in a large town misinterprets the cost of rent. Rents of course in the larger towns are very high, and it is my impression that many hardware merchants in the large towns are missing great opportunities looming before them because they are afraid to pay rent which will put them into the merchandising districts. It is false economy. When Mr. Liggett opened his store in the Grand Central Station in New York some of his friends told him that he was doing the most foolish thing he had done in his life. I do not recall what he pays but it is an enormous figure and looks staggering. Mr. Liggett had imagination and good judgment enough, however, and went ahead without hesitation, and the store was an immediate success. He told me his experience was that the more rent he paid the more money he made, not that high rent makes business but it enables one to obtain a proper merchandising location. In the main, large cities do not contain hardware stores in the shopping districts."

Actually this analogy to the experiences in the drug business has doubtful validity. While a high rent may not result in a high cost for a drug or similar-type store, where the turnover of merchandise is high, a combined hardware and sporting-goods store in the same location might well find that a part of its inventory moved too slowly to absorb the rental charge. As Winchester's announced policy was to handle only high-quality merchandise, its rate of turnover might be expected to be even lower than that of a conventional hardware store, or the hardware section of a large department store, selling lower-priced merchandise or handling only fast-moving items.

Within the first year and a half of the retail store operations, the Company discovered that hardware had a rate of turnover that was too slow to make it a profitable type of merchandise to handle in any of its stores, located as they were in high-rent districts. (For example, the New York store was located at the corner of 42d Street and Madison Avenue; in New Haven near the corner of Church and Chapel Streets; in Boston the three stores were on Tremont, Winter, and Summer Streets, respectively, in the heart of the downtown shopping district.)

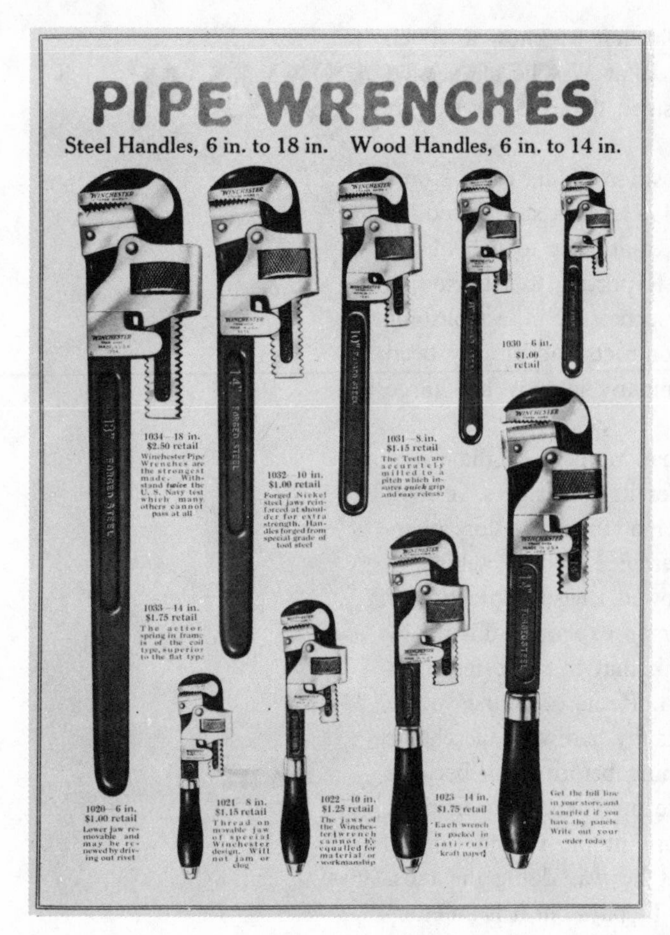

*Many Variations of the Same Type of Product Were Produced*

It was therefore decided to drop hardware from the lines carried in the retail stores and to concentrate on sporting goods and allied items that had a more satisfactory rate of turnover.

This decision meant that the sales of Winchester's new lines of hardware would be practically eliminated in the larger cities unless other outlets could be procured. The extension of the dealer-agencies into the urban areas came as a consequence.

By dropping hardware from its own retail stores, Winchester abandoned its original idea that these outlets would provide a substantial market for its new lines of products. To be sure, the Company's brands of sporting goods would continue to be handled, but financial success would not have to be measured largely in terms of its ability to carry on a merchandising venture that had little organic connection with the main functioning of the Winchester organization.

Judged by this standard, results of store operations for 1921 were disappointing. While sales had expanded to over $1.82 million the net loss amounted to more than $606,000. In spite of this record, the management had not yet lost its enthusiasm for the retail-store plan, at least in its modified form. In his annual report to the stockholders for December 31, 1921, Otterson stated: "These stores are developing at a satisfactory rate in spite of the business depression that has

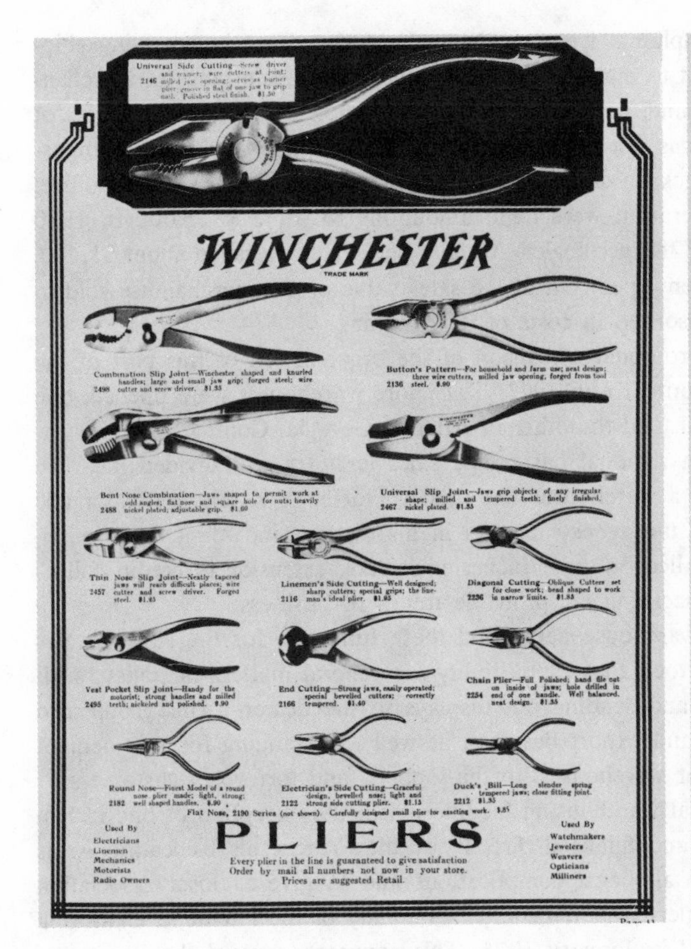


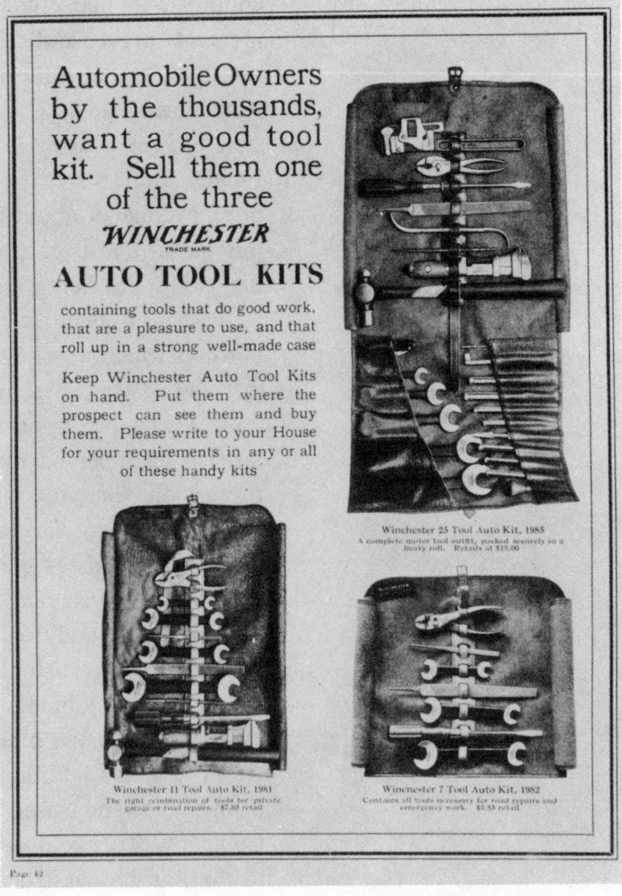


*Pliers and Automobile Tool Kits Were Also Offered*

affected all retail merchandising. They offer not only an excellent channel of distribution for our products, but are in themselves a splendid advertisement and serve to build up the good will and trade value of the name 'Winchester.' "

*Warehouses and Sales Organization*

Because of the decision to distribute the bulk of its new products directly to the dealer-agents and the retail stores, Winchester had to expand and reorganize its sales force and to provide additional facilities in order to assume the functions that would have otherwise been taken on by the jobbers. Among the more important of these functions were the physical storing and handling of merchandise, the employment of additional salesmen to call on the dealers, the analysis of credit risks, collection of accounts due, and the like.

Initially, it was planned to centralize most of these new functions in New Haven, where the Company had long maintained a warehousing and shipping organization. This was done during 1919 and 1920, although two additional warehouses were opened in 1919 to handle the physical distribution of goods, one in Chicago, and the other in San Francisco.

The Company soon discovered that under this arrangement it could not give its dealers service comparable with that offered by jobbers. Three warehouses were not enough to supply dealer-agents who were scattered throughout the entire country and many complaints were received about the delay in receiving shipments. It proved difficult to maintain adequate stocks of certain types of merchandise and, at the same time, to prevent the accumulation of excess inventories of slow-moving items. It was not easy to supervise the salesmen and almost impossible to keep a close check on credit analysis and collection from the central office. Finally the costs of operation were high, amounting to some $825,000 in 1920 or an average of about $285 per dealer. As sales per dealer averaged about $1,400, this meant that over twenty per cent of the sales value of the merchandise sold to the group was being absorbed in costs of distribution.

These difficulties prompted a revision of the organization of this part of the business which was begun early in 1921. Two more warehouses were opened, one in Kansas City, Missouri, and the other in Atlanta, Georgia. Controls were decentralized and put upon a regional basis. The sales territory was divided into five districts each served by a warehouse. The manager of each warehouse was made responsible for most of the agency matters in his district, including the supervision of salesmen who called on the Winchester dealers, extension of credit, collections, and estimates concerning the probable trends of business.

The New Haven warehouse performed these functions for the eastern sales district and in addition took the responsibility for general matters of policy, such as national advertising and sending out displays to the dealers. This group also supervised the jobbing and export business, as well as arranging for shipment of merchandise to the other warehouses, to the jobbers, and to foreign customers.

All of the additional warehousing facilities, with the exception of one in San Francisco, were leased and financed directly by the Winchester Repeating Arms Company. To avoid certain legal complications and to give a closer association to the Pacific Coast dealers, the Winchester Company of the Pacific, a California corporation, was formed in January 1921. This concern acquired the leases and other assets of the San Francisco warehouse plus some extra cash from the Winchester Repeating Arms Company in exchange for its entire issue of capital stock made up of $750,000 of $100 par value common stock and $250,000 of seven per cent preferred stock.

This stock was offered to Winchester dealers on the Pacific Coast in lieu of Winchester Company stock as a requirement of becoming dealer-agents and by 1922 some $150,000 worth of stock had been purchased. An added attraction was offered to stockholders in the form of a bonus-dividend based upon the value of purchases made from the Company by the stockholding dealers. The agents were given a further interest in the Winchester Company of the Pacific by the addition to the board of directors of three presidents of regional Winchester Clubs in the district.

Much was expected from the reorganization and decentralization of sales and warehousing function. Maycumber stated in April 1921: ". . . this new plan of distribution permits us to keep closer control of dealers' requirements, which results in lower inventories and more turnover . . . it enables us to give proper manufacturing orders to the factory in advance so that they will be in a position to manufacture goods which meet ready sale."

While these changes improved the situation somewhat, the number of distribution points was still too small to give adequate service to the dealers. An exclusive agent could easily be four hundred miles from the nearest Winchester warehouse and only fifty miles from the nearest jobber. Under these circumstances, the retailer was tempted to order merchandise from the more convenient source of supply. At the same time, the expansion of facilities and decentralization almost doubled the operating costs in 1921 over the previous year, amounting to over $1.5 million. The number of dealers had increased about twenty-five per cent but as sales per dealer averaged about the same as the preceding year, the average cost of servicing the dealer, approximately $425, now absorbed about thirty per cent of the value of his purchases.

These high costs of servicing the dealers were, of course, attributable to a considerable extent, to the limited sales during the 1921 depression. An expanded number of dealers and increased sales per dealer could conceivably help to lower the unit cost involved. That the management was not sanguine about operating its current distribution organization, even with the prospect of such an expansion, is shown by the discussions held early in 1922 with the Shapleigh Hardware Company, a prominent St. Louis jobbing house. A plan to join or absorb that concern was not carried through but, as will be shown, a merger with the Associated Simmons Hardware Company, of St. Louis, was later consummated.

*Summary*

From the foregoing discussion it is obvious that Winchester's general postwar program had undergone considerable revision by the end of 1921. In part, changes were imposed on the management by the advent of the business depression which came just as the program was getting under way. In part, the changes were made necessary by the discovery that the Liggett model had to be modified considerably before it could be adapted to the distribution of hardware and sporting goods.

Meanwhile, of course, Winchester was producing guns and ammunition.

# CHAPTER TWENTY-FOUR

# OLD-LINE PRODUCTS AND FINANCES

*New Model Guns and Ammunition*

In comparison with the new lines, the history of the production of guns and ammunition during the immediate postwar years was relatively prosaic. Like the well-behaved child in the family, this side of the business received rather little attention from a management that was having trouble with its new offsprings—hardware and sporting goods.

Because of its policy of keeping a number of commercial models in production during the war, the Company was able to convert to sporting arms and ammunition with comparative ease. Manufacturing was carried on with a minimum amount of difficulty. (*The Brill Report* for March 22, 1921, was critical of the new products development, but stated: "The methods of the Company for manufacturing guns and ammunition are wonderfully complete and efficient.")

The management was not so preoccupied with the new lines that it neglected to develop new-model firearms, and three new-model shotguns and one new-model rifle were brought out in 1920.

Of these, the *rifle* Model 52, was the most important addition to the Winchester line. Especially designed for the postwar demand for an accurate rifle suitable for shooting matches, the Model 52 had a bolt action with a detachable box magazine holding five cartridges and was chambered for caliber .22 long rifle rimfire ammunition.

During the war U.S. troops had used the modified Enfield rifle, and the returning soldiers were in general bolt-action conscious. But the .30-06 ammunition used in the service rifle had too great a velocity and range to be used conveniently in shooting matches. By shortening the ranges and reducing the size of the targets proportionately the .22 long rifle ammunition could be used in shooting matches that conformed to the standards set for military matches in which the heavier loads were required.

Actually the principal developmental work on the Model 52 was completed by early 1919. In order to introduce it quickly to the trade, twelve rifles were made up especially for the National Rifle Matches that were held at Caldwell, New Jersey, during August 1919. In these matches the Model 52 was used by several members of the U.S. team which beat a British team in an international match and was generally accepted with enthusiasm. Commercial production was started in 1920 and the first deliveries to the trade were made in September of that year.

The Model 52 became accepted as the standard rifle for all types of small-bore shooting matches. Listed at $70 during 1920 and 1921, only about five hundred had been sold by the end of the latter year. But the rifle experienced a gradually expanding demand, in part attributable to a drop in list price to $57.50 in 1922, and annual sales had reached around a thousand by 1924.

To meet the demand of target-shooters for ammunition of uniform quality and improved shooting qualities, Winchester brought out its Precision 75 and Precision 200/.22 long rifle cartridges. These were designed for the popular ranges for target shooting, 75 yards for indoor matches and 200 yards for those held outdoors.

The three shotguns introduced in 1920 were low-priced arms, adapted largely because they could be put into production at a relatively small cost and because it was hoped that their manufacture would utilize a part of the idle equipment in the gun department.

The first of these was the Model 20, a single-shot shotgun. It was a top-lever breakdown type with a visible hammer chambered for a .410-gauge, 2.5-inch shell. This model was designed as a small compact gun for small-game hunting and for practice shooting at midget clay targets. It was featured in a sales promotion plan to promote an interest among young people in trap-shooting. One of these guns was packed in each "Winchester Junior Trap Shooting Outfit," described in the catalog for 1920 as "The shooting novelty of the year for young and old." Included in the outfit was the "Winchester Midget Hand Trap with which the shooter can throw the little clay targets at which he shoots, or have them thrown for him by any companion of his outing."

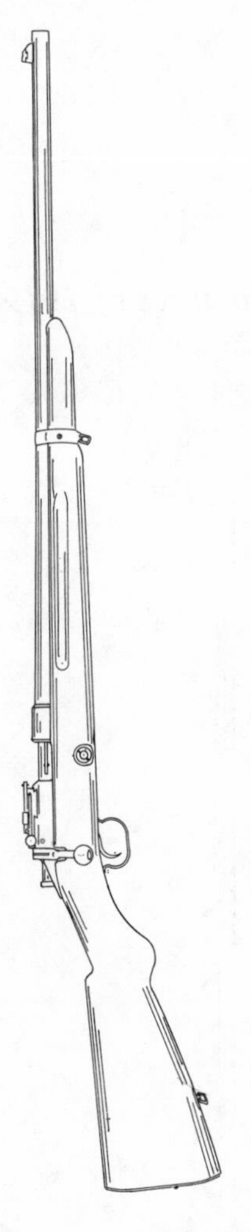

*Winchester Model 52 Rifle*

The Model 20 was initially listed at $30. At this price it was competitively out of line, and even when the price was dropped, in 1922, to $16.50, sales were not large, averaging around 1,600 a year. Its manufacture was dropped in 1924.

The second of the three shotguns introduced during 1920 was the Model 36. A single-shot, take-down weapon, it employed a bolt action which was cocked by pulling the firing pin to the rear. It was chambered interchangeably for 9mm. long and short shells and a 9mm. ball cartridge. It was expected that this gun would be popular in the Southern states for shooting rats and small game. Introduced at a list price of $13, later dropped to $7.50, this gun never became popular. It lacked firepower because of its small gauge and the short range of the ammunition. Sales averaged less than 600 a year and in 1927 it was dropped from the line.

The Model 41, introduced the same year, had a bolt action and was chambered for a .410-gauge, 2.5-inch paper shot-shell. Originally listed at $14, subsequently reduced to $13.25, its price was not low enough to make it an effective competitor in the field, although sales came to about 1,250 a year for the period 1921-24.

In sum, the Model 52 represented an important contribution to Winchester's old-line products. The shotguns, however, were not popular enough to attain the objective of taking over a large part of the low-priced shotgun market.

Although guns and ammunition received relatively little attention from the management during the 1919-21 period, it was the sales of the old-line products which helped to carry the financial load during these years. Compared to $15.6 million in 1919, these amounted to $15.4 million in 1920, and $9 million in 1921.

Largely because the new products were still in the developmental stage, the old-line products contributed some 98 per cent to the Company's total sales in 1919, 89 per cent in 1920, and 79 per cent in 1921. The sales of old-line products were substantial enough to ease, at least, the stress occasioned by the development of the new products.

*Finances of 1919-1921*

The Winchester management was, of course, prepared for a program of heavy expenditure as a necessary consequence of the adoption of the new program. The reorganization of the Company gave a clear mandate to Otterson and the other executives to avoid the losses which would accrue from a half-occupied plant. With substantial resources at its disposal at the beginning of 1920, the management had, too, the implicit undertaking of Kidder, Peabody & Company to support the development work. (Apart from an inventory valued at $9.7 million, the working capital at January 1, 1920, was $7.9 million, consisting of cash and receivables of $2.3 million, and a portfolio of securities whose book value was $5.6 million.)

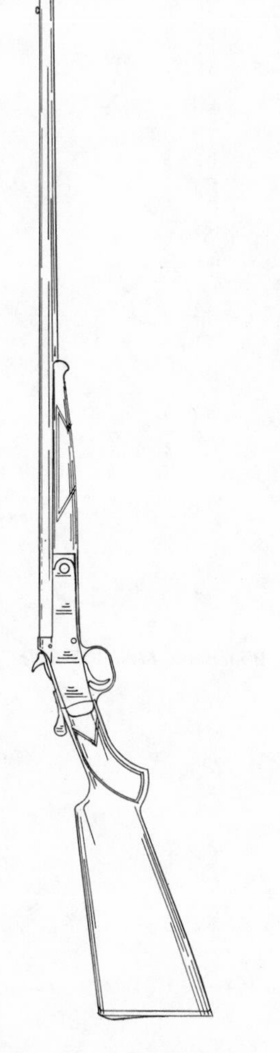

Winchester Model 20 Shotgun

Two tasks had to be performed: to equip the plant and that of the new companies acquired for the efficient handling of the new products; and to organize production so as, at once, to satisfy the demand being created by the new selling program and to achieve costs of production which would permit profitable operation.

From the records available it is difficult to distinguish the effects of these two aspects of the financial problem. As in any period of rapid and costly change, allocation of expenditure between capital investment and operating expenses would, at best, be somewhat arbitrary. Ideally, the expenditures added to capital would have been limited to a figure approximately the capitalized value of the earning power of the new facilities, with any excess expenditures treated as operating losses. While such a procedure would have been difficult in any case and perhaps impossible during the uncertainties of 1921, the Winchester management adopted a criterion which reversed the more normal approach. Under the accounting practices followed during the years 1920-21, all expenditures in excess of an arbitrarily determined specification cost were charged to capital or reserves.

In planning the new program, specification costs were determined in the following manner. A quality comparison was made of proposed Winchester products with those of rivals. The price of competitors' goods at the wholesale level was used as a base "jobbing" price which was considered as an index of 100. From this figure, 18 per cent was deducted to allow for selling costs, general overhead, and warehouse distribution. Thus 82 per cent of the base "jobbing" price was the amount which must provide the costs of raw materials, labor, factory burden, and a manufacturing profit. The manufacturing engineer was required to plan the production in such a way that these costs could be met and the production engineers had to meet the specifications imposed on them. (The term "specification cost" was used by the Winchester organization in a sense apparently analogous to the conventional "standard cost" but actually different from the latter in the following respects. *Standard cost* would be ascertained, for any product, by a process of experimentation with the material and labor elements in cost; that is, the article to be produced would be analyzed in terms of its content of raw materials and of the operations involved in changing those materials into the finished product. The elements would be priced and, as coupled with the wage rate, would give the permissible expenditure for this term. Winchester's *specification cost,* however, was arrived at by taking the competitive price of the article it was desired to produce, deducting therefrom an allowance for selling and warehouse expense and for fixed charges, leaving a price within which the factory was supposed to produce the article. Specification cost represented, therefore, an objective, rather than a standard determined empirically; a total sum which had to cover labor, material, and allocation of overhead as well as profit on the article in question.)

It would be difficult, under the circumstances of a policy of rapid expansion complicated by the adoption of the new marketing system, to suggest any better procedure by which manufacturing costs could be estimated. The success of applying this formula, however, depended upon the accuracy with which sales quotas were estimated and how close actual manufacturing costs would approach the figure established by the calculations made before the production was begun. These two elements would be interdependent. In setting up production facilities for any line, a rate of production had to be assumed and an amount of space and equipment allocated that would utilize these resources most efficiently, provided the production schedules were met. At the same time, it was possible that even at calculated rates of output, manufacturing costs would fail to reach competitive levels.

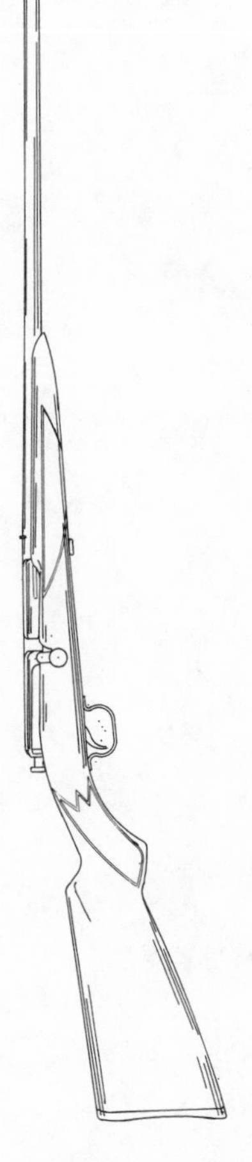

*Winchester Model 41 Shotgun*

A further complication was apparently introduced into the cost calculations at this point. In making its price comparisons, the management seems to have taken the prices of the highest quality and highest-priced competitive lines. Thus even if the Company were able to meet the specification costs established, those costs could be well above lines which were in fact competitive with the Winchester brand of merchandise.

The cost standard so determined became, in effect, the expense of production used in calculating the profit or loss on operations during 1920 and 1921. Any expenditures in excess of the cost allowance of 82 per cent of the base jobbing program were treated as a cost of the development of the program and either added to the fixed assets or charged off against earnings or reserves accumulated out of gun and ammunition profits of the past.

As a result of this approach, the net consolidated profits of the Winchester Company and its subsidiaries were reported to the stockholders as follows:

| | | |
|---|---|---|
| Year ended December 31, 1920 | Profit | $1,048,683 |
| Year ended December 31, 1921 | Loss | 1,165,514 |
| Net Loss for the two years | | $ 116,831 |

In addition, the directors in their report for the year ended December 31, 1921, drew attention to a sum of $3,100,000 charged to reserves, for losses on inventories and the cost of maintaining idle plant. The balance of the expenditures for the two years had been capitalized.

It is of interest to examine the details of the costs of the development program, actually incurred, which were in excess of the amounts charged as manufacturing costs during the two years ended December 31, 1921. These are indicated in the following tabulation (in thousands):

| | | |
|---|---|---|
| Development of new products | | |
| General | $ 851 | |
| Tools | 724 | |
| Engineering | 1,357 | |
| Patents | 37 | 2,969 |
| Establishing of the dealer-agency plan | | 928 |
| Cost of maintaining that part of plant which was unused | | 2,480 |
| Manufacturing costs in excess of those charged as operating costs: | | |
| (i) Unabsorbed burden | 513 | |
| (ii) Pre-pricing variance [a] | 2,442 | 2,955 |
| TOTAL | | $9,332 [b] |

[a] This loss results from the difference between the costs of materials and services purchased and the allowance for these items in the cost formula.
[b] Of this sum $5.9 million was spent in 1920 and $3.4 million in 1921.

Some of these costs undoubtedly represented the cost of acquiring technical skills and marketing experience, but it is difficult to regard the last item, of nearly $3 million, as anything more than an operating loss of which the stockholders could have been informed categorically.

The results of operations as recorded may be summarized as follows (in thousands):

| | *1920* | *1921* | *Total* |
|---|---|---|---|
| *Winchester Repeating Arms Company* | | | |
| Manufacturing profit | | | |
| Guns, ammunition | $4,482 | $2,593 | $7,075 |
| New products | 418 | 397 | 815 |
| | 4,900 | 2,990 | 7,980 |
| Less: Operating expenses | 4,059 | 3,879 | 7,938 [a] |
| Operating profit | 841 | | |
| Operating loss | | (889) | (48) |
| Income from U.S. contracts collected during the period | 298 | 458 | 756 |
| *Winchester Company* | | | |
| Operating loss | (60) | (606) | (666) |
| "Profit" for 1920 | 1,079 | | |
| "Loss" for 1921 | | 1,037 | |
| Net Profit, 1920–21 | | | 42 [b] |

[a] Including interest $1,411,000 and depreciation charged to operations $366,000.
[b] The difference between this figure and that shown on page 317 results from the technicalities of "consolidation."

In the light of the slight attention paid to guns and ammunition during the working out of the new plan, their contribution to the total business deserves especial attention. It is, of course, impossible to distribute the operating expenses, as recorded above, between the old and new lines, so as to ascertain the profit on guns and ammunition which would have been earned if there had been no new-products program; but they were credited with earning nearly 90 per cent of the manufacturing profit on a sales volume which accounted for 85 per cent of the total business done. The details are as follows (in thousands):

| | | *Guns and Ammunition* | *New Products* |
|---|---|---|---|
| 1920 | Sales | $15,405 | $1,866 |
| | Manufacturing profit [a] | 4,482 | 418 |
| 1921 | Sales | 9,034 | 2,514 |
| | Manufacturing profit [a] | 2,593 | 397 |

[a] In both cases the manufacturing profit is that obtained by the arbitrary allocation of costs between operating and development.

It will be noted that this operating loss of $42,000 as reported was arrived at after crediting to current income certain receipts, amounting to $756,000, representing final net payments to the Company by the U. S. Government, in respect of war contracts. In view of the use to which reserve created out of war-time profits had been put, it is astonishing that this item had not been added to surplus instead of being used to reduce the operating losses for 1920-21. (Certain inventory losses and costs of maintaining idle plant had been charged to reserves.)

In yet another respect were the operating losses understated when the statements are measured against today's accounting standards. While some depreciation had been charged as an operating cost, it represented less than 30 per cent of the full depreciation charge as established by reference to the Internal Revenue scale of allowance. A modern statement would, therefore, have recorded the loss for the two years as over $1.8 million by including a balance of $1.7 million of depreciation.

It is particularly in the light of this consideration that the payment of dividends during this period must be criticized. It will be recalled that the stockholders of Winchester Repeating Arms Company now held seven per cent first cumulative preferred stock in the Winchester Company and that Kidder, Peabody & Company had received second preferred and common stock in exchange for their contribution to the capital funds. Dividends were paid on the first preferred through April 15, 1921, and on the second preferred through June 30, 1921, the total payments being $829,000 in 1920 and $415,000 in 1921. Except, perhaps, for the purpose of maintaining the market in the stock, neither of these properties seems to have been justified, whether from the point of view of the impracticability of determining the true operating results or from that of the financial situation of the group.

The finances of 1920-21 can now be summarized (in thousands):

| | |
|---|---|
| Expenditures in development of new products | $5,924 |
| Other expenditures, chiefly in development of retail stores program | 2,689 |
| Cost of dealer-agency plan | 928 |
| Investments in manufacturing and other subsidiaries (net) | 1,133 |
| Increase in working capital (especially to carry increased inventories) | 2,590 |
| Maintenance of idle plant | 2,480 |
| Total development program expenditures 1920-21 | 15,744 |
| Income tax paid on war profits | 1,052 |
| Dividends paid to first and second preferred stockholders | 1,244 |
| Total expenditures | $18,040 |

It is evident from the size of the expenditures that the financial problem was far from simple. Having sold its portfolio of securities at a loss of over $200,000, the management resorted to the commercial banks and to Kidder, Peabody & Company. The aggregate of these bank loans exceeded $10 million at the end of 1920. The amount obtained from banks by direct loan amounted to over $1.5 million, of which $400,000 was secured by pledge of accounts receivable. Some $8.7 million represented the proceeds of accommodation notes, originating with the Winchester Company, endorsed by Winchester Repeating Arms Company and discounted with Kidder, Peabody & Company. These accommodations cost from seven to eight per cent per year, rates which appear to be in line with those ruling at the time.

This method of borrowing from Kidder, Peabody & Company made the securing of funds quite easy. Winchester had in effect a drawing account subject only to the willingness and ability of Kidder, Peabody & Company to supply money. As a long-range method of financing an expansion program, this type of loan might be questioned. At best, the physical assets and technical knowledge that were being acquired would be capable of earning an income sufficient to repay their cost over a time period considerably longer than the maturity dates of the loans which ranged between 30 and 180 days. Actually, of course, because of Kidder, Peabody and Company's position as a heavy equity holder in the Winchester organization, the loans advanced by that company were in the nature of a longer-term investment than the form of the borrowing suggests. Because the management had been unable or unwilling to make an estimate of its long-term capital requirements in 1919, this method of financing might be justifiably called a temporary measure until such time that the extent of the needs could be determined.

In March 1921 some of the loans were put on a long-term basis by the issue of a $7 million first mortgage, twenty-year gold bonds, bearing interest at 7.5 per cent. This issue, made in the name of Winchester Repeating Arms Company, was handled by Kidder, Peabody & Company, and netted Winchester some $6.439 million, which made the effective interest rate on the issue 8.2 per cent. Bank loans were reduced by $4.605 million leaving a balance of $1.834 million which represented the additional outside capital noted above. While this loan was undoubtedly necessary at the time, it did have the effect of increasing fixed charges against earnings by over a half million dollars per year.

While this funding operation enabled the Company to reduce bank loans, it by no means eliminated them. At the end of 1921, Winchester still owed the banks some $5.6 million. Of this amount $3.2 million was due Kidder, Peabody & Company, and the remainder of $2.4 million was owed to commercial banks in New York, Boston, San Francisco, Troy (New York), and New Haven. In other words, the proceeds of the bond issue were used to reduce the short-term loans of Kidder, Peabody & Company while at the same time loans from other banks were increased by about $900,000. Moreover, it is clear that the position of the first and second preferred stockholders' stock had been materially changed by the placing of prior charges requiring $525,000 a year between them and the payment of dividends on their holdings.

Summarizing these transactions, it will be seen that the total expenditures of $18.04 million had been financed as follows (in thousands):

| | |
|---|---|
| Net borrowings from banks | $5,615 |
| Proceeds of issue of $7 million, 20-year, 7.5 per cent gold bonds | 6,439 |
| Sales of securities | 5,210 |
| Total funds received from outside sources | 17,264 |
| Funds accumulated in depreciation reserves | 734 |
| Profits on operations as reported | 42 |
| | 18,040 |

The consolidated balance sheet of the Winchester Company and its subsidiaries at December 31, 1921, shown in Appendix G-9, indicates the financial difficulties faced at this time. Quick assets, in cash and receivables, were $3.454,000; bank loans amounted to $5,760,000; and other current liabilities to $1,701,000. While the organization had a large inventory, it must be remembered that this had increased by some $3 million, and though the management had written down its value to "cost or market, whichever [was] the lower," the business situation was still highly unpredictable. The management was, therefore, entirely at the mercy of the banks. Kidder, Peabody & Company could, no doubt, be relied upon to support their investment, but the attitude of the commercial banks which held $2.4 million of the organization's paper would not necessarily be as helpful.

The common stock had little or no cover in available assets if the hypothetical values ascribed to development expenditures and the deferred items be deducted from the net worth. Moreover, the Company had still to show that it could achieve earnings large enough to service the gold bonds, absorb the intangible values included on the balance sheet (or "valorize" them by earning a reasonable rate of return on the investment they represented) and resume dividends on the two issues of preferred stock. This could only be done by increasing the volume of sales of both old and new products and dealing with the problem of the manufacturing costs on a realistic basis.

By the end of 1921 the problems faced by the management were obvious. As has been noted, manufacturing costs on the new lines were high, the current methods used in distributing merchandise to the dealer-agents were both inadequate and expensive, the future of the retail stores was uncertain, and the Company's financial position had deteriorated. The principal question involved was to what extent these difficulties were attributable to the developmental phases of the postwar program and the effect of the 1921 depression and would be relieved with a recovery of business, and to what extent they were due to basic weaknesses in the policies initially adopted in 1919.

In all respects, the test of the Otterson management would come in the years that lay immediately ahead. Otterson's expressed opinion regarding the future of the Winchester organization is given in the following statement made to the stockholders at the end of 1921: "The Company faces the future with its house clean and in order, capable through the development and the economies that have been effected, of showing a profit on a comparatively small volume of business, and with its manufacturing and commercial development completed to the point where it can take immediate advantage of improved business conditions. Small stocks of our products in the hands of jobbers and retailers lead us to expect a more normal business in our lines during 1922."

CHAPTER TWENTY-FIVE

# WINCHESTER AND SIMMONS

## *Vote of Confidence*

Otterson's administration was subjected to some rather vigorous outside criticism during 1921. The occasion arose in connection with the financing of the Company's gold bonds in March of that year. Among the banking houses invited by Kidder, Peabody & Company to participate in the marketing of the securities was the Guaranty Trust Company of New York. As a condition for considering the securities, the Guaranty Trust Company asked that a consulting engineer, George M. Brill, be allowed to make an independent survey of the Winchester organization. A copy of Brill's report, which was highly critical, was sent to the Winchester board of directors in March 1921. The immediate reaction of the board was, "That the report was to a considerable extent based upon incomplete information as to the conditions and the steps being taken by the management to correct them."

Otterson was given full opportunity to reply to the criticisms in the Brill report and he made a good case for the charge that Brill had been unduly influenced by "outside rumors and propaganda" about the state of the Company's affairs and by his "preconceived ideas of management more than by his observations in our plant." While the board accepted his interpretation, Otterson must have begun to feel uncertainty during the following year as to whether his administration did, in fact, command the full confidence of the various groups interested—the directors, the bankers, and the preferred stockholders. The financial position of the organization at the end of 1921 would not have made him less sensitive to the possibility of criticism. Whatever his reasons he made a move in February 1922, to strengthen his internal position by requesting that a committee be appointed from among the directors of the Winchester Repeating Arms and the Winchester Company ". . . to investigate and report on all matters relating to company management; including management policy, its interpretation, application and administration; the organization with reference to its suitability as to character, form, and qualification of individuals occupying responsible positions; system with reference to its directness, simplicity, and economy; and the morale and administrative spirit."

A "vote of confidence" on the part of a selected group of directors would do much to strengthen Otterson's position by showing the other interested parties that his own organization was convinced of the soundness of the postwar plans and of his ability to manage the concern.

The committee collected their evidence principally from members of the management personnel. Some twenty-five individuals reported on the activities of their respective departments. Under the circumstances the materials submitted to the committee could hardly be completely objective. To a considerable extent each department head or subordinate was obliged to defend his own operations. Since the investigation had been prompted by Otterson and he took an active part in the proceedings, often assuming the role of the chief questioner of the witnesses, they were clearly inhibited from expressing any undue criticism of the general policies of the Company.

In spite of these limitations, the record of the proceedings gives considerable information about past and current operations. While no attempt was made to conceal the fact that mistakes had been made and difficulties encountered, the major emphasis was laid upon showing how these problems could be handled in the period that lay ahead.

For example, H. G. Knox, the factory manager, reported on some of the problems he was meeting in the manufacture of the new products. The "temperamental fishermen" were making it difficult to get high-enough quality and variety in fishing equipment to satisfy the demands. Cutlery prices were low because of German imports. The supply of hickory for hammer and hatchet handles was short. It had proved difficult to shift workers employed on seasonal items from one job to another.

More serious than these problems, which might be expected in the normal course of development and operations, was the level of manufacturing costs. No trouble was being experienced with guns and ammunition which were showing a satisfactory profit. On the new lines, Knox reported that while flashlights, batteries, baits, wrenches, hammers and chisels were being made at some profit, all others were barely breaking even, or were being produced at a loss. This latter group included fishing tackle, forged and edged tools, pliers, and cutlery. Of these cutlery presented the greatest problem, but according to Knox, with a fifty per cent increase in production all lines, except cutlery and reels, would immediately break even, and indeed, these lines would, in a few months, be produced within the specification costs allowed.

F. A. Maycumber, reporting on the marketing via the dealer-agents, admitted that Winchester's new products were in general higher-priced than competitors' lines, yet he felt that the exclusive features of the agency plan, plus the high quality of products, would insure a market. On the latter point he stated: "After comparing our lines of tools with other lines, I am convinced that our tool lines are not followers but leaders in quality. Our axes are standard in the great Northwest at the present time, and we have only been in the business one year. Our hammers are making a name for themselves even without advertising. Our chisels are in a class by themselves and are the highest priced chisels made today. I consider Robeson and ourselves are the standard makers of cutlery. Our prices are very close together. If anything, we are the highest priced cutlery manufacturers. . . . Under the sporting goods line, we have flashlights and batteries, which are better than Ever-Ready, which have been the standard. Our skates . . . are equal to any on the market."

Winchester's reels, baits, and rods, he felt, were equally high in quality compared with other lines.

He expressed an undiminished faith in the dealer-agency method of marketing, as fundamentally the correct method of distribution. "The Winchester Plan," he went on to say, "may be considered somewhat radical, but facts and figures show that it is not radical but built on sound business judgment."

For future, he thought that the existing dealer-agents would expand their purchases from 100 per cent to 150 per cent over 1920 figures. Furthermore, the Company could secure a total of some seven thousand agency-dealers during the coming two or three years. These agents would have a potential buying power of some $250 million, of which it was ". . . safe to assume that Winchester can secure from 20 to 25 million dollars." These were impressive figures. Even if the optimism of the witness were heavily discounted, the committee must have derived some encouragement from it.

William T. Birney, the assistant sales manager, gave a somewhat clearer picture of the plan for the immediate future. He outlined the system of sales quotas that had been set on the assumptions that general business conditions were going to improve and that the dealer-agents would purchase a large proportion of their requirements from Winchester than they had in the past. By this time, not only were more new lines in production, but the weaker dealers had been replaced by a group more enthusiastic about the plan. Pointing out that the sales of the dealers ranged between $35,000 and $75,000 per year, Birney forecast that, "We certainly are going to get at least 5 per cent of that business."

Frank Drew reported on the jobbing, export, and specialty business of the Company. He felt, on a basis of a recent trip in which he visited the trade, that the jobbers "who had spent from one year to fourteen months doing nothing but paying attention to the reduction of inventory," were now prepared to book all of the business they could get. He estimated that the business on shot shells for 1922 would increase at least fifty per cent over the preceding year, and the gun business would also improve. Because public sentiment was growing against the sale of pistols and revolvers and because legislation requiring permits to purchase cartridges seemed possible, he thought sales of metallic ammunition would not increase substantially.

He noted that the jobbers were still on the whole antagonistic to Winchester, but the Company had a list of some 755 jobbers who continued to purchase goods. A specialty division, under his charge, had been set up to sell Winchester's new products to the jobbers, either unbranded or marked with the latter's private brands. He was optimistic about this new department and suggested that with its facilities the Company could easily sell a million dollars' worth of tools, cutlery and the like to the jobbers.

Some improvement was expected in the export sales. H. F. Beebe, in charge of this department, indicated that a quota of $1.5 million had been set for 1922, and that there seemed a good chance that this figure would be met. Not only did the Company expect to sell its old lines in these markets, but it intended to push its new products as well.

Edwin Pugsley gave a rather full account of the operations of the retail stores. (In introducing him to the committee, Otterson said: "Mr. Pugsley's experience has been of a developmental nature. . . . It was my feeling at the time he was put in charge of the retail stores that he was just what the retail stores required. They didn't require necessarily a department store man who had had experience in running a department store in a routine way, but they needed a man with a promotional type of mind, who could take a new thing and analyze and shape it and build it up. Mr. Pugsley, I felt, had these qualities to a greater extent than any man whom we could get who happened to be a successful retail store operator in some restricted field not analogous to our own.")

He described the early difficulties with the stores and the subsequent changes in their organization, emphasizing the trend away from hardware and toward decentralization. A lack of working capital made it impossible for the stores to buy on a cash-discount basis; they had, indeed, been forced to go to the banks to finance their spring and Christmas business. He estimated that with sales of $2.5 million, the stores would about break even, and ". . . if we have any kind of business the stores should be able to sell $2.7 million and possibly $3 million worth of merchandise during 1922, which will return a profit on operations."

R. E. Anderson, treasurer, reported to the committee on financial matters. He made the astonishing disclosure that a strict budget control over purchases had been introduced for the first time during 1921. This, he explained, "was evolved because during the hectic time of 1920, we found that commitments were larger than they should be and required very drastic control."

He also touched upon the financial relations with the banks, stating that "practically all these banks have 90-day paper which they renew from time to time." Much of his time was apparently spent in negotiations with the banks, for he noted, "It has been one of my pleasant duties to visit all these banks (except Kansas City, Atlanta, and California), every few months, and keep informed of the Company's progress."

He reported also that interest rates on the Company's loans had gradually fallen during 1921, in some cases as the result of voluntary action by the banks and in other instances at his request.

Some measure of the shortage of working capital is given by Anderson's statement that "The increased activity of this spring has been partially financed through accounts payable, partially through allowing [payments on them] to slow down somewhat, and partially through making definite arrangements with large suppliers."

Under this last method, the Company arranged to buy copper, lead, powder, and coal on a ninety-day basis, giving notes bearing six per cent interest as security.

Anderson concluded his report with estimates of the amounts of business that would enable the Company to break even and to make a profit. The break-even point was fixed at $13.2 million; a sales figure of $16.5 million would permit dividends on first and second preferred stock; while $18 million would net an additional $300,000 to pay arrears of dividends on preferred stock or common stock. He felt that, at worst, the Company's business would not fall below the break-even point, and that prospects were good for reaching total sales of $16.5 million and possibly $18 million.

A general feeling of restrained optimism was apparent in the evidence of the management personnel. Almost every witness stated that an increased volume of business would solve the most pressing problems facing a particular department. The trends of business activity up to the time of the committee's investigation seemed to indicate that volume would pick up substantially during 1922 compared with 1921.

The committee's report to the directors, copies of which were sent especially to Kidder, Peabody & Company and Liggett, reflected in general the optimism expressed before it by the staff members. After reviewing with approval the initial reasons for the postwar program, the report stated: "It is unfortunate that our opening moves were made at a time that was so nearly coincident with not only a nation-wide but a world-wide period of business depression. This introduced a condition into the situation that affected the results upon which the judgment is to be passed. It is your committee's belief that under normal conditions the plan would have by this time been put to the point that its success would have been definitely established."

As to the prospects for increased business, the committee stated that it had received from the sales department ". . . convincing evidence that stocks of merchandise in the lines the Company manufactures are low throughout the country with both the retailer and the jobber. As a result of this condition there should be an improvement in our sales this year. This improvement should be augmented and accelerated if general business conditions improve." On the subject of the retail stores, the committee indicated that it ". . . had not had the opportunity to follow fully the development of these stores and therefore does not feel competent to pass upon the question of policy governing their initiation and development."

The committee did, however, express an opinion that the stores were currently being well supervised and managed. Improved business conditions would make it "at least not impossible" that sales would be such that the stores could carry their own financial weight and possibly pay interest on investment plus a profit. The committee approved of the trend toward decentralization of store management and the policy of confining sales to sporting goods. It also noted the possibility of combining the Winchester retail stores with nationally known sporting-goods stores to form a larger chain. The general management policy was viewed as being based on a thorough understanding of conditions under which the Company must exist. The organization appeared to be functioning smoothly. The morale and administrative spirit seemed good.

After a recording that the committee accepted the estimates of the management regarding the total sales that would enable the Company to break even or to pay dividends, the report concluded by urging that purchases be put on a cash basis as soon as possible, that all possible economies be practiced, and that further developments be undertaken only from earnings.

*Winchester-Simmons Merger*

The investigation was followed by a spectacular attack upon one of the major causes of difficulty disclosed by the evidence; i.e., the inter-related problems of costs, volume of sales, and distribution. The solution was sought in the combination of the interests of the Winchester group with those of one of the major objectors to the plan for direct distribution to the dealers, the Associated Simmons Hardware Companies of St. Louis.

The possible value to Winchester of such a combination is readily explainable.

The Company was having difficulty with its plan to assume the jobbing function for its dealer agents. Costs of operations were high, and the service rendered the dealers was still inadequate in spite of the increased number of warehouses. A greater volume of sales was needed to relieve the burden of overhead involved in manufacturing, and to reduce the unit costs of distribution. The merger offered not only a possible solution for these difficulties but the move would provide badly needed working capital through a sale of securities or through the utilization of new lines of credit with the banks.

In fact, negotiations had been begun early in 1922 with the Shapleigh Hardware Company, also centered in St. Louis, with a view to the joining of forces. Conversations were at the point where tentative plans for consolidation had been drawn up, when it was learned that Simmons was also receptive to such a plan. According to the minutes of the board of the Winchester Repeating Arms Company in April 1922: "Mr. Otterson stated that Simmons Hardware Company of St. Louis had approached this company with a proposition to sell its interests to this Company. Their motives were not clear. Balance sheets and statements showing profits and losses of the Simmons Company since 1921 were presented to the board. Their proposition to sell on the basis of common stock at par; namely $9,300,000, had been declined. Rough figures were presented to the board showing the possibilities of such a combination. After a thorough discussion of both the positive and negative sides of the Simmons proposition and related matters, the president was authorized to proceed with investigations and negotiations."

It is not astonishing that the motives of Simmons should be puzzling. The Simmons organization, it will be recalled, had been a bitter opponent of the Winchester marketing plan from the outset. A brief review of the history of Simmons will show, however, why that organization was willing to join forces with Winchester in 1922.

The business was founded by E. C. Simmons, who had started his career with a St. Louis jobbing house at the age of sixteen. In 1864, at twenty-five, he had formed his own organization, which was incorporated in 1873 as the Simmons Hardware Company of Missouri. All activities were centered in St. Louis until about 1905, when the concern began establishing branch warehouses in various cities in the Middle West and the East and acquiring control over certain of its suppliers. In 1911, the Associated Simmons Hardware Company organization was set up as a Massachusetts trust which took over the stock of the Simmons Hardware Company and the various subsidiary marketing and manufacturing concerns that had previously been established or acquired.

The development of the Simmons organization during these years reflected the rising importance of St. Louis as a distributing center, the changes that occurred in the general field of hardware distribution through the latter part of the nineteenth century, and the personality of the founder.

St. Louis in the late 1860s was recovering from the effects of the Civil War. Long an important port for river traffic, the city was about to emerge as a railway center and the focal point of a market network that spread north, west, and south. The Simmons organization grew with the city. Starting with a few traveling men, the company's salesmen numbered several hundred by 1900. Its catalog for 1890 listed some thousand items that it was prepared to supply to retailers. From handling the products of a few manufacturers or jobbers the company had come to control in part or entirely a number of its suppliers. About 1870, the company adopted the trade name Keen Kutter, which became famous in trade circles. E. C. Simmons was more than a passive agent in this development. Almost completely absorbed in the business, his drive and shrewdness as a marketer and as a judge of men, had brought the company to a leading position in the trade by 1900, a position it still maintained in the early 1920s.

In 1898 E. C. Simmons resigned as president and turned the management of the Company over to his three sons although he remained more or less active in the management until his death in 1920 at the age of eighty-three. The Simmons boys, Wallace, Edward, and George, had been raised in the tradition of the firm and had spent vacations working in the business. But the fact that all three had gone East to college and had not worked up through the organization in what was then the traditional manner, tended to alienate the members of the organization who had been with the firm.

Apparently the brothers assumed functions without much regard to the personality which each had developed. Wallace, as the eldest son, became president but because of his rather autocratic manner, he apparently had some difficulty in keeping his organization functioning well. Edward, the middle brother, took over the job of sales manager, although he had more capacity as a buyer, which position was assumed by George, the youngest, who had more the salesman's temperament.

The management by the Simmons sons was further complicated by the fact that E. C. Simmons and his associate, J. W. Morton, continued to serve in an advisory capacity. This caused a division in authority. According to Saunders Norvell, who was active in the company at the time ". . . if one referred some business question to any one of the Simmons boys and if the decision did not seem to be entirely satisfactory and the matter was taken over their heads to E. C. Simmons or to J. W. Morton, there naturally was feeling."

It was, perhaps, inevitable that the young men should wish to build up their own internal staff organization. To do this they brought in a considerable number of their Eastern college friends. This group did not mix well with the men who had been raised in the business. As Norvell puts it:

> Another thing that stuck in the craw of "us veterans" was the fact that while we were expected to be at our desks promptly at 8 o'clock every morning, our young college friends ambled in anywhere from 9:30 to 10:30.
>
> Then we had the pleasure also of reading all about them in the society columns. Upon their arrival they were immediately introduced into the "400", took out a special membership in the Country Club and after that no social function was complete without the brilliance of their presence. Us "roughnecks" of course were jealous.

As long as E. C. Simmons lived the company continued to occupy a leading place in hardware-trade circles. Apparently his advice and the loyalties of the old-line employees to him were sufficient to hold the organization together. After his death in 1920, however, there were increasing management troubles, and the two younger brothers, at least, were ready to consider a proposition that would get them out of the hardware jobbing business.



The negotiations actually were begun by George Simmons, with the cooperation of Edward while Wallace, president of the company, was away on vacation. (In a letter to the Simmons salesmen dated June 26, 1922, which explained the merger, Wallace Simmons stated that he had asked George to outline the plan ". . . because it is one which he started early in April before I returned from California, and when I returned and first learned of it, such progress had been made, including a definite commitment of our stocks [George's, Edward's, and mine], that it seemed proper that I should allow him and [his brother] to continue and consummate the deal.")

Festus J. Wade, president of the Mercantile Trust Company of St. Louis, acted as intermediary. He met with the representative of Winchester in a New York hotel in April 1922, and made the preliminary arrangements. In spite of Wallace Simmons's lack of enthusiasm for the proposition, he did not put any obstacles in the way after his return.

Events moved rapidly. Otterson announced to the stockholders of the Winchester Company and to the dealer-agents the formation of the Winchester-Simmons Company in a letter dated June 26, 1922:

*To the Preferred and Common Stockholders of*
*The Winchester Company and to Winchester*
*Stockholding Agents:*

The majority interests of The Winchester Company and the Associated Simmons Hardware Companies beg to announce that they have entered into a contract to combine the two interests under a common management and they will hereafter be operated jointly.

The Winchester Company will operate as the manufacturing organization and the Associated Simmons Hardware Companies will operate as the distributing organization:

The Associated Simmons Hardware Companies will continue the operation of their hardware jobbing business as heretofore and in addition will act as distributors of Winchester products to the Winchester stock-holding agents, and for this purpose the sales, warehousing and distributing organizations of Winchester and Simmons will be combined and hereafter be operated as one.

By this plan it is hoped to eliminate duplication of effort and to effect economies that have not been possible under separate operation.

The combined interests will be operated through a holding company to be known as THE WINCHESTER-SIMMONS COMPANY, the stock of which will be owned by the present Winchester and Simmons interests and both interests will have representation on the board of directors. The Winchester stock interests in the holding company referred to involve only the Winchester Company common stock. The common stockholdings of the majority interests will be exchanged for the common stock of the Winchester-Simmons Company and all The Winchester Company common stockholders will be given the same opportunity to exchange their stock upon the same terms. No action is necessary on the part of the preferred stockholders of the Winchester Company in this transaction, but the value and earning power of their preferred stock should be improved due to the distribution strength growing out of the affiliation with the Associated Simmons Hardware Companies. This should provide a greater market for Winchester products and result in a greater factory activity as well as sales and distribution economies. It should also result in greatly improved service to Winchester stockholding agents. The present management of the Winchester Company will manage the combined companies and their subsidiaries.

The Winchester stockholding agency plan started about two years ago, will be continued and developed. Its development should be greatly facilitated by combining the Winchester and Simmons interests.

On the same date a letter was also sent to the common stockholders of the Associated Simmons Hardware Companies, which stated in part:

As is well known to most of our stockholders, we have for many years been studying the evolution of the hardware business and adjusting our form of organization, so that we might take the greatest advantage of our opportunities. During the last ten or fifteen years we have established a number of distributing houses in various cities and have secured, in some cases, the control of factories, and in others the output of those which have manufactured some of our important lines of merchandise.

In accordance with this general policy, we have just taken what we believe is one of the most important steps in our history, one which offers very great possibilities for the future, in linking up our distributing facilities with those of one of the largest manufacturing organizations in the country.

The terms under which the stockholders of Simmons could exchange their stock were outlined. For each share of common stock, the holder would get $3.75 in cash or negotiable securities plus Winchester-Simmons preferred stock at par for the difference (later set at $2.50 per share) between $3.75 and the "net tangible value" of the Simmons stock. If the stockholder desired he could take the whole amount in Winchester-Simmons preferred stock.

The Winchester-Simmons Company was formed as a Delaware corporation in August 1922. The authorized capital was 100,000 shares of seven per cent preferred stock, par value $199, and 250,000 shares of no-par-value common stock. As had been announced, the new corporation was a holding company which would control the common stock of the Winchester Company and the Associated Simmons Hardware Companies.

As a majority of the Simmons common stock was owned by the Simmons family and the majority of the Winchester Company common stock was owned by Kidder, Peabody & Company, there was no difficulty in arranging an exchange or transfer of stock to the new corporation. Provision had to be made, however, to raise funds to pay the stockholders of Simmons in cash or negotiable securities. To supply this money, Kidder, Peabody & Company formed a syndicate in September 1922 which purchased from the Winchester-Simmons Company 34,120 shares of preferred stock for $3,412,000 and 20,000 shares of common stock for $20,000. This stock was sold to the public in blocks of three shares of preferred plus one share of common for $300.

The following is a summary of the disposition of the Winchester-Simmons securities stock issues:

| *Preferred Stock* | *Shares* | *Cash or Value* |
|---|---|---|
| Sold to Kidder, Peabody & Company for cash at par | 34,120 | $3,412,000 |
| Issued to Associated Simmons Hardware Companies stockholders against 912,250 common @ $2.50 | 22,806 | 2,280,625 |
| Issued against fractions | 30 | 3,000 |
| | 56,956.25 | 5,695,625 |

| Common Stock | Shares | Cash or Value |
|---|---|---|
| Sold to Kidder, Peabody for cash | 20,000 | 20,000 |
| Issued to Winchester Company stockholders | 90,913 | 9,091,300 |
| Incorporated Shares | 4 | |
| | 110,917 | $9,111,300 |

As this tabulation shows, the Simmons stockholders received some 22,800 shares of preferred stock of the new company. While this stock carried the same voting privileges as the common stock, the effective control of the Winchester-Simmons Company now rested with Kidder, Peabody & Company, which owned the large majority of the voting stock of the Winchester Company, which in turn now held some 54 per cent of the outstanding securities of Winchester-Simmons. This control was strengthened to the extent that Kidder, Peabody & Company may have held on its own account any additional stock acquired through its syndicate operations. The general corporate structure of the combined organization is indicated on the following page.

Because the payments of cash and negotiable securities to the Simmons stockholders amounted to some $3.42 millions out of the $3.43 million received from Kidder, Peabody & Company, the net capital addition to the Winchester-Simmons Company was negligible. But as will be shown, the Simmons bank credit was good and was utilized to secure additional short-term credit on a substantial scale.

The Winchester-Simmons merger permitted a division of functions along the lines indicated in Otterson's letter to the stockholders of the Winchester Company. Simmons assumed responsibility for the marketing and distribution of the Winchester-branded new lines to the dealer-agents in addition to carrying on its sales of Keen Kutter and other lines to its regular customers. Winchester concentrated on manufacturing, but at the same time kept control over its domestic sales of guns and ammunition and its foreign sales of both new and old lines.

This major division of functions was made effective by an exchange of facilities between the two companies. Winchester took over the manufacturing establishments controlled by Simmons. Simmons assumed the Winchester warehouses and inventories and either merged them with its own warehousing and wholesale subsidiaries, or in the case of the Chicago and San Francisco houses, formed new companies. Each of these subsidiaries operated as a separate wholesale hardware company, charged with the responsibility of supervising salesmen, inventories control, credit analysis of customers, and the like, subject only to the general policies laid down by the central management.

In October 1922, L. E. Crandall of the Simmons organization was made general sales manager for the Winchester-Simmons Company, with headquarters in New Haven. About the same time the buying department of Simmons was also moved to New Haven. The former Winchester salesmen were either discharged or employed by Simmons.

The first public announcement of the plan to merge Simmons and Winchester was made at the second annual convention of Winchester dealers, held in New Haven early in June 1922. Otterson appeared personally before the members and

CORPORATE STRUCTURE OF THE WINCHESTER-SIMMONS COMPANY

- THE WINCHESTER-SIMMONS COMPANY
  - THE WINCHESTER COMPANY
    - Winchester Repeating Arms Company
      - Barney & Berry, Inc.
      - Walden Knife Company
      - Mack Axe Company
      - Mound City Paint & Color Co.
      - Roanoke Spoke & Handle Co.
    - The Winchester Retail Stores Company, Boston
  - ASSOCIATED SIMMONS HARDWARE COMPANY
    - Simmons Hardware Company (Mo. Corp.)
    - The Winchester-Simmons Co. of Chicago
    - The Winchester-Simmons Co. of Atlanta
    - The Winchester-Simmons Co. of Boston
    - The Winchester-Simmons Co. of St. Louis
    - The Winchester-Simmons Co. of Minneapolis
    - The Winchester-Simmons Co. of Philadelphia
    - The Winchester-Simmons Co. (of Toledo)
    - The Winchester-Simmons Co. of Sioux City
    - The Winchester-Simmons Co. of the Pacific
    - The Winchester-Simmons Co. (of Wichita)

outlined the reasons for the move. He explained the expected advantages to be gained pointing out that with ten district warehouses and three branches, the Winchester-Simmons organization was prepared to give more effective service to the Winchester dealer-agents as well as the regular customers of the Associated Simmons Hardware Companies. The greater volume of sales now expected would give greater economies of operation. The merger, he emphasized, would not change the status of the dealer-agency plan. Winchester would, in fact, control the new organization and Winchester's new products would continue to be sold exclusively to Winchester dealers. As Simmons was now a part of Winchester he did urge the dealers to purchase Keen Kutter products to fill out their requirements for general hardware.

The announcement of the merger caused a considerable stir among the dealer-agents. Most of them had first-hand experience with Simmons's earlier attempts to undermine the dealer-agency plan. It required considerable mental adjustment to accept a situation where a Simmons salesman would be expounding the virtues of Winchester merchandise and where a Winchester dealer would be encouraged to buy the Keen Kutter brand. Upon reflection, however, the position of the Winchester dealer-agents appeared to be no less favorable than it had been prior to the merger. They still had the exclusive right to purchase the new lines of Winchester that carried the Company's trade mark, and would continue to receive merchandising services as before. They could expect better delivery service on orders. Finally the Winchester dealers could now purchase Simmons-branded merchandise with clear consciences because their buying would be helping the combined Winchester-Simmons organization.

There were some problems of adjustment from the Simmons side also. In a letter to the salesmen announcing the merger, George Simmons spoke in glowing terms of the Winchester organization and the abilities of its management, who, ". . . are men of high character and integrity and of great capacity and ability, both as manufacturers, and as clearly grasping the trend of the hardware business and methods that will insure success in the future."

Winchester had been assured of the hearty cooperation of the entire Simmons organization, and the Simmons brothers had promised in a letter to their salesmen on June 26, 1922, ". . . to explain the facts so clearly to all of our associates that every one of our officers and of our employees at all Houses and in all parts of our organization would arrive at the same conclusion that we have arrived at, namely: That under the new plans, the opportunities for every member of our business family are largely increased and are limited only by the personal ability of the individual and the amount of effort that he or she is willing to inject into the new organization to assure its success."

At the same time George Simmons felt called on to explain why he had changed his opinion, expressed two and a half years before, that ". . . the Winchester Plan might be a stock jobbing scheme and that the people in it were not experienced in the hardware business, and that it was not to the interest of the hardware trade that their Plan should be a success. My answer to that is that the record of the past two and one-half years has convinced me that my surmise was incorrect, and that this was not a stock jobbing proposition; also that there has not been, and is not now any affiliation with the other interests who have been identified with the stock jobbing operations in the past. Also it has been proved that while these gentlemen did not know from experience some of the things which our experience has taught us, still their ideas and ours are entirely in harmony as to the proper methods of distributing hardware; and furthermore that our chief objection that it was against the interest of the retailer to tie up with a concern which could not supply him promptly and in small quantities, and in the most economical way—as a jobber can—is entirely removed by the fact that we contribute to this consolidation exactly that factor, the absence of which we criticized in the original Winchester setup. I have discussed with several big manufacturers in the last five years just such an affiliation of producing and distributing organizations, and every one of them has been keen for it, but we have not found any other manufacturing concern big enough for us to tie up with because no other has the capacity for a broad variety of production that the Winchester Company has."

CHAPTER TWENTY-SIX

# TESTING THE MERGER

The Winchester group could not expect an immediate solution of its manufacturing problems as a result of the merger. The general competitive situation was unchanged. Only as an increased volume might come from a broader manufacturing and distributing basis and permit overhead costs to be spread, and only as economies could be introduced into the productive processes, would it be possible to reduce manufacturing costs and bring about profitable operations. It was to the task of achieving these results that the Winchester management devoted the succeeding two years.

*Absorption of Simmons's Production*

At the time of the merger Simmons had a controlling interest in three manufacturing establishments. These were the Walden Knife Company, Walden, New York; the Roanoke Spoke and Handle Company, Roanoke, Virginia; and the Mound City Paint and Color Company of St. Louis, which also had a branch plant in Philadelphia. One of the immediate tasks following the merger was to bring these companies under the Winchester management.

The easiest of the newly acquired manufacturing facilities to bring under the Winchester supervision was the Walden Knife Company. Operations were carried on at the plant in Walden until September 1923, when the tools, fixtures, equipment and machinery were moved to New Haven and installed in the Winchester plant. While the Walden concern had been producing knives and cutlery lines for Simmons, operations were not on a large scale. The total book value of the items moved to New Haven was less than $11,000—a comparatively small addition to Winchester's facilities.

No attempt was made to move the Roanoke Spoke and Handle Company from its location. In addition to handles for tools the plant was producing the well known Louisville Slugger brand of baseball bats. Winchester, as it happened, had just installed bat-making equipment at New Haven. The Company now found itself in the bat business on a considerable scale, producing the Louisville Slugger for distribution through Simmons and the Winchester bat for its dealer-agents. What on the surface appeared to be a simple problem of production turned out to have its complications. Every major-league player apparently wanted his own individually shaped bat and if his batting average fell off, wanted to change the shape. These changes in consumers' tastes made it difficult to maintain uniform production standards, especially on the Louisville Slugger, which was a favorite among professional ballplayers.



Even more serious was the fact that the Roanoke plant was in poor shape.

The equipment was run down and the morale of the workers low. A considerable effort was made to put the organization on a satisfactory basis but without much success and when a fire destroyed the entire property in July 1925, no attempt was made to replace it.

The main plant of the Mound City Paint and Color Company was maintained in St. Louis, but the equipment, machinery, and other equipment of the Philadelphia branch were moved to New Haven. This acquisition put Winchester into a new line of business, one that had little connection with existing types of production and one that had its own particular problems. The paint concern had been manufacturing a full line of paints but apparently the processes involved were more of an art than a science. The formulas used were the secrets of the foremen and on analysis it was discovered that the contents bore little relationship to the specifications printed on the labels. As this practice was illegal according to various state and federal laws, Winchester undertook at considerable expense to modernize the equipment and methods of paint manufacture. The resulting paint was a high-quality product which was marketed under both the Simmons and Winchester trade marks. The dealer-agents were urged to take on the line, but it proved difficult to compete with established brands. Furthermore, the costs of making an "honest" paint proved, over time, to be too high to yield a profit on operations. Winchester did not give up on paint, however, until 1927 when the capital stock of the Mound City Paint and Color Company was transferred back to Simmons and the manufacture of paint at New Haven was stopped.

In addition to the foregoing operation, Winchester undertook the manufacture of Keen Kutter brands of cutlery and hardware for distribution by Simmons. It was initially supposed that the addition of these lines to production at the Winchester plant would do much to utilize the remaining idle manufacturing space and equipment. These hopes were only partially realized. It turned out that Simmons's volume on these items was much smaller than anticipated. Furthermore there was a considerable cost involved in changing over or building new equipment to meet Simmons specifications. This proved to be a more or less continuing problem as the sales department made frequent requests for additional lines or changes in specifications.

Just how much additional business was added to Winchester by taking over the production of the Simmons brand goods is difficult to determine. An analysis of distribution through various sales outlets (*see Appendix I-2*) indicates that Winchester-Simmons purchases aside from goods going to the dealer-agents, amounted to 8.6 per cent of total sales in 1922 and 3.1 per cent in 1923. On new-line products the proportions were respectively 13 per cent and 10 per cent for the two years. Even allowing for the added sale of paint and products of the Roanoke Spoke and Handle Company marketed under the Winchester brand, the total addition to manufacturing at the Winchester plant was not very large.

While the evidence is not clear, there are grounds for believing that the assignment of sales policy to a Simmons executive resulted in the setting of prices which accentuated the production problem. It was to be expected that an aggressive salesman would be concerned about keeping and extending his market; but when he set prices at a "competitive" level, the factory found itself with a still greater discrepancy between its actual costs and those determined by "specification-cost" formula under which it continued to operate. It would seem, however, that the Simmons policy prevailed, at least by May 1923, when W. Drake, the factory manager, reported to Otterson: "No special concessions have been claimed or obtained by the factory over and above outside manufacturers, due to the inter-company relationships, but, on the contrary, special concessions to the Distributing Organization [Simmons] have been made on account of such relationship, it being considered that the factory should, in general, deal with the Distributing Organization on a strictly competitive basis and in individual cases of items where the arrangements above will result in selling goods at a loss, it was the factory's problem to reduce costs to meet prices which could be obtained elsewhere." [1]

*Retail Stores*

One possible way to offset the failure to add substantially to the new-line manufacturing operations through the acquisition of the Simmons facilities and lines, was to increase sales through the retail stores. Otterson's announced policy at the end of 1921 was to add to the chain as soon as business conditions improved. In reality this proved to be impracticable as it became increasingly clear after that date that the retail stores program was a failure.

No further effort was made to increase the eleven stores which were operating at the beginning of 1922. On the contrary, during that year two of the poorest-paying outlets, one in Boston and the store in Lawrence, Massachusetts, were closed. The Troy and Pawtucket stores were liquidated in 1923, and in January 1924 the Providence and a second Boston outlet were discontinued. Net sales on the remaining stores showed some improvement over the approximate $1.9 million in 1921, amounting to around $2.3 million in each of the succeeding two years. Despite this increase, however, there was a decline in both amounts and percentages (due in part to the dropping of hardware lines) of Winchester-branded merchandise sold through the stores. From $248,000 in 1921, the figures dropped to $106,000 in 1922, and $108,000 in 1923, or a decline from 13 per cent in 1921 to approximately 4.65 per cent in the following two years. As an outlet for Winchester's total manufactured products these quantities were truly insignificant, constituting 2.5 per cent in 1927, .64 per cent in 1922, and .58 per cent in 1923. Unless these rates could have been materially changed, a chain of fifty or more stores would have been needed to provide any substantial market for products manufactured in the Winchester plant.

Because of their obvious failure to provide an outlet for Winchester-manufactured products, the retail stores had to be judged financially on their operation as a subsidiary venture, almost entirely independent of the other functions performed by the Company. In this respect also the results were most disappointing. Operating losses alone for 1922 and 1923 came to over $970,000 while the expenses of liquidating the hardware inventories in the former year added another $372,000. Far from adding to the sales of Winchester-branded merchandise during 1922 and 1923, the stores were a severe financial drain which the Company could ill afford.

*Dealer-Agents*

Aside from the retail stores, the main opportunity for increasing sales was in expanding the amounts sold to the dealer-agents, either by increasing the average per dealer-agent or by increasing their numbers, or both. In this respect the management was more successful.



As of January 1922 the number of dealer-agents was around 4,100. During the succeeding two years some 1,500 more were added, 800 during 1922 and 700 during 1923, bringing the total to approximately 5,600 by January 1924. This was a noteworthy expansion, and although short of the initial goal of 8,000, brought about a quarter of the retail hardware merchants in the country under the plan.

In the campaign to expand the number of dealer-agents, the advantages of better distribution through the merger with Simmons were stressed. Otherwise there was no basic change in the merchandising services given the dealer. The Company continued to supply window displays, advised on the layout of stores at nominal cost, and made suggestions regarding effective merchandising methods.

The Company held its third annual convention of Winchester Clubs in Chicago in 1923. This was a four-day affair which was attended by some two thousand persons, including dealers and their families. The convention meetings were held in the coliseum at the Great Lakes Naval Training Station beginning on June 25. In general the proceedings followed the model established at the two previous occasions held in New Haven, but on a more elaborate scale. The guests were treated to a combination of educational and entertainment features. As a special attraction, Secretary of Labor James J. Davis addressed the group. Otterson and George W. Simmons spoke on various aspects of the business as it had developed since the merger while various dealers spoke on particular problems connected with hardware merchandising. On the lighter side there was a grand ball and sporting events. In the latter, Johnny Weismuller broke the world's swimming record for the 500-yard free style and Joie Ray ran an exhibition mile in near-record time. Enthusiasm on the part of those attending the convention apparently ran high and it was hailed by the management as a great success in building stronger relations with the dealer-agents.

One of the main concerns of the dealers during 1922 and 1923 was an expansion of the Winchester lines of hardware and sporting goods. This had proceeded rather slowly, and a number of dealers urged that the Winchester brand be put on additional lines and items, not manufactured by the Company, in order to increase the goods available for distribution. Otterson was understandably reluctant to take on merchandise which might ultimately be manufactured by the Company. In March 1923, he replied to this suggestion, by way of an open letter, stating that the management wanted to be "exceedingly careful about the use of the name Winchester and to confine it only to those products which will be a credit to it and upon which it will be significant." Urging patience upon the dealers he expressed satisfaction "in the rapidity with which the Winchester lines of products have been developed from nothing three years ago to their present state of completeness."

Work was pushed on the new lines during 1923 and on January 1, 1924, Otterson was able to report that about a thousand new products had been developed during the preceding twelve months. Winchester now had, he stated, "The most complete line of sporting goods placed on the market by any single manufacturer; also the most complete line of tools and hardware specialties. This development has been carried to the point where it is now possible for us to cease making additions to our lines for the time being and concentrate our attention on production and service on the lines which we have."

As a part of the policy emphasizing service, he announced the formation of a separate sales force made up of a group of old Winchester salesmen to be known as "Winchester missionaries." Like their counterparts in the selling of guns and ammunition these missionary salesmen were to cooperate with the regular salesmen of the Winchester-Simmons organization in promoting the sales of Winchester's new-line products and keeping up interest in the dealer-agency plan. This move may have been in response to a criticism acknowledged by George W. Simmons in a speech before the convention that the Simmons salesmen did not seem to be well posted on the Winchester line. It is also possible that the Winchester management wanted to be sure that the Simmons group was not pushing its brand at the expense of Winchester-manufactured products.

There was a noticeable increase in purchases by the dealer-agents. In 1922 the group absorbed some 43 per cent of the Company's total sales, over 35 per cent of the old and 60 per cent of the new. The following year combined purchases by the dealer-agents came to nearly 56 per cent of total sales, over 46 per cent of the old lines and 72 per cent of the new. What this meant in approximate average sales per dealer of Winchester products is shown in the following tabulation:

| *Year* | *1922* [a] | *1923* [b] |
|---|---|---|
| Old Lines | $915.00 | $1,013.00 |
| New Lines | 673.00 | 925.00 |
| Total | $1,588.00 | $1,938.00 |

[a] Assumed average number of dealer-agents, 4500.
[b] Assumed average number of dealer-agents, 5300.

Compared with the average total sales per dealer-agent of about $1,415 for 1920-21, this was a decided improvement. On the assumption, however, that the average dealer purchased $50,000 worth of merchandise annually it was still below the 5 per cent of those purchases which Birney, early in 1922, thought might be reached. It is also noteworthy that guns and ammunition continued to make up the greater part of the purchases by the dealer-agents, although by a smaller margin in 1923 than in 1922. Nevertheless, it was still possible that if a trend had been established in the purchases of the new lines over the 1922-23 year, the total volume going to the dealer-agents might be substantially increased in the future.

*Sales and Operating Results, 1922-1923*

At first glance the record of the Winchester organization for 1922 appears quite impressive. Total sales of Winchester products for the year came to a little over $16.6 million, to which the new products contributed approximately $5 million. (Sale of new products increased by almost 100 per cent, those of guns and ammunition increasing but 29 per cent.) This total, it will be recalled, was almost the exact amount the management had estimated some eleven months before, would enable the organization not only to break even, but to pay dividends as well on the preferred stock of the Winchester Company.

The results were in fact far short of the expected goal. The gross margin (i.e., the difference between the sales revenues and the costs allocated to the goods sold) was reported by the Winchester Company and its affiliated concerns at approximately $4.471 million. From this amount costs of administration and selling of $3.1 million and interest charges of $1.11 million were deducted, which gave a reported net profit of $248,000. Against this, the published accounts showed an operating and liquidating loss on the retail stores of $372,000, which was charged to surplus. Thus, on a basis of the published accounts, the net loss on operations for the year came to $124,000.

This figure, however, underestimates the true results of the year's operations in two major respects. Items were carried as assets or charged to old reserves, which, if a true financial picture had been shown, would have been treated as current operating losses. The expenditures in question were as follows:

| | |
|---|---|
| Operating losses on new products | $ 789,000 |
| Cost of new tools for "special" (i.e., new) products | 120,000 |
| Engineering development of new products | 121,000 |
| Costs of the dealer-agencies established during the year | 137,000 |
| Cost of maintaining idle plant | 133,000 |
| TOTAL | $1,300,000 |

Secondly, the accounts failed to recognize depreciation on the plant and equipment in the operations of the Company. At the normal rate used by the Company, this charge would have amounted to $1.24 million.

In sum, therefore, 1922 operations resulted in a loss of $2.664 million made up of:

| | |
|---|---|
| Loss as reported | $ 124,000 |
| Expenditures capitalized and later charged to reserves | 1,300,000 |
| Depreciation not charged | 1,240,000 |
| TOTAL | $2,664,000 |

These departures from sound accounting practice were, perhaps, justified so far as the so-called developmental costs were concerned. The cost of evolving new products and the establishment of new dealer-agencies might be considered as assets with a possible future earning capacity. The actual operating losses on the new products, depreciation and idle-plant charges, however, could hardly be put into the same category, and the failure to show them as operating losses undoubtedly gave a misleading impression of the Company's financial position. Even if the accounting treatment had been fully justified, there remained the inescapable fact that the Winchester organization failed by over $2.6 millions to gain a net profit on operations.

These results must have been disappointing to the management, although no recorded explanation of the failure to bring about more satisfactory financial returns was made either to the directors or the stockholders. In his report to the latter group covering the year 1922, Otterson spoke of the complex organization problems that had been encountered in connection with the Simmons merger and expressed his satisfaction with the smooth-running organization that had emerged. He continued: "The large development program that the company undertook at the end of the war in order to fill its war plants is thus brought nearer to completion. We find ourselves in a period of increased business activity with a well equipped plant. The improvement in general business conditions during the latter part of 1922 has continued into the early months of 1923 with resulting increased volume of sales and manufacturing activity and an improved earning situation. Stocks of merchandise are low with both the retailer and the jobber and the outlook is for improved demand for some time to come."

Otterson failed to point out, however, that a substantial proportion of the gross margin had been earned by the gun and ammunition departments or that those departments were, in effect, still subsidizing the new products.

The increase in the sales of the new products during 1922 was still inadequate to relieve the management of the pressing problem of the high costs of manufacture of the new lines. Only if these costs could be brought into line, either through reductions or by being spread out over a further increase in sales and only if the continued losses on retail stores could be eliminated would it be possible to return a real net profit on operations.

The management undertook a revaluation of the plan and equipment during 1922. There were two apparent motives for the step. It was, of course, in the interests of the stockholders to obtain the best possible terms in any scheme for merging their interests with those of another group, i.e., Simmons or Shapleigh. The book values of the fixed assets represented an accumulation of items having no very close affinity to a valuation based, for instance, on the capitalized value of expected earnings. They had been obtained by adding to the "insurance valuations" used as the basis for bringing in these assets at January 1, 1912, the expenditures on development of the property during and after World War I. A reappraisal was, therefore, essential before any financial agreement could be made with Shapleigh or Simmons. The appraisers, Messrs. Ford, Bacon, and Davis, recommended, in effect, the revaluing of the assets on the basis of replacement costs less depreciation from the date of actual purchase.

The result was the emergence of a "capital surplus" of some $13.6 million net. This surplus was of a debatable validity, even at the time it was created. It is true that it resulted from an expert calculation of providing, at current costs, an identical complex of buildings and machinery; the detailed schedules submitted by the appraisers show a most meticulous attention to the details of construction and equipment. There is, however, no indication that any attention was given at all to the capacity of the plant and machinery to earn, under the existing conditions, a reasonable rate of return. It is a commentary on contemporary financial attitudes that the net worth shown in the reorganized balance sheet could be accepted as the basis for an exchange of stocks.

The second—and probably less significant—motive behind the reappraisal was the provision of a reserve against which could be charged some of the development expenditures which, as suggested above, were not represented by earning assets. Whether the motive was explicit is, of course, not clear, but, in the event, some $5.1 millions of these unproductive development costs were actually charged off against the surplus arising from reappraisal.

Though the balance sheet had been, to some extent, "cleaned up" the result was to leave it with a heavy burden of capital assets upon which, as yet, there were no signs that the group could earn a positive rate of return, however small.

The total net sales of Winchester products came to a little over $18.37 million for 1923. The group reported a gross margin after deducting costs allocated to sales of some $4.3 million. The total sales, it may be noted, had exceeded the amount which the management had established, some two years before, as sufficient to permit payments not only to the preferred stockholders, but to common stockholders as well. Once more, however, the results fell far below expectations. The reported net income was approximately $141,000 after charging some $526,000 of development expense. This figure was arrived at as in the previous year by treating various expenditures as capital accounts or charging them off to surplus. The following summary of the pertinent items gives a more accurate picture of the current financial picture of the Company; while the management had included some depreciation as a cost, it represented a substantial reduction from its normal depreciation rates:

| | | |
|---|---|---|
| Profit as reported to stockholders | | *$141,000 Loss* |
| Current costs capitalized or charged to reserves | | |
| Costs of securing additional dealers agencies | 123,000 | |
| Development of new products | 135,000 | |
| Maintenance of idle plant | 113,000 | 371,000 |
| Operating loss before depreciation | | 230,000 |
| *Add* Balance of full depreciation for the year | | 1,037,000 |
| Total operating loss 1923 | | $1,267,000 |

The reasons for the unsatisfactory financial results are not hard to determine; the manufacturing departments were responsible for some $784,000 of the adjusted loss shown above, and the retail store organization for an additional loss of $519,000. The figures reflect, moreover, the increasing burden of the charge for interest which, in 1923, amounted to approximately $903,000.

Even for the benefit of the stockholders, Otterson could not draw any very optimistic conclusions as a result of the 1923 operations. In his report to the group for the year, he noted the increase of sales over the preceding year and the fact that some thousand new items had been added to existing lines of manufactured products, a further increase in the number of dealer-agents and increased emphasis on the policy of establishing agencies in the larger cities. He did not draw particular attention to the state of the Winchester group's finances which had now reached a deplorable state.

With current liabilities of $9.4 million (of which $8.3 million was owing to banks against ninety-day notes), the Winchester Company and its subsidiaries had but $4.1 million of cash and receivables. With $11.7 million of inventories it had, it is true, a net working capital of $6.5 million but it was clear that it had, by December 31, 1923, lost its freedom of action. The dividend on its first preferred stock was now in arrears of thirty-two months, involving a claim against future profits, if and when available for dividends, of over $1.8 million. Though the balance sheet showed capital, surplus and reserves amounting to $31.5 million (of which $8 million represented the balance of the reappraisal surplus set up in 1922), there was now every reason for the stockholders to doubt the reliability of this valuation as a guide to the future of their interests.

*Otterson's Resignation*

The unsatisfactory financial results of 1923 brought matters rapidly to a head. Early in 1924, Liggett, undoubtedly under orders—or at least pressure—from Kidder, Peabody & Company, sent two of his United Drug executives to New Haven to look into the management of the Winchester organization. Charles

McCallum was charged with investigating the Simmons part of the combination while William A. Tobler was to examine the Winchester management. Tobler, who reported orally to Liggett, was critical of the Winchester postwar program in general and of Otterson's management in particular. He especially questioned the wisdom of the marketing plan and he felt that Otterson had organized his staff on a much too elaborate basis for effective operation. The financial prospects of the Company were so unpromising, in his judgment, that he recommended an immediate receivership.

This recommendation was too strong for Liggett and for Kidder, Peabody & Company to accept, considering the heavy equity interest of the latter, but a change in management seemed to be indicated. The minutes of the board of directors of the Winchester Repeating Arms Company for June 1924, record that after taking care of routine affairs:

> The directors then went into executive session for a general discussion of the affairs of the Company, following which Mr. Otterson tendered his resignation as President of the Company.
>
> At the same time R. E. Anderson resigned as vice-president. Both resignations were immediately accepted with the proviso that Otterson's salary continue through the rest of the year.

To replace Otterson as president, the board promoted Frank Drew from his position as one of the vice presidents, and William A. Tobler and William T. Birney were elected vice presidents to fill the vacancies left by Drew's promotion and Anderson's resignation.

Otterson's departure marked the end of a chapter in Winchester's history. Developed with such high hopes some five years before, the plans laid out for the reorganization and expansion of the business had not only failed to live up to expectations, but had brought the Company to the verge of bankruptcy by the end of 1923.

# PART 8

# RETREAT FROM POSTWAR EXPERIMENT: 1924-1931

CHAPTER TWENTY-SEVEN

# LIGGETT'S ADMINISTRATION

*Management Personnel*

With the departure of Otterson the problem facing Kidder, Peabody & Company, as principal owners, was to choose a management group which might be able to put the combined operations of Winchester and Simmons on a paying basis. In this situation the bankers showed their continued faith in his ability and judgment by turning to Louis K. Liggett. He was immediately appointed president of the Simmons Hardware Company and succeeded T. G. Bennett as chairman of the board of the Winchester Repeating Arms Company when the latter resigned that position in August 1924. Liggett thus became responsible for general policies and attended the directors monthly meetings, held in New Haven, of the constituent companies.

Unlike Otterson, Liggett did not take over the active management of the business, the immediate responsibility for the operation of both Winchester and Simmons being delegated to others. The marketing activities, especially as they related to the dealer-agents, sales promotion, and the physical distribution of hardware and sporting goods, came under the direction of J. Clarke Coit, who was appointed general manager of Simmons Hardware Company. An experienced hardware jobber, Coit had spent some seventeen years in the buying and sales departments of the Lee, Clark, Anderson Company of Milwaukee, Wisconsin, prior to becoming vice president and sales manager in 1913. A few years later he became president of that company, a position which he held until January 1924, when he resigned to become the head of the Winchester-Simmons Company of St. Louis. It was his long experience in the hardware jobbing business that prompted Liggett and Kidder, Peabody & Company to appoint Coit vice president and general manager of the Winchester-Simmons Company in June 1924.

An announcement of Coit's appointment in the *Winchester Herald,* the house magazine that went to all Winchester dealer-agents, stated: "He brings the experience that has been won by merchandising through wars and through panics. Close contact and intimate friendship with many manufacturers have kept him in touch with sources and a wide acquaintance with retailers has given him an appreciation of merchandising tendencies throughout the country."

Frank Drew's election as president of Winchester Repeating Arms Company was primarily a move to strengthen the organization's ties with the jobbing trade. Generally credited with being responsible for continuing sales of guns and ammunition to the jobbers at the time of the reorganization in 1919, Drew was well

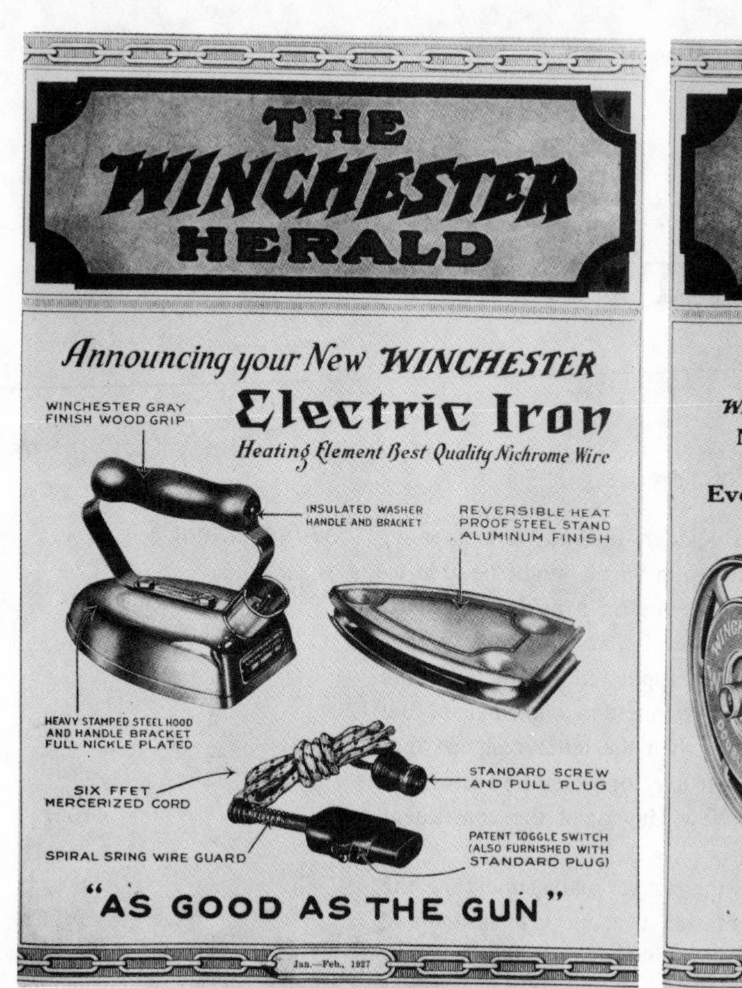

*Early Use of the Slogan "As Good as the Gun"*

known and liked in jobbing circles. His appointment was expected to overcome much of the antagonism raised by the adoption of the dealer-agency plan and to stimulate sales through these distribution channels.

William T. Birney's election as vice president was a move in the same direction. Despite his part in promoting the dealer-agencies, he too was popular among the jobbers. One of his first assignments on the new job was to join with Drew in making a good-will tour among the jobbers.

Neither Drew nor Birney was experienced enough in general administration to take general charge of the operations of Winchester Repeating Arms Company. For this position William A. Tobler was chosen. A native of Switzerland, Tobler had emigrated to the United States as a young man and for a time was engaged in the importing business in New York. He subsequently became associated with Liggett and the United Drug Company, specializing in the financial aspects of the business. Tobler served as vice president of Winchester Repeating Arms Company until August 1928, when he was made president, succeeding Drew, who was elected chairman of the board. (This shift was apparently in recognition of Tob-

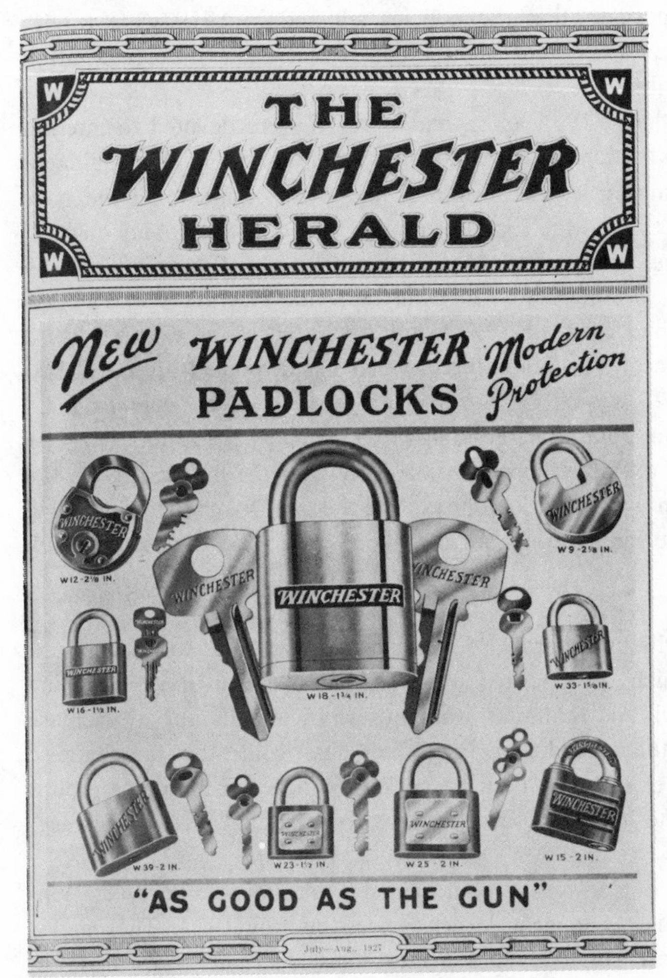

*Automobile Tires Resulted from the Merger with the Simmons Company*

ler's real function in the management. Liggett resigned only as chairman of the board in order to give Drew the title. When the latter was killed in an automobile accident in October 1928, Liggett resumed the chairmanship.)

The final key position at the Winchester plant, that of general superintendent, was filled by Edwin Pugsley, who aside from his assignment in connection with the Company's retail stores, already noted, had been associated for some thirteen years with the Company's developmental and manufacturing activities.

This management group, made up of both new and old-time employees, indicated the general character of the policies which were to be followed until the beginning of 1929. Liggett's position was an effective check on any rapid change in the plans adopted in 1919. Considerations of pride and prestige made him reluctant to admit that the Liggett methods of distributing drug-store items would not work equally well when applied to the marketing of sporting goods and hardware. It was hoped to revive the fortunes of the organization by increasing sales to the dealer-agents and the jobbers, by lowering manufacturing costs, and by more careful financial management. The succeeding four and half years were in effect a test of the proposition that the policies adopted in 1919 were fundamentally sound and under a different management could bring the organization out of its financial difficulties.

The remaining months of 1924 and a part of 1925 were devoted to internal reorganization and rehabilitation. The retail-stores program was finally liquidated by disposing of the remaining leases, furniture, and fixtures, including the New York store at 42nd Street and Madison. Inventories were reviewed, and obsolete and excessive items were sold, the total inventory account being reduced by nearly $2 million. About $500,000 was spent in replacing machinery and equipment in the plant which had been allowed to run down. Operating expenses were cut and bank loans reduced. The labor force which had averaged around 4,700 workers for 1922 and 1923 was cut to approximately 3,500. (*See Appendix J-1.*) Salaried personnel, totaling approximately 344 in 1923, had been reduced to 201 by 1926. These actions prompted one official to remark, "The change in the morale of the organization was magic. All of the old-timers throughout the factory, throughout the sales force, and throughout the offices said, 'We are getting back to old times.' "

*Marketing and Dealer-Agents*

J. Clarke Coit's merits as a hardware merchandiser were put to a stern test. Among the problems which he inherited was a large inventory of slow-moving merchandise in the Winchester-Simmons warehouses. In an attempt to increase sales during early 1924 the preceding management had "sold" this merchandise in large quantities in the expectation that the various Winchester-Simmons groups would be able to distribute it. It took over a year to get inventories into manageable proportions.

One difficulty of the dealer-agency plan, namely, the limited variety of Winchester-branded merchandise, had been largely solved by July 1924. The catalog issued that month contained some 7,584 separate items, distributed among tools, cutlery, flashlights, paint, steel goods, fishing tackle, baseball and football goods, skates, and other athletic supplies. Most of the athletic goods was purchased from outside suppliers but the large bulk of the rest was Winchester produced.

Despite this improvement, the morale of many of the dealer-agents was low during 1924 and 1925. The failure during preceding years to get a variety of merchandise at prices that were in line with competing items had weakened the loyalty to the Winchester plan. The National Executive Committee of Winchester Clubs, elected by the dealer-agents, took cognizance of this situation in January 1925. In an open letter the committee criticized the action of certain stockholding agency dealers who were ". . . lending, through publicity and moral support, aid and assistance to our competitors in their effort to establish competing lines [and were] writing testimonials for such competitors on stationery bearing 'Winchester Store' imprint to which national publicity is being given." Hope was expressed that the resolutions condemning these actions, which were published in the *Winchester Herald,* would be effective in checking such practices and ". . . those who have been consciously or unconsciously involved will refuse to aid such methods on the part of competitors."

Coit, along with Drew and other officials, spent a great deal of time during late 1924 and 1925 traveling about the country getting acquainted with the dealer-agents and attempting to sell them on the advantages of the plan.

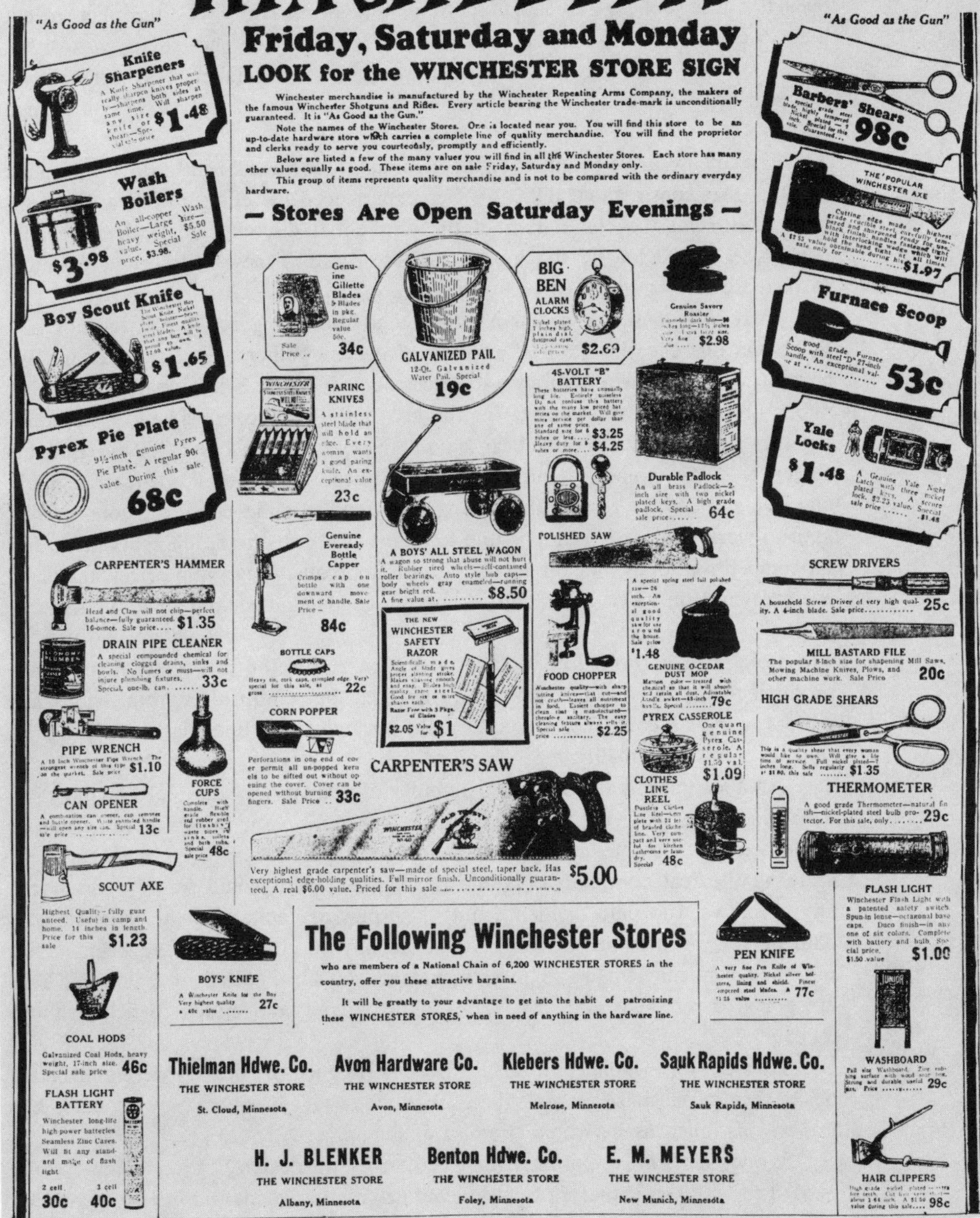

THURSDAY, FEBRUARY 3. THE ST. CLOUD DAILY TIMES PAGE FIVE

# Exceptional Introductory Values at THE WINCHESTER STORES

"As Good as the Gun" "As Good as the Gun"

## Friday, Saturday and Monday

### LOOK for the WINCHESTER STORE SIGN

Winchester merchandise is manufactured by the Winchester Repeating Arms Company, the makers of the famous Winchester Shotguns and Rifles. Every article bearing the Winchester trade-mark is unconditionally guaranteed. It is "As Good as the Gun."

Note the names of the Winchester Stores. One is located near you. You will find this store to be an up-to-date hardware store which carries a complete line of quality merchandise. You will find the proprietor and clerks ready to serve you courteously, promptly and efficiently.

Below are listed a few of the many values you will find in all the Winchester Stores. Each store has many other values equally as good. These items are on sale Friday, Saturday and Monday only.

This group of items represents quality merchandise and is not to be compared with the ordinary everyday hardware.

### — Stores Are Open Saturday Evenings —

Knife Sharpeners — $1.48

Wash Boilers — An all-copper Wash Boiler—Large size—heavy weight. $5.50 value. Special Sale price, $3.98. — $3.98

Boy Scout Knife — $1.65

Pyrex Pie Plate — 9½-inch genuine Pyrex Pie Plate. A regular 90c value. During this sale. — 68c

Genuine Gillette Blades — 34c

GALVANIZED PAIL — 12-Qt. Galvanized Water Pail. Special — 19c

BIG BEN ALARM CLOCKS — $2.60

Genuine Savory Roaster — $2.98

Barbers' Shears — 98c

THE POPULAR WINCHESTER AXE — $1.97

Furnace Scoop — A good grade Furnace Scoop with steel "D" 27-inch handle. An exceptional value at — 53c

Yale Locks — A Genuine Yale Night Latch with three nickel plated keys. A secure lock. $2.25 value. Special sale price — $1.48

PARING KNIVES — a good paring knife. An exceptional value — 23c

45-VOLT "B" BATTERY — $3.25, $4.25

Durable Padlock — An all brass Padlock—2-inch size with two nickel plated keys. A high grade padlock. Special sale price — 64c

Genuine Eveready Bottle Capper — Crimps cap on bottle with one downward movement of handle. Sale Price — 84c

A BOYS' ALL STEEL WAGON — A fine value at — $8.50

POLISHED SAW — $1.48

CARPENTER'S HAMMER — Head and Claw will not chip—perfect balance—fully guaranteed. 16-ounce. Sale price — $1.35

DRAIN PIPE CLEANER — A special compounded chemical for cleaning clogged drains, sinks and bowls. No fumes or muss—will not injure plumbing fixtures. Special, one-lb. can — 33c

BOTTLE CAPS — Heavy tin, cork caps, crimped edge. Very special for this sale, at gross — 22c

THE NEW WINCHESTER SAFETY RAZOR — $2.05 Value for $1

FOOD CHOPPER — $2.25

GENUINE O-CEDAR DUST MOP — 79c

PYREX CASSEROLE — $1.09

CLOTHES LINE REEL — 48c

SCREW DRIVERS — A household Screw Driver of very high quality. A 4-inch blade. Sale price — 25c

MILL BASTARD FILE — The popular 8-inch size for shapening Mill Saws, Mowing Machine Knives, Plows, and other machine work. Sale Price — 20c

HIGH GRADE SHEARS — This is a quality shear that every woman would like to own. Will give a life time of service. Full nickel plated—7 inches long. Sells regularly at $1.80, this sale — $1.35

PIPE WRENCH — A 10 inch Winchester Pipe Wrench. The strongest wrench of this type on the market. Sale price — $1.10

CAN OPENER — 13c

FORCE CUPS — 48c

CORN POPPER — Perforations in one end of cover permit all un-popped kernels to be sifted out without opening the cover. Cover can be opened without burning fingers. Sale Price — 33c

CARPENTER'S SAW — Very highest grade carpenter's saw—made of special steel, taper back. Has exceptional edge-holding qualities. Full mirror finish. Unconditionally guaranteed. A real $6.00 value. Priced for this sale — $5.00

THERMOMETER — A good grade Thermometer—natural finish—nickel-plated steel bulb protector. For this sale, only — 29c

SCOUT AXE — Highest Quality—fully guaranteed. Useful in camp and home. 14 inches in length. Price for this sale — $1.23

BOYS' KNIFE — 27c

PEN KNIFE — 77c

FLASH LIGHT — Winchester Flash Light with a patented safety switch. Spun-in lense—octagonal base caps. Duco finish—in any one of six colors. Complete with battery and bulb. Special price. $1.50 value — $1.00

COAL HODS — 46c

FLASH LIGHT BATTERY — 2 cell 30c, 3 cell 40c

WASHBOARD — 29c

HAIR CLIPPERS — 98c

## The Following Winchester Stores

who are members of a National Chain of 6,200 WINCHESTER STORES in the country, offer you these attractive bargains.

It will be greatly to your advantage to get into the habit of patronizing these WINCHESTER STORES, when in need of anything in the hardware line.

| Thielman Hdwe. Co. | Avon Hardware Co. | Klebers Hdwe. Co. | Sauk Rapids Hdwe. Co. |
|---|---|---|---|
| THE WINCHESTER STORE | THE WINCHESTER STORE | THE WINCHESTER STORE | THE WINCHESTER STORE |
| St. Cloud, Minnesota | Avon, Minnesota | Melrose, Minnesota | Sauk Rapids, Minnesota |

| H. J. BLENKER | Benton Hdwe. Co. | E. M. MEYERS |
|---|---|---|
| THE WINCHESTER STORE | THE WINCHESTER STORE | THE WINCHESTER STORE |
| Albany, Minnesota | Foley, Minnesota | New Munich, Minnesota |

*Example of Winchester-Dealer Cooperative Advertising*

This task was not made easier by a decision made at the end of 1924 to cancel the extra discount on guns and ammunition that Winchester dealers had enjoyed ever since the introduction of the agency program. In a letter sent to each of the agents, dated December 31, 1924, Liggett personally attempted to justify the change. He explained that the effect of the preferential discount had been to cause jobbers and manufacturers, who wanted to wreck the plan, to cut their discounts to the point that the business, especially on shot shells, was profitable ". . . today to neither manufacturers, jobbers or retailers." This letter was followed by a vigorous campaign to convince the dealers of the need for a change in policy.

The intense drive to put over the advantages of the change in discount policy suggests that considerable difficulty was experienced in selling the idea. It seems quite likely that the elimination of the differential discounts to dealers was the concession demanded by the jobbers of Drew and Birney who were attempting to increase sales through jobber outlets.

In respect to the prices of hardware and sporting goods, Coit was not sanguine. On one occasion he told a group of dealers gathered in New Haven, "We have made a battle with reference to prices but our desire is to give the consuming public ultimately the best article for the least price, quality considered." Contending that selling prices should bear no relative position to cost, Coit advised the dealers to "Take home to yourself and your business the one thought that supply and demand always govern the selling price and not the cost. Put your pricing man to work and see if it is possible to adjust five cents here, ten cents there, not on competitive goods, nor on goods that are 'footballs,'—carrying prices known to every layman in your community—but on goods that should yield you a fair profit."

Coit frankly recognized that it would be easier for the dealer to increase profits if the costs of merchandise were lowered, but until orders from the dealers increased, prices could not be cut. In the meantime the merchandise should be sold on a basis of quality.

Another thing that bothered a number of dealers was the fact that no dividends had been paid on the stock which they held. Coit informed the dealers: "You are not going to get any dividend at the present time. As business men, knowing the real condition of your organization, you would want to discharge any executive who paid dividends out of surplus or capital. Dividends should be paid out of earnings only. You haven't had any earnings—we have been in the red. You gentlemen made an investment and you are entitled to dividends. You are going to get them if it is possible for Mr. Drew and myself to deliver them to you."

He went on to point out that in lieu of dividends the dealers were still better off by being Winchester agents because of favorable treatment by jobbers, but this was as much as he would promise at that time.

While this frank approach appealed to many dealers, more tangible steps needed to be taken if the sales of Winchester-branded goods were to be increased. An attempt was made with moderate success to increase the number of dealers. Exact figures are not available for 1924, but the total at the end of that year was about 6,000. By June 1924, the number was reported at 6,300.



Meanwhile a good deal of effort went into aids to help the dealers in their

MODERN MERCHANDISING METHODS

# This Display Will Sell Lawn, Farm and Garden Tools for You in March

## MARCH WINDOW DISPLAY

Featuring the New Items in your Winchester Line such as Lawn Mowers, Grass Hooks, etc. This is also an ideal opportunity for you to show the New Wheel Barrow, Garden Plow and all other Lawn, Farm and Garden Tools. "Cash-in" by using this Display in connection with your March Drive.

Your Modern Merchandising Bulletin for March gives you a Retail Sales Campaign that will increase your Sales and Profits for this Month.

### Take Advantage of These Monthly Retail Sales Campaigns

Each month's plan is built around your 5 panel background screen. Make them work for your store. These seasonal drives are planned by Practical Hardware Men and will prove worth while if carefully followed.

### Constant and Consistent Advertising is necessary

For the success of your Retail Hardware Store. The realization of this fact marked the beginning of our co-ordinated monthly plans which are announced to you 30 days in advance of each campaign.

*"It Pays You to Advertise Winchester"*

*Suggested Window Display for Dealers*

*Variation of Window Display*

merchandising problems. In 1926, Winchester specials of first-quality merchandise were made available at prices which could be used for "get-acquainted" sales. During the same year a list of items was featured which could carry an added mark-up because of particular qualities which could be featured in advertising and selling. Agents were urged also to hold six special sales during the year for which they could get low prices on merchandise.

In 1927, the window-display service, store-arrangement, and accounting service, all of which had been dropped in 1924, were returned to the dealers on an optional basis. A new advertising slogan—"As Good as the Gun"—was adopted to describe Winchester-branded sporting-goods and hardware items. A plan of collective advertising by groups of Winchester dealers in urban centers proved quite popular. The Company also resumed national advertising in 1927 designed to tie in with a plan for the first nationwide Winchester store sale.

While these various activities may have served to restore some of the lagging spirits on the part of dealer-agents, they were apparently insufficient to increase the sales of Winchester-branded merchandise. Data on sales through the various marketing channels (*see Appendix I-2*) are available only for 1920-23, 1926 and 1929. These figures indicate that nearly 56 per cent of the Company's total sales went through dealer-agents in 1923, 46 per cent of the old-line products and 72 per cent of the new-line. In 1926, the total percentage amounted to around 36 per cent, 30 per cent of the old and about 59 per cent of the new. By 1929, the percentage in all categories only amounted to a little over 14 per cent. Average dollar-sales per store dropped from $1,938 in 1923 to $752 in 1926 and to $328 in 1929.

*Merchandise Was Sold in Packaged Lots*

There was some feeling on the part of the Winchester Repeating Arms Company management that the failure to increase sales was not entirely due to the weakness of the plan. There was a strong suspicion that Coit, despite his apparent vigor in promoting sales of Winchester brands, was actually pushing the sale of Simmons merchandise more effectively. In any event, by the end of 1928, there were serious doubts about the advisability of maintaining the dealer-agency plan.

*Exports and Sales to Jobbers*

A part of the decreased sales of new products to the dealer-agents was made up in expanded exports. This department, under the able direction of H. F. Beebe, had developed outlets in the foreign markets, especially for flashlights and batteries. Interestingly enough, these sales which were absorbing some 38.5 per cent of the new products in 1929, were not generally handled by domestic export jobbers. They were sold directly to various importing houses in the various foreign areas, chiefly Latin America.

For the domestic market, including Canada, however, the data in Appendix I-2 indicate the growing importance of jobber outlets after 1924. Handling only 28.1 per cent of the Company's total sales in 1923, the jobbers were absorbing nearly 52 per cent in 1929. Most of this expansion came in new lines which grew from 3 per cent to 37 per cent during the same period. The increased volume of new products handled by jobbers included a considerable amount of sporting goods and hardware, both in private brands and with trade marks other than Winchester, although beginning in 1929 the Company began selling Winchester brands in the open market.

*Winchester's Position in the Firearms and Ammunition Industry*

Excluding 1930-1931, dollar-sales of the Company's old-line products after 1919 averaged around $11 million annually compared with the $10.78 million average maintained during the five years ending 1914. (*See page below and Appendix F.*)

Although dollar-sales of guns and ammunition were approximately the same as prewar, there was a considerable drop in physical output, except for the peak year of 1919, when nearly 305,000 were sold, gun sales never reached prewar levels during the postwar period. The average annual number distributed was 306,500 for 1909-1914; during 1919-1929 the figure was approximately 171,600. (*See Appendix D-1*).

In ammunition the greatest reduction came in centerfire cartridges and the smallest in loaded shot shells, as shown in the following tabulation of average annual sales (in millions of units):

| | *1910-1914* | *1920-29* | *Percentage of decline* |
|---|---|---|---|
| Loaded shot shells | 249.6 | 180.2 | 28 |
| Rimfire cartridges | 681.0 | 362.4 | 47 |
| Centerfire cartridges | 45.6 | 12.1 | 73 |
| Pistol cartridges | 92.4 | 55.8 | 40 |

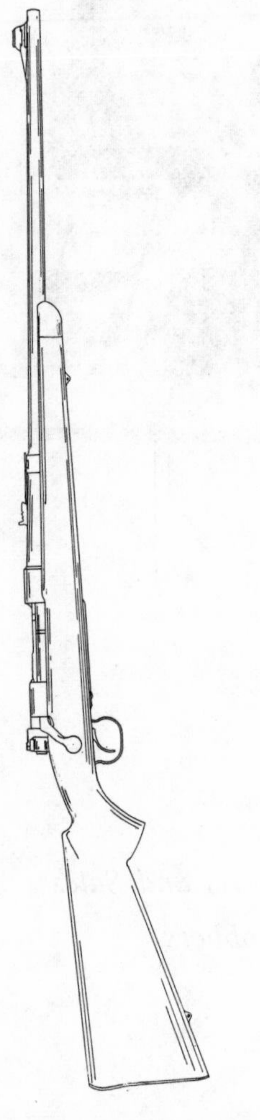
*Winchester Model 54 Rifle*

In the face of reduced physical output the Company was able to maintain its dollar volume from sales at approximately prewar levels because of the higher prices which prevailed during the latter period. By 1920 both gun and ammunition prices were more than double the levels of 1914. The impact of the 1921 depression brought about a reduction in 1922, which was followed by another drop in 1926 which still left the levels from 45 per cent to 60 per cent higher than prewar.

In part the Company's reduced physical output after 1920 confirms the belief of the management in 1914 that there would be a lower demand for guns and ammunition after World War I. In part, however, Winchester's decline was due to a loss of business to competitors. It is not possible to give an exact measure of the Company's changed relative position, but Winchester's total sales in 1914 constituted some 28 per cent of the value of the combined industry sales of guns and ammunition. By 1921 this percentage dropped to around 20 per cent and in the years following came to between 16 per cent and 17 per cent. (*See Appendix H.*) In other words, the Company's position in the industry by the beginning of 1923 had deteriorated some 40 per cent from what it had been in 1914.

It seems most likely that this drop in the percentage of industry sales was due principally to the antagonism on the part of jobbers and retailers to the Company's marketing plans adopted in 1919. If, in the absence of such a plan, Winchester had been able to maintain its prewar position, its total share of the industry's $69.2 million sales in 1923 would have amounted to approximately $18.6 million, some $3 million more than was received from both old and new products in that year. It is a small wonder that Drew and Birney, in 1924, were charged with the task of rebuilding jobber contacts. As was noted above, the percentage of sales through these channels was not sufficient to restore the prewar position of the Company in the industry.

It was no fault of the Company's gun department that sales of firearms were not larger after 1924. Under the direction of T. C. Johnson, who remained a fixture in charge of gun development throughout the various changes in management, this department brought out a total of nine new models between 1924 and 1931.

The first new rifles, in point of time, were the Models 53 and 55, introduced to the trade in August 1924. The Model 53 was essentially the same as the Model 92. The older gun had long been supplied in various styles of barrels and sizes of magazines, but sales no longer justified the manufacture of such a variety. The Model 53 was made therefore only with a round barrel 22 inches long and a tubular magazine holding six cartridges. With its introduction the Model 92, with the exception of the carbine, was dropped from production.

The Model 55 was a modified version of the Model 94. It too was put out in only one style, with a 24-inch, round barrel and a tubular magazine holding three cartridges. With its introduction, the manufacture of the Model 94, except for the carbine, was also dropped.

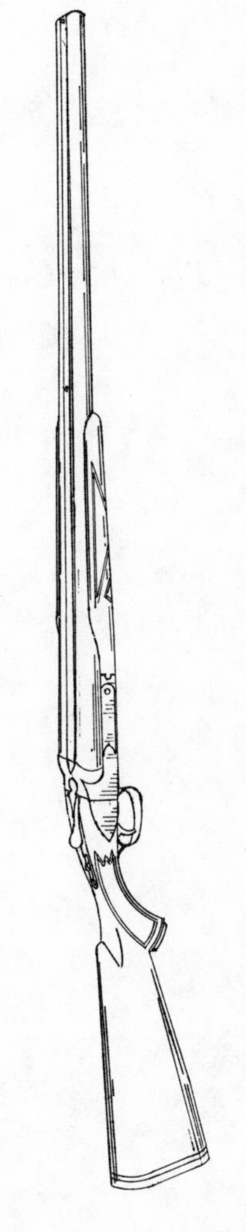

*Winchester Model 21 Shotgun*

The Model 54, introduced in 1925, was Winchester's first entry into the heavy-caliber, bolt-action field. This rifle was initially chambered for the Winchester .270 and the Government .30-06 cartridges. By 1931 it was being produced for the Winchester .30 (.30-30), 7mm, 7.65mm, 9mm, and the .250-300 Savage, all high-velocity cartridges. It was equipped with a nondetachable box magazine holding five cartridges. The rifle was reasonably popular, being adopted for large- and small-game hunting, varmint shooting, and shooting matches.

Two repeating rifles were brought out in 1926 to sell in the low-price field. One, Model 56, was a solid-frame, bolt-action, repeating rifle with a detachable box magazine holding five cartridges. It was chambered for .22 short and .22 long rifle cartridges. Sales were small and the gun was dropped from production two years later. The second, Model 57, was practically identical with the Model 56 except that it was designed for target shooting.

Also introduced in 1926 was the Model 58, a single-shot rifle, chambered (interchangeably) for .22 short, .22 long, and .22 long rifle cartridges. It was practically the same rifle as the Model 02, having a bolt action which was cocked by pulling the head of the firing pin to the rear. It was the lowest-priced gun in the Winchester line. Sales were not large and production was discontinued in 1931.

To replace the Model 58 in the low-price field the Company brought out two other guns in 1930. The Model 59 introduced in May 1930 was a bolt-action, single-shot, take-down rifle. The action was quite similar to the Model 58 and it was chambered (interchangeably) for .22 short, .22 long, and .22 long rifle cartridges. The model was not entirely satisfactory and it was replaced in December of the same year by the Model 60, an improved version of the same gun.

In many respects the Model 21 double-barreled shotgun, introduced in 1930, was among the finest firearms ever designed and produced by Winchester's gun department. The decision to put out the Company's first double-barreled shotgun was influenced by the growing movement toward game conservation that was gathering momentum during the 1920s.

Determined to make the finest double gun possible with the application of modern metallurgical and engineering methods, the Company made the barrels of chrome-molybdenum alloy steel. These barrels were joined together by a special vertical dovetail method, which permitted them to be heat-treated and brought to their ultimate strength without subsequent destruction of temper, which was impossible when barrels were joined together by brazing, as was the common practice. The Company made only one grade of gun; any differences in price being the difference in the cost of decorative work or finer woods in the stock and fore end. This too was contrary to common practice which was to increase the price of the barrels as the price of the guns went up. Made in 12, 16, and 20 gauges, the Model 21 was available in various barrel lengths and types of stocks. Selective ejection and single-trigger mechanisms were also available at an extra cost of $10 each.

*The U.S. Cartridge Company*

There were no important new developments in ammunition by Winchester during this period. Along with the other major ammunition concerns the Company was experimenting with noncorrosive priming mixtures, but it was not until after 1931 that this type primer was utilized in Winchester ammunition.

Through an arrangement with the U.S. Cartridge Company, however, the Winchester management was able to add substantially to its manufacturing activity in the production of ammunition. Early in 1926 William Tobler learned that the National Lead Company, which owned the U.S. Cartridge Company, was interested in getting out of the manufacture of ammunition. The immediate pressure came from the approaching termination of the lease on the U.S. Cartridge Company's plant in Lowell, Massachusetts. A more fundamental cause arose from the lack of integration in the production of loaded shot shells. Since about 1910, primed empty shells had been manufactured at Lowell and shipped to Perth Amboy, New Jersey, where the National Lead Company maintained a shot tower and loading plant.

After negotiations extending over several months an agreement was made in September 1926, under which Winchester acquired the physical assets, excluding finished products, of the U.S. Cartridge Company, plus patents covering the production of automobile radiator tubes. Under this agreement ammunition was to be manufactured in the Winchester plant for the U.S. Cartridge Company which would continue to distribute through its own marketing channels.

The U.S. Cartridge Company agreed to pay for deliveries of ammunition on a basis of specification-costs-plus-agreed-upon-percentages ranging from 5 per cent on shot shells to 25 per cent on centerfire ammunition. Specification costs included the cost of raw materials, direct labor, and an allowance for overhead. A ceiling was placed on these costs by a provision that they should in no case exceed the jobbers' price less 15 per cent (12½ per cent if Winchester paid advertising allowances).

Winchester paid $850,000 for the physical assets and radiator patents involved in the transaction, and some 83 freight-car loads of machinery were shipped from Lowell to New Haven, during the latter part of 1926, and installed in the Winchester plant.

In order to counteract rumors to the effect that the U.S. Cartridge Company had been "taken over" by Winchester, a letter was addressed to the Company's sales representatives on October 29, 1926, over the signature of H. F. Beebe, manager of the foreign trade department of Winchester. It was pointed out that while the U.S. Cartridge Company ammunition would be manufactured in New Haven, it would be

> . . . exclusively under the supervision of former U.S. Cartridge Company men and, as the Cartridge Company used processes and formulae which are and will be entirely different from ours, there can be no question as to the individuality of their products.
>
> Distribution of their goods and management will be their worry, not ours, therefore you will feel U.S. competition as keenly in the future as you have in the past.

On the whole the arrangement with the U.S. Cartridge Company was successful in adding substantially to Winchester's operations and sales. Full details are not available, but sales of U.S. Cartridge Company ammunition averaged over $2 million for the years 1927 and 1929. This made up nearly 30 per cent of Winchester's total ammunition sales for these two years and about 13 per cent of the aggregate net sales from all sources for the same two years.

There is some evidence that the gross margins on this business were lower than those realized on the Company's own brands. It is impossible to determine, however, whether this was due to lower prices or to higher manufacturing costs.

It had been the original intention to sell the patents covering the metal-extrusion process, acquired in the purchase of the assets of the U.S. Cartridge Company. When this proved impractical, Winchester started a small radiator manufacturing department. This turned out to be a small but profitable venture and among the customers in 1929 were the makers of Rolls Royce automobiles.

*Refrigerators*

The failure by the end of 1924 to get manufacturing volume up to the point of utilizing the entire Winchester plant led to the consideration of new products outside sporting goods and hardware, which might be produced on a scale to be profitable. It is noteworthy that in the case of the two major ventures into new products subsequently undertaken, the initiative was taken and the choice was made by Kidder, Peabody & Company and Liggett and not by the management at the Winchester plant.

During the early 1920s there was a considerable interest in mechanical refrigerators. In 1922 there were only an estimated 27,000 machines in use in the United States, but their early acceptance indicated a large potential market. When, in 1925, Kidder, Peabody & Company was approached by the inventor of an electric refrigerator, called the Ice-O-Lator, the banking house suggested to Liggett that he investigate its possibilities with a view of putting it into production at the Winchester plant. After a survey, which was cursory at best, Liggett made a favorable decision and in late 1925 a contract was made to acquire 55 per cent of the stock of the National Refrigerator Company, of Boston, which held the patents, at a price of $550,000.

Winchester's production engineers were presented with the blueprints and models of the new machine and instructions to work out plans to put it into production. It was soon apparent that the refrigerator thus acquired at a large cost was hardly developed beyond the experimental stage. The mechanism had to be completely redesigned into a gas-operated unit before production could even be started.

By the end of 1926 only 368 units, produced chiefly by hand labor, had been

*Iceboxes Distributed through Winchester Dealers*

manufactured at an operating deficit of over $155,000. During 1927, production was increased but so was the operating deficit which was reported at $560,000 at the end of the year. At this time it was stated that the machine was ready for volume production and the Company purchased $500,000 worth of new stock of the National Refrigerator Company (the minority stockholders having refused to subscribe) to provide additional working capital.

Within six months, however, it became increasingly clear that the refrigerator needed further development before it would operate with entire satisfaction. More serious were the marketing and servicing problems. Refrigerators were not an item that could be sold through hardware channels and the Company was faced with the prospect of establishing an elaborate servicing organization to back up sales through department stores and household supply houses.

Only a few machines were made during 1928 and in June the book value of the stock that had cost over $1 million was written down to $138,000. By the end of the year the project was abandoned and the entire investment, including $250,000 lent to the National Refrigerator Company, was wholly written off. A subsequent sale of the patents recouped a part of their loss, but the total cost of the venture came to an estimated $1,216,000.

*Washing Machines*

During 1926 there was still another attempt by the Company to expand output and sales by the introduction of a new product—in this instance a washing machine. The Savage Arms Company, which had suffered from immediate postwar financial difficulties, had brought out a highly successful washing machine, which was credited with saving the Savage concern from receivership and restoring dividend payments. When the inventor of the Savage model, George Dunham, approached Kidder, Peabody & Company with a new washing machine, allegedly superior to the original, the banking house provided for financial aid. A company, the George W. Dunham Corporation, was formed and production started in Utica, New York, in 1925.

In 1926, Kidder, Peabody & Company suggested to Liggett that this business, renamed the Whirldry Corporation, be acquired and added to the Winchester lines. A contract was made with the Whirldry Corporation, under which Winchester agreed to invest some $700,000 in that concern's class B stock. The machinery was to be moved from Utica to the Winchester plant in New Haven and put under the management of Winchester.

The transfer of machinery was completed and production started by the beginning of 1927. As had been the case with the refrigerators, it was found that the washing machine needed considerable further product development before it would operate effectively. Out of this development came a little Whirldry washer, suggested by Edwin Pugsley, which was well suited for household and apartment-house use.

Production of the washing machine consisted largely of assembling parts from outside suppliers and was carried on without serious trouble. The difficulty came in marketing the product. Washing machines, like refrigerators, were not a hardware jobbers' item but went largely to the department-store and household-appliance trade. Getting established in this market, especially with the competition of established manufacturers, proved difficult, although it was reported in December 1928, that operations are "now on a satisfactory basis and it is expected that no further losses will be sustained by Winchester." By that date the entire initial investment had been written off.

The hope that no further losses would be incurred was not realized. Through 1929 and 1930, Winchester advanced additional sums in excess of $1 million to keep the Whirldry Company going. By July 1931, the concern showed a complete loss of capital and owed creditors aside from Winchester over $500,000. The total expenditure by the Company in this venture amounted to approximately $1.75 million.

*Net Sales and Operating Profits*

The following tabulation shows the net sales of the Company from 1920 through 1931 (in millions):

| *Year* | *Old Line* | *New Line* | *Total* | *Index of Total* | *Percentage New Line* |
|---|---|---|---|---|---|
| 1920 | $15.40 | $1.87 | $17.27 | 100 | 11 |
| 1921 | 9.03 | 2.51 | 11.54 | 67 | 22 |
| 1922 | 11.64 | 5.00 | 16.64 | 96 | 30 |
| 1923 | 11.60 | 6.77 | 18.37 | 106 | 37 |
| 1924 | 8.97 | 2.98 | 11.95 | 69 | 25 |
| 1925 | 9.03 | 4.34 | 13.37 | 77 | 32 |
| 1926 | 9.35 | 3.77 | 13.12 | 76 | 29 |
| 1927 | 11.15 | 4.42 | 15.57 | 90 | 28 |
| 1928 | 12.57 | 4.60 | 17.17 | 100 | 26 |
| 1929 | 11.15 | 3.91 | 15.06 | 87 | 26 |
| 1930 | 8.35 | 2.95 | 11.30 | 65 | 26 |
| 1931 | 6.10 | 1.58 | 7.68 | 44 | 21 |

From the record it can be seen that the Company was unable to increase total net sales after 1924 above the levels established during the 1920-1924 period. The average for 1925-1930, was in fact, almost identical to that maintained during the preceding five years. The record for 1927 and 1928 was distinctly encouraging but the following year showed a recession, followed by the sharp declines during 1930 and 1931, reflecting the growing impact of the depression. The failure to expand the percentage of the new lines to old after 1923 is clearly demonstrated.

In the absence of increased sales it was possible that the financial position of the Company might be improved by cutting manufacturing costs. This responsibility was assumed by Edwin Pugsley in June 1924, when he became general superintendent of the plant. Some measure of his success is shown by the following data on the percentage of gross margins:

| *Year* | *Old Line* | *New Line* | *Year* | *Old Line* | *New Line* |
|---|---|---|---|---|---|
| 1924 | 28.2 | 9.0[a] | 1928 | 28.3 | 17.3 |
| 1925 | 26.3 | 4.9 | 1929 | 24.3 | 23.8 |
| 1926 | 33.1 | 4.7 | 1930 | 28.9 | 21.9 |
| 1927 | 23.6 | 13.5 | 1931[b] | 25.2 | 18.3 |

[a] Gross loss.
[b] Eleven months.

A further breakdown of the percentage returns on the new lines would show that electrical products (i.e., flashlights, and batteries) were in fact the only consistent producers of gross margins during the period. It was not until 1927 that cutlery, tools, and sporting goods began to return a small positive gross. The officials at New Haven had from time to time suggested that some of the lines which were not carrying their share of expenses be dropped, but Liggett and Kidder, Peabody & Company refused because of a fear that such a move would be interpreted by outsiders as a sign of internal weakness of Winchester.

Thus it may be concluded that by 1927, the management had succeeded in getting production problems under control. This, as shown by the record of sales, was evidently a result of economies of operation rather than through increased volume. Actually, if it had not been for the interest charges and amortization of funds, largely borrowed prior to 1924, the Company would have shown a net return over almost the entire period following 1924. Net profits before interest charges amounted to $3.83 million for these years, but interest charges totaled some $6.97 million, which brought operating losses to the figure of $3.14 million. If the years 1925-1929, which exclude the last year of the former administration and the latter effects of the depression are taken as a test, net profits before interest charges averaged over $1 million annually.

*Reorganization*

By the beginning of 1929, the management had given up on the dealer-agency plan. A survey of the retail hardware business indicated the Company could not expect to increase its sales through this outlet and would do better to sell in the open market. In order to effect this change and also to arrange for the funding of the Company's floating debt which amounted to more than $5.6 million by the end of 1928, it was decided to reorganize the Winchester Repeating Arms Company (Connecticut.)

A new firm, Winchester Repeating Arms Company of Delaware was incorporated on February 5, 1929. It acquired all of the assets of the Winchester Company and the old Winchester Repeating Arms Company, the latter being renamed Winchester Manufacturing Company.

The outstanding short-term loans were paid off out of the proceeds of a $6.5 million issue of five-year 6.5 per cent debentures, a claim against the newly formed Delaware corporation. These securities were purchased by Kidder, Peabody & Company at 95, plus accrued interest, which made the cost of carrying the loan around 7.9 per cent (including a straight-line proportion of the discount charges) compared with the 6 per cent interest rate paid to the banks. This may have been the necessary price to pay for securing a release from the pressure of bank-loan renewals, but the effect was to raise the already high interest charges being paid.

Immediately following the formation of the Delaware corporation, the officials (who were the same as those of the Connecticut concern) notified the dealer-agents that the new Company had decided not to take over the agency contracts. (The legal obligations involved are not clear. The original contracts had been with the Winchester Repeating Arms Company of Connecticut. The new Delaware corporation, in effect, refused to assume responsibility for these contracts. Apparently none of the dealer-agents felt it worthwhile to test the validity of cancellation in the courts.) At the same time the arrangement whereby Simmons had the

*Dealers' Convention, Chicago, 1923*

exclusive right to distribute Winchester-branded hardware and sporting goods was also terminated. Henceforth Winchester was to sell all of its merchandise in the open market.

It had taken just ten years to complete the cycle. As far as marketing channels were concerned the Company was back where it had been in 1919. The management hoped by this move to reestablish its cordial relations with the jobbers and to build up a satisfactory business with that group. The Company was also free to abandon the production of nonremunerative lines of merchandise. Whatever the advantages, the cost of the reorganization was high. The total expenditures immediately associated with the incorporation of the new company amounted to over $674,000. These, in round figures, included $351,000 for advertising, $30,000 for abandoning the dealer-agency plan, $96,000 for professional fees ($24,500 to Kidder, Peabody & Company), $32,000 for survey of the retail hardware business, $20,000 for an engineering firm's report on the plant, and $63,000 paid to Louis K. Liggett and Kidder, Peabody & Company for stock of the Winchester Repeating Arms Company, acquired during the reorganization in 1919. A dividend on the preferred stock of the newly formed corporation of $176,274, apparently for the purpose of supporting the market for debentures, should probably be added to the immediate costs connected with the organization, bringing the total expenditure above $850,700.

Judged by the available evidence, it is difficult to see how much, if any, the reorganization helped the Company's financial position. It is possible, of course, that funding the current debt made it possible to borrow additional short-term capital from the banks, which might have been used to increase output. The immediate effect, however, was to increase the interest charges against operations and to bring about a large expenditure of cash which the organization could ill afford to make.

*Financial Losses and Receiverships*

In some respects the outlook for the Company during 1929 was more favorable than at any time since 1924. The upward trend of sales and lowered manufacturing costs, already noted, were encouraging and a credit to the management. At the same time the organization was a long way from returning a net profit to the stockholders. The capacity to absorb further losses had been reduced by the ventures into refrigerators and washing machines as well as other expenditures connected with the business.

Some measure of the general financial deterioration of the Company is shown by the fact that for the seven years 1924-1931, the net worth had been reduced from around $22.5 million to a little over $8 million, a large part of which reduction occurred before 1930. The losses incurred during the period may be summarized as follows (in millions):

| | | |
|---|---|---|
| (1) Losses connected with changes made after Otterson's resignation in 1924: | | |
| Retail stores | $1.21 | |
| Inventory adjustment | 1.95 | |
| Dealer-agencies | 1.14 | |
| Sales of subsidiaries | .19 | $4.49 |
| (2) Losses on new ventures | | 3.38 |
| (3) Cost of 1929 reorganization | | .85 |
| (4) Settlement of World War I claims | | .92 |
| (5) Operating and miscellaneous losses | | 3.70 |
| (6) Costs of receivership, 1931 | | .23 |
| Total | | $13.58 |

The items, indicated under group (1), were book losses and represented expenditures made prior to 1924, which were written off after that date by charging them against reserves created for the purpose. The rest involved the actual disbursement of cash, and were financed, on balance, out of proceeds from the collection of receivables and the liquidation of inventories.

The Company was in no position to stand any further financial drain of any magnitude and the onset of the depression during the latter part of 1929 had the effect of bringing matters to a critical point by the end of 1930. Late in that year, Kidder, Peabody & Company informed Tobler that they were no longer in a position to advance funds to the organization. Tobler accordingly arranged to have the Company thrown into receivership, which was done on January 22, 1931, on a bill of complaint filed in the U. S. District Court for the District of Connecticut by unsecured creditors. Tobler and the Union New Haven Trust Company were appointed receivers by the court and provisions were made to continue the Company as a going concern by paying salaries and costs of raw materials and allowing orders to be taken from customers. By court order, interest on the first mortgage bonds due April 1, 1931, was deferred.

*Reorganization Committee and Sale to Western Cartridge Company*

Two committees, representing the holders of the Company's 7.5 per cent mortgage bonds and the 6.5 per cent debentures, were formed. These groups in turn appointed a reorganization committee which studied the prerequisites for continuing the business. The committee reported that ". . . a successful reorganization would require the raising of a substantial amount of new capital for (a) the readjustment of production facilities to affect operating economies, (b) a strong selling and advertising effort to regain sales lost in the period of financial stringency and receivership, and (c) additional working capital in sufficient amount to carry the Winchester Company through the present difficult period."

How greater economies of operation and increased sales might be achieved was not specified, but the impossibility of raising new capital was obvious. The committee therefore sought a solution to the difficulty through the sale as a going concern.

It was rumored among financial and business circles during July and August that the Remington Arms Company was going to purchase Winchester. At one point, Saunders Norvell, president of Remington, was reported as saying that negotiations were under way for such a purchase, but that the final date had not been settled.[1] It is doubtful if Remington was in any position to make such a purchase. Meanwhile an offer was received from the Western Cartridge Company which was acceptable to the reorganization committee, and the transfer of the property was made at the end of December 1931.

Under the terms of the agreement, the Western Cartridge Company took over the business with all "its properties, assets, business and good will" for $3 million in cash and $4.8 million par value of 6 per cent cumulative preferred stock of the Western Cartridge Company, plus the assumption of the current trading liabilities of the receiver and the expenses of the receivership up to $300,000. The first-mortgage bondholders received about 78 cents on the dollar for their claims, 50 cents in cash, and the rest in Western Cartridge Company preferred stock. The unsecured creditors, including the debenture holders, received approximately 38 cents on the dollar, all payable in preferred stock.

The stockholders, to the extent they had retained their original shares in the old Winchester Repeating Arms Company or its successor, the Winchester Repeating Arms Company of Delaware, received nothing. Whatever Kidder, Peabody & Company lost by its stock holdings was offset, at least in part, by a steady flow of earnings derived from the short-term financing undertaken during the whole 1920-1929 period and the fees collected from various reorganization and underwriting activities.

The purchase price brought the value of the fixed assets of the Winchester Repeating Arms Company down to about $3.45 million, compared with a net book value of over $24 million reported in 1931; or $18 million on a basis of original cost, less depreciation. The difference, in effect, represents the results of

# Gambill Bros. Proved There Was Room For Another Hardware Store

## Abilene crepe-hangers made another mistake—Modern fixtures installed in new building—Hundreds attend grand opening

"THERE is no room for another hardware store in Abilene. Gambill will never make a go of it," said the crepe-hangers in Abilene, Texas, when R. H. Gambill opened his Winchester Store three years ago. Those who were so pessimistic a few years ago now agree that the business is a great success.

A year ago, Mr. Gambill remodeled his store on the Winchester plan but his business grew so rapidly that he was forced to look for larger quarters. Just before the Convention in Chicago, he leased a building which was being built especially for the store.

While at the Convention, Gambill met Frank Mappes, store engineer of the Winchester Service Department at New Haven, and together they worked out a floor plan which is considered one of the best ever made by Winchester.

Immediately upon his return the work was started. Blueprints were furnished by the Service Department and Frederick Pfaff, Winchester service man in Texas, went to Abilene to assist with the work.

Gambill's store faces east on the corner of the block. The store occupies the Paxton building which was built by George L. Paxton, president of the Citizen's National Bank in Abilene. The building was constructed to meet the requirements of Gambill's.

There are one hundred and thirty-five feet of show windows facing on two streets. There is not a store in Texas with such a large space devoted to window displays.

The building has three entrances; vestibules being on the south and east with an alley entrance in the rear. A freight elevator conveys merchandise from the stock room, which occupies half the space on the second floor,

Looking across to the left side of Gambill Bros. new store in Abilene, Texas. Tools and builders' hardware neatly sampled on the panel doors by the Winchester service man assisted by the store force. Walking toward the rear, a turn to the left brings one to the side street entrance

*Example of Help to Dealers*

borrowing for a program of "development," which proved, in the event, to be a program of "dissipation."

It is of interest to note that a little over a year after T. G. Bennett died, on August 19, 1930, the Winchester Repeating Arms Company came under the ownership of the Western Cartridge Company, the concern that had, some forty years before, dared challenge the apparently impregnable position of Winchester in the ammunition industry.

CHAPTER TWENTY-EIGHT

# SUMMARY AND CONCLUSION

Advanced economic societies, whatever their political characteristics, are marked by extensive division of labor and by specialization. Indeed the ability of such societies to differentiate their economic activities is one basic factor for their comparatively higher standards of well being. At the same time this differentiation carries its own hazards, for without some integrating force it would lead to economic chaos.

In a capitalistic economy such integration is furnished principally by business managers or *entrepreneurs.* They supply the necessary discipline and direction within the individual producing units. Consciously through their effects on markets or unconsciously by their responses to the operations of a marketing mechanism, their decisions combine to bring about a balance between production and consumption. Moreover, they assume the main responsibility for introducing innovations without which the economy would lose its dynamic qualities.

All business executives operate in an environment which more or less limits their freedom of action. Even the most powerful are not immune to restrictions imposed by legal and social institutions; they are seldom in a position to exercise much individual influence on such factors as the phases of the business cycle or the general trends in the demand for various types of commodities and services. Less powerful executives find that they must modify their actions to meet a whole complexity of influences and limitations, including, to indicate only a few, such elements as the demands of stockholders or trade unions, the actions of competitors, changes in the cost of raw materials, and shifts in the methods of distribution.

Because this environment changes over time, it is difficult to generalize about the specific qualities that distinguish the successful from the unsuccessful executive. It is not even certain that any one individual can ever possess the qualities that would enable him to adjust to all conditions. The kind of policies that work brilliantly under one set of circumstances may prove disastrous under different conditions. An expanding market poses a different managerial decision from one that is stabilized or declining. The principal problem facing the executives of the same business concern may shift from production, to finances, to marketing, and back to production, all within a relatively short time. Policy decisions made at one point may seriously restrict the possibilities of action in the future.

In sum, the successful business manager must be skillful in adapting his organization to changing circumstances that affect its operation; his success will be conditioned by the rate at which adjustments must be made, his ability in deciding what policies should be followed, and the degree of freedom he has in putting his policies into action.

Either by force of circumstances or the character of the management personnel, this adaptation may be largely passive and consist in following policies pioneered by others in the same line. While this policy alone may be sufficient to maintain a going concern, it will not ordinarily bring the rewards, in the form of prestige, income, size or position in the market, and the like, which motivate many *entrepreneurs.* Such rewards generally go only to those who assume a more active role; who pioneer changes or are quick to see the application to their own business of innovations developed outside.

While active business leadership offers the greatest rewards it also carries the greatest risk. Success in performing this function seems to depend on a balance between conservatism and a boldness of vision. As one writer has put it, "Bitterest scepticism before making a choice, persistent and unerring faith in the choice when it is made—these are both necessary if decisions are to be the right ones and if the enforcement of them is to be carried to success." [1]

The changing character and position of business management in a single firm is well illustrated by the history of the Winchester Repeating Arms Company. Its chief executives not only differed in their personal qualities, but they functioned under varied circumstances in respect to the internal and external pressures that affected the concern's operations.

Of the half dozen individuals most prominent in the development of the Company, Oliver F. Winchester undoubtedly enjoyed the greatest freedom as far as internal management was concerned. At the same time he was subject to the pressure of changing external events and forces typical of a war and postwar period. A brief review of the policies adopted and followed during his administration shows that he kept a firm control over the internal management of the concern, that he was skillful in adapting it to changing external conditions, and that he maintained a close balance between conservativeness and boldness of vision that distinguishes the active, dynamic business executive.

The Civil War was a severe test of Winchester's managerial ability. Until the Henry rifle was perfected, he had serious doubts about continuing with the manufacture of firearms. Even after the new guns and ammunition were put into production, he was faced with problems of rising costs, scarcities of raw materials and labor, and of getting capital equipment. While the war had stimulated the demand for firearms and ammunition, the market for the Company's products was affected by the decisions of the military authorities over which Winchester could exercise little personal influence. Under these circumstances he followed a conservative policy and refused to expand operations on any substantial scale.

Convinced of the future possibilities of his product and with the war experiences behind him, Winchester decided to devote full time to the manufacture and sale of a repeating rifle. In 1866 when the outlook for gun sales was most unpromising, he chose to form a new corporation, build a new factory, and make the move back from Bridgeport to New Haven. His promotion of the Model 66 rifle was successful in securing the first Turkish contracts which kept the organization busy when domestic sales were slow. Quick to appreciate the potential market for factory-made ammunition and components, Winchester decided about 1872 to expand the Company's ammunition manufacture. This policy decision was exceptionally important in affecting the future fortunes of the concern. It not only paid off handsomely in the case of the second group of Turkish contracts, but it served to diversify operations by making the organization less dependent upon gun sales alone.

Throughout his administration Winchester maintained a firm hand on the internal functioning of the Company. His control rested initially on ownership of a majority share of the common stock. He improved his position by bringing members of his family into the managerial group and by following a conservative dividend policy which increased the organization's financial strength. Once free of financial pressures, Winchester had more freedom to take advantage of opportunities to buy up competing firms, like the Spencer Repeating Arms Company.

"Persistent and unerring faith" in his decision to promote the repeating rifle helped Winchester guide the Company through the postwar doldrums and the depression that affected industry generally for a decade after 1873. In 1865 the organization was relatively unimportant among several dozen arms manufacturers. By 1880 it had become the leading producer of repeating rifles and a major factor in the arms and ammunition industry. Under the guidance of the first president, the Company weathered the storms of its early history. Moreover, Winchester set a general course which was followed for nearly a quarter century after his death in 1881.

While the broad outlines of policy established by Oliver Winchester remained unchanged from 1880 to 1890, it would be inaccurate to describe his successor, William W. Converse, as a passive executive. Owning but a few shares of stock and related to the family only indirectly through marriage, Converse held his position because of the confidence placed in him by the principal owners. This confidence was justified by the Company's progress during his term in office. Like his predecessor, he was alert to capitalize on opportunities that would advance the firm's interests. He probably took no part personally in forming the important association with John M. Browning that resulted in an improvement and extension of the Company's gun line. He did, however, play a leading role in meeting the threat of cut-throat competition in the marketing of ammunition, which resulted in the formation of the Ammunition Manufacturers' Association. He was active in the negotiations leading to the purchase of the Whitney Arms Company and (with the Union Metallic Cartridge Company) the Remington Arms Company. During the ten years ending with 1889, the organization not only grew in absolute terms; even more impressive was the fact that the Company more than doubled its total share of the gun and ammunition business during the period.

Between 1889 and 1914, the arms and ammunition industry, measured in terms of employment and value of product, grew between three and four hundred per cent. The principal accomplishment of T. G. Bennett, the Company's third president, was to maintain the organization's relative position in the industry during this period. This was a noteworthy achievement, but it involved no important change in the major policies already established by 1889. With competitive relations fairly well stabilized and an expanding market, the main problem was to adjust the Company's internal organization to an expanding plant and to adapt gun and ammunition manufacture to the introduction of smokeless powder. His training as an engineer, long experience in the Company's development and manufacturing departments, conservative temperament, plus a complete devotion of time and energy to the Company, all combined to make Bennett efficient in this task. Married to one of the two principal owners of the common stock and brother-in-law of the other, with ample financial resources at his disposal, Bennett was able to dictate the policies of the organization with virtually no pressure from individuals or groups within or outside the organization.

As his successor T. G. Bennett had obviously picked his son, Winchester Bennett. The latter's training as an engineer and his work with the Company closely paralleled his father's career. It is quite likely that had it not been for World War I, Winchester Bennett would have continued to follow the management policies already established. In view of the expected stabilization of the arms and ammunition industry it is doubtful if such policies would have enabled the Company to grow much further in absolute terms. It is even possible that more vigorous competition from relative newcomers might have threatened the organization's relative position.

The outbreak of World War I prevented any such test. It radically altered the short-run demand for arms and ammunition and seemed to offer an opportunity for the Company to make sufficient profits out of war contracts alone to scrap the older buildings and construct a modern plant for postwar operations. As experienced gun and ammunition manufacturers, T. G. Bennett and his son could have had little doubt about the ability of the organization to meet the Russian, French, and British contracts without serious difficulty. With a substantial portion of the value of the contract paid in advance and the balance on delivery, even the financial problem looked comparatively simple.

There was little in the training or experience of either T. G. Bennett or Winchester Bennett to prepare them for management problems actually met during the early years of the war.

For some twenty-five years or more the Company had been remarkably immune to external pressures. Until around the turn of the century both costs and prices had generally declined. After 1900 advances were moderate and the substantial growth of the organization over a quarter century had been slow enough to permit an orderly and somewhat leisurely internal adjustment.

This background helps explain the failure to anticipate the rapidly rising costs of labor and materials during 1915 and 1916 which, along with the production difficulties associated with a mushrooming plant, practically wiped out the profits from the fixed-price Allied war contracts. It does not explain what can only be described as an almost incredible blunder in judgment, which resulted in scattering the new buildings among the old structures in such a way as to make it exceedingly difficult to scrap the latter at the end of hostilities. While the Company was able to retrieve its financial position after 1917, the excess manufacturing capacity remained and influenced the policies adopted in 1919.

Even at the end of the war it would have been possible to follow the original plan of returning to peacetime production of guns and ammunition, although this would have meant disposing or scrapping excess facilities at a large cost. While scarcely obvious at the time, as it turned out, the Company would have undoubtedly done better financially to have confined its activities to guns and ammunition. Such a decision would have been in keeping with the policies followed by the prewar management, and had a member of the family been available to assume executive responsibility it is not unlikely that it would have been made.

With no such person to turn to, T. G. Bennett, as the representative of the family, was almost of necessity forced to seek the advice and help of the outside interests now represented on the board of directors as a result of operations during the war. Thus out of the failure of the family to provide strong leadership to succeed T. G. Bennett, the availability of Otterson, the influence of Liggett, and the attraction of the reorganization plan and financial control of the Company for Kidder, Peabody & Company, came the decision to carry out a program of postwar expansion and diversification.

This decision marked a revolutionary change in the character of the Winchester management. Under all previous managements the success of the Company was the primary, if not sole, objective of anyone who had any voice in its operations. After 1919 this was no longer the case. A mere listing of the parties who helped formulate the reorganization plan indicates the diverse elements that affected the management after that date. This is not to suggest that Otterson, Liggett, and Kidder, Peabody & Company were indifferent to the fortunes of the organization. Otterson in particular had much to gain or lose. But for Liggett and the bankers, the Winchester Repeating Arms Company represented only one of a number of interests. It seems to have offered Liggett an opportunity to experiment with his marketing methods; his main interest remained with the United Drug Company. For Kidder, Peabody & Company, it offered a source of securities which could be sold to customers or held with the prospect of financial return. A failure of Winchester might weaken the financial position and reputation of the banking house, but not necessarily in either respect, if it were offset by an outstanding success with some other concern.

This situation, plus the optimism that affected business generally during the 1920s helps account for the willingness of the parties concerned to embark on a program that involved an extraordinary departure from the Company's previous operations and the investment of borrowed capital in large amounts.

Given this decision, involving as it did the extensive development of new products and the establishment of a marketing organization modeled on the Liggett organization, the basic question is whether any management, however skillful, could have made it work. To the extent that these over-all plans were not subject to considerable modification it seems doubtful. Looking back over the record it appears that the only way serious difficulties could have been avoided was for the management to have developed more slowly and conservatively and to have met conditions as they emerged by changes in the plan.

Winchester's financial success depended in the last analysis upon the profitable operation of the factory. Had developmental work on the new products initially been carried through to the point where it was clear that manufacturing costs could be brought to satisfactory levels, the management would have been in a much better position to decide whether the Company was prepared to supply its proposed dealer-agents and the retail stores with sufficient volume and variety of merchandise at costs which would justify the proposed changes in distribution methods. It could have tested one aspect of the plan at a time so that, if need be, it could continue as a manufacturing establishment concentrating on the production of guns and ammunition and such new products that had stood the test.

By launching the dealer-agency plan and the retail stores simultaneously with the new products program, however, the Company was committed at the outset to attempt the production of a rather wide variety of products, in volume large enough to make the investments in the marketing program worthwhile. This meant that the goods had to be produced even if manufacturing costs were at unsatisfactory levels. Once started, it was difficult to turn back or deviate from the original plans. The management, in effect, gambled on the possibility of setting up an organization which could make each part of the program operate successfully in a relatively short time through the expenditure of large amounts of money.

Some of the more immediate weaknesses in implementing the program are fairly clear. In choosing the types of new products for manufacture, it was decided, not illogically, to fabricate high-quality metal products that would utilize the skills and techniques developed during the Company's war and prewar experience. In selecting standard lines of hardware and sporting goods, however, the management failed to recognize that the Company's previous experience had only limited applications. Because of patent protection and the prestige of Winchester firearms and the control exercised over the marketing of ammunition, manufacturing costs had been of much less significance prior to 1914 than during the postwar period. Nor did the wartime production, especially that arising from the cost-plus contracts with the United States Government, give any adequate basis of comparison for peacetime manufacture. Under the circumstances, the management clearly overestimated its ability to get manufacturing costs down to satisfactory levels and underestimated the importance of long experience in the production of the new lines, sold for the most part under highly competitive conditions. Attempts made to purchase technical skills and experience largely failed to bring the desired results. With the exception of flashlights and batteries, none of the new lines ever showed more than negligible manufacturing profits at any time between 1919 and 1931, and until 1927 cutlery, tools, and sporting goods were all produced at a heavy manufacturing loss. As early as 1923, however, flashlights and batteries began returning a manufacturing profit which over the succeeding years became an important source of income. By getting into battery production when the techniques involved were undergoing important changes, Winchester was able to produce a high-quality product which could be marketed successfully.

This experience suggests that the management would have done better, as far as its manufacturing was concerned, to have selected more of the new items from products where further technical progress and patent protection were possible. Such opportunities were of course limited as long as the Company was committed to supplying the dealer-agents with standard lines of hardware merchandise, which were not generally susceptible to any great amount of technical advance.

It was in the marketing of its products that Winchester made the most radical departure from its prewar experiences. In deciding to sell its new lines directly to the dealers and through its own retail stores, the Company was alone among the gun and ammunition companies. By adopting this way of marketing, in which the influence of Liggett has already been shown, Winchester was, however, following a trend toward direct selling and chain-store operation that had already proved successful in other lines.

The primary purpose of the new marketing program was to assure a wide distribution of the Company's new products. Winchester recognized that by selling directly to the retail trade it would have to absorb the jobbing functions involved in getting the merchandise from the factory to the store and in servicing the dealers. In the case of its own retail stores, the Company undertook the merchandising functions as well. In both instances the management assumed that it could carry on these functions as efficiently as, if not better than, they were currently being performed.

Subsequent experience quickly demonstrated the errors in these assumptions. By early 1922 the jobbing problem had reached such serious proportions that a drastic change was necessary. It was clear by this time that the management had underestimated the costs of performing the jobbing functions. The dealer-agents were so widely scattered that the warehousing centers actually established were inadequate to give satisfactory delivery services. Inexperience on the part of the executives in this field no doubt further contributed to heavy financial losses.

The merger with Simmons, whatever its limitations, had the great advantage of getting Winchester out of the jobbing business. In the absence of Simmons's records it is not possible to determine how successfully, financially, the jobbing house operated as a part of the combined organization. In any event, Simmons's earnings were insufficient to permit the payment of any dividends on Winchester-Simmons stock.

Winchester's retail-stores experiment seems to have been ill-fated from the start. Two points had been stressed in the original arguments advanced for their establishment. One was the advantage to be gained by having a large outlet for the Company's own manufactured products in the cities where presumably the independent hardware dealer was not progressive enough to handle Winchester merchandise. The other was to have the Company's retail stores serve as models for the dealer-agents, thereby improving the latter's merchandising practices, and presumably the sales of Winchester goods.

If the Company, at this point, had acquired an existing chain of hardware and sporting-goods outlets and the experienced personnel that went with it, many of the subsequent difficulties that were encountered might have been avoided. Existing stores would presumably have occupied sites in the urban areas that were more suitable for hardware and sporting-goods establishments than the locations chosen, following the Liggett pattern, turned out to be. As it was the Company had to learn by experience that locations favorable for drug-store items were not suitable for sporting goods and hardware.

The Company-operated stores may have served as models for the dealer-agents, by providing an opportunity for the sales department to try out various merchandising plans and display methods which were passed on to the dealers. At best, however, they were an expensive laboratory for in all other respects the retail stores were a complete failure. The maximum amount of the Company's manufactured goods sold through the stores did not exceed two and a half per cent of Winchester's total sales. As a merchandising venture, largely independent of the other functions by the Company, the record was no brighter. At no time did the stores yield any operating profits.

It seems, in retrospect, that the Company was ill-advised to undertake an operation that was so remote from its previous experience. Initially, of course, the plan was conceived as an integral part of the whole postwar program, but this conception was based on a somewhat naïve acceptance of the Liggett model. Certainly, more consideration should have been given to the differences between selling drugs and sporting goods and hardware. Once launched, however, it was difficult to abandon the retail stores. The initial costs of development had been large and as long as there was a chance of making them pay, as it appeared in 1922, it seemed more desirable to continue than to take the added losses that liquidation would entail. Furthermore, the pride and prestige of the promoters of this innovation had to be reckoned with. It would have disrupted the organization to call attention too abruptly to the mistake in judgment of those responsible for this part of the program. Thus when Edwin Pugsley, soon after he was placed in charge of the retail stores, recommended to Otterson that the project be dropped, Liggett raised strenuous objections and it was decided to continue their operation.

There is no doubt that the depression that began in the latter part of 1920 added considerably to the management's problems in its attempts to carry out the postwar plans. The impact of the depression was severe, coming at a time when the whole program was just getting under way. More specifically, it brought the development of new products practically to a halt, it stopped further expansion of the retail-store chain, it retarded the campaign to add more dealer-agents, it revealed the difficulties with the warehousing and jobbing functions, and it weakened the financial position of the organization.

To some extent the depression served to reveal certain basic weaknesses in the postwar program more quickly than would otherwise have been the case. Had further investigation of new products been carried on, it is possible that the Company might have turned up another line, like batteries, which would have been a money-maker. It is equally possible that new lines might have added to manufacturing losses incurred. By stopping the expansion of the retail stores along with the lines projected in 1919 and early 1920, the depression probably saved the Company from a further financial drain which the establishment of fifty or one hundred such outlets might have caused.

The depression did not prevent a further expansion of the dealer-agency plan, which of the various parts of the postwar program came the closest to achieving the original objective. The total of some 6,300 Winchester dealers reached in 1926 gave the Company a direct tie with outlets handling merchandise valued at over $300 million (based on an assumed average annual sales per dealer of $50,000). By any standard, this number of dealers constituted an impressive chain. What percentage of the dealers' requirements might have been supplied by the items Winchester was manufacturing, is impossible to say. William T. Birney, in 1922, suggested a minimum of five per cent. The prospect of getting this comparatively small percentage share of the potential market was enough to cause the management to cling to the dealer-agents after the other phases of the postwar program were abandoned. Yet as far as the records show, Winchester was unable at any time to sell as much as four per cent of the total dealer requirements. Moreover, the larger part of these purchases were old-line products and of questionable value in adding to the Company's total sales.

The failure to increase sales of the new lines to the dealers was principally due to the inability to get manufacturing costs and prices on these items down to competitive levels. Although the quality was uniformly high, the prestige of the Winchester trade mark alone was not enough to attract sufficient retail buyers. The dealers consequently turned to handling other well-known brands or stocked lower-quality merchandise which sold better. While attempts were made to appeal to the self-interest of the dealers through the requirement of a purchase of stock, by conventions, advertising and merchandising services, and the like, the uncertainty of dividends (which indeed were not forthcoming after 1921), plus the continued high prices on most lines, made the dealers vulnerable to the persuasions of alert jobbers' representatives.

There was a fundamental difference between the Winchester dealer-agents and the United Drug-Rexall organization upon which the plan was modeled. The Rexall druggists owned the bulk of the stock of the United Drug Company which supplied them with a large portion of their needs. Furthermore, these items were not only competitively priced, but in many instances were of the cut-rate variety. The Rexall druggists stood to gain both as merchandisers handling popular items and as principal stockholders in the supplying company. The Winchester dealer-agents by contrast, had a comparatively small equity interest in the Winchester Company. Even if dividends had been paid, it is doubtful whether they would have been large enough to prompt the dealers to buy Winchester's new-line merchandise at premium prices.

It is idle to speculate what would have been the results if Winchester had been able to bring its manufacturing costs closer to competitive levels. It is reasonable to assume, however, that if this had been achieved, the postwar management would have effected a major long-run change in hardware distribution through its direct sales to retailers. Failing in this respect, the dealer-agency plan was dropped in 1929, leaving the Company just where it had been ten years before in its marketing practices.

Two by-products of the dealer-agency experiment should be noted. Several former Winchester dealers have commented to the author that the suggestions received from the Company which helped make their stores more attractive, and enabled them to improve their own merchandising practices more than made up for stock which they were required to purchase. Where a Winchester dealer took the lead in these matters, competitors in the same area were forced to improve their own practices. The result was an improvement in the merchandising practices of hardware dealers generally. A second result of the plan was to acquaint dealers with the advantages of group purchasing. This first came from concessions on prices which were offered to groups of dealers who ordered in large amounts from the Company. Their association with one another in the Winchester Clubs made it easier to continue and expand this practice after 1929.

To the extent that he helped formulate the reorganization plan of 1919, Otterson was a victim of his own failure to subject the proposal to the "bitterest scepticism before making a choice." Unfortunately, considering the weaknesses which later developed, the plan was followed with too much "persistent and unerring faith in the choice" once it had been made. Within the limits imposed by the program adopted in 1919, Otterson initially had a relatively free hand in the management of the Company although he was never completely free from the influence of Liggett and his tenure in office was dependent upon the decision of Kidder, Peabody & Company. As the organization became more deeply committed financially in new products, retail stores, jobbing, and the dealer-agency plan, the debt burden grew and fixed charges mounted. This situation was aggravated by the 1921 depression so that by the end of 1922, Otterson's financial independence was severely limited. When the financial situation failed to improve during 1923, the banking house, through Liggett, initiated the investigation that resulted in his retirement from office.

The management that succeeded Otterson at the Winchester plant undoubtedly had the least freedom of action of any of the Company's chief executives. Acting in this capacity, William Tobler not only operated within quite narrow financial limitations, but he was subject to the influence, if not the whims, of Liggett, to the decisions of the bankers, and to the demands of the Simmons side of the combined Winchester-Simmons organization. Little could be done about the legacy of a large debt, but within the plant Tobler and his associates did a remarkable job in cutting costs and showing operating profits. But they had no choice but to accept the addition of the washing machine and the refrigerator to the Company's manufacturing operations. Nor were they responsible for the failure by Liggett and the bankers to investigate more fully the technical development and limitations of these products as well as the amount of capital necessary to establish marketing outlets; a failure that resulted in a further drain on the Company's financial resources.

There was little chance of testing the merits of the decision reached in 1929 to separate completely from Simmons and the dealer-agents and to sell largely through jobbers. Continued total sales at the level established in 1928 plus the dropping of expensive cost items might conceivably have enabled the organization to pay off its large indebtedness, although this is doubtful. In any event the depression prevented any such test from being made and it remained for the new owners to demonstrate how well the Company could be operated in the absence of a large fixed debt and by concentrating on the production of firearms, ammunitions, and the new products which gave promise of continued profits—flashlights, batteries, and roller skates.

# EPILOGUE

## BY EDWIN PUGSLEY[1]

This epilogue is an account of some of the more important highlights in the history of Winchester since its acquisition at receiver's sale by the Olin interests of East Alton, Illinois.

The first Olin company was The Equitable Powder Manufacturing Company established at East Alton in 1892 by the late Franklin W. Olin. Originally a producer of black powder for the Illinois and adjacent coal fields, Equitable also made sporting powder for the loading of shotgun shells. Western Cartridge Company was founded in 1898 as an ammunition company which rapidly assumed size and importance as one of the leaders in its field. Through progressive management it had expanded to substantial stature by 1931, when it received word that the great Winchester Repeating Arms Company would be sold by a referee in bankruptcy to the highest bidder.

The Western management—F. W. Olin and his two sons, John M. and Spencer T. Olin—had been aware of the great advantage that Winchester possessed in manufacturing both sporting firearms and ammunition. Many times they had contemplated the purchase of various firearms companies and had even considered the possibility of developing a line of firearms of their own.

The Western management was also mindful of the rapidly changing competitive situation in the smokeless powder field and realized that this might well force the DuPont interests to seek a more certain outlet for their smokeless powder. There were strong rumors in the trade that DuPont might be interested in acquiring the Winchester properties, which tended to confirm the Western analysis of the situation. However, the nation's worst depression, which began in 1929 and which sealed the doom of Winchester, made new financing increasingly difficult and going concerns correspondingly more cautious as to how they expanded.

As the depression rapidly deepened, Western temporarily gave up the idea of purchasing the company and therefore released their New York banking connections from their agreement to supply the necessary funds for the possible purchase of Winchester. Meantime the competing companies made all the capital they could out of the situation to Winchester's detriment and raided the Winchester line of accounts.

As Winchester's position in receivership became progressively worse, the Olin interests began to view the possibilities of the purchase of Winchester more favorably and finally accepted the invitation of the receiver to have an audit made of Winchester assets.

On the basis of its auditors' report, Western offered to buy Winchester at receiver's sale for $8,122,837.67. The transaction is described in the February 20, 1932, report of Haskins & Sells, auditors:

> As of December 22, 1931, Western Cartridge Company acquired from the receivers for Winchester Repeating Arms Company (Delaware) all of the latter company's assets subject to assumption of its current liabilities. As of the same date a Maryland corporation was formed under the name of Winchester Repeating Arms Company with an authorized capital of 1,000 shares of $100.00 each. Western Cartridge Company thereupon acquired all the authorized capital of the newly formed company in consideration of transferring to the new company all the net assets acquired from the receivers for Winchester Repeating Arms Company (Delaware).
>
> The investment in the new company represents the following:

| | | |
|---|---|---|
| Paid to the receivers for distribution among the parties at interest in Winchester Repeating Arms Company (Delaware): | | |
| Cash | $3,000,000.00 | |
| Preferred stock of Western Cartridge Company—48,000 shares of $100.00 each | $4,800,000.00 | $7,800,000.00 |
| Paid to receivers for expenses of receivership and reorganization | | 300,000.00 |
| Total paid to receivers | | $8,100,000.00 |
| Expenses incurred by Western Cartridge Company in course of negotiations | | 22,837.67 |
| Total | | $8,122,837.67 |

The same report shows that at the end of the year 1931, Western owed on notes payable to banks and others an amount slightly more than $4 million, practically all of which was borrowed in November and December to raise the $3,300,000 in cash paid to the receivers of Winchester Repeating Arms Company, and to provide funds to restore the going value of the Winchester concern.

The borrowing of more than $4 million in the fall of 1931 was a formidable task. The Western plant at East Alton was ample security for the issuance of $4,800,000 of preferred stock of Western Cartridge Company, but the raising of more than $4 million in cash was another matter. Banks were collapsing all over the nation, and investment bankers were particularly hard hit by the progress of the depression.

The loan was finally arranged by the First National Bank of St. Louis which in turn farmed out portions within the limited lending power of other St. Louis institutions as laid down by the Federal Reserve Bank. Not only was Western Cartridge Company involved in the transaction but the Olin Corporation, which had been organized for the express purpose of providing cash in emergencies, pledged its resources, as did F. W. Olin and his two sons, John M. and Spencer T. Olin.

Only those who passed through the financial depression can realize the courage of these three men in staking practically their entire fortune upon their judgment.

Fortunately, as soon as Western was in actual control of Winchester, refinancing of these obligations in New York was a comparatively simple matter. Members of the Olin family were released from their personal obligations in connection with the purchase, and other encumbrances were assumed by Western Cartridge Company, much to the benefit of Olin Corporation.[2]

The dead hand of receivership had gradually but inexorably strangled the Winchester organization. Every employee whose services could be dispensed with, even to the detriment of the organization, had been reluctantly laid off and those who remained were given successive reductions in pay. This pay reduction was universal, starting from the top management and going down to the lowliest office boy. No new work could be started and only those projects which would show immediate return could be considered. The great momentum of the company was slowing down very rapidly.

One of the assets of the company, however, was the designing staff headed by T. C. Johnson. As has already been related, Johnson had been with the company over fifty years and in the beginning had, along with William Mason, successfully translated the crude models submitted by the Browning brothers into producible and successful weapons. At the termination of the Browning contracts he headed the Winchester inventive staff, and had produced many outstanding weapons, such as the Model 12 shotgun, the most copied arm in the country; the .22 caliber model 52 rifle that holds all of the world's records for accuracy; the Model 21 shotgun, which is now recognized as the finest of all double-barrel guns; and the Model 54, which later became the Model 70, which enjoys the top place in the country's bolt-action heavy rifles.

To dissipate such a staff as Johnson had surrounding him would have meant losing one of the greatest assets of the company. The receivers very wisely chose to retain that staff; however, on reduced pay. During the years immediately preceding the receivership the design staff had been busily at work on several new models. Because of the large make-ready cost and the ever-present risk that the product might not be profitable, the receivership definitely put an end to any thought there might have been of putting them on the market.

The purchase of the company by the Olin interests brought a breath of life to the institution and brought to Winchester many things. First of all was the end of management by people who were not familiar or sympathetic with the gun and ammunition business. It brought to the company the very able and astute business management of the Olin group. It brought financial stability and also commercial confidence. Western Cartridge Company over the years had built up a group of loyal jobbing connections and had developed a reputation for honest transactions so that the trade was willing to accept at face value the statements of the Olin management. This was the great asset in clearing up the muddled relationship which had existed between Winchester and the trade in the latter years of the former regime.

Immediately on its purchase, the Olins sent representatives to the company with instructions to start operations; raw materials were purchased, production orders placed and the machinery began to hum once more. All was not easy, however, because the country was still in the depths of its worst depression and it took great courage on the part of the Olin family to continue to pour money into inventories under such circumstances. Nevertheless, they were willing to proceed and the plant began to produce.

The acquisition of Winchester made Western Cartridge Company the largest owner of patents covering firearms and ammunition developments in the industry and permitted the pooling of manufacturing and technical knowledge to the benefit of both organizations.

When John M. Olin, now President of Olin Industries, and at that time First Vice President of Western Cartridge Company, came to New Haven to find out just what he and his associates had purchased, he found the stored-up accumulation of new gun models and ideas which had been developed by Johnson and his engineers. Having been an admirer of Winchester firearms from boyhood, John Olin was not only able to make an accurate appraisal of each model, old and new, but was also in a position to introduce a number of revolutionary ideas he had in mind.

Johnson, despite his advanced age, gave unstintingly of his time, during evenings and weekends, pointing out what had been planned for each firearm; also, his own ideas regarding the potentialities of each type of firearm manufactured by Winchester. With the passing of Thomas C. Johnson on June 4, 1934, the job of modernizing the Winchester line of firearms was put under my supervision.

Many now-famous sporting firearms were soon introduced. One of the most important of these was a .410 pump-action repeating shotgun which was practically ready to go into production at the end of 1932. John Olin, having been the pioneer of the Super-X, the heavy game load which had so successfully captured the American shot shell market, had also been considering a very much longer and more efficient .410 shell. Although the standard shell at the time was two inches long, Winchester had designed the new gun to handle a 2½-inch shell. Mr. Olin insisted that the gun be made to handle three-inch shells which necessitated a complete redesign. This decision delayed the development of the arm, but subsequent success of the model amply justified his judgment.

The Model 21 double-barrel shotgun, first introduced on January 2, 1931, had not sold very well. This was because of the time it appeared and the meager advertising which the nearly defunct Winchester organization was able to devote to the gun's promotion. Seeing that this arm had possibilities of being developed into America's finest shotgun, Mr. Olin gave orders to increase its production and also the variations in which it was offered. The Model 21 not only achieved all of the early expectations for its eminence but became generally acknowledged as the foremost example of American fine gun-making, with a fool-proof single trigger, mechanical dovetailing of the barrels and other improvements long demanded by American sportsmen for a double-barrel shotgun.

Another gun which T. C. Johnson and his engineers had ready for consideration was a new hammerless .22 caliber slide-action repeater. This gun was approved by the new management and the Model 61 was delivered to the warehouse in 1932. Twenty-two caliber rifle competition was extremely strong and Winchester modified several of its existing .22 caliber models, issuing them promptly after the termination of the receivership. The stock, forearm design and mechanism of the familiar Model 90 slide-action .22 hammer repeater were changed and the rifle was brought out as the Model 62 in June of 1932. In August of the same year the Model 60A Target rifle was added to the list, using the basic Browning bolt-action, single-shot mechanism which Winchester had used so successfully.

The Model 1903 .22 Automatic was the first successful automatic on the market but at the time it was developed required a special cartridge loaded with

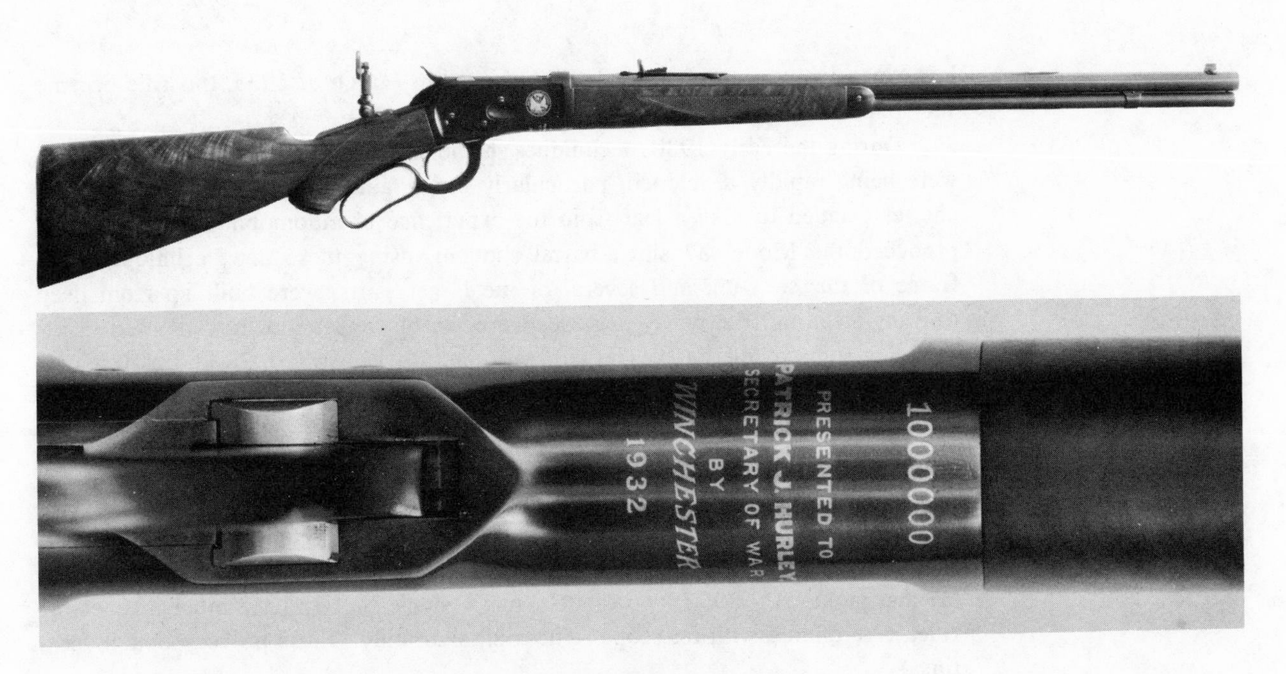


*One-millionth Winchester Model 1892 Presented to Secretary of War Patrick J. Hurley*

smokeless powder to prevent fouling the mechanism. By 1933, however, the development in .22 ammunition was such that it was no longer necessary to have the gun chambered only for the special cartridge, and models had been worked up to handle the popular standard .22 Long Rifle. The Model 63 was put on the slightly altered Model 1903 mechanism to handle this popular cartridge. This gun was immediately popular and became the highest grade .22 automatic on the market.

Unquestionably the most successful center-fire lever-action model ever produced by Winchester was the Model 1894, the first Winchester to pass the million mark in manufacture and which is still a "best seller" in the lightweight carbine style. The Model 1894 rifle was revised in 1925 as the Winchester Model 55, and again in 1933 as the Model 64, the de luxe model of which became widely known as the "deer rifle," with its sling swivels, beaver-tail fore-end, and appropriate checkering on both pistol grip and fore-end.

The Model 54, predecessor of the Model 70, was first announced by Winchester in 1925. This bolt-action model was specifically intended to handle the .30-06 Springfield cartridge, and a new cartridge, the .270 Winchester, which has since become one of the most popular big-game cartridges in the United States. Additional calibers were added and in the January 1, 1937, price list the Winchester Model 70 superseded the original Winchester Model 54. The new developments in the gun included a hinged floor plate, new speed lock with short pull, new safety that does not interfere with telescope sight, bolt stop independent of the sear and trigger, and other devices calculated to make the Model 70 the best bolt-action rifle on the market.

Changes in the .22 caliber single-shot line were continued, in line with general competition and development of this type of rifle, and a new version, the Model 68, was brought out in May, 1934. The Model 56, having proved too high-priced for general acceptance, the Model 69 was brought out as a simplified and less expensive version of this rifle. First issued in March of 1935, this rifle became very popular.

During the early 1930s techniques in the welding and brazing of sheet metal were being rapidly developed, particularly in the automobile field. In 1936 Winchester decided to take a leaf from the experience of automobile companies, and produced the Model 37 single-barrel shotgun, using these new techniques. The frame of this shotgun, and several of the larger parts, were built up from deep drawing steel and the newly developed process of copper brazing was used in assembling some of the parts. The gun was made in 12, 16, 20, 28 and .410 gauge. It was an all-steel answer to the low-priced, cast-iron shotguns. It was given the same general stock dimensions as the popular Model 1912 and the mechanism was semi-hammerless.

In the middle 1930s the low-priced telescope had struck the fancy of .22 caliber rifle buyers, and a number of such scopes with very good optics were on the market. Winchester was among the leaders in this development and went so far that in January 1938, two models, one a single-shot and the other a repeating rifle, were offered with telescope sight equipment only. These proved popular for a time.

In 1938 Winchester brought out the Model 72, a lower-priced, bolt-action repeating .22 rifle. This rifle did not have the refinements of the Model 52 but was still an excellent shooting arm. A year later it was refined into the highly accurate Model 75 target and sporter model.

In 1939 Winchester pioneered the first of a line of .22 automatic rifles in the Model 74 made in both Short and Long Rifle. This lead was quickly followed by all competitors.

Also in 1939 a double-barrel gun known as the Model 24, built along the lines of the Model 37, but using new techniques, was put on the market in 12, 16 and 20 gauge.

With the increase in popularity of the then rising trapshooting game of Skeet, there was an insistent demand for an automatic shotgun. After a general study of the situation, Winchester decided to revamp the Model 1911 into a streamlined version and produced the Model 40 automatic repeating shotgun as a stopgap. This was made in the skeet model only and its production was curtailed by the war.

About 1934 there had been considerable publicity on a German development known as the Halger rifle, reported to be an ultra-high-speed rifle. The rifle had been developed by a German named Harold Gerlich who was brought to the United States for the purpose of testing his gun by the United States Army's Ordnance Department. A more or less confidential test was held at Aberdeen and the unofficial reports were that in loading this gun to a velocity of 2500 feet per second the bullet would simply splash against a steel plate; while in loading the same rifle to a velocity of 5,000 feet per second, the bullet would punch a hole through the armor plate and the punching would be found back of it. Thus the mere change of velocity had changed the behavior of matter.

A characteristic of the gun was a taper-bored barrel using a bullet with folding skirts, which started out as a .50 caliber and, due to the tapered barrel, came out of the muzzle as a .30 caliber, the skirts being folded up like an umbrella during its travel down the barrel. The large base, on which the powder gases acted, theoretically imparted sufficient energy to produce the additional velocity. As reports on this gun gradually leaked out it was determined to ask Gerlich to come to the Winchester plant.

He and his wife were met on the train leaving Aberdeen and persuaded to come to New Haven for two or three days' conference. Gerlich brought his rifle and two or three of his cartridges which were submitted to ballistic tests. The expected phenomenal velocities did not materialize and Winchester engineers concluded that whatever additional velocity obtained was due to excessively high pressure, approximating 80,000 or 90,000 pounds per square inch. These pressures were too unpleasant to shoot commercially and Winchester was considerably disappointed.

Gerlich claimed, however, he could design a cartridge which could be handled by the Model 86, Winchester's strongest lever-action model, and which would impart increased ballistics to that arm without undue pressure increase. He promised to develop such a cartridge after his return to Germany. Winchester therefore started to make changes in Model 86 in anticipation of such a cartridge, and also to develop a heavier cartridge along more or less standard lines. Gerlich died shortly after returning home, without having developed his ideas. Winchester, nevertheless, brought out the new gun with its own cartridge and, as a result, in November of 1935 the Model 71 in caliber .348 appeared and was an immediate success. The .348 was the heaviest cartridge yet handled in a lever-action rifle.

Gerlich's visit, however, started a line of research in the company's ballistic laboratory that had far-reaching results. Experiments with large-powder-volume-small-caliber-bullet combinations resulted in the production of three new and revolutionary cartridges: the .220 Swift, the .219 Zipper, and the .218 Bee. The .220 Swift was a 43-grain bullet with an initial velocity of 4,160 feet per second, the fastest commercial cartridge ever produced. The Zipper and Bee were smaller versions of the Swift and adapted to the new Models 55 and 64. These cartridges added materially to the rapidly accumulating fund of knowledge of the now generally realized lethal effect of mere high velocity.

As it afterward turned out both Western and one of its principal competitors were working on the improvement of soft-nosed bullets. The competitors announcement came at a time when John and Spencer Olin were attending a sales conference at Winchester early in 1940. They immediately put pressure on Western engineers to complete their experiments with the result that the now famous Silvertip bullet was born. Production was rushed so that the new bullet was available in the principal big-game cartridges for the 1940 fall hunting season. The bullet was immediately popular and its principle of delayed expansion became firmly established with hunters within a single year, an accomplishment unique in American ammunition manufacture. The combination of the 130-grain Silvertip bullet in the .270 cartridge and the Winchester Model 70 gave sportsmen one of the most efficient and hence most popular game rifles thus far produced.

Another Western ammunition development, through which Winchester profited both in firearms and ammunition, consisted of tests at East Alton which resulted in Super-Match .22 cartridges originally designated as Mark I, and later, modified as the Super-Match Mark II and Mark III cartridge.

Convinced that "sonic velocity" was just another term as far as .22 caliber ammunition was concerned, Western loaded its .22 match cartridges with smokeless powder to a velocity approximately 80 foot seconds in excess of the old-time

Lesmok cartridges which had been termed "standard velocity" by all manufacturers. Cartridges which did not meet Western's exacting specifications for .22 Super-Match ammunition were called Xpert and classified as "intermediate velocity."

Super-Match .22s at once proved so popular as to revolutionize the habits of competitive target shooters throughout the country, especially in combination with the Winchester Model 52 heavy-barrel target rifle, with which many of the original tests were made. The first cartridge, designated as Mark I, completely ignored "sonic velocity" in that it was loaded to the middle of a "flat" established by the trial firing of thousands of rounds in a mechanical rest named "Oscar." This rest, designed by Western shooters to simulate the stresses of prone shooting on the stock and fore-end of a modern .22, quickly established the middle of the "flat" at about 1160 feet per second. However, it developed that even the slight difference of 2½ granules of powder—not grains—upon occasion would send a "flier" out of the top of the "flat," and therefore, Super-Match Mark II with slightly reduced velocity was introduced.

Winchester followed Western's lead in abandoning the old Lesmok target cartridge, originally designated as EZX in the Winchester brand. Smokeless EZXs of "intermediate velocity" soon took their place alongside Western's Super-Match, and soon all manufacturers had discontinued so-called "standard velocity" cartridges entirely. As part of the simplification program of the industry, the term "intermediate velocity" was changed to "standard velocity," and thus a combination Western-Winchester development resulted in a complete change in loading practices within the industry.

Another outstanding example of Western-Winchester teamwork was in the development of the original metal-piercing cartridges made available in both brands in .38 Special, .45 Automatic and .357 Smith & Wesson Magnum calibers.

Winchester followed the Western pattern in the development of modern shotgun loads since new facilities for the production of modern shot shells constantly were being developed at East Alton under the personal eye of John and Spencer Olin. The original Super-X development, of which John Olin was the acknowledged father, immediately was extended to the Winchester line. When Super-X became a brand name instead of a load designation, Winchester retained all Western high-speed loadings in a shell called the Super Speed.

Winchester is credited with the development of the 12-gauge Magnum shot shell carrying 1⅝ ounces of shot, originally intended for use in the Model 12 repeating shotgun, converted into a heavy duck gun for use in conjunction with this load.

While these changes and additions to the gun and ammunition lines were in progress, the Olin management was faced with many other problems. Winchester had developed during the "Agency" days many lines completely unrelated to either gun or ammunition manufacture. During the latter years of the former management many of these had been dropped as being unprofitable but the end of the receivership saw the company still manufacturing radiator tubes, radiators, flashlights, dry-cell batteries, roller skates, tools and cutlery.

After reviewing the various items, the new management decided to continue only the extruded tube and heat exchanger department, flashlights and batteries, and roller skates. At the same time it was decided to add brass specialties which had been successfully developed at Western. These decisions, easy to record here, were only arrived at after careful investigation, and called for the liquidation of both inventory and special equipment created for their manufacture. Subsequently the electrical activities of the company were expanded by the acquisition of the Bond Electric Corporation.

The extrusion process became the most active of these products prior to World War II. In 1938 a contract was entered into with a British concern to set up machinery in England for the manufacture of tubes by this process under a license agreement. During the war this company produced tubes for 75% of the British liquid-cooled aircraft engines. As liquid-cooled engines disappeared from the air, the tubes were used for oil coolers and other necessary auxiliary equipment.

For some years following the termination of World War I, and during the early 1930s the U. S. Army's Ordnance Department had been relatively inactive largely because of the refusal of Congress to appropriate funds. With the clouds of war beginning to gather in the late 1930s the Department became more and more activated and more interested in discussing the problem of producing military weapons with commercial firms. Winchester kept in close touch with the changing situation and was prepared to cooperate whenever called upon.

The military development from the Winchester standpoint took on two major aspects, one being the heated discussions attendant to the adoption of the semiautomatic .30 M1 (popularly known as the Garand rifle) and the development of educational and production orders for this arm; and, concurrently, the development of a new cartridge and the new arm destined to become the .30 Army carbine. Winchester was able to play a very important part in both of these developments.

The semiautomatic Garand rifle, invented by John C. Garand of the Springfield Armory, had been selected in January 1936 as the rifle to replace the 1903 bolt-action Springfield as the official infantry weapon of the United States. A considerable delay in putting the Garand rifle into production was occasioned in part by an extended discussion both within and without government circles over the relative merits of the gun. It was finally determined to push ahead on the Garand and the manufacture of the rifle was begun at the Springfield Armory in early 1937. The Ordnance Department, however, felt that it was desirable to provide for additional production facilities. About this time the Educational Order bill, which gave the Ordnance Department the privilege of placing educational orders on badly needed and technically complicated war material with firms which, in their judgment were best fitted to handle such work, was passed by Congress. Taking advantage of this act the Ordnance Department issued requests for bids on the first Educational Order for 500 Garand rifles to various commercial gunmakers, including Winchester. Winchester's bid was lowest and the Company was awarded the contract.

This first educational order was a mixed blessing as it called for only one tool, one gauge and one fixture for each operation and included only one machine of each type required. It was necessary, for example, to set up all of the milling cuts on a single milling machine and the small number of pieces called for (500 in this case) had to be run on this one machine, the set-up being changed for each operation. This procedure placed a tremendous burden on the organization but the work was nevertheless undertaken and eventually completed.

When the educational contract was approximately half finished, the government decided to issue requests for bids on the manufacture of the gun in quantity in plants other than the Springfield Armory. Winchester again entered a bid, and using the knowledge so far acquired on the Educational Order, was able to offer a price approximately $100 a gun cheaper than the nearest competitor and to save approximately a year in the initial delivery. As a result of these advantages, the Ordnance Department felt that the Educational Order had been amply justified, and accordingly signed a contract with Winchester for 65,000 Garand rifles.

The first Garand rifles were delivered by the Company in 1940, well in advance of Pearl Harbor. Thus, Winchester started on a production run of this gun which was to continue throughout the war and was the only manufacturer producing the rifle outside of the government arsenal at Springfield. In all, 513,582 Garands were produced by the Company in addition to those made in the government's own facilities for manufacture of this weapon.

Winchester's second major contribution to improved American military weapons came out of a need for a lighter arm and a lighter cartridge that could be used by many of the special military personnel who were already so overloaded with special equipment that it was physically impossible for them to carry a full-weight rifle. Such a light-weight rifle would be a more effective weapon than a pistol which in many cases it could supercede. Winchester representatives sat in on early discussion of this problem with the Ordnance Department and assured the Ordnance officials that a 5-pound semiautomatic arm was entirely feasible. About 1940 the Government crystallized its ideas and told Winchester engineers that it wanted a cartridge developed that would be between a .276 which it felt was too heavy, and a 7.65 Mauser, which it believed was too light. Winchester, on a basis of long experience in building the Model 94 .30-30 carbine and the Winchester Model 92 carbine, recommended that it design for the Government a cartridge somewhat like the ammunition developed for these rifles, around which an arm could be developed.

As a result of these negotiations, in November 1940, Winchester submitted samples of a proposed cartridge made to the specifications outlined by the Ordnance Department. Subsequently, small experimental lots of the cartridge were manufactured for the Government. It was this cartridge which was finally accepted as standard for the U. S. Carbine M1, which Winchester also designed.

About the same time the new cartridge was being tested the Ordnance Department sent out invitations to gun designers the country over, asking them to submit models of the proposed carbine and giving indications of the type of gun that was wanted. At the time the Company was entirely engaged in the production of the Garand and other experimental work, and was unable to enter the competition, with the result that the first trials, which were held in May and June, 1941, included no Winchester entrant. The rifles in this trial were in general unsatisfactory and none was accepted.

For several years, however, Winchester had been experimenting with a new device for the operation of semiautomatic rifles, developed by David Marshall Williams, employed as a gun designer by the Winchester organization. This device became known as the short-stroke piston. Tests of this device in a rifle at the Marine Corps base in San Diego in the fall of 1940 convinced the Winchester engineers that the short-stroke piston was sound not only in theory but in practice. Over the following several months the Company was able to develop a 7.5-pound rifle which used the short-stroke piston and which fired the standard .30-06 cartridge.

Upon being informed that the Company felt certain it could produce a 5-pound carbine based on its new 7½ pound rifle, the Ordnance officials asked Winchester to submit a sample gun. In just 13 days after the order was received, a 5-pound carbine was produced and was ready for a firing test at Aberdeen on August 11, 1941. Following this demonstration, the Ordnance Department ordered Winchester to put a gun into the general competition which was set for Monday, September 15, which allowed only 34 days to perfect a design and to complete the second model.

During 1918, working from a sample gun, Winchester engineers had produced a test model of the Browning machine gun in 39 days. But it was questionable whether the staff could better that performance 23 years later on an entirely new model firing a new cartridge. By working around the clock, including Sundays, the parts of the new gun were assembled on the afternoon of Friday the 13th of September. On Saturday morning a call from the Ordnance Department informed Winchester that the gun must be in Aberdeen by the noon of the following day in order to undergo a firing test of 1,000 rounds before being submitted to the Test Board on Monday. It was not until nearly midnight on Saturday that the gun was operating satisfactorily. Six hours later it was on its way to Aberdeen.

On arrival at Aberdeen about 1:30 p.m. Sunday the gun was rushed through the preliminary trials required of all guns to be entered in the test. These consisted of photographs and description of all components, demonstration of disassembling and reassembling, and firing of 1000 rounds including the dust test. All of these were successfully completed by 6:00 p.m. Sunday night, although the Ordnance personnel were prepared to work all night if necessary. The gun was entered in competition on the following morning and by Wednesday of that week the competition was rapidly narrowing down to the Government model and the Winchester model. As the test progressed, the Winchester gun pulled away from the field and at the end of the test, by unanimous choice, became the now worldwide known U. S. Carbine, Caliber .30, M1 of the U. S. forces and, under Lend-Lease, that of our many allies.

After being officially notified on October 1, 1941, that the gun had won the test, Winchester was asked to make five experimental carbines by hand. The first one of these was delivered on November 8, 1941, and the remaining four on December 14. At the same time conferences started between Winchester engineers and those at Springfield Armory, looking toward getting Government drawings and other necessary information required for manufacture. The first set of Winchester blueprints was sent to Springfield Armory on October 13, 1941, and these formed the basis of official Ordnance drawings which were being prepared currently at Springfield. As additional contractors came into the picture, the conferences included representatives of the new companies, with the result that gradually the Carbine Production Committee was set up. From this grew the Carbine Industry Integration Committee with an executive committee, engineering and other subcommittees. The first meeting of this new committee was held in New York City on July 14, 1942. This committee continued to function until its services were no longer needed and it was placed in an inactive status by General James Kirk on May 1, 1944.

From this it will be seen that all of the mass production referred to was primarily engineered by Winchester which furnished all the original data and was looked to continually as a guiding hand on the basic design.

Winchester itself could take but a comparatively small part in the manufacture of these guns. The Government was naturally anxious to build up as many sources of supply as it could and needed all available tooling equipment to establish these factories. It was therefore decided by the Ordnance Department that no additional equipment or machine tools could be bought for the Winchester Repeating Arms Company and that it would have to manufacture as its quota only such as it could on the equipment which had been available for its commercial manufacture. On August 27, 1942, Winchester turned out its first ten carbines. Winchester was given an initial order for 350,000 carbines on November 24, 1941. The Company's total production of the U. S. Carbine, Caliber .30, M1, was 818,059.

In spite of the handicaps imposed by the machinery not especially procured for this carbine manufacture, Winchester was told that it produced the carbine at the lowest cost to the Government. The Company resorted to every device that management could think of in the way of split shifts, conservation of help and the use of women on jobs never before thought possible for women to accomplish in this country. Winchester was able to go through the emergency with no stoppages due to lack of material or labor, and industrial relations were excellent throughout the period.

While the carbine was developed with a speed heretofore unknown in the arms industry, there were fewer changes made on it than is generally experienced in new-gun development. There were no structural changes necessary, the only changes required being dimensional in nature to aid quantity production in plants that had never before made guns.

In the early part of the war Winchester was approached to develop a new, heavier type of ammunition. Winchester, having developed the first .50 caliber cartridge in World War I, together with the first successful machine gun to fire it, had followed this development over the years and felt that the .50 caliber was too small for the larger airplanes already in use. The management for some time had urged the Government to consider a larger, higher-velocity round and accompanying guns. The Ordnance Department was working along these lines with the result that on August 6, 1942, the Company was asked to develop a new .60 caliber round and was given an outline of the government requirements. Winchester developed the new round, produced a thousand cartridges and turned the experimental rounds and the test barrel which it had made to do the test firing over to Aberdeen. The .60 caliber, as it is known, was the result of this development.

Soon after the United States entered the war the Washington representatives of the Company, sensing the gravity of the situation, recommended that the Company volunteer to stop all commercial production and devote its entire facilities to government work. Such an offer was made and on January 13, 1942, the Company ceased all commercial manufacture. This lead was shortly followed by all of its principal competitors.

While the firearms division of the Winchester plant at New Haven was busy making Garand rifles and Winchester carbines, the ammunition division was more

WORLD WAR II EFFORT STATISTICS—OLIN INDUSTRIES

| *Item* | *Quantity* |
|---|---|
| CARTRIDGES | |
| Rim Fire | 1,456,217,620 |
| Center Fire Rifle .30-06 Class | 8,362,290,537 |
| Center Fire Pistol | 1,718,320,461 |
| .50 Caliber | 3,052,913,818 |
| .20 Millimeter | 54,851,309 |
| Shot Shells | 346,873,585 |
| Miscellaneous | 268,657,924 |
| *Total Rounds Ammunition* | 15,260,125,254 |
| WINCHESTER CARBINES | 818,059 |
| GARAND RIFLES | 513,582 |
| MISCELLANEOUS RIFLES & SHOTGUNS | 116,587 |
| *Total Firearms* | 1,448,228 |
| OTHER ITEMS FURNISHED | |
| Radiator Tubes | 1,000,000,000 |
| Radiators | 50,000 |
| Batteries | 2,212,777 |
| Ignition Cartridges, Primers, Detonators, Clips and Traps and Trap Targets * | |
| Targets | 162,229,210 |
| Bulk Powder & Other Explosives | 10,220,667 Lbs. |
| Brass | 1,587,254,979 Lbs. |
| Aluminum | 105,610,534 Lbs. |
| Alumina | 2,711,252 Lbs. |

* Used in Army Air Forces training program.

EMPLOYMENT

| | *Peak* | *Total Hired* |
|---|---|---|
| New Haven | 13,667 | 45,413 |
| East Alton | 12,805 | 28,283 |
| St. Louis | 34,338 | 86,294 |
| Alumina & Aluminum | 600 | 1,700 |
| Powder & High Explosives | 275 | 750 |
| TOTAL | 61,685 | 162,440 |

than swamped with demands for military ammunition for the United States and the Allies.

The first order for ammunition in the beginning of World War II hostilities was taken from the Finnish Government for their rifle cartridge. The Finnish Legation in the United States at the time of Russia's invasion of Finland in 1939 had no drawings or specifications for the cartridge, but Winchester happened to have some cartridges that would do and submitted a bid to the Finnish military attaché in Washington. As it turned out the price quoted was less than the cartridges cost the Finnish Government to make in peacetime, a fact greatly appreciated by the Finnish representative.

John Olin, as active head of the Winchester manufacturing organization, was especially proud of the ability of the Winchester factory to convert its machinery intended to manufacture the .30-06 cartridge to turning out of great quantities of .303 British cartridges during the war. By reason of its versatility as a commercial manufacturer, Winchester was able not only to continue the production of huge quantities of the .303 British cartridges, but to furnish in addition many special-purpose cartridges and training ammunition for the United States and its Allies.

Winchester put to good use in World War II its experience in the production of radiator tubes and assembled radiators. More than one billion of the former and fifty thousand of the latter were included in the war effort items furnished by the New Haven factory to the United States Government. As mentioned before, the greatest number of tubes were used for radiators in liquid cooled engines but as these became obsolete the tubes were necessary for oil coolers and various other intercoolers on the new aircraft so that they were a vital contribution to American supremacy in the air in the latter days of the war.

The total military production achievements of Olin Industries, including the Winchester plant, during World War II is shown in the table on the preceding page.

Nearly a century has passed since Oliver Winchester and his associates incorporated the Volcanic Repeating Arms Company in June 1855. This survey of the years since 1932 shows that Winchester, under its new management and as an important part of the expanding Olin organization, has carried on the pioneering tradition of its founder, Oliver F. Winchester, devoted to the primary task of developing superior firearms and ever ready to assist the nation in times of military emergency.

# NOTES

## PREFACE

1. John A. Kouwenhoven, *Made in America: The Arts and Modern Civilization,* 5.

## CHAPTER ONE

1. John G. W. Dillin, *The Kentucky Rifle,* 11-16.

2. *Cf.* Townsend Whelen, *The American Rifle,* 5. Some authorities have argued that the effective range of the Kentucky rifle was more nearly 200 yards than 100 yards. Describing the Battle of New Orleans, Harlow Pease tells of one British officer being killed by a shot from a Kentucky rifle nearly 300 yards away, but concludes, ". . . it is probable that at and under 200 yards was practical extreme range for most of the [American] riflemen." ("The Kentucky at the Plain of Chalmette," *The American Rifleman,* December 1937.)

The matches of the National Muzzle Loading Rifle Association infrequently produce groups of .89 inches at 50 yards *from a rest,* rarely produce groups of 2 inches at 100 yards, and never yet have grouped 4 inches at 200 yards.

As far as velocity goes, Lucian Cary reports these chronograph figures for six Kentucky rifles (*True,* November 1949): "The average was 1,923 feet per second at the muzzle—lowest was 1,708, highest 2,042. . . . [one rifle] started its ball at 1,979 feet a second, but the velocity had fallen off to 1,387 at 50 yards, 1,021 at 100 yards and 681 at 200 yards. . . . the familiar 170-grain .30-30 has a muzzle velocity of 2,200—only about 10% more than the round ball. But at 100 yards the speed of the relatively long bullet is 1,930, at 200 yards 1,680."

3. T. B. Tryon, "The Percussion Plains Rifle," *The American Rifleman,* November 1936.

4. Paul B. Jenkins, "Old Reliable," *The American Rifleman,* December 1931. Dr. Jenkins was for many years Historian and Advisor on Arms to the famous Rudolph J. Nunnemacher Firearms Collection, Milwaukee Public Museum, Milwaukee, Wisconsin. He became one of the leading American historians of firearms development and was known as a careful, accurate scholar.

5. V. D. Stockbridge, *Digest of Patents Relating to Breech-Loading Magazine Small Arms (Except Revolvers) Granted in the United States from 1836 to 1873 Inclusive.*

6. Claud E. Fuller, *The Breech-Loader in the Service.*

7. Stockbridge, *op. cit.,* 173–176.

8. Joseph W. Roe, *English and American Tool Builders,* 4.

9. Roe, *op. cit.,* 4-5.

10. Felicia Deyrup, *Arms Makers of the Connecticut Valley*, 220.

11. Colt had started manufacture of his revolver in Paterson, N.J., in 1836, but this company failed. He was later encouraged by the interest shown in his weapons by Captain Walker of the Texas Rangers and made an arrangement with Eli Whitney to produce the famous Walker Colts in the latter's plant in 1847. The returns from this gave Colt some much-needed capital, and in 1848 he started a new plant on a small scale in Hartford. Five years later he constructed a large factory which marked an epoch in American manufacturing. (Roe, *op. cit.*, 167-168.)

12. The invested capital for the Colt's and Sharps establishments in Hartford in 1860 was $1.75 million. (U.S. Census 1850, *Manufacturers*, 39.) This figure, however, must be used with caution because of inconsistencies in reporting "invested capital" to the Census.

## CHAPTER TWO

1. See "Sewing Machines," *Encyclopedia Britannica*, 11th ed.

2. According to Guy Hubbard, "This loaded ball acted just like the Minié in expanding into the rifling upon firing, and while not primarily designed for this purpose it is said to have thus accidentally antedated Col. Minié's famous invention." (*The Beginning of Smith and Wesson*, manuscript in archives of the Winchester Repeating Arms Company, 4.)

3. U.S. Patent Office, *In the Matter of the Application Sarah E. Allen, Executive, for the Extension of Letters Patent Issued to Ethan Allen, Etc.*, 103-107.

4. The products manufactured by the partnership are shown in Appendix A-1.

5. *Patent Right Deed and Covenant between Courtlandt Palmer and Horace Smith and Daniel B. Wesson*, June 20, 1854. The apparent inclusive features of this agreement raised several questions regarding the right of its successive holders to use patents subsequently made or acquired by Smith & Wesson.

6. According to the Veader-Earle account, the three sold some 700 shares of this stock between September 1855 and September 1856. (D. H. Veader and A. W. Earle, *The Story of the Winchester Repeating Arms Company*, unpublished manuscript, hereafter referred to as *Veader-Earle Story*, 6.)

7. He is listed in the New Haven directory for 1856-57 as treasurer of the New England Carving Company, president of the Volcanic Repeating Arms Company, and shipping merchant.

8. An advertisement in the New Haven *Journal-Courier* of July 1, 1856, places him in business in New Haven at the time. The notice reads: "Wm. C. Hicks & Company, Mechanical Engineers, Designers, and Draughtsmen, No. 73 College St., N.H. All kinds of mechanical designing, drawings, specifications, and models for patents, calculations for steam engines, water wheels, shafting, gearing, etc., executed practically, accurately, and promptly. Governor cut off attachment put on old or new engines and warranted. The construction of all kinds of machinery superintended on reasonable terms."

9. According to *Veader-Earle Story*, 7, work was done for the Company by the Whitney Arms Company and the Northford Manufacturing Company.

10. The foregoing information was obtained from payroll records of the Volcanic Repeating Arms Company on deposit in the Winchester Repeating Arms Company archives. The data are not complete enough to warrant any more detailed statistical analysis.

11. The author is indebted to Mr. Paul Beem for this analysis, which also included the following ballistic table comparing the Volcanic performance with a modern Colt .45 automatic. "Mid-Range Trajectory" means height of bullet above a horizontal plane along the line of sight halfway between the firing point and the target.

VOLCANIC BALLISTIC TABLE

Assume Muzzle Velocity of 500-ft-sec. Caliber .38, Weight 100 grains.

| | VELOCITIES FT-SEC. (range in yards) | | | | MID-RANGE TRAJECTORY (in inches) | | |
|---|---|---|---|---|---|---|---|
| | *Muzzle* | *100* | *200* | *300* | *100 yds.* | *200 yds.* | *300 yds.* |
| Volcanic | 500 | 410 | 330 | 275 | 20 | 100 | 290 |
| Colt .45 | 860 | 750 | 650 | 570 | 6.4 | 31.1 | 81 |

ENERGIES (FT.-LBS.)

| | *Muzzle* | *100 yds.* | *200 yds.* | *300 yds.* |
|---|---|---|---|---|
| Volcanic | 56 | 38 | 24 | 17 |
| Colt .45 | 378 | 288 | 216 | 166 |

12. Calvin Goddard, "An American Heritage," Part II, *Army Ordnance,* May-June 1938.

## CHAPTER THREE

1. Mrs. Fanny Winchester Hotchkiss, *Winchester Notes,* 3.
2. Specifications of Letters Patent No. 5,421, February 1, 1848, U.S. Patent Office.
3. Edward E. Atwater, *History of New Haven to the Present Time,* 628.
4. Winchester seems at first to have been unimpressed by the possibilities of the sewing machine. According to one account, "early in 1852 Wheeler (of the firm of Wheeler & Wilson) took one of his machines to O. F. Winchester of New Haven, who was at that time a manufacturer of shirts. Winchester was so skeptical that he refused to try the "contrivance," but when Wheeler actually caused a shirt to be made with the machine in his presence, operated by the wife of the inventor, skepticism gave way to wonderment. The speed and perfect workmanship developed led Winchester to consent to take some on trial. Within two months he had purchased the patent rights for New Haven County." (Norris Galpin Osborn, ed., *History of Connecticut,* iv, 347.)
5. *U.S. Census Report, 1860;* New Haven Registrar's reports on file at State Library, Hartford, Connecticut.
6. Some impression of Winchester's financial status in 1860 can be obtained from the fact that his half-interest in the partnership with Davies in that year amounted to $200,000. In addition, he had $20,000 invested in the New Haven Arms Company (although at this time the investment had a doubtful value) and an additional $20,000 that he had realized from the sale of the Volcanic assets to the same concern.
7. Apparently work was resumed in the former Volcanic plant even before the new company was organized. *Veader-Earle Story,* 17, reports a payroll covering the earnings of 29 employees for the three weeks ending April 30, 1857.
8. The account of Henry's career prior to his association with the New Haven Arms Company is drawn principally from an unpublished manuscript by Guy Hubbard, *The Beginning of Smith and Wesson and Winchester,* on file in the archives of the Winchester Repeating Arms Company.
9. *U.S. Census Report, 1860;* New Haven Registrar's reports, on file at State Library, Hartford, Connecticut.
10. A full account of the Company's early history is lacking, but the following letter, dated October 17, 1862, from O. F. Winchester to E. B. Martin, gives a good summary of the problems encountered up to that date:

"Mr. C. F. Shelton made some inquiry of me in your interest in reference to the N.H. Arms Co., and in a conversation with him this morning, it was thought best that I should make such explanations of the position and operations of the Company as might be of interest to you.

"Five years ago last May the Company commenced manufacturing the Volcanic Firearms, starting a large lot of each size, and in about 18 months thereafter began to turn out finished arms, and put them into the market. They at once found a strong prejudice against them among the dealers, and after a few months vain efforts to sell them became satisfied that there were radical defects which would prevent their ever becoming a saleable article. We of course had no way but to finish up those we had commenced, as they would have been a total loss to have dropped them. This involved a large outlay. Most of that stock has been sold at a heavy loss; and nearly all of the costly tools and machinery for making them were rendered useless. While finishing up these arms (taking about three years) we perfected and patented certain improvements (Dec. '60) obviating the objections to the old arms, and making a perfect thing as applied to the rifle.

"At this point we were too much exhausted, as we felt, to proceed in getting up the tools and fixtures to manufacture the rifle; but let them lay, and took a contract to make 3,000 revolvers for a party in New York, calculating to clear some eight thousand dollars upon the same; (amounting to $26,000.) but when the pistols were finished, the party failed to respond. We now have them on hand, and consequently the capital they cost locked up in a lawsuit.

"Eighteen months ago, we commenced the construction of the tools and fixtures for making our improved rifles. We have had them in the market about three months.

"From the commencement of our organization, till within the last three months (5 years and a half) there has not been a month in which our expenditures have not exceeded our receipts. Consequently we have accumulated a very large indebtedness, the principal items of which are:

| | |
|---|---|
| Cash advanced by O. F. Winchester | $22,000 |
| Bills payable (Bank accommodation) | 36,687 |
| Savings Bank (Endorsed by Directors) | 10,000 |
| Due B. T. Henry, Superintendent | 2,500 |
| Borrowed of Stockholders (other than O.F.W.) | 6,250 |
| | $77,437 |

"The assets of the Company cannot be sold for enough to pay its indebtedness. I have repeatedly offered to give all of my stock to other stockholders, if they would reimburse my advances, and relieve me from my responsibility for the Company, which covers its whole indebtedness.

"So much for the present value of the stock, which you will see is nothing. The stock, however, has a value, but, it is entirely prospective. It arises from the fact that our new rifle is a success, and will, in time, if pressed with vigor, retrieve our past losses; but to do this, further aid and support will be needed from the stockholders.

"Your absence has prevented our calling upon you for assistance heretofore. We shall be glad to hear from you as to your disposition. There has been but one sale of the stock, to my knowledge, and this was made recently upon this prospective value, at 25 cents on the dollar. If you wish to sell, I think you can get 25 cents for the stock. We should prefer to have you hold on, and help us.

"If you sell, however, it will help us indirectly, as the parties offering to buy, do so with the purpose of seeing the thing through, if money will do it. . . ."

This shows clearly that Winchester and his associates had become painfully aware of the limitations of the Volcanic arms by the fall of 1858. While experiments were being made to remedy the trouble, the Company continued to operate at a loss.

11. French. *Brevet d'Invention,* No. 843, old series.

12. W. W. Greener, *The Gun and Its Development,* 131-132.

13. Greener, *op. cit.,* 133.

14. L. D. Satterlee, "The Model 1866 Winchester," *The American Rifleman,* December 15, 1924.

15. U.S. Patent Office, *Specifications Forming Part of Letters Patent No. 27,433, April 17, 1860. Horace Smith and Daniel B. Wesson, of Springfield, Massachusetts. Improvements in Filling Metallic Cartridges.*

16. Testimony of B. Tyler Henry, *Winchester Repeating Arms Company—Union Metallic Cartridge Company: Cartridge Arbitration, April 12, 1882,* 200.

17. On this point, a letter written by Winchester to John W. Brown, Columbus, Ohio, November 26, 1862, is of interest. Referring to a lot of Smith & Wesson cartridges he had recently examined, he commented: "They are larger than ours, with a larger ball, and a heavier charge of powder. This, of course, gives more force and penetration. To have made our gun to use this length of cartridge in the first place would have been better, I have no doubt, and I now regret that it was not done, though it would have reduced the number of charges to 13 or 14 and increased the length and depth of the frame, and thus increased its weight."

18. "In the matter of the application of B. TYLER HENRY, for an extension of Letters Patent, granted to him October 16, 1860, reissued December 8, 1868, for magazine Firearms." (*Brief on the Part of Applicant, Before the Hon. Commissioner of Patents, September 21, 1874,* 1-3.) There is no record that the extension of the patent was granted.

19. George Morgan Chinn, Jr., and Bayless Evans Hardin, *Encyclopedia of American Hand Arms,* 248.

## CHAPTER FOUR

1. Letter, Lieutenant W. Mitchell to Bureau of Ordnance, May 20, 1862, reproduced in the New Haven Arms Company catalog, 1862, 4-5.

2. Letter quoted by Claud E. Fuller in *The Breech-Loader in the Service,* 199-200.

3. Letter, Oliver F. Winchester, November 27, 1863, to Hon. T. C. Watson, Assistant Secretary of War:

"We offer to make for the United States Government as follows:

"First: We will manufacture and sell the Government Forty Thousand (40,000) Henrys Patent Repeating Carbines for Twenty Six ($26.00) each. The first delivery of 200 to be made in six months from the final agreement upon the exact details and (200) for each working day thereafter until the order is completed.

"Second: We will make and furnish Twenty Thousand (20,000) Henrys Patent Repeating Carbines at Twenty Seven ($27.00) Dollars each, the first delivery of 100 to be made six months after the final agreement upon the exact details and One Hundred (100) per day for each working day thereafter until the order is completed.

"Third: We will manufacture and sell to the Government Ten Thousand (10,000) Henrys Patent Repeating Carbines for Twenty Eight ($28.00) Dollars each, the first delivery of Fifty (50) to be made eight months after the final agreement, upon the exact details, and fifty (50) per day for each working day thereafter until the order is completed.

"All the carbines proposed to be made as above to be 44/100 bore, of the usual lengths used in the Cavalry and of the same material and quality of workmanship shown in a model, which we propose to make for the examination of the government, open, however, to such change in the material as may be agreed upon and such length of cartridge and weight of powder and ball as may be ordered by the government. We further propose to furnish Cartridges for the Carbine 1⅜ inches long with a charge of thirty (30) grains of powder, and ball of 240 grains lead, at Fourteen ($14.00) dollars per thousand. And we also propose to furnish Cartridges of any length required, and a corresponding increase of the charge, at the rate of $1.50 per thousand for each addition of 10 Grains of Powder (equal to ¼ inch increase in length of cartridge).

"If either of the first or second offers are accepted, the Arms will be manufactured by the Colt's Patent Fire Arms Co. whose extensive facilities and high reputation for good workmanship are good guarantees for the promptness and fidelity with which the Orders will be executed. If the third proposition only should be accepted we propose to manufacture them at our Armory in Bridgeport."

4. *Cf.* Fuller, *op. cit.,* 140.
5. *Ordnance Contracts,* 277.
6. *Ibid.,* 277, 842.
7. Fuller, *op. cit.,* 226.
8. *Ibid.*
9. He wrote to George D. Prentice of Louisville, on March 10, 1863: "I enclose an article from the Scientific American. Will you please have it copied in your 'Daily and Weekly Journal' and charge to our account."
10. Charles Winthrop Sawyer, *Our Rifles,* iii, 279.
11. Charles Minor Blackford, III (Susan Leigh Blackford, ed.), *Letters from Lee's Army,* 7.
12. Even running a relatively small business during this period presented many difficulties. Winchester felt under constant pressure to expand his capacity, and in letter after letter during 1862 and 1863 he expressed regret at not being able to fill orders for rifles that were running from thirty to ninety days ahead of delivery. But even getting a moderate expansion presented difficulties. On May 23, 1863, he wrote to John W. Brown, of Columbus, Ohio: "We are doing all we can to increase our production, but our effort will not tell for some time to come as we have to wait a long time to get our machines made at big prices and hire hands at extravagant wages."

Four months later, on September 7, 1863, he noted in a reply to an inquiry of Messrs. Tyron & Brothers, of Philadelphia, about purchasing a second-hand jigging machine:

"We have had occasion within the last few weeks to buy some Ten Thousand Dollars worth of *Gun Machinery* and have been through the whole market and know that there is not now a machine of the kind in the market.

"We bought two of the jigging machines, all we could find new, of the Massachusetts Arms Co., Chicopee Falls, Mass. They are good machines and they probably can get them up for you as soon as any one."

The Company was able to supplement the New Haven plant's capacity by getting other concerns to make parts. For example, there was an order given on November 18, 1863, to the Arcade Malleable Iron Works of Worcester, Massachusetts, for 5,000 levers to be made ". . . from our patterns, same as last, and make four shipments of 1,250 each. We should like the first shipment of 1,250 at the earliest possible moment, all to be made of the best stocks."

Colt's Patent Fire Arms Company of Hartford supplied 2,500 swivels December 5, 1863.

For a number of items such as powder, priming mixtures, blanks to be drawn into cartridge cases, and barrels, the organization depended entirely upon outside sources of supply. These suppliers contributed on occasion to production problems or the bottlenecks experienced by the New Haven Arms Company. An acknowledgment of November 16, 1863, of a shipment of cartridge blanks from Brown Brothers of Waterbury, Connecticut, ended with the comment that the size was all right, but ". . . the quality of metal does not seem to be quite as good as the last, they do not draw so well." On September 30, 1863, the Company wrote Messrs. A. G. Potter, Gay, and Tollman of Boston:

"We telegraphed you this morning for powder to be sent by Express. We are very disappointed in not receiving the powder ordered before this.

"We are now entirely out. We are using from 40 to 50 pounds a day. Please see that we are kept with about that supply until further order."

On another occasion, November 12, 1863, Winchester wrote English & Atwater of New Haven:

"We placed with you the 2nd of July last an order for 500 steel Barrels equivalent to 5,500 pounds. The last of September we received 5,721 pounds being a few pounds in excess of the order.

"August 12th we placed another order for 5,000 Barrels equivalent to 5,500 pounds, 600 Barrels to be delivered October 1st and 400 Barrels the first of November and 400 the first of each month thereafter. Two shipments 1,000 Barrels are past due, and nothing has been received upon this order, in the meantime we are out of work for our machinery and may add the delay is a serious loss and inconvenience to us and we write to urge the utmost possible dispatch in getting the order out to us to save us further loss."

In general, the situation was not so tight in respect to cartridge production as it was for rifles. Except for occasional delays in the shipment of powder and relatively minor production difficulties, the Company had little trouble filling orders for ammunition. This was probably because Winchester went ahead with the proposal, outlined on April 20, 1863, in the letter to Smith & Wesson.

Even in this instance, some trouble was experienced in obtaining equipment. On October 15, 1863, the Company stated in a letter to S. Crispin, Captain of Ordnance, in New York, that ". . . [cartridge] machinery which was to be done 30 days ago to enable us to make 20,000 a day, is not yet finished and it looks now as if it will take 30 days longer to get it running."

13. No exact figure can be fixed, but Winchester stated in 1867 that about 10,000 rifles had been sold during the last two years of the war, ". . . while orders for at least 100,000 which were received during that time could not be filled." *Cf. Winchester Repeating Arms Company catalog, 1867,* 7. That production was somewhat in excess of 10,000 is indicated by the fact that one of the Henry rifles in the collection of the Winchester Repeating Arms Company bears the serial number 10,331.

14. Cf. Deyrup, *op. cit.,* 202.

15. How active Winchester had been in the partnership of Winchester and Davies during the 1860s is impossible to determine. There are no available records indicating what that company did during the war years. Davies filed a return for the Census of 1870 which showed a considerable reduction in size of plant and annual output.

16. The change in the corporate title suggests that the relationships between B. Tyler Henry and Winchester had become strained during 1865 and 1866. But the record is completely blank beyond the fact that when the new company was formed and the plant moved to Bridgeport, Henry remained in New Haven where he ran a small gun and machine shop until his death in 1898.

17. "Spirit Guns: A True Story of the First American Repeating Rifles and Their Use in a Fight on the Western Frontier," *The American Rifleman,* February 1929.

18. Neill C. Wilson, *Treasure Express: Epic Days of Wells Fargo,* 112-113. Copyright 1936. The quotation is used by permission of The Macmillan Company, publishers.

## CHAPTER FIVE

1. These were the patents and the covenant signed by Smith and Wesson, that had been assigned to him when the Volcanic Repeating Arms Company was liquidated.

2. According to the report made by the Company in 1869 for the Census of 1870, the labor force totaled 260, of whom 236 were men and 24 were women. Of this number, 38 were employed in ammunition production. The monthly payroll averaged $15,000 and the capital investment was set at 500,000. The equipment listed included 3 power saws, 15 drill presses, 40 lathes, 100 milling machines, 8 drawing machines, and 4 cartridge-loading machines.

3. The loading arrangements on the new model were covered by a patent (U.S. 55,012) issued to Nelson King, May 22, 1866, and assigned to O. F. Winchester. King, who was employed as plant superintendent in 1867, at Bridgeport, was a resident of that city. There is no available information about his background or how he came to be employed by the Company. By authorization of the board of directors, February 16, 1868, King was paid $5,000 for his patent, $1,000 in cash and the remainder in stock purchased for him by the Company. At the same time his salary as superintendent was raised from an undisclosed amount to $3,000 a year.

4. *Cf.* Fuller, *op. cit.*, 227-228.

5. *Ordnance Memoranda No. 15, Small Arms,* 28-35.

6. *Ibid.*, 96.

7. Frazier and Robert Hunt, *I Fought With Custer: The Story of Sergeant Windolph, Last Survivor of the Battle of the Little Big Horn,* 92.

8. *Ibid.*, 91.

9. The Swiss later adopted the Vetterli (or Vetterlli) repeating rifle, which had a tubular magazine under the barrel but used a bolt action.

10. The results of these trials are contained in *Reports on Breech-Loading Arms by a Special Sub-Committee of the Ordnance Select Committee, War Office, 1868.*

11. Addis retired from the Company in 1901, and died in New Haven eight years later. He was buried in Evergreen Cemetery in the same city and his grave is marked by a tombstone which he had ordered, bearing the inscription, "In Memory of Thomas Emmet Addis, Traveler, 1840–1909." His personal fortune of over $340,000 was willed to the New Haven City Library, the New Haven and Grace Hospitals, and the Masonic Home.

12. The account that follows of the negotiations between the Winchester Repeating Arms Company and Oscanyan is drawn principally from *Records of the U.S. Circuit Court, Southern District of New York, Christopher Oscanyan* v. *Winchester Repeating Arms Company, Law Docket,* Vol. 4, 1847–1881, 84-95.

13. Deposition taken in the case of *Christopher Oscanyan* v. *Winchester Repeating Arms Company.*

14. *Oscanyan* v. *Winchester Repeating Arms Company, Federal Cases, Circuit and District Courts, 1874–1880,* Vol. 18, Case No. 10,600; *Oscanyan* v. *Winchester Repeating Arms Company, United States, Reports, Supreme Court,* Vol. 103, 261-278. For the place this case occupies in Procedure, see Charles E. Clark, *Cases on Pleading and Procedure,* 2d ed., 432-435.

15. A recapitulation of the contracts made on November 9, 1870, and August 19, 1871, including the ammunition which was not involved in Oscanyan's suit, shows the following: 46,000 Winchester muskets at $28 less 5 per cent, $1,223,600; 5,000 Winchester carbines at $20 less 5 per cent, $95,000; 4 million cartridges at $12 per thousand, $48,000; 16 million empty shells at $26 per thousand, $96,000; total $1,462,-600. (*Veader-Earle Story,* 56.)



The Company had cabled its terms to the Turkish authorities via Western Union.

In transmission the quotation for the carbines was stated at $20 instead of $27 which had been filed by the Winchester Repeating Arms Company. In March 1871, the Company put in a claim for $35,000 against Western Union, but after considerable correspondence the matter was dropped. (*Veader-Earle Story,* 55-56.)

16. It is not possible to determine exactly how much the Turkish contracts contributed to the aggregate income of the Company for the period or what proportion foreign sales made up of the total business of the firm, but a rough approximation can be made. The records of the Winchester Repeating Arms Company show the following data on sales and profits for the period under consideration:

| *Year* | *Guns Sold* | *Guns-and-Ammunition Net Sales* | *Profits Before Depreciation* |
|---|---|---|---|
| 1869 | 10,930 | $ 323,531 | $ 80,058 (*loss*) |
| 1870 | 22,365 | 809,393 | 218,920 |
| 1871 | 34,589 | 1,015,652 | 279,580 |
| 1872 | 22,680 | 591,449 | 159,440 |
| TOTALS | | | |
| 1870–72 | 89,634 | 2,416,494 | 657,940 |
| 1873 | 8,535 | 335,321 | 132,326 |

The sharp drop in gun sales and total receipts in 1873 suggests that the Turkish contracts had been completed by the end of 1872. If this was the çase, these two contracts absorbed nearly two thirds of the guns sold and contributed some 60 per cent to the income of the Winchester Repeating Arms Company during the three-year period ending 1872. The 6,000 arms and 4.5 million cartridges sold to the French plus the $36,000 Peruvian order during 1870 would raise the percentage of foreign business to a total even higher.

17. An agreement, dated August 22, 1870, and recorded April 8, 1878, in the U.S. Patent Office gives some information on the nature of the patent rights acquired. Involving Patent 27,393, which was the basic patent granted to Spencer on his repeating rifle, the Winchester Repeating Arms Company agreed to pay Spencer one dollar on every gun manufactured under his patent and to that extent assumed a contract which had been made on July 12, 1861, between Spencer and Charles Cheney. At the same time the Company waived any claims on future inventions made by Spencer on single-shot rifles, or single or repeating shotguns and pistols, but reserved "full and complete right to all present and future inventions of the said Spencer in repeating rifles or carbines." (U.S. Patent Office, *Liber N–22,* 356.)

An auction of the equipment of the Spencer Repeating Rifle Company was held in Boston on September 28, 1869. The sale was widely publicized and well attended and some $138,000 worth of machinery was sold. (*Cf.* L. D. Satterlee, "The Spencer Repeating Rifle," Part II, *The American Rifleman,* May 15, 1926.) Whether this auction was conducted by the Winchester Repeating Arms Company as a result of the purchase of the entire assets or by the Spencer concern was not reported. But on December 11, 1869, *The Scientific American* carried an advertisement offering for sale 2,000 Spencer muskets, 30,000 Spencer carbines, and 500 Spencer sporting rifles by the Winchester Repeating Arms Company.

18. In this instance the details of the purchase are more extensive. There is a record in the U.S. Patent Office, dated September 22, 1868, in *Liber W–20,* 176, of an assignment by Valentine Fogarty and the American Repeating Rifle Company to the Winchester Repeating Arms Company of "All machinery, tools, fixtures, gun materials, supplies, notes, book debts, cash, patent rights, and assets and property of every name

and description now belonging to the American Repeating Rifle Company, or to which they may become entitled hereafter by virtue of any contracts with Valentine Fogarty or other parties."

19. Winchester at various times held considerable holdings of real estate in New Haven. In 1859 he had bought the area between Prospect and St. Ronan, extending between what are now Edwards and Canner Streets. Later he purchased land to the west of this area, a part of which became the location of the Winchester Repeating Arms Company.

20. The increase in net worth had been built up in this manner:

| | | |
|---|---|---|
| SURPLUS REINVESTED IN BUSINESS: | | |
| Profits from operations | $885,602 | |
| Realized profits on sale of assets of American Repeating Rifle Company | 32,128 | $917,730 |
| LESS: | | |
| Dividends paid | 215,625 | |
| Dividends declared, payable 2/1/73 | 25,000 | 240,625 |
| NET SURPLUS INVESTED IN BUSINESS | | 677,105 |
| PLUS AMOUNT RECEIVED FROM SALE OF STOCK | | 50,000 |
| | | 727,105 |
| THE INCREASE IN NET WORTH HAD BEEN INVESTED IN | | |
| Real estate, plant, and machinery | | 495,930 |
| Patents | | 81,175 |
| Working capital | | 150,000 |
| TOTAL | | $727,105 |

Despite the improved financial position of the Company, it was apparently easier or less expensive for the management to borrow on notes endorsed by the directors in their individual capacity. On October 7, 1872, the board voted to issue a mortgage to Oliver F. Winchester, Edward A. Mitchell, and Jeremiah A. Bishop, to secure them ". . . for present and future endorsements for the accommodation of this Company which they may make to said Company for its accommodation to an amount not exceeding $400,000."

21. Page 208.

## CHAPTER SIX

1. The best description of the methods used in ammunition production for this period is to be found in Charles H. Fitch, "The Manufacture of Ammunition," *Tenth Census of the United States, 1880, Manufacturers,* 640-648.

2. Henry O. Dwight, *Turkish Life in War Time,* 163.

3. It is stated by Norton in *American Inventions and Improvements in Loading Small Arms* that the Providence Tool Company subsequently manufactured some 600,000 Martini-Peabody rifles for the Turkish Government. There is no evidence that these later orders were secured through the Winchester Repeating Arms Company.

4. Captain E. C. Crossman, "With Captain Crossman at the Big Winchester Factories," *The Sporting Goods Dealer,* January 1920.

5. N. H. Roberts, "The Rifles of Yesterday," *The American Rifleman,* April 1935.

6. *Annual Report of the Chief of Ordnance to Secretary of War, 1878,* v-vi.

7. *Report of the Chief of Ordnance, 1880,* xv-xvi.

8. These were manufactured under U.S. patents 103,504 issued May 24, 1870, and 125,988 issued April 23, 1872. Both patents were granted to O. M. Robinson.

9. *Marcellus Hartley: A Brief Memoir.*

10. The sources of the increase in the net worth were:

| | | |
|---|---|---|
| PROFITS FROM OPERATIONS 1873–1880 | | $2,566,996 |
| LESS: Distributed as dividends | $700,000 | |
| Repayment of loans made by Davies and O. F. Winchester in 1871 | 99,425 | 799,425 |
| SURPLUS INVESTED IN BUSINESS | | $1,767,571 |

11. His estate was made up of 4,000 shares of Winchester Repeating Arms Company stock valued at approximately $1.2 million (there had been a dividend of 100 per cent in 1878), other securities worth $44,105 and real estate totaling $184,000, and personal property valued at $3,400. *Cf. Will of Oliver F. Winchester,* probated in New Haven, December 10, 1880.

## CHAPTER SEVEN

1. "American Arms and Ammunition," *Scribner's Monthly,* January 1880.

2. Deyrup, *op. cit.,* 43, 101.

3. References to the contract system will be found in J. L. Bishop, *A History of American Manufacturers;* C. M. Greene in H. F. Williamson, *Growth of the American Economy;* and J. Richards, *The Making of America.*

## CHAPTER EIGHT

1. *Report of the Chief of Ordnance, 1886,* 5.

2. Clarence E. Mulford, *Hopalong Cassidy,* 90 *et seq.*

3. The early contracts between Browning and the Winchester Repeating Arms Company have not been preserved, but this figure of $8,000 was supplied by George E. Browning, a younger brother of John Moses Browning, in August 1946.

4. The Sharps Rifle Company had been organized to take over the manufacture of the rifle after the failure of Robbins & Lawrence some years before. *Cf.* Winston O. Smith, *The Sharps Rifle,* 23-44.

5. J. M. and M. S. Browning Company, *A History of Browning Guns from 1831,* 11.

6. Paul B. Jenkins, "Wild Life of Yesterday, and the First Successful Repeating Shotgun," *The American Rifleman,* October 1935.

7. Interview, George E. Browning, August 1946.

8. U.S. 208, 589. John Gardner had started work with the Company around 1868. In 1881 he became superintendent of the cartridge shop, a position which he held until his retirement in December 1908. He took out a large number of patents, all assigned to the Company, covering ammunition design and manufacture.

9. "Wild Life of Yesterday, and the First Successful Repeating Shotgun," *loc. cit.*

10. *Cf.* William G. Lathrop, *The Brass Industry in the United States.*

## CHAPTER NINE

1. Three of these models utilized the right-hand, swing-out cylinder, with simultaneous ejection, features which were not introduced by Colt's and Smith & Wesson until some years later.

2. *Cf.* L. P. Satterlee, *A Catalogue of Firearms for the Collector,* 189-192.

3. Charles Lee Karr, Jr., and Carroll Robbins Karr, *Remington Handguns,* 4. This work has an excellent sketch of the early history of the Remington company.

4. While ammunition was sold through the same channels as guns, the relationships with the trade after 1883 were worked out through an association of ammunition manufacturers, to which Winchester belonged. This association and the marketing of ammunition is described in Chapters Ten and Seventeen.

5. It is not known whether the dealers sold to retail customers at list prices; but as the Company insisted that the discounts by jobbers to dealers remain uniform, the latter were not under pressure to change any previously established relationships between retail and list prices. For this reason it seems most likely that the reduction of prices to consumers was proportionate to the drop in list prices.

6. The improved position of the jobber because of the increase in rebates is clearly indicated. Even more striking is the reduction in net prices of guns to the Company, which is reflected in the indices of the A jobbers' net price. The drop of 46 per cent during the period overstates the decline somewhat because of the sales to other classes of jobbers and direct to dealers in foreign markets. But because some 85 to 90 per cent of sales were probably made to the domestic market and the large jobbers in turn handled the bulk of the domestic business, the reduction in the average price per gun received by the Company was substantial.

7. James Kerr was the inventor of the Kerr rifle and the Kerr revolver, which were manufactured for the London Armoury Company and shipped in considerable numbers to the Confederacy during the Civil War.

8. This volume will hereafter be referred to as *Foreign Contract Book.*

9. The following simple calculation will demonstrate the validity of this approach. Taking the Model 73, which was the best seller, as typical, and basing the labor cost on the payments to the labor contractors for work on this model as also typical, the following table shows the changes between 1880 and 1889:

| | *Net selling price to company* | *Labor cost* |
|---|---|---|
| 1880 | $16.58 | $4.84 |
| 1889 | 8.83 | 3.56 |

The number of guns sold increased from 26,400 in 1880 to 72,000 in 1889. If material and overhead be taken as MO (combined material and overhead costs) in both years, the *profits* would have been:

1880: 26,400 ($16.58 – $4.84 – MO) = $309,936 – MO
1889: 72,000 ($ 8.83 – $3.56 – MO) = $379,440 – MO

If MO were constant throughout the period, the increase in profits would have been under 23 per cent. Any increase in the costs of materials and of overhead would, of course, have affected the increase in profit in a downward direction.

10. The gross investment in production assets at the end of 1880 was $1,500,345. During the nine years ending December 31, 1889, it increased by $1,133,099, or by over 75 per cent. While depreciation was not, at this time, charged as a cost, it would seem reasonable to expect an increase in the costs of operating the physical equipment which, if not, indeed, proportionate to the increase in the capital cost, would have been significant.

11. It is not possible to measure the proportion of the total industry sales of firearms contributed by Winchester, owing to the limitations of the Census data for 1880 and 1890 which include only a total-dollar volume for all types of firearms including pistols.

## CHAPTER TEN

1. *Cf. Report of the Industrial Commission on Trusts and Industrial Combinations,* xiii, *Commission Reports,* 474.

2. Some states had passed legislation prohibiting pooling within their jurisdiction and under the Interstate Commerce Act of 1887, they had been declared illegal among railroads.

3. For the history of the Phoenix Metallic Cartridge Company, see J. R. Cole, *History of Tolland County.*

## CHAPTER ELEVEN

1. The increase in net worth had been invested in the business in the following forms:

| | |
|---|---|
| Real estate, plant and machinery | $1,133,099 |
| Patent expenditures | 99,458 |
| Working capital | 1,108,520 |
| Invested in Remington Arms Co. | 178,000 |
| Total | $2,519,152 |

2. This includes a total of 20 per cent declared for 1889 at the board meeting of January 22, 1890. At this meeting the large extra dividend was explained as resulting from "surplus cash."

3. Converse held 150 shares at the end of 1884. His holding fell to 41 shares in 1885 and to 20 by April 1887. This stock was apparently sold, 100 shares being transferred in 1885 to Ezekiel H. Trowbridge and his son, E. Hayes Trowbridge, West India merchants of New Haven.

4. T. G. Bennett's regular salary was maintained at $6,500 from 1884 through 1889, his share of the Company's prosperity coming indirectly through his wife's holdings.

## CHAPTER TWELVE

1. "The Contract System," *Brewer Notes.* Brewer had started to work for Winchester following his graduation from Yale Sheffield Scientific School in 1894. He served a two-year apprenticeship in the shops and about 1898 began specializing in ballistics. In 1906 he became superintendent of the cartridge shop, in 1914 was elected a director, and in 1915 became a vice president, which position he held until his retirement in 1922. Some years later Brewer, at the suggestion of Edwin Pugsley, wrote out a series of memoranda on various phases of the Company's history with which he was familiar.

## CHAPTER THIRTEEN

1. Townsend Whelen, *Small Arms Design and Ballistics,* 246.
2. Townsend Whelen, *The American Rifle,* 338.

## CHAPTER FOURTEEN

1. Sharpe, *op. cit.,* 240.
2. The author is indebted to Mr. W. W. Wallis of the London Armoury Company, Ltd., of London, for this information.

3. This gun was based on U.S. Patent 441,390, which had been issued to the Browning brothers in November 1890.

4. The report of this case is contained in *Federal Reporter,* Vol. 85, first series, U.S. Circuit Court of the Southern District of New York.

5. Bannerman carried the case to the U.S. Superior Court of Appeals of the Second District, but that court sustained the verdict of the lower court on January 5, 1900. *Cf. Federal Reporter,* Vol. 99, first series, 294-298.

6. These improvements were covered by patents taken out by William Mason, T. G. Bennett, and T. C. Johnson.

7. Crossman, *op. cit.*

8. Paul B. Jenkins, "The Trench Gun of the A.E.F.," *The American Rifleman,* November 1935.

9. *Cf.* Julian W. Feiss, "Steel in Modern Firearms," *The American Rifleman,* May 1932.

10. The added strength in the breech was provided by ". . . a vertically moving block which covers the whole reach of the breech bolt. The firing pin is automatically retracted and the trigger locked until the parts are in firing position." T. C. Johnson, *History of the Repeating Gun and the Winchester Repeating Arms Company,* unpublished manuscript on file in archives of the Winchester Repeating Arms Company.

11. The barrel-drilling machinery was a carefully guarded secret of the Company for a number of years. Brewer recalled how T. G. Bennett was unwilling to have the Springfield Armory officials visit the plant because the latter would not guarantee that the information about the developmental work in barrel-drilling might not be passed on to competitors.

12. The effectiveness of the Winchester .30–30 cartridge as compared with the black-powder Winchester .44–40 and the black-powder Government .45–70–405 is shown in this ballistics table. "Mid-range trajectory" refers to the height of a bullet above a horizontal plane at a point midway between the muzzle of the gun and the target. (*Statistics from Winchester Repeating Arms Company Catalog,* 1909.)

| *Cartridge* | *Weight of bullet (grains)* | *Muzzle velocity (f.p.s.)* | *Energy at 50 feet (ft.-lbs.)* | *Mid-range trajectory 300 yards (inches)* |
|---|---|---|---|---|
| .44–40 WCF | 200 | 1300.6 | 688 | 37.39 |
| .45–70–405 Govt. | 405 | 1317.6 | 1486 | 29.00 |
| .30–30 WCF | 170 | 2008.3 | 1449 | 15.23 |

13. R. F. Chatfield-Taylor, "Rifles and Pistols in the Southwest," *The American Rifleman,* June 1934.

14. *Cf.* S. R. Truesdell, *The Rifle: Its Development for Big Game Hunting.* Truesdell has made careful analysis of the guns used by prominent big-game hunters from 1834 through 1946.

15. S. E. White, *Camp and Trail,* 68-69.

16. Sharpe, *op. cit.,* 245.

17. *Federal Reporter,* Vol. 97, Circuit Court of the Southern District of New York, 634-635.

18. U.S. Court of Claims, *Reports,* Vol. 51, 118-125.

19. Bennett did not let the criticism of the Company's ammunition go unchallenged. On August 6 he answered Browning on this point: "With regard to misfires in Winchester cartridges, would say that to the best of our belief, our primers are more regular than any other. We do not believe anybody pays so much attention to the testing

with known blow and after the primer is stuck in shell and loaded in the chamber than we do. Not only do we test extensively for sensitiveness after being stuck in the shell, but we also test for the heat developed. We do not believe anybody else has apparatus for this test. The primers used in the Climax shells are more sensitive than ours. We believe they are too sensitive. The primers made by the United States Cartridge Co. are generally more sensitive than ours. We believe these are too sensitive. Otherwise, there are none on the market more sensitive."

20. These were U.S. 659,507 (February 8, 1900), U.S. 689,283 (March 18, 1901), and U.S. 710,094 (January 11, 1902).

## CHAPTER FIFTEEN

1. For a description of these various models, see Sharpe, *op. cit.*, 308-318.
2. Letter, copy in Winchester Archives.
3. *Cf.* Saunders Norvell, *Forty Years of Hardware*, 385 *et seq.*, for a more complete description of this movement.
4. Corwin D. Edwards, *Maintaining Competition*, 66. The cases were *Dr. Miles Medical Company* v. *John B. Park and Sons*, 22 U.S. (1911) and *Bauer & Cie.* v. *O'Donnell*, 229 U.S. (1912).
5. *Cf.* New Haven *Journal-Courier*, April 28, 1930. Stetson left Winchester and entered Yale Medical School at the age of thirty-seven, graduating with the class of 1881. He began practicing in New Haven and became a distinguished physician. He died in 1930 at the age of eighty-four.
6. Ernie Pyle, *Home Country*, 380-382.
7. *Loc. cit.*
8. Buffalo Bill (Hon. W. F. Cody), *The Story of the Wild West and Camp Fire Chats*, 508. The subtitle of this work is *A Full and Complete History of the Renowned Pioneer Quartette: Boone, Crockett, Carson, and Buffalo Bill, Including a Discription of Buffalo Bill's Conquest of England.*

## CHAPTER SIXTEEN

1. *Hunting and Fishing*, September 1948.
2. This last must have been one of the English-made double-barrel shotguns imported by Winchester and sold during the 1880s.
3. Chapel, *op. cit.*, 41.

## CHAPTER SEVENTEEN

1. *Cf. Winchester Repeating Arms Company* v. *Peters Cartridge Company*, Circuit Court of the United States, Southern District of Ohio, Western Division, No. 4527.
2. Letter, American Buckle and Cartridge Company to Peters Cartridge Company, June 14, 1889; *Winchester Repeating Arms Company* v. *Peters Cartridge Company*, Circuit Court of the United States, Southern District of Ohio, Western Division, No. 4527, Defendant's Record, 164; testimony of Orrin E. Peters, President of Peters Cartridge Company, in *Winchester Repeating Arms Company* v. *Peters Cartridge Company, loc. cit.*
3. *Olin Security Company* v. *Commissioner of Internal Revenue*, U.S. Board of Tax Appeals Hearings, May 1939, Docket No. 80133; testimony of F. W. Olin, 38.

4. These were purchased, 12.75 per cent from U.S. Cartridge and 43.75 per cent each from Winchester and Union Metallic Cartridge; *ibid.*, 41.

5. *Cf.* "Important Letter," June 8, 1900, Simmons Hardware Company to salesmen.

6. Ammunition Manufacturers' Association, *Certificate of Extension of Corporate Existence*, September 24, 1903.

## CHAPTER EIGHTEEN

1. Mrs. William Wirt Winchester deposited 2,000 shares, keeping out the 777 which she had owned prior to the division of the trust set up by Oliver F. Winchester.

## CHAPTER NINETEEN

1. *Cf.* U.S. Senate, Seventy-Fourth Congress, Second Session, *Hearings on Resolution 5206* (*Seventy-Third Congress*), part 9, December 4 and 5, 1934.

2. Court of Claims of the United States, *Winchester Repeating Arms* v. *United States*, D 842, etc.; defendant's printed testimony, 2.

3. U.S. Senate Investigation of the War Department, *Hearings Before Committee on Military Affairs, Sixty-Fifth Congress, Second Session*, part 2, December 18-29, 1927, *passim*.

4. Court of Claims of the United States, *Winchester Repeating Arms* v. *United States*, D 843, etc.; defendant's printed testimony (Henry Brewer), 4.

5. Earl of Oxford and Asquith, *Memories and Reflections, 1852–1927*, 90. The Cabinet meeting at which this plan was disclosed took place on May 11, 1915.

6. This cancellation was closely tied with the cancellation of the Enfield contracts which occurred about the same time.

7. Colonel W. G. Lyddon, CMG, *British War Missions to the United States, 1914–1918*, 151.

8. U.S. Senate, *Munitions Industry Hearings Pursuant to Senate Resolution 206*, part 25, January 7–8, 1936, *World War Financing and Company*, exhibit 2091, page 7725 (hereafter referred to as *Senate Hearings, Resolution 206*).

9. *Ibid.*, exhibit 2098, page 7732.

10. *Ibid.*, exhibit 2105, page 7739.

11. *Loc. cit.*

12. *Ibid.*, exhibit 2113, page 7746.

13. *Ibid.*, exhibit 2119, page 7753.

14. In his book, *Time Studies as a Basis for Rate Setting*, Merrick acknowledges the "unparalleled opportunities afforded in the development of the time study and the introduction of author's methods of rate setting in the plant of the Winchester Repeating Arms Company, by the management of that plant" (page xiv).

15. Court of Claims of the United States, *Winchester Repeating Arms* v. *United States*, D 842, etc.; defendant's printed testimony, x4.

16. Court of Claims of the United States, *Winchester Repeating Arms* v. *United States, General Brief* (February 28, 1930), x125.

## CHAPTER TWENTY

1. Benedict Crowell and Robert F. Wilson, *The Armies of Industry;* Vol. I: *Our Nation's Manufacture of Munitions for a World in Arms, 1917–1918*, 230. The

foregoing account of the circumstances affecting the choice of the modified Enfield is drawn largely from this source.

2. *Ibid.*, 232.

3. *Loc. cit.*

4. Investigation of War Department, *Hearings, op. cit.*, 411-412.

5. Crowell and Wilson, *op. cit.*, 244-248.

6. The Navy contract, made as a result of a competitive bid, was an exception to the general position taken by the Company. *Cf.* Investigation of War Department, *Hearings, op. cit.*, 413.

7. *Ibid.*, 157.

8. In 1925 the Company brought suit in the U.S. Court of Claims for the payment by the Government of amounts sufficient to cover these items. In testimony brought out in this case it was stated that the intention of the contracts to allow the Company as a cost the difference between the cost of the special plant and equipment and its postwar value in the market for commercial plants of this description. The Company fought the Government on this issue until 1931, when its petition for a writ of *certiorari* was denied by the Supreme Court. The references to the Supreme Court decisions are: 52 S.Ct. 21; 284 United States 633; and 54 S.Ct. 47; 290 United States 628.

9. Court of Claims of the United States, *Winchester Repeating Arms* v. *United States*, D 844; plaintiff's exceptions to Commissioner's report, 145.

10. E. S. Bright to J. E. Otterson, September 24, 1917.

11. This was the committee of the House on Urgent Deficiency Appropriations, 1918. *Cf. Hearings* (July 17, 1917), 859 *et seq.*, and *Congressional Record* (September 15, 1917), 7865 *et seq.*

12. *Congressional Record* (September 16, 1917), 7869.

13. Crowell and Wilson, *op. cit.*, 234. This figure is confirmed by Otterson's testimony taken in 1925. *Cf.* Court of Claims *Hearings, op. cit.*, 152.

14. *Ibid.*, 206.

15. *Ibid.*, 207-208.

## CHAPTER TWENTY-TWO

1. Samuel Merwin, *Rise and Fight Again*, 62.

2. *Ibid.*, 89.

3. The Company's policy on this matter is explained by the following: "Under our dealer's arrangement it will be the dealer's obligation simply to give Winchester preference and to meet demands in his territory for goods of the character that Winchester produces. It is also his obligation to do what he can to stimulate that demand, and it is our obligation to stimulate it ourselves. We do not desire a dealer to come into this who thinks we are proposing a plan which means substitution. If, for example, a man comes into your store and asks for a Disston Saw, and wants a Disston Saw, we hope you will sell him a Disston saw even though you have Winchester saws on your shelves also. If he comes into your store and asks for a saw, then it would be your obligation to sell him a Winchester saw and we believe you will find it to your interest to sell him a Winchester saw, but we do not wish to substitute Winchester when the demand is for something else. We want to make this clear because it is to become part of our policy. We are not entering any destructive campaign whatever."

4. The number of retail hardware stores in the United States for 1919 is not available. In 1930 the Census reported some 25,330 such stores in operation during 1929. The number ten years earlier probably did not exceed this figure by any large amount. (*Fifteenth Census of the United States, Distribution*, Vol. I, Part 1, 49 *et seq.*)

5. W. E. Freeland, "The Winchester Plan of Management," *Iron Age,* January 3, 1918.

6. *Ibid.,* 129.

## CHAPTER TWENTY-THREE

1. *Hardware Age,* October 16, 1919.

## CHAPTER TWENTY-FIVE

1. Saunders Norvell, in his *Forty Years of Hardware,* says, ". . . They were active youngsters and worked hard (during vacations), but I have often wondered if it ever occurred to them that it was somewhat unusual for so many boxes to unexpectedly fall on their heads."

## CHAPTER TWENTY-SIX

1. Factory manager's report to J. E. Otterson, May 2, 1923, quoted in Arthur Young & Company, *Report on Inter-Company Transfer and Relations, 1922–23,* schedule 7, page 3.

## CHAPTER TWENTY-SEVEN

1. *Journal of Commerce,* August 5, 1931.

## CHAPTER TWENTY-EIGHT

1. Maurice Dobb, *Capitalist Enterprise and Social Progress,* 33.

## EPILOGUE

1. In charge of Winchester firearms research, 1932-1950; Vice President, Winchester Repeating Arms Company, 1932-1938; Assistant Secretary, Western Cartridge Company, 1939-1944, and of Olin Industries, Inc., 1944-1952; Director, Western Cartridge Company, 1941-1944, and Olin Industries, Inc., 1944-1952.

2. Winchester was operated as a Maryland corporation until December 31, 1938, when its corporate identity was discontinued, and the name was changed to Winchester Repeating Arms Company, Division of Western Cartridge Company. This arrangement was continued until December 30, 1944, when Winchester became a division of Olin Industries, Inc. The latter change was at the time of the merger of Olin Corporation into Western Cartridge Company as of December 31, 1944, and the change of Western's corporate name to Olin Industries, Inc., as of that date. In January 1952, the arms and ammunition operations of the Winchester plant were joined with the Western ammunition operations of the Olin East Alton plant, as the Arms and Ammunition Division of Olin Industries, Inc.

# BIBLIOGRAPHY

Until the end of 1931, the bulk of Winchester's records no longer needed for current operation were transferred to dead storage in a large basement. In some instances department heads and individuals kept a selected number of historical records pertaining to their own activities in desks and various safes scattered throughout the plant. Under the blanket order issued in 1932 not to preserve material longer than seven years, the records in dead storage were destroyed. Fortunately, the order did not apply generally to records which had not been transferred, and these were made available for the preparation of the history of the Company. Because the need for historical data varied widely among departments and individuals, rather little of the preserved material covers any long-time periods. Detailed information was available for some topics for short periods; in other instances the record was a complete blank. Wherever possible these gaps were filled by reference to other sources.

Unless otherwise noted, all statistical material and statements pertaining to the history of the Company have been drawn from Company records. No attempt has been made to footnote these sources, as most of the records have been returned to the departments or individuals from whom they were borrowed and are not generally accessible.

The list of archive materials in the bibliography do not include the many hundred individual items which were consulted. The materials indicated are typical of the kinds of documents which provided useful information and may give a clue to sources available in the records of other business concerns.

## I. PRIMARY SOURCES

### 1. ARCHIVE RECORDS

#### MANUSCRIPTS

Brewer, Henry, *Historical Notes.* Based on personal observation by an official, this covers a variety of topics in the history of the Company.

Earle, A. W., *The Ammunition Manufacturers' Association.* A general account based on personal observation.

Hubbard, Guy, *The Beginning of Smith and Wesson and Winchester.* An account of the early history of the Volcanic Repeating Arms Company.

Johnson, Thomas C., *History of the Repeating Gun and Winchester Repeating Arms Company.* Covers the technical development of the Company's guns down through 1908, including production data for individual models.

Veader, D. H., and Earle, A. W., *The Story of the Winchester Repeating Arms Company.* By two long-time officers of the Company, this deals largely with financial and corporate history.

BOUND VOLUMES, COMPLETE SETS

Catalogs, New Haven Arms Company, 1863, 1865.

Catalogs, Winchester Repeating Arms Company, 1867–1931.

Minute books, Winchester Repeating Arms Company: Directors, Stockholders, and Financial Statements, 1867-1931.

Minute Books, The Winchester Company: Directors, Stockholders, and Financial Statements, 1919–1931.

Minute Books, Winchester-Simmons: Directors, Stockholders, and Financial Statements, 1922–1929.

Stock transfer books, Winchester Repeating Arms Company.

Stock transfer books, The Winchester Company.

Stock transfer books, Winchester-Simmons.

Patent records: copies of all patents owned by the Winchester Repeating Arms Company, 1848–1931.

*Winchester Herald,* Volumes I-VII (1921–1927).

*Winchester Record,* Volumes I-III (1918–1920).

BOUND VOLUMES, BROKEN SETS

Cartridge Arbitration Hearings, Sessions 28-57, 1880–1882.

Circular Letter Book. Letters to salesmen and customers, 1888–1918.

Contract record books, 1881–1904.

Discount sheets, guns, ammunition shot shells, 1898–1919.

*Foreign Contract Book,* 1883–1895.

Labor book-payroll records of contract workers, 1876–1904.

Labor records, Volcanic Repeating Arms Company and New Haven Arms Company, 1856–1867.

Letter book, New Haven Arms Company, 1857–1862.

LOOSE RECORDS AND MISCELLANEOUS PAPERS

File boxes, containing documents relating to lawsuits and patent appeals.

Files (about 40 filing cases), records of Winchester Repeating Arms Company production, contracts, etc., during World War I.

OUTLINE OF THE WINCHESTER PLAN, 1919

Papers relating to organization of: Volcanic Repeating Arms Company; New Haven Arms Company; Winchester Repeating Arms Company; Winchester Repeating Arms Company subsidiaries; The Winchester Company; Winchester-Simmons; Winchester Repeating Arms Company (Delaware).

PROCEEDINGS OF NATIONAL ASSOCIATION OF WINCHESTER CLUBS, 1920

REPORTS TO INVESTIGATING COMMITTEE, 1922

Reports of public accounts (Arthur Young & Company), 1914–1931.

SURVEY OF HARDWARE DISTRIBUTION, 1919

## 2. WINCHESTER REPEATING ARMS COMPANY (SPECIAL STUDIES, NOT FOR OUTSIDE CIRCULATION)

Watrous, George, *Sale of Winchester Arms, 1904–1944.*

——. *Standardization and Simplification of Paper Shot Shells.*

——. *Winchester Ammunition.* A listing and description of Winchester metallic ammunition and shot shells.

——. *Winchester Rifles and Shotguns.* A complete listing and description of the Company's firearms.

## 3. COURT RECORDS


PROCEEDINGS

*Christopher Oscanyan* v. *W.R.A.Co.*, depositions taken Taylor, Douglas, Prentice, New York, 1877.

*Christopher Oscanyan* v. *W.R.A.Co.*, records of U.S. Circuit Court, Southern District of N.Y., Law Docket, Vol. 4, 1874–1881. U.S. National Archives.

*Christopher Oscanyan* v. *W.R.A.Co.*, Federal Cases, Circuit and District Courts, 1874–1880. Case No. 10,600.

*Winchester* v. *American Buckle and Cartridge Company*, Docket files of 1877 at Circuit Court Office in New Haven. Case No. 630.

——. Case No. 676.

——. Case No. 677.

——. Case No. 678.

*Winchester* v. *Marlin Fire Arms*, docket files of 1878 at Circuit Court office in New Haven. Case No. 458.

*Bannerman* v. *Sanford*, 99 C.C.A. 2, 294-298.

——. 85 C.C., 448-449.

DECISIONS

*Winchester Repeating Arms Co.* v. *U.S.*, 51 Ct.Cl. 118.

——. 60 Ct.Cl. 815.

——. 270 U.S. 611.

——. 284 U.S. 633.

——. 290 U.S. 628.

*Winchester Manufacturing Company* v. *U.S.*, 72 Ct.Cl. 106.

GOVERNMENT DOCUMENTS AND REPORTS

Great Britain. Committee on Machinery in the United States, *Report 32*. Parliamentary Papers. 1854–1855. L.

——. War Office. *Reports on Breech-Loading Arms by a Special sub-committee of the Ordnance Select Committee*. London 1868.

United States. Board of Ordnance, *Officers' Report, Ordnance Memorandum 15, The Proper Calibre for Small Arms*, 1873.

——. Bureau of the Census, *Biennial Census of Manufacture*, 1921–1931.

——. Bureau of the Census, *Census of Manufacturers*, 1899, 1904, 1914, 1919.

——. Bureau of the Census, *Decennial Reports, Manufacturers, or Industry and Wealth*, 1850–1930.

——. Bureau of the Census, *Fifteenth Census (1930)*. Distribution, Vols. I-II.

——. *Federal Census of Manufacturers Enumerators' Reports for Hartford, Middlesex, and New Haven Counties, Conn. 1850, 1860, and 1870.*

——. *Hearings Before the Select Committee on Expenditures in the War Department*, House of Representatives, 66th Congress, *War Expenditures*, Serial 1, Part 9 (1919).

——. Senate, 65th Congress, 2d Session, Committee on Military Affairs, Investigation of War Department *Hearings*, Part 2.

——. Senate, 74th Congress, 2d Session, *Hearings on Resolution 5206 (73d Congress)*, part 9.

——. Senate, 74th Congress, 2d Session, *Munitions Hearings Pursuant to Resolution 206*, part 25.

——. United States Council on National Defense, *Readjustment and Reconstructive Information*, part II (1919).

——. War Department, *Annual Reports of Chief of Ordnance to Secretary of War*, 1872–1931.

## II. SECONDARY SOURCES

### 1. PERIODICALS

Anonymous. "American Arms and Ammunition," *Scribner's Monthly*, Vol. 19, (1880).

Chapel, Charles Edward. "The Guns of Teddy Roosevelt," *Hunting and Fishing*, Vol. 25, No. 9 (September 1948).

Chatfield-Taylor, R. F. "Rifles and Pistols of the Southwest," *The American Rifleman*, Vol. 82, No. 6 (June 1934).

Crossman, Captain E. C. "With Captain Crossman at the Big Winchester Factories," *The Sporting Goods Dealer*, January 1920.

Feiss, Julian W. "Steel in Modern Firearms," *The American Rifleman*, Vol. 80, No. 5 (May 1932).

Freeland, W. E. "The Winchester Plan of Management," *Iron Age*, Vol. 150 (1918).

Goddard, Lt. Col. Calvin. "An American Heritage," Part II, *Army Ordnance*, Vol. 18, No. 108 (May-June 1938).

Jenkins, Paul B. "Old Reliable," *The American Rifleman*, Vol. 79, No. 12 (December 1931).

——. "The Trench Gun of the A.E.F.," *The American Rifleman*, Vol. 83, No. 11 (November 1935).

——. "Spirit Guns: A True Story of the First American Repeating Rifles and Their Use in a Fight on the Western Frontier," *The American Rifleman*, Vol. 77, No. 2 (February 1929).

——. "Wild Life of Yesterday, and the First Successful Repeating Shotgun," *The American Rifleman*, Vol. 83, No. 10 (October 1935).

Pease, Harlow. "The Kentucky at the Plain of Chalmette," *The American Rifleman*, Vol. 88, No. 12 (December 1937).

Roberts, N. H. "The Rifles of Yesterday," *The American Rifleman*, Vol. 83, No. 4 (April 1935).

Stevens, William S. "The Powder Trust, 1872–1912," *Quarterly Journal of Economics*, Vol. 26 (1911–1912).

Satterlee, L. D. "The Model 1866 Winchester," *The American Rifleman*, Vol. 62, No. 14 (December 15, 1924).

——. "The Spencer Repeating Rifle," Part II, *The American Rifleman*, Vol. 73, No. 24 (May 1926).

Simmons, George W. "The Winchester Plan," *Hardware Age*, Vol. 105, No. 8 (February 1920).

Soule, Roy F. "Winchester Chain Stores Promise Fireworks," *Hardware Age*, Vol. 104, No. 21 (December 1919).

——. "The Manufacturers' Side of the Winchester Plan," *Hardware Age*, Vol. 104, No. 22 (December 1919).

——. "The Wholesalers' Side of the Winchester Plan," *Hardware Age*, Vol. 105, No. 1 (January 1920).

——. "The Retailers' Side of the Winchester Plan," *Hardware Age*, Vol. 105, No. 2 (January 1920).

Tryon, T. B. "The Percussion Plains Rifle," *The American Rifleman*, Vol. 84, No. 11 (November 1936).

2. BOOKS

Anonymous. *Marcellus Hartley: A Brief Memoir.* New York: privately printed, 1903.

Askins, Charles. *Modern Shotguns and Loads.* Marshallton, Delaware: Small Arms Technical Publishing Company, 1929.

Atwater, Edward E. *History of New Haven to the Present Time.* New York: W. W. Munsell & Company, 1887.

Blackford, Charles Minor (Blackford, Susan Leigh, ed.). *Letters From Lee's Army.* New York: Charles Scribner's Sons, 1947.

Browning, J. M., and Browning, M. S. *A History of Browning Guns From 1831.* Ogden, Utah: J. M. & M. S. Browning Company, 1942.

Cole, J. R. *History of Tolland County.* W. W. Preston Company, 1898.

Crowell, Benedict, and Wilson, Robert F. *How America Went to War;* Vol. I, *The Armies of Industry.* New Haven: Yale University Press, 1921.

Chinn, George Morgan, Jr., and Hardin, Bayless Evans. *Encyclopedia of American Hand Arms.* Huntington, West Virginia: Standard Printing and Publishing Company, 1942.

Clarkson, Grosvenor B. *Industrial America in the World War.* Boston: Houghton Mifflin Company, 1923.

Cleveland, H. W. S. *Hints to Riflemen.* New York: D. Appleton & Company, 1864.

Cody, W. F. (Buffalo Bill). *The Story of the Wild West and Camp Fire Chats.* Richmond: B. F. Johnson & Company, 1888.

Deyrup, Felicia. *Arms Makers of the Connecticut Valley.* (Smith College Studies in History, Vol. 33.) Menasha, Wisconsin: George Banta Publishing Company, 1948.

Dillin, John G. W. *The Kentucky Rifle.* Washington: National Rifle Association, 1924.

Dobb, Maurice. *Capitalist Enterprise and Social Progress.* London: George Rutledge & Sons, 1926.

Dwight, Henry O. *Turkish Life in War Time.* New York: Charles Scribner's Sons, 1881.

Earl of Oxford and Asquith. *Memories and Reflections, 1852–1927.* Boston: Little, Brown & Company, 1928.

Edwards, Corwin D. *Maintaining Competition.* New York: McGraw-Hill Book Company, 1949.

Fitch, Charles H. *Report on Manufacturing of Interchangeable Mechanisms.* (Extra Census Bulletin.) Washington: Government Printing Office, 1883.

Fuller, Claud E. *The Breech-Loader in the Service.* New York: Arms Reference Club of America, 1933.

——, and Steuart, Richard D. *Firearms of the Confederacy.* Huntington, West Virginia, Standard Publications, Inc., 1944.

"Gloan" (pseudonym). *Breech-Loaders.* New York: Orange Judd & Company, 1873.

Gould, A. C. *Modern American Rifles.* Boston: Bradlee Whidden, 1892.

Greener, W. W. *The Gun and Its Development,* 9th ed. New York: Cassell & Company, Ltd., 1910.

Grey, Zane, and Wetmore, H. C. *The Last of the Great Scouts.* New York: Grosset & Dunlap, 1913.

Hotchkiss, Mrs. Fanny Winchester. *Winchester Notes.* New Haven: The Tuttle, Morehouse, and Taylor Company, 1912.

Hunt, Frazier, and Hunt, Robert. *I Fought With Custer: The Story of Sergeant*

*Windolph, Last Survivor of the Little Big Horn.* New York: Charles Scribner's Sons, 1947.

Johnson, Melvin M., Jr., and Haven, Charles T. *Automatic Arms.* New York: William Morrow & Company, 1941.

Karr, Charles Lee, Jr., and Karr, Carroll Robbins. *Remington Handguns,* Harrisburg, Pennsylvania: Military Service Publishing Company, 1947.

Kouwenhoven, John A. *Made in America: The Arts and Modern Civilization.* New York: Doubleday & Company, 1948.

Lyddon, Colonel W. G. *British War Missions to the United States, 1914–1918.* London: Oxford University Press, 1938.

Maurice, Major Frederick Barton. *The Russo-Turkish War of 1877.* London: Swan, Sonnenschein & Company, Ltd., 1905.

Merrick, Dwight V. *Time Studies as a Basis for Rate Setting.* New York: The Engineering Magazine Company, 1919.

Merwin, Samuel A. *Rise and Fight Again.* New York: Albert & Charles Boni, Inc., 1935.

Mulford, Clarence E. *Hopalong Cassidy.* New York: A. C. McClurg & Company, 1910.

Norman, C. B. *Armenia and the Campaign of 1877.* London: Cossell, Petter, and Golpin, 1878.

Norton, Charles B. *American Inventions and Improvements in Breech Loading Small Arms. . . .* Springfield, Massachusetts: Chapin & Gould, 1880.

Norvell, Saunders. *Forty Years of Hardware.* New York: Hardware Age, 1924.

Osborn, Norris Galpin, ed. *History of Connecticut,* Vol. IV. New York: The States History Company, 1925.

Pyle, Ernie (Ernest Taylor). *Home Country.* New York: William Sloane Associates, Inc., 1947.

Roe, Joseph Wickham. *English and American Tool Builders.* New Haven: Yale University Press, 1916.

Roosevelt, Theodore. *African Game Trails.* New York: Charles Scribner's Sons, 1920.

——. *Hunting Trips of a Ranchman.* New York: G. P. Putnam's Sons, 1885.

——, and Grinnell, George Bird. *Hunting in Many Lands.* New York: Forest and Stream Publishing Company, 1895.

Satterlee, L. D. *Catalogue of Firearms for the Collector,* 2d ed. Detroit: privately printed, 1939.

Sawyer, Charles Winthrop. *Our Rifles,* Vol. III. Boston: The Cornhill Company, 1920.

Sharpe, Philip B. *The Rifle in America.* New York: Funk & Wagnalls Company, 1947.

Shields, G. O. (ed.). *The Big Game of North America.* Chicago: Rand, McNally & Company, 1890.

Smith, Winston O. *The Sharps Rifle.* New York: William Morrow & Company, 1943.

Stockbridge, V. D. *Digest of Patents Relating to Breech-Loading and Magazine Small Arms (Except Revolvers) Granted in United States from 1836 to 1873 Inclusive.* Washington: Government Printing Office, 1875.

Thorp, Willard L., and Mitchell, Wesley C. *Business Annuals.* New York: National Bureau of Economic Research, Inc., 1926.

Truesdell, S. R. *The Rifle: Its Development for Big Game Hunting.* Harrisburg, Pennsylvania: Military Service Publishing Company, 1947.

Walsh, Richard J. *The Making of Buffalo Bill: A Study in Heroics.* Indianapolis: The Bobbs-Merrill Company, 1928.

Whelen, Townsend. *The American Rifle.* New York: The Century Company, 1918.

——. *Small Arms Design and Ballistics.* Plantersville, South Carolina: Small Arms Technical Publishing Company, 1945.

White, Stewart Edward. *Camp and Trail.* New York: Doubleday, Page & Company, 1913.

Wilson, Neill C. *Treasure Express: Epic Days of the Wells Fargo.* New York: The Macmillan Company, 1936.

Wright, William H. *The Grizzly Bear.* London: T. Werner Laurie, Cliffords Inn, 1909.

# APPENDIXES

## DETAILED CONTENTS OF APPENDIXES

# APPENDIX A-1

## FORERUNNERS OF THE TRUE WINCHESTER

*By Thomas E. Hall and John Peck*

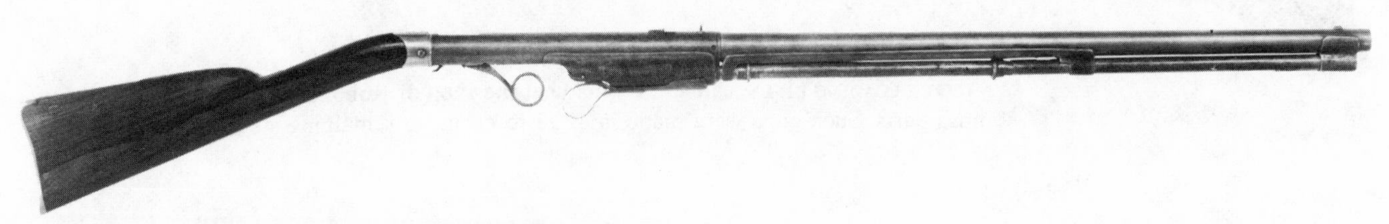

HUNT REPEATING RIFLE, caliber .54. Patent model 1849.

HUNT CARTRIDGE. Patented, 1848. Used in Jennings breech loading rifles, 1850 to 1852.

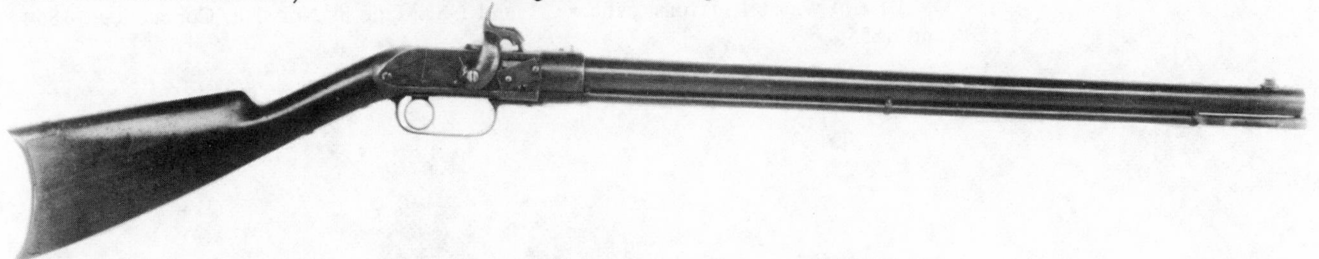

JENNINGS BREECH LOADING RIFLE, caliber .54. Made as single shot, 1850 and 1851. Manufactured by Robbins and Lawrence of Windsor, Vermont.

JENNINGS REPEATING RIFLE, caliber .54, manufactured 1851 and 1852.

> In establishing the dates given in connection with the illustrations in Appendix A, the first and last listings in Winchester catalogues have been given wherever possible. Those calibers marked with an asterisk have been discontinued although the model may still be in the line.

MUZZLE LOADING RIFLE, caliber .54, made at the shop of Robbins and Lawrence from Jennings parts. Such guns were made in 1852 to clean up remaining stock.

SMITH AND WESSON PISTOLS, caliber .31 and .38. Made at Norwich, Connecticut, 1854 and 1855.

CARTRIDGE for above pistols, caliber .38.

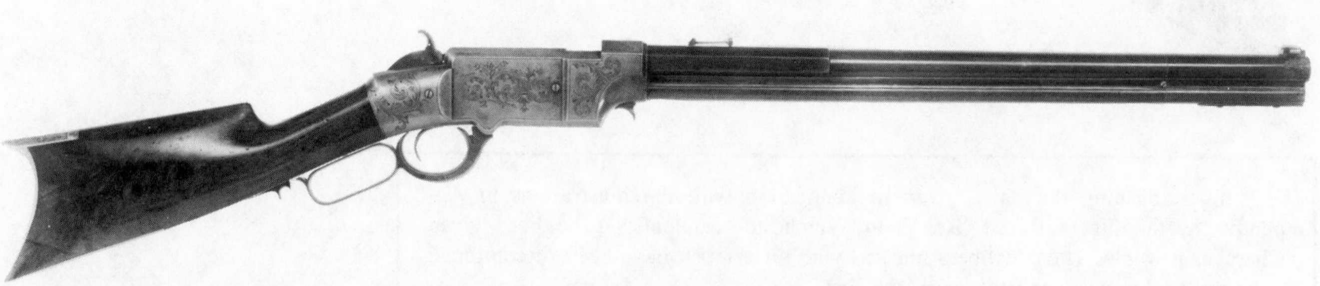

SMITH AND WESSON EXPERIMENTAL RIFLE made at Norwich, Connecticut, in 1854 or 1855. This rifle is chambered for a .50 caliber rimfire cartridge.

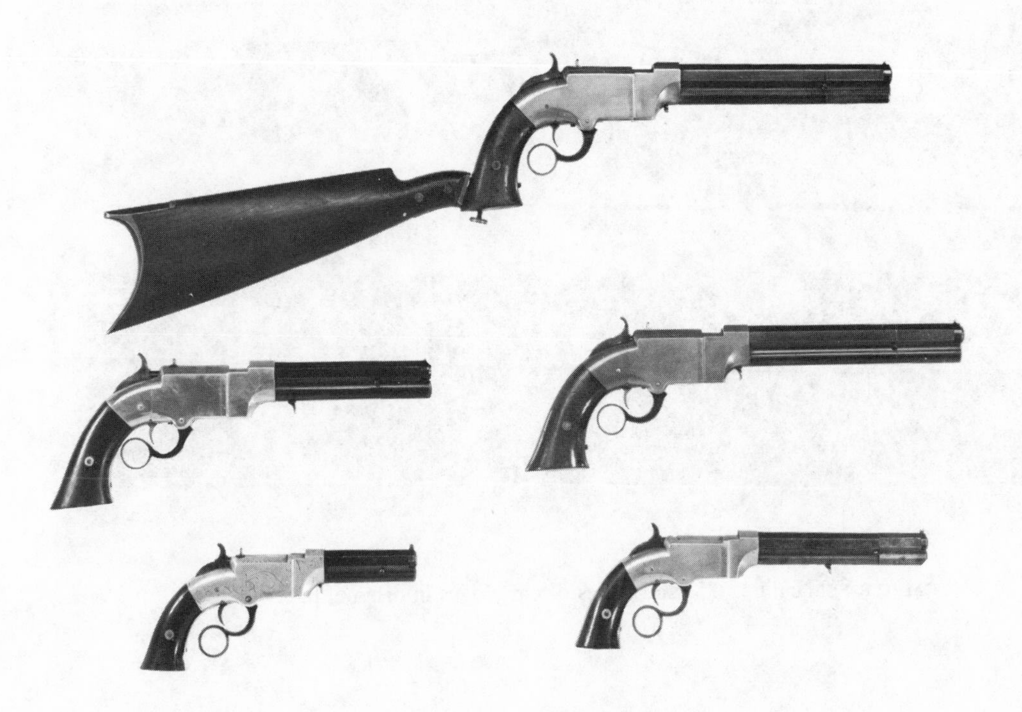

VOLCANIC PISTOLS, caliber .31 and .38. Made by the Volcanic Repeating Arms Company and the New Haven Arms Company, 1856 to 1860.

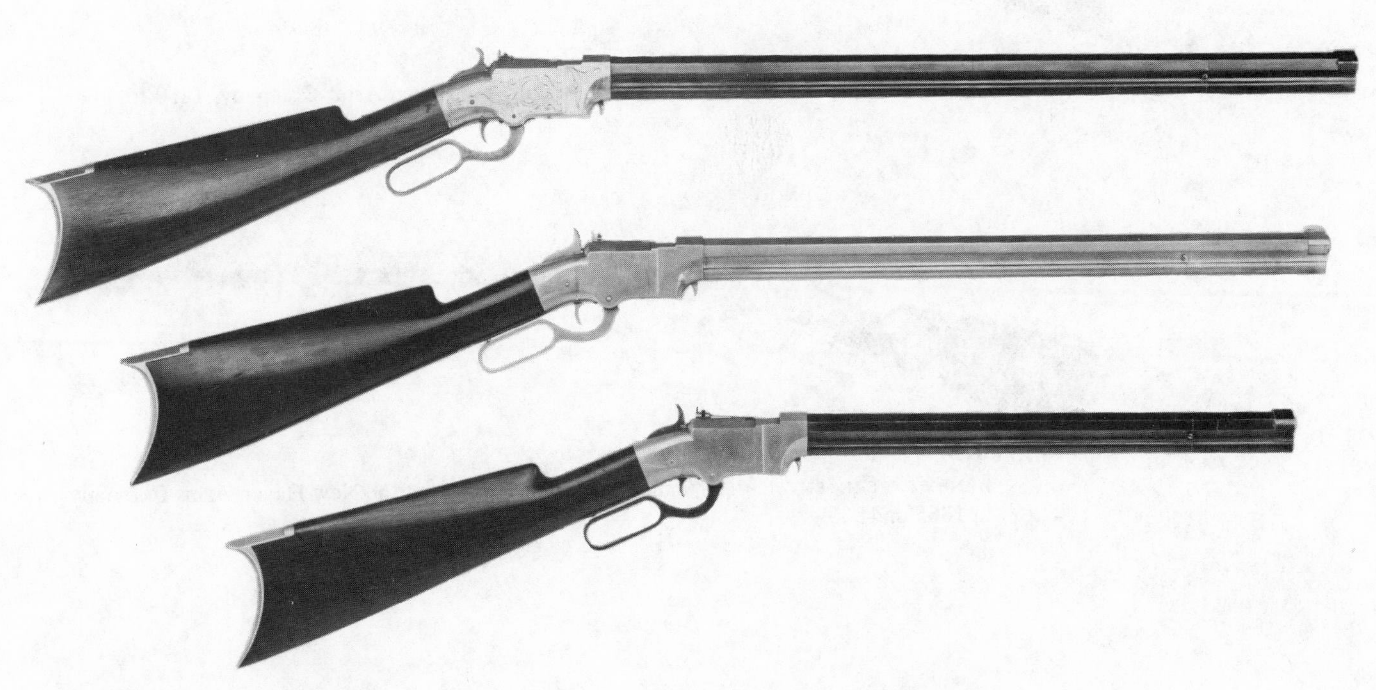

VOLCANIC RIFLES, caliber .38. Made by the Volcanic Repeating Arms Company and the New Haven Arms Company, 1856 to 1860.

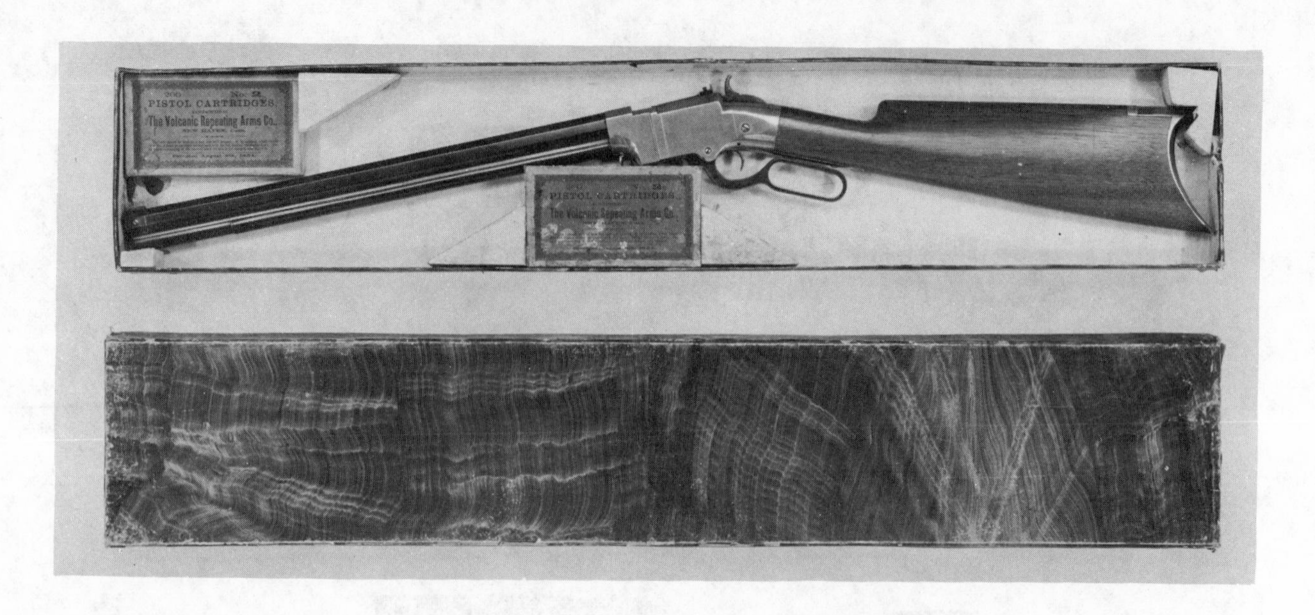


VOLCANIC RIFLE, caliber .38, and boxes of cartridges in original packing box.

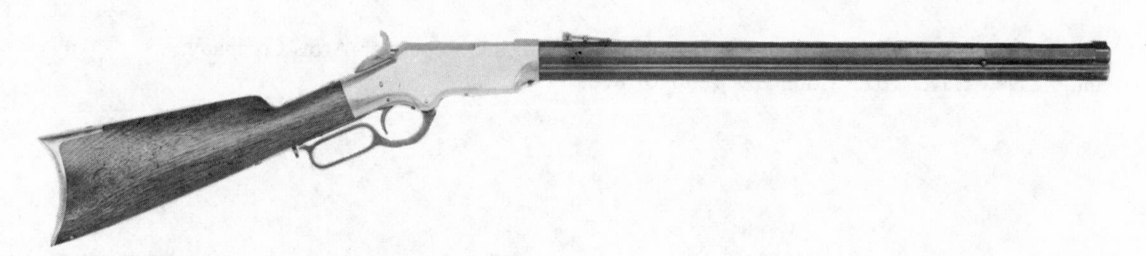

HENRY RIFLE, caliber .44 rimfire. Made by the New Haven Arms Company, 1860 to1866.

HENRY EXPERIMENTAL RIFLE, caliber .44 rimfire. Made at the New Haven Arms Company in 1865 or 1866.

# APPENDIX A-2

## LIST OF ALL MODELS MANUFACTURED BY THE WINCHESTER REPEATING ARMS COMPANY

*By Thomas E. Hall and John Peck*

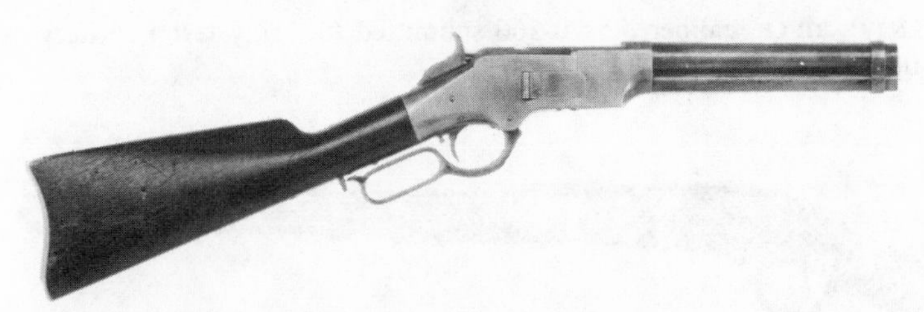

ORIGINAL PATENT MODEL with King's improvement, 1866. (Loading gate in side of receiver).

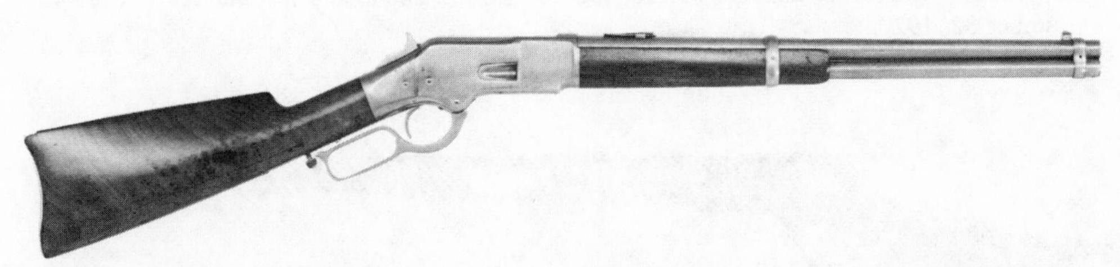

MODEL 1866 CARBINE, caliber .44 rimfire. Listed in catalogues 1873 to catalogue number 61 dated March 1898. Was left out of catalogues dated 1875 and 1876, but reappeared in 1878. The model 1866 Winchester had been made since 1867, but was not so called in catalogues until 1873.

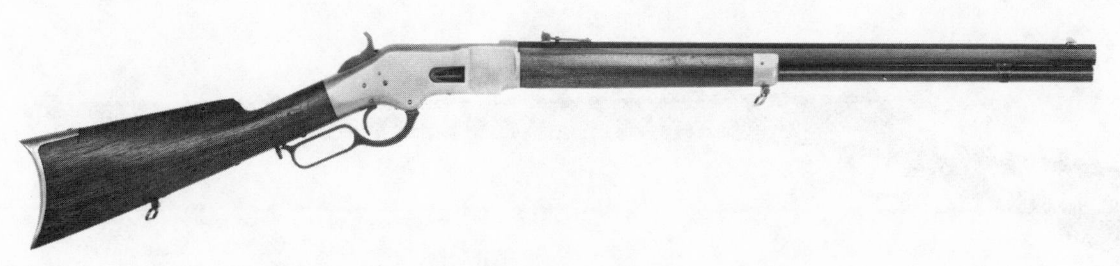

MODEL 1866 RIFLE, caliber .44 rimfire. Same listing as above.

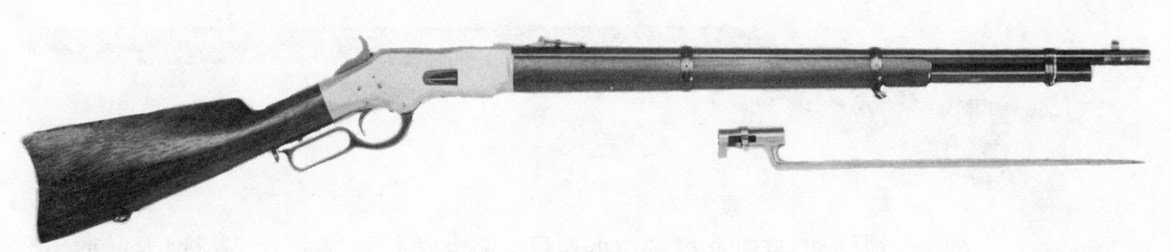

MODEL 1866 MUSKET, caliber .44 rimfire. Same listing as above.

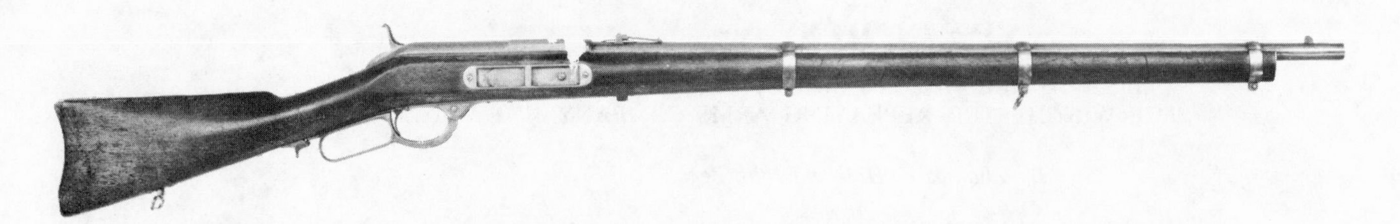

WINCHESTER EXPERIMENTAL RIFLE, caliber .45-70-360 submitted to Army test February 1873. Magazine held 10 rounds.

MODEL 1873 CARBINE, calibers .44-40, .38-40 and .32-20. Listed in catalogues 1875 to number 82, 1920.

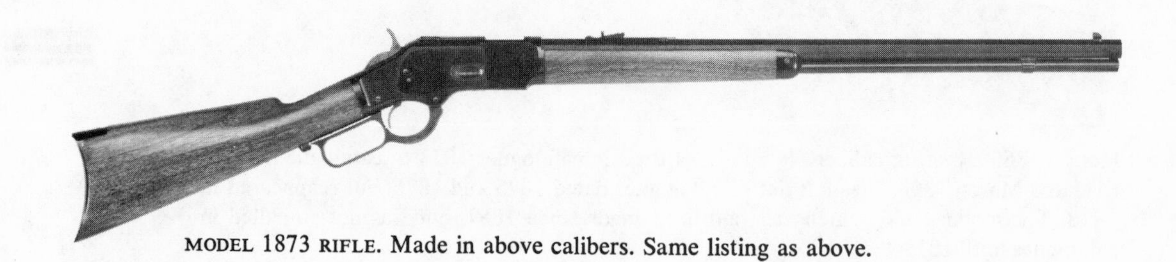

MODEL 1873 RIFLE. Made in above calibers. Same listing as above.

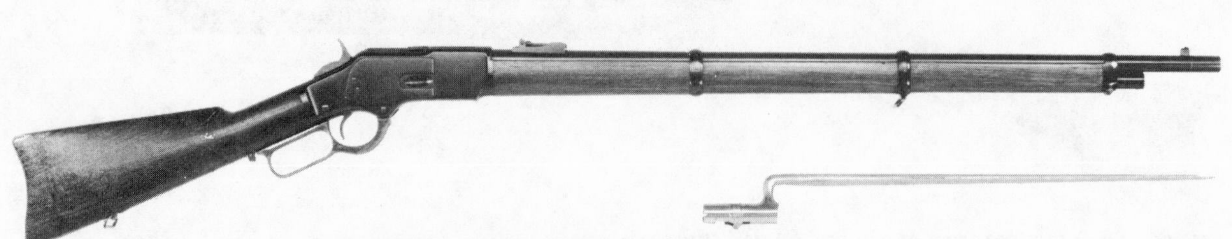

MODEL 1873 MUSKET with angular bayonet. Also made for saber bayonet. Listed in .44-40 only. Listed in catalogues 1875 to number 80, 1916.

MODEL 1873 RIFLE, caliber .22 rimfire. Chambered for .22 short or .22 long (not interchangeable). Listed in catalogues September 1884 to number 71, 1904.

MODEL 1873 CARBINE, caliber .44-40. Spanish contract. Guns shipped from plant in 1878 and 1879.

MODEL 1876 CARBINE, calibers .45-75, .45-60 and .40-60. Listed in catalogues 1878 to December 1892.

MODEL 1876 RIFLE, calibers .45-75, .45-60, .40-60 and .50-95 Express. Listed in catalogues 1878 to October 1893.

MODEL 1876 RIFLE, half magazine. Made in above calibers. Same listing as above.

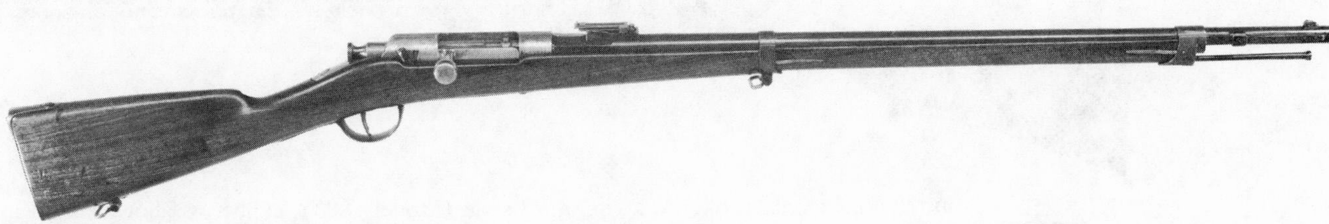

HOTCHKISS, FRENCH MODEL. Forerunner of Winchester-Hotchkiss.

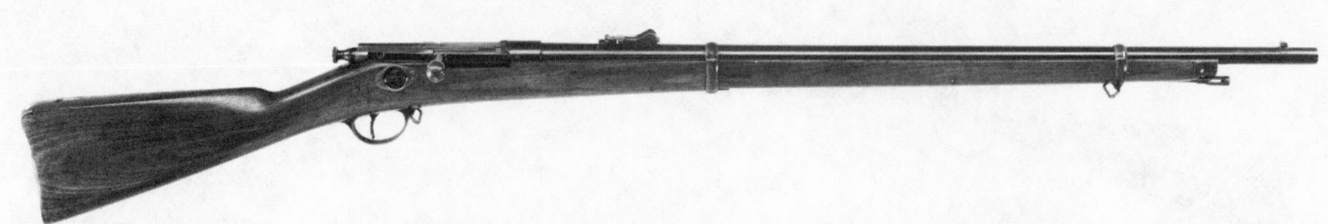

HOTCHKISS MUSKET, first style, caliber .45-70-405 United States Government. Listed in 1880 to May, 1881 catalogues.

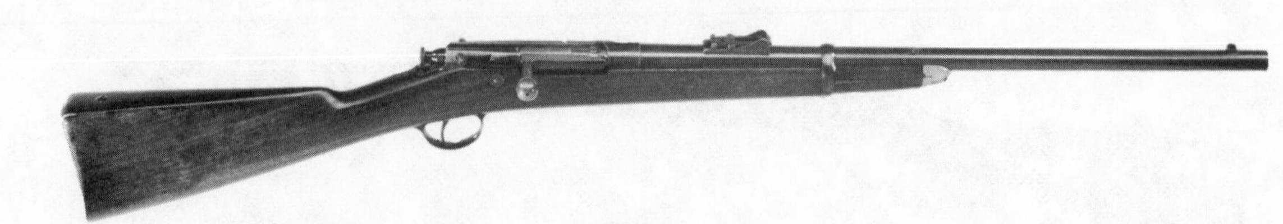

HOTCHKISS CARBINE, second style, caliber same as above. Listed in catalogues April 1882 to June 1883.

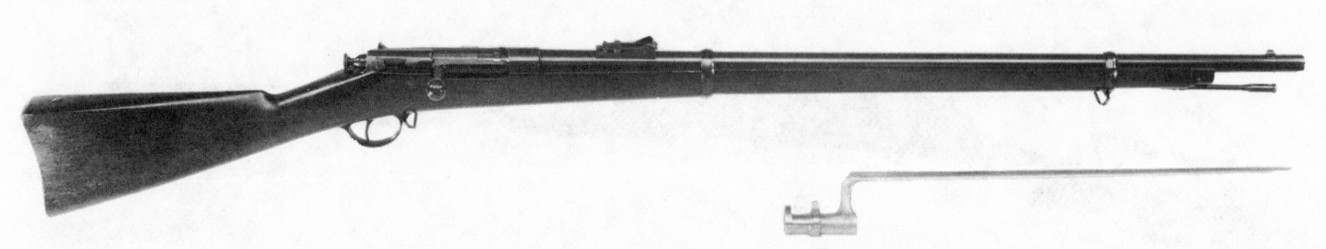

HOTCHKISS MUSKET, second style, caliber and listing same as above.

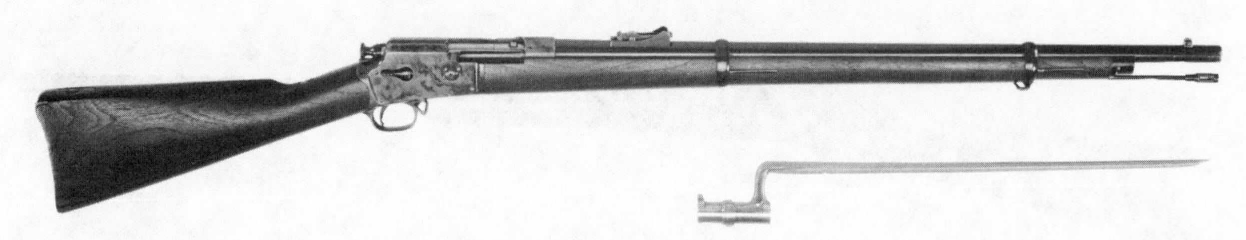

HOTCHKISS MUSKET, third style (Model 1883), caliber same as above. Listed in catalogues January 1884 to June 1902.

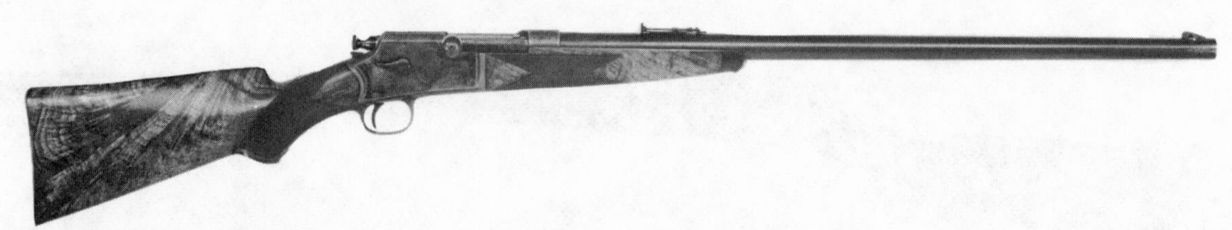

HOTCHKISS FANCY SPORTING RIFLE, third style (Model 1883), caliber as above. Listed in catalogues January 1884 to February, 1890.

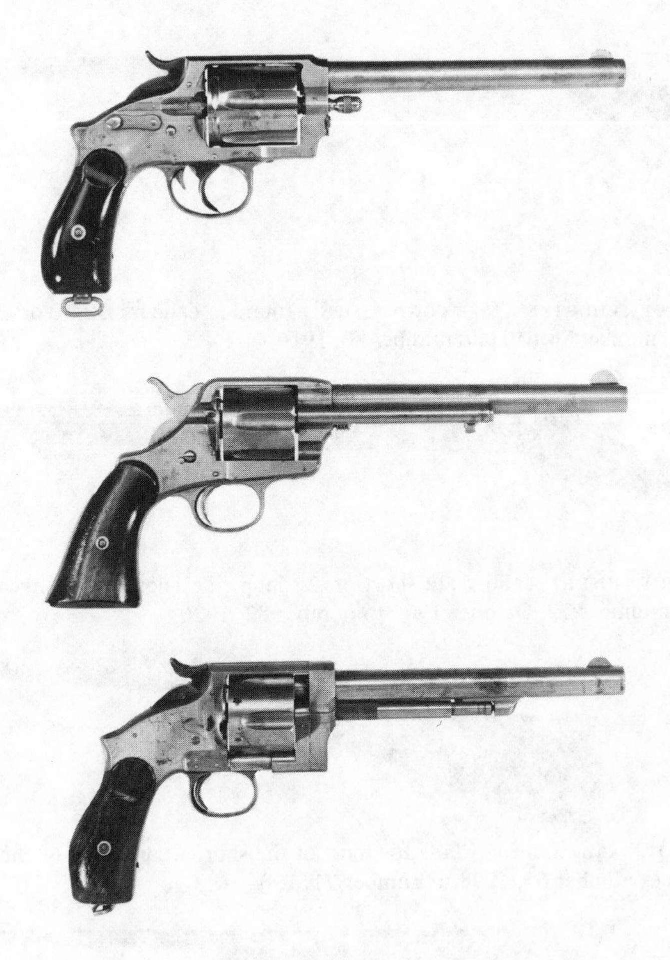

WINCHESTER EXPERIMENTAL REVOLVERS. Top and center made in 1884, bottom in 1876.

SINGLE SHOT RIFLE, patented by John Browning, manufactured by Browning Brothers, Ogden, Utah. Forerunner of Winchester Single Shot.

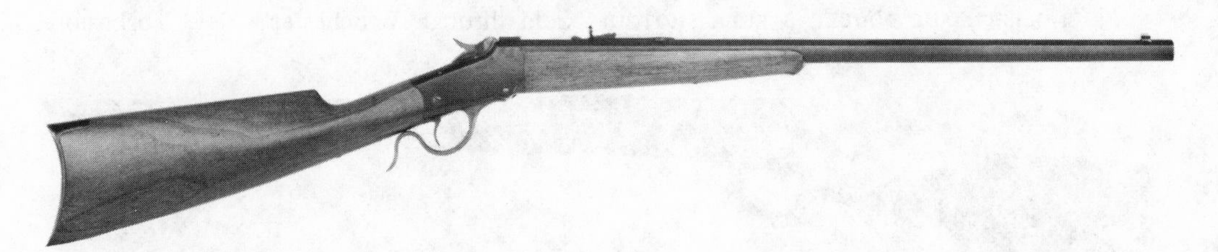

WINCHESTER SINGLE SHOT RIFLE, Model 1885. Barrel size number 1. Made in all desirable calibers of the time from .22 to .50. Listed in catalogues November 1885 to number 81, 1919.

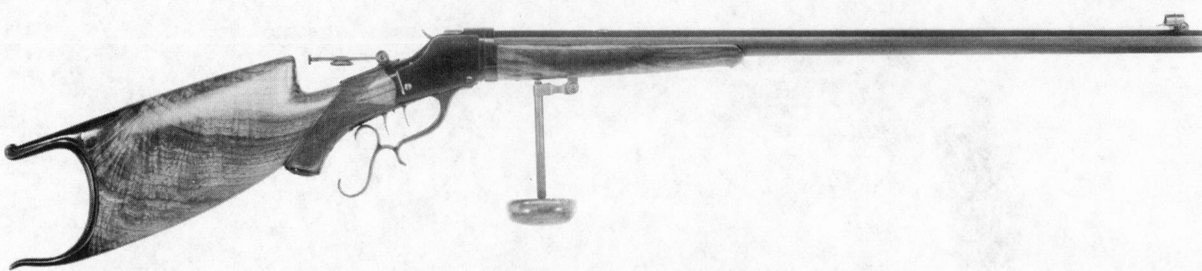

SINGLE SHOT, SCHUETZEN, take down. Usually found in calibers .32-40 or .38-55. Listed in catalogues number 76, 1910 to number 80, 1916.

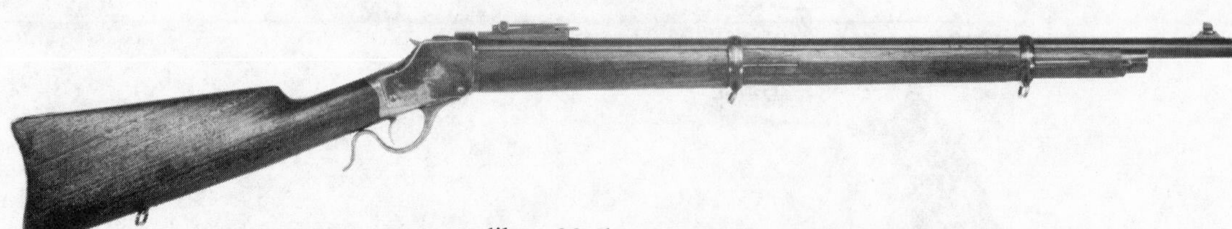

SINGLE SHOT MUSKET, caliber .22 short or .22 long rifle (not interchangeable). Listed in catalogues number 72, October 1905 to number 82, 1920.

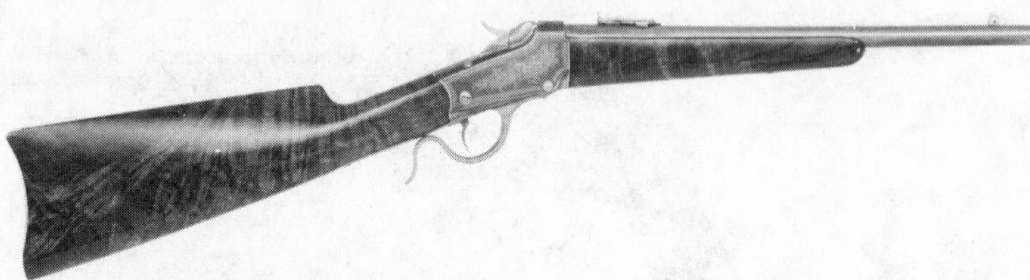

SINGLE SHOT, BABY CARBINE. Made for most of the shorter cartridges of the period. Listed in catalogues number 61, 1898 to number 71, 1904.

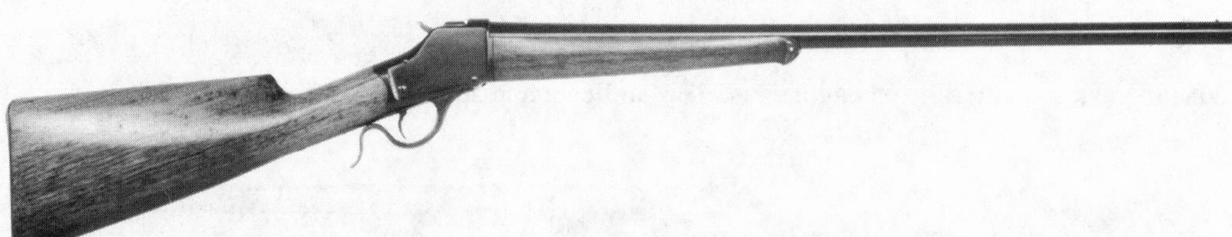

SINGLE SHOT, 20-GAUGE SHOTGUN. Listed in catalogues number 79, 1914 to number 80, 1916.

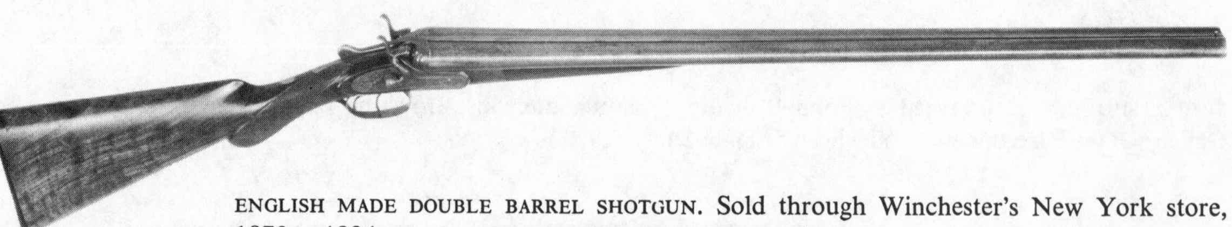

ENGLISH MADE DOUBLE BARREL SHOTGUN. Sold through Winchester's New York store, 1879 to 1884.

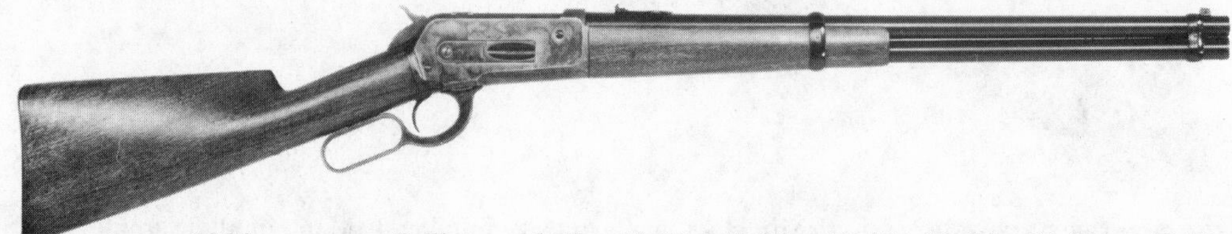

MODEL 1886 CARBINE. Calibers .45-70, .45-90, .40-82, .40-65, .38-56, .50-110, .40-70, .38-70, .50-100, .33 W.C.F. Listed in catalogues of June 1889 to number 81, 1919.

MODEL 1886 RIFLE, take down. Made in above calibers. Listed in catalogue number 52, 1894 and discontinued 1935.

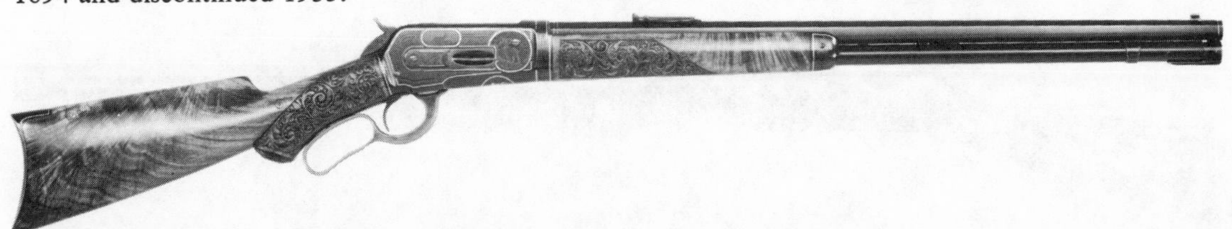

MODEL 1886 RIFLE, take down. An example of the engraving, wood carving, and gold inlay work available at extra cost. Engraving by John Ulrich, a Winchester engraver.

MODEL 1887 LEVER ACTION SHOTGUN. 10 and 12 gauge. Listed in catalogues June 1887 to number 67, 1901.

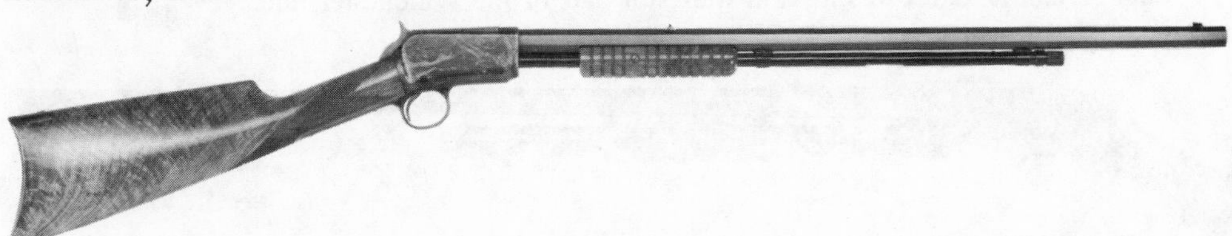

MODEL 1890 RIFLE. Calibers .22 short, .22 long, .22 long rifle or .22 W.R.F. Listed in catalogues November 1890 to October 1892.

MODEL 1890 RIFLE, take down. Calibers as above. Listed in catalogues December 1892, to number 89, 1934.

MODEL 1892 CARBINE. Calibers .25-20, .32-20, .38-40, and .44-40. Listed in catalogue July 1892, discontinued 1941.

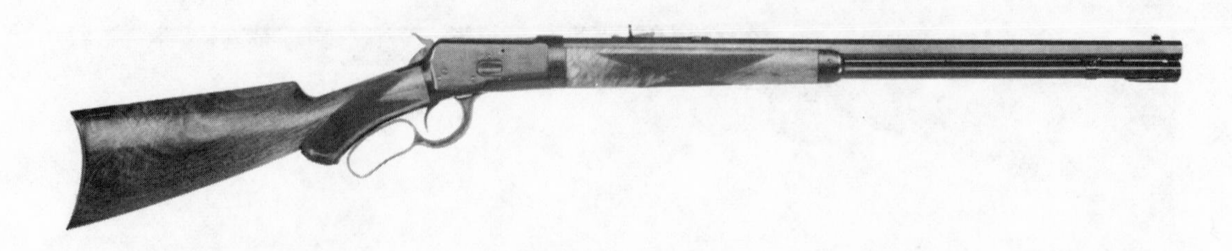

MODEL 1892 RIFLE, take down. Made in above calibers. Listed in catalogues October 1893, to number 89, 1934.

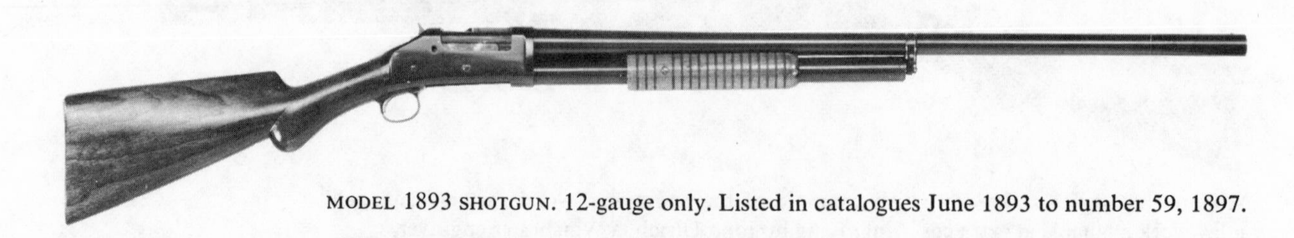

MODEL 1893 SHOTGUN. 12-gauge only. Listed in catalogues June 1893 to number 59, 1897.

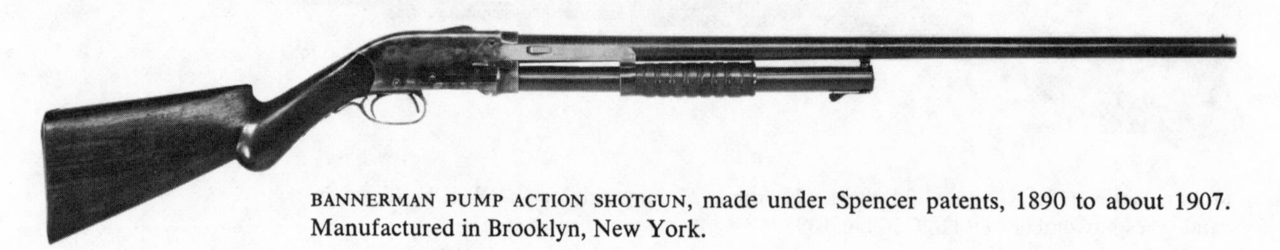

SPENCER PUMP ACTION SHOTGUN. Made at Windsor, Connecticut by the Spencer Arms Company, 1882 to 1889. This and the four illustrations that follow were used in the Bannerman *v.* Sanford suit, and were not part of the Winchester line.

BANNERMAN PUMP ACTION SHOTGUN, made under Spencer patents, 1890 to about 1907. Manufactured in Brooklyn, New York.

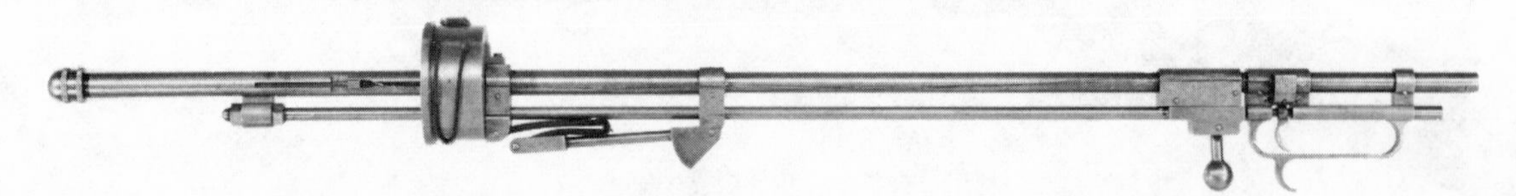

MODEL OF CURTIS PUMP ACTION RIFLE, patented in England July 10, 1866.

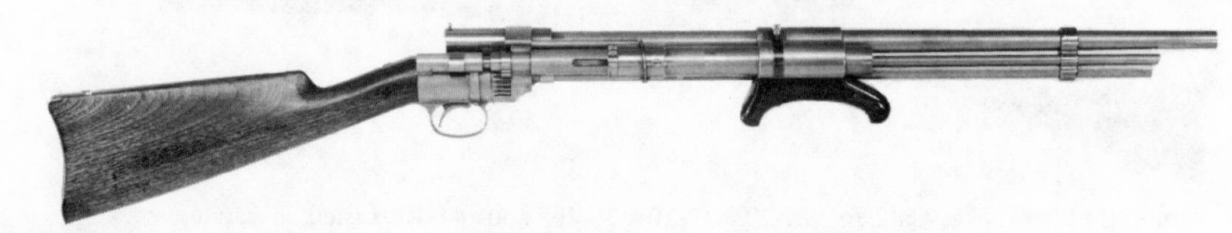



MODEL OF KRUTZSCH PUMP ACTION RIFLE, patented in England August 27, 1866.

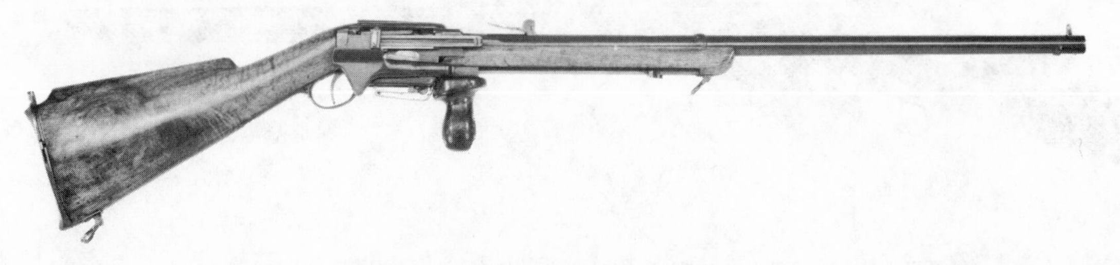

MARGOT PUMP ACTION RIFLE, patented in France October 5, 1880.

MODEL 1894 CARBINE. Calibers .32-40*, .38-55*, .25-35*, .30-30 Winchester, and .32 Winchester Special. Listed in catalogue number 53, 1894, still in the line.

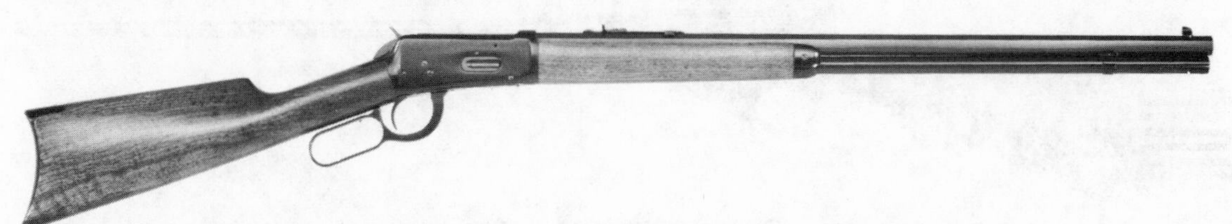

MODEL 1894 RIFLE. Calibers as above. First listed in catalogue number 53, 1894, discontinued in 1936.

MODEL 1894 RIFLE, take down. Half magazine and fully engraved. The take down style was first listed in catalogue number 55, 1895 and was discontinued in 1936.

MODEL 1895 CARBINE. Calibers .30 Army, .303 British, .30-'03, .30-'06. Listed in catalogues number 62, 1898, to number 89, 1934.

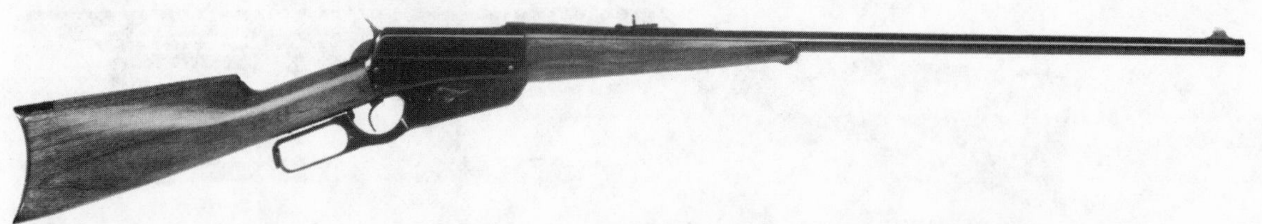

MODEL 1895 RIFLE. Calibers .30 Army, .38-72, .40-72, .303 British, .35 Winchester, .405 Winchester, .30-'03, and .30-'06. Listed in catalogues number 57, 1896, to number 89, 1934.

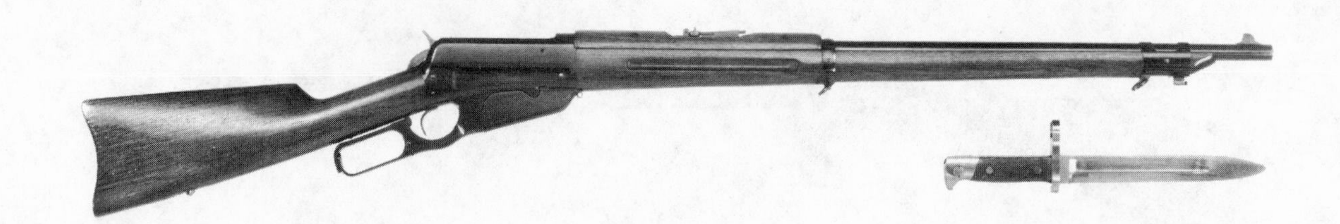

MODEL 1895 MUSKET. Calibers .30 Army, .30-'03, and .30-'06. Listed in catalogues number 62, 1898 to 1924.

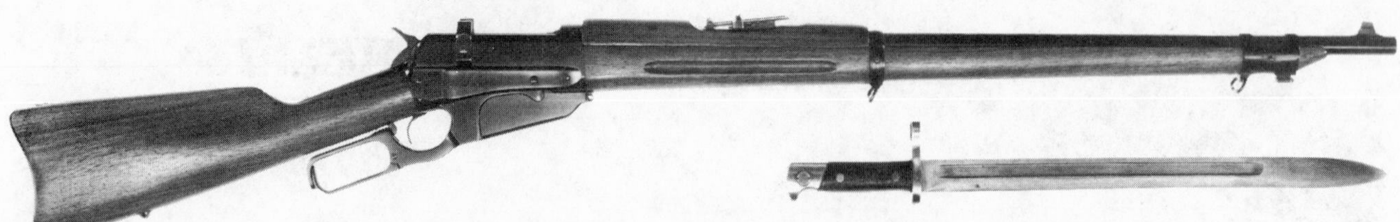

MODEL 1895 MUSKET. Caliber 7.62 mm. Made for Imperial Russian Government during 1915 and 1916.

LEE SPORTING RIFLE. Caliber 6 mm (.236). Listed in catalogues number 60, 1897 to number 69, 1902.

LEE NAVY MUSKET. Caliber 6 mm (.236). Listed in catalogues number 60, 1897 to number 69, 1902. This was the rifle adopted by the U. S. Navy during the Spanish-American War.

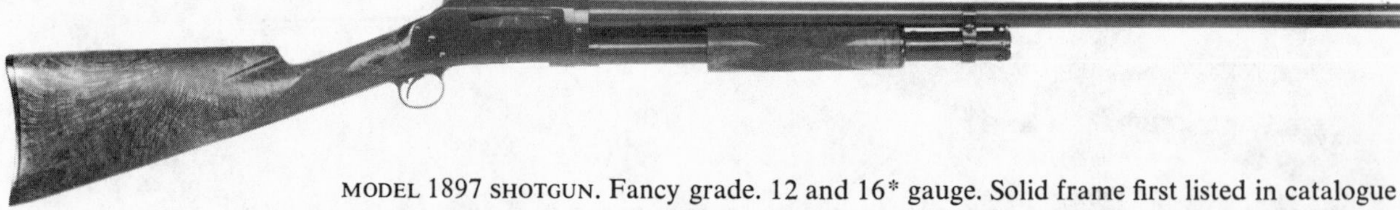

MODEL 1897 SHOTGUN. Fancy grade. 12 and 16* gauge. Solid frame first listed in catalogue number 60, 1897; last listed in catalogue number 81, 1919. Take down first listed in catalogue number 62, 1898; still in the line.

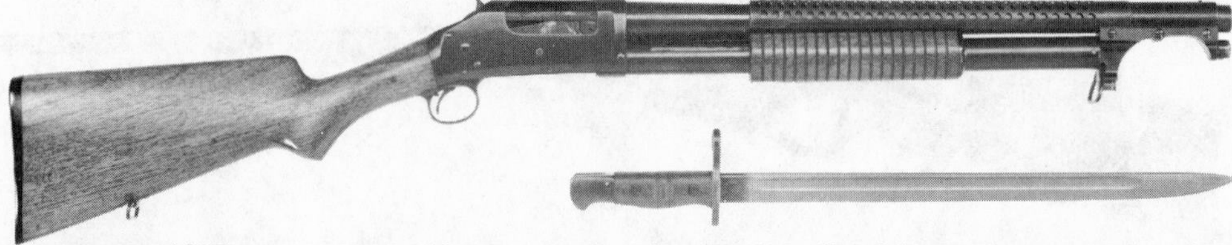

MODEL 1897 TRENCH GUN. 12 gauge only. Riot gun first listed in catalogue number 61, 1898; Trench gun introduced in 1917; still in the line.

WINCHESTER BREECH LOADING CANNON (MODEL 98). 10 gauge blank only. First listed in catalogue for March 1903; still in the line.

MODEL 1900 RIFLE. Caliber .22 short or long. Listed in catalogues number 65, 1900 to number 69, 1902.

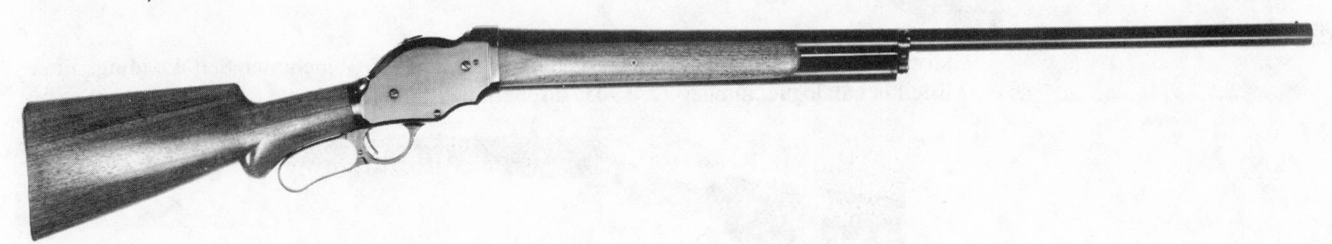

MODEL 1901 SHOTGUN. 10 gauge only. Listed in catalogues number 68, 1902 to number 82, 1920.

MODEL 1902 RIFLE. Caliber .22 short, long, long rifle, and extra long. Listed in catalogues March 1903 to 1930.

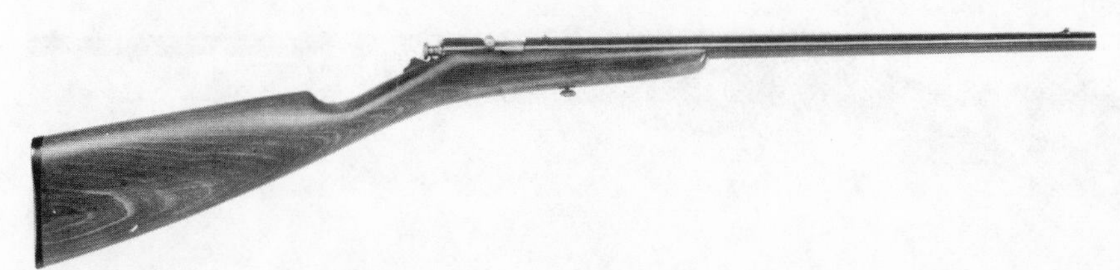

THUMB TRIGGER RIFLE (MODEL 99). Caliber .22 short, long, and long rifle. First listed in catalogue number 71, 1904; discontinued in 1923.

MODEL 1903 RIFLE. Caliber .22 Winchester Automatic. First listed in catalogue number 71, 1904; discontinued in 1932.

MODEL 1904 RIFLE. Calibers .22 short, long, extra long, and long rifle. Listed in catalogues number 71, 1904 to 1930.

MODEL 1905 SELF LOADING RIFLE. Calibers .32 and .35 Winchester Self Loading. First listed in catalogue number 72, 1905; discontinued in 1920.

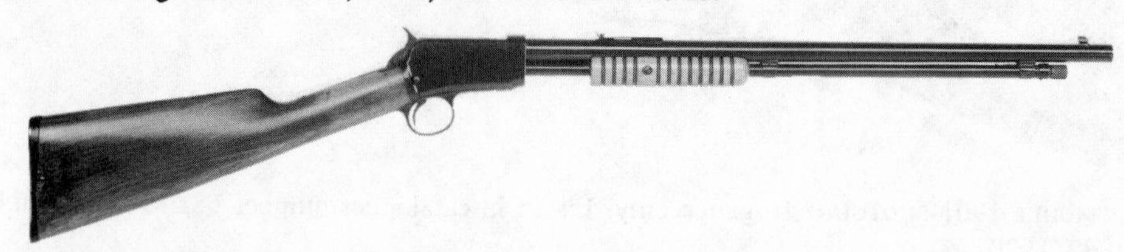

MODEL 1906 RIFLE. Caliber .22 short, long, and long rifle. Listed in catalogues number 73, 1907 to number 89, 1934.

MODEL 1907 SELF LOADING RIFLE. Caliber .351 Winchester Self Loading only. First listed in catalogue number 73, 1907. Still in the line.

MODEL 1910 SELF LOADING RIFLE. Caliber .401 Winchester Self Loading only. First listed in catalogue number 76, 1910; discontinued in 1936.

MODEL 1911 SELF LOADING SHOTGUN. 12 gage only. First listed in catalogue number 77, 1911; discontinued in 1925.

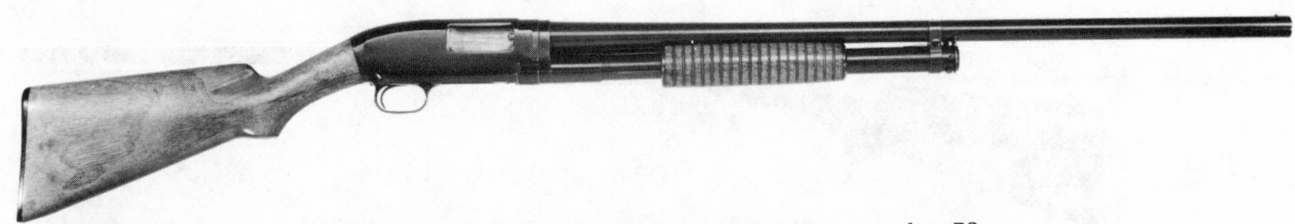

MODEL 1912 SHOTGUN. 12, 16, 20, and 28* gauge. First listed in catalogue number 78, 1913; still in the line.

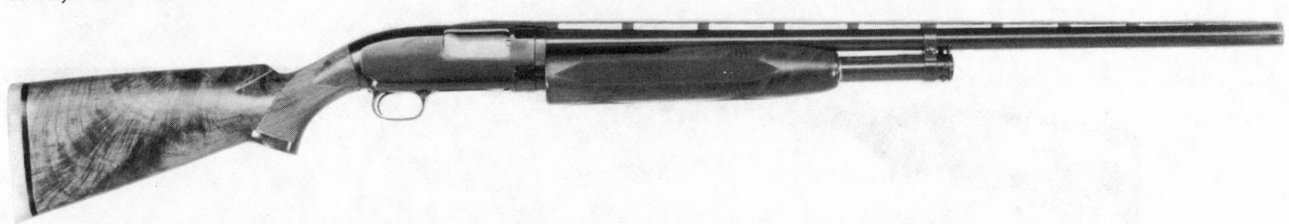

MODEL 1912 SHOTGUN. Engraved trap gun. 12 gauge.

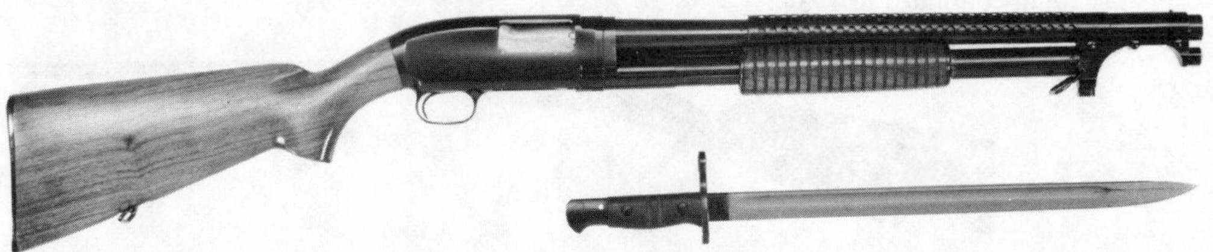

MODEL 1912 TRENCH GUN. 12 gauge only. Riot gun. First listed in catalogue number 81, 1918; Trench gun introduced in 1917; still in the line.

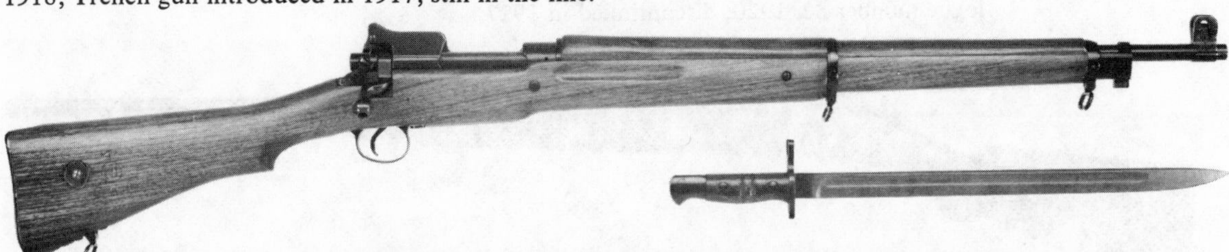

PATTERN '14. Caliber .303 British. Made for British Government, 1915 to 1917.

U. S. RIFLE, caliber .30 Model of 1917. Caliber .30-'06. Made for U. S. Government, 1917-1918.

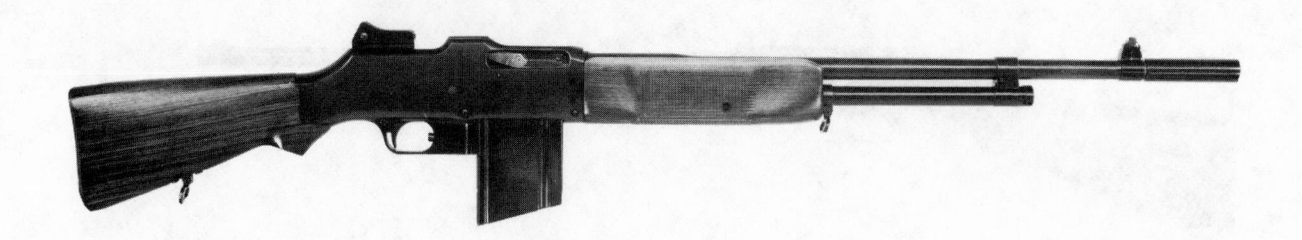

BROWNING AUTOMATIC RIFLE, Model of 1918. Caliber .30-'06. Made for U. S. Government 1918.

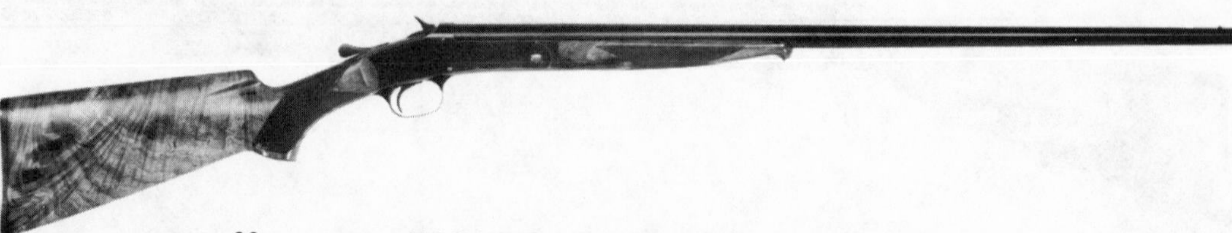

MODEL 20 SHOTGUN. .410 bore, 2½ inch shell only. Listed in catalogues number 82, 1920 to 1927.

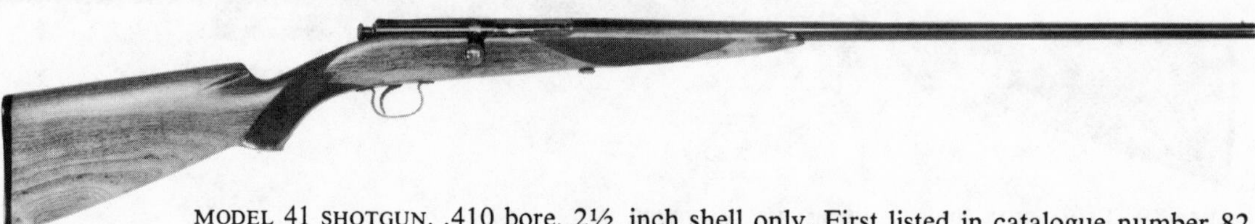

MODEL 41 SHOTGUN. .410 bore, 2½ inch shell only. First listed in catalogue number 82, 1920; discontinued in 1934.

MODEL 36 SHOTGUN. 9mm long or short shot or 9mm ball cartridge. First listed in catalogue number 82, 1920; discontinued in 1927.

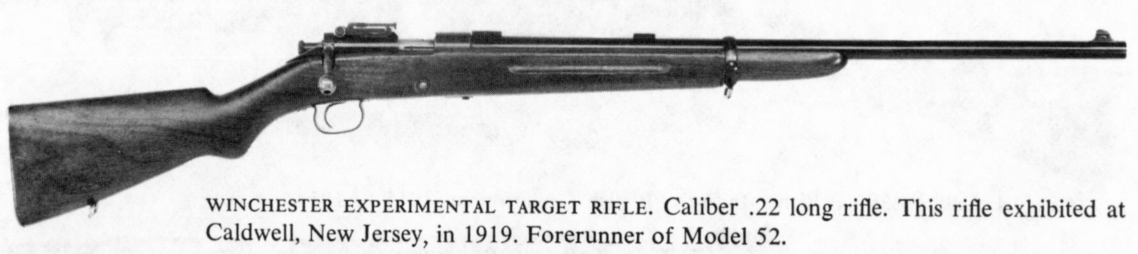

WINCHESTER EXPERIMENTAL TARGET RIFLE. Caliber .22 long rifle. This rifle exhibited at Caldwell, New Jersey, in 1919. Forerunner of Model 52.

MODEL 52 TARGET RIFLE. Caliber .22 long rifle. First listed in catalogue number 82, 1920; still in the line.

MODEL 52 SPORTING RIFLE. Caliber .22 long rifle. Authorized February 5, 1934. Still in the line.

MODEL 53 RIFLE. Calibers .25-20, .32-20, and .44-40. Listed in catalogues 1924 to number 89, 1934.

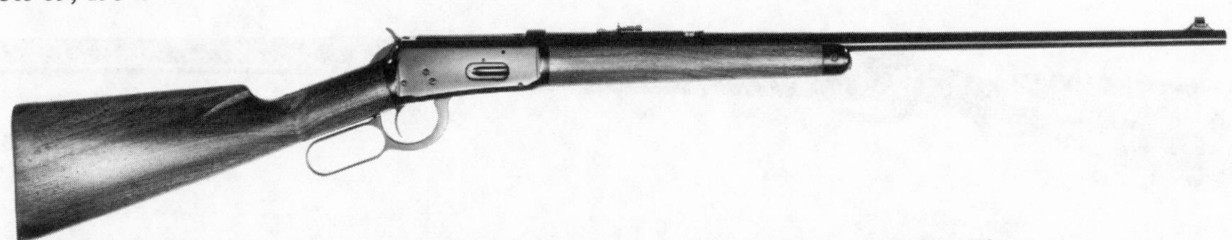

MODEL 55 RIFLE. Calibers .25-35, .30-30 Winchester, and .32 Winchester Special. First listed in the catalogue for 1924; discontinued in 1932.

MODEL 54 RIFLE. Calibers .22 Hornet, .220 Swift, .250 Savage, .257 Roberts, .270 Winchester, 7mm, 7.65mm, .30-30 Winchester, 30-'06, 9mm. First listed in catalogue number 83, 1925; discontinued in 1936.

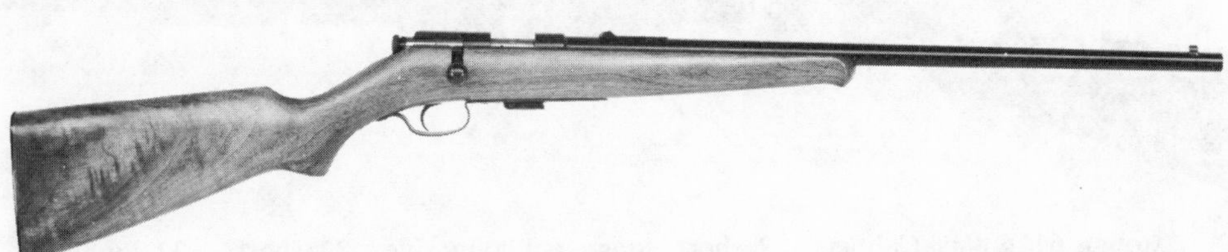

MODEL 56 RIFLE. Caliber .22 short and .22 long rifle. Introduced in 1926. Last listed in 1930.

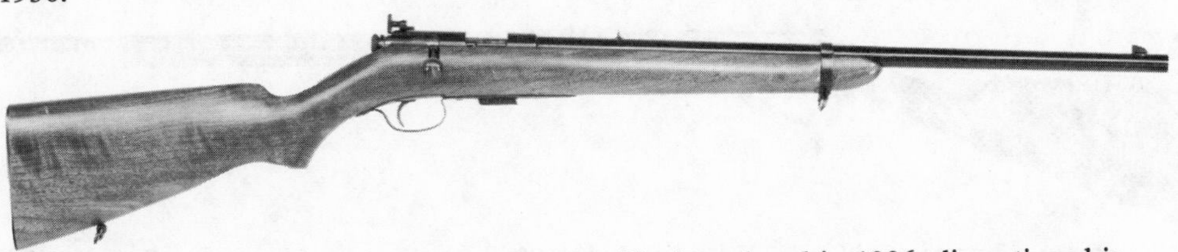

MODEL 57 RIFLE. Caliber .22 short and .22 long rifle. Introduced in 1926; discontinued in 1936.

MODEL 58 RIFLE. Caliber .22 short, long, and long rifle. Introduced in 1928, last listed in 1930.

MODEL 59 RIFLE. Caliber .22 short, long, and long rifle. Introduced in 1930, discontinued same year.

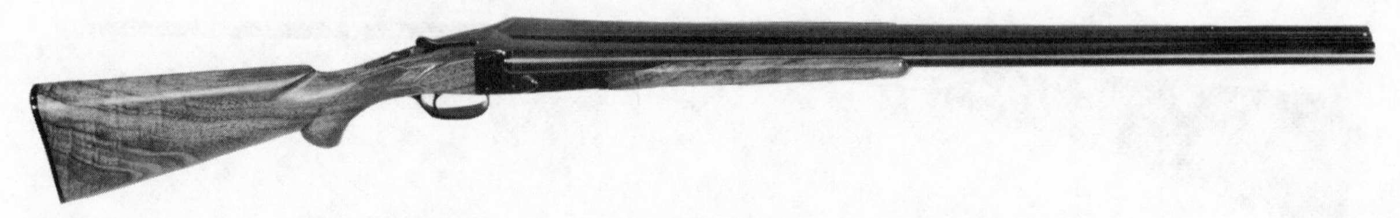

MODEL 21 SHOTGUN. 12, 16, 20, and 28* gauge. First listed in catalogue for July 1931. Still in line.

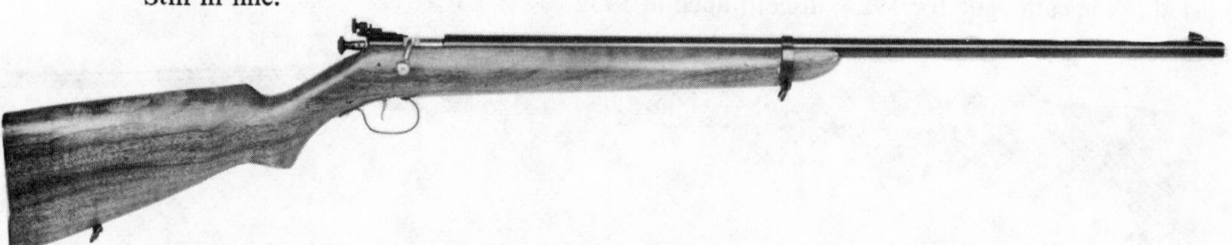

MODEL 60 A RIFLE. Caliber .22 long rifle. First listed in 1933. Discontinued in 1939.

MODEL 61 RIFLE. Calibers .22 short, long, and long rifle, .22 short*, .22 long rifle*, .22 W.R.F.*, .22 long rifle shot*. First listed in 1933. Still in line.

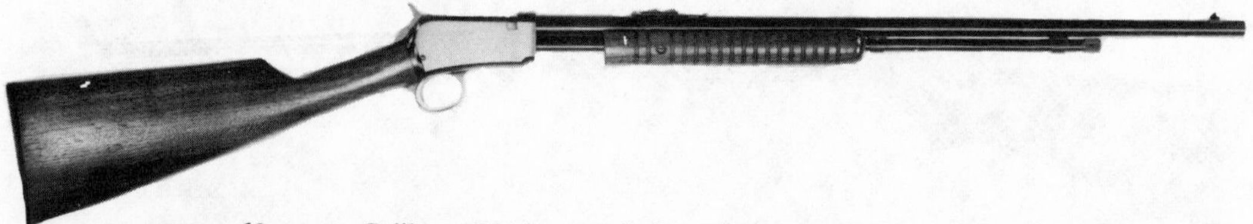

MODEL 62 RIFLE. Calibers .22 short and also .22 short, long, and long rifle. First listed in 1933 catalogue. Still in the line.

MODEL 63 SELF LOADING RIFLE. Caliber. 22 long rifle. First listed in 1933 catalogue. Still in the line.

MODEL 64 RIFLE. Calibers .219 Zipper*, .25-35*, .30-30 Winchester, .32 Winchester Special. First listed in 1933 catalogue. Still in the line.

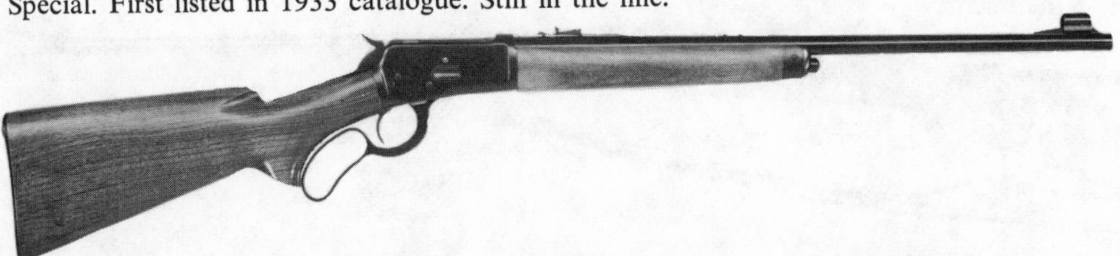

MODEL 65 RIFLE. Calibers .218 Bee, .25-20, .32-20. First listed in 1933 catalogue. Discontinued in 1947.

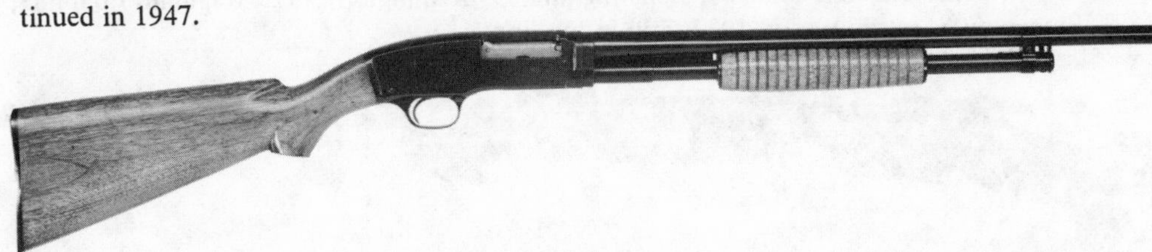

MODEL 42 SHOTGUN. .410 bore, 2½ or 3 inch shell. First listed in 1934 catalogue, still in the line.

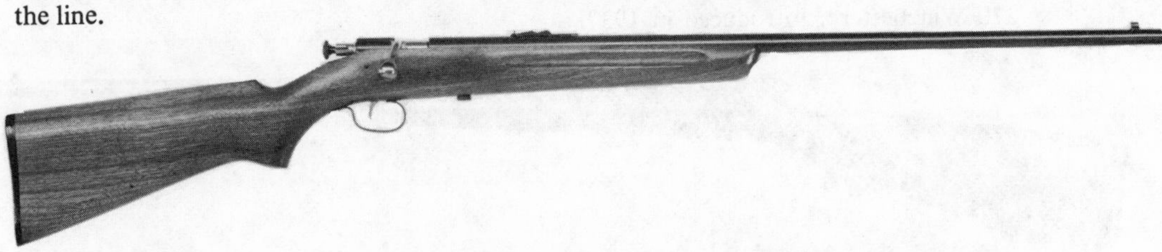

MODEL 67 RIFLE. Calibers .22 short, long, and long rifle, .22 W.R.F., .22 long and long rifle shot*, .22 long rifle shot. First listed in 1934 catalogue, still in the line.

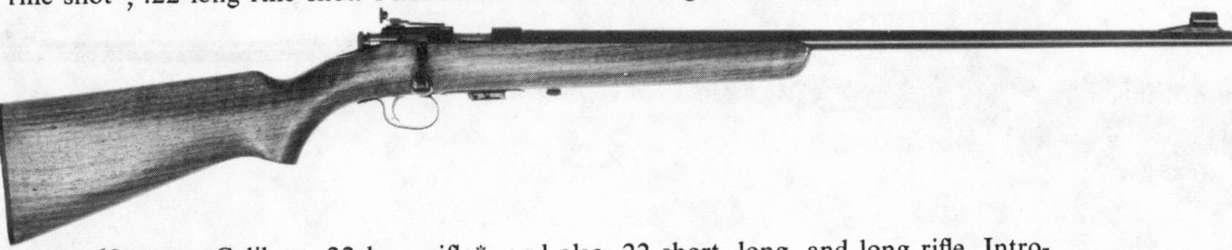

MODEL 69 RIFLE. Calibers .22 long rifle*, and also .22 short, long, and long rifle. Introduced in 1935. Discontinued in 1938.

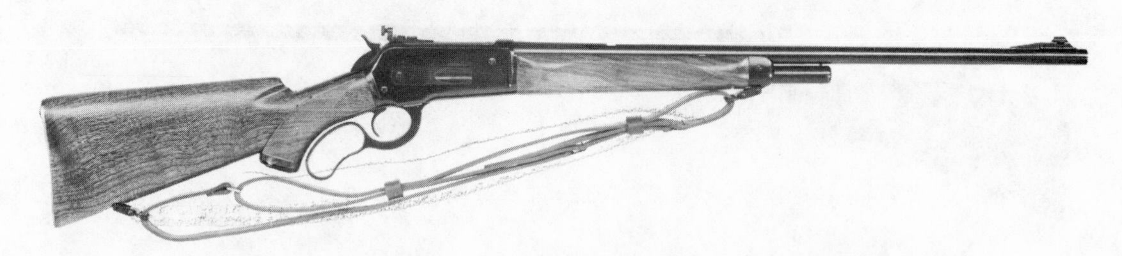

MODEL 71 RIFLE. Caliber .348 Winchester. Introduced in 1935. Still in the line.

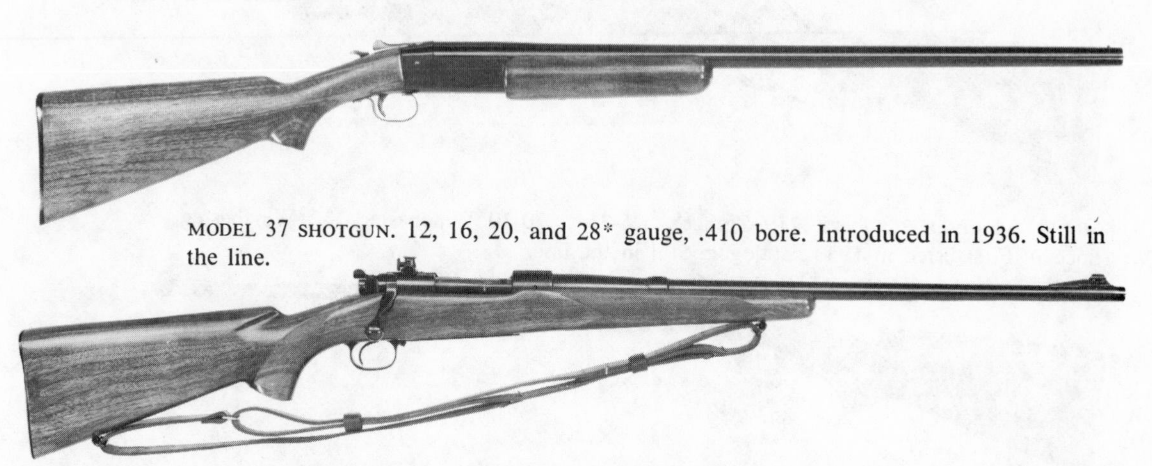

MODEL 37 SHOTGUN. 12, 16, 20, and 28* gauge, .410 bore. Introduced in 1936. Still in the line.

MODEL 70 SPORTING RIFLE. Calibers .22 Hornet, .220 Swift, .250 Savage*, .257 Roberts, .270 Winchester, 7mm*, .30-'06, .300 Magnum, .35 Remington*, .375 Magnum, 7.65mm*, 9mm*, .308. Introduced in 1937. Still in the line.

MODEL 70 TARGET RIFLE. Calibers .220 Swift*, .257 Roberts*, .30-'06, .300 Magnum*, .270 Winchester*. Introduced in 1937.

MODEL 72 RIFLE. Caliber .22 short, long, and long rifle. Introduced in 1938. Still in the line.

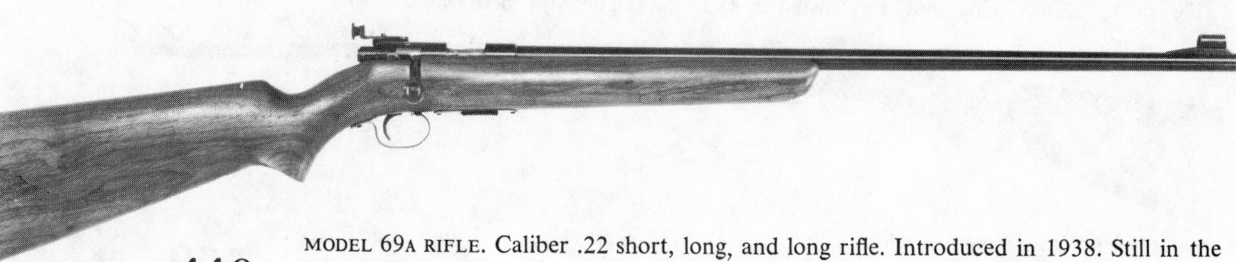

MODEL 69A RIFLE. Caliber .22 short, long, and long rifle. Introduced in 1938. Still in the line.

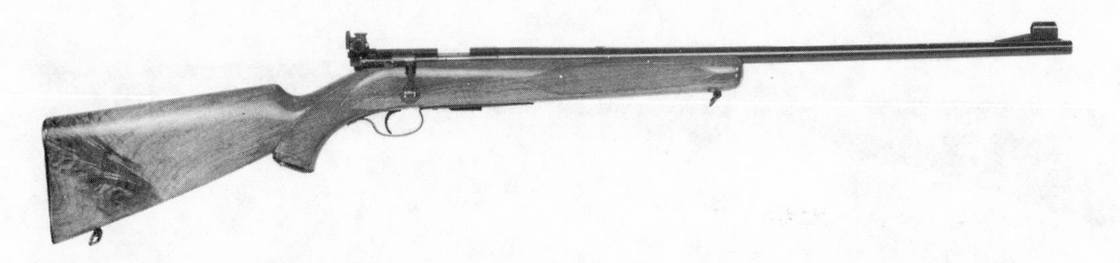

MODEL 75 SPORTING RIFLE. Caliber .22 long rifle. Introduced in 1938. Still in the line.

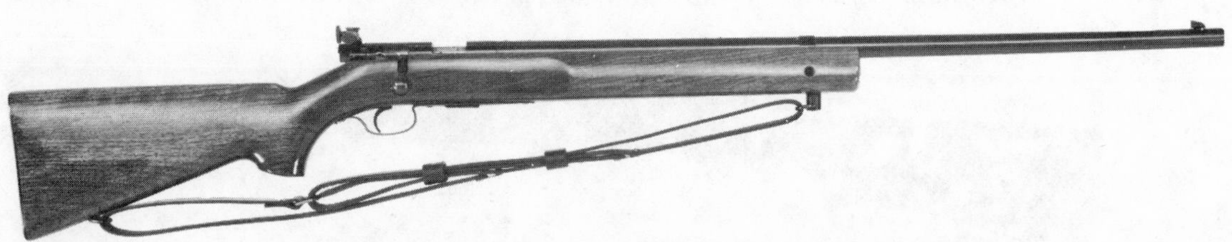

MODEL 75 TARGET RIFLE. Caliber .22 long rifle. Introduced in 1938. Still in the line.

MODEL 74 SELF LOADING RIFLE. Caliber .22 short* and .22 long rifle. Introduced in 1939. Still in the line.

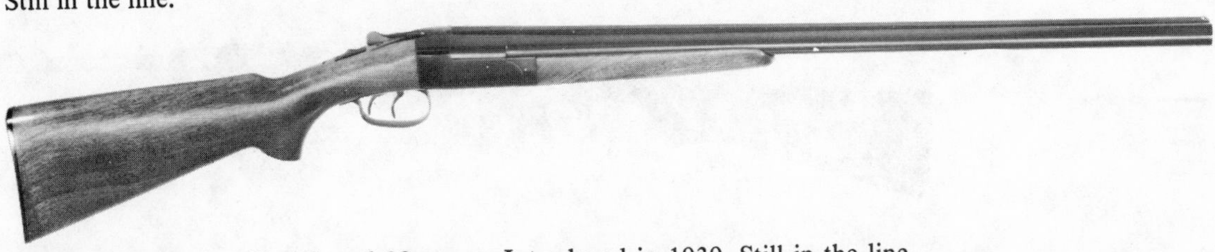

MODEL 24 SHOTGUN. 12, 16, and 20 gauge. Introduced in 1939. Still in the line.

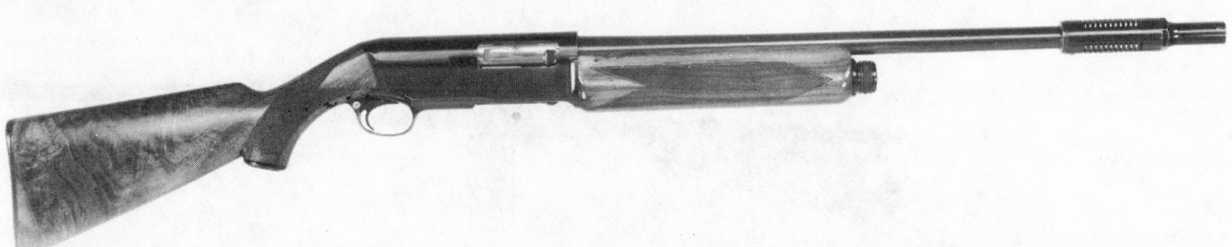

MODEL 40 SELF LOADING SHOTGUN. 12 gauge only. Introduced in 1940. Discontinued in 1941.

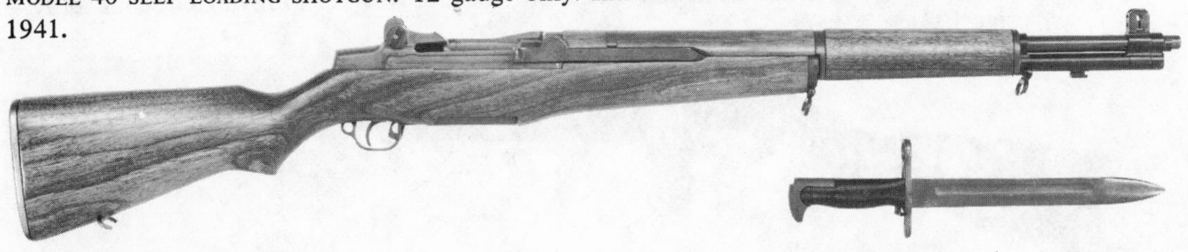

U. S. RIFLE. Caliber .30 M 1 (Garand) Caliber .30-'06. First deliveries in 1940. Made only for U. S. Government.

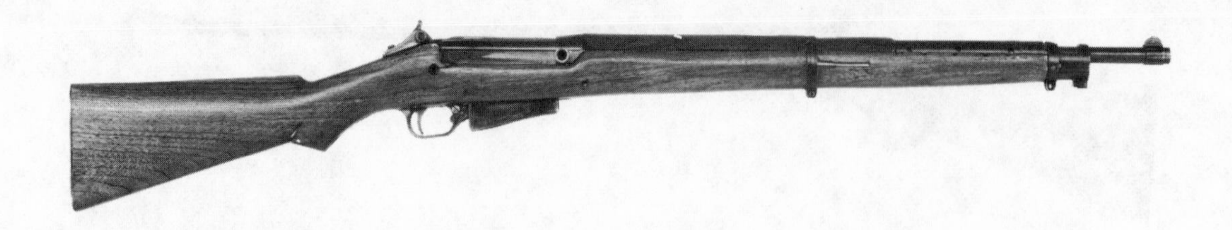

JONATHAN EDMUND BROWNING EXPERIMENTAL SEMI-AUTOMATIC RIFLE. Caliber .30-'06. Brought to Winchester by Mr. Browning in 1939.

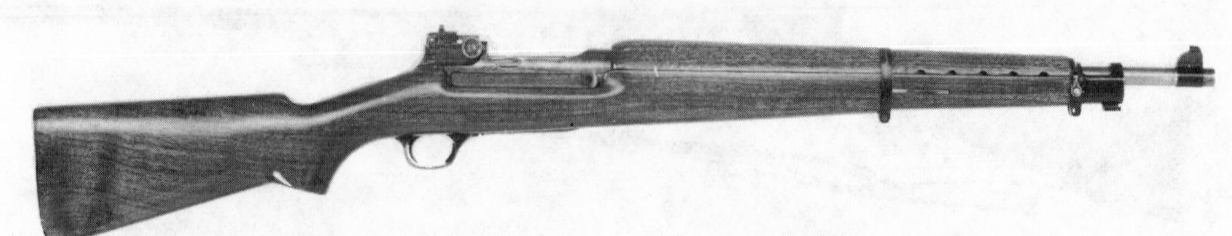

WINCHESTER EXPERIMENTAL SEMI-AUTOMATIC RIFLE. Caliber .30-'06. Based on Browning action. Williams piston. Submitted to Marine Corps trials in 1940.

U. S. RIFLE, Caliber .30 M 1. Modified to use Williams piston and trigger mechanism.

FIRST WINCHESTER EXPERIMENTAL CARBINE. Caliber .30.

SECOND WINCHESTER EXPERIMENTAL CARBINE Sent to Aberdeen Proving Grounds for testing 1941.

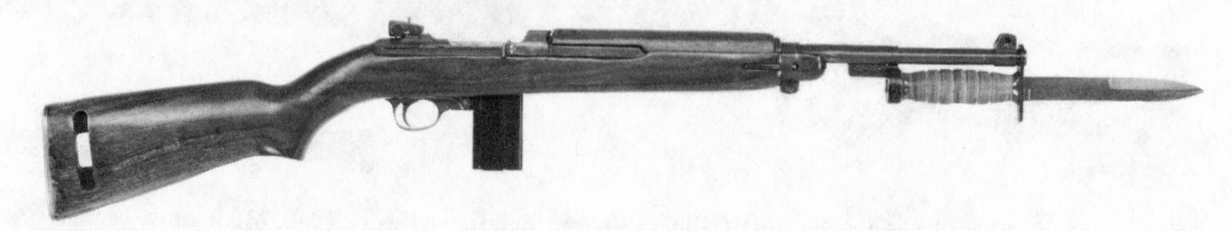



U. S. CARBINE, Caliber .30 M 1. Manufactured for U. S. Government during World War II.

MODEL 43 RIFLE. Calibers .218 Bee, .22 Hornet, .25-20*, .32-20* Winchester. First listed in 1949. Still in the line.

MODEL 47 RIFLE. Calibers .22 short, long, and long rifle. First listed in 1949. Still in the line.

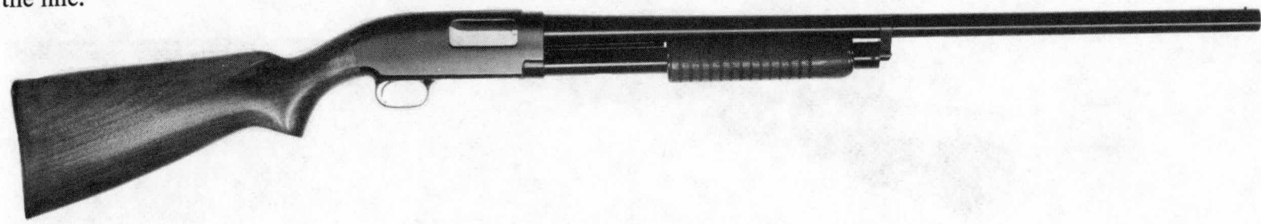

MODEL 25 SHOTGUN. 12 gauge. First listed in 1950. Still in the line.

# APPENDIX A-3

## RIFLES AND SHOTGUNS MANUFACTURED BY COMPETITORS BOUGHT OUT BY WINCHESTER, 1869-1898

*By Thomas E. Hall and John Peck*

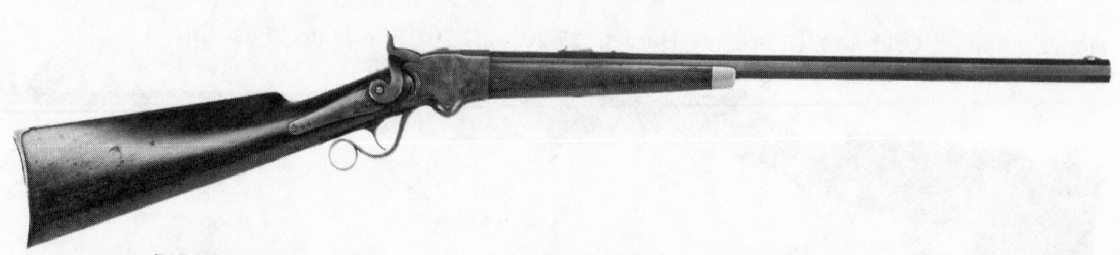

EARLY SPENCER SPORTING CARBINE, Caliber .36 rimfire. Made at Hartford, Connecticut 1861 or 1862.

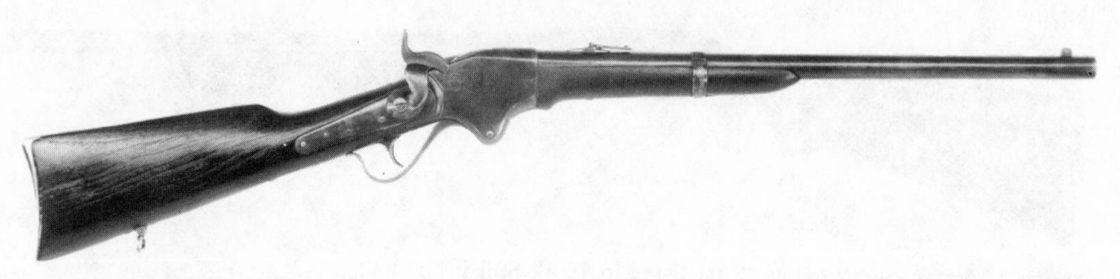

SPENCER CARBINE, Caliber .56-52 rimfire. Manufactured by the Spencer Repeating Rifle Company, Boston, Massachusetts 1862 to 1865.

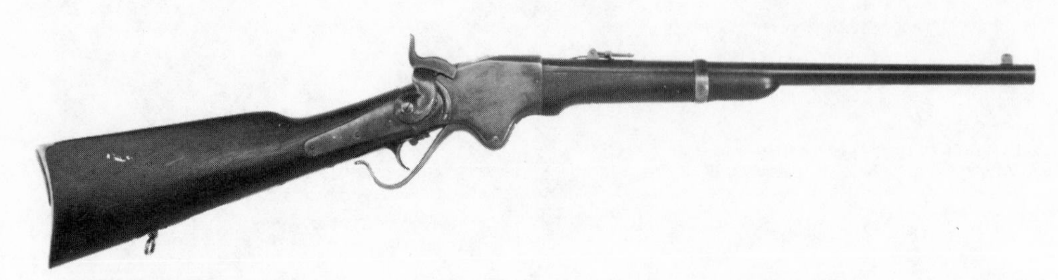

SPENCER CARBINE with Stabler cut-off, Caliber .56-50 rimfire. Manufactured by the Spencer Repeating Rifle Company, Boston, Massachusetts. Model 1865.

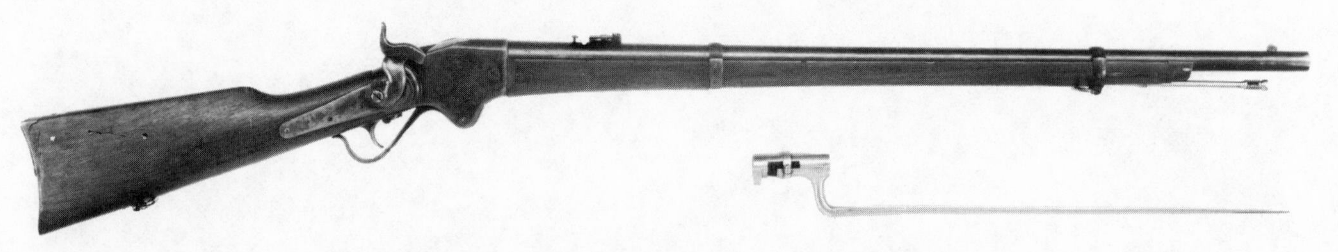



SPENCER MUSKET, Caliber .56-50 rimfire. Manufactured by the Burnside Rifle Company, Providence, Rhode Island, 1865.

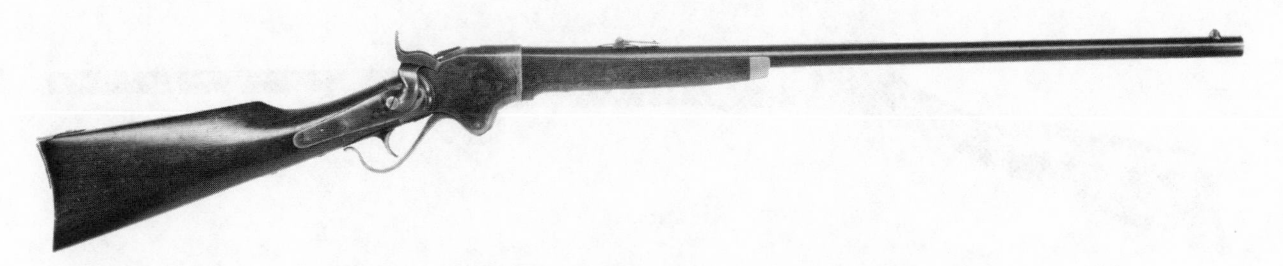

SPENCER SPORTING RIFLE, Caliber .56-46 rimfire. Model 1867. Manufactured by the Spencer Repeating Rifle Company, Boston, Massachusetts, 1867 to 1869.

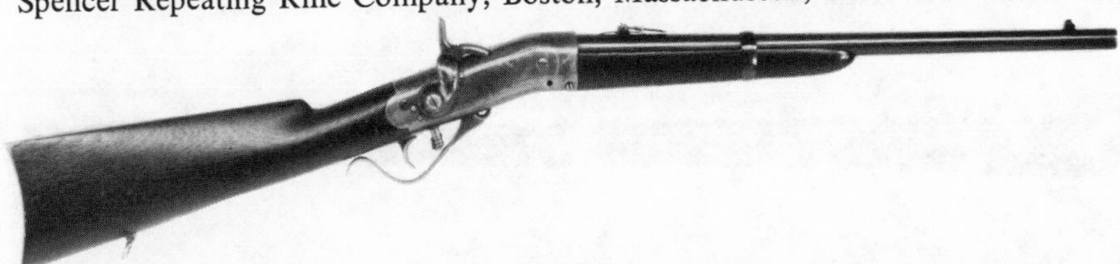

FOGERTY CARBINE, Caliber .45 rimfire. Manufactured by Fogerty Rifle Company, Boston, Massachusetts, 1865 to 1867. The name of this company was changed to the American Repeating Rifle Company—1867 to 1869.

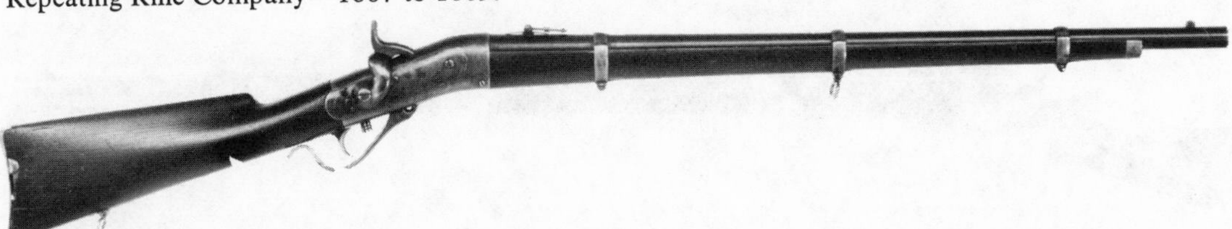

FOGERTY MUSKET, Caliber .50 rimfire. For company name and dates see above.

FOGERTY SPORTING RIFLE, Caliber .40 rimfire. For company name and dates see above.

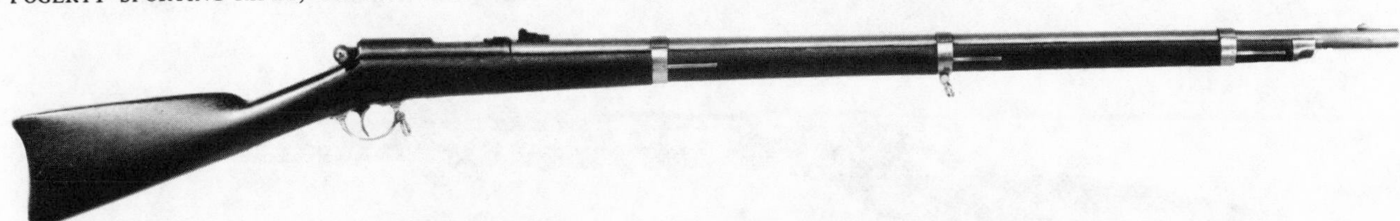

FOGERTY EXPERIMENTAL MILITARY RIFLE, Caliber .58 centerfire. Patented July 25, 1871.

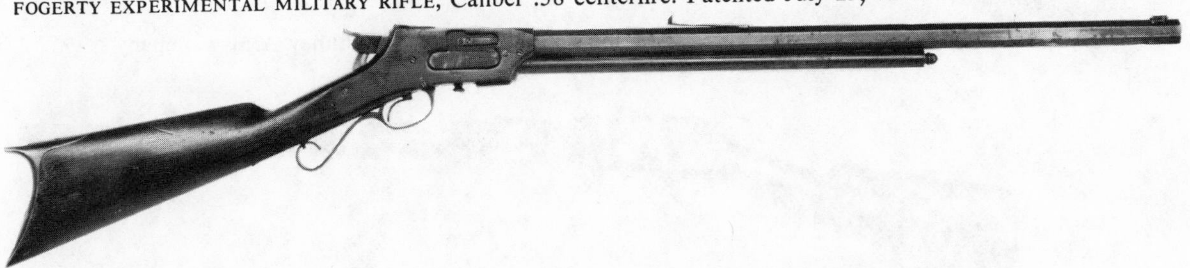

ROBINSON RIFLE, Caliber .44 rimfire. Manufactured by A. S. Babbit, Plattsburgh, New York, 1870 to 1872.

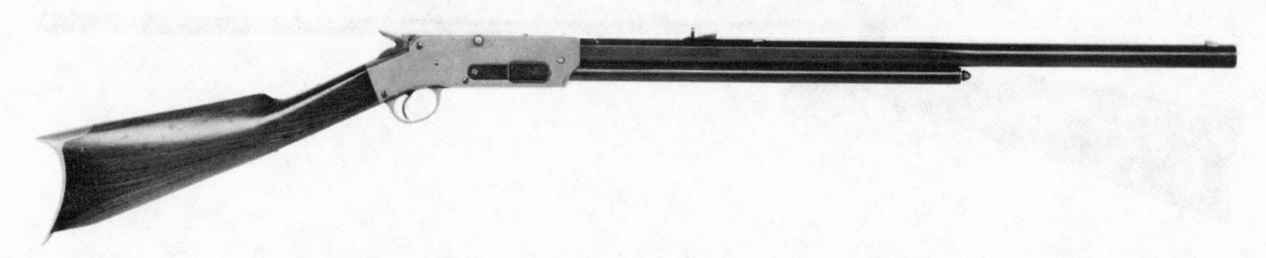

ROBINSON RIFLE, Caliber .44 rimfire. Manufactured by the Adirondack Fire Arms Company, Plattsburgh, New York, 1872 to 1874.

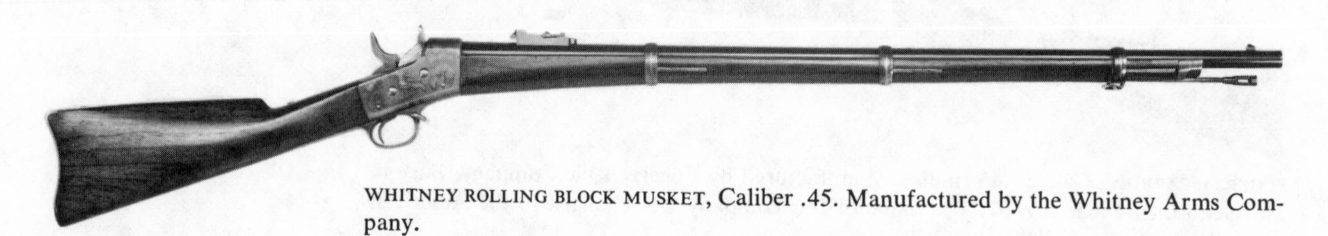

WHITNEY ROLLING BLOCK MUSKET, Caliber .45. Manufactured by the Whitney Arms Company.

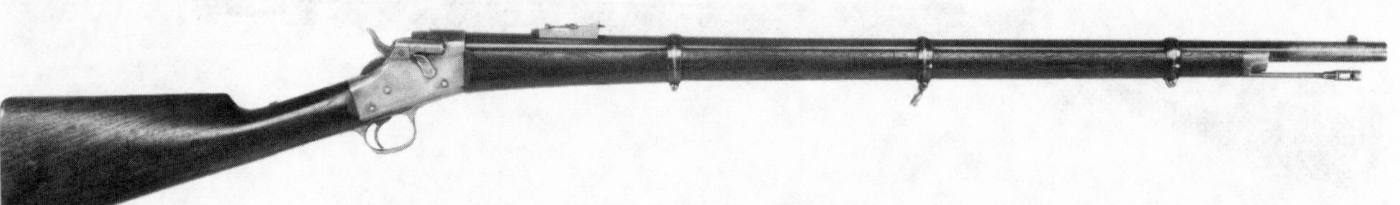

PHOENIX RIFLE, Caliber .45-70. Manufactured by the Whitney Arms Company.

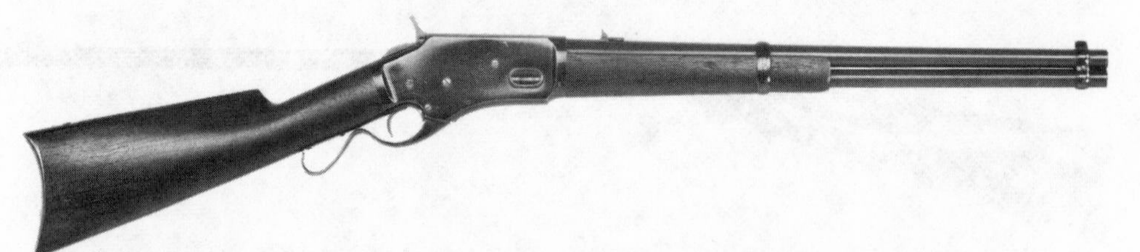

KENNEDY CARBINE, Caliber .44. Manufactured by the Whitney Arms Company.

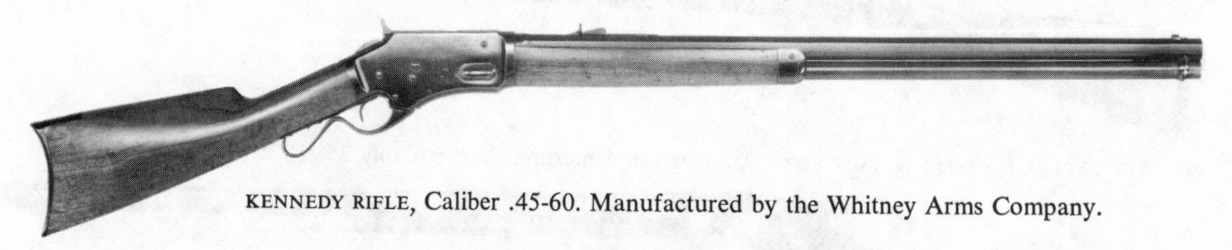

KENNEDY RIFLE, Caliber .45-60. Manufactured by the Whitney Arms Company.

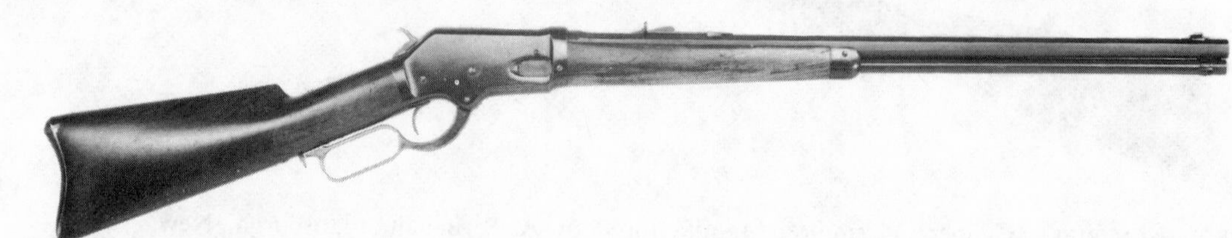



BURGESS SPORTING RIFLE, Caliber .32. Manufactured by the Whitney Arms Company.

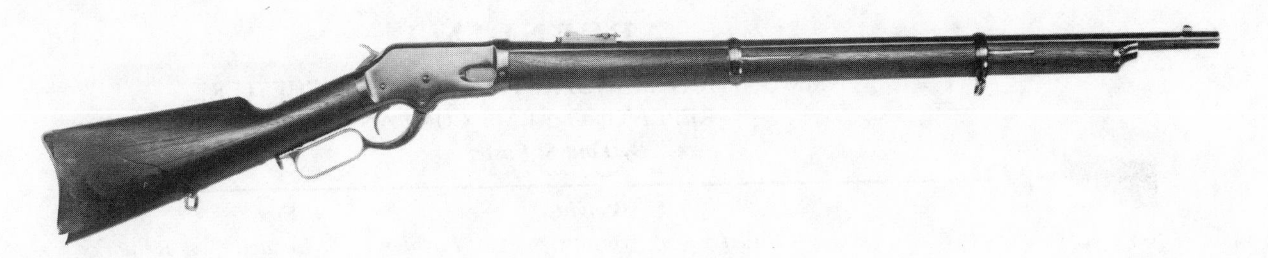

BURGESS MUSKET, Caliber .38. Manufactured by the Whitney Arms Company.

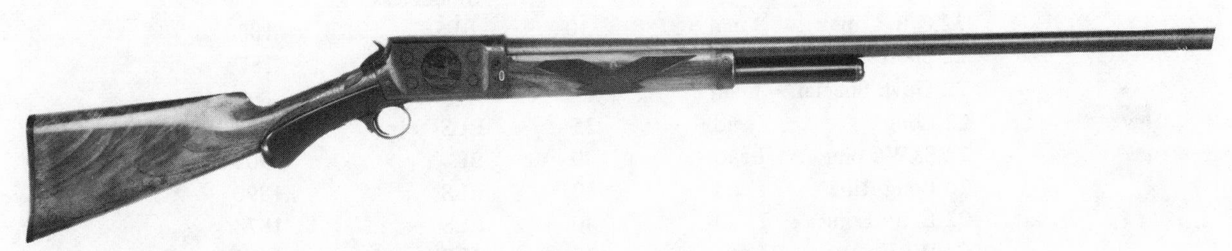

BURGESS SHOTGUN, 12 gauge. Manufactured by the Burgess Gun Company, Buffalo, New York, 1892 to 1898.

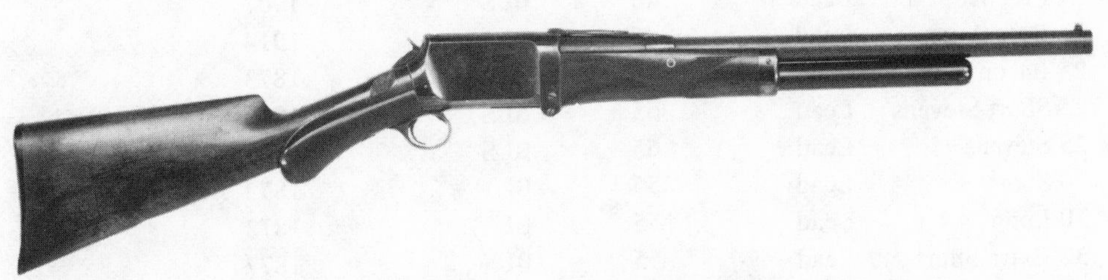

BURGESS SHOTGUN, folding take down, 12 gauge. Manufactured by the Burgess Gun Company, Buffalo, New York, 1894 to 1898.

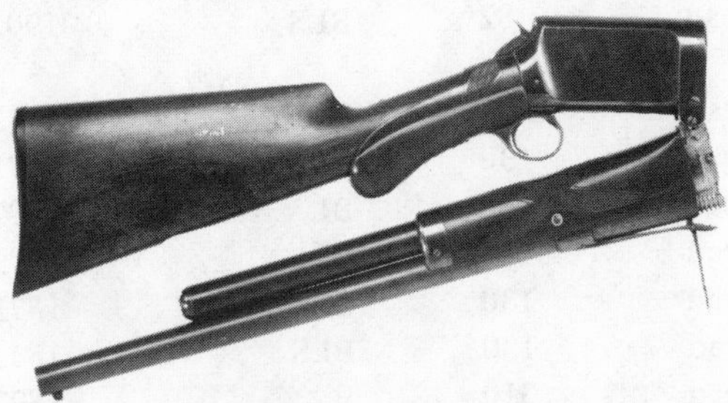

BURGESS SHOTGUN, folding take down, 12 gauge. Same as above.

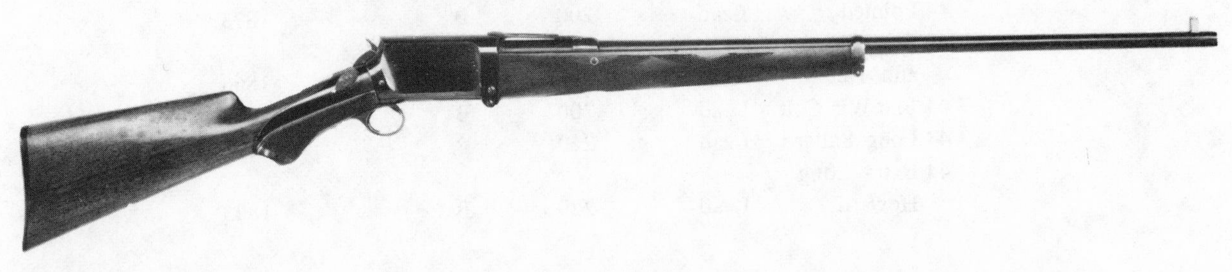

BURGESS RIFLE, folding take down, .30-30 Winchester. Manufactured by the Burgess Gun Company, Buffalo, New York, 1892 to 1898.

## APPENDIX B

### AMMUNITION MANUFACTURED BY WINCHESTER REPEATING ARMS COMPANY

*By Paul S. Foster*

| | Bullet | Weight (grains) | Powder | First Loaded | Remarks |
|---|---|---|---|---|---|
| | | | RIM FIRE | | |
| 22 B.B. Cap | Lead | 18 | Black, Lesmok Smokeless | 1878 | |
| 22 C.B. Cap | Lead | 30 | BLS | 1886 | |
| 22 Short | Lead | 30 | BLS | 1873 | |
| 22 Govt. Special | Lead | | | | |
| 22 Long | Lead | 35 | BLS | 1873 | |
| 22 S&W Long | Lead | 40 | BL | 1903 | |
| 22 Long Rifle | Lead | 40 | BLS | 1890 | |
| 22 Extra Long | Lead | 40 | BLS | 1878 | |
| *22 WRF | Lead | 45 | BLS | 1890 | |
| *22 Win Auto | Lead | 45 | Smokeless | 1904 | |
| 22 U.S. Armory Practice | Lead | 40 | BLS | 1907 | |
| 22 Rem Auto | Lead | 45 | S | 1914 | |
| 25 Bacon Bliss | Lead | 38 | BL | 1873 | |
| 25 Short Stevens | Lead | 65 | BLS | 1902 | |
| 25 Stevens | Lead | 65 | BLS | 1890 | |
| 30 Short | Lead | 55 | BL | 1873 | |
| 30 Long | Lead | 55 | BL | 1873 | |
| 32 Extra Short | Lead | 55 | BLS | 1877 | |
| 32 Short | Lead | 82 | BLS | 1873 | |
| 32 Long | Lead | 90 | BLS | 1873 | |
| 32 Long Rifle | Lead | 82 | BLS | 1901 | Case .937 OL 1.215 |
| 32 Extra Long | Lead | 90 | BL | 1873 | |
| 38 Short | Lead | 130 | BL | 1873 | |
| 38 Long | Lead | 148 | BL | 1873 | |
| 38 Extra Long | Lead | 148 | BL | 1873 | |
| 41 Short | Lead | 130 | BLS | 1873 | |
| 41 Long | Lead | 130 | BLS | 1873 | |
| 41 Swiss Vetterli | Lead | 310 | BS | 1877 | |
| 44 Short | Lead | 200 | B | 1873 | |
| 44 Pointed | Lead | 200 | B | 1873 | |
| *44 Flat Win and Henry | Lead | 200 | B | 1866 | |
| 44 Flat Win Colt | Lead | 200 | B | 1873 | |
| 44 Long Ballard | Lead | 220 | B | 1873 | |
| 44 Extra Long Howard | Lead | 220 | B | 1873 | |

| | Bullet | Weight (grains) | Powder | First Loaded | Remarks |
|---|---|---|---|---|---|
| 45 Danish | Lead | | B | 1877 | |
| 45 Peabody | Lead | | B | 1877 | |
| 46 Short | Lead | 230 | B | 1873 | |
| 46 Long | Lead | 300 | B | 1873 | |
| 50 Pistol | Lead | 290 | B | 1877 | |
| 50–60 Peabody | Lead | 320 | B | 1877 | |
| 50–70 | Lead | 450 | B | 1878 | |
| 50–70 Sharps | Lead | 425 | B | 1878 | |
| 52 Carbine | Lead | 400 | B | 1878 | |
| 52–70 Sharps | Lead | | B | 1878 | |
| 56–46 Spencer | Lead | 330 | B | 1873 | |
| 56–50 Spencer | Lead | 350 | B | 1873 | |
| 56–52 Spencer | Lead | 386 | B | 1873 | |
| 56–56 Spencer | Lead | 350 | B | 1873 | |
| 58 Carbine | Lead | 530 | B | 1878 | |
| 58 Gatling | Lead | 575 | B | 1884 | |
| 58 Joslyn | Lead | 350 | B | 1884 | |
| 58 Miller | Lead | | B | 1886 | |
| 58 Springfield | Lead | 530 | B | 1878 | |
| 58 Roberts | Lead | 480 | B | 1878 | |

CENTER FIRE

| | Bullet | Weight (grains) | Powder | First Loaded | Remarks |
|---|---|---|---|---|---|
| *218 Bee | HP | 46 | S | 1939 | |
| *219 Zipper | HP | 46<br>56 | S | 1938 | |
| 22 Extra Long | Lead | 45 | BL | 1890 | |
| *22 Hornet | SP HP | 45, 46 | S | 1932 | |
| 22 Savage | SP FP | 70 | S | 1913 | |
| *22 WCF | Lead | 45 | BLS | 1885 | |
| *220 Swift | SP HP | 48 | S | 1936 | |
| | | 56 | | | |
| 25 Auto. | FP | 50 | S | 1908 | |
| 25–20 SS | Lead SP | 86 | BLS | 1890 | |
| *25–20 WCF | Lead SP | 86 | BLS | 1895 | |
| | HP FP | 60 | | | |
| 25–20 Marlin | Lead SP | 86 | BLS | 1895 | |
| 25–21 Stevens | Lead | 86 | BS | 1905 | |
| 25–25 Stevens | Lead | 86 | BS | 1894 | |
| *25–35 WCF | Lead SP | 86 | S | 1895 | |
| | FP | 100 | | | |
| | | 117 | | | |
| 25–36 Marlin | SP FP | 117 | S | 1896 | |
| | | 86 | | | |
| 250–3000 | SP HP | 87 | S | 1913 | |
| | FP PP | 100 | | | |
| | ST | | | | |

| | Bullet | Weight (grains) | Powder | First Loaded | Remarks |
|---|---|---|---|---|---|
| 257 Roberts | SP HP | 87 | S | 1936 | |
| | PP ST | 100 | | | |
| | | 117 | | | |
| *270 Win | SP HP | 100 | S | 1925 | |
| | PP ST | 130 | | | |
| | | 150 | | | |
| 280 Ross | PP | 150 | S | 1914 | |
| 30 Rook | — | — | — | — | |
| 30–30 Wesson | Lead | 165 | B | | |
| *30 WCF | SP HP | 110 | S | 1895 | |
| (30–30) | FP ST | 150 | | | |
| | | 170 | | | |
| 30 Marlin | SP | 170 | S | 1896 | |
| 30 Rem | FP SP | 160 | S | 1907 | |
| | | 170 | | | |
| 30 Savage | FP SP | 190 | S | 1896 | |
| 30–40 (30 Army) | SP FP ST | 100–180 | S | 1894 | |
| | HP PP | 150–220 | | | |
| 30 Govt. M03 | FP SP | 220 | S | 1905 | |
| 30–06 Springfield | FP HCT | 145, 150 | | | |
| | HP SP | 172 | S | 1908 | |
| | PP ST | 180, 220 | | | |
| 300 Savage | SP HP | 150 | S | 1927 | |
| | PP ST | 180 | | | |
| 300 H&H | FP SP | 180 | S | 1937 | |
| | HP ST | 220 | | | |
| 303 Savage | HP SP | 100 | S | 1897 | |
| | FP ST | 190 | | | |
| 303 British | HCT FP | | | | |
| | SP | 174 | S | 1897 | |
| | PP | 215 | | | |
| 308 WCF | ST | 110, 150 | S | 1952 | |
| | | 180 | | | |
| 310 Cadet | Lead | 120 | S | 1908 | |
| 32 Browning Auto | Lead | 74 | S | 1899 | |
| 32 Colt Auto | FP SP | 74 | S | 1903 | |
| 32 Colt | Lead | 90 | BS | 1878 | |
| 32 Colt New Police | Lead | 98 | BLS | 1896 | |
| 32 CLMR | Lead | 100 | BLS | 1895 | |
| 32 Short | Lead | 82 | B | 1878 | |
| 32 Short Colt | Lead | 80 | BLS | 1905 | |
| 32 Long | Lead | 90 | B | 1878 | |
| 32 Long Colt | Lead | 90 | BLS | 1905 | |
| 32 Long Colt IL | Lead | 90 | BL | 1901 | |
| 32 Long Rifle | Lead | 82 | BL | 1910 | Case .937<br>OL 1.215 |
| 32 Extra Long | Lead | 105 | BL | 1879 | |
| 32 H&R | Lead | 88 | B | 1884 | Case .885<br>OL 1.225 |

| | Bullet | Weight (grains) | Powder | First Loaded | Remarks |
|---|---|---|---|---|---|
| 32 MH | Lead | 88 | BL | 1904 | |
| 32 Ideal | Lead | 150 | BL | 1894 | |
| 32 Protector | Lead | 40 | BLS | 1892 | |
| 32 S&W | Lead | 85 | BLS | 1878 | |
| | FP | 55 | | | |
| 32 S&W Long | Lead | 98 | BLS | 1896 | |
| 32 S&W Rifle | Lead | 100 | BL | 1884 | |
| (Name changed to 32 S&W Revolving Rifle in 1914) | Lead | 100 | BL | 1914 | |
| *32 WCF | Lead SP | 80 | BLS | 1882 | |
| (32–20) | FP HP | 100 | | | |
| | | 115 | | | |
| 320 | Lead | 94 | B | 1919 | |
| 320 | Lead | 80 | BS | 1919 | |
| 32–20 Marlin | Lead SP | 100 | BLS | 1895 | |
| 32–44 S&W | Lead | 85 | BL | 1887 | |
| | | 55 | | | |
| 32 Rem Auto | SP FP | 165 | S | 1908 | |
| *32 WSL | SP FP | 165 | S | 1905 | |
| *32 Win Spl | SP FP ST | 170 | S | 1902 | |
| *32–40 WCF | Lead SP FP | 165 | BS | 1885 | |
| 32–40 Ballard | Lead | 165 | B | 1886 | |
| 32–40 Bullard | Lead | 150 | B | 1885 | |
| 32–40 Rem | Lead | 150 | B | 1904 | |
| 32–70 USN | FP | 240 | S | 1893 | |
| 32–70 USN | FP | | S | | |
| *33 WCF | SP | 200 | S | 1903 | |
| *345 AR | FP Lead | 150, 173 | S | 1917 | |
| *348 Win | SP ST | 150 | S | 1936 | |
| | | 200 | | | |
| | | 250 | | | |
| 35 S&W Auto | FP | 76 | S | 1914 | |
| *35 WSL | SP FP | 180 | S | 1905 | |
| *351 WSL | SP FP | 180 | S | 1907 | |
| 35 Rem | SP FP HP ST | 200 | S | 1907 | |
| *35 WCF | SP | 250 | S | 1903 | |
| 357 Magnum | Lead | 158, 150 | S | 1936 | |
| 375 H&H | FP SP | 235 | S | 1936 | |
| Magnum | PP | 270 | | | |
| | | 300 | | | |
| 380 Revolver | Lead | 130 | BS | 1919 | |
| 38 Auto Colt | FP SP | 130 | S | 1899 | |
| 38 Colt Spl | Lead | 158 | BLS | 1910 | |
| 38 Short Colt | Lead | 130 | BLS | 1876 | |
| 38 Long Colt | Lead | 150 | BLS | 1876 | |

| | Bullet | Weight (grains) | Powder | First Loaded | Remarks |
|---|---|---|---|---|---|
| 38 Extra Long | Lead | 160 | BL | 1876 | |
| 38 M&H | Lead | 145 | B | 1883 | |
| 38 S&W | Lead | 145 | BLS | 1878 | |
| | FP | | | | |
| 38 S&W | L LB | 150, 158 | BLS | 1900 | |
| Special | FP | | | | |
| *38 WCF | Lead SP | 180 | BLS | 1879 | |
| | FP HP | 165 | | | |
| 38–40 Marlin | Lead SP | 180 | BLS | 1895 | |
| 38–40 Rem | Lead | 245 | B | 1909 | |
| 38–44 S&W | Lead | 70 | BL | 1895 | |
| | | 146 | | | |
| 38–45 Bullard | Lead | 190 | B | 1885 | Case 1²⁵⁄₃₂ |
| 38–50 Rem | Lead | 245 | B | 1904 | |
| 38–55 Ballard | Lead | 255 | B | 1884 | Case 2¹⁄₁₀ |
| *38–55 WCF | L, SP | 255 | | 1886 | |
| | FP, BS | | | | |
| *38–56 | L, SP | 255 | BS | 1887 | |
| | FP | | | | |
| *38–70 | L, SP | 255 | BS | 1894 | Case 2⁵⁄₁₆ |
| *38–72 | L, SP | 275 | BS | 1896 | Case 2⁶⁄₁₀ |
| | FP | | | | |
| *38–90 Ex. | Lead | 217 | B | 1886 | Case 3¼ |
| 380 Colt Auto | FP | 95 | S | 1909 | |
| 40–50 Sharps | Lead | 285 | B | 1876 | Case 1¹¹⁄₁₆ |
| 40–50 Sharps | Lead | 265 | B | 1879 | Case 1⅞ |
| Straight | | | | | |
| 40–60 Marlin | Lead | 260 | B | 1884 | Case 2¹⁄₁₀ |
| *40–60 WCF | Lead | 210 | B | 1884 | Case 1⅞ |
| *40–65 WCF | Lead SP | 260 | BS | 1887 | Case 2¹⁄₁₀ |
| 40–65 Sharps | Lead | 330 | B | | Case 2½ |
| and Rem | | | | | |
| 40–70 Ballard | Lead | 330 | B | 1883 | Case 2⅜ |
| 40–70 Bullard | Lead | 232 | B | 1884 | Case 2⅜ |
| 40–70 Sharps | Lead | 370 | B | 1876 | Case 2¼ |
| 40–70 Sharps | Lead | 330 | B | 1879 | Case 2½ |
| Straight | | | | | |
| 40–70 Peabody | | | | | |
| Martini | | | | | |
| What Cheer | Lead | 380 | B | 1878 | Case 1¾ |
| *40–70 WCF | Lead | 330 | BS | 1894 | Case 2⁴⁄₁₀ |
| *40–72 WCF | Lead SP | 330 | BS | 1896 | Case 2⁶⁄₁₀ |
| *40–75 WCF | Lead | 260 | B | 1887 | Case 2⁴⁄₁₀ |
| *40–82 WCF | Lead SP | 260 | BS | 1885 | Case 2¹⁵⁄₁₆ |
| 40–85 Ballard | Lead | 370 | B | 1885 | Case 2¹⁵⁄₁₆ |
| 40–90 Ballard | Lead | 370 | B | 1884 | Case 2¹⁵⁄₁₆ |
| 40–90 Bullard | Lead | 300 | B | 1884 | Case 2¹⁄₃₂ |

| | Bullet | Weight (grains) | Powder | First Loaded | Remarks |
|---|---|---|---|---|---|
| 40–90 Sharps and Rem | Lead | 370 | B | 1878 | Case 2⅝ |
| 40–90 Sharps Straight | Lead | 370 | B | 1884 | Case 3¼ |
| 40–90 Peabody Martini What Cheer | Lead | 500 | B | 1879 | Case 2¹⁄₁₆ |
| *40–110 Win Ex | Lead | 260 | B | 1886 | Case 3¼ |
| *401 WSL | SP FP | 200<br>250 | S | 1910 | |
| *405 WCF | SP FP | 300 | S | 1904 | |
| 41 Cal | Lead | 130 | BL | 1878 | |
| 41 Short Colt | Lead | 160 | BLS | 1884 | |
| 41 Long Colt | Lead | 200 | BLS | 1876 | |
| 42 Russian | Lead | 370 | B | 1876 | Case 2¼ |
| 42 Russian Carbine | Lead | 370 | B | 1878 | Case 1⅞ |
| 43 Carbine | Lead | 400 | B | 1878 | Case 1⅞ |
| 43 Egyptian | Lead | 400 | B | 1878 | Case 1¹⁵⁄₁₆ |
| 43 Greek (11mm. Gras) | Lead | 395 | B | 1878 | |
| 43 Mauser | Lead | 375 | B | 1878 | |
| 43 Peabody | Lead | 395 | B | 1878 | |
| 43 Spanish | Lead | 395 | B | 1876 | Case 2¼ |
| 44 Bulldog | Lead | 168 | BL | 1884 | |
| 44 Colt | Lead | 210 | BL | 1876 | |
| 44 CLMR | Lead SP | 217 | BLS | 1895 | |
| 44 Evans OM | Lead | 215 | B | 1878 | |
| 44 Evans NM | Lead | 280 | BL | 1883 | |
| *44 Henry CF | Lead | 200 | B | 1891 | |
| 44 Game Getter | Lead | 115 | BLS | 1910 | |
| 44 Long | Lead | 250 | B | 1876 | |
| 44 MH | Lead | 220 | BL | 1882 | |
| 44 Rem | Lead | 200 | B | 1878 | |
| 44 SW American | Lead | 205 | BLS | 1876 | |
| 44 SW Russian | Lead | 255<br>105<br>115 | BLS | 1876 | |
| 44 S&W Special | Lead | 246 | BLS | 1909 | |
| 44 Webley | Lead | 200 | BL | 1876 | |
| *44 WCF (44–40) | Lead SP<br>FP HP | 200<br>180 | BLS | 1873 | |
| 44–40 Marlin | Lead SP | 217 | BLS | 1895 | |
| 44–60 Sharps | Lead | 395 | B | 1877 | Case 1⁹⁄₁₀ |
| 44–77 Sharps | Lead | 470 | B | 1876 | Case 2¼ |
| 44–90 Rem Creedmore | Lead | 520<br>550 | B | 1876 | |

| | *Bullet* | *Weight (grains)* | *Powder* | *First Loaded* | *Remarks* |
|---|---|---|---|---|---|
| 44–90 Rem Special | Lead | 470 | B | 1876 | |
| 44–90 Rem. and Sharps Special | Lead | 520 | B | 1876 | |
| 44–90–105 Sharps | Lead | 520 | | 1876 | |
| 44–95 Peabody Martini What Cheer | Lead | 550 | B | 1878 | |
| 45 S&W | Lead | 250 | BL | 1876 | |
| 45 Van Choate | Lead | 420 | B | 1879 | Case 2¼ |
| *45–60 WCF | Lead | 300 | B | 1879 | |
| 45–70 Govt | Lead FP SP | 500, 405 300, 200 | BS | 1876 | Case 2 1/10 |
| *45–70 WCF | Lead SP FP | 350, 330 | BS | 1886 | |
| 45–70 Marlin | Lead SP | 405 | B | 1884 | Case 2 1/10 |
| 45–75 Sharps | Lead | 420 | B | 1885 | Case 2 1/10 |
| *45–75 WCF | Lead | 350 | B | 1876 | Case 1⅞ |
| *45–82 WCF | Lead | 405 | | 1887 | Case 2 4/10 |
| 45–85 Bullard | Lead | 285 | B | 1884 | Case 2 1/10 |
| 45–85 Colt | Lead | 290 | B | 1914 | |
| 45–85 Marlin | Lead | 285 | B | 1885 | Case 2 1/10 |
| *45–85 WCF | Lead | 300 | B | 1896 | Case 2 4/10 |
| *45–90 WCF | Lead FP SP | 300 | BS | 1886 | Case 2 4/10 |
| 45–90–450 Winchester Special Long Range Model 1876 | Lead | 450 | B | 1878 | |
| *45–125 Win Ex | Lead | 300 | | 1886 | Case 3¼ |
| 450 WR #1 Musket | Lead | | B | 1886 | Case 2¼ |
| 45 Colt | Lead | 255 | BLS | 1876 | |
| 45 Colt Govt | Lead | 255 | B | 1914 | |
| 45 Colt Auto | FP | 200 230 | S | 1905 | |
| 45 Auto Rim | Lead FP | | S | 1931 | |
| 45 Danish | Lead | 380 | B | 1878 | Case 1⅝ |
| 45 Martini Henry | Lead | 480 | B | 1876 | Case 2 5/16 |
| 45 Turkish Peabody | Lead | 480 | B | 1879 | Case 2 3/10 |
| 45 Peabody Martini Carbine | Lead | 400 | B | 1879 | Case 1⅝ |
| 45 Roumanian | Lead | 380 | B | 1876 | Case 1 15/16 |
| 45–70 Sharps | Lead | 420 | B | 1885 | Case 2 1/10 |
| 45 Sharps 2 4/10 | Lead | 500 | B | 1884 | Case 2 4/10 |
| 45 Sharps 2 6/10 | Lead | 500 | B | 1884 | Case 2 6/10 |
| 45 Sharps 2⅞ | Lead | 550 | B | 1878 | Case 2⅞ |

| | Bullet | Weight (grains) | Powder | First Loaded | Remarks |
|---|---|---|---|---|---|
| 45 Sharps 3¼ | Lead | 550 | B | 1884 | Case 3¼ |
| 45 Peabody Sporting | Lead | 290 | B | 1876 | Case 1³⁷⁄₆₄ |
| 450 Cal | Lead | 230 | BS | 1919 | |
| 455 Eley | Lead | 265 | BS | 1901 | |
| 455 Colt | Lead | 265 | BS | 1904 | |
| 450 Colt | Lead | 265 | BS | 1901 | |
| 50 Carbine | Lead | 400 | B | 1876 | Case 1¹¹⁄₃₂ |
| 50 Pistol | Lead | 425 | B | 1876 | |
| 50 Sporting Sharps | Lead | 425 | B | 1876 | Case 1¾ |
| 50–70 Musket | Lead | 450 | B | 1876 | Case 1¾ |
| 50–90 Sharps | Lead | 473 | B | 1878 | Case 2½ |
| *50–90 WCF (50–95) | Lead SP HP | 300, 312 | BS | 1879 | |
| *50–100–450 | Lead | 450 | BS | 1895 | |
| *50–105 | Lead | 300 | B | 1886 | |
| *50–110 | HP FP SP | 300 | BS | 1887 | |
| *50–140 | Lead | 300 | B | 1886 | |
| Cal. 50 M1918 & 19 | FP | 700 | S | 1918 1919 | |
| Cal. 50 Browning M1921 | Ball AP Tracer Explosive | | S | | |
| 58 Carbine | Lead | 530 | B | 1877 | Case 1⅛ |
| 58 Musket | Lead | 530 | B | 1877 | Case 1¾ |
| 58 Roberts | Lead | 480 | B | 1884 | Case 1⅜ |
| 58 Turkish | Lead | 480 | B 85 | 1875 | |
| *70–150 | Lead | | B | 1888 | |
| 50 Sharps 3¼ | Lead | 700 | B | | |
| Cal. 60 | FP | 1100 | S | 1939 | |
| 1-in. Gatling | Lead | | B | | |
| 5.5 Velo Dog | FP | 45 | S | 1919 | |
| 6mm. Lee Rimless | FP SP | 112 135 | S | 1894 | |
| 6mm. Lee rimmed | FP | 135 | S | 1894 | |
| 6.5 Mann Schoe | SP | 160 | S | 1914 | |
| 6.5 Dutch Mann | FP | 160 | S | 1914/15 | |
| 7mm. Mauser | FP HP SP | 139, 175 | S | 1899 | |
| 7.5 Reichger (Swiss) | FP | 180 | S | 1921 | |
| 7.62 Russian | FP HCT | 145 | S | 1914 | |
| 7.63 Mauser | FP SP HP | 86 | S | 1900 | |
| 7.65 Roth Sauer | FP | 71 | S | 1908 | |

| | Bullet | Weight (grains) | Powder | First Loaded | Remarks |
|---|---|---|---|---|---|
| 7.65 Luger | FP | 93 | S | 1902 | |
| 7.65 Mauser | FP | 215 | S | 1900 | |
| | SP | 219 | | | |
| | | 154 | | | |
| 7.65 Argentine Navy Match | FP | 180 | S | 1914 | |
| 7.92 Mauser (8mm.) | FP | 227, 170 | S | 1914 | |
| 8mm. Mann-Schoe | FP SP | | S | 1904 | |
| 8mm. Mann-Mauser | FP SP | 227, 236 | S | 1905 | |
| 8mm. Siamese | FP | 180 | S | 1924 | |
| 9mm. Luger | FP HP | 125, 115 | S | 1908 | |
| 9 x 57 Mauser | FP SP | 280 | S | 1905 | |
| 9.8 Colt AP | FP | 130, 150 | S | 1910 | |
| 10.4 Italian | FP | | B | | |
| 11mm. Mauser | Lead | 370 | BS | 1878 | |
| 11mm. Brazilian Comblain | Lead | | B | | |
| 11mm. Montenegrin Revolver | Lead | | B | 1912 | |
| 11mm. Jap Murata | Lead | | B | | |

* Developed for Winchester Rifles.

*Abbreviations*

B — *Black*
L — *Lesmok*
S — *Smokeless*
HP — *Hollow Point*
SP — *Soft Point*
FP — *Full Patch*
ST — *Silver Tip*
PP — *Protected Point*
HCT — *Hollow Copper Tube*
LB — *Lead Bearing*

No attempt has been made to list all the bullet weights and types in every caliber.

Factory records of cartridge manufacture prior to 1877 are extremely sketchy. Dates given for first manufacture are as accurate as can be determined from existing records.

# APPENDIX C

## SERIAL NUMBERS AND SHIPPING DATES; SELECTED WINCHESTER RIFLE AND SHOTGUN MODELS, 1875–1900

*By Thomas E. Hall*

### MODEL 1866

No record of sales available prior to 1875.

| *Serial Number* | *Year* | *Serial Number* | *Year* |
|---|---|---|---|
| 125,000 to 125,600 | 1875 | 162,401 to 163,700 | 1884 |
| 125,601 to 131,900 | 1876 | ———— | 1885 |
| 131,901 to 148,200 | 1877 | 163,701 to 165,000 | 1886 |
| 148,201 to 150,500 | 1878 | 165,001 to 165,900 | 1887 |
| 150,501 to 152,100 | 1879 | 165,901 to 167,100 | 1888 |
| 152,101 to 154,200 | 1880 | 167,101 to 167,400 | 1889 |
| 154,201 to 155,700 | 1881 | 167,401 to 167,900 | 1890 |
| 155,701 to 159,500 | 1882 | 167,901 to 169,000 | 1891 |
| 159,501 to 162,400 | 1883 | 169,001 to 170,100 | 1892–98 |

### MODEL 1873

| *Serial Number* | *Year* | *Serial Number* | *Year* |
|---|---|---|---|
| 1 | 1873 | 26 | 1873 |
| 2 | " | 27 | " |
| 3 | " | 30 | " |
| 6 | " | 32 | " |
| 7 | " | 33 | " |
| 9 | " | 36 | " |
| 10 | " | 41 | " |
| 23 | " | 43 | " |
| 24 | " | 49 | " |

The above listed numbers were actually shipped from the plant in the year 1873. It will be noted that some numbers that should be included in this group were held back. The reason for this cannot be explained.

| *Serial Number* | *Year* | *Serial Number* | *Year* |
|---|---|---|---|
| 4 to 2,780 | 1874 | 253,804 to 282,435 | 1888 |
| 2,781 to 9,996 | 1875 | 282,436 to 321,717 | 1889 |
| 9,997 to 13,225 | 1876 | 321,718 to 362,104 | 1890 |
| 13,226 to 15,008 | 1877 | 362,105 to 404,549 | 1891 |
| 15,009 to 22,177 | 1878 | 404,550 to 440,765 | 1892 |
| 22,178 to 40,550 | 1879 | 440,766 to 465,948 | 1893 |
| 40,551 to 62,177 | 1880 | 465,949 to 480,714 | 1894 |
| 62,178 to 81,313 | 1881 | 480,715 to 499,299 | 1895 |
| 81,314 to 107,492 | 1882 | 499,300 to 507,534 | 1896 |
| 107,493 to 139,060 | 1883 | 507,535 to 513,403 | 1897 |
| 139,061 to 168,403 | 1884 | 513,404 to 525,299 | 1898 |
| 168,404 to 195,448 | 1885 | 525,300 to 540,648 | 1899 |
| 195,449 to 221,832 | 1886 | 540,649 to 550,250 | 1900 |
| 221,833 to 253,803 | 1887 | | |

**MODEL 1876**

| Serial Number | Year | Serial Number | Year |
|---|---|---|---|
| 1 to 1,258 | 1877 | 55,826 to 58,708 | 1887 |
| 1,259 to 7,965 | 1878 | 58,709 to 60,485 | 1888 |
| 7,966 to 8,950 | 1879 | 60,486 to 62,025 | 1889 |
| 8,951 to 12,050 | 1880 | 62,026 to 62,322 | 1890 |
| 12,051 to 20,050 | 1881 | 62,323 to 62,783 | 1891 |
| 20,051 to 31,100 | 1882 | 62,784 to 63,678 | 1892 |
| 31,101 to 36,214 | 1883 | 63,679 to 63,788 | 1893 |
| 36,215 to 42,600 | 1884 | 63,789 to 63,868 | 1894–97 |
| 42,601 to 49,720 | 1885 | 63,869 to 63,871 | 1898 |
| 49,721 to 55,825 | 1886 | | |

**HOTCHKISS**

| Serial Number | Year | Serial Number | Year |
|---|---|---|---|
| 1 to 3,100 | 1879 | 56,972 to 67,200 | 1890 |
| 3,101 to 4,492 | 1880 | ———— | 1891 |
| 4,493 to 15,392 | 1881 | 67,201 to 68,077 | 1892 |
| 15,393 to 19,769 | 1882 | 68,078 to 70,879 | 1893 |
| 19,770 to 22,550 | 1883 | 70,880 to 77,939 | 1894 |
| 22,551 to 43,170 | 1884 | 77,940 to 84,229 | 1895 |
| 43,171 to 53,070 | 1885 | 84,230 to 84,428 | 1896 |
| 53,071 to 54,798 | 1886 | ———— | 1897 |
| ———— | 1887 | 84,429 to 84,551 | 1898 |
| ———— | 1888 | 84,552 to 84,555 | 1899 |
| 54,799 to 56,971 | 1889 | | |

**MODEL 1885 SINGLE SHOT**

| Serial Number | Year | Serial Number | Year |
|---|---|---|---|
| 1 to 272 | 1885 | 59,801 to 65,798 | 1893 |
| 273 to 6,543 | 1886 | 65,799 to 69,086 | 1894 |
| 6,544 to 16,330 | 1887 | 69,087 to 73,771 | 1895 |
| 16,331 to 29,695 | 1888 | 73,772 to 76,197 | 1896 |
| 29,696 to 36,951 | 1889 | 76,198 to 78,872 | 1897 |
| 36,952 to 44,047 | 1890 | 78,873 to 82,256 | 1898 |
| 44,048 to 52,398 | 1891 | 82,257 to 85,086 | 1899 |
| 52,399 to 59,800 | 1892 | 85,087 to 87,544 | 1900 |

**MODEL 1886**

| Serial Number | Year | Serial Number | Year |
|---|---|---|---|
| 1 to 2,082 | 1886 | 83,199 to 92,534 | 1894 |
| 2,083 to 12,034 | 1887 | 92,535 to 103,102 | 1895 |
| 12,035 to 28,494 | 1888 | 103,103 to 109,594 | 1896 |
| 28,495 to 37,299 | 1889 | 109,595 to 113,945 | 1897 |
| 37,300 to 49,122 | 1890 | 113,946 to 118,433 | 1898 |
| 49,123 to 63,019 | 1891 | 118,434 to 120,568 | 1899 |
| 63,020 to 72,473 | 1892 | 120,569 to 122,826 | 1900 |
| 72,474 to 83,198 | 1893 | | |

| *Serial Number* | *Year* | *Serial Number* | *Year* |
|---|---|---|---|
| | MODEL 1887 L. A. SHOT GUNS | | |
| 1 to 6,928 | 1887 | 54,327 to 56,210 | 1894 |
| 6,929 to 20,351 | 1888 | 56,211 to 57,699 | 1895 |
| 20,352 to 24,443 | 1889 | 57,700 to 59,960 | 1896 |
| 24,444 to 28,620 | 1890 | 59,961 to 62,620 | 1897 |
| 28,621 to 38,222 | 1891 | 62,621 to 64,842 | 1898 |
| 38,223 to 48,660 | 1892 | 64,843 to 64,855 | 1899 |
| 48,661 to 54,326 | 1893 | | |

LEE NAVY

| *Serial Number* * | *Year* |
|---|---|
| 1 to 1,917 | 1896 |
| 1,918 to 10,512 | 1897 |
| 10,513 to 20,000 | 1898 |

* No receivers numbered from 11,719—12,002, 13,701—13,733, 14,980—15,000. Rifles numbered from 13,734 to 14,979 were held at the plant and sold between 1901 and 1908.

## APPENDIX D-1

### WINCHESTER GUN SALES
(in thousands)

| *Year* | *Number* | *Year* | *Number* | *Year* | *Number* | *Year* | *Number* |
|---|---|---|---|---|---|---|---|
| 1869 | 10.9 | 1885 | 51.1 | 1901 | 172.9 | 1917 | 221.7 |
| 1870 | 22.6 | 1886 | 46.5 | 1902 | 193.9 | 1918 | 182.5 |
| 1871 | 34.6 | 1887 | 61.4 | 1903 | 198.3 | 1919 | 304.6 |
| 1872 | 22.7 | 1888 | 64.4 | 1904 | 225.4 | 1920 | —— |
| 1873 | 8.5 | 1889 | 72.0 | 1905 | 246.3 | 1921 | 70.2 |
| 1874 | 7.2 | 1890 | 79.1 | 1906 | 346.0 | 1922 | 123.1 |
| 1875 | 9.8 | 1891 | 80.5 | 1907 | 309.6 | 1923 | 152.3 |
| 1876 | 9.9 | 1892 | 82.8 | 1908 | 228.8 | 1924 | 133.7 |
| 1877 | 19.5 | 1893 | 71.5 | 1909 | 262.6 | 1925 | 144.4 |
| 1878 | 9.8 | 1894 | 75.4 | 1910 | 316.8 | 1926 | 162.9 |
| 1879 | 18.7 | 1895 | 71.0 | 1911 | 288.9 | 1927 | 185.1 |
| 1880 | 26.5 | 1896 | 60.2 | 1912 | 324.5 | 1928 | 183.7 |
| 1881 | 41.5 | 1897 | 78.2 | 1913 | 310.8 | 1929 | 165.8 |
| 1882 | 44.9 | 1898 | 108.9 | 1914 | 292.4 | 1930 | 99.1 |
| 1883 | 41.4 | 1899 | 113.0 | 1915 | 265.7 | 1931 | 112.8 |
| 1884 | 49.1 | 1900 | 163.7 | 1916 | 184.5 | | |
| | | | | | | TOTAL | 8062.2 |

*Note.* Sales data for 1915–1919 do not include 771,019 service rifles and 19,796 BARs for the British and American governments.

## APPENDIX D-2

### PRODUCTION FIGURES OF OBSOLETE WINCHESTER MODELS TO 1945

*By Thomas E. Hall*

| *Year Model Introduced* | *Year Model Discontinued* | *Total Number Manufactured* | |
|---|---|---|---|
| Model 1866 | 1898 | 170,101 | |
| (This total includes 1,000 rifles which, in 1891, were chambered for .44 Henry C.F. cartridges) | | | |
| Model 1873 | 1924 | 720,610 | |
| (Model 1873 caliber 22 rifles, included in above total 19,552.) | | | |
| Model 1873 | One of One Thousand | 135 | |
| Model 1876 | 1897 | 63,871 | |
| Model 1876 | One of One Thousand | 47 | |
| Hotchkiss 1879 1st type | 1880 | 6,419 | } 84,555 |
| Hotchkiss 1880 2nd type | 1883 | 16,102 | } 84,555 |
| Hotchkiss Model 1883 | 1899 | 62,034 | } 84,555 |
| Model 1885 Single Shot | 1920 | 139,725 | |
| Model 1886 | 1935 | 159,994 | |
| Model 1890 | 1932 | 849,000 | |

| Year Model Introduced | Year Model Discontinued | Total Number Manufactured |
|---|---|---|
| Model 1892 | 1941 | 1,004,067 |
| Lee Navy 1895 | 1900 | 20,000 |
| (This Lee Navy total includes 1,700 Sporter rifles.) | | |
| Model 1895 | 1931 | 425,881 |
| (This Model 1895 total includes 293,816—7.62 m/m rifles, sold to Russia in 1915–1916.) | | |
| Model 1900 | 1902 | 105,000 |
| Model 1902 | 1931 | 640,299 |
| Model 1903 | 1936 | 126,000 |
| Model 99 Thumb trigger 1904 | 1923 | 75,433 |
| Model 1904 | 1931 | 302,859 |
| Model 1905 | 1920 | 29,113 |
| Model 1906 | 1932 | 848,000 |
| Model 1910 | 1936 | 20,786 |
| 1914 British Enfield (1915) | 1917 | 245,866 |
| 1917 U.S. Enfield (1917) | 1918 | 545,511 |
| B.A.R. (1918) | 1918 | 47,123 |
| Model 53 (1924) | 1932 | 24,916 |
| Model 55 (1924) | 1932 | 20,580 |
| Model 54 (1925) | 1936 | 50,145 |
| Model 56 (1926) | 1929 | 8,297 |
| Model 57 (1926) | 1936 | 18,600 |
| Model 58 (1928) | 1931 | 38,992 |
| Model 59 (1930) | 1930 | 9,293 |
| Model 60 (1930) | 1934 | 165,754 |
| Model 60-A (1932) | 1939 | 6,118 |
| Model 65 (1933) | 1947 | 5,704 |
| Garand (1940) | 1945 | 513,582 |
| M-1 Carbine (1942) | 1945 | 818,059 |
| | WINCHESTER SHOTGUNS | |
| Model 1887 | 1899 | 64,855 |
| Model 1893 | 1897 | 34,050 |
| Model 1901 | 1920 | 13,500 |
| Model 1911 | 1925 | 82,774 |
| Model 20–1919 | 1924 | 23,616 |
| Model 36–1920 | 1927 | 20,306 |
| Model 41–1920 | 1934 | 22,146 |
| Model 40–1940 | 1941 | 12,000 |
| TOTAL | | 8,471,264 |

# APPENDIX E

## STOCKHOLDERS OF VOLCANIC REPEATING ARMS COMPANY

CAPITAL STOCK: $150,000, 6000 shares, par $25.00.

| INCORPORATORS: | Horace Smith | Norwich, Connecticut |
|---|---|---|
| | Daniel B. Wesson | Norwich, Connecticut |
| | Courtlandt Palmer | New York, New York |

SUBSCRIBERS TO STOCK:

| | *Name* | *Address* | *Business* |
|---|---|---|---|
| 1. | Adams, James N. | 41 St. John St., New Haven | Clockmaker |
| 2. | Alcott, John E. | 95 Wallace St., New Haven | Joiner |
| 3. | Bates, Charles B. | 41 St. John St., New Haven | Clockmaker |
| 4. | Bishop, George B. | 37 Hamilton St., New Haven | Carriage maker |
| 5. | Bowditch, E. B. | 41 St. John St., New Haven | Clockmaker |
| 6. | Bryant, C. B. | 41 St. John St., New Haven | Clockmaker |
| 7. | Buchanan, R. N. | | |
| 8. | Bushnell, H. T. & C. S. | State-Crown, New Haven | Grocers |
| 9. | Camp, Hiram | 76 Wooster St., New Haven | Pres., N. H. Clock Co. |
| 10. | Campbell, James B. | | |
| 11. | Converse, Paschal | 41 St. John St., New Haven | Clockmaker |
| 12. | Dickerman, Charles | Howe & George, New Haven | Coach manufacturer |
| 13. | Gaston, Nelson H. | 137 Orange St., New Haven | Shipping merchant |
| 14. | Gilbert, Sachett | 43 Crown St., New Haven | Saddle mfr. |
| 15. | Harris, Charles S. | | |
| 16. | Hicks, William C. | New Haven | Machinist |
| 17. | Hooker, Henry | 96 York St. | Carriage manufacturer |
| 18. | Kendrick, Green | | |
| 19. | Linsley, James N. | | |
| 20. | Perry, Silas R. | 84 Hamilton St. | Clockmaker |
| 21. | Post, J. W. | | |
| 22. | Robertson, Wm. H. | | |
| 23. | Sherman, Thaddeus | 20 High St., New Haven | |
| 24. | Stannard, Ruben | | |
| 25. | Stock, I. C. | 68 Wooster St., New Haven | Conductor of NH RR |
| 26. | Strong, Wm. | | |
| 27. | Talcott, Samuel L. | | |
| 28. | Tyler, Morris | 77 George St., New Haven | Shoe business |
| 29. | Winchester, O. F. | 57 Court St., New Haven | Shirt manufacturer |

## APPENDIX F

WINCHESTER NET SALES, PROFITS, PROFITS AS PERCENTAGE OF SALES, DIVIDENDS, DIVIDENDS AS PERCENTAGE OF PROFITS: 1869–1914

| *Year* | *Net sales (in thousands)* | *Profits* [1] *(in thousands)* | *Profits as precentage of net sales* | *Dividends (in thousands)* | *Dividends as percentage of profits* |
|---|---|---|---|---|---|
| 1869 | $ 323.5 | (80.1) [2] | | $ 70.0 | 21.6 |
| 1870 | 809.4 | 219.0 | 27.0 | 50.0 | 6.2 |
| 1871 | 1015.7 | 280.0 | 27.7 | 25.0 | 2.5 |
| 1872 | 591.5 | 160.0 | 27.0 | 50.0 | 8.5 |
| 1873 | 355.3 | | | 50.0 | |
| 1874 | 1834.7 | 265.0 | 12.1 | 50.0 | 37.9 |
| 1875 | 1067.0 | 444.1 | 41.9 | 50.0 | 11.5 |
| 1876 | 1812.5 | 444.5 | 24.5 | 50.0 | 11.2 |
| 1877 | 2802.6 | 668.4 | 23.7 | 100.0 | 15.0 |
| 1878 | 1319.8 | 221.0 | 16.7 | 75.0 | 31.6 |
| 1879 | 919.4 | 206.3 | 22.4 | 50.0 | 24.2 |
| 1880 | 1235.3 | 319.0 | 25.9 | 100.0 | 31.4 |
| 1881 | 1799.0 | 238.0 | 13.2 | 50.0 | 21.0 |
| 1882 | 1662.0 | 353.0 | 21.3 | 80.0 | 22.6 |
| 1883 | 1868.0 | 385.0 | 20.6 | 130.0 | 33.8 |
| 1884 | 2011.0 | 493.4 | 24.5 | 150.0 | 30.4 |
| 1885 | 1840.1 | 419.6 | 22.8 | 170.0 | 40.5 |
| 1886 | 1743.0 | 401.3 | 23.1 | 170.0 | 42.0 |
| 1887 | 1909.0 | 432.1 | 22.6 | 220.0 | 51.0 |
| 1888 | 1994.3 | 466.0 | 23.4 | 250.0 | 53.5 |
| 1889 | 2503.0 | 696.2 | 27.8 | 400.0 | 57.5 |
| 1890 | 2716.4 | 688.0 | 25.3 | 490.0 | 77.0 |
| 1891 | 2910.0 | 776.0 | 26.7 | 500.0 | 64.0 |
| 1892 | 3066.0 | 856.3 | 28.0 | 510.0 | 59.5 |
| 1893 | 2447.0 | 596.3 | 24.3 | 440.0 | 73.5 |
| 1894 | 2833.0 | 714.0 | 25.2 | 520.0 | 73.0 |
| 1895 | 2891.0 | 706.0 | 24.4 | 460.0 | 65.0 |
| 1896 | 2608.0 | 448.1 | 17.2 | 350.0 | 78.0 |
| 1897 | 3343.0 | 667.0 | 20.0 | 505.0 | 75.0 |
| 1898 | 5150.0 | 1308.0 | 25.4 | 900.0 | 69.0 |
| 1899 | 4846.0 | 1086.0 | 22.4 | 855.0 | 79.0 |
| 1900 | 4924.0 | 1130.3 | 23.0 | 880.0 | 78.0 |
| 1901 | 6237.0 | 1390.0 | 22.3 | 1180.0 | 78.0 |
| 1902 | 7044.4 | 1385.4 | 19.7 | 725.0 | 52.5 |
| 1903 | 7080.1 | 1295.0 | 18.3 | 825.0 | 64.5 |
| 1904 | 7521.4 | 1231.3 | 16.4 | 725.0 | 58.5 |
| 1905 | 8210.0 | 1335.0 | 16.2 | 625.0 | 47.0 |
| 1906 | 10136.0 | 1681.0 | 16.7 | 725.0 | 43.0 |
| 1907 | 10050.2 | 948.2 | 9.4 | 200.0 | 21.0 |
| 1908 | 9442.0 | 1334.0 | 14.1 | 450.0 | 33.5 |
| 1909 | 9782.0 | 1447.0 | 14.8 | 425.0 | 29.4 |
| 1910 | 10192.0 | 1802.0 | 17.7 | 650.0 | 36.0 |
| 1911 | 9948.0 | 1673.0 | 16.8 | 650.0 | 39.0 |
| 1912 | 11059.1 | 1874.2 | 16.9 | 650.0 | 34.5 |
| 1913 | 10898.3 | 1713.1 | 15.7 | 550.0 | 32.0 |
| 1914 | 11782.0 | 2153.3 | 18.3 | 450.0 | 21.0 |

[1] Profits before depreciation. [2] Loss.

# APPENDIX G-1

## NEW HAVEN ARMS COMPANY

*Approximate Balance Sheet December 1866*

| | | | |
|---|---|---|---|
| ASSETS | | | |
| Cash | | $ 1,374.65 | |
| Accounts Receivable | | 182,234.20 | |
| Inventory | | | |
| Guns | $58,311.53 | | |
| Ammunition | 14,136.21 | 72,447.74 | |
| Machinery, Tools, Fixtures | | 150,000.00 | |
| Other Assets | | 136,000.00 | $542,056.59 |
| TOTAL LIABILITIES (detail not available) | | | 188,493.58 |
| NET WORTH | | | 353,563.01 |

(*Note.* Book value per share of 1,940 shares outstanding—$182.25.)

# APPENDIX G-2

## WINCHESTER REPEATING ARMS COMPANY

*Estimated Balance Sheet, April 1, 1867*

| | | |
|---|---|---|
| CURRENT ASSETS | | |
| Cash | $ 1,374.65 | |
| Accounts Receivable from New Haven Arms Company | 182,234.20 | |
| Inventory | 72,447.74 | |
| Chilean-Peruvian Assets | 57,000.00 | |
| Stock Subscription Receivable (payable April 1–December 1, 1867) | 82,936.99 | $395,993.58 |
| LESS: CURRENT LIABILITIES | | |
| Accounts Payable from New Haven Arms Company | 188,493.58 | |
| Due Stockholders of New Haven Arms Company | 136,500.00 | 324,993.58 |
| NET WORKING CAPITAL | | 71,000.00 |
| FIXED ASSETS | | |
| Value of New Haven Arms Company Plant | 150,000.00 | |
| Other Assets | | |
| Burnside Rifle Claim [1] | 21,000.00 | |
| Mexican Matter [2] | 58,000.00 | |
| Patent Rights | 150,000.00 | 379,000.00 |
| NET WORTH (represented by Capital Stock) | | $450,000.00 |

[1] The nature of this claim is not revealed in the Company records.
[2] Amount due from sale of arms and ammunition to Mexico.

# APPENDIX G-3

## WINCHESTER REPEATING ARMS COMPANY

*Balance Sheet at December 13, 1872*

| | | | |
|---|---|---|---|
| CURRENT ASSETS | | | |
| Cash | $ 83,624.17 | | |
| Bills receivable | 2,783.09 | | |
| Sundry renewables | 29,467.98 | | |
| "Merchandise" (Presumably inventories) | 183,618.53 | | |
| Imperial Ottoman Government | 318,992.57 | $618,416.34 | |
| LESS: CURRENT LIABILITIES | | | |
| Sundry credit balances | 34,084.33 | | |
| Bills payable | 104,050.00 | | |
| Azarian Pere et Fils | 55,856.66 | | |
| Dividend payable 2/1/73 | 25,000.00 | 218,990.99 | |
| NET WORKING CAPITAL | | | $399,425.35 |
| FIXED ASSETS | | | |
| Value of Real Estate, Plant & Machinery, 4/1/67 | 150,000.00 | | |
| Estimated Total expenditure, 4/1/67 to 12/31/72 | 495,930.00 | | |
| Patents | | | |
| Acquired from O. F. Winchester | 150,000.00 | | |
| Estimated total expenditure, 4/1/67 to 12/31/72 | 81,175.00 | 877,105.00 | |
| DEDUCT: LOAN LIABILITIES | | | |
| Estate of J. M. Davies | 85,000.00 | | |
| O. F. Winchester | 14,425.35 | 99,425.00 | |
| NET FIXED CAPITAL | | | 777,680.00 |
| ESTIMATED NET WORTH AT DEC. 13, 1872 | | | $1,177,105.35 |

(*Note.* No account has been taken of depreciation; nor is it safe to assume that the additions to plant, machinery, *etc.* represent exclusively "capital" items, since accounting practice during the period often failed to distinguish adequately between addition to plant and the repair and maintenance expenditures necessary to keep the plant in full operating efficiency.)

# APPENDIX G-4

## WINCHESTER REPEATING ARMS COMPANY

*Balance Sheet at December 31, 1880*

| | | |
|---|---|---|
| CURRENT ASSETS | | |
| Cash | $ 76,851.98 | |
| Bills Receivable | 101,153.40 | |
| Sundry Receivable | 241,130.80 | |
| Inventories | 628,456.92 | |
| Investments—Time Deposits | 200,000.00 | |
| Other | 5,212.61 | $1,252,805.71 |
| LESS: CURRENT LIABILITIES | | 99,767.15 |
| NET WORKING CAPITAL | | 1,153,038.56 |
| FIXED ASSETS | | |
| Value of Real Estate, Plant and Machinery, 4/1/67 | 150,000.00 | |
| Estimated total expenditures from 4/1/67 to 12/31/80 | 1,350,345.00 | |
| Patents | | |
| Acquired from O. F. Winchester | 150,000.00 | |
| Estimated total expenditure from 4/1/67 to 12/31/80 | 240,718.00 | |
| NET FIXED CAPITAL | | 1,891,063.00 |
| ESTIMATED NET WORTH AT DEC. 31, 1880 | | 3,044,101.56 |

(*Note.* This balance sheet reflects the estimated *total* expenditures on fixed capital assets, no account being taken of depreciation or of the probability that certain expenditures of a capital nature were charged off as an expense. [*Cf.* note to Appendix G-6.] The book value of the real estate and plant and machinery was to December 31, 1880, $950,000, suggesting an implicit depreciation fund of over $550,000 which would appear to be more than adequate.

# APPENDIX G-5

## WINCHESTER REPEATING ARMS COMPANY

*Balance Sheet at December 31, 1889*

| | | |
|---|---|---|
| CURRENT ASSETS | | |
| Cash | $ 575,676.09 | |
| Bills Receivable | 83,768.81 | |
| Sundry Receivables | 145,706.14 | |
| Inventories | 915,963.69 | |
| Investments | 630,998.75 | $2,352,113.48 |
| LESS: CURRENT LIABILITIES | | 90,555.48 |
| NET WORKING CAPITAL | | 2,261,558.07 |
| FIXED ASSETS | | |
| Real Estate, Plant and Machinery, 4/1/67 | 150,000.00 | |
| Estimated total expenditure from 4/1/67 to 12/31/89 | 2,483,444.00 | |
| Patents | | |
| Acquired from O. F. Winchester | 150,000.00 | |
| Expenditures from 4/1/67 to 12/31/89 | 340,176.00 | |
| Investment | | |
| Remington Arms Co. | 178,075.00 | |
| TOTAL FIXED CAPITAL | | 3,301,695.00 |
| ESTIMATED NET WORTH AT DECEMBER 31, 1889 | | $5,563,255.07 |

(*Note.* As in previous balance sheets the figures above include *total* expenditures on capital assets without allowance for depreciation.)

## APPENDIX G-6

### WINCHESTER REPEATING ARMS COMPANY

*Balance Sheet at December 31, 1914*

| | | | |
|---|---|---|---|
| CURRENT ASSETS | | | |
| Cash | $ 726,505 | | |
| Bills Receivable | 93,682 | | |
| Accounts Receivable | 222,236 | | |
| Inventories | 7,258,807 | | |
| Securities | 248,375 | | |
| Other Debit Balances | 220,652 | $8,770,257 | |
| LESS: CURRENT LIABILITIES | | 621,897 | |
| NET WORKING CAPITAL | | | $ 8,148,360 |
| FIXED ASSETS | | | |
| Value of real estate, plant, and machinery and patents, 4/1/67 | 150,000 | | |
| Value of patents acquired from O. F. Winchester | 150,000 | | |
| Estimated total expenditure 4/1/67 to 12/31/14 | 12,643,705 | 12,943,705 | |
| LESS: DEPRECIATION [1] | | 4,247,752 | |
| BOOK VALUE OF FIXED ASSETS | | | 8,695,953 |
| NET WORTH AT DECEMBER 31, 1914 | | | $16,844,313 |

[1] The Company introduced "depreciation reserves" into its accounting system on January 1, 1912, in connection with a re-appraisal of its assets. These changes were required to meet the situation arising from the introduction of the federal income tax on corporations which first applied to the Company on its profits for 1912. By December 31, 1914, the annual charge for depreciation had resulted in the accumulation of a reserve of $1,618,109.08. The difference between this figure and that shown arises from the fact that the basis of valuation used at January 1, 1912, resulted in a new book value of less than the original cost. This implicit depreciation of the assets acquired through December 31, 1911; it is roughly equivalent to the cost of the fixed assets acquired through December 31, 1889. It should be noted that the valuations used, at January 1, 1912, were, as regards land, those adopted by the Board of Tax Assessors and, for other property, the values at which the assets were insured at December 31, 1911. This suggests a probable tendency towards undervaluation.

# APPENDIX G-7

## WINCHESTER REPEATING ARMS COMPANY

*Balance Sheet at June 30, 1918*

### *ASSETS*

| | |
|---|---|
| CURRENT ASSETS AND INVENTORIES | |
| Cash | $ 1,449,246.38 |
| Accounts Receivable | 5,299,601.15 |
| Notes Receivable | 73,117.66 |
| Investments | 3,618,857.67 |
| Inventories | 13,692,809.66 |
| Total Current Assets and Inventories | 24,133,632.52 |
| DEFERRED DEBITS | 1,370,094.85 |
| FIXED ASSETS | |
| Plant and Equipment | 13,854,845.21 |
| | $39,358,575.58 |

### *LIABILITIES AND CAPITAL*

| | | |
|---|---|---|
| CURRENT LIABILITIES | | |
| Accounts Payable | | $ 2,442,477.95 |
| Accrued Taxes | | 1,558,557.26 |
| Accrued Interest | | 190,576.64 |
| Advances: | | |
| From U. S. Gov't | 4,139,086.62 | |
| From Customers | 941,000.30 | 5,080,086.92 |
| Total Current Liabilities | | 9,271,698.77 |
| NOTES PAYABLE | | 8,013,000.00 |
| DEFERRED CREDITS | | 370,918.29 |
| CAPITAL STOCK | | 1,000,000.00 |
| SURPLUS | | 20,765,958.52 |
| | | $39,358,575.58 |

## APPENDIX G-8

### THE WINCHESTER COMPANY AND SUBSIDIARIES

*Consolidated Balance Sheet at December 31, 1919*

*ASSETS*

| | | |
|---|---|---|
| CURRENT ASSETS AND INVENTORIES | | |
| Cash | $1,545,404.16 | |
| Accounts and Notes Receivable | 2,253,445.71 | |
| Investments in Securities | 5,568,417.02 | |
| Inventories | 9,800,806.92 | $19,168,073.81 |
| FIXED ASSETS | | |
| Land, Buildings, Equipment | 19,547,558.79 | |
| Less: Reserves for Depreciation | 9,149,860.67 | |
| Total Fixed Assets | | 10,397,698.12 |
| INVESTMENTS IN OUTSIDE COMPANIES | | 225,000.00 |
| DEFERRED ITEMS | | 413,817.29 |
| PATENTS | | 113,400.00 |
| | | $30,317,989.22 |

*LIABILITIES AND CAPITAL*

| | | |
|---|---|---|
| CURRENT LIABILITIES | | |
| Accounts Payable | $969,677.86 | |
| Accrued Payrolls | 195,801.88 | |
| Accrued Interest | 1,487,256.15 | $2,751,036.06 |
| MISCELLANEOUS RESERVES | | 1,636,184.06 |
| CAPITAL STOCK | | |
| 1st Preferred, 7% Cumulative | 9,754,700.00 | |
| 2nd Preferred, 6% Non-Cumulative | 2,000,000.00 | |
| Common Stock | 1,000,000.00 | 12,754,700.00 |
| CAPITAL SURPLUS | | |
| Appropriated for expenses connected with war termination | | 2,800,000.00 |
| Unappropriated | | 8,627,794.60 |
| EARNED SURPLUS (April 16, 1919—Dec. 31, 1919) | | $30,317,989.22 |

# APPENDIX G-9

## THE WINCHESTER COMPANY AND SUBSIDIARIES

*Consolidated Balance Sheet at December 31, 1921*
*(in thousands)*

| | | | |
|---|---|---|---|
| CURRENT ASSETS | | | |
| Cash, receivables and securities | | $ 3,454 | |
| Inventories | | 12,515 | |
| | | 15,969 | |
| Less: current liabilities and bank loans | | 7,461 | |
| NET WORKING CAPITAL | | | $ 8,508 |
| INVESTMENTS IN OUTSIDE COMPANIES | | | 136 |
| FIXED ASSETS | | | |
| Real estate, plant and machinery | $21,430 | | |
| Less depreciation reserve | 7,377 | 14,053 | |
| Development expenditures | | | |
| Tools, etc., for new products | 1,488 | | |
| Retail stores | 2,592 | | |
| Warehouses and other development and marketing | 3,662 | 8,102 | |
| DEFERRED ITEMS | | 842 | |
| | | 22,997 | |
| LESS FIRST MORTGAGE, 20-YEAR, 7.5% GOLD BONDS | | 7,000 | 15,997 |
| NET WORTH, DECEMBER 31, 1921 | | | 24,641 |
| Represented by: | | | |
| First preferred 7% cumulative stock | | | 9,755 |
| Second preferred 6% non-cumulative stock | | | 2,000 |
| Common stock | | | 10,000 |
| Reserves | | | 2,804 |
| Surplus | | | 82 |
| | | | $24,641 |

# APPENDIX G-10

## THE WINCHESTER COMPANY AND SUBSIDIARIES
## CONSOLIDATED BALANCE SHEET AT DECEMBER 31, 1924

*ASSETS*

| | | |
|---|---|---|
| CURRENT ASSETS AND INVENTORIES | | |
| Cash | $ 608,056.67 | |
| Accounts and Notes Receivable | 674,188.07 | |
| Inventories | 8,610,822.02 | |
| Total Current Assets | | $9,893,066.76 |
| FIXED ASSETS | | |
| Plant, Land, Buildings, Equipment | 37,331,376.05 | |
| Retail Stores: Leaseholder, Fixtures | 109,548.00 | |
| | 37,440,924.05 | |
| Less: Reserve for Depreciation | 8,631,038.14 | |
| | | 28,809,885.91 |
| DEFERRED ITEMS AND ADVANCES | | 797,439.62 |
| | | $39,500,392.29 |

*LIABILITIES AND CAPITAL*

| | | |
|---|---|---|
| CURRENT LIABILITIES | | |
| Accounts and Notes Payable | 470,213.27 | |
| Due Simmons Hardware Co. | 236,352.99 | |
| Bank Loans | 5,926,000.00 | |
| Accrued Interest and Taxes | 497,654.43 | $7,130,220.69 |
| MISCELLANEOUS RESERVES | | 1,117,654.36 |
| GENERAL RESERVES (NET) | | 514,110.98 |
| FIRST MORTGAGE 20-YEAR 7½% GOLD BONDS MATURING 1941 | | 6,582,000.00 |
| MINORITY INTEREST IN SUBSIDIARIES | | 960,231.34 |
| CAPITAL STOCK | | |
| 1st Preferred 7% Cumulative Stock | 9,754,700.00 | |
| 2nd Preferred 6% Non-Cumulative Stock | 2,000,000.00 | |
| Common | 10,000,000.00 | 21,754,700.00 |
| SURPLUS | | 1,441,474.92 |
| | | $39,500,392.29 |

## APPENDIX G-11

### WINCHESTER REPEATING ARMS COMPANY (DELAWARE) AND SUBSIDIARIES

*Consolidated Balance Sheet at December 31, 1929*

*ASSETS*

| | | |
|---|---|---|
| CURRENT ASSETS | | |
| Cash | $1,037,480.48 | |
| Accounts Receivable | 696,774.44 | |
| Inventories | 6,400,008.89 | $8,134,263.81 |
| FIXED ASSETS | | |
| Buildings, Equipment, Leaseholds, etc. | 34,943,248.16 | |
| Less: Reserve for Depreciation | 10,271,470.67 | $24,671,957.49 |
| ADVANCES—Whirldry Corp. (Less Reserves) | | 266,235.32 |
| DEFERRED ITEMS AND ADVANCES | | 444,821.28 |
| | | $33,517,277.90 |

*LIABILITIES AND CAPITAL*

| | | |
|---|---|---|
| CURRENT LIABILITIES | | |
| Advances, Accrued Interest and Taxes | | $1,434,355.25 |
| RESERVE FOR REORGANIZATION EXPENSES | | 829,148.95 |
| FIVE YEAR 6½% NOTES, DUE JAN. 1, 1932 | | 850,000.00 |
| FIVE YEAR 6½% DEBENTURES, DUE FEB. 1, 1934 | | 6,500,000.00 |
| FIRST MORTGAGE TWENTY YEAR 7½% GOLD BONDS DUE 1941 | | 5,887,000.00 |
| CAPITAL STOCK | | |
| Preferred 7% Cumulative Stock | $5,036,400.00 | |
| Class "A"—No par $6.00 Dividend | | |
| Common Stock—No Par | 8,134,000.00 | $13,170,400.00 |
| SURPLUS | | 4,846,373.70 |
| | | $33,517,277.90 |

# APPENDIX H

## COMPARATIVE POSITION OF WINCHESTER REPEATING ARMS COMPANY IN FIREARMS AND AMMUNITION INDUSTRY: EMPLOYMENT AND VALUE OF SALES

| *Date* | *1869* | *1879* | *1889* | *1899* | *1909* | *1914* | *1921* | *1923* | *1925* | *1927* | *1929* |
|---|---|---|---|---|---|---|---|---|---|---|---|
| INDUSTRY * | | | | | | | | | | | |
| Value (in millions of dollars) | 8.06 | 7.65 | 9.4 | 18.4 | 34.0 | 41.3 | 45.2 | 69.2 | 56.8 | 65.1 | 65.8 |
| Employment (in thousands) | 3.29 | 5.93 | 5.03 | 10.1 | 14.7 | 19.8 | 13.1 | 16.7 | 12.3 | 13.7 | 13.43 |
| WINCHESTER REPEATING ARMS COMPANY | | | | | | | | | | | |
| Value (in millions of dollars) | .32 | .92 | 2.5 | 4.8 | 9.8 | 11.8 | 9.0 | 11.6 | 9.0 | 11.1 | 11.1 |
| Percentage of industry | 4 | 12 | 27 | 26 | 28 | 28 | 20 | 17 | 16 | 17 | 17 |
| Employment (in thousands) | .26 | .61 | 1.26 | 2.78 | 4.56 | 6.16 | — | — | — | — | 2.46 |
| Percentage of industry | 8 | 10 | 27 | 29 | 32 | 31 | — | — | — | — | 18 |

* Including pistols and revolvers.
[*Sources:* U. S. Decennial Census of Manufacture; U. S. Biennial Census of Manufacture; Winchester Repeating Arms Company records.]

# APPENDIX I-1

## WINCHESTER GUN LINE AND SALES: 1890–1914

| *Model* | *Years listed in catalog* | *Approximate total sales (thousands)* |
|---|---|---|
| RIFLES: SINGLE-SHOT | | |
| Single-shot | 1890–1914 | 69.6 |
| 1900 | 1899–1903 | 105.0 |
| 1902 | 1903–1914 | 355.2 |
| 1904 | 1904–1914 | 121.4 |
| Thumb trigger | 1904–1914 | 59.3 |
| RIFLES: REPEATING | | |
| 66 | 1890–1899 | 3.0 |
| 73 | 1890–1914 | 374.0 |
| 76 | 1890–1894 | 4.0 |
| 83 (Hotchkiss) | 1890–1903 | 19.8 |
| 86 | 1890–1903 | 117.4 |
| 90 | 1890–1914 | 532.4 |
| 92 | 1892–1914 | 736.6 |
| 94 | 1895–1914 | 707.3 |
| 95 | 1895–1914 | 67.4 |
| Lee straight-pull | 1897–1903 | 21.7 |
| 06 | 1907–1914 | 422.8 |
| RIFLES: SELF-LOADING | | |
| 03 | 1904–1914 | 93.0 |
| 05 | 1905–1914 | 26.2 |
| 07 | 1907–1914 | 30.9 |
| 10 | 1910–1914 | 12.3 |
| SHOTGUNS: STANDARD STYLES | | |
| Lever Action (1887) | 1890–1901 | 33.7 |
| 1893 | 1893–1897 | 35.3 |
| 1897—12-gauge | 1897–1914 | 622.3 |
| 1901—10-gauge | 1902–1914 | 11.2 |
| 1911—12-gauge | 1911–1914 | 40.0 |
| 1912—12-gauge | 1913–1914 | 79.7 |
| GRAND TOTAL GUNS SOLD | | 4,701,500 |

# APPENDIX I-2

## PERCENTAGE DISTRIBUTION BY SALES OUTLETS

| | *1920* | *1921* | *1922* | *1923* | *1926* | *1929* |
|---|---|---|---|---|---|---|
| **TOTAL SALES** | | | | | | |
| Export | 19.1% | 5.2% | 5.4% | 8.9% | 16.5% | 17.9% |
| Jobbers | 56.0 | 46.3 | 38.6 | 28.1 | 46.0 | 51.9 |
| Dealer-agency | 23.5 | 45.1 | 43.0 | 55.8 | * | * |
| Winchester-Simmons | | | 8.6 | 3.1 | 35.5 | 14.3 |
| Retail stores | 1.4 | 1.7 | 0.5 | 0.3 | — | — |
| Specialty | — | 1.7 | 3.9 | 3.8 | — | — |
| U. S. Cartridge | | | | | 0.5 | 13.1 |
| Refrigerators | | | | | 1.0 | — |
| Radiators | | | | | 0.5 | 2.8 |
| **OLD LINE PRODUCTS** | | | | | | |
| Export | 21.0 | 6.0 | 6.5 | 10.5 | 13.6 | 10.5 |
| Jobbers | 58.0 | 55.0 | 51.0 | 43.0 | 55.4 | 57.2 |
| Dealer-agency | 20.0 | 38.0 | 35.5 | 46.5 | * | * |
| Winchester-Simmons | — | — | 7.0 | — | 30.3 | 14.5 |
| Retail | 1.0 | 1.0 | — | — | — | — |
| U. S. Cartridge | | | | | .7 | 17.8 |
| **NEW LINE PRODUCTS** | | | | | | |
| Exports | 3.0 | 2.0 | 3.0 | 6.0 | 23.7 | 38.5 |
| Jobbers | 36.5 | 15.5 | 10.0 | 3.0 | 22.9 | 37.0 |
| Dealer-agency | 55.5 | 70.0 | 60.0 | 72.0 | * | * |
| Winchester-Simmons | | | 13.0 | 10.0 | 48.5 | 14.0 |
| Retail | 5.0 | 5.5 | 1.0 | 1.0 | — | — |
| Specialty | | 7.0 | 13.0 | 10.0 | — | — |
| Refrigerators | | | | | 3.3 | — |
| Radiators | | | | | 1.6 | 10.5 |

* Dealer agency sales made through Winchester-Simmons.

# APPENDIX J-1

WINCHESTER REPEATING ARMS COMPANY
AVERAGE ANNUAL EMPLOYMENT: 1870–1931

(Excluding salaried personnel)

| *Year* | *Workers* | *Year* | *Workers* | *Year* | *Workers* | *Year* | *Workers* |
|---|---|---|---|---|---|---|---|
| 1870 | —— | 1886 | 1074* | 1902 | 3547* | 1918 | 18142 |
| 1871 | 244 | 1887 | 1260* | 1903 | 3747* | 1919 | 8130 |
| 1872 | 198 | 1888 | 1457* | 1904 | 4893* | 1920 | 8780 |
| 1873 | 197 | 1889 | 1232 | 1905 | 4127* | 1921 | 4166 |
| 1874 | —— | 1890 | 1430 | 1906 | 4702 | 1922 | 4324 |
| 1875 | 563 | 1891 | 1675 | 1907 | 5218 | 1923 | 5213 |
| 1876 | 689 | 1892 | 1751* | 1908 | 4775 | 1924 | 3669 |
| 1877 | 1208 | 1893 | 1586* | 1909 | 4566 | 1925 | 3453 |
| 1878 | 751 | 1894 | 1767* | 1910 | 4653 | 1926 | 3694 |
| 1879 | 609 | 1895 | 1867* | 1911 | 4870 | 1927 | 4260 |
| 1880 | 688 | 1896 | 1769* | 1912 | 5095 | 1928 | 4790 |
| 1881 | 883* | 1897 | 2095* | 1913 | 5803 | 1929 | 3802 |
| 1882 | 964 | 1898 | 2896* | 1914 | 6166 | 1930 | 3099 |
| 1883 | 1089 | 1899 | 2781* | 1915 | 11516 | 1931 | 2439 |
| 1884 | 1162 | 1900 | 2689* | 1916 | 16387 | | |
| 1885 | 1200 | 1901 | 3110* | 1917 | 12546 | | |

* Estimated by the following method: Total payroll of Winchester Repeating Arms Company divided by average annual wages per employee to get total number of employees. Average annual wages found by adjusting Paul Douglas, *Real Wages in United States, 1880–1920,* data on Foundry and Machine Shops and Brass, Bronze and Copper (pp. 271, 279) combined to fit the Winchester Repeating Arms series 1888–1890 and 1906–1910.

# APPENDIX J-2

NUMBER OF GUN SHOP CONTRACTORS; PERCENTAGE GUN SHOP PAYROLL (1881–1896) AND PERCENTAGE TOTAL COMPANY PAYROLL PAID TO GUN SHOP CONTRACTORS AND THEIR WORKERS (1881–1913)

| *Year* | *Number of Contractors* | *Percentage Gun Shop* | *Percentage Total* | *Year* | *Number of Contractors* | *Percentage Total ** |
|---|---|---|---|---|---|---|
| 1875 | 11 | — | — | 1897 | 18 | 28 |
| 1878 | 9 | — | — | 1898 | 17 | 32 |
| 1881 | 15 | 57 | 40 | 1899 | 17 | 32 |
| 1882 | 15 | 55 | 38 | 1900 | 17 | 35 |
| 1883 | 16 | 57 | 39 | 1902 | 19 | 28 |
| 1884 | 15 | 57 | 38 | 1903 | 18 | 33 |
| 1885 | 15 | 55 | 37 | 1904 | 18 | 32 |
| 1886 | 16 | 45 | 32 | 1905 | 17 | 26 |
| 1887 | 16 | 53 | 40 | 1906 | 14 | 19 |
| 1888 | 17 | 57 | 43 | 1907 | 10 | 11 |
| 1889 | 19 | 54 | 37 | 1908 | 8 | 11 |
| 1890 | 20 | 54 | 36 | 1909 | 7 | 7 |
| 1891 | 18 | 56 | 39 | 1910 | 6 | 7 |
| 1892 | 18 | 56 | 37 | 1911 | 6 | 8 |
| 1893 | 20 | 55 | 38 | 1912 | 6 | 7 |
| 1894 | 19 | 52 | 33 | 1913 | 5 | 6 |
| 1895 | 19 | 44 | 28 | | | |
| 1896 | 18 | 43 | 27 | | | |

* Comparable data are unavailable for ammunition shop.

# APPENDIX J-3

GUN SHOP: EMPLOYMENT; PERCENTAGE WORKER UNDER CONTRACT; ANNUAL INCOMES FOR CONTRACTORS, CONTRACT WORKERS, AND NON-CONTRACT WORKERS; PERCENTAGE GUN SHOP WORKERS TO TOTAL EMPLOYMENT; 1881–1896

| *Year* | *Total employment gun shop* | *Percentage gun shop workers under contract* | *Average Annual Income* | | | *Percentage gun shop workers to total employment* |
|---|---|---|---|---|---|---|
| | | | *Contractors* | *Contractors' workers* | *Non-contract workers* | |
| 1881 | 507 | 48 | $1862 | $731 | $565 | 57 |
| 1882 | 540 | 44 | 2298 | 733 | 536 | 56 |
| 1883 | 603 | 49 | 2726 | 699 | 572 | 56 |
| 1884 | 646 | 48 | 3247 | 716 | 564 | 55 |
| 1885 | 689 | 49 | 2727 | 666 | 600 | 57 |
| 1886 | 672 | 40 | 2439 | 642 | 599 | 63 |
| 1887 | 811 | 48 | 2859 | 688 | 626 | 64 |
| 1888 | 966 | 52 | 3393 | 662 | 618 | 66 |
| 1889 | 710 | 49 | 2132 | 664 | 608 | 58 |
| 1890 | 817 | 49 | 2291 | 674 | 624 | 57 |
| 1891 | 995 | 52 | 2772 | 661 | 624 | 59 |
| 1892 | 976 | 52 | 2815 | 658 | 628 | 56 |
| 1893 | 898 | 51 | 2667 | 635 | 605 | 57 |
| 1894 | 860 | 45 | 2325 | 673 | 589 | 49 |
| 1895 | 966 | 47 | 3089 | 603 | 666 | 52 |
| 1896 | 899 | 42 | 1862 | 603 | 648 | 51 |

* Includes payment of Winchester Repeating Arms Company foremen which may in part account for change in last two years.

## APPENDIX J-4

COMPARISON OF CONTRACTORS IN GUN SHOP, 1876–1889

| | *Large* | *Medium* | *Small* |
|---|---|---|---|
| Average number of jobs under contract (1876–89) | 5 | 8 | 5 |
| Total number of contractors (1876–89) | 17 | 14 | 14 |
| Average number of workers (1881–89) | 43 | 11 | 2 |
| Average annual pay of workers (1881–89) | $700 | $650 | $570 |
| Average annual income of contractors (1881–89) | $4800 | $1740 | $1430 |
| Percentage change in price indices (1876–89) | −37% | −50% | −54% |
| Average number of price changes per contract (1876–89) | 10 | 9 | 5 |
| Average magnitude of individual price changes (1876–89) | 7% | 8% | 14% |

[*Source:* WRA payroll books; contractor record books; contractor price books.]
(*Note.* Processes under large contracts include: receivers, small parts, drilling barrels, stocking, and the water shop; under medium contracts, machining barrels, boxes and cases, polishing parts, muzzle filing, screw job, projectiles and reloaders; under small contracts, rifling, bluing, browning, polishing and leading barrels, case hardening, and bayonets. A few contractors, for whom information is lacking, were omitted in the construction of these indices.)

## APPENDIX J-5

INDEX OF PAYMENTS TO LABOR CONTRACTORS 1880–1907 (1880 = 100) *

| *Year* | *Index* | *Year* | *Index* |
|---|---|---|---|
| 1880 | 100 | 1894 | 61.0 |
| 1881 | 97 | 1895 | 61.5 |
| 1882 | 98.3 | 1896 | 59.5 |
| 1883 | 91.5 | 1897 | 59.5 |
| 1884 | 92.3 | 1898 | 55.5 |
| 1885 | 84.7 | 1899 | 52.5 |
| 1886 | 78.8 | 1900 | 51.0 |
| 1887 | 79.7 | 1901 | 48.5 |
| 1888 | 78.4 | 1902 | 49.0 |
| 1889 | 73.3 | 1903 | 48.5 |
| 1890 | 71.6 | 1904 | 48.0 |
| 1891 | 68.5 | 1905 | 55.0 |
| 1892 | 67.0 | 1906 | 69.0 |
| 1893 | 64.0 | 1907 | 55.0 |

(*Note.* The following estimates of the total labor cost of the Model 73 carbine will be of interest: 1876, $6.68; 1880–1, $4.84; 1889–90, $3.56.)

* The index has been derived from individual indices of rates paid to contractors weighted by reference to annual volume of work done by them as measured by dollar payments. Contract rates for *receivers* were changed separately from other rates and with less regularity and an independent index for these parts was compiled and combined with the other indices.

# APPENDIX K

## WINCHESTER REPEATING ARMS COMPANY

### BRASS MILL AND AMMUNITION PRODUCTION

1890–1914 (in millions)

| *Year* | *Brass mill Production (pounds)* | *Loaded paper shot shells* | *Military & sporting cartridges* | *pistol cartridges* | *Rimfire cartridges* |
|---|---|---|---|---|---|
| 1890 | 1.9 | 23.2 | | | |
| 1891 | 3.1 | 22.9 | | | |
| 1892 | 3.3 | 33.2 | | | |
| 1893 | 2.8 | 32.4 | | | |
| 1894 | 3.4 | 48.4 | | | |
| 1895 | 4.1 | 67.5 | | | |
| 1896 | 3.3 | 60.1 | | | |
| 1897 | 4.6 | 78.9 | | | |
| 1898 | 7.5 | 93.2 | | | |
| 1899 | 6.0 | 94.1 | | | |
| 1900 | 4.6 | 91.9 | | | |
| 1901 | 6.7 | 144.0 | | | |
| 1902 | 8.0 | 189.9 | | | |
| 1903 | 6.8 | 149.6 | | | |
| 1904 | 7.2 | 171.3 | | | |
| 1905 | 8.5 | 191.6 | | | |
| 1906 | 10.3 | 219.7 | 51.7 | 97.8 | |
| 1907 | 11.0 | 243.4 | 29.1 | 105.3 | |
| 1908 | 9.3 | 258.8 | 22.7 | 75.9 | |
| 1909 | 10.9 | 258.1 | 25.0 | 96.2 | 531.7 |
| 1910 | 11.2 | 247.4 | 23.6 | 99.5 | 741.5 |
| 1911 | 11.1 | 251.0 | 30.2 | 94.0 | 630.2 |
| 1912 | 10.6 | 263.3 | 37.3 | 90.7 | 652.1 |
| 1913 | 12.8 | 236.6 | 53.0 | 97.3 | 690.6 |
| 1914 | 14.7 | 249.3 | 83.7 | 80.1 | 690.6 |

In the absence of production data for metallic cartridges prior to 1906, the best index of the Company's over-all ammunition production is shown by the figures on the output of brass, which was used exclusively in primers, shot-shell heads, and cartridge cases. This is not to suggest that the amount of ammunition components from a pound of brass remained constant, but the changes were probably not great enough to make the margin of error very large. According to these data the trend of ammunition production moved up impressively from 1890 to about 1907. After that date output leveled off for five years, followed by another increase during 1913 and 1914 which reflected preparation for World War I. With the exception of the last two years the production of loaded paper shot shells followed the same general trend only at an accelerated rate.

Just why Winchester's production of ammunition should become relatively stabilized after about 1907 is not clear. One explanation may be that the general demand had become stabilized. It is also probable that the Company was meeting stronger competition. The Ammunition Manufacturers' Association was dissolved in 1907 and two important new ammunition concerns had become established by that date.

The data for brass production and paper shot shells as well as the later figures for metallics show considerable year-to-year fluctuation. The sudden jump in brass production in 1898 reflected the impact of the Spanish-American War during which Winchester supplied the U. S. Government with military ammunition. There is some evidence of the effects of general business depressions of 1893, 1903, and 1908.

The very large production of rimfire cartridges deserves special mention. These were principally caliber .22 which sold at a low price and were used in shooting galleries, small game hunting, and target practice.

# INDEX

**B**

N



O

**S**

**Y**